# ANDALUCIA

B. Kaufmann/MICHELIN

**Executive Editorial Director** David Brabis
**Chief Editor** Cynthia Clayton Ochterbeck

## THE GREEN GUIDE - ANDALUCIA

**Editor** Gwen Cannon
**Principal Writer** Paul Glassman
**Production Coordinator** Allison M. Simpson
**Cartography** Alain Baldet, Peter Wrenn
**Photo Editor** Cecile Koroleff, Lydia Strong
**Proofreader** Gaven Watkins
**Layout & Design** Tim Schulz
**Cover Design** Ute Weber, Laurent Muller

**Contact Us:**

The Green Guide
Michelin Maps and Guides
One Parkway South
Greenville, SC 29615
USA
☎ 1-800-423-0485
www.michelintravel.com
michelin.guides@us.michelin.com

Michelin Maps and Guides
Hannay House
39 Clarendon Road
Watford, Herts WD17 1JA
UK
☎ (01923) 205 240
www.ViaMichelin.com
travelpubsales@uk.michelin.com

**Special Sales:**

For information regarding bulk sales,
customized editions and premium sales,
please contact our Customer Service
Departments:
USA 1-800-423-0485
UK (01923) 205 240
Canada 1-800-361-8236

**Note to the reader**
While every effort is made to ensure that all information printed in this guide is correct and up-to-date, Michelin Maps and Guides (Michelin Tyre PLC; Michelin North America, Inc.) accepts no liability for any direct, indirect or consequential losses howsoever caused so far as such can be excluded by law.

# One Team …
# A Commitment to Quality

There's just one reason our team is dedicated to producing quality travel publications—you, our reader. We want you to get the maximum benefit from your trip—and from your money. In today's multiple-choice world of travel, the options are many, perhaps overwhelming.

In our guidebooks, we try to minimize the guesswork involved with travel. We scout out the attractions, prioritize them with star ratings, and describe what you'll discover when you visit them.

To help you orient yourself, we provide colorful and detailed, but easy-to-follow maps. Floor plans of some of the cathedrals and museums help you plan your tour.

Throughout the guides, we offer practical information, touring tips and suggestions for finding the best views, good places for a break and the most interesting shops.

Lodging and dining are always a big part of travel, so we compile a selection of hotels and restaurants that we think convey the feel of the destination, and organize them by geographic area and price. We also highlight shopping, recreational and entertainment venues, especially the popular spots.

If you're short on time, driving tours are included so you can hit the highlights and quickly absorb the best of the region.

For those who love to experience a destination on foot, we add walking tours, often with a map. And we list other companies who offer boat, bus or guided walking tours of the area, some with culinary, historical or other themes.

In short, we test and retest, check and recheck to make sure that our guidebooks are truly just that: a personalized guide to help you make the most of your visit. After all, we want you to enjoy traveling as much as we do.

**The Michelin Green Guide Team**

# PLANNING YOUR TRIP

# INTRODUCTION TO ANDALUCÍA

## SYMBOLS

-    **Tips to help improve your experience**
-    **Details to consider**
-    **Entry Fees**
-    **Walking tours**
-    **Closed to the public**
-    **Hours of operation**
-    **Periods of closure**

# CONTENTS

## DISCOVERING ANDALUCÍA

# HOW TO USE THIS GUIDE

## Orientation

To help you grasp the "lay of the land" quickly and easily, so you'll feel confident and comfortable finding your way around the region, we offer the following tools in this guide:

- Detailed table of contents for an overview of what you'll find in the guide, and how it is organized.
- Map of Andalucía at the front of the guide, with the principal sights highlighted for easy reference.
- Detailed maps for major cities and villages, including driving tour maps and larger-scale maps for walking tours.
- Map of Driving Tours in Andalucía, each numbered and color-coded.
- Principal Sights ordered alphabetically for easy reference.

## Practicalities

At the front of the guide, you'll see a section called "Planning Your Trip" that will help you make the most of your visit, with information about the best time to go, different ways of getting to the region and getting around, and basic facts and tips. You'll find driving and themed tours, and suggestions for outdoor fun. There's also a calendar of popular annual events in Andalucía. Information on shopping, sightseeing, kids' activities and sports and recreational opportunities is also included.

## LODGINGS

We've made a selection of hotels and arranged them within the cities by price category to fit all budgets *( see the Legend on the cover flap for an explanation of price categories)*. For the most part, we selected accommodations based on their unique regional quality, their Andalusian feel, as it were. So, unless the individual hotel embodies local ambience, it's rare that we include chain properties, which typically have their own imprint. If you want a more comprehensive selection of accommodations in Andalucía, see the red-cover **Michelin Guide España & Portugal**.

## RESTAURANTS

We thought you'd like to know the popular eating spots in Andalucía. So we selected restaurants that capture the Andalusian experience—those that have a unique regional flavor and local atmosphere. We're not rating the quality of the food per se. As we did with the hotels, we selected restaurants for many towns and villages, categorized by price to appeal to all wallets. If you want a more comprehensive selection of dining recommendations in the region, see the red-cover **Michelin Guide España & Portugal**.

## Attractions

Principal Sights are arranged alphabetically. Within each Principal Sight, attractions for each town, village, or geographical area (such as Granada) are divided into local Sights or Walking Tours, nearby Excursions to sights outside the town, or detailed Driving Tours—suggested itineraries for seeing several attractions around a major town. Contact information, admission charges and hours of operation are given for the majority of attractions. Unless otherwise noted, admission prices shown are for a single adult only. Discounts for seniors, students, teachers, etc. may be available; be sure to ask. If no admission charge is shown, entrance to the attraction is free.

If you're pressed for time, we recommend you visit the three- and two-star sights first: the stars are your guide.

## STAR RATINGS

Michelin has used stars as a rating tool for more than 100 years:

| | |
|---|---|
| ★★★ | Highly recommended |
| ★★ | Recommended |
| ★ | Interesting |

## SYMBOLS IN THE TEXT

Besides the stars, other symbols in the text indicate tourist information ⓘ; wheelchair access ♿; on-site eating facilities ✕; camping facilities △; on-site parking 🅿; sights of interest to children Kids; and beaches ⌂.

See the box appearing on the Contents page for other symbols used in the text. See the Maps explanation below for symbols appearing on the maps.

Throughout the guide you will find peach-coloured text boxes or sidebars containing anecdotal or background information. Green-coloured boxes contain information to help you save time or money.

## Maps

All maps in this guide are oriented north, unless otherwise indicated by a directional arrow. See the map Legend at the back of the guide for an explanation of other map symbols. A complete list of the maps found in the guide appears at the back of this book.

Addresses, phone numbers, opening hours and prices published in this guide are accurate at press time. We welcome corrections and suggestions that may assist us in preparing the next edition. Please send your comments to:

Michelin Maps and Guides
Hannay House
39 Clarendon Road
Watford, Herts WD17 1JA
UK
travelpubsales@uk.michelin.com
www.michelin.co.uk

Michelin Maps and Guides
Editorial Department
P.O. Box 19001
Greenville, SC   29602-9001
USA
michelin.guides@us.michelin.com
www.michelintravel.com

**Tourist town, city**
⚐ Spa
♨ Seaside resort
❄ Winter sports resort
⚓ Marina
⛳ Golf course

1
2
3

**5** The river Guadalquivir in the province of Córdoba

**6** Art and history in the province of Sevilla

**7** Horses, bulls and wine

**8** A land of bandits

**9** Wine and cured ham

**10** The legacy of the nasrids

0          50 km

# WHEN AND WHERE TO GO

## Driving Tours

We've put together 10 different itineraries for visitors who wish to spend a few days exploring Andalucía by car. *See the Driving Tours map on pages 11-13.*
You may also wish to refer to the map of **Principal Sights**, which are described in the **Discovering Andalucía** section of this guide.

---

### ① LAND OF THE OLIVE TREE

#### Round trip of 225km/141mi from Jaén

This tour through the Jaén countryside is punctuated with dramatic mountain scenery, hills shaded by olive trees, and historic villages and towns embellished with some of the region's most important Renaissance buildings.
After exploring the provincial capital, **Jaén**, famous for its Moorish fortress (Castillo de Santa Catalina), its awe-inspiring Renaissance cathedral and magnificent Arab baths, head east to **Baeza** and **Úbeda**. These delightful towns, just 9km/5mi apart, have two of the most stunning and superbly preserved monumental centres in Andalucía. From Úbeda, continue to **Sabiote** to admire its splendid castle and wander narrow streets lined by elegant mansions. The itinerary then heads the short distance south to

*Olive groves*

B. Kaufmann/MICHELIN

**Torreperojil**, its centre dominated by the Gothic-style Iglesia de la Asunción. After a brief stop in **Villacarrillo**, where the highlight is undoubtedly its Renaissance church, the route winds to picturesque **Cazorla**, a mountain village crowned by the craggy relief of its imposing castle, and the ideal departure point for the spectacular **Parque Natural de las Sierras de Cazorla, Segura y las Villas**. Return to Jaén through **Jódar**, site of an information centre for the **Parque Natural de Sierra Mágina**.

---

### ② TROGLODYTE LANDSCAPES

#### Round trip of 272km/170mi from Guadix

The Sierra Nevada and Sierras de Cazorla y Segura are separated by valleys and mountain chains rich in archaeological interest. An outstanding feature of local villages is the abundance of troglodyte dwellings built into the clay.
The journey starts in **Guadix**, a town overlooked by one of the finest areas of troglodyte houses. Nearby **Purullena** is an unusual village where "cave dwellings" and pottery shops line both sides of the main road. The tour skirts the River Farbes as far as the spa of **Baños de Alicún** before heading southeast along the Gor Valley. **Gorafe**, halfway along the valley, is marked by some 200 dolmens dating from Neolithic times, and an impressive series of troglodyte dwellings. After a short section along the A 92 heading northeast, the tour veers into the mountains, to **Zújar**, at the foot of Monte Jabalcón, close to the Negratín Resevoir, whose waters have been renowned since Antiquity. Continuing north, the route borders the southern section of the **Parque Natural de las Sierras de Cazorla, Segura y las Villas** before reaching picturesque **Castril**, a village nestled beneath an imposing cliff, and just a stone's throw from the scenic **Parque Natural de la Sierra de Castril**. The main feature of

interest in **Huéscar**, a short distance to the east, is without doubt its attractive main square (plaza Mayor). As the road descends south, it is worth stopping in **Galera** to admire the remains of an Iberian necropolis, the vestiges of its Moorish quarter and a group of cave dwellings in the upper reaches of the town. Just 8km/5mi to the southeast, nestled in an delightfully bucolic landscape, is **Orce**, famous in the 1980s for the discovery of a child's remains dating back one and half million years. The last stage of the tour before returning to Guadix is **Baza**, an important Iberian settlement dating from the 4C BC where the famous Dama de Baza sculpture was discovered. Bordering the **Parque Natural de la Sierra de Baza**, the town is the main centre of interest in the Baza valley, with an interesting architectural heritage that includes Moorish baths dating from the caliphal period and a sober, fortress-like collegiate church, the Colegiata de Santa María de la Encarnación.

## ③ THE DESERT AND BEACHES OF THE PROVINCE OF ALMERÍA

### Round trip of 254km/159mi from Almería

This tour through stunning and somewhat surprising desert landscapes also encompasses charming isolated beaches, unexpectedly verdant orchards, infinite mountain vistas, summer coastal resorts and Almería's picturesque inland villages – all beneath the renowned clear azure sky of southeastern Andalucía.

**Almería**, crowned by its magnificent Moorish fortress, is the starting-point. Head southeast to the **Parque Natural de Cabo de Gata**, with its strikingly beautiful beaches, dunes and reefs. After **Níjar**, a small whitewashed town built around a 15C parish church on the fold of a hill, return to the coast for splendid views of the Mediterranean along the road linking **Agua Amarga** and Mojácar, and the occasional view of an old watchtower. **Mojácar**, perched on a rocky promontory just 2km/1.2mi

inland, is one of the most enchanting small towns in the province of Almería, with an old quarter that preserves an unmistakable Moorish air. The tour then penetrates into the Almerian desert, characterised by a rugged, arid landscape of rocks and low-lying hills. Continuing west, the road passes on the right the impressive **Paraje Natural de Karst en Yesos**, a nature reserve made up of thousands of limestone caves formed by erosion, before reaching **Sorbas**, an attractive small town built on a clay escarpment on a meander of the River Aguas. The A 370 then continues 30km/18mi further west to **Tabernas**, at the foot of a Moorish castle, and **Mini-Hollywood**, a reconstructed American Wild West town used as a set for spaghetti westerns. Before returning to Almería, it is well worth a short detour to **Los Millares**, the most important Copper Age settlement ever discovered in Europe.

## ④ THE VILLAGES OF THE PARQUE NATURAL DE LA SIERRA SUBBÉTICA

### Round trip of 175km/109mi from Lucena

This route through the Sierra Subbética in the province of Córdoba is characterised by dramatic viewpoints, hillsides carpeted in olive groves, and attractive villages clinging to mountain slopes, some crowned by fortresses hewn out of rock.

After exploring the centre of **Lucena**, including its main church of interest, the Iglesia de San Mateo, head up to the **Santuario de la Virgen de Araceli** for the impressive view from its esplanade. On returning to Lucena, pass through **Rute**, a village renowned for its anise-flavoured liqueur, and then enjoy superb views along the way the **Iznájar Dam**; the picturesque village of Iznájar overlooks the lake from atop a hill. The next stop is the delightful town of **Priego de Córdoba**, the somewhat surprising capital of Cordoban Baroque. From here, head west to **Carcabuey**, at the foot of a castle in ruins, then Luque, before reaching **Zuheros**, a charming village straddling a rocky outcrop beneath the remains of a stone castle. A scenic road then winds it way to the **Cueva de los Murciélagos**, a cave renowned for its chambers of impressive stalactites and stalagmites, as well as the remnants of Neolithic wall paintings and engravings. Return to Zuheros, before continuing to **Baena**, one of Spain's leading towns for olive oil and home to several churches of interest. Heading southwest, the A 316 leads to **Cabra**, a tranquil town spread out in a swathe of white across the sierra of the same name. Before heading back to Lucena, be sure to visit the **Ermita de la Virgen de la Sierra**, a sanctuary which enjoys a superb setting offering expansive views of the Subbética range and the Cordoban countryside.

## ⑤ THE RIVER GUADALQUIVIR IN THE PROVINCE OF CÓRDOBA

### Round trip of 241km/151mi from Montoro

The Guadalquivir winds its way through the province of Córdoba, reflecting picturesque villages and occasional imposing castle or ruins that recall past glories.

This drive begins in **Montoro**, a charming and elegant whitewashed town huddled around a meander in the river. From here, head northwest away from the river to **Adamuz**, situated amid a vast expanse of olive groves, before following a minor road skirting the river west to **Córdoba**. A visit to the Mezquita and a stroll through the city's Jewish quarter are the high points of this magnificent city teeming with art and history, delightful small squares and charming flower-decked patios seemingly at every turn. A visit to **Las Ermitas**, a group of 13 hermitages on the northern outskirts of Córdoba, will provide a delightfully bucolic contrast with the hustle and bustle of the centre of the provincial capital; set in a wild mountainous landscape, the hermitages afford memorable views. The next stage of the tour encompasses **Medina Azahara**, and the remains of a

sumptuous palace city built at the end of the 10C and destroyed early in the 11C; this caliphal complex is without doubt one of the finest examples of Hispano-Moorish architecture. Some 20km/12mi southwest, on the banks of the river is **Almodóvar del Río**, huddled at the foot of a hill crowned by a majestic castle. Continue west along the Guadalquivir to visit the attractive gardens in the village of **Moratalla**, before reaching the whitewashed town of **Palma del Río**, on a plain between the Guadalquivir and Genil, where the main sights of interest are the vestiges of Almohad defensive walls and several noteworthy churches. After returning to the A 4 after Córdoba, stop briefly at **El Carpio**, straddling a hill dominated by an imposing Mudéjar brick tower.

## ⑥ ART AND HISTORY IN THE PROVINCE OF SEVILLA

### Round trip of 278km/174mi from Sevilla

This tour, centred on the area close to the A 4 – E 5 and A 92 highways, includes some of the finest and most elegant towns and villages in the province. Impressive churches and magnificent civic buildings stand alongside historic palaces and vestiges from the Roman and Moorish occupation.

The departure point is **Sevilla**, capital of Andalucía and a city with myriad attractions. Set out eastwards to historic **Carmona**, where the main sights of interest are its fortress-palace (*alcázar*) and Roman necropolis. The next stop is elegant **Écija**, renowned for its churches and palaces. Numerous Baroque towers stand proudly above the rooftops. A fine monumental centre is the highlight of historic **Osuna**, perched on a hill 34km/21mi further south. Seat of the House of Osuna, this ducal town has inherited a rich architecture, which includes a number of fine palaces, seigniorial mansions and predominantly Baroque churches. The tour then continues to **Estepa**, another hilltop town, where the highlights are the vestiges of the old Moorish walls and several impressive churches, convents and towers. From here, head directly west past Osuna and then north along the A 364 to **Marchena**, renowned for the outstanding works of art within the walls of the Iglesia de San Juan Baptista, and the museum devoted to Zurbarán inside the same church. Pass through **Paradas**, which owes its name to the caravans that passed through here in olden times (*parada* translates as halt or stop), before reaching **El Arahal**, a charming village of Moorish origin subsequently embellished with an interesting mix of Baroque and neo-Classical buildings. Before heading back to Sevilla, it is well worth making a final stop in **Alcalá de Guadaira**, impressively sited at the foot of an imposing Almohad fortress.

## 7 HORSES, BULLS AND WINE

### Round trip of 216km/135mi from Cádiz

This driving tour through the western reaches of the province of Cádiz takes in picturesque coastal and inland towns and villages, in addition to rural landscapes where the traditions of the *feria*, Andalusian horsemanship, bullfighting, guitar music and sherry-making continue to influence daily life. The first port of call on this fascinating tour is **Cádiz**, a city of wonderful light jutting into the Atlantic with an interesting mix of elegant Baroque and neo-Classical buildings and picturesque narrow streets and squares

*Casa de los Visires, Medina Azahara, Córdoba*

H. Champollion/MICHELIN

with an attractively neglected air. **El Puerto de Santa María**, a summer resort across the Bay of Cádiz, is a lively and pleasant town dotted with well-preserved buildings from the 18C and 19C. Just 23km/14mi northwest of here, at the mouth of the River Guadalquivir, stands the coastal town of **Sanlúcar de Barrameda**, the home of *manzanilla*, where the upper town has an abundance of wine cellars and attractive monuments, while the riverfront, in the lower section of town, is teeming with restaurants specialising in fish and seafood. Return inland across a fertile landscape to the noble and refined town of **Jérez de la Frontera**, whose medieval heart, constructed after the Christian Reconquest, is embellished by several fine churches, in addition to impressive monuments such as the fine Baroque cathedral; the Renaissance-style former town hall (Casa del Cabildo); Iglesia de San Miguel, a remarkable clock museum (Museo de Relojes); the Royal Andalusian School of Equestrian Art; and – not to forget – the town's ubiquitous sherry *bodegas*. From Jérez, head inland along the A 382 to **Arcos de la Frontera**, a delightful town characterised by steep, narrow streets lined by whitewashed houses adorned with wrought-iron grilles; the views from the spectacular natural setting on a ridge overlooking the valley of the River Guadalete will offer a lasting reminder of your time spent in the town. The road south winds its away through the rural heart of the province to **Medina Sidonia**, a small hilltop town offering expansive views of the surrounding countryside. The main features of interest here are the remains of the town's Roman underground galleries, its old quarter, including the Iglesia de Santa María la Mayor, and the fortifed Christian fortress (*alcázar*). Continuing south, the A 393 skirts the exquisite, impressively located whitewashed hilltop town of **Vejer de la Frontera** before continuing north to **Chiclana de la Frontera**, a popular holiday base bordered to the east by a network of saltpans, and to the west by the Playa de la Barrosa, a magnificent 7km/4.5mi-long beach, and the tourist complexes of Sancti Petri and Novo Sancti Petri. The last stop on this tour before returning to Cádiz is **San Fernando**, a town that has had strong links with the Spanish Navy since the 18C.

## ⑧ A LAND OF BANDITS

### Round trip of 256km/160mi from Algeciras

This itinerary penetrates deep into spectactular and isolated mountain landscapes and on to picturesque villages and territory made famous by Andalusian bandits of the past before returning to sea level and some of the Costa del Sol's most famous resorts. The starting-point of the tour provides an opportunity to enjoy a superb view of the Rock of Gibraltar from the busy port of **Algeciras**, before heading inland to **Castillo de Castellar**, a charming village-fortress of Moorish origin nestled amid the wooded landscapes of the Parque Natural de los Alcornocales and overlooking the Guadarranque Reservoir. The next stop is **Jimena de la Frontera**, whose whitewashed houses and narrow cobbled streets extend in a swathe across a hill. Like Castillo de Castellar, Jimena was the scene of fighting between Christians and Moors for control of this area in the 15C. As the itinerary heads further into the Serranía de Ronda mountain range and past **Gaucín**, tucked against the hillside, the road starts to gain altitude as it winds its way up to **Ronda**, a romantic mountain town that was the cradle of modern bullfighting and the home of many bandits in the past. Ronda enjoys a formidable site, perched on the top of a steep rock, where it is cut in two by a deep ravine with the River Guadalevín at its base. The steep, winding descent to the Mediterranean is even more spectacular, particularly beyond the Alájar Pass, leading to **San Pedro de Alcántara**, a well-established resort with the additional bonus of a number of interesting archaeological remains. **Puerto Banús**, just 6km/4mi to the east, is home to the most famous

marina on the Costa del Sol, and is followed by **Marbella**, the cosmopolitan centre of tourism along this *costa* and famous as the preferred anchorage and playground of the international jet-set during the summer months. To return to Algeciras, head west past San Pedro de Alcántara to **Estepona**, yet another lively and busy resort, and **La Duquesa**, with its modern marina. As Gibraltar comes into view once more, the road skirts to the north of **Sotogrande**, passing a series of luxury tourist developments built close to Valderrama, one of the world's most famous golf courses.

## ⑨ WINE AND CURED HAM

### Round trip of 338km/211mi from Huelva

This driving tour through the province of Huelva starts off along the coast before heading inland to visit the area's major wine-producing area and then climbing towards the Sierra de Aracena, where the best-quality cured ham in the whole of Spain is produced.

From **Huelva**, hemmed in to the west and east by the mouths of the Tinto and Odiel respectively, make the short journey south to the **Monasterio de la Rábida**, whose name is indelibly linked with that of Christopher Columbus and the epic poem relating to the discovery of America. After visiting the monastery, continue along the coast road, skirting the long and sandy **Playa de Mazagón**, before arriving in **Matalascañas**, a lively and popular summer resort. Then leave the coast behind you as you head 16km/10mi north to the small town of **El Rocío**, on the edge of the **Parque Nacional de Doñana**, which during Whitsun weekend every year at the end of May is the destination for the largest and most popular religious pilgrimage in Spain. Directly north of El Rocío, the tranquil and elegant wine-producing towns of **Almonte**, **Bollullos del Condado** and **La Palma del Condado** are known for their white and sweet wines of the Condado de Huelva appellation. The HV 5131 then heads north into the sierra, joining up with the N 435 to reach **Zalamea la Real**, renowned for its anise-flavoured liqueurs. From here, a winding road to the east skirts mountainous terrain as far as **Minas de Riotinto**, whose unusual landscapes have been sculpted by mining since Antiquity. The spectacular open-cast mining area exploited here and the "English" district of Bellavista are the main sights of interest in and around the town. An attractive mountain road leads from Minas de Riotinto deep into the **Parque Natural de la Sierra de Aracena y Picos de Aroche** as far as **Aracena**, a charming small town standing in the shadow of its castle. Not to be missed on the southern outskirts of the town is the spectacular Gruta de las Maravillas (Cave of Marvels), which more than lives up to its name. The tour continues through the wooded landscapes within the boundaries of the park to villages such as **Jabugo**, famous for its cured hams, **Cortegana**, an important arts and crafts centre dominated by a medieval castle, and **Almonaster la Real**, which has preserved the remains of a 10C mosque. As you retrace your steps to Huelva, make a brief stop in **Valverde del Camino**, known across Spain for its high-quality boots, and **Niebla**, a delightful medieval fortified village.

## ⬜0⬜ THE LEGACY OF THE NASRIDS

### Round trip of 330km/206mi from Granada

This driving tour explores the lands of the former Nasdrid kingdom of Granada, passing through a region of mountainous landscapes, attractive towns and villages and a significant stretch of the Mediterranean coastline in the provinces of Málaga and Granada.

Following your visit to the Alhambra, one of the world's most breathtaking monuments located in the capital of the former Nasrid kingdom, **Granada**, begin your journey west to **Santa Fé**, where the Catholic Monarchs and Christopher Columbus signed their historic agreement, before continuing to **Loja**, towering above the Genil Valley on a low promontory. The next stage of the journey leads to **Archidona**, nestling at the foot of the Sierra de Gracia amid a landscape of verdant olive groves, where the main attraction is an unusual octagonal plaza. **Antequera**, 19km/11mi further west, a town of whitewashed houses fronted by wrought-iron grilles and with several monuments of interest including its former Moorish castle, is the ideal base from which to explore the stunning natural landscapes of the area. The busy route to the coast climbs steeply before descending dramatically to **Málaga**, the capital of the Costa del Sol, and a city with an interesting historical heritage which bears witness to its prominence since Roman times. The city's most noteworthy monuments are the remains of the Gibralfaro and fortress, which highlight the defensive system of the Moorish settlement known as Malaka. The tour then heads east along the coast of the **Axarquía** area, home to several popular summer resorts, to the **Cueva del Tesoro**, a cave formed by maritime erosion, close to Rincón de la Victoria, and the spectacular **Cueva de Nerja**. From **Nerja**, a lively tourist centre, it is well worth a detour inland to visit the picturesque whitewashed village of **Frigiliana**, with its well-preserved architecture bearing the undeniable mark of its Moorish past. Continuing east, the corniche road provides further fine views of the indented coastline along this stretch of the Mediterranean, before reaching **Almuñecar** and then **Salobreña**, a charming village on a hill dominated by the remains of its Nasrid castle, from where the tour veers directly north to return to Granada, briefly leaving the N 323 to discover the charming village of **Guajar de Faragüit**, to the west, and **Nigüelas**, at the western edge of the Alpujarras mountain range.

## ROUTES IN AL-ANDALUS

The Moorish Legacy *(El Legado andalusí)* initiative has been developed by the Junta de Andalucía and the Spanish government to provide information for visitors on the Moorish presence in the Iberian peninsula. This effort includes a series of exhibitions; the creation of official tourist routes through **al-Andalus** (Andalucía, Murcia, Portugal and North Africa); the publication of works relating to this period; and the detailed cataloguing of all aspects of Moorish architecture. The tourist routes explore areas away from the tourist centres and offer an in-depth look at the historical and artistic heritage of one of the most brilliant civilisations in history, as well as its gastronomy and handicrafts. The routes provide visitors with a comprehensive introduction to this culture, whose influence is so strongly felt in the region.

In 1998 the European Council awarded the **European Cultural Itinerary** label to the tourist routes in al-Andalus. This label is given to routes which promote cultural tourism and further the understanding of the different strands that have come together to forge the modern identity of Europe. Four signposted routes have been created in Andalucía:

### The Route of the Caliphate

This route links Córdoba and Granada, the two main cities of Moorish Spain and heirs to a vast cultural, political

*Iberian pigs*

*Salobreña*

and social legacy from the civilisation of al-Andalus. This itinerary offers a comprehensive insight into this region of stunning villages, impressive castles and myriad legends.

**Route:** Córdoba, Fernán Núñez, Montemayor, Montilla, Aguilar de la Frontera, Lucena, Cabra, Carcabuey, Priego de Córdoba, Espejo, Castro del Río, Baena, Zuheros, Luque, Alcaudete, Castillo de Locubín, Alcalá la Real, Moclín, Pinos Puente, Colomera, Güevejar, Cogollos Vega, Alfacar, Viznar, Granada.

### The Washington Irving Route

This route closely follows the itinerary taken in 1829 by the American Romantic writer Washington Irving, who was fascinated by the exuberant and exotic nature of the Moorish monuments in Andalucía. Linking the towns of Sevilla and Granada, this historical route once served as an important communication channel between the Nasrid kingdom and the Christian authorities.

**Route:** Sevilla, Alcalá de Guadaira, Carmona, Marchena, Écija, Osuna, Estepa, La Roda de Andalucía, Fuente de Piedra, Molina, Humilladero, Antequera, Archidona, Loja, Moraleda de Zafayona, Alhama de Granada, Huétor Tájar, Montefrío, Illora, Chauchina, Fuente Vaqueros, Santa Fe, Granada.

## The Nasrid Route
Straddling the provinces of Jaén and Granada, this route is dedicated to the last chapter of the Moorish history in Spain. The itinerary starts in the hills of the Sierra Morena. It was in Las Navas de Tolosa, near Despeñaperros, that the famous battle took place (1212) which led to the Christian reconquest of Andalucía, finalised by the capture of Granada in 1492.

**Route:** Las Navas de Tolosa, La Carolina, Baños de la Encina, Bailén, Mengíbar, Andújar, Arjona, Porcuna, Torredonjimeno, Martos, Torredelcampo, Linares, Baeza, Úbeda, Mancha Real, Jódar, Jimena, Jaén, La Guardia de Jaén, Cambil, Huelma, Guadahortuna, Piñar, Iznalloz, Deifontes, Albolote, Maracena, Granada.

## The Almoravid and Almohad Route
This route runs from Tarifa through the provinces of Cádiz and Málaga to Granada, crossing superb nature parks and the lovely White Villages of the province of Cádiz.

**Route:** Tarifa, Algeciras, Castellar de la Frontera, Jimena de la Frontera, Casares, Gaucín, Banalauría, Algatocín, Benadalid, Atajate, Alcalá de los Gazules, Medina Sidonia, Cádiz, Puerto de Santa María, Jerez de la Frontera, Arcos de la Frontera, Grazalema, Zahara de la Sierra, Algodonales, Olvera, Setenil, Ronda, Teba, Campillos, Vélez Málaga, Alcaucín-Zafarraya, La Mala, Las Gabias, Granada.

## Information
El Legado Andalusí, Calle Mariana Pineda, Edif. Corral del Carbón, 18009 Granada, ☎ 958 22 59 95; fax 958 22 86 44; www.legadoandalusi.es and http://legadoandalusi.andalucia.org; info@legadoandalusi.es

# When to Go

## BEST TIME

Spring and autumn are the best seasons for touring inland Andalucía, as temperatures can exceed 40°C/104°F in summer. Winters are generally mild, although temperatures can dip dramatically at higher altitudes. The coastal resorts of the Mediterranean enjoy mild temperatures and plentiful sunshine even in winter.
For up-to-date information on **weather** in Andalucía log onto the Spanish Meteorological Office Web site at www.inm.es.

| | Jan | Feb | Mar | Apr | May | Jun | Jul | Aug | Sep | Oct | Nov | Dec |
|---|---|---|---|---|---|---|---|---|---|---|---|---|
| **Almería** | 16 | 16 | 18 | 20 | 22 | 26 | 29 | 29 | 27 | 23 | 19 | 17 |
| | 8 | 8 | 10 | 12 | 15 | 18 | 21 | 22 | 20 | 16 | 12 | 9 |
| **Cádiz** | 15 | 16 | 18 | 21 | 23 | 27 | 29 | 30 | 27 | 23 | 19 | 16 |
| | 8 | 9 | 11 | 12 | 14 | 18 | 20 | 20 | 19 | 16 | 12 | 9 |
| **Córdoba** | 14 | 16 | 19 | 23 | 26 | 32 | 36 | 36 | 31 | 24 | 19 | 14 |
| | 4 | 5 | 8 | 10 | 13 | 17 | 19 | 20 | 17 | 13 | 8 | 5 |
| **Granada** | 12 | 14 | 18 | 20 | 24 | 30 | 34 | 34 | 29 | 22 | 17 | 12 |
| | 1 | 2 | 5 | 7 | 9 | 14 | 17 | 17 | 14 | 9 | 5 | 2 |
| **Huelva** | 16 | 18 | 20 | 22 | 25 | 29 | 32 | 32 | 29 | 25 | 21 | 17 |
| | 6 | 7 | 9 | 11 | 13 | 16 | 18 | 18 | 17 | 14 | 10 | 7 |
| **Jaén** | 12 | 14 | 17 | 20 | 24 | 30 | 34 | 34 | 29 | 22 | 16 | 12 |
| | 5 | 5 | 8 | 10 | 13 | 17 | 21 | 21 | 18 | 13 | 9 | 5 |
| **Málaga** | 16 | 17 | 19 | 21 | 24 | 28 | 30 | 30 | 28 | 24 | 20 | 17 |
| | 8 | 8 | 10 | 11 | 14 | 17 | 20 | 20 | 18 | 15 | 12 | 9 |
| **Sevilla** | 15 | 17 | 20 | 23 | 26 | 32 | 36 | 36 | 32 | 26 | 20 | 16 |
| | 6 | 6 | 9 | 11 | 13 | 17 | 20 | 20 | 18 | 14 | 10 | 7 |

**Temperature chart** (maximum temperatures in normal text; minimum temperatures in italics).

# KNOW BEFORE YOU GO

## Useful Web Sites

**www.andalucia.org:** The Andalusian Tourist Board provides comprehensive information on the region including transport, accommodation and real-time booking, sport and leisure.

**www.spain.info:** The official visitors' information site for tourism in Spain.

**www.okspain.org:** Spain's site for visitors from the United States.

**www.fco.gov.uk:** The UK's Foreign and Commonwealth Office provides information on global travel.

**www.state.gov:** American visitors should check the US State Department Web site for worldwide travel advice.

## Tourist Offices

Contact your nearest **Spanish Tourist Office** for up-to-date information.

### SPANISH TOURIST OFFICES

**London:**
22-23 Manchester Square, London W1U 3PX, ☎ (020) 7486 8077; londres@tourspain.es; www. tourspain.co.uk

**New York:**
666 Fifth Avenue, New York, NY 10103, ☎ 212-265-8822; oetny@tourspain.es@tourspain.es; www.okspain.org

**Chicago:**
Water Tower Place, Suite 915 East, 845 North Michigan Avenue, Chicago, IL 60611, ☎ 312-642-1992; chicago@tourspain.es

**Los Angeles:**
8383 Wilshire Blvd, Suite 960, Beverly Hills, CA 90211, ☎ 323-658-7188; losangeles@tourspain.es

**Miami:**
1395 Brickell Avenue, Miami, FL 33131, ☎ 305-358-1992; miami@tourspain.es

**Toronto:**
2 Bloor St West, 34th Floor, Toronto, Ontario M4W 3E2, ☎ 416-961-3131; toronto@tourspain.es; www.tourspain.toronto.on.ca

### TOURIST INFORMATION CENTRES

**International Tourism Centre of Andalucía** (Centro Internacional de Turismo de Andalucía), Ctra. Nacional 340, km 189.6, 29600 Marbella (Málaga). ☎ 952 83 87 85,.

**Tourist Board of Andalucía** (Dirección General de Turismo de Andalucía), Av. República Argentina 25, 41011 Sevilla. ☎ 954 55 84, info@andalucia.org.

**Local Tourist offices** are indicated on maps and plans by the 🄑 symbol. Their addresses and telephone numbers are listed for each town and city in the *Discovering Andalucía* section.

**Tourist information hotline (in English):** ☎ 901 300 600 (Mon-Thu, 8.30am-7.30pm; Fri, 8.30am-2.30pm).

## International Visitors

### SPANISH EMBASSIES AND CONSULATES

**Spanish Embassy:**
39 Chesham Place, London SW1X 8SB, ☎ 0171 235 5555.

**Spanish Consulate:**
20 Draycott Place, London SW3 2RZ, ☎ 0171 589 8989; consulates also in Manchester and Edinburgh.

### Embassy of Spain:
2375 Pennsylvania Avenue NW, Washington DC 20007; ☎ (202) 452 0100; www.spainemb.org; consulates in Boston, Chicago, Houston, Los Angeles, Miami, New Orleans, New York and San Francisco.

## FOREIGN EMBASSIES AND CONSULATES

### American Embassy:
Serrano 75, 28006 Madrid, ☎ 91 587 2200; www.embusa.es
Consular agencies in Málaga (☎ 952 47 48 91) and Sevilla (☎ 954 23 18 85).

### Australian Embassy:
Plaza del Descubridor Diego de Ordás 3, 28003 Madrid, ☎ 91 441 60 25; www.embaustralia.es
Consulate in Sevilla (☎ 95 422 09 71).

### British Embassy:
Calle Fernando el Santo 16, 28010 Madrid, ☎ 91 700 82 00; www.ukinspain.com
Consular office in Málaga (☎ 952 35 23 00).

### Canadian Embassy:
Calle Núñez de Balboa 35, 28001 Madrid, ☎ 91 423 32 50; www.canada-es.org
Consulate in Málaga (☎ 952 22 33 46).

### Embassy of Ireland:
Ireland House, Paseo de la Castellana 46, 4°, 28046 Madrid, ☎ 91 436 4093; embajada@irlanda.es
Honorary Consulates in Málaga (☎ 952 47 51 08) and Sevilla (☎ 954 21 63 61).

## DOCUMENTS

Visitors must have a **passport** valid for their entire trip. British, Irish and US passport holders need no visa to stay less than 90 days. Others, and those planning to stay longer than 90 days, should enquire at a Spanish consulate. US citizens should view *Your Trip Abroad* online (travel.state.gov/travel/tips/brochures/brochures_1225.html) for general information on visas, customs regulations, etc.

Motorists usually need only a current driving licence from home and vehicle documentation and insurance to drive in Spain. In certain situations an International Driving Permit is required. Check with the AA or RAC (UK), the AAA (US) or CAA (Canada).

## CUSTOMS

UK residents may bring home goods on which taxes have been paid (Canary Islands excluded). Contact HM Customs and Excise, ☎ (0845) 010 9000; www.hmce.gov.uk. US citizens can obtain a pamphlet, **Know Before You Go**, from the US Customs Service, ☎ 202-354-1000; www.customs.gov
**Pets (cats and dogs)** – Carry a health certificate and proof of rabies vaccination from your vet.

## HEALTH

British citizens should apply for the European Health Insurance Card (www.ehic.org.uk or at a post office) to obtain free or low-cost treatment in the EU. All visitors should consider insurance for uncovered medical expenses, lost luggage, theft, etc.

# Accessibility

*Wheelchair access to sights in this guide is indicated by the ♿ symbol.*
**Turismo@Polibea** *(Ronda de la Alvutarda, 3, 28043 Madrid, ☎ 917 59 53 72, www.polibea.com/turismo)* provides information on facilities and activities for visitors with disabilities.
For information on facilities in Andalucía, contact the **Confederación Andaluza de Minusválidos Físicos**, Alfarería, 126 A, 41010 Sevilla, ☎ 954 33 60 36.
**Rompiendo Barreras Travel** (Roncesvalles, 3, 28007 Madrid, ☎ 915 52 84 07; fax 915 52 62 07, rbtravel@senda.ari.es), specialises in holidays for disabled travellers.

# GETTING THERE

## By Air

A number of Spanish and international airlines operate direct scheduled services to airports in Andalucía. These include:

### Iberia Airlines:

Iberia House, 10 Hammersmith Broadway, London, W6 7AL; ☎ 0870 609 0500; www.iberia.com; direct flights from London Heathrow to Sevilla, connections elsewhere.
Reservations within the US and Canada: ☎ 800-772-4642

### British Airways:

Waterside, PO Box 365, Harmondsworth, UB7 0GB, England; ☎ 0870 850 9850; www.ba.com; flights to Málaga, Sevilla and Gibraltar, some of which are operated by their franchise holder GB Airways. Reservations within the US and Canada: ☎ 1-800-772 4642.

A number of low-cost airlines also offer inexpensive flights to Andalusian cities from the UK. Some airlines only allow bookings to be made via the Internet, while others offer small discounts for Internet bookings:

### EasyJet:

☎ 0871 244 2366 charged per minute (90 229 99 92 in Spain); www.easyjet.com

### Bmibaby:

☎ 0871 224 0224 (34 902 10 07 37 in Spain); www.bmibaby.com

### MyTravel:

☎ 0870 241 5333; www.mytravel-lite.com

### Ryanair:

☎ 0871 246 0000; www.ryanair.com

Hundreds of weekly charter flights also operate to Andalusian cities, particularly Málaga and Almeria, from all over the UK.

## By Sea

Brittany Ferries and P&O Ferries both operate services to northern Spain.

**Brittany Ferries** run a ferry service between Plymouth and Santander (leaving Plymouth on Sundays and Wednesdays, returning from Santander on Mondays and Thursdays; journey time: 24hr). Motorists need to allow a further two days to reach Andalucía from northern Spain. For reservations contact:

### Brittany Ferries:

Millbay Docks, Plymouth PL1 3EW, Devon, England ☎ 08703 665 333; www.brittany-ferries.com
Estación Marítima, 39002 Santander, Spain ☎ 942 36 06 11.

**P&O Portsmouth** offer a twice-weekly crossing from Portsmouth to Bilbao (leaving Portsmouth on Tuesdays and Saturdays, returning from Bilbao on Mondays and Thursdays; journey time: 30hr). For reservations contact:

### P&O Portsmouth:

Peninsular House, Wharf Road, Portsmouth P02 8TA, England ☎ 08705 980 333; www.poportsmouth.com
Muelle Vizcaya, Espigón 3, Santurtzi 48980 (Bilbao), Spain ☎ 902 02 04 61.

## By Rail

### Eurostar

(☎ 08702 649 899; www.eurostar.com) operates high-speed passenger trains to Paris, from where overnight train-hotel services operate to Madrid, with connections to destinations across Andalucía. Services can be booked through the Spanish State Railway Network's (RENFE) UK agent, the **Spanish Rail Service**, ☎ 0207 224 0345; www.spanish-rail.co.uk Alternatively, visit www.renfe.es

## By Car 🚗

From the UK, an alternative to the cross-Channel ferry services is the **Channel Tunnel**.The high-speed undersea rail link ferries motorists and their cars through the tunnel (**Eurotunnel** – 35min) on specially designed double-decker carriages. The Calais terminal is linked to the French motorway network (the distance to Madrid by road is about 1 600km/just under 1 000mi, from where it is a farther 550km/344mi to either Sevilla or Málaga). For information, contact Eurotunnel, ☎ 08705 353 535; www.eurotunnel.com

Michelin is able to work out driving routes from 43 European countries to Spain on the Web site, www.ViaMichelin.com. Details listed include the total distance, journey time, and tourist sights of interest, as well as a selection of Michelin-recommended hotels, restaurants and campsites. Fees for using motorways along the route are also indicated.

## By Bus

Regular long-distance bus services operate from London to major towns and cities in Andalucía. For information, contact **Eurolines,** ☎ 08705 80 80 80; www.eurolines.co.uk

# GETTING AROUND

## Driving in Andalucía 🚗

The Andalusian road network has improved considerably in recent years. Today, the region has over 24 000km/15 000mi of motorways (*autopistas*), dual carriageways (*autovías*) and other roads of varying categories. The most important road in Andalucía is the A 92 dual carriageway which crosses southern Spain from east to west, connecting, either directly or via other *autovías*, every provincial capital in the region. ♿ Roads in Andalucía are being renumbered; some numbers may have changed by the time of your visit. Due to the excellent condition of roads in the region and, with the exception of some of the roads along the Mediterranean during the summer months, the relatively low volume of traffic, private car is the best means of transport for those with time to spare.

The maximum speed limits in Spain are as follows:
120kph/75mph on motorways and dual carriageways;
100kph/62mph on national roads;
90kph/56mph on minor roads;
50kph/31mph in built-up areas.

### ROAD INFORMATION

**The National Traffic Agency** (Dirección General de Tráfico) provides information in English on road conditions, driving itineraries, regulations etc. For further information telephone ☎ 900 12 35 05 (toll-free) or consult the agency's Web site at www.dgt.es

### MAPS AND PLANS

To help you plan your holiday and choose the most appropriate route, consult the ♿**Maps and plans** section at the back of the guide.

## ROADSIDE ASSISTANCE

**RACE** (Spanish Royal Automobile Club) ☎ 902 40 45 45 and 902 30 05 05 (roadside assistance); www.race.es

## PETROL/GAS

The cost of petrol – *normal* (92 octane), *super* (97 octane) and *sin plomo* (unleaded) – varies (€1.10 to €1.14 per litre approximately) according to the maximum price fixed by the government. This is also the case for *gasóleo* (diesel), which is considerably cheaper (around €0.85 per litre).

## RENTAL CARS

Vehicles in Andalucía can be reserved through the offices of all major car hire companies around the world. Alternatively, cars can be hired at major airports, train stations and large hotels around Andalucía:

- Avis ☎ 902 18 08 54; www.avis.es
- Europcar ☎ 913 43 45 12; www.europcar.es
- Hertz ☎ 915 09 73 00; www.hertz.es

Most companies will only rent out vehicles to drivers over the age of 21. A valid driving licence is required.

## By Train

The rail network is operated by **RENFE** (Spanish State Railways). Information is available 24hr a day; reservations are from 5.30am to 11.50pm; ☎ 902 24 02 02; www.renfe.es In general prices are inexpensive, with a number of discounts available:

- Travellers between 12 and 26 years old holding a Spanish or foreign **youth card (carnet joven)** receive a discount of 20-25%.
- The **Eurailpass**, available to visitors from abroad, offers unlimited use of the rail network and is priced in line with the number of days purchased (15, 25, 30, 60 or 90 days). The **Spain Rail Pass** provides unlimited travel for a set period. For information, contact www.raileurope.com or www.eurail.com

The **AVE** (*Alta Velocidad Española*) high-speed train links Madrid with Córdoba (1hr 45min) and Sevilla (2hr 15min). Speedy **Talgo** trains run from Madrid to Córdoba and Granada; the **Talgo 200**, running at speeds of 200km/125mi per hour, links Málaga and Córdoba with Madrid in a few hours. For information and reservations, call ☎ 902 24 02 02.

## GREEN STATIONS

Several "green stations" (*estaciones verdes*) have been designated, due to their proximity to the region's nature reserves, or because of their relevance for hikers, mountain-bikers or for nature-lovers wishing to discover the beauty of rural Andalucía. Information is available from railway stations in provincial capitals. Additional tourist information can be obtained at www.renfe.com/empresa/mundo/medio_ambiente

| Province | Green station | Line |
|---|---|---|
| Almería | Gádor | Linares-Almería |
| Cádiz | Jimena de la Frontera | Bobadilla-Algeciras |
| Córdoba | Aguilar de la Frontera | Córdoba-Málaga |
| Granada | Guadix | Linares-Almería |
| Huelva | San Juan del Puerto-Moguer | Sevilla-Huelva |
| Jaén | Andújar | Alcázar-Sevilla-Huelva |
| Málaga | Ronda | Bobadilla-Algeciras |
| Málaga | Fuente de Piedra | Córdoba-Málaga and Sevilla-Málaga |
| Sevilla | Cazalla-Constantina | Mérida-Sevilla |
| Sevilla | Lebrija | Sevilla-Cádiz |

## TOURIST TRAINS

### Train and visit to Isla Mágica

This package includes a return train ticket from various stations around Andalucía to Santa Justa station in Sevilla, plus entry to the Isla Mágica theme park. Discounts are available for children and those over age 65. Information can be obtained from any RENFE station in Andalucía.

### Al Andalus Express

This magnificent train, consisting of carriages from the 1920s and 1930s which have been refurbished to a luxurious standard, has every comfort the traveller could possibly imagine for this unforgettable journey through Andalucía. Facilities on board include two dining cars, a lounge and recreation car, a bar, five sleeping cars, two shower cars and one car for staff.

During the course of the one-week journey (departures from either Sevilla or Madrid), passengers visit Jerez de la Frontera, Carmona, Ronda, Antequera, Granada and Córdoba. Meals not eaten on board the train are taken in the region's very best hotels and restaurants.

The train operates from April to June and from September to November. Prices vary according to the date of travel, category of accommodation and the itinerary chosen, but range from about €24.40 to €41.20 per person.

For reservations and information, contact Al Andalus Expreso, Capitán Haya 55, 28020 Madrid, ☎ 917 88 83 15, www.alandalusexpreso.com.

## By Coach/Bus

Travelling by bus is an efficient and inexpensive way of getting around the region. A large number of bus companies operate services within Andalucía. The address and telephone numbers of bus stations and major bus companies are listed in the **Address Books** of major towns and cities in the *Discovering Andalucía* section of this guide.

## By Air

Contact numbers for airports:
Almería ☎ 950 21 37 00/950 21 37 01.
Córdoba ☎ 947 21 41 00.
Granada ☎ 958 24 52 00.
Jerez de la Frontera ☎ 956 15 00 83.
Málaga ☎ 952 04 84 84.
Sevilla ☎ 954 44 90 00.

### MAIN SPANISH AIRLINES:

**Iberia** ☎ 902 400 500 (information and reservations); www.iberia.com
**Air Europa** ☎ 902 401 501 (information and reservations); www.air-europa.com
**Spanair:** ☎ 902 13 14 15; www.spanair.com

## By Boat

Andalucía's main ports for commercial traffic are in Algeciras, Cádiz, Málaga and Almería. **Trasmediterránea** is the largest ferry company in the country, with a weekly service from Cádiz to the Canary Islands and daily crossings to Ceuta and Melilla from Almería, Málaga and Algeciras. ☎ 902 45 46 45 (information and reservations); www. trasmediterranea.es

### Port authorities:

Recinto del Puerto – 11201 Algeciras.
Parque Nicolás Salmerón, 19 – 04002 Almería.
Avenida Ramón Carranza, 26 – 11006 Cádiz.
Estación Marítima Recinto del Puerto. Local E1 – 29016 Málaga.

*A Trasmediterránea fast ferry in the port of Algeciras*

G. Bludzin/MICHELIN

# WHERE TO STAY AND EAT

Hotels and Restaurants are described in the Address Books which you will find throughout the **Discovering Andalucía** section of the guide. Within these Address Books we have listed a selection of hotels, restaurants and useful addresses that will enhance your stay and enable you to make the most of your holiday. A conscious effort has been made to cover all budgets, although some parts of the region, in particular the resorts along the Mediterranean, are more expensive than others. *For coin ranges, also see the Legend on the cover flap.*

## Where to Eat

The restaurants described in the Address Books have been chosen for their surroundings, ambience, typical dishes or unusual character. Prices specified correspond to the average cost of both an inexpensive and expensive meal, but are given as a guideline only. Restaurants are classified into three categories based on price: (*meals under €14*), (*between €14 and €25*), (*between €25 and €40*), and (*over €40*).

### A TYPICAL MEAL

Traditionally, a Spanish meal comprises a first course (*primero*) or appetiser (*entremeses*), such as a salad, soup or selection of cured meats; a main course (*segundo*), consisting of meat (*carne*) or fish (*pescado*); followed by a dessert (*postre*), usually fruit (*frutas*), a pastry (*pastel*) or ice cream (*helado*). Small local restaurants often offer an inexpensive menu *de la casa*, which normally includes reasonable quality house wine (*vino de la casa*).

### DRINKS

In restaurants, tap water (*agua del grifo*) will be provided in a carafe (*jarra*) if required, although most people tend to drink bottled **mineral water** (*agua mineral*), either sparkling (*con gas*) or still (*sin gas*). The excellent selection of Spanish wine (*vino*) usually on offer will include white (*blanco*), red (*tinto*) or rosé (*rosado*), available in carafes (*frasca*) as well as bottles (*botella*). **Beer** (*cerveza*) is available either draught (*caña*) or bottled; the main brands are San Miguel, Mahou, Águila and Damm. **Sangría** is normally served as an aperitif, accompanied by a selection of tapas. Visitors are often surprised by the large measures used in cocktails such as the popular **Cuba libre**, a mix of rum (*ron*) and Coke, usually served in a tall glass with lots of ice.

### TAPAS

Given the region's reputation for *tapas*, we have included a list of tapas bars where visitors can enjoy an aperitif or meal throughout the day and late into the evening. Prices of *tapas* and the larger *raciones* are often not listed, although as a general rule the cost of a tapas lunch or supper should be relatively inexpensive.

### TIPPING

Even if service is included, it is customary to leave an additional tip in bars, restaurants and hotels of up to 10 percent if you consider the service satisfactory. Passengers are also expected to leave a small tip for taxi-drivers.

### THE MICHELIN GUIDE

The **Michelin Guide España & Portugal** recommends a selection of restaurants that will allow you to discover and sample the best that Andalucía has to offer. Those restaurants recognised for the exceptional quality of their cuisine are highlighted by Michelin's renowned stars (one, two or three).

# Where to Stay

Address Books present a selection of hotels, *hostales* and *pensiones* divided into categories based on the price (excluding VAT) of a double room in high season, generally without breakfast unless otherwise indicated. The difference in rates between high and low season can be significant, particularly on the coast and islands, so it is always advisable to ask for confirmation of prices in writing at the time of booking. These recommendations have been chosen for their location, comfort, excellent value for money and in some cases for their charm. Prices for a double room in high season are denoted by the following symbols: ⊖ (*under €40*), ⊖⊖ (*between €40 and €65*), ⊖⊖⊜ (*between €65 and €100*), ⊖⊖⊜⊜ (*over €100*).

## HOTELS

The Spanish Tourist Board also publishes an accommodation guide, with hotels rated from one- to five-star. Hotel prices vary according to location and time of year — higher toward the coast and during the summer months. Many hotels can be booked online through www.andalucia.org (click *Organize Your Travel*).

## DISCOUNTED RATES

Many chains and hotels offer reduced rates at weekends. It is also possible to purchase vouchers for one or several nights at advantageous prices. For further information on these special offers, contact the following:
**NH Hoteles:** ☎ 902 11 51 16 (24hr) and www.nh-hoteles.com. Weekend rates with activities from €99 nightly per person, Sleep and Go rates for under-30s for €29 per person.
**Bancotel:** ☎ 915 09 61 22 and www.bancotel.com Booklets of five vouchers on sale exclusively at travel agencies and on its Web site. Three-, four- and five-star hotels with good discounts on standard rates.
**Halcón Viajes:** ☎ 807 22 72 22 and www.halconviajes.com Vouchers for discounted weekend hotel stays as well as Web specials.
**Hoteles Meliá:** ☎ 902 14 44 40 and www.solmelia.com Discounts via the MAS loyalty card and special weekend offers.

## PARADORS

Almost all of the state-run network of luxury hotels are in restored historic monuments (castles, palaces, monasteries etc) set in magnificent locations. The average price for a double room is generally between €100 and €150 (plus VAT). Out of season the network introduces special offers for guests, although this varies according to the location. In addition, with the "Tarjeta Amigos de Paradores" loyalty card, guests are able to accumulate points which can be exchanged for free stays. For more information, contact Paradores de Turismo, calle Requena, 3, 28013 Madrid ☎ (00 34) 902 54 79 79; www.parador.es The official UK representative is Keytel International, 402 Edgware Road, London W2 1ED, ☎ (020) 7616 0300; www.keytel.co.uk Special weekend **offers** are often available, in addition to a five-night "go as you please" **accommodation card**. *Paradors are indicated on Michelin maps by the symbol* ⌂

## RURAL ACCOMMODATION

The Andalusian Network of Rural Accommodation (**Red Andaluza de Alojamientos Rurales**) or RAAR, is a private owners' association offering a

B. Kaufmann/Paradores

*Parador, Castillo de Santa Catalina, Jaén*

choice of over 350 addresses to those interested in a holiday in the heart of the Andalusian countryside. The RAAR publishes a practical guide listing details of every type of accommodation available, including rooms in private houses, hostels for groups, entire houses for rent and farm campsites. Reservations can be made directly with the individual owners, through travel agents or via the RAAR reservations centre, ☎ 902 44 22 33 (Mon-Fri, 10am-2pm and 5-7pm); fax 950 27 16 78; www.raar.es and info@raar.es

The Association of Rural Hotels in Andalucía **(Asociación de Hoteles Rurales de Andalucía)** or AHRA, is a group of over 100 small **rural hotels** dotted around the region. The association operates a system of rural vouchers *(bonos rurales)* that can be bought for €33 each. Contact the AHRA reservations centre, ☎ 807 51 72 06; www.hvsl.es/Trural/Ahra.htm Some rural hotels may be booked through www.andalucia.org

## YOUTH HOSTELS (ALBERGUES JUVENILES)

The **Inturjoven** organisation, set up by the regional parliament (Junta de Andalucía), manages a large network of youth hostels and organises a wide range of sporting, cultural and tourist activities. The 20 youth hostels belonging to this association are located at strategic centres in cities, along the coast and in the mountains across Andalucía.

An individual or group hostelling card, obtainable from any hostel or from the Inturjoven reservations centre, is required to stay in any of the hostels within the network. Cards issued to members of the IYHF (International Youth Hostel Federation) are also accepted. Reservations can be made via phone, fax, e-mail or online: **Red de Albergues Juveniles de Andalucía**, Central de Reservas, Miño, 24, 41011 Sevilla; ☎ 902 51 00 00; www.inturjoven.com; informacionitj@ juntadeandalucia.es

## CAMPING AND CARAVANNING

The Junta de Andalucía *(⏻ see Books, below)* publishes a comprehensive camping and caravanning guide listing the facilities available at every accredited site in the region. Camping outside of authorised sites is permitted in some areas. Contact individual town halls for further information.

## THE MICHELIN GUIDE

The annually updated red-cover **Michelin Guide España & Portugal**, is an indispensable complement to this guide with hotel recommendations based on category, price, level of comfort, setting and facilities (such as swimming pool, tennis court, golf course, garden etc).

# WHAT TO DO AND SEE

## Outdoor Fun

Andalucía's diverse landscapes and excellent climate make it possible to enjoy outdoor sporting activities all year round.

### HIKING AND MOUNTAIN-BIKING

It is often said that if there's an abundance of anything in Andalucía, it is nature and sunshine. What is certain is that walkers and cyclists are spoiled for choice in one of Spain's best regions for these two pursuits. Details of over 200 walking itineraries and 120 cycling routes are listed in the following guides published by the Andalucía Tourist Board: *Bicycle; Rural Andalucía;* and *Hiking (& see Books: Travel).* Information can also be obtained on-line at www.andalucia.org

**Andalusian Cycling Federation** (Federación Andaluza de Ciclismo): Edificio La Compañía 4, 11403 Jerez de la Frontera (Cádiz), ☎ 956 34 88 12; fax 956 34 86 17, fac@andaluciaciclismo.com, www.andaluciaciclismo.com

### WATER SPORTS

From sailing to scuba-diving and water-skiing to windsurfing, Andalucía offers a whole range of sporting options for beginners and more experienced water sports enthusiasts alike.

**Andalusian Sailing Federation** (Federación Andaluza de Vela): Avenida de la Libertad, Puerto Sherry, 11500 El Puerto de Santa María (Cádiz), ☎ 956 85 48 13; fax 956 87 48 05, info@fav.es, www.fav.es

**Andalusian Water-Skiing Federation** (Federación Andaluza de Esquí Náutico): Calle Relator 73 A, 41003 Sevilla, ☎ 954 90 27 13.

### MARINAS

Andalucía's seafaring tradition spans the centuries. Today, there are over 30 marinas along the region's 836km/522mi of Atlantic and Mediterranean coastline, in addition to two river ports in Sevilla.

Many marinas have sailing, scuba-diving and windsurfing schools; some even have rowing and canoeing facilities.

Two guides published by the Junta de Andalucía – *Nautical Guide* and the *Pleasure Craft Harbours* brochure – list information on every port and marina in Andalucía, as well as the facilities available (& see Books: Travel).

An online marina directory may be viewed at www.puertosdeandalucia.com

### SCUBA-DIVING

In addition to the schools located at various marinas along the Andalusian coast, the region has six scuba-diving clubs for more experienced divers. It should be noted that the areas renowned for diving in the Atlantic and Mediterranean are very different. The waters of the Atlantic are relatively cold, visibility varies between 15m/50ft-20m/65ft and almost nothing. Dangerous currents make it advisable to dive with a local instructor. By contrast, the Mediterranean is characterised by warmer

*Hiking in the Alpujarras*

B. Kaufmann/MICHELIN

temperatures, good visibility and more tranquil sea conditions. Further information can be obtained from the **Andalusian Scuba-Diving Federation** (Federación Andaluza de Actividades Subacuáticas): Playa de las Almadrabillas 10, 04007 Almería, ☎ 950 27 06 12; fax 950 27 62 99; www.faasub.com

## RIVER FISHING

Jaén and Granada are the two most popular provinces for fishing in Andalucía. Rivers and lakes teem with trout and, in some areas, carp and crayfish. In general, the season starts on 15 March and ends on 15 August, although some areas are open all year. Fishing enthusiasts must be in possession of a relevant fishing licence. For further information, contact the **Andalusian Sport Fishing Federation** (Federación Andaluza de Pesca Deportiva): Calle León Felipe 2 - bajo (Apartado 157 04080), 04007 Almería, ☎ 950 15 17 46; fax 950 25 74 86; www.fapd.org

## HORSEBACK RIDING

The horse has long been a part of Andalusian culture. This tradition continues today throughout the region, perhaps most visibly during the pilgrimage to El Rocío, at the "mares' auction" *(saca de las yeguas)* held on 26 June every year in the Parque Natural de Doñana, the rounding-up of the bulls contests in Villamanrique and

*La Duquesa (Costa del Sol)*

B. Kaufmann/MICHELIN

Sevilla (April), and the horse races on the sands of Sanlúcar de Barrameda. Mention should also be made of the mule- and horse-drawn carriage exhibitions in Andalucía's main bullrings as part of the region's annual fair.

Major international **competitions** in Andalucía include the Trofeo del Sol show-jumping competition, organised over the winter in a number of locations along the Costa del Sol, and the polo tournaments in Sotogrande (Cádiz), played during July and August.

The annual Jerez Horse Fair *(Feria del Caballo de Jerez)* held in May, and the SICAB, an international show in Sevilla every November, are the two most important events in the Andalusian equine calendar. The Royal Andalusian School of Equestrian Art, also in Jerez, has weekly shows featuring its magnificent Cartujana horses.

For those who prefer participating to spectating, Andalucía offers excellent options, including cross-country **treks** lasting several days and stays on horse farms, in country houses and rural hotels; as well as courses on breaking in horses and equestrian techniques. The *Horse* brochure *( see Books: Travel)*, available from tourist offices and the organisations below, provides further information on horse riding in the region.

**Andalusian Equestrian Federation** (Federación Hípica Andaluza): O'Donnell 16-3°, 41001 Sevilla, ☎ 954 56 16 33; fax 954 56 16 33, www.federacionhipicaandaluza.com **Association of Andalusian Equestrian and Rural Tourism Companies** (Asociación de Empresas de Turismo Ecuestre y Rural de Andalucía): Isla de la Cartuja, 41092 Sevilla, ☎ 954 48 89 00; fax 954 48 89 11.

## HUNTING

The hills and mountains of Andalucía offer rich pickings for hunters. Very few parts of Europe are home to such a variety of large game, including wild boar (Doñana), mountain goat (Cazorla, Sierra Nevada, Ronda), deer (Serranía de Cádiz) and mouflon, the latter raised in enclosures. Smaller game is also hunted, such as hare (traditionally on horseback accompanied by hunting dogs), quail and partridge. Further information is contained in the *Hunting* brochure (*see Books: Travel*), available from regional offices (*delegaciones provinciales*) of the Ministry of Agriculture and Fisheries (*Consejería de Agricultura y Pesca*) and from provincial hunting federations (*federaciones provinciales de caza*).

**Andalusian Hunting Federation** (Federación Andaluza de Caza): Los Morenos, 29300 Archidona (Málaga), ☎ 95 271 48 71/65; fac@fac.es, www.fac.es

## GOLF

Golfers are attracted to Andalucía in the tens of thousands by the superb golfing conditions and the high quality of the 60 courses scattered around the region. The majority are along the Costa del Sol – one of which, Valderrama, hosted the 1997 Ryder Cup – although excellent courses can also be found close to the cities of Sevilla, Huelva, Cádiz, Granada and Almería. Details on the specific aspects of each course are listed in the *Golf* brochure (*see Books: Travel*) published by the Andalusian Tourist Board.

**Andalusian Golf Federation** (Federación Andaluza de Golf): Sierra de Grazalema, 33 – 5, 1ºB, 29016 Málaga, ☎ 952 22 55 90; fax 952 22 03 87; www.fga.org

*Stunning scenery for a round of golf*

G. Bludzin/MICHELIN

## WINTER SPORTS

The Sierra Nevada ski resort, one of the most popular in Spain, is easily accessible by car (just 30min from Granada along Europe's highest road), bus (local services and a daily Madrid-Sierra Nevada service), train (the nearest railway station is just 33km/21mi away) and plane (Granada, Málaga and Sevilla airports). Sierra Nevada has 84km/43.7mi of marked runs and all the facilities expected of a major ski resort. Information on skiing in the Sierra Nevada is available from the resort operator, **Cetursa,** Plaza de Andalucía, 18196 Sierra Nevada, Monachil, Granada, ☎ 902 70 80 90; fax 958 24 91 46; agencia@cetursa.es; www.cetursa.es

**Andalusian Winter Sports Federation** (Federación Andaluza de Deportes de Invierno): Avenida de la Constitución, 27- 1˚ A, 18014 Granada, ☎ 958 13 57 48; fax 958 13 57 49, fadi@serinves.es, www.fadiandalucia.com

# Spas

The region's spa resorts offer rest and relaxation, cultural activities and health treatments in beautiful natural surroundings. Four are located in the province of Granada, two in Málaga and Almería, and one in and Jaén and Cádiz. In addition, five "Curhoteles" (four in Málaga province and one in Almería) offer a high level of comfort and provide guests with the very latest techniques in health treatment. For further details, contact the **Andalusian Spa Association** (Asociación de Balnearios de Andalucía), Avenida Mariana Pineda 16, 18500 Guadix (Granada) ☎ 958 69 40 22, info@balneariosdeandalucia.com, www.balneariosdeandalucia.com. Additional information can be found in the *Guide to Spas and Spa Hotels* (*see Books: Travel*) or on-line at www.andalucia.org or www.balnearios.org

**Balneario San Nicolas**, Alhama de Almería, Almeria, ☎950 64 13 61,

www.grupoalessa.com/nextel/bal-
nearios/andalucia/sannicolas.htm
**Balneario Sierra Alhamilla**, Almeria,
☏ 950 31 74 13
**Balneario Alicun de las Torres**, Gra-
nada, ☏ 958 69 40 22, www.arrakis.
es/~alicun/
**Balneario Alhama de Granada**,
Granada, ☏ 958 35 00 11, www.bal-
nearioalhamadegranada.com/
**Balneario Graena**, Granada, ☏ 958
67 06 81, www.balneario-graena.com/
**Balneario Lanjarón**, Granada, ☏ 958
77 01 37, www.aguasdelanjaron.es/
**Balneario San Andrés**, Jaen, ☏ 953
77 00 62, www.balneariosanandres.
com/
**Balneario Carratraca**, Carratraca,
Malaga, ☏ 952 45 80 71
**Balneario Fuente Amarga**, Tolox,
Malaga, ☏ 952 48 70 91
**Balneario Fuente Amarga**, Chiclana,
Cadiz, ☏ 956 40 05 20

# Activities for Children

Sights of particular interest to children
are indicated in this guide with a
Kids symbol. Some attractions offer
discounted fees for children. Leisure
facilities for children are available
close to major towns, along the Costa
del Sol and even in national parks and
nature reserves. Families in particular
will enjoy spending a few hours at the
many water parks, zoos, fun-fairs and
botanical gardens scattered across the
region. The following three attractions are some of the most popular in
Andalucía:
**Isla Mágica theme park**, in Sevilla.
**Interactive Science Museum**, in
Granada.
**Oasys theme park**, near Almería: this
desert theme park, including the Mini-
Hollywood film sets where a number
of the most famous spaghetti westerns have been filmed, is a must for
families visiting this part of Andalucía.
Further information on activities for
children can be obtained from tourist
offices and in publications such as the
free weekly English newspaper, **Sur in
English**.

# Calendar of Events

Practically every day something is
celebrated or commemorated somewhere in Andalucía.
The list below includes some of the
more well-known events, although
exact dates should be checked with
the appropriate tourist office.

## JANUARY

Jan 2: **Commemoration of the
capture of Granada** Granada

## FEBRUARY/MARCH

Feb 2: **Candlemass processions** In
many towns and cities
Week prior to Ash Wednesday
(between 5 February and 4 March):
**Carnival** Cádiz and elsewhere in
Cádiz province; Isla Cristina and
Ayamonte (Huelva)

## HOLY WEEK

**Processions** throughout Andalucía,
particularly in Sevilla, Málaga,
Córdoba and Granada

## APRIL (AFTER HOLY WEEK)

**Fair** Sevilla
Last Sunday in April: **Virgen de la
Cabeza pilgrimage** Andújar
(Jaén)

## MAY

First fortnight in May: **International
Theatre Festival** Granada
7-11 May: **Spring and Fino Sherry
Fair** El Puerto de Santa María
10-17 May: **Horse Fair** Jerez
19-24 May: **Manzanilla Fair** Sanlúcar
de Barrameda (Cádiz)
Throughout May: **May Crosses, Patio
Competition, Annual Fair.
National Flamenco Contest**
(held every three years) Córdoba

## WHITSUN (MAY OR JUNE)

**El Rocío pilgrimage** Almonte
(Huelva)

CARRERAS DE CABALLOS

H. Champollion/MICHELIN

*Horse racing poster, Sanlúcar de Barrameda*

### JUNE-JULY

Corpus Christi: **Processions, Flamenco Festival (the oldest in Spain)** Granada

June-July: **International Music and Dance Festival** Granada

16 July (Virgen del Carmen): **Seafaring processions** Several towns and villages along the Mediterranean, particularly Almería

22-27 July: **Nerja Caves Festival** Nerja (Málaga)

Third week in July: **Festivities commemorating the Battle of Bailén** Bailén (Jaén)

### JULY-AUGUST

**Columbus Festival** Huelva

### AUGUST

**Horse races on the beach** Sanlúcar de Barrameda

**International Music and Dance Festival** Priego de Córdoba (Córdoba)

13-21 Aug: **August Fair** Málaga

22-31 Aug: **Virgin del Mar Festival** Almería

Penultimate Sunday in August: **Moors and Christians Festival** Bubión (Granada)

### SEPTEMBER/OCTOBER

4-8 Sept: **Nuestra Señora de Regla Fair** Chipiona (Cádiz)

First Sunday in September: **Wine Harvest Festival** Montilla (Córdoba)

8 Sept: **Virgen de Setefilla pilgrimage** Lora del Río (Sevilla)

First week in September: **Goya bullfights, Flamenco Singing Festival** Ronda (Málaga)

Second fortnight in September and first fortnight in October: **Autumn Festivals (Wine Harvest and Horse Week)** Jerez (Cádiz)

### OCTOBER

**St Luke's Fair** Jaén

### DECEMBER

28 Dec: **Los Verdiales Festival** Málaga

# Shopping

Andalucía's handicrafts cover a wide range. Although many vary considerably from area to area, particularly pottery and ceramics, a lot of the region's traditions are common to most provinces. Over the past few years, strenuous efforts have been made to rediscover old techniques and decorative motifs that have been in danger of disappearing; sadly, however, some aspects of ornamental art, such as decorative work on silk – a common feature during Moorish times – have been lost forever.

## POTTERY AND CERAMICS

Andalucía's pottery and ceramics industries produce an almost unlimited choice, ranging from items of everyday use (pitchers, jars and bowls) to those used for decorative purposes only, such as the high-quality Pickman-La Cartuja de Sevilla porcelain, with its delightful grey, pink and green decorative motifs.

The kilns used in the Almerian villages of Albox, Níjar and Sorbas are almost identical to those used in times past; the province of Granada retains many of its 19C wood-fuelled kilns; while the potters' wheels in Guadix remain as active as ever.

The numerous workshops in the Triana district of Sevilla still produce their traditional blue, yellow, orange and purple pottery and ceramics, while the village of Sanlúcar la Mayor to the west specialises in the reproduction of lustre ceramics with Hispano-Moorish designs.

Jaén is renowned for the blue and white ceramics of Andújar. Not to be outdone, the province of Córdoba has made its name with Caliphal ceramics decorated with geometric, plant and animal motifs.

## WOODWORK

The manufacture of furniture has become a feature of Andalusian industry, establishing itself alongside sculptural art with a tradition dating back several centuries and whose work is inspired by the creations of sculptors such as Martínez Montañés and Pedro Roldán.

In the 19C, following the arrival of a number of English wine and sherry producers, the coopers of Sanlúcar de Barrameda and San Fernando near the city of Cádiz, who had hitherto concentrated on barrelmaking, found it easy to develop their work to English tastes and create a range of high-quality mahogany furniture. Further to the east, the town of Ronda has made a name for the production of a more rustic style of furniture.

H. Champollion/MICHELIN

*A shop that sells carpets*

Granada is famous for its inlaid (marquetry with inlaid bone, mother-of-pearl, amber or marble) and gilded work. Over the course of time, some villages within the province have also developed an excellent reputation for furniture produced in the Mudéjar (Capileira) and Renaissance styles (Baza).

So-called "Sevilla chairs", with their bright colours and flower motifs, are manufactured in several towns and villages in the province of Huelva, including Valverde, Galorza and Zalamea.

## LEATHER GOODS

Because of the huge importance of horses to the region's economy, a large equestrian equipment industry has developed in Andalucía which produces saddles, riding breeches, leather pouches and other items used for horse riding and hunting. The leading leather centres are found in Jerez de la Frontera, Alcalá de los Gazules and Villamartín (Cádiz); Almodóvar del Río (Córdoba) and various towns and villages in Huelva, particularly Almonte and Zalamea la Real.

Ubrique and Prado del Rey (Cádiz) have developed into capitals of leather fashion accessories. A number of workshops produce a range of bags, belts and gloves for leading companies around the world.

Shoes are also important to the local economy, as seen in Valverde del Camino (boots) and Montoro (hand-made shoes).

This list is not complete, however, without mentioning the magnificent cordovans (embossed leather) with their traditional and modern decoration produced, as the name would suggest, in the workshops of Córdoba.

## IRON AND METALWORK

In many areas, iron is still worked by traditional methods, using the forge and anvil to produce grilles, fences and staircases. The towns of Arcos de la Frontera (Cádiz) and Torredon-jimeno (Jáen) are both reputed for this type of metalwork. Some smaller towns in the province of Málaga, such as Arroyo de la Miel, Cártama and Estepona all specialise in the production of artistic locks.

Also worthy of mention are imaginative tin and glass lamps from Úbeda, the unusual cowbells made in Cortegana (Huelva), and attractive carriages from Bollulos del Condado with their combination of iron and woodwork.

# Sightseeing

## OPENING TIMES AND FEES

Opening times (🕒) and entrance fees (👛) for monuments, museums, churches, etc. are listed in the **Discovering Andalucía** section of this guide. This information is given as a guideline only, as times and prices are liable to change without prior warning.

Prices are listed for individual visitors and do not take into account discounts for groups, who may also benefit from private visits. As many monuments require frequent maintenance and restoration, it is always advisable to phone ahead to avoid disappointment.

Information for churches is only given if the interior contains a sight of particular interest, including specific opening times or if an entrance fee is payable. In general, religious buildings should not be visited during services, although some only open for mass, in which case visitors should show appropriate respect.

## WORLD HERITAGE SITES

Andalucía holds several UNESCO World Heritage Sites including:
The **Historic Center of Córdoba**
The **Alhambra, Generalife** and **Albayzín** in Granada
The **Catedral, Alcázar** and **Archive of the Indies** in Sevilla
**Parque Nacional de Doñana**
The Renaissance cities of **Úbeda** and **Baeza**

## THE COASTS

Andalucía has the geographical advantage of bordering both the Atlantic and the Mediterranean. This setting, coupled with the 25 protected areas along its two coasts, ensures a diversity of landscape and beaches unique in Spain.

### Atlantic coast

This coastline, which is also known as the **Costa de la Luz** (Coast of Light), extends from the Portuguese border to the Straits of Gibraltar, a total length of 330km/206mi, in the provinces of Huelva and Cádiz. In general, its beaches are popular with Spanish visitors, particularly families. Days are hot, the evenings cooled by ocean breezes, and the sea temperature cooler than that of the Mediterranean. The 15 beaches in **Huelva** province are characterised by golden sand, clear water, surf, sand dunes and pine forests. A number of resorts, such as **Isla Canela**, have excellent sporting and sailing facilities, while other wild and isolated stretches of coast are only accessible on foot from the larger resorts. Some of the Atlantic coast's best-known beaches include **Isla Cristina**, with a long fishing tradition; **La Antilla**, a 22km/14mi stretch close to Lepe; **El Rompido**, with its enormous dunes and pine forests offering superb views; **Punta Umbría**, famous for its marina; **Mazagón**, with its steep cliffs; and the renowned **Matalascañas**, bordering El Rocío and the Parque Nacional de Doñana.

The **Cádiz coast**, the most southerly in Spain, stretches 200km/125mi. Its beaches of fine, golden sand are lined by some of Spain's most historic towns and cities such as Sanlúcar de Barrameda, Rota, El Puerto de Santa María and Cádiz, so visitors can combine time on the beach with cultural visits to these fascinating places. To the south of the beach at **Bajo de Guía**, where horse races are held in summer, the resort of **Chipiona** has four beaches which have been popular for many years. El Puerto de Santa María, within the boundaries of

*San José, Cabo de Gata*

H. Champollion/MICHELIN

which lies the glitzy **Puerto Sherry** marina, has some excellent beaches of its own, such as **La Puntilla** and **Valdelagrana**, while those close to Cádiz (**La Victoria**, **La Caleta** and **Cortadura**) are thronged during the summer months with inhabitants of the city. Also worthy of mention are the recently created tourist complex of **Sancti Petri**, and the series of delightful beaches near Conil (**Caños de Meca**, **Zahara de los Atunes** and **Bolonia**) which have thus far escaped the blight of mass tourism. The only drawback for sun-worshippers on this coast is the strong wind, a feature of the local climate that attracts thousands of windsurfers every year.

## Mediterranean coast

This coastline includes areas with differing geographical characteristics, but all have a similar hot and dry climate. The waters of the Mediterranean are generally calm, warm and crystal clear.

**Costa del Sol** – The section of the Sun Coast in the province of Málaga is the leading tourist destination in Andalucía (🕭 *see Costa del Sol*). The western section, from Gibraltar to the city of Málaga, contains over 50% of all hotel accommodation along the Andalusian coasts. Paradoxically, the majority of the beaches here are pebbly. Tourist development is less pronounced along the eastern stretch, in an area also known as La Axarquía (🕭 *see La Axarquía*), where accom-

modation tends to be more apartment-based. Major resorts along this coastline, with its small beaches and numerous cliffs, are **El Rincón de la Victoria**, **Nerja** and **Torre del Mar**.

**Costa Tropical** – The shores of Granada province are known as the Tropical Coast; the sub-tropical climate results from the protection afforded by the Sierra Nevada. The beaches along this stretch range from coves protected by high cliffs to enormous beaches such as those in **Almuñécar**. Tourism is concentrated in Almuñécar; Salobreña, with its two large beaches; the more developed **Playa del Peñón** and the wilder **Playa de La Guardia**; in Motril (**Playa de Poniente** and **Playa de Granada**); and in Castell de Ferro and La Rábita.

**Costa de Almería** – The Almeria Coast represents a quarter of the entire Andalusian coastline. Most development here is between Adra – including the immense sandy beaches of **Balanegra** and **Balerma** and the resort of **Almerimar** – and Aguadulce. The onward stretch from Aguadulce to Almería comprises an impressive series of steep cliffs. To the east of the provincial capital, the Mediterranean is bordered by the Parque Natural de Cabo de Gata, with its superb beaches, such as **Morrón de los Genoveses**, and the attractive small resort of **San José**.

## NATIONAL AND NATURAL PARKS

Over the past few decades, the regional government *(Junta de Andalucía)* has increased its efforts to protect the natural environment. Today, Andalucía has two national parks, 20 nature parks and a number of protected areas covering 18 percent of the region's area.

For further information contact the **Andalusian Environment Council** (Consejería de Medio Ambiente – Junta de Andalucía), Avenida Manuel Siurot, 50, 41071 Sevilla, ☎ 955 00 34 00/35 00; fax 955 00 37 75; www. juntadeandalucia.es/medioambiente Those interested in environmental

| | Provinces | Ha/acres | ☎ Information |
|---|---|---|---|
| **National parks** | | | |
| Doñana | Huelva-Sevilla-Cádiz | 50 720/124 217 | 959 44 23 40 |
| Sierra Nevada | Granada-Almería | 86 208/213 020 | 950 51 35 48 |
| **Natural Parks** | | | |
| Cabo de Gata-Níjar | Almería | 33 663/83 181 | 950 38 97 42 |
| Sierra María-Los Vélez | Almería | 22 500/55 597 | 950 52 70 05 |
| La Breña y Marismas de Barbate | Cádiz | 3 797/9 382 | 956 59 09 71 |
| Bahía de Cádiz | Cádiz | 10 000/24 710 | 956 59 02 43 |
| Los Alcornocales | Cádiz-Málaga | 170 025/420 132 | 956 41 33 07 |
| Sierra de Grazalema | Cádiz-Málaga | 51 695/127 738 | 956 71 60 63 |
| Sierra de Cardeña y Montoro | Córdoba | 41 245/101 916 | 957 45 32 11 |
| Sierra de Hornachuelos | Córdoba | 67 202/166 056 | 957 45 32 11 |
| Sierras Subbéticas | Córdoba | 31 568/78 004 | 957 33 40 64 |
| Sierra de Baza | Granada | 52 337/129 324 | 958 86 10 13 |
| Sierra de Castril | Granada | 12 265/30 307 | 958 53 76 00 |
| Sierra de Huétor | Granada | 12 428/30 710 | 958 54 04 26 |
| Sierra de Aracena et Picos de Aroche | Huelva | 184 000/454 664 | 959 12 84 75 |
| Despeñaperros | Jaén | 6 000/14 826 | 953 12 50 18 |
| Sierras de Andújar | Jaén | 60 800/150 236 | 953 50 02 79 |
| Sierras de Cazorla, Segura y Las Villas | Jaén | 214 336/529 624 | 953 71 30 40 |
| Sierra Mágina | Jaén | 19 900/49 172 | 953 78 76 56 |
| Montes de Málaga | Málaga | 4 762/11 766 | 952 04 11 69 |
| Sierra de las Nieves | Málaga | 16 564/40 930 | 952 87 77 78 |
| Sierras de Tejeda y Almijara | Málaga-Granada | 40 600/100 323 | 952 04 11 48 |
| Sierra Norte de Sevilla | Sevilla | 164 840/407 320 | 955 95 20 49 |

issues may consult the council's library or contact it at ☎ 955 00 38 04; biblioteca@cma.juntadeandalucia.es

# Discounts

## DISCOUNTS FOR YOUNG PEOPLE

For information in Andalucía, contact the **Instituto de la Juventud**: calle Muñoz Olivé 1, 3°, 41001 Sevilla, ☎ 955 03 50 00; fax 955 03 50 41. The **EURO<26 Card**, issued in 39 countries, entitles young people between ages 14 and 25 to a series of discounts on travel, cultural events, and accommodation. In Spain, some 50 000 outlets participate in the pro-

gram. For details, and to obtain a card in Andalucía, search for "*carnet joven*" on www.andaluciajunta.es
The **Student Card**, available to those aged 12 and over, also provides numerous discounts.

## DISCOUNTS FOR SENIOR CITIZENS

Persons aged 65 and over qualify for significant discounts on transport, entrance fees to monuments, and events and shows. Many museums offer half-price entry, with free entrance to a number of national monuments. RENFE (Spanish State Railways) also offers reductions for passengers aged 60 and over who hold a senior citizen card.

# Books

## HISTORY

**A Concise History of the Spanish Civil War** by Paul Preston *(Fontana 1996)*

**Imperial Spain 1469-1716** by JH Elliott *(Penguin Books 1990)*

**Infidels: The Conflict between Christendon and Islam 638-2002** by Andrew Wheatcroft *(Viking 2003)*

**Moorish Spain** by Richard Fletcher *(Phoenix Press 1994)*

**Spain 1516-1598** by John Lynch *(Blackwell Publishers 1994)*

**The Arab Conquest of Spain 710-797** by Roger Collins *(Blackwell Publishers 1994)*

**The Inquisition** by Michael Baigent & Richard Leigh *(Viking 1999)*

**The Hispanic World in Crisis and Change, 1598-1700** (A History of Spain) by John Lynch *(Blackwell Publishers 1994)*

**The Sephardim** by Lucien Gubbay and Abraham Levy *(Carnell Ltd 1992)*

**The Spanish Civil War** by Alun Kenwood (Ed) *(Berg Publishers 1993)*

**The Spanish Inquisition** by Cecil Roth *(WW Norton 1964)*

**The Spanish Labyrinth** by Gerald Brenan *(Cambridge University Press 1990)*

**The Spanish Seaborne Empire** by JH Parry *(University of California Press 1990)*

## TRAVEL

**A Parrot in a Pepper Tree** by Chris Stewart *(Penguin Books 2002)*

**A Rose for Winter** by Laurie Lee *(Penguin Books 1971)*

**Driving Over Lemons: an Optimist in Andalucia** by Chris Stewart *(Penguin Books 1999)*

**Duende: A Journey into the heart of flamenco** by Jason Webster *(Broadway Books 2003)*

**Wines of Spain** by Jan Read *(Mitchell Beazley 1997)*

**On the Shores of the Mediterranean** by Eric Newby *(Picador 1985)*

**South from Granada** by Gerald Brenan *(Penguin Books 1992)*

**Spain** by Jan Morris *(Penguin 1986)*

**Tales of the Alhambra** by Washington Irving *(Everest de Ediciones y Distribucion, S.L. 1995)*

**Tapas & More Great Dishes from Spain** by Janet Mendel *(Santana Books 1997)*

**The Face of Spain** by Gerald Brenan *(Penguin Books 1987)*

**The Factory of Light: Life in an Andalucian Village** by Michael Jacobs *(John Murray 2003)*

**The Houses and Palaces of Andalusia** by Monteros, Venturi *(Cartago 1998)*

**The Pillars of Hercules** by Paul Theroux *(Penguin Books 1996)*

## POETRY

**Gypsy Ballads** – Federico García Lorca *(Aris & Phillips 1990)*

**Lorca: a Dream of Life** by Leslie Stainton *(Bloomsbury 1999)*

**Selected Poems as Trueblood** by Antonio Machado *(Harvard University Press 1988)*

**Selected Poems of Luis Cernuda** by Luis Cernuda, Reginald Gibbons (Ed) *(Sheep Meadow Press 2000)*

## THEATRE AND OPERA

**Blood Wedding** by Federico García Lorca, David Johnston (Trans) *(Hodder & Stoughton Educational 1989)*

**"Carmen" and Other Stories** by Prosper Merimée, Nicholas Jotcham (Trans) *(Oxford Paperbacks 1998)*

**The House of Bernarda Alba** by Federico García Lorca, Rona Munro (Ed) *(Nick Hern Books 1999)*

**The Three-cornered Hat** by Pedro Antonio de Alarcon, Alexander Tulloch (Ed) *(Everyman Paperbacks 1995)*

**The Barber of Seville & The Marriage of Figaro** by Beaumarchais, John Wood (Trans) *(Penguin Books 1972)*

## TRADITIONS AND CUSTOMS

**Flamenco: Gypsy Dance and Music from Andalusia** by Claus Schreiner (Ed), Mollie Comerford Peters (Trans) *(Amadeus Press 1990)*

# BASIC INFORMATION

## Business Hours

### OPENING HOURS

Shops are open mornings to 2pm; after lunch and *siesta,* they are open 5-8pm or 8.30pm. Larger stores do not close for lunch. Most shops close on Sundays, a few on Saturday afternoon. Dinner is served after 9pm. Andalusians stay up late to make the most of cooler temperatures.

### BANKS

Banks are generally open 8.30am-2pm, Monday to Saturday and close on Saturdays in summer.

### POST

Post offices are open 8.30am-2.30pm, Monday to Friday, 9.30am-2pm on Saturdays. Stamps *(sellos)* can also be purchased at tobacconists *(estancos)*. The **Michelin Guide España & Portugal** gives the postcode for every town and city in Andalucía.

## Electricity

220 volts AC (110V in some older establishments). Plugs are two-pin.

## Emergencies

**Emergency services**:
✚ ☎ 112 or 902 50 50 61.

## Money

The currency in Spain is the **euro** (€). In September 2006, the exchange rate was €1.46 to the pound, €0.78 to the US dollar. There are no restrictions on taking currency into or out of Spain. **Exchange travellers' cheques** or cash at banks and exchange offices *(cambios)*; or obtain euros from bank machines using credit or debit cards.

Major **credit cards** are accepted in most shops, hotels and restaurants. In the event of a **lost or stolen credit card**, contact the issuer as soon as possible: **Visa/Mastercard**: ☎ 91 362 62 00; **American Express** ☎ 91 572 03 03; **Eurocard** ☎ 91 519 60 00; **Diners Club** ☎ 91 547 40 00.

## Newspapers and Television

English newspapers are widely available on publication day, some in European editions. Sky News, CNN and Eurosport TV channels are available in better hotels.

## Public Holidays

Towns and cities have their own festivals and feast days. The following are national public holidays:

- 1 January (New Year's Day)
- 6 January (Epiphany)
- Holy Thursday
- Good Friday
- 1 May (Labour Day)
- 15 August (Assumption of Our Lady)
- 12 October (Virgin of the Pillar: Hispanic Day)
- 1 November (All Saints)
- 6 December (Spanish Constitution Day)
- 8 December (Immaculate Conception)
- 25 December (Christmas Day).

## Telephone

**Directory enquiries**: ☎ 1003. **International enquiries**: ☎ 025. Public telephones accept coins or phonecards *(tarjetas telefónicas)*, sold at tobacconists and post offices. For For **international calls** dial 00 plus the following country codes:

- 61 for Australia
- 44 for the UK

- ◆ 1 for Canada
- ◆ 64 for New Zealand
- ◆ 1 for the USA

For **calls within Spain**, dial the full 9-digit number; **from abroad**, dial the international access code, then 34 for Spain, then the full 9-digit number.

## Time

Andalucía is 1hr ahead of GMT. The Andalusians keep very different hours from either the British or North Americans. As a general rule, restaurants serve lunch from 1:30pm to 3:30pm and dinner from 9pm to 11pm.

# USEFUL WORDS & PHRASES

For vocabulary relating to hotels and restaurants, please refer to the **Michelin Guide España & Portugal**.

| Common Words | | Time | |
|---|---|---|---|
| yes, no | **Sí, no** | when? | **¿cuándo?** |
| good morning | **Buenos dias** | at what time? | **¿a qué hora?** |
| good afternoon | **Buenas tardes** | today | **hoy** |
| goodbye | **Hasta luego, adiós** | yesterday | **ayer** |
| please | **Por favor** | tomorrow morning | **manãna por la manãna** |
| how are you? | **¿qué tal?** | tomorrow afternoon | **manãna por la tarde** |

| On the road, in town | | Correspondence | |
|---|---|---|---|
| car | **coche** | post box, letter box | **buzón** |
| petrol, gasoline | **gasolina** | post office | **correos** |
| on the right | **a la derecha** | telephone | **telégrafos, teléfonos** |
| on the left | **a la izquierda** | letter | **carta** |
| road works | **obras** | post card | **(tarjeta) postal** |
| dangerous | **peligroso** | post office box | **apartado (de correos)** |
| beware, take care | **cuidado** | stamp | **sello** |
| to go round, tour | **dar la vuelta a...** | telephone call | **conferencia, llamada** |
| after, beyond | **después de...** | tobacco shop | **estanco** |
| to go round, to circle | **girar** | | |

| Shopping | | | |
|---|---|---|---|
| thank you (very much) | **(muchas) gracias** | how much? | **¿cuánto (vale)?** |
| excuse me | **Perdone** | (too) expensive | **(demasiado) caro** |
| i don't understand | **No entiendo** | a lot, little | **mucho, poco** |
| sir/mr, you | **Señor, usted** | more, less | **más, menos** |
| madam, mrs | **Señora** | big, small | **grande, pequeño** |
| miss | **Señorita** | credit card | **tarjeta de crédito** |

| Places and things to see | | | |
|---|---|---|---|
| **bodega** | wine cellar/store | **puerta** | door, gate, entrance |
| **calle** | street | **puerto** | pass, harbour, port |
| **campanario** | belfry | **romano, románico** | Roman; Romanesque |
| **capilla** | chapel | **talla** | carrved wood |
| **carretera** | main road | **tapiz** | tapestry |
| **casa consistorial** | town hall | **techo** | ceiling |
| **castillo** | castle | **tesoro** | treasury, treasure |
| **castro** | Celtic village | **torre** | tower, belfry |
| **ciudad** | town, city | **torre del homenaje** | keep |
| **collado, alto** | pass, high pass | **valle** | valley |
| **cruz** | cross, Calvary | **vidriera** | window: plain or stained |
| **cuadro** | picture | | glass |
| **cueva, gruta** | cave, grotto | | |

**Places and things to see** (See also Architectural terms in the **Introduction** section)

| English | Spanish | Spanish | English |
|---|---|---|---|
| where is? | ¿dónde está? | desfiladero | defile, cleft |
| may one visit? | ¿se puede visitar? | embalse | reservoir, dam |
| key | llave | ermita | hermitage, chapel |
| light | luz | excavaciones | excavations |
| sacristan | sacristán | fuente | fountain |
| guide | guia | garganta | gorge |
| porter, caretaker | guarda, conserje | lago | lake |
| open, closed | abierto, cerrado | mezquita | mosque |
| not allowed, no entry | prohibido | monasterio | monastery |
| entrance, exit | entrada, salida | nacimiento | source, birthplace |
| head toward | dirigirse a | palacio (real) | (royal) palace |
| wait | esperar | pantano | marsh |
| storey, stairs, steps | piso, escalera | paseo | avenue, esplanade, promenade |
| | | plaza | square |
| alcazaba | Muslim fortress | plaza mayor | main square |
| alcázar | Muslim palace | plaza de toros | bullring |
| ayuntamiento | town hall | portada | portal, west door |
| balneario | Spa | presa | dam |
| barranco | gully, ravine | pueblo | village, market town |
| barrio | quarter | puente | bridge |

*Casares*

B. Kaufmann/MICHELIN

# NATURE

Spain's most southerly autonomous community *(comunidad autónoma)* **covers 87 300km²/33 706sq mi and is similar in size to Portugal and Switzerland. This figure represents 17.3% of the country's total area. Over seven million people (18% of the Spanish population) live in this historic region, which acts as a bridge between Europe and Africa and between the East and West.**

The lands of Andalucía, which for centuries were a source of fascination for successive waves of colonisers, extend southward from the Sierra Morena – a range of mountains separating the region from the communities of Extremadura and Castilla La Mancha – to the Mediterranean coast; and eastward from the River Guadiana – a natural border with Portugal – to the community of Murcia.

## Landscape

Contrary to popular belief, Andalucía is a land of sharp contrasts, in terms of both its climate and its landscape. The fertile Guadalquivir Valley, which has always been considered the region's most representative area, is set between two high mountain ranges, the Sierra Morena to the north and the Cordilleras Béticas to the south, while Andalucía's coastal areas, lapped by the waters of the Atlantic and the Mediterranean, have their own varied landscapes.

### SIERRA MORENA

The modern-day name of this mountain range remains something of an enigma. There are those who believe that the name evolves from the Sierra Mariana (from Marius, a praetor in Roman Hispania), while others are of the opinion that the name alludes to the dark colour

of its landscape, with its predominance of slate.

Yet despite its rugged, mountainous appearance, it is not a true sierra or cordillera, but the southern extension of the Castilian Meseta, which descends sharply into the Guadalquivir depression. It begins to the north of Jaén, where it reaches its maximum altitude (Sierra Madrona – 1 323m/4 339ft) and extends west to form the Sierra de Hornachuelos in the province of Córdoba, the Sierra Norte in the province of Sevilla and the Sierra de Aracena in the province of Huelva.

Through the ages, the approach to Andalucía from the Meseta has been via the **Despeñaperros pass**, a defile cut by the river of the same name in an area of astonishing geological formations covered with cork, holm and gall oaks. As a result of work carried out in recent years, the road traversing the pass is much less arduous than in times past, and is almost as spectacular as the route created by the French architect, Le Maur, in 1779.

In addition to its significant game, especially deer and wild boar, the Sierra Morena is home to a wealth of protected fauna such as wolves, Iberian lynx, imperial eagles, and black and tawny vultures. The mountain range contains three nature parks. **Despeñaperros** and the **Sierras de Andújar** are in the province of Jaén. **Sierra de Aracena y Picos de Aroche** in northern Huelva province is one of the largest in Andalucía (184 000ha/ 454 664 acres), encompassing a varied vegetation and 28 small communities

### Geology

In geological terms, Andalucía is a young region covering the large sea once situated between the continental masses of Eurasia and Goswana. The Cordilleras Béticas, which rose up as a result of Alpine movements during the Tertiary Era, and the River Guadalquivir, slowly sedimenting, cut off the sea, leaving just a 14km/8mi-wide stretch of water, the Straits of Gibraltar, which, with the exception of the Suez Canal, is the only navigable gateway to the Mediterranean.

*Castril*

with a total population of 41 000. Each community prospers from harvesting cork, raising black pigs (the best hams in Spain are produced in Jabugo, Cortegana and Cumbres Mayores) and, in recent years, from rural tourism (mainly from the province of Sevilla), which is increasing in importance throughout the region.

The Parque Natural de las Sierras de Andújar occupies the heart of the Sierra Morena and is an excellent example of a Mediterranean ecosystem with varied, abundant vegetation and large swathes of forest and Mediterranean scrub.

## GUADALQUIVIR DEPRESSION

The spine of Andalucía, as it is known, runs from the Sierra Morena in the north to the Cordilleras Béticas in the south. This former area of Tartessian settlement forms a triangle of flat landscapes whose highest point is found to the east, in the province of Jaén, descending to the lowest part of the depression along the Gulf of Cádiz, where the Atlantic exerts its considerable influence.

The whole valley, which covers 65% of Andalucía, is a densely populated, predominantly agricultural area owing to its deep, fertile black soil, which is irrigated

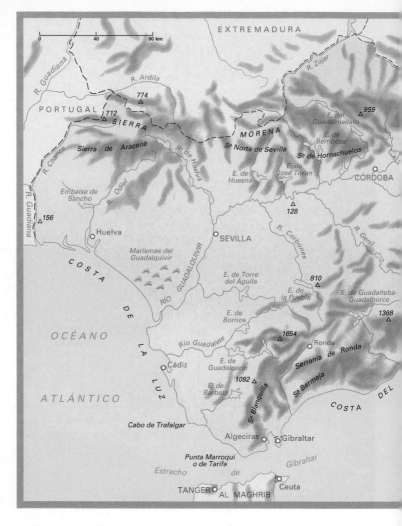

to advantage by water from the tributaries of the Guadalquivir. As a result, the valley is home to fruit and vegetable farms, with large areas devoted to cereal crops, olive groves and vineyards.

The Guadalquivir depression is also home to two of Spain's most historic cities, namely **Córdoba** and **Sevilla**, as well as one of Europe's most impressive national parks, the **Parque Nacional de Doñana**, with its abundance of flora and fauna.

### River Guadalquivir

The Romans called it Betis, while to the Moors it was known as the Great River (Guad-al-Quivir in Arabic); irrespective of its name, however, it has always been the soul of Andalucía, and is the only river (670km/419mi) which flows exclusively through the region. Due to the thrust of the powerful Cordilleras Béticas to the south, its path has gradually shifted northwards, to such an extent that it now flows at the very foot of the Sierra Morena.

The Guadalquivir rises in the **Sierra de Cazorla** (Jaén), at an altitude of 1 600m/5 248ft. After a brief journey through the mountains, it then enters the Baetica depression, gently flowing from an altitude of 100m/328ft in the province of Córdoba to just 10m/32ft in Sevilla. With the additional waters of its

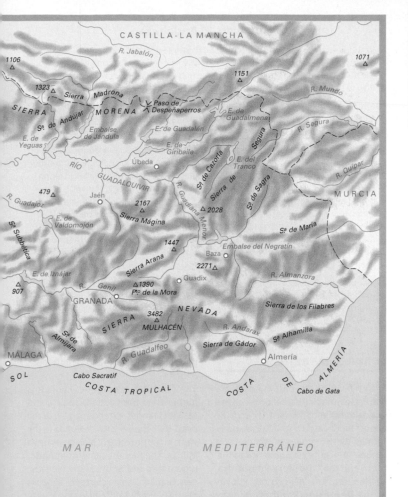

tributary, the Genil, the river is navigable from the city of Sevilla to the Atlantic, where it forms a huge marshland area (Doñana), which the Romans named Lacus Ligustinus.

Although the Guadalquivir's tributaries flowing down from the Sierra Morena (the Viar, Bembézar and Guadiato) all follow a short course and are particularly erosive, those rising in the Cordilleras Béticas, the Guadiana Menor and Genil in particular, carry a far greater volume of water.

Ch. Sappa/HOA QUI

*River Guadalquivir*

# The rivers of Andalucía

In addition to the Guadalquivir basin, the region's hydrographic network consists of a variety of rivers, the volume of which can vary enormously from one season to the next. The reservoirs built during the second half of the 20C have enabled their flow to be regulated, thus increasing areas under cultivation.

Andalucía's major Atlantic rivers, such as the Guadiana, Tinto, Odiel and Guadalete, are all of significant length, carry relatively large volumes of water, and form estuaries and sand bars where they flow into the ocean.

The rivers descending to the Mediterranean coast (Guadiaro, Guadalhorce, Guadalfeo, Adra, Almería and Almanzora) rise in the Cordilleras Béticas, are shorter in length, and, in general, form deltas at their point of entry into the sea. During periods of low water in the provinces of Granada and Almería, the wide, deep gullies known as *ramblas*, which are in fact the beds of rivers, remain empty of water, to such an extent that during longer periods of drought, local people often use these ramblas for planting crops and even as building sites. Needless to say, during periods of heavy rain, the torrents of water cascading down these bare depressions destroy everything in their path, resulting in huge material losses and even loss of life.

Mention should also be made of Andalucía's large wetland areas, including the Ría del Tinto-Odiel, the Bay of Cádiz, Adra and Doñana National Park, as well as the region's salt marshes and lagoons, underground aquifers, and inland areas dotted with lakes, such as Fuente de Piedra (Málaga).

## CORDILLERAS BÉTICAS

This chain is the steepest in Andalucía and acts as a natural barrier between the Guadalquivir and the coast. It occupies almost all of eastern Andalucía and is formed by two groups of Alpine-type ranges: the Cordillera Subbética to the north and the **Cordillera Penibética** to the south. An inner corridor, known as the **Depresión Penibética**, runs between the two.

This depression widens out to the east, forming the **Depresíon de Granada**, irrigated by the Genil, continuing along to the **Guadix** and **Baza** basins, before skirting either side of the **Sierra de Filabres**, forming the Almanzora Valley and the Almería depressions.

The **Sistema Subbético**, which connects with the Sierra Morena to the east, is less well defined, however. The highest sections of this chain are the **Sierras de Cazorla**, **Segura and Las Villas** (600m/1 968ft-2 100m/6 888ft), which together have been designated a nature park. This particular area, dotted with oak, arbutus (strawberry tree) and rowan trees, is a haven for birds of prey, mountain goats and various types of game.

The Cordillera Penibética, which is higher than the Cazorla, Segura and Las Villas ranges, extends parallel to the coast from the Serranía de Ronda to the west, in the province of Málaga, as far as Murcia. The highest summits in Andalucía are found in the Sierra Nevada, near Granada, with a cluster of 14 peaks over 3 000m/9 840ft, including Monte Veleta (3 392m/11 125ft) and Mulhacén (3 481m/11 418ft), the highest peak on the Iberian Peninsula. On its southern flank is the historic Alpujarras region, renowned for its wilderness and difficult access. To the east, behind the Sierra de Los Filabres and the Sierra de Gádor in the province of Almería, lies a large volcanic region, the Cabo de Gata-Níjar, with its spectacular landscapes which provide a dramatic contrast with the deep blue sea.

## THE COAST

Andalucía's 900km/562mi of coastline constitute one of Europe's most visited tourist areas. Its beaches, where many centuries ago merchants from the East

## 10th labour of Hercules

To commemorate his victory over Geryon, a winged monster with a huge herd of oxen, Hercules created two gigantic columns alongside the waters of the Ocean River. One of these, Abila, rose up on the present-day promontory of Ceuta; the other, Calpe, dominated the Rock of Gibraltar.

and invaders from North Africa first set foot on European soil, are now the domain of visitors with more peaceful intentions from Spain and abroad, who wish to spend an enjoyable holiday in the sun or retire away from the colder climates of Northern Europe.

The coastline extending from the Portuguese border to the Straits of Gibraltar is known as the **Costa de la Luz** (Coast of Light), and enjoys the slightly cooler influence of the Atlantic. Until recently, these vast beaches of fine sand were deserted apart from a handful of small resorts such as La Antilla and Matalascañas in Huelva, which were popular with Spanish families, particularly from Sevilla. Over the past few years, a number of new large tourist complexes have begun to attract more foreign visitors, such as Zahara de los Atunes, Caños

de Meca and Tarifa, a town popular with surfers from around the world.

The beaches of the Mediterranean are neither as long nor as open as their Atlantic counterparts; they are, however, far better known, undoubtedly because visitors can be guaranteed fine weather almost all year round. The beaches around Marbella, the capital of the famous **Costa del Sol** (Sun Coast), are not as attractive as those in Rincón de la Victoria, also in the province of Málaga; however the luxurious infrastructure and sporting facilities of this glamorous resort more than make up for this. The **Costa Tropical**, to the south of Granada, is rocky with crystal-clear water perfect for snorkelling and scuba diving. The **Costa de Almería,** further east, attracts nature lovers with its quieter beaches, some of them protected, such as Los Genoveses and Cabo de Gata.

# Climate, Vegetation and Fauna

## CLIMATE

In general terms, the climate of Andalucía is Mediterranean in nature with dry summers and relatively mild win-

*Cabo de Gata headland*

H. Champollion/MICHELIN

*Cork oak*

*Cork oak bark*

ters, during which the region receives the majority of its somewhat scarce and irregular precipitation. The region's average annual temperature is 16.8°C/63°F. Because of the size of Andalucía and the presence of high mountain ranges skirting an extensive stretch of coastline along two huge bodies of water, closer analysis of the Andalusian climate shows significant differences between areas. As an example, although the Guadalquivir Valley has a climate that could be described as typically Mediterranean, neighbouring mountain areas are much colder and receive far greater precipitation. Along the coast, a marked contrast can also be seen between the beaches of the Mediterranean, with its calm, warm waters, and those of the more open Atlantic coast, characterised by colder waters and frequent strong winds, particularly around Tarifa on the Straits of Gibraltar, a paradise for windsurfers, where the average wind strength is 30.6kph/19mph.

Specific areas clearly demonstrate the region's climatic differences; this can be seen along a line stretching from Andújar through Córdoba to Sevilla, where temperatures in summer often exceed 40°C/104°F and where spring, considered to be the best time of the year, starts at the end of February. The most westerly parts of the Sierra Morena, such as the Sierra de Cádiz and the Sierra de Málaga, in the Cordilleras Béticas, are the wettest areas of Andalucía due to the influence of Atlantic winds, while the Sierra de Grazalema registers precipitation levels above 4 000l per year, the highest in Spain. The region's coldest temperatures have been recorded in the Sierra Nevada, where snow remains on the highest peaks all year round and where the ski slopes stay open until May. In complete contrast, the startling Campo de Níjar area in the province of Almería is arid, volcanic and desert-like, with temperatures to match.

## VEGETATION

Andalucía is home to a huge variety of plants and flowers. Perhaps the most representative landscapes of the region are the mountain ranges skirting the Mediterranean, with their small shrubs and bushes such as rockrose, lentisk (mastic tree) and juniper; aromatic plants (thyme, lavender and rosemary); and trees belonging to the Quercus family, including evergreen, gall and cork oak. Carobs, chestnuts, and wild olives, the latter occasionally attaining an impressive size, can often be seen in areas covered by forests of oak.

Pine trees are more prevalent at higher altitudes, as well as in coastal regions. Several species, including umbrella and maritime pines, are used to prevent sand dune erosion along the Atlantic coast. The resistant holm oak and larch are also found in this area. Many of these trees, along with the ubiquitous eucalyptus, are the result of reafforestation schemes undertaken at a time when little thought was given to vegetation native to these areas. The **Spanish fir**, a tree considered a relic from the Tertiary Era, is also common to the region, although it is generally only found in the woods around Grazalema (Cádiz), and in the Sierra de las Nieves and Sierra Bermeja in the province of Málaga.

Forests of ash, willow and poplar all grow alongside rivers, streams and lakes, while wetland areas are the natural habitat for various species of reeds, salt cedars and coarse grasses – ideal nesting grounds for aquatic birds.

Andalucía's myriad protected habitats are also home to a breathtaking variety of vegetation (the oak forests of Sierra Quintana, near Andújar, and the cork oak groves in the province of **Cádiz**), much of which is endemic to the region and has already disappeared from the rest of Europe.

## FAUNA

The region has an equally rich and varied fauna, which includes a number of protected species, some of which are either extinct or dying out in the rest of the world, such as the monk seal, found on the Chafarinas islands (Almería), and the malvasia duck, whose habitat is the lakes of the Sierra Subbética in the province of Córdoba.

In addition to species of game such as wild boar, stag, deer, mountain goat and the mouflon (particularly abundant in the Sierra de Cazorla and Sierra de Segura), large populations of **lynx** and **ichneumon**, both of which are stringently protected, are also found in the region.

Andalucía's birdlife warrants special mention, given the 184 different species which nest in the region, in addition to the fifty or so others which spend their winters here. The area's numerous aquatic birds include the **pink flamingo**, which flourishes only in Fuente de Piedra (Málaga) and the French Camargue, and the eastern glossy ibis, found only in Andalucía. Birds of prey, such as the magnificent **imperial eagle**, the Egyptian vulture and the black vulture tend to nest in the more inaccessible parts of the region.

## A profusion of plants and flowers

A lack of plants and flowers is not a criticism that can be levelled against Andalusian houses. Around the region, patios, balconies and terraces are bedecked in greenery, while streets and squares carry the scent of citrus blossom in spring and the enchanting aroma of jasmine in summer.

The patios of noble houses are resplendent with plants of every type, from leafy ferns to hyacinths, gladioli, tuberose and violets. In smaller abodes, the simplicity of the accommodation is often hidden behind whitewashed walls covered with myriad species of plants such as single, double, scented and ivy geraniums, carnations and jasmine.

The selection of the most suitable plants for different times of the year and their ground and wall arrangement is an art form which has been completely mastered by Andalusian women. Dark corners are ideal for aspidistras, while sun traps are perfect places for geraniums; carnations and other plants which are not particularly attractive when not in flower are left to grow on terraces and then brought onto patios when in bloom. As a general rule, plants are not purchased; instead, seeds and cuttings are passed on by friends and neighbours and then nurtured in pots of every description, from jam jars to magnificent ceramic flowerpots.

# HISTORY

The mythical kingdom of Tartessus; a long period of splendour dominated by the civilisation of al-Andalus before its slow destruction by the Reconquest; and the golden age brought about by the discoveries of the New World. These are the key points in the history of a region which subsequently experienced a long and painful decline marked by poverty, occasionally violent conflict over land and nostalgia for its glorious past. That decline has now been checked by the advent of the post-industrial society and the region's evolution into an autonomous community which is quite distinct from the rest of Spain.

## Timeline

### THE PHOENICIANS

Towards the end of the second millennium BC, at the same time as the first Indo-European tribes were crossing the Pyrenees, navigators from the far east of the Mediterranean were landing on the southern coast of Spain. The discovery of riches in the south of the peninsula (silver, gold, copper and tin) led the Phoenicians to found their first colonies here.

**1100 BC** — Foundation of Gadir (Cádiz), the largest Phoenician colony in the Western Mediterranean. Minerals extracted and exported from the Riotinto and Aznalcóllar mines.

**8C-7C BC** — The apogee of the kingdom of Tartessus, which traded with Phoenician and Greek colonies in the southern part of the peninsula.

### THE CARTHAGINIANS

**BC**

**6C-4C** — Various **Iberian tribes** continue to inhabit the peninsula. Andalucía remains the most homogenous region. The Carthaginians gradually settle in southern Spain, replacing the Phoenicians. Cádiz develops into a major port and a prosperous city, while the Mediterranean coast of Andalucía experiences increasing growth.

*Conquest of Toledo by Alfonso VI on 25 May 1085*

H. Belmenouar/MICHELIN

## The Kingdom of Tartessus (?13C-6C BC)

This kingdom, which later came to be identified with the biblical Tarsis, and whose legendary status is equal to that of Atlantis, reached its pinnacle in the 9C and 8C BC and died out in the 6C BC, either a victim of the Carthaginian invasion or simply as a result of the major crisis which affected the Mediterranean after the conquest of the city of Tyre by Nebuchadnezzar (573 BC). The wealth of this kingdom dazzled the Greeks and Phoenicians and has amazed modern archaeologists, who have discovered numerous remains of this civilisation in Huelva, Sevilla and Córdoba.

Greek and Latin writers date the mythical foundation of Tartessus to around the year 1200 BC. Others believed that the Tartessian monarchy had two different dynasties. The first was founded by Geryon – a creature with three heads and three bodies – who was defeated by Hercules, and the second by Gargoris and his son Habis, the inventor of agriculture.

Modern researchers believe the Tartessian civilisation evolved from the Megalithic culture of southern Spain. The civilisation developed to such a degree that it had its own written laws, a well-organised society comprising seven social groups and an excellent knowledge of techniques for transforming metal. The dynasty's only historical king was Arganthonios, who ruled during the 7C BC and was praised by writers such as Herodotus, Anacreon and Pliny. Despite the many archaeological findings, the exact location of the civilisation's capital is still uncertain, although it is thought to have been situated close to Sanlúcar de Barrameda (Cádiz).

---

**264-241 — First Punic War**. Rome defeats Carthage and significantly reduces its freedom of movement and its income in the Mediterranean.

**237 —** The Carthaginian general Hamilcar Barca lands in Cádiz, makes a pact with the Iberians and establishes an operational base against the Romans in southern Spain. He is followed by Hasdrubal, who commandeers richer lands in the region and founds his capital at Nova Carthago (Cartagena, Murcia). The Carthaginians improve agricultural techniques in the Guadalquivir Valley, which they transform into an important grain-producing area. Carthaginian fishing boats ply the Andalusian coast and set up a flourishing salting industry.

**218-201 — Second Punic War**. Rome is victorious once more and the Carthaginians are forced to relinquish their Spanish territory.

## ROMAN DOMINATION

**197 —** The Romans conquer Cádiz, the last Carthaginian stronghold in Spain.

**83-45 —** Hispania is the stage for the civil war between Sertorius and Sulla and for the Pompeyan wars, which are brought to an end by Caesar's

*Roman mosaic, Casa del Planetario, Itálica*

H. Champollion/MICHELIN

| | |
|---|---|
| **Emirate of Córdoba** (borders at the end of the Emirate in 929) | **Nasrid kingdom (Granada)** |
| | (1230) Date of reconquest |
| **Almohad empire in 1212** | Current borders of Andalucia |

victory in Munda (Montilla) in 45 BC.

**40 —** Caius Octavius **Augustus** is declared Roman Emperor. This heralds the integration of Hispania into the Roman sphere.

## ROMANISATION

With the rise of Julius Caesar to power, Rome begins to establish a policy of determined colonisation, which involves the founding and regeneration of cities. Augustus divides the peninsula into three large provinces: Tarraconensis, Lusitania and Baetica (Andalucía). As a result of its greater degree of Romanisation, the latter comes to depend on the Senate even though the other provinces remain under the control of the Emperor. Perhaps in order to compensate for the bloodshed suffered in prior years, as well as to house veterans of the civil wars, many cities in Baetica receive special treatment, including Corduba (the capital), Gadir, Hispalis (Sevilla), and Itálica. The region quickly adopts Roman habits and customs: Roman sol-diers are granted land, become farmers and marry Iberian women. In order to facilitate the movement of troops and trade to the cities (metals, wine, oil and salted products) a number of roads are built; one of these is the Via Augusta, which runs parallel to the Mediterranean coast and crosses Baetica from east to west. Andalucía enjoys a period of peace spanning several centuries.

## AD

**14-37 —** During the rule of Tiberius a number of Hispanic patricians obtain Roman citizenship and move to Rome. Inhabitants of Baetica who later became famous were among them, such as the philosopher Seneca, born in Córdoba in 4 BC, and his nephew Lucan (b 39). Both men committed suicide in the imperial city in 65, on the orders of Nero.

**74 —** **Vespasian** grants the right of citizenship to Hispanics in recognition of the part played by the peninsula during the

## The pantry of Europe

During their occupation of Hispania, the Romans exploited the mines of the Sierra Morena and Riotinto (Huelva), and the marble quarries at Macael (Almería), and encouraged the development of agriculture in Baetica. Wines from Cádiz were exported to various parts of the Empire (especially to Italy and the south of France), olive oil was sold in the markets of Rome, Gaul, Germania and Britain, and there was growth in the raising of livestock in the north of Huelva and on the mud flats of the Guadalquivir. In addition, the fish-salting industry in Hispalis and Córdoba experienced great development as a result of the many marine species found along the Andalusian coast. Despite its wealth, Baetica, along with the rest of the peninsula, tended to export the majority of its products and resources.

crisis which followed Nero's assassination.

**98-117** — Rule of Marcus Ulpius **Trajan**, born in Itálica in 53, the first Emperor to be neither Roman nor Italian.

**117-38** — Rule of **Hadrian**, also originally from Itálica. Baetica and the rest of Hispania reach their zenith.

**3C** — The arrival of Christianity, probably from North Africa. Rome moves its commercial axis to the East and the slow decline of Hispania begins.

**300-14** — Council of the Hispanic bishops in Elvira (Granada).

**395** — Death of **Theodosius**, the last great Roman Emperor, probably born in Itálica.

## VISIGOTHIC DOMINATION

**411-25** — The Vandals and Alans occupy Andalucía for a short period until the Visigoths, allied with Rome, and led by Athaulf, succeed in expelling them to North Africa.

**441** — The Swabian king Rekhila conquers Sevilla.

**484-507** — The Visigothic occupation of Andalucía is consolidated during the reign of **Alaric II**.

**522** — The Byzantine Emperor **Justinian** establishes a Byzantine province in the southeast of the peninsula, which is later reconquered by the Visigoths.

**568-86** — During the reign of Leovigild, Andalucía supports the revolt of **Hermenigild** against his father.

**589** — Third Council of Toledo and the conversion of the Goths to Catholicism.

**615** — **Sisebut** implements the first official attempt at eradicating Judaism from the Iberian Peninsula.

**7C** — During this period, under the influence of **St Leander** († 600) and **St Isidore** († 636), who dedicates his *Etymologies* to King Sisebut, Baetica is the only sizeable cultural region in Latin Christendom. Syrian and Greek merchants trade with the south of the peninsula.

Jews begin to settle in Córdoba, Sevilla and Málaga. Roman Law is abandoned and the patricians are replaced by bishops and judges.

**710** — Death of **King Witiza**. Faced with the claims to the throne of **Roderick**, Duke of Baetica, Witiza's followers turn abroad for assistance.

## MUSLIM ANDALUCÍA OR AL-ANDALUS (8C-15C)

At the beginning of the 8C the Umayyad Caliphate from Damascus conquers the Berber lands of North Africa. This Caliphate had outgrown the lands of the Arabian Peninsula and the concept of holy war enabled it to divert its aggression from Berber chiefs and towards an external enemy. The dominant tribes adhere to the Islamic faith and join together with the powerful Muslim forces.

711 — An army of 7 000 men under the command of the Berber **Tarik-ibn-Zeyad**, the governor of Tangiers, crosses the Straits and defeats King Roderick near the River Guadalete, or the La Janda lagoons. They march north to conquer Toledo, the capital of the Visigothic kingdom, marking the beginning of Muslim domination in Spain.

712 — 18 000 soldiers land in Andalucía led by the governor Musa, Tariq's superior. Damascus increases in size as a result of the Arab conquests. The Caliphs respect the local governments set up in the conquered territories. In 719 troops of the Caliphate attempt to conquer the south of France but are repulsed in Poitiers by Charles Martel. The Arabs settle in the Guadalquivir Valley and leave the Berbers the less productive lands of Castilla, León and Galicia.

740-50 — Confrontations between the various ethnic groups of Islamic faith occupying the peninsula. In Arabia the Abbasid dynasty murders the Umayyads and seizes power from them.

## The Emirate of Córdoba (756-929)

The al-Andalus kingdom is created, eventually embracing almost the entire Iberian Peninsula. Although theoretically subject to the authority of the new Abbasid capital of Baghdad, the Andalusian Emirs are practically independent.

755 — Abd ar-Rahman, the only remaining member of the Umayyad family, lands in southern Spain and in a short period succeeds in uniting all Muslims. A year later he settles in Córdoba and proclaims himself emir. **Abd ar-Rahman I** lays the foundation of the kingdom of al-Andalus.

784 — Construction of the Mezquita in Córdoba begins.

788-929 — On the death of Abd ar-Rahman I, the seemingly resolved tensions explode and conflict breaks out between ethnic groups (Arabs, Berbers, Jews and Christians converted to Islam [muladíes]). The Emirate is weakened and the Christian kingdoms of the north strike a number of major blows against the army of al-Andalus.

## The Caliphate of Córdoba (929-1031)

The new Caliphate, which had finally broken all ties with Baghdad, becomes the most powerful kingdom in the West and its court the most cultured and refined. Spain regains its commercial impetus in the Mediterranean, which had practically been paralysed during Visigothic domination. Muslims and Christians mount raids on each other's territory throughout the peninsula and a network of castles and watchtowers is built to keep an eye on the enemy.

929 — Beginning of the rule of **Abd ar-Rahman III** (912-61) who declares himself Caliph and Commander of the Believers, brings peace to his kingdom and reinforces the frontier provinces of Toledo, Badajoz and Zaragoza.

936 — Construction of the city of Medina Azahara begins.

978 — General **Almanzor** seizes power and establishes himself as Prime Minister. The Caliph becomes a figurehead.

1002 — The death of Almanzor in Calatañazor. The first skirmishes in a civil war destabilise the Caliphate.

1031 — End of the Umayyad dynasty. Rebellion of the Cordoban nobility and the destruction of Medina Azahara. The provinces and cities exert their-

*Detail on the east door of the Mezquita, Córdoba*

## St James the Moorslayer

Tradition has it that St. James the Apostle was decapitated on Herod's orders in Palestine after seven years of preaching in Spain. Centuries later, in 834, the tomb of St James was found in the diocese of Iria (Galicia). He was soon adopted as the patron saint of the troops of the Christian Reconquest and earned the sobriquet of Moorslayer (Matamoros) after he appeared on a white horse at the Battle of Clavijo (844?) to secure the Christian victory. Some say this battle never took place. Nevertheless, "Santiago and strike for Spain" became the Christian battle cry.

independence and a number of autonomous kingdoms are created.

### First Taifa kingdoms and Almoravid supremacy (1009-1110)

The taifa (group or faction in Arabic) kingdoms which appeared at the beginning of the 11C organise according to ethnic criteria. Berbers control the coast from the River Guadalquivir to Granada and the Arabs hold power in Córdoba and Sevilla.

At first the taifa kingdoms make alliances with their neighbours, although some also enter into pacts with the Christians where necessary, even to the extent of paying tribute in order to remain on their own land.

The Christian monarchs exploit their enemies' weaknesses and succeed in conquering a number of large towns.

1042 — Construction of the Alcázar begins in Sevilla.

1064 — Work begins on the Alcazaba in Málaga.

1085 — **Alfonso VI** of Castilla and León conquers Toledo. Lengthy Christian campaigns are waged against Sevilla and Badajoz.

**Al-Mutamid**, king of Sevilla, feels threatened and calls upon the Almoravids of North Africa for assistance. Yusuf Ibn Tashunin responds to the plea, crosses the Straits of Gibraltar and in a short time manages to assume control of all the taifa kingdoms.

1118 — The expeditions of **Alfonso I** (El Batallador) in Andalucía expose the weakness of the Almoravids at a time when the Almohad movement is beginning to gain ground in Morocco.

### Second Taifa kingdoms (1144-70) and Almohad supremacy

For a short period of time the taifa kingdoms reappear, taking advantage of the decline of the Almoravids, but they fall once again, this time as a result of the Almohad invasion led by Abd al-Mumin (the Miramamolin of Christian chronicles).

**1147** — Almohad troops occupy Marrakech, Tarifa and Algeciras. Overcoming resistance by Christians and some Moorish kings in the eastern provinces, the Almohads manage to take control of southern Spain.

**1163** — Sevilla becomes the capital of Al-Andalus.

**1184** — Work starts on the Great Mosque (Mezquita Mayor) in Sevilla, whose minaret is later known as the Giralda.

**1195** — The Battle of Alarcos (Ciudad Real), in which Al-Mansur is victorious over the Castilian king Alfonso VIII, is the last great triumph of the Almohad army. The decline of the Muslim invaders is to follow.

## Almoravids and Almohads

The **Almoravid** religious movement developed at the beginning of the 11C when a Berber chieftain in Mauritania founded a monastery to prepare soldiers for holy war against the infidels. This institution was the origin of an empire which extended along the Atlantic and North African coasts. After founding the city of Marrakech (1070), which they subsequently turned into their capital, the Almoravids occupied Fez and extended their power across the whole of what is now Morocco.

The **Almohad** empire was founded by Abd al-Mumin (1130-63), the follower of a Berber religious leader who instituted far-reaching legal and religious reforms based on the strict observance of the Koran. By the middle of the 12C the Almohad dominions stretched from the Atlantic coast to Libya and from the River Tagus to the Sahara.

**1212** — **Battle of Las Navas de Tolosa**. The armies of Castilla, Aragón and Navarra inflict a decisive defeat on the Almohads.

### The Nasrid kingdom (1232-1492)

During the last phase of declining Almohad power, Mohammed I, of the Banu Nasr or Nasrid dynasty, succeeds in uniting the territories of Granada, Málaga and Almería to create a kingdom that is to last for two and a half centuries, protected by sea and mountains. In order to secure power, he willingly acts as vassal of the Castilian kings and even joins them in the conquest of Sevilla. However, he subsequently takes advantage of the expulsion of the Moors from Christian lands to build up a highly populated and productive kingdom.

The reigns of the 23 Nasrid kings were often beset with interminable internal strife, and the kingdom fell amid violent disputes between the Cegri and Abencerraje families.

**1237** — Work starts on the Alcazaba, the oldest part of the Alhambra palace.

**1248** — The **conquest of Sevilla** by Christian troops establishes a frontier which remains unchanged until the 15C.

**1313** — Construction of the Generalife begins.

**1410** — Don Fernando, the ruling Castilian prince, takes Antequera.

**1462** — **Enrique IV** conquers Gibraltar and Archidona. The Nasrids appeal in vain for assistance from Muslim lands.

**1464-82** — Reign of **Muley Hacén** (Abu I-Hasan in Arabic), who provokes the animosity of his people by introducing high taxes.

**1482-92** — **Boabdil**, son of Muley Hacén, deposes his father and accedes to the throne. He decides to attack Lucena but is taken prisoner by the Catholic Kings, who release him in exchange for his continuing opposition to his father.

Muley Hacén dies and is succeeded by his brother, El Zagal.

The Nasrids suffer a series of defeats.

**1492** — Boabdil surrenders and retires to the Alpujarras estate placed at his disposal by the victors. Shortly after he moves to the Maghreb and settles in Fez.

## THE RECONQUEST (12C-15C)

The breakup of the Caliphate and the proclamation of the Kingdom of Taifas weakens Moorish power. Muslim troops from the various kingdoms concentrate their efforts on fighting over territory rather than holding back the Christian advance.

**1158-1214** — Reign of **Alfonso VIII**. Beginning of the Christian campaigns in Andalucía. Castilla seizes the Sierra Morena. The Almohads are defeated at Las Navas de Tolosa.

**1217-52** — **Fernando III the Saint**, King of Castilla, takes a decisive step towards the reconquest of Andalucía by first seizing eastern Andalucía, culminating in his entry into Córdoba in 1236, and then western Andalucía (including Sevilla in 1248).

**1252-84** — Fernando III's son, Alfonso X the Wise, conquers the kingdom of Niebla (Huelva), consolidates the Castilian dominions in Lower Andalucía, suppresses revolts in Cádiz and Jerez and expels large numbers of Muslims.

**1284-1469** — The Reconquest advances slowly and is halted from the middle of the 14C to the beginning of the 15C. The 15C sees Christian victories during the reigns of Juan II and Enrique IV.

**1469** — The marriage of **Isabel of Castilla** to **Fernando of Aragón**, to whom the Valencian pope

Alexander VI grants the title of the Catholic Monarchs in 1496. Beginning of the unification of the Christian kingdoms.

**1481** — The Inquisition holds the first auto-da-fé in Sevilla.

**1482-92** — The Catholic Monarchs begin their major offensive against the Nasrid kingdom of Granada. Muslim cities fall to the Christians one after the other, Ronda in 1485, followed by Málaga (1487), Baza (1489), Almería and Guadix (1489).

**2 January 1492** — **Boabdil** hands over the keys of the city of Granada to the **Catholic Monarchs**. The victorious Christian monarchs agree to respect the religion, laws and customs of those Muslims who wish to remain.

## CONSEQUENCES OF THE RECONQUEST

In the 13C the repopulation of Andalucía took place in two stages: the first during the reign of Fernando III and the second during that of Alfonso X; those Moors who resisted were forced to emigrate. It is thought that between 1240 and 1270 more than 300 000 Muslims fled their homes in order to settle, almost exclusively, in Granada. Immediately after the revolt of 1262 and the resulting expulsion of Muslims, the workforce was substantially reduced and the region saw an increase in the development of huge estates *(latifundios)*.

The reconquest of the kingdom of Granada had very similar consequences. However, on this occasion the majority of inhabitants remained in their towns and villages as a result of the agreement signed by the Catholic Monarchs promising to respect their religion, laws and customs. The breaking of this promise by the Christians provoked two rebellions in the Alpujarras mountains, which were violently put down. In 1570 the Moors were forced to disperse throughout Castilla. The final expulsion was ordered in 1609.

F. Arborio Mella/Archivi Alinari, Firenze

*The caravels of Christopher Columbus*

## THE GOLDEN AGE OF ANDALUCÍA

Trade with **America** brought wealth to Sevilla and the surrounding region, including Córdoba and Málaga. Sevilla, which benefited from the monopoly, was transformed into a major Spanish city and a paradise for powerful merchants, adventurers and those on the margins of society. The situation in the rest of Andalucía was different. The arrival of new products from the Indies (cochineal, indigo) had an effect on the region's traditional textile industry, while Granada's silk industry, which produced satin, velvet and damask, suffered immeasurably from the austere clothing policy imposed on the Spanish Empire by the Habsburgs. However, Córdoba began to specialise in the production of harnesses and cordovans made from American leather, while mercury from the mines of Almadén, used in the production of silver amalgams, became indispensable for exploiting the silver of Mexico and Peru. On the other hand, continuous increases in taxes and the relentless demand for agricultural produce helped to concentrate land in the hands of the most powerful.

1492 — **Christopher Columbus** sets sail from the port of Palos de la Frontera (Huelva) on 3 August. On 12 October he arrives at Guanahani Island (Bahamas).
**Expulsion of the Jews** who have not converted to Christianity. More than 150 000 people are forced to leave Sefarad (Spain). The majority settle in Mediterranean countries, where they form Sephardic communities in which some of the inhabitants continue to speak the Spanish of that period *(ladino)*.

1499-1501 — **First Alpujarras rebellion**. The intransigence of Cardinal Cisneros provokes an uprising by Muslims from the Albaicín in Granada. It soon spreads to the Alpujarras region, the Sierra de los Filabres and the Serranía de Ronda.

1502 — Publication of a decree which forces the Muslim rebels to convert to Christianity or leave the country. The majority opt for baptism. Moors who convert become known as **Moriscos**.

1503 — The Casa de Contratación, which monopolises the colonial market, is founded in Sevilla.

1516 — **Carlos I**, later to become Emperor under the name Carlos V, inherits the Spanish throne on the death of his grandfather Fernando the Catholic.

1530 — Construction of Carlos V's palace begins in the Alhambra.

1556 — Carlos V abdicates in favour of his son **Felipe II**.

**1568-71 — Second Alpujarras rebellion.** Afraid that the Moors would ally themselves with the Turks and Berbers, Felipe II outlaws the use of Arabic and the observance of the Islamic religion. Revolts erupt throughout the region. The Moors from Granada disperse throughout Spain.

**1599 —** The painter **Diego Velázquez** is born in Sevilla, where he will work until 1622.

## THE CRISES OF THE 17C-18C

The first half of the 17C witnessed the beginning of Andalucía's decline. One of the causes was the drop in population, decimated by four major plagues (in 1649 the population of Sevilla was reduced by half) and by the final expulsion of the *moriscos*, whose labor was of fundamental importance to agriculture. In the next few years the situation in the Andalusian countryside continued to decline, with most of the land falling into the hands of large landowners. More than 80% of agricultural workers were day labourers and only 7% of land belonged to those who worked it. Gradually the wealthy created a powerful rural oligarchy closely connected to the municipal administration which completely controlled the life of the people. Industry in Sevilla, closely bound to maritime trade, collapsed after the silting up of the Guadalquivir at Sanlúcar, preventing large ships from navigating upstream.

*Felipe IV by Velázquez, Galleria Palatina, Florence*

Archivi Alinari, Firenze

**1610 — Decree of expulsion** of the morisco population.

**1621 — Felipe IV** ascends to the throne.

**1641 —** Riots in the region's main towns and cities are the result of the economic crisis.

**1680 —** Cádiz becomes an Atlantic trading port, taking over the role previously held by Sevilla.

**1700 — Carlos II**, the last monarch of the House of Austria, dies in Madrid.

**1702 —** Beginning of the **War of the Spanish Succession** between Felipe V and Carlos of Habsburg. In the course of the struggle, the British, who supported the Archduke Carlos, take **Gibraltar**. The Treaty of Utrecht (1713)

## The Spanish Inquisition

The Court of the Inquisition was set up in 1468 in order to punish converted Jews who continued to practice their religion in secret; although soon it was used to suppress any kind of moral or heretic deviation. Its extensive and complex organisation was made up of a council of the Supreme Inquisition and local, fiscal and domestic inquisitors. All methods were considered suitable for extracting a confession from the accused; however, once condemned, the offender was handed over to the secular branch of the organisation which carried out the sentence. During the four centuries of the Inquisition (it was abolished by the Cádiz courts in 1813) this highly effective tool of suppression was used by both the Church and the State, especially in the period up to the 18C.

ratifies English control of the Rock.

**1767** — **Carlos III** begins the repopulation of the Sierra Morena.

**1788** — The colonial monopoly of Cádiz is abolished.

## THE SOCIAL CONFLICTS OF THE 19C

At the beginning of the century there was little industrial development in Andalucía. The mining of natural resources began towards the middle of the century, although in 1868 the mining industry was taken over by foreign monopolies, in particular the British. At the same time, the shipbuilding industry experienced significant growth in Cádiz, agricultural produce began to be sold commercially and large sections of the railway network were built. Continued trade with the colonies, which was to last until 1898, also enabled exchanges with a number of European countries. As a result of these contacts, groups of middle-class liberals began to develop in major towns and cities.

**1808** — The French army enters Spain. Beginning of the **War of Independence** (Peninsular War). On 19 July General Dupont is defeated at **Bailén**, in the province of Jaén, by Spanish troops under the command of General Castaños.

**1812** — During the French invasion the **Cortes de Cádiz** (Cádiz Parliament) is convened and the liberal Constitution of Cádiz is drawn up.

**1814** — End of the War of Independence.

**1820** — **Rafael del Riego** leads a liberal revolt in Andalucía and forces King Fernando VII to reinstate the 1812 constitution.

**1835-37** — Minister Mendizábal orders the disentailment (*desamortización*) of the property of the Church and town councils.

**1840** — Andalusian peasants, the victims of liberalism and dis-

entailment, organise themselves in order to improve their living conditions.

**1863** — Pérez del Álamo, a veterinary surgeon, starts a major Republican uprising which spreads to Málaga, Granada, Jaén and Almería.

**1873** — Proclamation of the **First Republic**. Tentative efforts at land redistribution.

**1875** — **Restoration** of the monarchy (Alfonso XII).
Andalusian anarchism develops into terrorism. Labor strife and strikes increase.

## 20C

**1900-31** — Strikes and social struggles continue unabated, led by the trade unions, particularly the CNT and FAI.

**1931** — Proclamation of the **Second Republic** and minor attempts at agrarian reform which do not satisfy Andalusian farm workers, who are beset by hunger and unemployment.

**January 1933** — The **Casas Viejas** incident in Cádiz. The revolutionary general strike which started in Cádiz comes to a tragic end when the Civil Guard and riot police set fire to the house in which the anarchist leaders had taken refuge. This brings about the Socialists' defeat in the elections of the same year.

**1936-39** — In the early days of the **Civil War**, most of Andalucía falls into the hands of military garrisons based in the region's cities (Cádiz, Granada, Córdoba and Sevilla), while the east of the region remains loyal to the Republic.

**1960** — This decade sees an increase in **emigration** to the more industrialised regions of Spain (Basque Country and Catalunya) and to a number of European countries (West Germany, France and Switzerland).

*AVE high-speed train, Santa Justa station, Sevilla*

**1975** — Death of Francisco Franco. **Juan Carlos I** is declared king.

**1977** — The Spanish Socialist Workers Party (PSOE) wins the elections in Andalucía.

**1978** — The government of Adolfo Suárez approves the pre-autonomous status of the region and the Junta de Andalucía is established.

**1980** — Andalusian autonomy is approved by referendum.

**1982** — The **Statute of Autonomy of Andalucía** comes into force.
First elections for the Andalusian Parliament. **Rafael Escuredo** becomes the first President of the Junta de Andalucía.

**1984** — Presidency of Juan Rodríguez de la Borbolla.

**1990** — Presidency of Manuel Chaves.

**1992** — Universal Exposition (Expo) at Sevilla. Inauguration of the Madrid-Sevilla high-speed train (AVE).

**1999** — World Track and Field Championships are held in Sevilla.

**2002** — World Equestrian Championships are held in Jérez de la Frontera.

**2005** — Mediterranean Games are held in Almería.

**2006** — Andalucía experiences record high temperatures and tourist arrivals.

# Al-Andalus

For almost eight centuries, from 711 to 1492, Muslim Andalucía or al-Andalus was the backdrop for the incredible cohabitation of two completely contrasting religious, architectural and cultural worlds: Islam and Christianity. The imprint left by those Muslims who inhabited this southern tip of Spain is immense.

R. Corbel/MICHELIN

## THE POPULATION

The inhabitants of al-Andalus were of different origins and therefore had different physical characteristics. As the years passed the distinction between natives and foreigners lessened as the newcomers imposed their structures on the conquered territories. The natives were Hispano-Roman Visigoths, both Christian and Jewish, of Latin culture and organised according to a feudal system. The foreigners were Arabs and Berbers, of Muslim faith and Arab culture.

The process of islamisation and arabisation imposed by those in authority gave rise to a relatively uniform Moorish society which was both Arabic and Muslim. Initially this society comprised two main social groups: the upper (*jassa*) and lower (*amma*) classes. These groups differed greatly, even in legal matters; a member of the nobility was not punished in the same way as a member of the lower class. A middle class, which continued to increase in size, came into existence around the 11C. The poor (miskin) survived through taking on occasional work as labourers on farms and during harvests. The clients or maulas were free servants who were bound to a master, from whom they could take their name. The largest number of slaves belonged to the siqlabi group (*esclavos*), who were purchased on the international market or taken prisoner in times of war; these people usually worked for the most important nobles. Negro slaves (*abid*), who worked mainly in the army, originated from the African slave market.

## ORIGINS

### Arabs

They arrived in the peninsula in two main waves – the first in the 8C and the second during the Almohad period in the 12C – and always occupied the most powerful positions. Their aim from the beginning was to islamise the native population. In the later period, in order to be recognised as an Arab, it was enough to bear a suitable name, which could be acquired relatively easily by those with the right contacts.

### Berbers

The first large contingent of this North-African ethnic group crossed the Straits of Gibraltar in the 8C, led by the generals Tarik and Musa. In the second half of the 10C and beginning of the 11C, many of the same faith followed and eventually found themselves in control of some of the taifa kingdoms, including Granada. Although many obtained positions of responsibility, the vast majority worked as agricultural labourers, cattle breeders and craftsmen.

### Mozarabs

The Christians used this term to describe the arabised Christians who stayed on their land and remained true to their religion after the arrival of the Muslims. The Arabs referred to them as nazarenos (naara).

## Muladíes

These were Christians who converted to Islam and, in a number of cases, managed to obtain prominent positions. During the 11C they altered their family tree in order to create an ostensible Arab line that would allow them to retain their privileged position in society.

## Jews

Badly treated by the Visigoths, they greeted the arrival of the Muslims with delight. They integrated into Islamic culture perfectly and experienced no major problems until the Almohad invasion.

## DAILY LIFE

### Towns

The Moors made profound changes to Hispano-Visigothic society which, having experienced a long period of decline, was extremely rural in character. This eminently urban Islamic civilisation founded a number of towns, some of which were quite sizeable; Córdoba, for example, became the largest and one of the most important cities in Europe at the time, both in terms of population and cultural activity. It should be noted that Andalusian cities of the period were equipped with sewerage systems, public lighting and various communal services. In fact, they were blessed with far more amenities than their contemporary Christian counterparts.

The Moorish **medina** (al-Madinat), the old walled centre of the city, followed an organised pattern within the chaos of its narrow streets and alleyways which developed as a result of a lack of building regulations. The districts (harat) were inhabited by craftsmen of the same guild or by families of the same religion (Jews and Mozarabs). The interior of the medina housed markets now known in Spanish as zocos (from the Arabic suq), public baths (hamam), mosques and restaurants, and even included a university or madrassa in larger towns and cities.

More modern districts or **arrabales** (al-Rabad) were situated around the medina and were soon walled. The **cemetery** (maqbara) was located outside the city walls, not far from the roads leading into the city, as was the sa'ría, a large esplanade that was occasionally used as a military training area (musalla), and sometimes as a meeting place for the faithful (musara) to celebrate the end of Ramadan; this often replaced the main mosque in smaller settlements. During the Christian period these esplanades were subsequently used to thresh grain and were known as eras (threshing floors).

The civil and military authorities, as well as the army and their families, lived in the **alcazaba** (al-Qasaba), an independent walled fortress equipped with its own services which was never a part of the main city.

### Living quarters

In general only one Moorish family lived in each house. The wealthy could afford to have many wives, but for the rest of the population monogamous marriage was the norm. The surface area of those Moorish houses which have been excavated by archaeologists varies from 50 to 300m²/538 to 3 229sq ft.

R. Corbel/MICHELIN

The most obvious feature of Moorish houses is the desire for privacy. Each individual built his house to meet his own needs, but nearly all houses were away from the road in order to avoid noise. Only the Jews built houses grouped together around a yard, with a joint entrance situated at the end of a cul-de-sac. Protected by a very plain façade, with few openings covered with shutters, Moorish houses were organised around a patio which was reached across a hallway. All houses had a privy, a kitchen and one or more rooms, as well as a barn. Water was stored in a cistern or drawn from a well in the patio. Fireplaces were not common as the houses were heated with braziers and the women cooked over fires contained in

Cold room

Hot room

R. Corbel/MICHELIN

Warm room  Boilers

earthenware pots.

Household furnishings were simple: ceramic and earthenware utensils, chests and carpets, as well as tapestries and cushions which could be made from cotton, wool or silk depending on the financial standing of the family.

## The market or souk

Although it also existed in rural areas, the souk or *zoco* was mainly an urban feature. Cities had specialised markets which sold and even manufactured products which came from the countryside. Articles of high quality and value were sold in special markets known as *alcaicerías*. These were also centres of export to much larger areas, such as the Mediterranean, Islamic countries, the Maghreb and other African markets. The market overseer, known as the *almotacén*, controlled commercial activity, which was regulated down to the smallest detail, in order to limit illegal practices and abuse.

*Alhóndigas* were used to store products and to house merchants. The Spanish word fonda, meaning inn, has evolved from the Arabic word for this particular building (funduq). The Corral del Car-

bón in Granada is a reconstructed old alhóndiga.

## Baths

Every district in the towns and cities of al-Andalus would have had its own hamam or public bath (it is said that Córdoba had over 600), to meet the demands of a population with a great penchant for water and a desire to fulfil the Islamic obligations of spiritual and bodily cleanliness. As well as centres of hygiene with specialised staff, baths also acted as a place in which to meet and relax – in the mornings for men, and the afternoons for women and children.

The exteriors of the baths were topped with vaults with small skylights to enable the diffusion of a thin, but pleasant, light. The interior, covered with azulejos, was divided into four main areas whose temperature progressively increased. In the first, visitors would undress once they had obtained towels and the obligatory wooden shoes. They would then enter a second section, a cold room, housing the latrines, where the bathing process would begin, before continuing to the remaining two rooms, one hot, the other warm. The purpose of the hot room was to open up the pores, while the warm room would have been used for massages. Men would take advantage of their visit to the baths to have their hair cut and beard trimmed, while women would apply a range of beauty products, such as depilatory creams, jasmine-scented perfume, henna to colour the hair and kohl to darken the area around the eyes.

## The mosque

The mosque (*mezquita*) is not a temple inhabited by God, but a house of prayer to which Muslims over the age of 16 were called to midday prayer on Fridays. Towns would have small, local mosques, as well as larger ones, known as aljamas, as in Córdoba. In line with other parts of the Islamic world, mezqui-

Prayer room

Alminar or minaret

R. Corbel/MICHELIN

Patio or shan

tas in al-Andalus were also used as large civic centres, similar to the Roman forum and the public squares of the Middle Ages. Here, documents of interest to the community could be read and flags would be blessed prior to the departure of a new military expedition. Initially, the mezquita would have also have been used as a teaching centre and the office of the town's treasury.

The layout of the mezquita was inspired by the house in Medina where the prophet Muhammad lived and imparted his teaching. As a result, in keeping with the design of a traditional house, it consisted of two clearly defined areas: the **covered area** or prayer room *(haram)*, with its floor covered in matting, and the **patio** *(shan)*, with a fountain or pool *(sabil)* for ritual ablutions. Other basic features included:

The **kiblah**, or main wall of the room, facing Mecca. Strangely, mezquitas in al-Andalus faced southwards rather than southeast, which would have been the direction towards Mecca from Andalucía. Some experts believe that this was due to Syrian influence, while others consider that the route to Mecca would first have involved a journey south.

The **mihrab**, an empty niche in the centre of the kiblah to remind the faithful of the place where Mohammed prayed.

The **maqsura**, an area surrounded by latticework screens located in front of the mihrab. It would appear that this area was reserved for the Caliph.

The **mimbar**, a type of wooden pulpit used by the imam to conduct Friday prayers *(jutba)*.

The **alminar** or minaret, the most symbolic feature of Islamic architecture, is a tower attached to one of the walls of the patio, the upper part of which is used by the muezzin to call the faithful to prayer. A typical Andalusian alminar would be crowned with three gilded spheres *(yamur)* of decreasing sizes and a fleur-de-lis.

## THE COUNTRYSIDE

The outskirts of large cities were dotted with farms known as *almunias*. The beauty of these luxurious mansions with their own gardens, orchards, pools and fountains was said to rival that of some of the most sumptuous royal palaces. A fine example of this was the almunia of al-Rusafa, to the northeast of Córdoba. Although sovereigns and leading figures in Islamic life owned extensive land farmed by labourers, independent farmers and cattle breeders were also commonplace in al-Andalus. They lived within small communities known as **alquerías** which were generally protected by a castle. These hamlets included houses, outbuildings, farmland and barns. Larger ones were often surrounded by fortifications and had their own common amenities similar to those found in urban areas.

## Agriculture

The introduction of sophisticated hydraulic techniques had a significant effect on the Mediterranean ecosystem of Andalucía. Although some of these techniques originated from the Roman period, such as the river water-wheel, it is undeniable that the Moors were superbly skilled at extracting water from below ground and channeling it to extensive areas of farmland. In fact, modern-day Spanish contains a number of agricultural terms which directly descend from Arabic.

In addition to terrace farming, the Moors introduced animal-powered wheels and an irrigation system of Oriental origin consisting of boring holes in the ground until a spring was discovered; the wells were used to control the pressure of the water which was then channelled to those areas requiring irrigation.

Islamic law controlled the provision of water, which was considered an asset in common. The *zabacequia* would settle disputes and would establish an irrigation timetable which was scrupulously respected. If a farmer failed to make use of his slot, it would be channelled to other land; nobody, however, had the right to pass on water as a gift, sell it or exchange it.

Alongside the region's traditional crops (olives, cereals and vines), the Moors also grew other products imported from the East including rice, pomegranates, cotton and saffron, as well as what were considered to be luxury items, such as spices or mulberry trees to feed silkworms. The fertile irrigated land *(huertas)* overflowed with high-quality products, many of which had been introduced by the Moors, such as the aubergine, artichoke, chicory and asparagus. Meanwhile, the magnificent gardens traditionally associated with Moorish culture were a feast of colour with violets, roses, honeysuckle and jasmine.

## Animal breeding

The Moors were great breeders of animals which were used for riding, as draft animals, and for the table. As an illustration of their importance, the **Andalusian horse**, whose origins can be traced back to the Moors, is now famous the world over. The leather industry was one of the most flourishing sectors of the region's economy. Documentary evidence has also shown that flocks of sheep were of enormous size during the period of Arab domination. It is also strange to note that although Muslims were prohibited from eating pork, old texts refer to the breeding of pigs and of payment to farmers for them. The main breeding areas were the marshlands of the lower Guadalquivir and the area to the east of Córdoba.

## DEFENSIVE ARCHITECTURE

The Moors built numerous military installations both for defence and as bases from which to attack their Christian and fellow Muslim rivals. Many of these constructions were reused after the Reconquest and some are still standing today.

Besides the alcazaba, the most typical defensive buildings were the castles erected along the border with Christian-held territory. As a general rule, they were built with an east-west orientation and comprised two clearly defined sections: the alcázar or **fortress**, organised around a central patio, and a large esplanade in which the barracks for troops would have been located. On the outer limits of the central castle, and separate from it, there would have been a series of smaller fortresses in constant communication with a number of **watchtowers**.

The **walls** were strengthened by the construction of towers, used as garrisons and strategic points from which to harass the enemy, as well as pyramid-shaped merlons. Communication around the walls was via an inner circular path.

The 11C saw the construction of the first **barbicans**, defensive walls positioned in front of the main walls, and the first moats. Later on, during the period of Almohad domination, **turrets**, such as the Torre del Oro in Sevilla, began to appear. These defensive constructions were independent of the main fortified area, but connected to it via a wall with a narrow path **(coracha)**.

In the early days of Moorish rule, the gateways along the walls were strengthened using metal plates and leather. In the 11C, however, these gateways began to be built in the towers themselves, while later refinements saw the introduction of **machicolations** and platforms consisting of small raised structures erected on the external façade of the defensive wall.

Obviously, construction techniques evolved over the centuries. During the Caliphate of Córdoba, for example, ashlar stone was predominantly used, to be subsequently replaced by the more resistant clay mortar, a mixture of sand, lime and gravel made into moulds and then covered with brightly coloured plaster to physically dazzle the enemy.

## A LAND OF SCHOLARS, POETS AND PHILOSOPHERS

For eight centuries al-Andalus was an important centre of artistic and scientific culture. While sovereigns elsewhere on the Iberian Peninsula were living in sombre castles, in which they were surrounded by men interested in nothing but warfare, Moorish emirs, caliphs and monarchs were inhabiting luxurious palaces and encouraging cultural development. Scientists, philosophers, poets and artists acted as the best possible ambassadors for the power and refinement of their Moorish rulers. Nor should it be forgotten that those at the vanguard of Andalusian culture were

R. Corbel/MICHELIN

not isolated figures, for they carried out their work alongside a team of assistants within the Court itself. This research would have taken place either in large libraries, such as the one created by Al-Hakam II, with over 300 000 volumes, or in the madrassas (religious academies) created for this very purpose.

From the 11C onwards, Arabic was the most widely used language across the entire peninsula; and although Christians and Jews preserved their own languages, they used Arabic in daily life and in their artistic and scientific work. Another feature of Moorish culture was the constant interchange with other areas, from the eastern boundaries of Islamic influence – on journeys to and from Mecca – to North Africa, particularly during the Almoravid and Almohad periods.

Much of the credit for the preservation of Muslim knowledge, which was highly valued by the Western world throughout the Renaissance and even beyond, is due to the efforts of Alfonso X. With the cooperation of Mozarabs and Jews alike, this Christian monarch had Arabic manuscripts copied and corrected following his conquests and those of his father, Fernando III.

R. Corbel/MICHELIN

## The sciences

Moorish scientists took an interest in every conceivable aspect of science. Alchemists studied the behaviour of metallic substances and slowly discovered their basic processes; agronomists wrote agricultural papers including detailed information on the rearing of carrier pigeons, which at the time were the fastest and most efficient form of communication; **naturalists** created zoos housing unusual species; while **mathematicians**, such as Avempace, who was also a great astronomer, were noted for their work on trigonometry.

The field of **medicine** reached new heights through the work of specialists who published their scientific findings in encyclopaedia. Through these publications, it is known that they were able to perform somewhat complex surgery and were aware of illnesses such as haemophilia. As well as the most famous physician of them all, **Averroës**, who

was also a great philosopher, mention should also be made of the five generations of the **Avenzoar** family. Medical science was strictly linked with **botany** – another field in which spectacular advances were made. An example of this can be seen in the work of Ibn al-Baytar, from Málaga, the author of a compendium in which he lists 1 400 plant- and mineral-based medicines which were of great importance during the Renaissance.

The extensive knowledge of Moorish scientists resulted in the development of **inventions** revolutionary in their time. These ranged from the construction of astrolabes and quadrants – fundamental to navigation – to refrigeration systems, lighting effects created via bowls of mercury, anaphoric clocks (moved by water) – very useful for fixing the hours of prayer – and even mechanical toys. The Moors also adopted Chinese paper-manufacturing techniques, resulting in the production of paper in Córdoba from the 10C onwards, and were responsible for introducing so-called **Arabic numerals**. It should also be noted that the Spanish words *guarismo* (a number or figure) and *algoritmo* (algorithm) derive from the name of the mathematician al-Khuwarizmi.

## Literature

In Arabic literature, poetry was of greater importance than prose. Arab writers improvised; in other words they composed their poetry out loud, and on many occasions forced their slaves to learn poems by heart in order to sell them at a higher price.

Early divans (collections of poems) solely consisted of **qasidas,** classical, mono-rhymed love poems made up of three parts: the evocation of the beloved, the description of a journey and an elegy of the poem's subject. At the end of the 9C, a poet from Cabra invented the moaxaja, with one part written in classical Arabic, the other in Romance vernacular (jarcha). The romantic couplets which appeared as **jarchas** in Arabic moaxajas are the oldest European lyrical poetry. The **zejel**, apparently invented by **Avempace**, was the other type of poem frequently used in al-Andalus; these were written in the vernacular and were generally narrative ,

**Al-Mutamid**, king of Sevilla during the taifa period, was one of the finest Moorish writers, although the poet cited most by critics was the Cordoban Ibn Zaydun, lover of Wallada, an Umayyad princess, who herself was also a brilliant poet.

In terms of literary prose, during the Caliphal period the most significant written work was the *El collar único* (The Single Necklace), by Abd al-Rabbini, who also wrote many epistles. However, the best-known writer of the period was the jurist and theologian **Ibn Hazm**, to whom we owe *The Dove's Necklace* on poetic diction and psychological truth, which has been widely translated. In it, he narrates amorous adventures set in the court of Córdoba, but always with exemplary, moral zeal. The 14C saw the rise to prominence of **Ibn Zamrak**, whose verses are engraved in the walls of the Alhambra.

It is highly probable that Greek philosophy, particularly that inspired by Aristotle, would not have reached us without **Averroës** (Ibn Rusd), the intellectual heir to Avicenna. This great Cordoban (1126-98), who was a magistrate in Sevilla and Córdoba and who even became physician to the court, relied on the texts of Greek thinkers to develop his own philosophy out of the pre-ordained ideas of Islamic religion. This physician, musician, astronomer, mathematician and poet was without doubt the most outstanding figure in Moorish culture.

## Religions

**Islam** – The Umayyad rulers who invaded Spain in the 8C were noted for their tolerance towards other religions; however, this did not prevent them from attempting to islamise the country's native inhabitants from the very outset, offering them incentives such as exemption from the payment of religious taxes. It would appear that in the 10C, 50% of the region's inhabitants were Muslims, increasing to 90% two centuries later. The al-Andalus kingdom of three religions only really existed during the first four hundred years of Moorish rule, after which non-Muslims were in the minority.

**Christianity** – Those who opted to retain their own religion were placed into the category of tributaries (dimmí). They had their own hierarchies but were subject to Muslim authority and had to pay a special tax (yizya).

The crisis enveloping Christianity in al-Andalus began with the arrival of the Almoravids. This period saw the initiation of compulsory conversions, emigration to Christian territories, and even deportations to various parts of the Maghreb.

**Judaism** – In line with Christians, Jews could continue to practise their religion after the arrival of the Moors, provided they paid tribute; as can be seen in the Jewish quarters of Andalucía today, they generally lived in enclaves in the heart of towns and cities. Following the decree implemented by the first Almohad king forcing Jews to convert to Islam or face expulsion, many settled in other Jewish communities across the Maghreb and in Egypt. Those who converted and remained in al-Andalus were forced to wear distinctive clothing or signs such as a yellow cap and a special belt.

# ART AND CULTURE

## Architecture

While the popular architecture of Andalucía is as varied as its landscape, many towns and villages have a number of features in common, such as narrow streets, whitewashed façades, niches with statues of saints or the Virgin Mary, and windows with wrought-iron grilles, as well as balconies, sun porches and drying galleries. Beyond the main door, access to the house is often via a hallway through to the patio; these two parts of the entrance area create an air circulation system which helps to temper

the extreme heat of high summer. The kitchen and lounge are normally found on the ground floor; the bedrooms on the first floor. The attic or *soberao* is used as a storeroom and an area for drying hams and sausages at the very top. Those with both the means and space may have two types of sleeping quarters: bedrooms on the ground floor for the summer and others on the upper floors for the winter months. Roofing varies from one province to the next; flat roofs (used as terraces), particularly in Almería, are as common as those with slopes.

In the countryside of Córdoba and Sevilla, where large estates or *latifundios* are the norm, *cortijos* (homesteads), haciendas and *lagares* (wine and olive estates) dot the landscape, and are now wrongly perceived as the archetypal *"casa andaluza"*. These large rural units usually consist of a spacious patio surrounded by stables, storehouses and the accommodation provided for staff and some farm workers, and a smaller patio at the center of the owner's house.

Up until the 19C, towns and cities were comprised of individual houses. However emigration from the countryside and smaller towns resulted in the construction of new types of housing. It was from this time that the so-called

R. Mattes/MICHELIN

## A familiar sight in the Spanish countryside

For the past three decades and more the lofty silhouette of this impressive metal bull has graced the tops of Spanish hillsides, establishing itself as one of the most characteristic features of the country's road network. Originally erected in 1956 as part of an advertising campaign for the Osborne sherry and brandy company, they were on the point of disappearing from the Spanish landscape altogether in 1988, when roadside advertising was banned outside of urban areas. Although the company subsequently removed its name, leaving only the bulls in place, the controversy remained. Legal moves to have the bulls removed sparked a debate that received widespread media coverage, resulting in the signing of petitions and the formation of associations to preserve them. Their defenders were of the opinion that these black bulls had gone beyond their original marketing purpose and had become a decorative feature which was now an integral part of the Spanish landscape and a national symbol. The regional parliament (Junta de Andalucía) was moved to classify the bulls as official historical monuments, thus enabling them to fight another day!

H. Champollion/MICHELIN

*A flower-decked patio, Córdoba*

"neighbourhood corrals" *(corrales de vecindad)* evolved, occasionally created in abandoned convents and monasteries. Today, following substantial renovation, some of these corrals have been converted into expensive seigniorial residences popular with artists and high-earning professionals. At the lower end of the economic scale, blocks of flats began to be built at the beginning of the 20C.

Andalucía also contains a number of unique types of housing such as caves in Granada, Almería and in particular Guadix; the humble homes of the Doñana National Park, built of wooden frames covered with rushes; the houses of the Alpujarras (Granada and Almería), the direct inheritors of Moorish architecture; the small houses tucked away down alleyways and under the arches of villages in the Axarquía region (Málaga); and the incomparable beauty of the pueblos blancos (white villages) of Cádiz and Málaga.

## Architectural Terms

**Alcazaba**: fortified military settlement.

**Alcázar**: Moorish royal palace.

**Alfiz**: rectangular surround to a horseshoe-shaped arch in Muslim architecture.

**Alicatado**: technique of Persian origin consisting of cutting sheets of ceramic tiles *(azulejos)* in such a way as to form geometric patterns.

**Altarpiece**: retable. Decorative screen above and behind the altar.

**Apse**: far end of a church housing the high altar; can be semi-circular, polygonal or horseshoe-shaped.

**Arabesque**: a Romantic term used to express the ornamental effect of Islamic art.

**Archivolt**: each of the concentric ornamental mouldings on the outer edge of a splayed arch.

**Artesonado**: marquetry ceiling in which raised fillets outline honeycomb-like cells in the shape of stars.

**Ataurique**: stylised plant ornamentation inspired by the acanthus leaf, a feature of Moorish art.

**Azulejo**: glazed, patterned, ceramic tiles.

**Cabecera**: east (apsidal) end of a Christian church, housing the chancel.

**Caliphal**: architectural style developed in Córdoba under the Caliphate (8C-11C) of which the finest example is the Mezquita.

**Camarín**: small chapel on the first floor behind the altarpiece or retable. It is elaborately decorated and very often contains a lavishly costumed statue of the Virgin Mary.

**Capilla Mayor**: area of the high altar containing the retablo mayor or monumental altarpiece which often rises to the roof.

**Churrigueresque**: in the style of the Churrigueras, an 18C family of architects. Richly ornate Baroque decoration.

**Coro**: chancel in Spanish canonical churches often built in the middle of the nave. It contains the stalls *(sillería)* used by members of religious orders. When placed in a tribune or gallery it is known as the coro alto.

**Crucero**: transept. The part of a church at right angles to the nave which gives the church the shape of a cross. It consists of the transept crossing and arms.

**Cuerda seca**: glazed ceramic technique.

**Estípite**: pilaster in the shape of a truncated inverted pyramid.

**Grotesque**: typical Renaissance decoration combining vegetation, imaginary figures and animals.

**Kiblah**: sacred wall of a mosque from which the *mihrab* is hollowed, facing towards Mecca.

**Kufic**: Arabic script originating from the city of Kufa, characterised by large angled letters.

**Lacerías**: geometric decoration formed by intersecting straight lines making star-shaped and polygonal figures. Characteristic of Moorish architecture.

**Lantern**: an architectural feature in the highest part of a cupola admitting light to the area below.

**Madrassa**: a Moorish university or religious academy.

**Mihrab**: richly decorated prayer-niche in the sacred wall *(kiblah)* in a mosque.

**Minaret**: tower of the mosque *(mezquita)*, from which the muezzin calls the faithful to prayer.

**Mocárabes**: decorative motifs of Muslim architecture formed by assembled prisms ending in concave surfaces. They resemble stalactites or pendants and adorn vaults and cornices.

**Modillion**: a bracket or console used to support a cornice, the springing of an arch etc.

**Mozarabic**: the work of Christians living under Arab rule after the Moorish invasion of 711. On being persecuted in the 9C, they sought refuge in Christian areas bringing with them Moorish artistic traditions.

**Mudéjar**: the work of Muslims living in Christian territory following the Reconquest (13C-14C).

**Plateresque**: term derived from *platero* (silversmith), and used to describe the early style of the Renaissance characterised by finely carved decoration.

**Predella**: the lower part of an altarpiece.

**Presbytery**: the space in front of the main altar, separated from the nave by steps or a partition.

**Sagrario**: chapel containing the Holy Sacrament. May sometimes be a separate church.

**Sebka**: type of brick decoration developed under the Almohads consisting of an apparently endless series of small arches forming a network of diamond shapes.

**Stucco**: type of moulding mix consisting mainly of plaster, used for coating surfaces. It plays a fundamental role in the wall decoration of Hispano-Muslim architecture.

**Trasaltar**: back wall of the *capilla mayor* in front of which sculptures or tombs are often found.

**Trascoro**: the wall, often carved and decorated, which encloses the *coro*.

**Triforium**: arcade above the side aisles which opens onto the central nave of a church.

**Tympanum**: inner surface of a pediment. This often ornamented space is bounded by the archivolt and the lintel of the doors of churches.

**Yesería**: plasterwork used in sculptured decoration.

# Pre-Muslim Art

Although the Moors embellished Andalucía with its most emblematic monuments, the land they conquered was far from being virgin territory. From the Palaeolithic period onwards civilisations succeeded each other on Andalusian soil, each leaving its indelible mark.

## PREHISTORY AND ANTIQUITY

Of prime importance from the **Palaeolithic Era** (30000-9000 BC) are the **Pileta caves** at Benaoján (Málaga), with their miles of galleries decorated with paintings of animals and symbolic drawings, and the caves at Nerja (Málaga). The Ambrosio cave in Vélez Blanco (Almería), holds an unusual decorative engraved frieze.

The **Neolithic Era** saw the development of more schematic human and animal figures alongside drawings of the sun, idols and various symbols. Drawings in the caves at Tajo de las Figuras (Cádiz), La Graja (Jaén) and Los Letreros (Vélez Blanco, Almería) all date from this period.

The third millennium BC saw the influx of civilisations from the Mediterranean, heralding early **Megalithic culture**, which reached its zenith in the second millennium; the most striking example of this period is at **Los Millares** (Gádor, Almería). This large complex of walls and collective sepulchres shows that its builders not only knew how to work metals, but also had significant knowledge of ceramics, basket-making and weaving. The collective Menga, Viera and Romeral dolmens at Antequera, those at Castilleja de Guzmán and the 4C-3C BC Dolmen del Soto at Trigueros are the finest Megalithic constructions found anywhere in Spain, in terms both of size and level of development.

### Oriental influences

**The Phoenicians** – Oriental art came to Andalucía via the Phoenicians who, having founded Gades (Cádiz), established

*Ephebus of Antequera*

### What about the Greeks?

Cádiz and Huelva contain the richest examples of Greek ceramics in Andalucía, despite the fact that neither province was home to Greek settlements of any importance. It is highly probable that many of these were in fact gifts that the Phoenicians bestowed upon the native inhabitants to win their friendship.

outposts on either side of the Straits of Gibraltar in preparation for further advances along the Mediterranean coast. The oldest Phoenician remains discovered are from the settlement at Morro de Mezquitilla (Málaga), dating from the 9C BC. Other Phoenician vestiges have also been unearthed in the provinces of Cádiz, Málaga (the tombs at Trayamar) and Almería (Sexi necropolis).

### The Tartessians

The kingdom of Tartessus (9C-4C BC), aligned with the Phoenicians, pro-

B. Kaufmann/MICHELIN

duced a variety of objects made from bronze and ceramic (jugs, water pitchers, amphorae), as well as delicate pieces of goldware (diadems, belts, pendants) decorated with distinctive motifs, undoubtedly linked to the worship of various divinities.

## The Iberians

The earliest Iberian **sculpture** dates from the 5C BC and shows clear influences from Greek and Phoenician art, with rigid figures represented frontally. These artefacts were generally used to protect the dead, whose remains were cremated and deposited in urns or sarcophagi placed in large stone mausoleums, as can be seen at La Toya (Jaén), Baza (Granada) and Villaricos (Almería). The apogee of local sculptural art was from the 5C-4C BC, during which works with clear Hellenic influences were created, such as the magnificent **Dama de Baza**. Iberian **ceramics** also copied the red glaze used by the Phoenicians and Greek vases. Their varied designs evolved from primitive bands and circumferences to complex drawings of leaves and flowers interspersed with geometric motifs.

## Roman art in Spain

In accordance with their custom, the Romans who came to Hispania in the 2C BC immediately introduced the official art from their imperial capital. Although, with the passing of time, many of these works were created entirely on the Iberian peninsula, it is not possible to talk of truly Hispano-Roman art, but of Roman art created in Hispania.

Baetica, the most advanced region on the Iberian peninsula during the Roman period, began to experience significant growth with the development of new settlements along the River Guadalquivir (Betis), planned according to the Roman grid system. Córdoba, the capital, could not match the splendour of **Itálica**, which attained maximum development under emperors Trajan and Hadrian, both of Andalusian extraction. The cities of **Hispalis** (Sevilla), **Carmona** and **Acinipo** (Ronda la Vieja) also contained opulent patrician mansions

and large public buildings that used marble from Macael (Almería).

In Roman **sculpture**, representations of emperors (Trajan, Hadrian and Vespasian) and their families were common, as were sculptures of goddesses (Venus in Itálica, for example). The decoration of patrician mansions also imitated that of Rome. **Mosaics** and small bronze figures reproduced the work of slaves brought from Africa (standard-holders, candelabra). Tiny statues of household gods (lares) governed daily activities .

Lastly, the layout and design of **rural villas** would later provide inspiration for popular Andalusian architecture.

## HISPANO-VISIGOTHIC ART (6C-8C)

The Visigoths who invaded Spain in the 5C were nomads without an architectural tradition. Consequently, palaeo-Christian forms, which had already absorbed Byzantine and Oriental influence, persisted throughout Roman Baetica until the end of the 6C.

The third Council of State in Toledo (589), which proclaimed the unity of the kingdom, marked the start of new architectural forms which consolidated to acquire undisputed uniformity.

In religious buildings, the classical basilican plan, slightly modified, as in Alcalá de los Gazules, developed into a cruciform shape. Aisles were separated by columns supporting **horseshoe arches**. Vaults were generally semicircular, while aisles often had a wooden framework. Decoration on walls, imposts and capitals showed a marked **Oriental influence** with mostly **geometric motifs** as opposed to vegetal and a few human figures. The exteriors were devoid of buttresses of any kind.

Given that almost every Visigothic temple was later modified, the original plan can now be recognised in just a few buildings, such as in San Pedro de Alcántara (Málaga), El Germo (Córdoba) and Gerena (Sevilla).

The most recognisable feature of Visigothic art is its **gold** and **silverwork**, which reached a level of perfection in the 7C. Craftsmen produced two types of work, namely liturgical items (processional crosses and votive objects such as their famous crowns) and articles of a personal nature (clasps, bracelets, necklaces and pendants). Some pieces now exhibited in museums, such as those from **Torredonjimeno** (Jaén), belong to treasure buried by the Visigoths in the face of the advancing Moors.

# Hispano-Muslim Art (8C-15C)

The Moorish invasion, which may initially have appeared a tragedy, was in reality the beginning of a magnificent era of creativity and vitality as the inhabitants of Andalucía came into contact with the aesthetics of Islam.

However, through eight centuries of Moorish occupation, Andalusian art always retained basic artistic characteristics which clearly distinguished it from all other artistic trends of the period.

## MOORISH ART

### Arches

During the early days of Moorish rule, the **horseshoe arch**, with its Visigothic and Oriental influence and alternating red (brick) and white (plaster with lime) voussoirs, was the main feature of Moorish buildings. The arches had a dual purpose: as an element of support and as decoration, for example as a border for a blind arch. The development of intersecting arches gave rise to the pointed horseshoe-shaped arch, used extensively from the 12C onwards.

As time passed, the **foliated arch**, already in evidence in the Mezquita in Córdoba, evolved into the highly complex **multifoil arch**.

The **alfiz**, the rectangular moulding surrounding the arch, was another recurrent theme of Moorish art, and was to have a major influence on Mudéjar art in subsequent centuries.

### Vaults, armatures and artesonado work

Hispano-Moorish vaults took their influence from Oriental Islamic art. Unlike those in Christian art (arris and fan vaults), their ribs do not cross at the centre. Perhaps one of the best examples is the enclosure of the mihrab in Córdoba's Mezquita.

Despite the uniqueness of Andalusian vaults, it is undoubtedly the widely used wooden armature which can be considered the architectural feature which best displays the Moor's technical and aesthetic expertise. Wooden coverings evolved from simple paired and knuckle armatures to the most sophisticated of

*Arcades, Patio de los Loenes, Alhambra, Granada*

B. Kaufmann/MICHELIN

artesonado work decorated with stars to form attractive *lacería* ornamentation.

## Decoration: materials and motifs

Behind austere outer walls, the interiors of Andalusian palaces were often of extraordinary splendour. Sometimes resplendent facing completely masked humble construction materials.

The refined aesthetic sense of the Hispano-Moors managed to successfully combine techniques as disparate as **azulejos** and **alicatados** (decorative sections of tiling), panels of stone or sculpted plasterwork, mosaics with Oriental influence, wood worked to form latticework, and exquisite *artesonado*, to create surprisingly sumptuous effects. The decorative motifs used can be classified into three main groups:

*Ataurique motifs, Medina Azahara, Córdoba*

**geometric designs**, mainly used in the decoration of glazed ceramic friezes and in the ornamentation of wood (doors, latticework and artesonados), in which the lines are broken up by polygons and stars;

**plant motifs**, known as **atauriques**, used to decorate sculpted stone or plaster wall panels. Over time, these motifs (palm leaves, grapevines) were styled to create extremely complex designs. A common technique was the stylisation of the tree of life – vegetal decoration arranged around a vertical axis. Mocárabes, decorative motifs resembling stalactites, were used to decorate arches and cupolas;

**epigraphs** fulfilled the same informative function as images used by other architectural styles, with **Kufic script**, characterised by its large, angled lettering, and **Nesjí script**, with its more free-flowing characters, the most widely used.

## Applied arts

Andalusian decorative art produced a variety of elaborate objects which can be classified as household or luxury items. The latter were created to satisfy the demand of a more refined ruling class who afforded importance to interior decoration and who took great pleasure in bestowing unique and sumptuous gifts on foreign visitors.

In terms of **ceramics**, the following stand out: the earthenware known as **green and manganese**, the so-called **cuerda seca** ceramics (azulejos) used as wall decoration, and the gilded work known as **reflejo metálico** (lustre work). The latter, production of which began in Córdoba in the 9C, attained its full glory during the Nasrid period in the production centres in and around Málaga.

In addition to Córdoba, where Abd ar-Rahman II founded the Casa del Tiraz or Royal Silk Factory, Almería specialised in the production of exquisite **fabrics**; during the 14C and 15C, the workshops of Granada also produced impressive silk fabrics entwined with gold thread. Intense colours predominated in these fabrics, which were decorated with inscriptions and architectural motifs.

Nasrid **gold** and **silversmiths** showed a special predilection for ceremonial swords, the hilts and guards of which were decorated with extraordinary combinations of marble, filigree and polychrome enamel.

To complete the full picture of Hispano-Moorish artistry, mention should also be made of the highly delicate marble carvings, which were popular decorative features used by the Caliphate, *taraceas* (wood inlaid with **marble** and woods of varying colours) used to decorate Nasrid furniture, and leatherwork (**cordovans** made from goatskin and embossed sheepskin **guadamecies**).

Many of these items were to remain in use by the Christians, who praised their quality and value. In fact, the sculpted marble boxes and chests in which Muslim women kept their jewels and perfume were subsequently used to preserve the relics of saints.

## Cordoban caliphate (8C-10C)

The Mezquita in Córdoba and the Medina Azahara palace, the two great monuments from this period, contain all the features associated with early Hispano-Moorish art, which developed during the three centuries in which Córdoba was the capital of al-Andalus.

In accordance with their custom of assimilating the culture of those they conquered, the Moors used techniques and features from both Visigothic and Roman art, skilfully combined with the traditions of the Arabian Peninsula.

The major imports from Caliphal art were the **foliated arch** and the **alfiz**, the rectangular surround of a horseshoe arch. In decoration, early geometric motifs containing squares and diamonds gradually evolved into designs encompassing floral motifs (vine leaves, bunches of grapes, acanthus leaves, palm trees and rosettes) inspired by the Umayyads; these were later replaced by heart-shaped floral drawings which took their inspiration from the Abbasids.

The Caliphate's economic prosperity was reflected in the materials used (ashlar stone and worked marble) and the opulence of the metallic lustre of Byzantine mosaics created by foreign craftsmen.

B. Kaufmann/MICHELIN

*Caliphal capital, Medina Azahara, Córdoba*

## Taifa period (11C)

Despite the political dispersion which was a feature of the taifa (faction) kingdoms, Andalusian art of the period showed great unity, given that Andalucía had become isolated from the rest of Islam. Artists from the erstwhile Caliphate of Córdoba emigrated to the courts of various taifas where they continued the Cordoban tradition.

Economic decline resulted in the abandoning of noble materials such as ashlar stone on walls, and columns and pillars made from marble in favour of **brick**, **plaster** and **mortar**. To compensate for this, **decorative motifs** attained unexpected heights (epigraphic, geometric and plant designs) and combinations of **arches (foliated, mixtilinear**, semicircular, pointed, intercrossing etc) came into use to form arabesque features. During this period, religious architecture was less important than both civil (numerous **public baths** such as the so-called Bañuelo de Granada) and military architecture (the alcazabas in Málaga, Granada and Almería).

## Almoravid period (12C)

Following the arrival of the Almoravids, Andalusian art spread throughout the Maghreb. Marrakech and Sevilla developed into the capitals of a new kingdom on either side of the Straits of Gibraltar, gradually introducing new trends result-

## Other caliphal buildings

During the Caliphal period, other constructions included the minarets of San Juan and Santa Clara (Córdoba), El Salvador (Sevilla) and San José (Granada), in addition to the fortifications in Tarifa and the Pinos Bridge (Granada).

*Iglesia de San Lorenzo, Córdoba*

H. Champollion/MICHELIN

ing from mutual influence between the peoples of the two continents.

Arches began to develop ever more complicated styles, as did **cupolas**, some of which contained openwork; others which were decorated with mocárabe motifs. This era heralded the appearance of geometric decoration in the form of networks of **sebka** or diamond-shaped designs; combinations of epigraphic and lacería motifs also increased in complexity.

Almost all buildings dating from this period have either disappeared or been swallowed up beneath additions introduced by the Almohads, although experts recognise features of the Almoravid style in the mihrab in one of the mezquitas in Almería (the present-day Iglesia de San Juan).

## Inscriptions

Buildings in the kingdom of Granada contained three types of inscriptions: those of an informative nature relating to the origin of the building; religious inscriptions, taken from the Koran; and literary and poetic inscriptions.

### Almohad period (13C)

The basic religious principles of the Almohads, which were based on **purity** and **austerity**, were reflected in the simplicity and monumental nature of their buildings, the majority of which were defensive in character, such as the Alcázar and the Torre del Oro in Sevilla. This type of fortified construction, with its delimiting gateways and defensive towers *(albarranas)* separated from the fortified buildings, would later be adopted by the Christians as a model for their own castles.

The new arrivals used the same construction materials as their predecessors, namely brick, mortar, plaster and wood, but opted for more sober decoration, with large empty spaces and geometric adornments replacing plant motifs. The traditional horseshoe arch was practically abandoned, except in exceptional circumstances, and replaced by **pointed horseshoe** and foiled arches.

Without doubt, the most representative monument from this period is the Giralda in Sevilla which, in its day, was the minaret for the main mezquita in the capital of the Almohad kingdom.

*Torre del Oro, Sevilla*

H. Belmenouar/MICHELIN

## The use of water in the architecture of al-Andalus

Throughout the kingdom of al-Andalus, that scarce commodity – water – played a fundamental role in architecture. Water had a triple function: practical, religious and aesthetic. Practical, because of its necessity for life (the irrigation of fields and the supply of bath water); religious, because the Koran states that a series of ablutions must be carried out prior to prayer; and aesthetic, because water stored in pools and basins reflected the elegant decoration of the walls and ceilings, while water running through channels, fountains and gutters produced a relaxing murmur and cooled the air. Water also enabled the creation of gardens that were so well integrated into the surrounding architecture that it is difficult to know where nature ends and where the works created by man begin.

## Nasrid period (13C-15C)

In the eyes of many specialists, this represents the greatest period in Andalusian art. For many years, these experts highlighted the poverty of the materials used in Nasrid art, and their contrast with their abundance of decoration. Nowadays it is known that the function of the building determined the choice of materials. Consequently, in baths, as well as fortresses such as the Alcazaba in Granada, ashlar stone, bricks and mortar (of characteristic red colour) were used. Palaces such as the Alhambra used **marble** on the floors and for its columns, **glazed ceramics** (azulejos) in areas exposed to friction, **elaborate plaster and stucco decoration**, wooden vaults and artesonados and **mocárabe vaults**.

**Capitals** were generally of two types: the first had a cylindrical base decorated with plain leaves which supported a parallelepiped adorned with additional foliage; the second type were mocárabe in style and derived from Asian art.

Although less spectacular nowadays due to weathering, **colour** was the other main feature of Nasrid buildings, the interiors of which, in their prime, must have looked like an Impressionist painting. In addition to the friezes of azulejos, the plaster and wood used to cover walls were painted in red, blue, green and gold tones, at a time when different-coloured marble was also used for capitals and columns. Given that the present-day appearance of the Alhambra continues to impress and amaze millions of visitors, we can only imagine how impressive it must have looked during its period of maximum splendour.

## MEDIEVAL ANDALUSIAN ART

### Mudéjar art (13C-16C)

Following the conquest of Córdoba and Sevilla in the first half of the 13C, Christian models were imposed on those buildings under the yoke of the kingdom of Castilla, although their construction was entrusted to skilled Muslim craftsmen. This resulted in the development of the typically Spanish Mudéjar art, the fusion of Islamic and Western artistic concepts.

Mudéjar architecture evolved over the centuries, adapting to the dominant features of each area, in such a way that the Mudéjar style in Andalucía is different from that of other Spanish regions. Despite these differences, in general it can be said that it remains loyal to Muslim traditions in terms of the materials used (plaster, brick and wood), its con-

H. Champollion/MICHELIN

*El Cervatillo, Museo Arqueológico Provincial, Córdoba*

struction techniques (walls, horseshoe arches and wood ceilings) and decoration (fine artesonado work, the use of alfiz, and complicated plasterwork).

In the main, the churches of Sevilla (San Marcos, San Pablo and Santa Marina) are built using brick, with artesonados and traditional features of Almohad decoration. Major examples of civil architecture, in which roofs with two or four slopes predominate, include the Alcázar in Sevilla, which Pedro I rebuilt in 1366, the Torre de Don Fadrique (Sevilla), the Torre de El Carpio (Córdoba), the Castillo de San Romualdo (San Fernando, Cádiz) and the Casa de Pilatos (Sevilla).

## Gothic art (13C-15C)

Early Andalusian Gothic art, which was inspired by the Cistercian model (large rose windows on the façades and a central nave with two side aisles of lower height with ogival vaults), produced works of great interest such as the so-called Fernandina churches of Córdoba (Santa Marina, San Miguel and San Lorenzo).

The construction of Sevilla Cathedral started in 1401. This is the largest Gothic building in Andalucía and one of the last Spanish Gothic churches to be built. The Flemish artists who worked on this ambitious project introduced a series of innovations, such as a rectangular floor plan, a flat apsidal end with a small apse, slender fasciated pillars,

*East façade, Mezquita, Córdoba*

complex star-shaped vaults and abundant decoration.

During the reign of Isabel the Catholic, the **Isabelline** style developed, halfway between Gothic and Renaissance, exuberantly combining Flamboyant and Mudéjar features. The Capilla Real in Granada, a work by Enrique Egas, is the best example of the Isabelline style.

Foreign artists who came to Sevilla in the 15C brought Flemish influence, with its deep realism, to Andalusian sculpture. **Lorenzo Mercadante**, who was born in Brittany, is one of the best exponents of this Andalusian Gothic style. He worked mainly on the cathedral in Sevilla and introduced the technique of terra cotta, which was later used by numerous local artists. Spanish artists of the period worthy of mention include **Pedro Millán**, creator of the statue of the Virgin of the Pillar (Virgen del Pilar) in the same cathedral.

*Azulejos, Alcázar, Sevilla*

# Renaissance and Baroque

The arrival on Spanish shores of seemingly limitless bounty from the Americas coincided with the introduction in the country of new artistic forms inspired by the Renaissance. This flowering of the arts, led by the appearance of leading artists of the time, saw Sevilla, Córdoba, Granada and many other towns and cities across the region establish themselves as centres of artistic creation. This expansion reached its zenith during the two centuries that followed, a period that saw the full expression and glory of Andalusian Baroque.

## THE RENAISSANCE (16C)

### Architecture

The arrival of the Renaissance in Spain coincided with a new period of splendour in Andalucía. The monopoly on trade with the New World held by Sevilla resulted in the amassing of huge fortunes in the region's capital and other main towns and cities, which were soon embellished with myriad religious and secular monuments.

However, the magnificence of late-Gothic architecture and Mudéjar tradition initially prevented the total adoption of Renaissance ideas; in fact, the first three decades of the 16C saw the development of the **Plateresque style**, similar in style to Isabelline, and so called because of its lavish, refined decoration which was reminiscent of silverwork (plata: silver). Although the masterpiece of this genre is undoubtedly the town hall (ayuntamiento) in Sevilla, a work by **Diego de Riaño**, a number of other fine examples of the style can be found across Andalucía: the gracious Lonja of the Chapel Royal and Diego de Siloé's doorway of the church at the Monasterio de San Jerónimo, both of which are found in Granada; a number of palaces in Baeza and Úbeda, in the province of Jaén; and the façade of the Iglesia de Santa María de la Asunción, by Alonso de Baena, in Arcos de la Frontera.

As the century evolved, greater importance was attributed to proportions than ornamentation, resulting in the total abandonment of Gothic ideas. Barrel, oval and oven vaulting became predominant features, along with the almost exclusive use of the semicircular arch; decorative motifs also increased in size at a time when the trend was for the concentration of decoration in specific areas to allow for the development of vast open areas.

Three names stand out in Renaissance architecture in the region. Diego de Siloé (1495-1563) completed the work on Granada Cathedral, having modified the Gothic plans conceived by Enrique de Egas. The edifice, one of the most significant from this period, served as a model for the cathedrals in both Málaga and Guadix. De Siloé was also active

*Cupola, Capilla del Sagrario, Priego de Córdoba*

H. Champollion/MICHELIN

## Andrés de Vandelvira, The Andalusian Brunelleschi

This brilliant architect (1509-75), a disciple of Diego de Siloé, enjoyed great prestige in his lifetime for the monumental aspect that he brought to Andalusian Renaissance architecture. Vandelvira's style blends in perfectly with the barrenness of Jaén's landscapes, where his ornamental features are reduced to a minimum of expression, yet at the same time embracing a taste for large, bare and luminous spaces.

elsewhere in the region, in particular Guadix, Montefrío (Iglesia de la Villa) and across the province of Jaén, where he worked in close collaboration with his disciple, Andrés de Vandelvira, who left his audacious mark on Jaén Cathedral and other buildings in the same province, particularly in Úbeda (Iglesia del Salvador) and Baeza.

Lastly, the architect and painter **Pedro Machuca** (d 1550) always remained faithful to his Italian training, which he received alongside Michelangelo. Carlos V's palace in Granada's Alhambra, his most impressive work, is a work of extreme simplicity (a circle built within a square) and total innovation which was completely misunderstood at the time.

The most important figures of the Renaissance in Sevilla were **Martín Gaínza**, the architect for the chapel royal in the city's cathedral, and the Cordoban **Hernán Ruiz**, who was responsible for the modern-day appearance of the Giralda.

The last third of the 16C in Spain also saw the forceful imposition of the **Herreran** style created by **Juan de Herrera**, as seen at El Escorial. Sevilla is also home to a work by Felipe II's favourite architect: the Archivo de Indias which, with its sober, rectilinear façade, encompasses all the characteristic features of Counter Reformation art.

### Sculpture

Realism and expression are the dominant sculptural themes from the Renaissance period, which was already providing a foretaste of Baroque imagery. Given that most projects were commissioned by the Church, religious figures predominate. It should also be remembered that the Counter Reformation was initiated in the last third of the century, on behalf of which Felipe II was determined to mount a strong defence. More often than not, these sculptures were carved in polychrome wood; marble, alabaster and stone were only used for rare secular figures, funereal and monumental art. As was the case during the Gothic period, the Renaissance in Andalucía saw an abundance of altars decorated with large-dimensioned retables.

Of the numerous Italian artists who worked in the region, the following stand out: **Domenico Fancelli** (1469-1518), the sculptor of the tombs of the Catholic Monarchs in the Chapel Royal in Granada Cathedral; **Jacobo Florentino** (1476-1526), who created the Burial of Christ (Entierro de Cristo) exhibited in the Museo de Bellas Artes in the city; and **Pietro Torrigiano**, whose Penitent St Jerome (Museo de Bellas Artes, Sevilla) was to exert great influence on Sevilla's Baroque sculptors. The Burgundian **Felipe Vigarny** (d 1543) mainly worked in Castilla in collaboration with Berruguete; however, he created one of his

*Palacio de Carlos V, Alhambra, Granada*

H. Champollion/MICHELIN

H. Champollion/MICHELIN

*Tomb of Juana the Mad, Capilla Real, Granada*

best works in Granada, namely the altarpiece for the city's Chapel Royal.

Although he died young, the most important Spanish sculptor of the period was **Bartolomé Ordóñez** (d 1520), born in Burgos but trained in Italy, who died in Carrara after working on the tombs of Juana la Loca (Joan the Mad) and Felipe el Hermoso (Philip the Handsome) for the Capilla Real in Granada.

## Painting

As with the sculpture of the period, religious rather than secular themes dominated Renaissance painting. It could be said that in the whole of Andalucía, the only city to stand apart was Sevilla, where several families with large fortunes decorated their mansions with secular, mythological and allegorical canvases (Casa de Pilatos). During the early decades of the century the Flemish influence, with its characteristic taste for concrete images, remained ever present. However, Tuscan mannerism and Raphael's classicism gradually paved the way for the arrival of Venetian painting.

The best exponent of the early Sevillian Renaissance was **Alejo Fernández** (?1475-1546), an artist of German extraction who adopted the Spanish surname of his wife. In line with the themes popular with Flemish painters, he was first attracted by the effects of perspective and by the arrangement of space. During this period, when his studio was in Córdoba, he painted his

famous *Flagellation* (Museo del Prado, Madrid) and *Christ Tied to the Column* (Museo de Bellas Artes, Córdoba). When he moved to Sevilla, his interest evolved to the human form, with works such as the *Virgin of the Rose* (Iglesia de Santa Ana) and the *Virgin of the Navigators*, his most famous painting of the period, on display in the Alcázar in Sevilla.

The Sevillian artist **Luis de Vargas** (1506-68), who trained in Italy with a disciple of Raphael, took his inspiration from the mannerism of Vasari and the delicate touch of Correggio. His most renowned work is the *Generación temporal de Cristo* in the city's cathedral, which was given the nickname of La Gamba due to the beauty of Adam's leg (*gamba* in Italian). In the eyes of many, **Luis de Moraleis** (?1520-?86), an artist from Extremadura who had close ties with Andalucía, is the most interesting painter of his era; his highly personal works manifest both Flemish and Italian influence. The gentleness of his feminine characters and the expressiveness of his ailing Christs (*Ecce Homo* in the Academia de San Fernando, Madrid) made him the most admired artist of the time and subject to imitation by his peers.

During the 16C, Sevilla became popular with many Flemish artists who were attracted by the wealth and riches of the city and hope of commissions in America. These included Peter Kempeneer, known as **Pedro de Campaña** (1503-63), who painted the impressively

## Italian Ceramics in Andalucía

Glazed and painted ceramics from Italy, which co-existed with those created according to Mudéjar traditions, were brought to Andalucía at the beginning of the 16C by the Pisan, Francisco Niculoso, who was responsible for two interesting works in Sevilla, namely the portal of the church of the Convento de Santa Paula and the altarpiece in the oratory of the Alcázar. This type of decoration was inspired by the work of the Della Robbia family.

large *Descent from the Cross* in the city's cathedral, and **Hernando Sturbio** (d 1577), the creator of the Retable of the Evangelists in the same edifice.

## BAROQUE (17C-18C)

Spanish Baroque shone forth in every aspect of art. During the first half of the 17C, the influence of the Herreran style remained: churches with a very simple rectangular plan, ornamental plaster motifs and occasionally façades decorated with panels of azulejos (Hospital de la Caridad, Sevilla). This austerity gradually softened, as buildings started to be covered with more ornate decoration, even though the structures themselves remained simple in design and many cupolas were deceptive in that they were often composed of a wooden arcature with a plaster facing instead of being made of stone.

It was during the course of this century that the architect, sculptor and painter **Alonso Cano** created the main façade of Granada Cathedral.

However, it was not until after the rise to power of the Bourbons that Andalusian Baroque entered into its most sumptuous phase, with the development of trade with the Americas (due to the silting up of the River Guadalquivir, Cádiz replaced Sevilla as the main trading port with the Americas in 1717), resulting in a period of frenetic construction across the entire region. Numerous small towns were soon embellished with seigniorial mansions and Baroque churches, such as Osuna (bell tower of the Iglesia de la Merced and Palacio de los Marqueses de la Gomera), Écija (Palacio de Benamejí, Palacio de Peñaflor and the bell tower of the Iglesia de San Juan), Lucena (Capilla del Sagrario), Priego de Córdoba, Alcalá la Real, Guadix (bell tower and façade of the cathedral), Carmona (Convento de las Descalzas) and Estepa (doorway of the Iglesia del Carmen).

The overflowing imagination of artists knew no bounds. Concave and convex structures gave undulating movement to façades, while decorative motifs such as volutes, floral bands and Solomonic columns adorned every surface. Beneath the common denominator of exuberance, architects felt free to interpret Baroque according to their own personal preferences. Moorish influence and a fantasy of colour were the prime influences behind the ostentatious Sagrario in the Carthusian monastery (Cartuja) in Granada, designed by **Francisco Hurtado** (1669-1725); in the same city, the extraordinary decor of the Iglesia de San Juan de Dios stands out for the rich ornamentation of its façade. Meanwhile, **Vicente Acero**, the architect of the Real Fábrica de Tabacos (Royal Tobacco Factory), was inspired by Siloé's Renaissance cathedral in Granada, when he embarked upon Spain's last great cathedral, in Cádiz, built between 1722 and 1729.

The Sevillian **Leonardo de Figueroa** (1650-1730), the creator of a number of important civic buildings in his native city such as the Palacio de San Telmo (originally built as a school for future navigators and today the seat of the Andalusian parliament) and the Hospital de los Venerables, was also responsible for several fine churches, including the Iglesia del Salvador and the Iglesia de San Luis de los Franceses; the latter, with its central plan and Solomonic columns, demonstrates his great ability to combine brick, ceramics and coloured plaster.

### Sculpture

Although marble and bronze statues inspired by allegorical and mythological themes were popular in both Italy and France, in Andalucía as in the rest of Spain sculpture was used as a tool of the Counter Reformation, with realism as its dominant theme.

At the beginning of the 20C, the region became a fundamental focal point for religious sculpture – times were difficult and people were looking towards religion as a solution to their problems. Communities of monks and nuns developed, multiplying the need for sculpted images and groups of statues, both to be venerated at the altar and held aloft in street processions such as those during Holy Week. These increasingly realistic and expressive works continued to be carved from polychrome wood, although the colours became increasingly natural. In many cases fabric covered the whole body, so that only the face and hands were carved; it was also known for glass eyes and tears, added as a final touch of authenticity.

Known to his contemporaries as the "god of wood", **Juan Martínez Montañés** (1568-1648), born in Alcalá la Real, was the true founder of Sevilla's sculptural school and the finest representative of the zenith of the art in Andalucía. More influenced by Renaissance ideas than his contemporaries, this masterful sculptor only evolved towards the Baroque style towards the end his career. The creator of numerous polychrome works (whose colours were often adopted by the artist Francisco Pacheco), he was able to confer great serenity upon the expressions depicted in his faces. As well as numerous Mannerist-inspired retablos (Santos Juanes in the Iglesia de San Leandro), he also created countless images of Christ and saints (his best work is without doubt his Christ of Clemency in Sevilla Cathedral), including tiny marble figurines. From his Baroque period, particular attention should be paid to the extraordinary retable of the Battle of Angels (Iglesia de San Miguel, Jérez de la Frontera) and the magnificent, reflective Immaculate Conceptions in Sevilla Cathedral. Among the disciples of Montañés, mention should be made of the Sevillan **Alonso Martínez** (d 1668), who collaborated on a number of masterpieces by his master, the Cordoban **Juan de Mesa** (1583-1627),

*Detail, Capilla del Sagrario, Priego de Córdoba*

H. Champollion/MICHELIN

whose style was considered more dramatic; the latter was the creator of the venerated Jesús del Gran Poder (Jesus of Great Power), nowadays exhibited in the modern Templo de Nuestro Padre Jesús del Gran Poder, built in 1965.

The Sevilla School was headed by the multi-faceted **Alonso Cano** (1601-67), an architect, artist and sculptor born in Granada and who trained alongside Martínez Montañés. His simple, delicate figures would later be reinterpreted by his numerous pupils, such as **Pedro de Mena** (1628-93), the sculptor of the choir stalls in Málaga Cathedral, and José de Mora (1642-1724), whose psychological imbalance – he was to die insane – remain entrenched in his often striking works.

During the course of the 17C, and particularly at the beginning of the 18C, Italian influence began to manifest itself, inspired by the style employed by Bernini. Agitation, movement and a sense of the dramatic in the scenes portrayed are the dominant features of this style subsequently copied by Andalusian artists. Alongside **José de Arce** (d 1666), who introduced this new trend, other artists who stand out include **Pedro Roldán** (1624-1700), who mainly worked in Sevilla (creating the Entombment in the Hospital de la Caridad), and **Pedro Duque Cornejo** (1677-1757), the creator of many works for Carthusian monasteries in and around Sevilla and the fine choir stalls in Córdoba Cathedral.

P. Feria Fernandez/ Museo de Bellas Artes, Sevilla

*St Hugh and Carthusian Monks at Table, Zurbarán*

The long list of Baroque sculptors from the Granada School should also include **Torcuato Ruiz del Peral**, who carved highly expressive heads of saints and the choir stalls in Guadix Cathedral.

## THE GOLDEN AGE OF ANDALUSIAN PAINTING

The 17C is without doubt the Golden Age of Andalusian painting, which started out loyal to the dominant Flemish tradition of the 16C before developing its own expression through opulence and light. From the middle of the century onwards, Sevilla and Madrid became the undisputed capitals of Spanish painting.

The renown of Sevillian artists in the early decades of the 17C, such as **Francisco Pacheco**, the father-in-law of Velázquez, has remained obscured by the brilliance of three undisputed masters: Velázquez, Zurbarán and Murillo.

**Diego Velázquez** spent the majority of his professional life in Madrid as a portrait painter to the Court. However, neither fame nor the influence of Italian artists whom he admired greatly, in particular Titian, could bring him to forget his training in Sevilla. It was during this period (1617-23), before he left the city of his birth, that he painted works with predominantly religious themes and or in the costumbrismo genre (Adoration of the Kings, Museo del Prado, Madrid).

**Francisco de Zurbarán** (1598-1664), from Extremadura, interpreted themes of monastic life, but also painted more popular themes, representing reality as

### La Roldana's Cribs

The tradition of cribs (nacimientos), which would appear to have been started by St Francis of Assisi, has always been very popular in Spain. During the Baroque period, many sculptors created, and inspired through their work, a huge variety of popular figures made from polychrome fired clay, which became part of the country's cultural heritage. La Roldana, the daughter of Pedro Roldán, was one of the finest exponents of this art form in the Andalusian School. One of her most notable works is the Virgen de las Angustias (Virgin of Anguish), in Cádiz.

accurately as possible, with an economy of means and a deliberately limited range of colour which emphasises the play of light and, in his portraits in particular, sees his characters burst forth from the canvas. His academy rapidly developed into one of the largest in Sevilla, exporting more works to the Americas than any other in the city.

**Bartolomé Esteban Murillo** (1617-82), whose works of a religious nature (Virgin Mary, Infant Jesus) have been reproduced time and time again, was the most famous Spanish artist of the period. Through his academy, he also exported innumerable canvases destined for the churches of the New World. The delicate touch and warmth of these occasionally bland paintings cannot hide the qualities of an extraordinary painter who was a great master of both technique and colour, and highly skilled in the portrayal of genre scenes.

In complete contrast, **Juan Valdés Leal** (1662-95) concentrated on expression and the macabre with a striking power and realism that at times touched on the morbid, as seen in the frescoes painted for Sevilla's Hospital de la Caridad.

In Granada, the aforementioned **Alonso Cano** (1661-67), a great friend of Velázquez, was the most classical of all Baroque painters. His most famous work is a series of canvases representing the Life of the Virgin (Granada Cathedral), showing the major influence of the Venetian masters, whose work he became familiar with when he worked under the protection of the favourite of Felipe IV, the Count-Duke of Olivares.

## 19C-20C Art

After several centuries of artistic splendour, Andalusian creativity appeared to run out of steam as it entered the 19C. The severe economic crisis in the region was reflected in a dearth of commissions and the absence of prestigious projects. Despite this, a few Andalusian artists still managed to make their mark in Spain.

### PAINTING

In Romantic painting, several Sevillian artists stand out. These include Antonio Martínez Esquivel, José Gutiérrez de la Vega and **Valeriano Domínguez Bécquer**; the latter, the brother of the poet Gustavo Adolfo Bécquer, was inspired by costumbrismo, with its joyful scenes so alien to his personal experiences of sadness. **Manuel Rodríguez de Guzmán** is worthy of special interest as a result of the huge excitement generated by his excellent sketches of Andalusian life. His warm portrayals of life in southern Spain, which were greatly admired by foreigners, helped to perpetuate the romantic image of Andalucía.

In the last quarter of the century, the realist **Julio Romero de Torres** (1880-1930) was born in Córdoba. This artist specialised in painting Andalusian women of great beauty and restrained sensuality (Oranges and Lemons). Although his work was criticised in certain quarters, such was his popularity that shortly after his death a museum was created in the house in which he was born.

Very different from Romero de Torres, both in terms of his style and his life

### Alonso Cano, The Complete Artist

This Granada-born architect, sculptor, designer and creator of numerous altarpieces and canvases is now recognised as one of the key figures of the Spanish Golden Age. His irascible character, which sullied his reputation while he was alive, continued to blight him even after his death. Cano arrived in Sevilla at the age of 13, linking up with Velázquez, his fellow student in the workshop of Pacheco, before pursuing his training under Montañés. Financial worries (he even went to prison due to unpaid debts) saw him head north to Madrid in 1637, where he enjoyed the patronage of the Count-Duke of Olivares. His lifestyle remained largely unsettled, as borne out by his involvement in several duels and the accusation levelled against him of having ordered the murder of his wife. His return to Granada in 1651 saw the full flowering of his talents in the work carried out on the city's cathedral.

*Puente de la Barqueta, Sevilla*

outside Spain, was the Málaga-born **Picasso** (1881-1973) who is undoubtedly the most famous figure of contemporary Spanish pictorial art. Although he lived in his native Andalucía for just eight years, he maintained close ties with his own region and kept alive his passion for bullfighting from afar.

Two artists who made their names in the early part of the 20C were **Daniel Vázquez Díaz** (1882-1969), who took his inspiration from Cubism to create works such as the frescoes in the Monasterio de la Rábida (Huelva), and **Rafael Zaba-**

*Contradiction, by Julio Romero de Torres*

**leta** (1907-60), an artist known for his stylised, rustic expressionism.

Other artists born towards the middle of the 20C include Luis Gordillo (1934) and Guillermo Pérez Villalta (1948), both involved in the renewed trend towards figurative representation, as well as Alfonso Fraile, Vicente Vela, Alfonso Albacete, Carmen Laffon, Chema Cobo and the Granada-born José Guerrero.

## SCULPTURE

**Mateo Inurria** (1869-1924), the creator of the statue of El Gran Capitán in Córdoba, and **Jacinto Higueras** were the leading Andalusian sculptors from the first half of the 20C. **Miguel Berrocal** (1933), who in his early works manifested his keen interest in abstract forms, later moved on to more figurative subjects.

## ARCHITECTURE

The widespread changes within the field of architecture were slow to take root in Andalucía. Modernismo merely produced a few strange examples of the genre within bourgeois society (the interiors of houses and small shops), particularly in the province of Cádiz. At the same time, and inspired by the Costurero de la Reina lodge (Sevilla, 1893), the historicist and revivalist movement was born, and came to the fore at the 1929 Ibero-American Exhibition, with its ornate pavilions. Other official buildings, such as the Palacio Provincial in Jaén and a number of cinemas and theatres, including the Teatro Falla in Cádiz and the Aliatar in Granada are further examples of this movement.

The architecture of recent decades, which has openly embraced these new trends, is a clear reflection of the positive development of the Andalusian economy. Since the sixties, during which the School of Architecture was created in Sevilla, a number of public buildings, tourist complexes and housing developments have been built, designed by the best architects from Andalucía and elsewhere in Spain (Saénz de Oiza, Moneo, de La-Hoz, García de Paredes, Cano Lasso etc).

The urban projects completed for the 1992 World Expo in Sevilla are further proof of the architectural renaissance which has taken place in the region.

# Literature, Music and Cinema

Andalucía has produced countless figures of renown in the world of culture. From the Roman philosopher Seneca to Nobel Prize-winning authors such as Juan Ramón Jiménez and Vicente Aleixandre, and writers of the stature of Luis de Góngora, the list of celebrities is long. Some remained on their home soil or maintained close ties; others labored far from their region of birth. And there are those from afar who have had a deep attraction for the soul of this complex region. We can mention just a few of those who have found inspiration in this magnificent land.

## LITERATURE

**Tirso de Molina** (1579-1684), the probable author of *Don Juan*, set the conquests of the legendary rake Don Juan Tenorio on the banks of the Guadalquivir. Alongside Don Quixote and Faust, this great lover was to become one of the signature figures of world literature thanks to the playwright José Zorrilla. The latter, a prolific Romantic author, was a contemporary of a group of foreign writers who found their sought-after exoticism and mystery in Andalucía. Among the first foreign tourists to travel to the south of Spain were British writers such as **Richard Ford**; **Théophile Gautier**, Victor Hugo and Latour from France; the American **Washington Irving**; and Italy's Edmundo d'Amicis. Between them they created the myth of Andalucía – land of brigands, bullfighters, gypsies and carefree people – which had little in common with reality but met with great success. Elsewhere, Sevillian poet **Gustavo Adolfo Bécquer** was penning

---

## Highwaymen of the Sierra Morena

Given the irregular profile of the Sierra Morena, it is easy to understand how, over the centuries, it became a refuge for those on the edge of the law.

Romantic writers, particularly English and French, were deeply attracted to the outlaws of the 18C and 19C, depicting them in many tales. Thus was born the archetype of the Andalusian highwayman, a seeker of justice and defender of the oppressed. Although it is true that on occasion peasants considered these bandoleros heroes, for the most part they protected them through fear.

In Spanish history, two influential characters personified the Spanish highwayman. The first was **Diego Corrientes** (1757-81), who specialised in the theft of horses from farms and homesteads, and who was executed in Sevilla. The second, and perhaps the most famous bandit of them all, was **José María el Tempranillo** (1805-35). Having killed a man to defend his honour, he joined the famous gang of the Niños de Écija (Children of Écija), devoting his life to extracting tribute from travellers passing through the Sierra Morena, as well as offering sporadic help to exiled liberals. Bowing to popular opinion, the king pardoned his crimes shortly before this young hero died from natural causes.

his famous *Rimas* (Rhymes) which some writers considered the perfect union of German *lied* and Andalusian *siguiriyas* and fandango.

The poetry of Andalucía reached its headiest heights early in the 20C, through the writing of members of the Generation of '27. **Antonio Machado** (1875-1939), author of *Cantares*, and forever nostalgic for his childhood in Sevilla, and his brother **Manuel Machado**, who wrote *Cante Jondo*, both reflected the true nature of the region. **Federico García Lorca** (1898-1936) lifted Andalusian lyricism to its peak with the *Gypsy Ballads*, *Blood Wedding* and *The House of Bernarda Alba*. The poems of painter and poet **Rafael Alberti** (1902-99) were highly personal, gracious and popular in style, as well as typically Andalusian (*Marinero en tierra*).

Notable figues of Andalusian literature in the second half of the 20C include **Félix Grande**, **José Caballero Bonald**, **Antonio Muñoz Molina** and, above all, **Antonio Gala**, the Cordoban writer who perhaps painted a better picture than anyone of the realities of modern Andalucía and the grandeur of its past.

## MUSIC

Three great Spanish classical composers who drew their inspiration from popular music reflected the Andalusian soul perfectly. Strangely, just one of them was a native of the south; the other two were Catalan.

**Manuel de Falla** (1876-1946), born in Cádiz, is surely the most illustrious Spanish composer of the 20C. He took a studied approach to musical ethnography, and avoided being merely a conveyor of picturesque folklore. The passion of gypsy song and the brilliance of flamenco are both present in his two most famous works, *El amor brujo* (Love, the Magician) and *The Three-Cornered Hat*.

Gerona-born **Isaac Albéniz** (1860-1909), a major exponent of the Spanish nationalist movement, dedicated some of his best works to Andalucía, such as *Caprichos andaluces* and a major part of his *Iberia*. Lastly, **Enrique Granados** (1867-1916) dedicated one of his three Spanish Danzas to Andalucía.

Great operas set in the region include Bizet's *Carmen* and Mozart's *Don Giovanni*.

## CINEMA

Since its earliest days, Spanish cinema has often found inspiration in Andalusian themes, which are considered some of the most authentic in Spain. This trend, caricatured by Berlanga in his unforgettable *Bienvenido Mr Marshall* (1952), was

Archivi Alinari, Firenze

*Carmen*

*An Andalusian bandit*

Museo di Storia della Fotografia Fratelli Alinari, Firenze

to wane until Carlos Saura put Andalusian folklore back on the screen with works such as *Bodas de sangre* (1981), *Sevillanas* (1991), and *Flamenco (1995)*.

In recent times, following his success with *Solas* (1995), critics pronounced **Benito Zambrano** the standard bearer of new Andalusian cinema.

## Popular Traditions

Andalusians are renowned for their fiestas, uniquely celebrated by entire villages, towns and cities. Through the course of the year over 3 000 festivals are held around the region, the majority of a religious nature (processions and *romerías*), although mention needs to be made of the famous fairs (*ferias*), carnivals and Moorish and Christian fiestas.

### HOLY WEEK (SEMANA SANTA)

Gold-embroidered capes glistening in candlelight, sumptuous statues lit by the moon borne reverently along streets lined by orange trees, the beating of drums, sacred flamenco *saetas* sung from a balcony as Virgin and Child pass below… such is the image of Semana Santa (Holy Week), the most important fiesta in the Andalusian calendar.

Towns, cities and villages across Andalucía all commemorate the Passion and the Death of Christ in their own way, carrying in procession works of art created by famous sculptors such as Alonso Cano, Martínez Montañés and Pedro de Mena. These images are transported on floats known as **pasos** in Sevilla and **tronos** in Málaga, all of which are decorated with richly sculpted wood, engraved silver and a multitude of flowers. Hidden by velvet gowns, the bearers or **costaleros** advance slowly with their load, weighing around three tonnes. Each carrier supports a weight of approximately 80kg/176lb. To prepare for this arduous task, teams train for

*A bullfight*

J. Malburet/MICHELIN

97

three months between Christmas and Semana Santa, during which younger members cover the route to be taken with a structure similar in weight and size to the one they will bear on the day of the procession.

Andalucía has close to a thousand Confraternities or Brotherhoods of the Passion, responsible for the creation and maintenance of these floats. Donations and raffles ensure that these pasos are impeccable and increasingly sumptuous. The statues of the Virgins themselves have an extensive wardrobe from which the *santera* (statue keeper) will choose as appropriate.

As the processions wind their way, onlookers take up strategic positions to admire the floats – illuminated as they negotiate a darkened lane – as well as the skill of the carriers beneath. Amid this endless shuffle, the outdoor terraces of bars are quickly swamped with people caught up in the sometimes surprising bustle that is so charactistic of religious expression in Andalucía.

"Al cielo con Ella"! (To heaven with Her!), rises the cry as the float is lifted and the procession advances.

## RELIGIOUS PILGRIMAGES (ROMERÍAS)

Devotion to the Virgin is without doubt the most characteristic feature of Andalusian religious fervour, to the extent that it is said that "Andalucía is the land of the Blessed Mary". Countless sanctuaries advocate every possible veneration of the Virgin: de la Cabeza (the head), de la Bella (the beautiful) de la Regla (the rule), del Sol (the sun), de la Luna (the moon), de la Peña (cliff) and de la Sierra (the mountain), to name but a few.

Every *romería* (religious pilgrimage) has its idiosyncratic features, some particularly odd, but in general each consists of a pilgrimage to a church, often on decorated carts and horseback, and a religious ceremony with a procession, followed by dinner outdoors with dancing and singing until dawn, or beyond. The most famous *romería* is to the **Virgin of El Rocío**, an event attracting close to one million pilgrims and visitors from

El Rocío pilgrimage

around Spain as well as from other European countries (*see El ROCÍO*).

## MAY CROSSES (CRUCES DE MAYO)

The Festival of the Crosses (cruces), held on 3 May every year, celebrates the Discovery of the Holy Cross. According to tradition, in the 4C the mother of the Emperor Constantine discovered the cross *(Lignum crucis)* on which Christ had died and distributed fragments throughout the Christian world.

The Cruces de Mayo are celebrated all over Andalucía, although veneration varies from province to province. In some areas, the crosses are fixed and venerated all year round, as in La Palma del Condado in the province of Huelva, while in others crosses are erected specifically for the celebration, as in Conil de la Frontera (Cádiz). In every case, the crosses are adorned with branches of rosemary and flowers. Religious ceremonies are followed by singing and dancing well into the night. In Córdoba, Cruces de Mayo erected around the city are particularly renowned for their imagination and stunning beauty.

## CARNIVAL

In most Andalusian towns and cities, the *fiestas* during Carnival have a long tradition, initiated by Sevilla during its Golden Age and further developed by **Cádiz**, nowadays the site of the most spectacular celebrations. Carnival is a time of excess for the imagination and an opportunity for extravagant celebration. It is the culmination of months of hard practice and costume design. The main participants are known as *comparsas* – groups dressed in similar costume who make their way through the streets singing ironic and humorous songs based on political and current affairs.

Carnival celebrations near the Meseta and the borders with Castilla tend to be more restrained in nature. More importance is attributed to the so-called "burial of the sardine", in reference to fish eaten during Lent.

## THE FERIA

The Andalusian feria is a celebration encompassing all the colour, music, dance and exuberance of the region. Its origins lie in the spring and autumn cattle fairs which were first held, as in the rest of Spain, during the Middle Ages. As these fairs developed over the centuries, they evolved into general celebrations where everyone would dress up in finery, bring out their finest horses and carriages, and above all, enjoy themselves to the full. Although every feria has its specific characteristics, they also have many features in common.

Strangely, Sevilla's April Fair, the best-known of all Andalucía's festivals and one which was to serve as a model for other important modern ferias such as those held in Córdoba, Málaga and Jerez, is relatively recent, created in 1847.

The area used to host the feria is generally enclosed with access via a large entrance gateway decorated with myriad coloured lights. Inside, the fairground is separated into distinct zones: the so-called **calle del Infierno** (literally, the Street of Hell); the **Recreo** (entertainment area); **Los Cacharritos**, home to typical fairground attractions (Ferris wheel, roller coaster, shooting ranges, tombolas etc); the shopping area, or Rastro, (only generally found in small towns and villages); and the feria's **Real** area, with its succession of flimsy, ephemeral entertainment booths known as **casetas**. The booths are decorated with lamps, pictures and furniture designed for the simple pleasures of eating, drinking and dancing, day and night; some are private, with entrance strictly reserved for members or for those with tickets, while others are open to everyone.

Although it may not appear obvious to first-time visitors, there is a strict programme for the feria, as is the case with every traditional celebration in Andalucía. From noon until around four in the afternoon, everyone gathers in the Real dressed in traditional costume. As music starts up in the casetas, encouraging the more energetic early birds to dance a *sevillana* or two, others parade through the streets on magnificent horses with elaborately decorated harnesses and saddles or in elegant open carriages. The period after the siesta or the traditional bullfight is the time for children to make the most of the festivities. As darkness falls, more visitors return to the feria, in everyday dress, for more eating, drinking and dancing until the early hours of the morning. Such is the typical routine during feria week – a time for little sleep and significant reserves of energy.

*R. Mattes/MICHELIN*

*Illuminated casetas at the Sevilla Fair*

## BULLFIGHTING

The world of bullfighting, which excites the passions of its enthusiastic followers and staunch opponents alike, is indelibly associated with Andalusian life.

Whether the event is a full-fledged *corrida de toros* featuring leading matadors, a *novillada*, at which aspiring bullfighters take on three-year-old bulls, or a bullfight on horseback *(corrida de rejoneo)*, the bullfight is the highlight of the feria in every Andalusian town and city.

In general, a bullfight comprises the killing of six bulls by three matadors.

Each combat is divided into three acts (or *tercios*): the mounted picador thrusts his lance into the bull's neck; the bandilleros plunge their decorative darts into the bull's back; and lastly, the matador himself performs his *faena* with his red cape *(muleta)* to demonstrate his art, technique and bravery, before finally putting the bull to the sword.

If the faena is performed successfully and the kill (*estocada*) is clean, swift and effective, aficicionados in the stands will wave their white handkerchiefs to implore the presiding judge to award one ear, two ears or even the bull's tail to the matador in recognition of his skilful performance.

The expertise and warmth of spectators in Andalucía makes the region the ideal centre in which to discover the world of the corrida, preferably in the architecturally stunning plazas de toros in Sevilla and Ronda, or alternatively in the bullrings of Antequera, El Puerto de Santa María, or Sanlúcar de Barrameda, or during the annual ferias held in Jerez, Córdoba, Granada, Almería and Jaén.

## FLAMENCO

Flamenco was created towards the middle of the 19C from a combination of musical forms present in Andalucía, including Jewish, Byzantine, Moorish and even Hindu. Experts fail to agree on the scale of this influence, but what does seem clear is that it developed in Lower Andalucía (Jerez, Utrera, Lebrija, Cádiz) among families who passed the art from generation to generation. Though in no way of gypsy origin, it is generally acknowledged that the *gitanos* have incorporated their own personality and their considerable talents into flamenco.

For a long time considered to be an art form associated with "low lifes" – a view expressed at the turn of the century by writers such as Miguel de Unamuno – initiatives led by leading cultural figures such as Federico García Lorca and Manuel de Falla elevated flamenco to the status of the cultural expression of the Andalusian people.

Flamenco has seen the rise to fame of singers such as Antonio Mairena, Fosforito, la Niña de la Puebla and, in more recent times, **Camarón de la Isla**, renowned guitarists such as Paco de Lucía and dancers of the quality of Cristina Hoyos.

The new generations have demonstrated that flamenco remains a living art and that it is capable of evolving and assimilating new rhythms. Purists do not agree, but groups such as Ketama and Navajita Plateá, guitarists such as Raimundo Amador and dancers of international renown such as Joaquín Cortés and Antonio Canales are ready to show that flamenco can explore new avenues.

Although to many observers and listeners the individual aspects of flamenco may be somewhat difficult to comprehend and interpret, it is impossible not to be moved by the passion of this truly Andalusian art form.

## TRADITIONAL COSTUME

Each of Andalucía's provinces has its regional costume, which varies significantly from one area to the next. In Málaga, for example, part of the **verdiales** costume consists of a garish hat totally covered with flowers and a variety of coloured bands; this contrasts with the **piconera** costume in Cádiz, with its satin skirt, white blouse, black apron and hairnets of arbutus flowers; and the costume of the Alpujarras mountains (Granada), with its multicoloured striped skirt, long-sleeved blouse and flowery shawl.

R. Mattes/MICHELIN

*A traditional flamenco performance*

However, what is considered to be the Andalusian costume par excellence is the one traditionally worn in Córdoba and Sevilla which saw various modifications during the second half of the 20C. In fact, the so-called Andalusian costume is perhaps the only one in the world with its own fashion, which varies from year to year in colour, number and length of pleated ruffles, the shape of the sleeves etc.

Variations apart, the **traje de faralaes** or flamenco costume worn by women is characterised by bright colours and a tight fit which highlights the figure. A wide neck and and a skirt ruffled at the bottom complete the look. The costume is sometimes accompanied by a shawl, earrings and bracelets to match, as well as real or artificial flowers in the hair. The country version, worn on horseback, consists of a riding skirt, a blouse with a lace apron, and a black jacket.

The men's costume, generally black, grey or dark brown in colour, includes a short jacket, white shirt without a tie, tight-fitting trousers and leather boots. The traditional headgear is either the wide-brimmed *sombrero cordobés* or the lower-crowned *sombrero sevillano*.

# ANDALUCÍA TODAY

As an autonomous region within the Spanish state, Andalucía now possesses the political institutions necessary to ensure its own development. For years held back by the vagaries of history and by occasionally archaic social structures, the region is now blessed with a major asset in the form of tourism which, in its different forms, brings wealth to Andalucía without destroying its soul.

## Government

### AN AUTONOMOUS REGION

Once democracy was restored to Spain after the death of General Franco in 1975, Andalucía was the fourth *comunidad* to be recognised within the Spanish state, which is now made up of 17 autonomous communities.

The Statute of Autonomy, approved in 1981, was a response to the wishes of the Andalusian people as expressed in the referendum on 28 February 1980.

### Blas Infante (1885-1936)

During the Second Republic, this politician made his name as the leader of the Andalusian Movement. He participated in the drafting of the preliminary bill for the Statute of Andalucía (1933) and presided over the assembly formed to ensure the recognition of the Confederate Andalusian State. The author of *El ideal andaluz* (1915) among other works, he was shot shortly after the outbreak of the

### Political organisation

The **Junta de Andalucía** is the autonomous executive body that coordinates and manages the administration of the region. Its president works in collaboration with the *Consejo de Gobierno* (Cabinet), currently made up of 13 ministers each responsible for a separate department.

Legislative functions are performed by the **Andalusian Parliament** *(Parlamento de Andalucía)*, the seat of which is in Sevilla. Its 109 members are elected by universal suffrage every four years. The region's highest court is the **Tribunal Superior de Justicia** in Granada. Centralised administration is the responsibility of the government's delegate for Andalucía *(Delegado del Gobierno)*, whose office is based in Sevilla, and beneath whom affairs are managed by a network of provincial subdelegates *(subdelegados)*.

### THE SYMBOLS OF ANDALUCÍA

Although definitively approved by the Andalusian Parliament as part of the new democratic process, the three symbols of Andalucía are not new. In fact, the Statute of Andalucía (1982) clearly stated that the anthem, coat of arms and green and white **flag** would be those defined by the Assembly of Ronda in 1918 and by the Juntas Liberalistas de Andalucía in 1933.

The **coat of arms**, inspired by the escutcheon of the city of Cádiz, shows Hercules between two columns subduing two lions. Above him is the Latin inscription *Dominator Hercules Fundator* and at his feet the motto *Andalucía, por sí, para España y para la Humanidad* (Andalucía itself, for Spain and for Humanity). The **anthem**, the third symbol of Andalusian nationality, embraces the traditional claims of its people, reaffirming their love of peace and their desire for a future in which they regain the privileged position they occupied in the past.

R. Corbel/MICHELIN

## Economy

To express his admiration for the immense natural riches of Andalucía, the Greek geographer Strabo compared the region with the Elysian Fields. How is it possible, therefore, that in centuries to follow, peasants were plunged into starvation and then forced to emigrate? Agricultural decadence began with the expulsion of the Moors. Land was abandoned while new settlers, fewer

G. Bludzin/MICHELIN

*Palacio de San Telmo, the seat of the Andalusian Parliament in Sevilla* in number than those who had already left, showed greater enthusiasm for warfare and the colonisation of America than for agricultural labor. In years to come, large landowners *(caciques)* and the ruling classes did little to improve the situation. However, there are those who believe that the "traditional" underdevelopment of Andalucía is in reality a relatively new phenomenon which began in the second half of the 19C. In fact, at the beginning of the 19C, the distribution of wealth was reasonably uniform across the whole country. The development of the Hispanic capitalist society had an extremely detrimental effect on the lands of southern Spain, to the extent that in 1935 per capita income in Andalucía was just 717 pesetas, against 1 307 pesetas in the rest of the country. The problems intensified in the post-war period, when the most impoverished felt obliged to emigrate to other Spanish regions (mainly Catalonia and the Basque Country) and to various European countries (particularly Germany, France and Switzerland). During the 1960s, over 900 000 Andalusians left their native region.

This situation slowly began to improve during the 1970s, although the endemic problems remained: the unequal distribution of land into large estates *(latifundios)*, low levels of industrial investment and poor professional training for workers. During the second half of the 1980s, the region enjoyed another economic revival, particularly in the provinces along the Mediterranean coast.

1992 was to be a key year in Andalucía's economic development. The **World Expo** in Sevilla, which received 40 million visitors, brought tremendous economic benefits to the region's capital and coastal towns and cities, and had a positive effect on other provinces. This included the construction of the motorway linking Sevilla, Córdoba, Granada and Málaga, and the creation of the AVE high-speed rail link between Madrid and Sevilla via Córdoba.

Following the euphoria of 1992, a new industrial crisis hit the region, exacerbated by problems linked to drought, forest fires and unemployment.

In recent years, the growth rate in Andalucía has been similar to the national average, while the official unemployment rate, although the highest in Spain, has been significantly reduced to 13%.

## AGRICULTURE AND LIVESTOCK

**Agriculture** is the mainstay of the region's economy. Cereal production is concentrated in the province of Sevilla (which leades the country in production), Cádiz, Almería and Granada; fruits (particularly citrus fruits) and vegetables are mainly produced in the fertile lowlands of Granada; olives in Jaén and Granada;

*Agricultural land near Jerez de la Frontera*

vines in Jerez, Montilla and Málaga; and cotton in Córdoba and Sevilla. Over the past few years, the provinces of Huelva and Almería have become covered with a sea of plastic, used to protect early - season produce and winter crops.

**Livestock** raising is concentrated on the pasturelands of the Sierra Morena, the Sierra de Cádiz and the Cordillera Subbética. In the main, these fenced lands have been stripped of their low bushes and scrub and, in places, of their natural vegetation of holm and cork oak. These areas constitute an agro-forestry system which is unique in Europe, where in addition to animal breeding, firewood, cork and honey are produced. Traditional livestock operations are extensive and take advantage of natural pasture to raise select and, in many cases, uniquely Andalusian, breeds, such as the Cartujana horse, Merino sheep, Iberian pig and the fighting bull.

The **food-processing** industry is also worthy of note given the widespread production and excellent quality of Andalusian wines (particularly around Jerez, Montilla and Málaga), and the reputation of the region's olive oil. Andalucía is also the country's second most important region for fish and seafood, in particular tuna, sardines, clams, cockles, shrimp and prawns.

## INDUSTRY

Andalucía is a region with limited industry, with the exception of the province of Huelva and the area around La Rábida, where a number of chemical and petrochemical plants and factories have been established. Andalucía's traditional **mining** has declined dramatically and is now a mere shadow of its former self. Gone are the days when, at the end of the 19C, the English company which acquired the mines at Riotinto (Huelva) employed over 10 000 workers or when, in the time of the Phoenicians, the kingdom of Tartessus prospered from mineral and metal deposits. Despite this decline, the extensive open-cast pits at Ríotinto are still operational, lead is still mined in the provinces of Jaén, Almería and Córdoba, pyrite and manganese dioxide in

Huelva, and iron in Granada, Sevilla and Almería.

## TOURISM

In a surprising twist of fate, the tourist industry now brings wealth to regions and countries that were overlooked by the industrial revolution two centuries ago. Every year, more than 15 million tourists visit Andalucía, which is now the third most popular destination in Spain for foreign holiday-makers.

The region's many attractions appeal to a wide range of visitors. The mild climate and beaches of the Andalusian coast attract visitors in search of sea and sunshine, with the majority of tourists heading to the **coastline** between Málaga and Estepona on the Costa del Sol. This stretch caters to everyone, with package tours filling many of the hotels in Torremolinos and Benalmádena. The Spanish and international jet-set head for the more upmarket resorts of Marbella and Puerto Banús. Today, hotels, restaurants, nightclubs and marinas stand side by side along the seafront, changing forever the face of former fishing ports. Less crowded is the Atlantic coast of the provinces of Huelva and Cádiz, known as the Costa de la Luz (Coast of Light), whose long, sandy beaches are particularly popular with surfing enthusiasts. The indented, tropical coastline of the province of Granada has also retained much of its original charm, as has the Almería coast, especially around the protected areas of Cabo de Gata.

However, Andalucía has much more to offer than its coastline, as demonstrated by the increasing number of Spanish visitors attracted by the **outdoor activities** and **mountain tourism** on offer in inland areas. Footpaths criss-cross the region, allowing visitors to discover its flora and fauna and to enjoy the relative cool of the mountains, whether they are exploring the Serranía de Ronda with its whitewashed villages; the Sierra de Cazorla, where the distant call of a stag can often be heard; the Sierra de Aracena, with its lakes and forests; the Sierra Morena or the Sierra Subbética. The scenery is varied and ever-changing, ranging from luxuriant vegetation to desert landscapes, from olive groves stretching as far as the eye can see to extensive sugar cane plantations, and from snowcapped mountain peaks to vast sun-scorched plains.

Finally, **cultural tourism** attracts visitors to the historical centres of Andalucía – not just the famous cities of Sevilla, Granada and Córdoba, but also to the lesser-known towns of Ronda, Carmona, Écija, Guadix, Úbeda and Baeza.

## A GENTLE PACE OF LIFE

As you explore delightful towns and villages, you will undoubtedly stumble upon a typical Andalusian scene: a small cobblestoned square surrounded by dazzling whitewashed houses, an ornate fountain, the emblazoned façade of an aristocratic mansion, a Baroque church and a bar frequented in the early evening by locals of all ages, the women sitting in the shade playing with their fans. This indolent, seemingly timeless scene encompassing both the modern and the archaic is repeated throughout the region, providing a picture of Andalucía that is clichéd and yet authentic, full of the contrasts that make up this complex region.

Visitors soon adapt to the summer rhythm of life in Andalucía, with its long afternoon siestas, late nights, disconcerting meal times and the constant noise of activity that reigns in the region's lively streets and public squares. Lottery ticket sellers calling "para hooy", locals relaxing with the newspapers at outdoor cafés, seemingly oblivious to the *limpiabotas* shining their shoes, the sharp click of a fan expertly handled – all these details contribute to the gentle Andalusian way of life that slowly charms and delights visitors.

## Food and Wine

The highly colourful cuisine of Andalucía is distinctly Mediterranean in character. Regional gastronomy is based on the wealth of local produce, with pride of place given to its olive oil, the key ingredient in many of the region's recipes. Another key component in Andalusian

S. Ollivier/MICHELIN

*A café terrace in an Alpujarran village*

cuisine is wine, and in particular its world-famous sherries, which provide the perfect accompaniment to the typical dishes of southern Spain.

Eight centuries of Moorish presence have had a profound effect on Andalusian culture, including the region's cuisine. New agricultural techniques, based on making the best use of water through irrigation networks made it possible to grow crops on hitherto uncultivated land, thus enabling the region to produce fruits and vegetables throughout the year. The Moors brought with them a whole range of new crops (rice, aubergines, artichokes and asparagus) as well as spices which at the time were

### Gazpacho

This chilled, refreshing and healthy soup is by far Andalucía's most famous dish. Its basic ingredients are tomatoes, cucumber, peppers, oil, vinegar, garlic and salt, the quantities of which vary from family to family; many people will also add croutons, onions and even sliced hard-boiled egg. Despite their different flavours, salmorejo (bread mashed with tomatoes, garlic, oil, vinegar and salt), *ajo blanco* (similar to *salmorejo* but made with almonds instead of tomatoes and served with grapes or melon) and *porra antequerena* are considered to be variations on the gazpacho theme, perhaps because all three are also served chilled.

*Gazpacho*

Mimos/STOCK PHOTOS

unknown in the western world (pepper, cinnamon and cumin).

The Moors also introduced the modern-day order for the presentation of dishes which, until then, had been served at the same time.

Yet, despite its deep influence on on southern Spain, Arab cuisine failed to displace traditional Mediterranean cooking, centred on wine and olive oil, which remains very much alive. Nowadays, the wines of Andalucía have a well-deserved worldwide reputation while the region's olive oil, including two quality Denominación de Origen labels – Baena (Córdoba) and Sierra de Segura (Jaén) – currently enjoys great popularity.

The dominant features of Andalusian cuisine differ according to whether you are on the coast, where fish and seafood predominate, or inland, where the cooking is dominated by meat dishes, vegetables, hearty soups and stews.

Although fried fish (*pescaíto frito*) is a popular dish in bars along the coast, Andalusian cuisine is mainly based on its stews (*guisos*), which may also be known as *cocido andaluz*, *olla* or *puchero*. These can be found in every province, with variations according to local ingredients. Dishes with either pork or chicken, vegetables and chickpeas and/or various type of beans (*judías*) are also popular across Andalucía. The local meat stew known as *pringá* is a popular tapa in the bars of Sevilla.

In the more mountainous parts of inland Andalucía, game stews are an important part of the local cuisine, providing calories and warmth on a cold winter's night. This contrasts with lighter fish dishes,

prepared in every manner possible along the Mediterranean and Atlantic coasts; these may be boiled (*cocido*); grilled (*a la plancha*), particularly the shrimp and prawns from Sanlúcar de Barrameda; served in stews (*guisados*), such as the seafood stews (*guisos marineros*) from Cádiz; fried (*frito*), including anchovies, squid and cuttlefish; or barbecued (*asado*), an ideal way of grilling sardines caught off the Málaga coast.

Another important aspect of Andalusian gastronomy is the wide choice of cured hams and sausages (embutidos). Local products include *morcón*, a type of blood pudding; the cured legs of hams (*cañas*) from Jabugo (Huelva), one of Spain's main areas for the rearing of acorn-fed pigs for the famous *jamón ibérico*; *morcilla* (black pudding) from

## Tapas

The tradition of eating tapas is synonymous with Spain, Andalucía and, more particularly, Sevilla, where they originated. Although tapas originally consisted of no more than just a thin slice of cured ham, a single prawn or a small piece of Spanish omelette to accompany a glass of wine, as time has passed, tapas have increased in size to such an extent that a selection of tapas or the larger raciones are often eaten instead of a full meal. The choice is seemingly endless, with a whole range of cured hams (including the famous jamon ibérico), cheeses, prawns either grilled (*a la plancha*) or with a garlic sauce (*al ajillo*), squid, tortillas *(omelettes)*, fried fish *(pescaítos fritos)* etc on offer. Locals will often be seen enjoying tapas standing at the bar or even out on the street at busy times, with refreshment taking the form of a chilled glass of draught beer or a glass of *fino* or manzanilla. Visitors are often somewhat daunted by this hectic scene, but it's well worth fighting your way to the bar to order local specialities which are usually posted on a board. If all else fails, point at what you want and hope for the best! Above all, make sure you enjoy the friendly atmosphere of this unique gastronomic art!

Ronda (Málaga) and the renowned sausages and hams from Trévelez, in the province of Granada.

## BREAKFAST

In most bars and cafeterias you can try a typical Andalusian breakfast *(desayuno)* consisting of toasted bread with olive oil and manteca *colorá*, a reddy-coloured dripping. If this traditional delicacy fails to whet your appetite, try deep-fried *churros*, long strips of doughnut, traditionally served with thick, sweet hot chocolate.

Andalucía's cheeses are generally made from goats' or sheep's milk, although cows' milk is used on rare occasions. Although these predominantly strong-flavoured cheeses are little known outside of the region, they are an ideal accompaniment to a glass of chilled fino, manzanilla or oloroso sherry, but are never eaten after the main course. The main areas of cheese production are the mountains of Almería and Granada, the Serranía de Ronda (Málaga) and in the Sierra de Grazalema (Cádiz).

Moorish and Jewish influence is very evident in the tremendous variety of regional cakes and pastries. Some of the best- known, flavoured with cinnamon, almonds and anise, include the *polvorones* and *mantecados* from Estepa (Málaga), which are eaten throughout Spain at Christmas; the delicious *tocinos de cielo* (literally "bacon from heaven"), a custard pudding from Jerez de la Frontera; and flaky round cakes known as *roscos* in a variety of guises such as millefeuilles (*milhojas*) and honeyed fritters (*pestiños*). Nowadays, many of these cakes are produced by nuns according to traditional recipes dating back many centuries. Perhaps this is why many of them have evocative names such as *huesos de santo* (saint's bones), *cabello de ángel* (angel hair), *suspiro de monja* (nun's sigh) and the aforementioned tocino de cielo.

## LOCAL SPECIALITIES

Each province has its signature dishes. The specialities in the province of Granada include *habas con jamón* (broad beans with ham), *sopita de ajo* (garlic soup), a range of omelettes, including *tortilla del Sacromonte*, also known as *tortilla granaína* (with ham, brains and pig's kidneys), *rabo de toro* (oxtail), and the hearty *potaje de San Antón*, a soup made with broad beans, bacon, black pudding and pig's ears, which is traditionally eaten on 17 January. Flour, cod, potatoes and peppers are the main ingredients of *gurupina*, a speciality of the town of Baza, in the mountainous east of the province, where *testuz*, a dish comprising broad beans, white haricot beans, black pudding, bacon and pig's ears is also a local favourite.

Córdoba is known for its excellent grilled meats (*churrascos*), in particular pork, and *alcachofas a la montillana* (artichokes from Montilla).

In the province of Jaén, meanwhile, make sure you try the meat-based *croquetas de collejas*, asparagus (*espárragos*) coated in a variety of sauces, *empanadas del viernes*, literally "Friday pasties", and broad bean and aubergine soup (*potaje de habas con berenjenas*).

*Specialties of the region*

## The solera method

The solera blending process, which is applied to most Andalusian sherries, enables a constant quality to be maintained from one year to the next and is based on a system in which between four and eight levels of barrels are positioned one on top of the other. Once fermentation has taken place in accordance with normal wine-producing methods, and pure alcohol added, the new wine is pumped into the top barrel. The sherry to be bottled is taken from the solera (the barrel closest to the floor) and is immediately replaced by sherry from the barrel immediately above it (criadera primavera); this process continues until every barrel in the chain has been refilled. By following this method, quality is maintained from one harvest to the next.

The Sierra de Cazorla, in the same province, is known for its *talarines*, a type of tart stuffed with partridge or rabbit, its game dishes, marinated partridge, and the extraordinary bitter orange fish soup which has developed into the speciality of the town of Baena.

Lastly, arroz marinero, the Andalusian variant of paella, is far more moist than its Valencian cousin, and can be widely found along the region's Mediterranean and Atlantic coasts.

## WINE AND SHERRY

Andalucía has 86 000ha/212 500 acres of vineyards producing wines which have a superb reputation around the world. Almost all of this land is found within certified designations of origin (*denominación es de origen*).

### Denominaciones de Origen

Four *denominaciones de origen* (D.O.) currently govern the quality of Andalusian wines: Jerez, Montilla-Moriles, Condado de Huelva and Málaga. Each of these areas concentrates on the production of full-bodied wines, although recent diversification has seen their range expand towards young, light and fruity table wines.

### D.O. Jerez

The sherries of the Jerez area, which include the famous *finos* and *manzanillas*, are Andalucía's best-known and most prestigious wines. Sherry, as the name suggests (the word sherry is the anglicised form of the town's name), can only be produced in the designated area around Jerez, while *manzanillas* are the exclusive preserve of Sanlúcar de Barrameda. The Jerez appellation also produces sweet and dry *olorosos*, sweet wines *(vinos dulces)* such as Moscatel and Pedro Ximénez, and *amontillados*, which undergo a longer oxidisation in the barrel.

### D.O. Montilla-Moriles

These excellent wines produced in the area south of Córdoba have a high alcohol content. Although they are classified according to the same criteria as those wines produced in Jerez, Montilla-Moriles wines are very different from those produced further west.

### D.O. Málaga

Up until a century ago, sweet Málaga wines could be enjoyed on the finest tables in Europe. Despite their slight decline in fortune due to changing tastes, they are still the perfect accompaniment for dessert or afternoon tea.

J. Malburet/MICHELIN

*Bodega, González Byass, Jerez de la Frontera*

H. Champollion/MICHELIN

*A bottle of Montilla-Moriles*

### D.O. Condado

The pale and fruity Condado wines are produced from the Zalema grape. There are two types of Condado: Condado Pálido, reminiscent of the sherries of Jerez and manzanilla; and Condado Viejo, similar to an *oloroso*, which can attain an alcohol content of 23 per cent.

In addition to these leading regions, Andalucía also has other, smaller areas of vineyards producing wines rarely seen elsewhere in Spain or abroad. These include Aljarafe and Los Palacios (Sevilla); Villaviciosa de Córdoba (Córdoba); Bailén, Lopera and Torreperogil (Jaén); Costa-Albondón (Granada) and Laujar (Almería).

### Serving suggestions

The sherries of Andalucía are produced according to a special solera blending process which guarantees uniform quality over a period of years.

These wines are traditionally served in *catavinos* – narrow, tall glasses which enable the superb qualities of the wine to be enjoyed to the full.

Each variety of sherry should be drunk at a different temperature:

♦ *finos* are generally chilled to between 8°C and 10°C. Once opened, a bottle should be drunk as quickly as possible;

♦ *amontillados* should be ideally served between 12°C and 14°C;

♦ *olorosos* are at their best at a temperature of 18°C.

## Brandies and liqueurs

Brandies and liqueurs are also an important feature of the Andalusian economy. Anise, brandy and rum produced in Andalucía are sold throughout Spain and are increasingly being exported.

The early **aniseed**-based liqueurs originated from Ojén (Málaga), next to Spain's very first blast furnace, at a time when it was thought that aniseed had a beneficial effect on respiratory tracts affected by the mining, iron and steel industries. Today, the main areas for anise are in Montilla (Córdoba), which produces liqueurs with a smooth aroma and high alcohol content; Cazalla and Constantina (Sevilla), famous for their strong *cazalla*; and Zalamea la Real and Alosno (Huelva), with its dry and potent aguardiente.

Most of the **brandy** served in bars around Spain comes from Jerez de la Frontera, Sanlúcar de Barrameda and Puerto de Santa María, all of which belong to a regulatory body for brandy quality, the Consejo Regulador del Brandy. However, it is also distilled in Rute and Montilla (Córdoba), Málaga and in La Palma del Condado (Huelva).

It should also be remembered that the distilling and production techniques for **rum**, which is now considered to be a typically Caribbean drink, and its main ingredient – sugar cane – were exported to Cuba from Spain. Centuries later, when Fidel Castro came to power on the island, some Cuban producers transferred their production plants to Andalucía, particularly to Málaga and Granada, the only parts of Europe where sugar cane is grown.

# AGUILAR DE LA FRONTERA★

POPULATION: 13 397.

Historic, whitewashed Aguilar extends across a hill above green vineyards, preserving mansions and Baroque churches in its charming old quarter. Moorish Bulay, in the borderlands (*de la Frontera*) of the kingdom of Granada, was reconquered in the 13C. The Fernández de Córdoba family became lords of Aguilar in 1370. ▯ *Cuesta de Jesús, 2, 14920 Aguilar de la Frontera, ☎ 957 66 00 00.*

▶ **Orient Yourself:** In southern Córdoba province, Aguilar is reached via A 45 from the city of Córdoba (51km/32mi N), and Lucena (to the SE).
⊙ **Organizing Your Time:** Allow a couple of hours to discover Aguilar at leisure.
▦ **Especially for Kids:** See the ducks at nearby Laguna de Zóñar.
⚲ **Also See:** CABRA, LUCENA, MONTILLA and CÓRDOBA (51km/31mi N).
▣ **Parking:** Leave your car in the central llano de las Coronadas.
⊚ **Don't Miss:** The 17C and 19C mansions in **calle Arrabal** (nos 5, 11 and 13).

## Walking Tour

▶ *Head towards placilla Vieja, then climb the cuesta de Jesús hill.*

### Nuestra Señora del Soterraño★
⊙ *Visits by prior arrangement. ☎ 957 66 00 14.*
The main church, honoring Aguilar's patron saint, dates from the 16C.

**Exterior** – The Baroque left portal originates from an earlier church. It is similar to other doorways in Aguilar. The finely sculpted doorway to the right is Plateresque.

**Interior** – The chapel decoration is surprisingly rich. Ogival arches on cruciform pillars separate the aisles. The church has a straight triple apse. The main nave has a Mudéjar *artesonado* ceiling, while the high altar is crowned by a Gothic pointed vault. A large Baroque altarpiece in the presbytery honors the town's patron saint. An 18C lectern and attractive walnut **choir stalls** are at the rear of the central aisle. Medallions on seat backs show primitive yet expressive saints and Apostles.
The **Capilla del Sagrario★** and the **Capilla de la Inmaculada** (*left and right of the Capilla Mayor*) hold notable 17C stuccowork. A **high relief of the Last Supper** in the Capilla del Sagrario is particularly worthy of note. Also note the venerated statue of Jesus of Nazareth in the mid-18C **Capilla de Jesús Nazareno★** in the Epistle nave. Stuccowork completely covers the cupola. Note the rear prayer niche.
The ruins of a castle, the Castillo de Poley, lie on a small hill behind the church.

▶ *From llano de las Coronadas, follow calle Santa Brígida.*

### Iglesia del Hospital de Santa Brígida
This 16C church was rebuilt in the 17C and 18C. Note the central tower flanked by simple Baroque doorways. Unusually for the area, the 18C tower is neo-Classical.

▶ *Return to llano de las Coronadas and take calle Moralejo.*

### Aguilar's famous pastries
During your visit, try the delicious *risaos* made with almonds, sugar, egg yolk and lemon, or the equally tasty coffee or strawberry meringues (*merengas*).

### Monasterio de San José y San Roque

This Carmelite *convento* (convent) was built from 1668 to 1761. The interior *(☾only open during services)* is Aguilar's Baroque masterpiece,with sumptuous retables, oil paintings, stucco foliage, volutes and angels.
Note the fine mansions on calle Moralejo and calle Carrera.

▶ *From calle Moralejo, take calle Granada or calle Mercaderes.*

### Plaza de San José★

This unusual octagonal square, plain and harmonious, is dominated by the town hall *(ayuntamiento)*.

▶ *Leave plaza de San José via calle Don Teodoro.*

### Torre del Reloj★

This 18C Baroque tower on the plaza de los Desamparados, built for civil use, became a model for contemporaneous belfries. Features include a cupola with *azulejo* decoration and a turret.

### Calle del Carmen

This street off calle Desamparados affords views of surrounding vineyards. In **placita del Carmen**, a small square, stands a Christ of the Lanterns, similar in style to the one found in Córdoba.

B. Kaufmann/MICHELIN

*Detail, Torre del Reloj*

▶ *Return to calle Moralejo and head along calle Vicente Núñez.*

Note, at n° 2, **Casa Señorial del Caballo de Santiago**, a mansion named for the horse of St James, depicted on the central balcony.

## Excursions

### Laguna de Zóñar

*Follow A 309 towards Puente Genil.* The **Centro de Visitantes Zoñar** (km 77) has an interactive exhibition on the lagoon, home to the **malvasia duck**, threatened with extinction until a few decades ago. ▯ *For information, call ☎ 957 33 52 52.*

### Puente Genil

*18km/11mi along A 309.* A pleasant walkway runs alongside the river of this village, named for its 16C bridge. This region is renowned for its quinces, a fruit used to produce a variety of local specialities. In the centre are old mansion houses, particularly in calle Don Gonzalo, and the **Museo Arqueológico y Etnográfico**, a small archaeological and ethnographical museum displaying

### Holy Week

As you wander through the streets of Puente Genil, you will perhaps notice the strange signs outside some of its houses such as *Imperio Romano, Cien Luces, Los Levitas* etc. These are the headquarters of the 65 associations or brotherhoods that participate in the Holy Week festivities. The processions displaying characters from the Old and New Testaments are a feature of Aguilar's Semana Santa.

local finds. ◷ *Open Tue-Sun, 10.30am-1.30pm.* ◷ *Closed Mon.* ⊜ *No charge.* ☎ *957 60 29 34.*

Churches include the 17C **Nuestra Señora de la Concepción**, with its tower-flanked portal and polychrome stucco main altarpiece; the **Iglesia de la Purificación**, with its attractive 19C bell tower and spire, and an Immaculate Conception by Pedro Duque Cornejo; the **Iglesia del Convento de San Francisco**, with its fine sculptures; and the **Iglesia de Jesús Nazareno**, decorated with paintings by local 19C artists, and housing a venerated image of Jesus of Nazareth, Puente Genil's patron saint.

# ALCALÁ LA REAL ★

POPULATION: 21 493

**Hilltop Alcalá la Real is overlooked by the Fortaleza de la Mota, an imposing fortress offering magnificent views of the surrounding olive groves.**
Birthplace of poet Juan Ruiz, known as the **Arcipreste de Hita**, and medieval sculptors **Juan Martínez Montañés** and **Pablo de Rojas**, Alcalá today is an agricultural and commercial centre. 🛈 *Paseo de los Álamos, Fortaleza de la Mota, 23680 Alcalá la Real,* ☎ *953 58 22 17.*

▸ **Orient Yourself:** Alcalá lies between Granada and Jaén in Jaén province.
🚫 **Don't Miss:** The Fortaleza de Mota for a sense of medieval Alcalá.
◷ **Organizing Your Time:** Take two hours, or more if you enjoy old fortresses.
🧒 **Especially for Kids: La** La Mota is interesting for grown-ups, fun for kids.
👁 **Also See:** PRIEGO DE CÓRDOBA (24km/15mi W), MONTEFRÍO (24km/15mi S), GRANADA (52km/32mi SE) and JAÉN.

## Visit

### Fortaleza de la Mota★★
This majestic fortress blends into the crags and rocks of La Mota hill. The Puerta de la Imagen is similar to the notable Puerta de la Justicia in the Alhambra.
The original Moorish *alcazaba* is a castle with three towers: the Torre de Mocha, Torre de la Campana and Torre del Homenaje, built on the remains of the former

## Address Book

### WHERE TO EAT
⊜ **El Curro** – *Ramón y Cajal, 6 –* ☎ *953 58 30 50 –* ▭ . ◷ *Closed Wed and in September.* This is first and foremost a bar popular with locals. Although there is a somewhat nondescript dining room, regulars tend to eat in a more attractive room with a low ceiling and fireplace. Specialities here include grilled meats and ham.

### WHERE TO STAY
⊜ **Hospedería Zacatín** – *Pradillo, 2 –* ☎ *953 58 05 68 – www.hospederiazacatin.com -* ▭ *– 15 rooms.* ⊠ €3.

Basic, but with a certain charm from both the personal attention of the owner and its location. Attractive rustic dining. Restaurant (⊜).

⊜ **Hotel Torrepalma** – *Conde de Torrepalma, 2 – www.hoteltorrepalma.com -* ▭ ♿ – ☎ *953 58 18 00 – 38 rooms.* Comfortable, modern, on one of Alcalá's busiest and noisiest shopping streets. Ask for an inside room.

### LOCAL SPECIALITIES
Typical local dishes include *pollo a la secretaria*, chicken with peppers, peas and an onion and saffron sauce.

*Fortaleza de la Mota, Alcalá la Real*

mosque. Inside, the **Iglesia de Santo Domingo**★, a Gothic-Mudéjar church built by Alfonso XI, retains the tower of the former minaret – one of the most characteristic features of Alcalá – and holds a fine 15C retable. The **Iglesia de Santa María la Mayor**, on an esplanade of the fortress, was badly damaged in the War of Independence. Diego de Siloé is known to have worked on its attractive Renaissance **façade**, Plateresque in style. This monumental complex also houses the interesting **Museo Arqueológico**, inside the Torre del Homenaje, with its collection of archaeological exhibits from Alcalá region. ◷ *Open daily 10.30am-1.30pm and 3.30-6.30pm (4.30-6.30pm, Sat-Sun and public hols); Jun-Sep daily Mon-Fri, 10.30am-1.30pm and 5-8pm.* ☞ *€1.50.* ☎ *639 64 77 96.*

### A border town

The town's origins date back to prehistoric times; however, due to its strategic position on the border between Christian- and Muslim-held lands, it became synonymous with fierce battles between the two adversaries. During the period of Moorish domination, which lasted over 600 years, *Qalat*, (a fortified settlement in Arabic), as it was then known, reached the pinnacle of its splendour, until its reconquest by Alfonso XI in 1341.

### Nuestra Señora de las Angustias
This impressive octagonal 13C church built by Ventura Rodríguez holds exceptional medieval painted **tablets**★.

### Ayuntamiento
The charming 18C Baroque town hall is on pleasant **plaza del Arcipreste de Hita**, flanked by two towers, opposite an artistic **sundial**★ by Fernando Tapia.

### Palacio Abacial
The abbot's palace, in front of the attractive Los Álamos fountain at an end of the paseo of the same name (☝ *see below*), is soberly neo-Classical. The façade has a Renaissance-inspired balcony and an elegant doorway with reliefs and coats of arms.

### Paseo de los Álamos

This delightful avenue is the ideal place to relax at the end of a long day and enjoy a chilled glass of the local wine on the outdoor terraces of its numerous tapas bars.

## Excursions

### Castillo de Locubín

*12km/8mi north.* The road winds to the Puerto del Castillo pass and this whitewashed settlement, with superb **views**★ of the River San Juan and Víboras Reservoir. Visit the remains of the **Moorish castle**, part of a system of border defenses.

### Alcaudete

*26km/16mi northwest along N 432.* Nestled amid olive groves on a promontory, amid olive groves. Alcaudete was conquered by the Infante Don Fernando de Antequera in 1408, and became one of Granada's border bastions. Its fame today rests on its pastry: *hojaldrinas,* cider *empanadillas* and *roscos de vino,* doughnut-like cakes made by the nuns from the Convento de Santa Clara.

**Castle ruins** – The Moorish *alcazaba* was built on the site of a Roman fortress and has preserved several vestiges of its walls and keep.

**Iglesia de Santa María** – This Gothic church with its Plateresque side portal stands at the foot of the castle. Inside, note the fine *artesonado* **ceiling**, the Renaissance grilles in front of the high altar, and the doors of the sacristy.

**Iglesia de San Pedro** – This 16C Mudéjar-style church has a fine altarpiece.

**Plaza Mayor** – The main square is situated at the heart of a labyrinth of narrow streets with a number of shops and bars. The 18C town hall comes into view after passing through an archway known as the Arco de la Villa.

# ALGECIRAS

POPULATION: 109 000.

Its strategic location, facing the Rock of Gibraltar, has exerted a major influence on Gibraltar since Moorish troops landed in the 8C. In modern times Algeciras bustles with commerce, links Europe and Africa, and is Spain's leading passenger port. 🚹 *Juan de la Cierva, 11207 Algeciras,* ☎ *956 57 26 36.*

▶ **Orient Yourself:** Algeciras and Gibraltar are magnificently sited at the southern tip of mainland Spain, in sight of North Africa, at opposite ends of a wide bay.

⊘ **Don't Miss:** The mix of Spain, North Africa and distant lands in and around the Market and at the ferry docks.

🕐 **Organizing Your Time:** Allow a morning or afternoon for the main sights.

🐾 **Also See:** TARIFA (21km/13mi SW), JIMENA DE LA FRONTERA (43km/27mi N) and COSTA DEL SOL.

### Paco de Lucía

Born Francisco Sánchez Gómez in Algeciras on 21 December 1947, **Paco de Lucía** is widely recognised as one of Spain's greatest ever flamenco guitarists, accompanying singers such as "Camarón de la Isla" and developing worldwide recognition for his improvisations in the company of renowned jazz musicians such as of John McLaughlin and Al Di Méola.

## Historical notes

Known to the Moors as *al-Yazirat al-jadra*, meaning 'green island', Algeciras reached its greatest splendour during a period that coincided with the period of Arab domination (711-1344). During that time it was one of two administrative districts of the Cádiz region. In the 18C, following the capture of Gibraltar by the British, it regained its strategic importance, resulting in the growth of its population and development as Spain's counterpoint to British domination in the Straits. In 1906 the city played host to the **Algeciras Conference**, at which the major European powers confirmed the division of Morocco into separate zones of influence.

# Visit

## Museo Municipal
🕐 *Open daily (except Sat-Sun), mid-Jun to late Sep, 10am-2pm; otherwise, daily (except Sun), 10am-2pm and 5-8pm.* 🕐 *Closed on public hols.* ☎ *956 57 06 72.*
This large house in Parque de las Acacias park displays Roman amphorae, which bear witness to significant trade in the Bay of Algeciras. Other exhibits relate to the Siege of Algeciras (1342-44), when Alfonso XI employed the first firearms, known as truenos (thunderclaps).

## Market
This iron and concrete structure in the plaza Palma has an innovative roof supported at just four points.

## Plaza Alta
Note the attractive 1930s Mudéjar-style azulejo and brick fountain surrounded by palms in this landmark square. Nearby are the 18C Iglesia de Nuestra Señora de la Palma, a mixture of Baroque and neo-Classical styles, and the smaller Baroque Iglesia de Nuestra Señora de Europa.

## Merenid Baths (Baños Meriníes)
These 13C Moorish baths in Parque María Cristina were originally part of a Merenid dynasty residence. A Moorish wheel and well have been reconstructed.

# Excursions

## The road to Tarifa
The 21km/13mi of the southmost road in Europe offer stunning **views**★★★ of North Africa. Cars can stop at the Mirador del Estrecho, 13km/8mi along, though views are better near Algeciras. Note the modern wind turbines.

## La Línea de la Concepción
*17km/11mi west of Algeciras.* One of the youngest towns in Spain was part of a defensive line against the British. It was formally incorporated in 1870 as La Línea de la Concepción, to honour the Virgin Mary, at that time the patron saint of the army.
The town has little to offer tourists. The heavily built-up centre is laid out around calle Real and the Iglesia de la Inmaculada Concepción, built in 1879.

### WHERE TO STAY

🛏🛏🛏 **AC La Línea de la Concepción** – *Los Caireles, 2 – La Línea de la Concepción* - ☎ *956 17 55 66* - *www.ac-hotels.com* - 🍽 - *80 rooms* - 🛏 €8. Sleek, well-equipped rooms in this modern hotel overlook the pool or the Rock of Gibraltar.

*Rock of Gibraltar*

B. Kaufmann/MICHELIN

## Gibraltar★

*Plan in Michelin Guide España & Portugal.* ⓘ *Casemates Square,* ☎ *9567 749 82; Cathedral Square (Duke of Kent House),* ☎ *9567 749 50, tourism@gibraltar.gi.*
Gibraltar is most famous for its Rock, rising a mere 423m/1 388ft above the sea, but visible from all around the bay. It acquires even greater substance close-up.
The history of Gibraltar is its position. **Tarik-ibn-Ziyad**'s army of Moors landed here in 711. In antiquity, it was Calpe, a Pillar of Hercules; today it is literally 'Tariq's Mountain' (from the Arabic *Djebel Tarik*). Christians and Moors con-

### ⊙ A Bit of Advice ⊙

**Gibraltar**★ *(20km/12mi east of Algeciras)* is a British Crown Colony and requires a passport for entry. Visitors are advised to check the entry situation before arrival as long queues (1hr or more) occasionally develop for motorists entering and leaving Gibraltar. On these occasions, it is worth leaving your car on the Spanish side and walking across the border.

tested the Rock, until the Duke of Medina Sidonia took it in 1462. The British took permanent but disputed control during the 18C **War of the Spanish Succession**.

## Gibraltar Museum

ⓞ*Open Mon–Fri, 10am–6pm; Sat, 10am–2pm.* ⊚*£2.* ☎ *350 74289; www.gib.gi/museum/museum.htm*
Close to the tourist office in the town centre, the museum is housed in a simple colonial building above 14C **Moorish baths**★. Exhibits on the history of the Rock range from the 1848 discovery of the **Gibraltar skull,** that of a Neanderthal woman, to Gibraltar's role in the Second World War. The enormous **model**★ (1865) of the Rock is also worthy of note.

## Main Street

Gibraltar's main thoroughfare is lined by hundreds of shops, banks and bars that operate on the Gibraltar pound, though most also accept the euro. Check out **St Mary's Catholic Cathedral,** built above the former main mosque, and the Convento, the residence of Gibraltar's governor since 1728, where the changing of the guard occurs several times daily.

## Upper Rock

*The top of the rock is accessible via cable car, car or taxi. Follow Main Street and then signs to the Upper Rock: 9.30am–7pm. Entrance includes Moorish castle, Upper Rock, Nature Reserve, Great Siege Tunnel, Apes' Den and St Michael's Cave.* ⊚*£7 (vehicle access: £1.50).* ☎ *350 74950.*

The Upper Rock, designated a Nature Reserve, is home to some of Gibraltar's more interesting sights, including the famous Barbary apes, brough here by British troops from North Africa at the end of the 18C. *The reserve can be reached via the cable car station at the foot of the rock.* ◷*Open 9.30am-5.15pm (last descent at 4.15pm).* ⬤*£9 (round trip).*

Don't miss the **Moorish castle**, the **Great Siege Tunnels** or **St Michael's Cave**, all included in the price of admission to the Upper Rock.

# ALHAMA DE GRANADA★

POPULATION: 5 894.

With its whitewashed houses and narrow streets literally overhanging a gorge, Alhama de Granada inspires both poets and travellers. The Moors named it Al-Hamma ('hot spring'), and during the Reconquest, Christians paid enormous sums to take the waters.

▶ **Orient Yourself:** Alhama lies beside the River Alhama, 60km/37mi southwest of Granada along the A 338.

⬡ **Don't Miss:** The Moorish Quarter is redolent of times past.

◷ **Organizing Your Time:** Two hours are sufficient, more to stroll, relax over drinks, or take the waters.

⬥ **Also See:** LOJA (32km/20mi N), ANTEQUERA, MÁLAGA, NERJA, ALMUÑÉCAR and GRANADA.

## Walking Tour

### Moorish Quarter★

Alhama's interesting Moorish quarter is easily explored on foot. Start with the **view**★ from behind the **Iglesia del Carmen** over the famous gorge of the River Alhama. Walk around the church to the delightful Baroque Capilla de Jesús Nazareno, past

*Moorish cistern, Hotel Balneario*

B. Kaufmann/MICHELIN

## A valuable prize

Alhama was captured from the Moors by Christian troops under the Castilian **Ponce de León** in 1482, signalling the start of the **War of Granada**, which ended with the capture of the Nasrid capital ten years later. Due to its magnificent, almost impregnable position, the fertile fields surrounding it and, above all, its springs of thermal water, the qualities of which have been known since Roman times, Alhama was considered one of the jewels in the Nasrid crown. As such, its capture by the Christians was a mighty blow.

an Arab fortress restored in the 19C. Head up calle Baja de la Iglesia to the imposing tower of the **Iglesia de la Encarnación**, rising above whitewashed houses.

### Iglesia de la Encarnación★
🕐 *Open Tue-Thu, noon-2pm.* €1. ☎ *958 36 06 86.*
The church stands on a former mosque. The Baroque portal conceals an early Gothic façade of plant motifs and fantastic animals. The sober interior is topped by a complex pointed vault. In the sacristy museum are valuable 16C priests' vestments *(ternos)*. Upon leaving the church, admire the Isabelline **Casa de la Inquisición** (House of the Inquisition, *right*), rebuilt in the 1950s. The enchanting plaza de los Presos is on the other side of the tower with, to the right, the former 17C **prison**, and opposite, the intact façade of the 16C **granary**. Calle Vendederas leads to the kingdom of Granada's first military field hospital, now the **tourist office**.

▶ *Walk around the Tourist Office and follow calle Caño Wamba.*

An unusual 16C fountain and the ruins of the **Iglesia de las Angustias** are farther along.

▶ *Head down calle de la Mina.*

The unusual **Moorish dungeons** *(mazmorras árabes)*, excavated out of rock, were once used as both a prison and silos for grain.

### WHERE TO STAY

🛏🛏 **Hotel Balneario** – *3km/2mi north toward Granada* – ☎ *958 35 00 11* – *www.balnearioalhama-degranada.com* - *Open Mar-Nov* – ☎ *958 35 00 11* – 🅿 – *106 rooms.* These springs date to Roman times, and were famed under the Caliphs. Thermal waters gush at 47°C/116°F into the *aljibe,* or **Moorish cistern**★ in a room with an octagonal vault supported by 11C Caliphal arches. The owners have a second hotel, the **Baño Nuevo** (🛏), nearby. The clientele here tends to be elderly.

# ALMERÍA

POPULATION: 168 025.

The whitewashed town of Almería spreads out between the sea and the arid hill of its impressive fortress *(alcazaba)*. Once isolated, it is now a leader in Spanish agriculture. Its superb climate has led to a tourism boom.  *Parque Nicolás Salmerón, 04002 Almería, ☎ 950 27 43 55, otalmeria@andalucia.org.*

- ▶ **Orient Yourself:** The Gulf of Almería was the city's only link with the outside, before the relatively recent development of inland and coastal links.
- ◷ **Organizing Your Time:** Spend most of a day seeing Almería, including the indispensable Alcazaba.
- ⌀ **Also See:** Parque Natural de CABO DE GATA-NÍJAR, COSTA DE ALMERÍA, TABERNAS (30km/19mi N) and GUADIX (109km/68mi NW).

## A Bit of History

Almería was founded in the 9C by Abd ar-Rahman II. Abd ar-Rahman III built the *alcazaba* and walls in the 10C, creating the key port. Later the capital of a taifa kingdom, and a textile centre, it was attacked by Christian Aragón. Almería became part of Nasrid Granada, and fell to the Catholic Monarchs in 1489.

16C Berber attacks and the expulsion of the *moriscos* (converts from Islam) weakened Almería. The 1522 earthquake destroyed the entire city.

Almería began to recover in the 19C, as mining grew. Old walls were demolished. Foreign mining companies withdrew after the First World War, but in recent years, agriculture and tourism have taken up the slack.

*Alcazaba and town of Almería*

B. Kaufmann / MICHELIN

# Sight

## Alcazaba★

○ *Open 9.30am-8.30pm (6.30pm Nov-Mar).* ○ *Closed Mon, 1 Jan and 25 Dec.* ⊜ *€2; no charge for citizens of the European Union.* ☎ *950 27 16 17.*

Abd ar-Rahman III had this superbly sited hilltop fortress built in the 10C. It was enlarged by Almotacín, and by the Catholic Monarchs.

*Access is via an arch and a ramp leading to three walled enclosures.*

The **first enclosure** *(recinto)* holds gardens and cistern *(aljibe)*. The bell tower once warned of pirate attacks. Walls connect the fortress with San Cristóbal hill.

The **second enclosure** housed the Caliphal residence, including the cistern room (now an exhibition hall), a Mudéjar hermitage, a pool and baths used by troops. The esplanade was a parade ground. The baths of the Caliph's wife are in one corner.

In the **third enclosure**, to the west, is the castle of the Catholic Monarchs. The large parade ground is dominated by an imposing keep with a Gothic doorway.

The impressive **view**★ from the battlements takes in city and port, the working-class district of **La Chanca**, and a backdrop of arid hills and shimmering azure sea.

# Walking Tour

## City Centre 🕭 *See city plan.*

### Cathedral★

◦➤ *Guided tours 10am-5pm. No visits during services.* ⊜ *€2.* ☎ *950 23 48 48.*

The fortress-like cathedral on the site of a mosque in the 16C, when Barbary pirates regularly raided. A large 17C tower is crowned by a small belfry.

The Renaissance **main doorway**★ contrasts with the austere façade, its rich decoration unable to disguise classical lines. The escutcheon of the founding bishop is on the door pediment, and that of Carlos I, with two-headed eagle, on the upper floor. Before entering the cathedral, admire the unusual relief of the **Portocarrero sun**★ – an animated sunburst, the symbol of the city – at the east end.

**Interior** – Three Gothic aisles are topped with star vaults on fasciated pillars. The chancel, tabernacle, retable and ambulatory arches were remodelled in the 18C. Renaissance **choir stalls** have exceptional profile medallions in the upper stalls and full-bodied lifelike reliefs; the neo-Classical back wall, in multi-hued marble, was designed by Ventura Rodríguez. The transept door is Flamboyant Gothic.

The **ambulatory** has three chapels: the Gothic axial houses the venerated statue of Cristo de la Escucha. St Indalecio, patron of Almería, can be seen in the right-hand Renaissance chapel, and various canvases by Alonso Cano in the chapel to the left.

The late-19C Palacio Episcopal (Bishop's Palace) and the Iglesia de las Puras, part of an old convent founded in the 16C, front the **plaza de la Catedral**.

*Detail, choir stalls*

### Iglesia de las Puras

The church and tower are both 17C. The escutcheon on the doorway is flanked by the heads of two lions and urns decorated with the sun and the moon. The Baroque altarpiece has an Immaculate Conception by Alonso Cano.

## Address Book

For coin ranges, see the Legend on the front cover flap.

### WHERE TO EAT

**Asador La Gruta** – *5km/3mi west toward Aguadulce* – *www.asadorla-gruta.com* – *dinner only* – ☎ *950 23 93 35* – *Closed Sun, two weeks in Feb and Oct*. The huge caves of this ex-quarry are a unique setting for a menu of prime grilled meats prepared in simple, time-honoured fashion.

**Real** – *Real, 15* – ☎ *950 28 02 43 – closed Sun* – . This 19C mansion retains its original floor plan, with dining rooms decorated with antiques in the fashion of Almerian districts. Seafood and updated regional dishes are offered.

### TAPAS

**Casa Puga** – *Jovellanos, 7 (old city)* – ☎ *950 23 15 30* – *Closed Sun and public hols (except Holy Week), and 1-21 Sep*. Almería is teeming with tapas bars, of which Casa Puga is the oldest. A huge choice of tapas, excellent wines and sausages.

**El Quinto Toro** – *Juan Leal, 6* – ☎ *950 23 91 35* – *Closed Sat night and Sun* – . Close by the central market, this is a tapas classic. The skewers bar has its own seating area. A specialty is *patatas a lo pobre* (poor man's potatoes).

### WHERE TO STAY

The centrally situated placita de Flores is the best area to look for accommodation as it is fronted by hotels of different standards (**Torreluz II** and **AM Torreluz**), a restaurant and a tapas bar.

**Torreluz II** – *Plaza Flores, 6* – ☎ *950 23 43 99* – *www.torreluz.com* – – *24 rooms* – €5.70 - Restaurant (). A modern hotel with spacious rooms. Nearby Torreluz hotels, of differing standards, have the same owners.

**Hotel Costasol** – *Paseo de Almería, 58* – ☎ *950 23 40 11* – *www.hotelcostasol.com* – – *55 rooms* – €5.70. A sixties hotel on the busiest street in Almería. Rooms are large and comfortable, some with balcony.

**Hotel AM Torreluz** – *Plaza Flores, 5* – ☎ *950 23 49 99* – *www.amhoteles.com* – *105 rooms*. A comfortable, recently renovated hotel in the heart of the city. Facilities include a private garage, piano-bar, swimming pool and fitness room. One restaurant specializes in grilled meats, the other in regional specialties.

### SPA

**Lanjarón Spa** - ☎ *958 77 01 37; www.aguasdelanjaron.es*. Located just north of Lanjarón.

## Plaza Vieja (Plaza de la Constitución)

The **town hall** dominates this lovely, arcaded 19C square, on the site of Moorish bazaars. A column commemmorates the 1824 liberal revolt against Fernando VII.

## Iglesia de las Claras

This small, 17C church, hidden behind a simple, yet elegant doorway, is noteworthy for its cupola above the transept decorated with stuccowork and escutcheons.

## Iglesia de San Pedro

The present neo-Classical church was built in the 18C. The length of its central nave is accentuated by the balcony beneath the lunette-adorned barrel vault.

## Iglesia de Santiago

The 16C church, one of the city's smallest, is in narrow calle de las Tiendas ("street of shops"). A **Renaissance portal**★ , similar to the cathedral doorway, magnificently depicts St James the Moorslayer *(Santiago Matamoros)*. Scallop shells and crosses of St James decorate the space between the columns. The solid tower is pierced by arches in its lower section.

### Ajibes de Jayrán
The nearby 11C **Moorish cisterns** in calle Tenor Iribarne, with their brick cannon vaults, are worth a visit.

### Puerta de Purchena
This square, a busy crossroads, is at the very heart of Almerian life. Many of its seigniorial buildings date from the late 19C.

### Paseo de Almería
The main avenue is fronted by a mixture of 20C buildings and modern tower blocks. The **Círculo Mercantil**, with 1920s ceilings, stuccowork and *azulejo* panelling, is one of its most attractive buildings; behind it, the landmark **Teatro Cervantes** opened in 1921. The nearby **Basílica de Nuestra Señora del Mar** houses Almería's venerated patron saint; its 18C cloister is now home to the city's **Arts and Crafts School**.

▸ *Return to paseo de Almería.*

The former casino (n° 64), a 19C building with a central patio and seigniorial rooms, is the headquarters of the **Delegación del Gobierno de la Junta** (provincial government). At the end of the street, by the plaza Emilio Pérez, is the surprising and unusual Casa Montoya, built in a style associated with Santander in northern Spain.

### Parque de Nicolás Salmerón
This pleasant strip of greenery with its fountains and pools runs parallel to the port in a former warehouse district.

### Hospital Real
Although the hospital was founded in the 16C, the façade and doorway of this large 18C building are distinctly neo-Classical in style.

### Iglesia de San Juan
The church's exterior, with sober portal of ringed columns, a pediment and coat of arms, has a distinctly civic air. The surprising interior contains a 12C *mihrab* and *qibla* wall – vestiges of a 10C mosque.

## Visit

### Museo Arqueológico de Almería
☺ *The new museum building is about to open; inquire locally.* The collection extends from prehistory through the Islamic era, with finds from El Argar and Los Millares.

### Railway Station
The late-19C brick *estación* has attractive ceramic and wrought iron details.

### Cable Inglés
The "English Cable" is an early 20C rail line from the terminus to the docks. It consists of a stone bridge and an iron mechanism which was used for loading.

## Excursion

### Los Millares★
*19km/12mi north, to the west of Benahadux (reception hut at km 42).* ◷ *Open 10am-2pm.* ◷ *Closed Mon and Tue.* ☎ *677 90 34 04 or 670 94 59 76.*
Europe's most important Copper Age settlement was occupied from 2700 to 1800 BC. Perhaps 1 000 to 1 500 people lived a settled urban life at Los Millares. Its inhabitants included arable and livestock farmers, as well as artisans of copper and ceramic ritual

objects. The site, dominating the Andarax Valley, had a wetter climate than today, with abundant game and copper available in the nearby Sierra de Gádor.
The defensive wall is the longest known from this period. Dwellings were circular. In the **necropolis** are a perfectly preserved tomb with atrium, a corridor with perforated slate tiles, and a chamber covered with a false cupola.
**Balneario San Nicolas**, a spa, is located here.

# ALMUÑÉCAR

POPULATION: 20 997.

Hilltop Almuñécar was once Hins-al-Monacar ("fortress city" in Arabic). Protected from cold by a mountain ridge and warmed by North African winds, Almuñécar is a year-round holiday destination. Fruits, vegetables and flowers proliferate all year. ⓘ *Av. Europa, Palacete La Najarra, 18690 Almuñécar,* ☎ *958 63 11 25.*

▶ **Orient Yourself:** Almuñécar is at the southern tip of Granada province, at the mouth of the fertile River Verde valley, along the N 340 – E 15 east of Málaga.

ⓒ **Organizing Your Time:** Allow a morning or afternoon to see Almuñécar, more to wander the coast and return to town.

ⓒ **Also See:** COSTA DEL SOL, La AXARQUÍA, MÁLAGA and ALMERÍA.

## Visit

### Palacete de la Najarra
ⓒ *Open mid-Jun to mid-Sep, 10am-2pm and 6-9pm; mid-Sep to mid-Mar, 10am-2pm and 4-7pm; mid-Mar to mid-Jun, 10am-2pm and 5-8pm.* ⓒ *Closed 1 Jan and 25 Dec.* ☎ *958 63 11 25.* ⓒ *Only the garden and entry are open to visitors.*
This small, late-19C neo-Moorish palace houses the tourist office and is the ideal starting point for a tour of Almuñécar. Note the exotic garden inside the palace.

---

## Address Book

### WHERE TO EAT
⌂ **Vizcaya** – *Paseo de las Flores (Playa de San Cristóbal)* – ☎ *958 63 57 12* – ⓒ *Closed in November, and Wednesday in winter.* On a pebbly beach, Vizcaya offers paellas, and grilled meats and fish in the style of the Biscay region, from which it takes its name. Atmospheric by day, romantic by night.

⌂ **Mar de Plata** – *Paseo San Cristóbal (Edificio Mar de Plata)* – ☎ *958 63 30 79 – www.restaurantemardeplata. com* – ⓒ*Closed Tuesdays and in May.* This restaurant banks on a beachside location and value for money. The

menu offers paellas, seafood, and regional *pescado a la sal* (whole fish cooked in a block of salt).

### WHERE TO STAY
⌂ **Hotel Casablanca** – Plaza San Cristóbal, 4 – ☎ *958 63 55 75 – www. almunecar.info/casablanca* - 🖻 ♿ – *35 rooms.* With its raspberry-coloured façade and impressive dome, the hotel's theme is resolutely Moroccan, enhanced by tasteful marble features and crystal chandeliers in the bedrooms. Advance booking recommended.

### Castillo de San Miguel★

🕓 *Open in summer, 10.30am-1.30pm and 6.30-9.30pm; otherwise, 10.30am-1.30pm and 4-6pm; Sun and public hols 10.30am-1.30pm.* 🕓 *Closed Mon, 1 Jan and 25 Dec.* ∞€2. ☎ 958 63 11 25.

This Roman castle lay in ruins from the war against the French in 1808 until recent times. A dungeon and house remain from service as a Nasrid palace. The entry towers were built under Charles V. The museum displays **models** of the Almuñécar area.

### Cueva de los Siete Palacios (Museo Arqueológico)

🕓 *Open in summer, 10.30am-1.30pm and 6.30-9pm, Sun and public hols, 10.30am-1.30pm; otherwise, 10.30am-1.30pm and 4-6pm, Sun and public hols, 10.30am-2pm.* 🕓 *Closed Mon, 1 Jan, 25 Dec.* ∞€2.10. ☎ 958 63 11 25.

The archaeological museum in a Roman basement exhibits artefacts from Phoenician burials, including an outstanding Egyptian **funerary urn**★ of Apophis I, in grey marble, containing the oldest written document found in Spain.

### Parque "El Majuelo"

This botanical garden contains 400 species of palm tree, among other species, as well as the ruins of a **Phoenician salting factory**.

## Excursions

## Costa Tropical

The Tropical Coast is the 100km/60mi stretch between La Herradura and La Rábita, characterised by mountains swoop down to the sea forming delightful coves.

### La Herradura

*8km/5mi west of Almuñécar.* This spectacular horseshoe beach lies between the watchtowers of **La Punta de la Mona** and **Cerro Gordo**. Rugged seaside mountains create an extraordinary setting. **Puerto Deportivo Marina del Este** is a marina at La Punta de la Mona. Stunning **views** abound toward Cerro Gordo.

### Salobreña★

*15km/9mi east of Almuñécar.* Hilltop Salobreña, a cluster of whitewashed houses, is the most attractive town on this stretch of coast. Visit the imposing **castle**, the **Iglesia de la Virgen del Rosario**, and splendid beaches, such as **Playa de El Peñón**. **Castle** – *The best view is from the Almuñécar road.* 🕓 *Open in summer, 10.30am-2pm and 5-9.30pm; in winter, daily (except Mon), 10.30am-2pm and 4-7pm.* ∞€2 (€2.55 including entry to museum). ☎ 958 61 27 33/03 14.

---

## Address Book

### WHERE TO STAY

⊜⊜ **Best Western Salobreña** – *On N 340, 3km/2mi toward Málaga* – ☎ 958 61 02 61 – *www.hotelsalobrena.com* – 📗🔄 – *195 rooms*. This large tourist complex, with its gardens and swimming pool, comprises several modern buildings with rooms overlooking the sea or the rocky coastline. The views of the Mediterranean are superb and the complex is built away from the road so that the only sound here is of the waves breaking on the shore.

### SCUBA DIVING

**La Herradura** has developed into an important centre for scuba diving. A number of dive companies operate here, offering courses for all levels.

**Buceo La Herradura** - *Puerto deportivo de Marina del Este* – ☎ 958 82 70 83 – *www.buceolaherradura.com.*

## A Castle of Legends

**Washington Irving** wrote that the princesses Zaida, Zoraida and Zorahaida, daughters of King Mohammed IX of Granada, were confined to this sumptuous palace for many years by their father who, on the advice of his astrologers, decided to protect them from everyday temptation, not least that of meeting an undesirable suitor. The three princesses lived here surrounded by luxury, their every need attended to, until their father took them to his palace at the Alhambra. Destiny dictated that they encountered their predicted temptation on the journey to Granada, when the party fell upon three Christian prisoners who immediately fell in love with the young princesses.

The original 10C castle was transformed into a luxurious residence - and royal prison - under the Nasrids. Access is via a corner doorway to the first enclosure. Continue to the *alcazaba* (fortress), with its two underground caverns and keep.

### Motril

*21km/13mi east of Almuñécar and 6km/4mi east of Salobreña.* This community of 50 000 is the largest town along the Costa Tropical, a centre of sugar cultivation since the 18C, and before then, a backwater where the mother of the last king of Granada lived. The few tourists flock to hotels along the **Playa de Poniente** *(4km/2.5mi SE).*
From **Motril**, a coastal road passes through Torrenueva, **Carchuna**, **Calahonda** and Castell de Ferro. Beaches are long and wide. Medieval watchtowers – Torre de Carchuna, Torrenueva and La Rábita – are visible. From La Rábita, detour (5km/3mi) to **Albuñol**, a *pueblo blanco* nestled in the Sierra de la Contraviesa.

# LAS ALPUJARRAS★

The Alpujarras (from the Arabic *al-bucharrat*, 'pastures') is a region of whitewashed villages, rugged mountains and fertile valleys straddling Granada and Almería provinces. It was the final stronghold of the Nasrids. This magnificent range was rediscovered by 19C Romantic travellers, and today is one of Andalucía's most popular destinations. ▯ *Oficina de Información del Legado Andalusí, avenida de Madrid, Lanjarón, ☎ 958 77 02 82.*

▸ **Orient Yourself:** This rugged and varied region extends across the southern slopes of the Sierra Nevada, inland from the Costa Tropical and Motril.
◔ **Organizing Your Time:** Allow two days or more to explore by car.
◔ **Also See:** GRANADA, SIERRA NEVADA, GUADIX, Sierra de los FILABRES and ALMERÍA.

## A Bit of History

**Arab presence in the Alpujarras** – Berbers arrived with the Moors in 711, and began to grow olives and vines and breed silkworms. The Alpujarras prospered under the Nasrids between the 13C and 15C, when industry, espcially textiles, flourished. After the fall of Granada, the Catholic Monarchs ceded this area to Boabdil. Intolerance led to revolts, the last in 1568 led by Don Fernando de Córdoba (known as **Abén Humeya**). The expulsion of the *moriscos* led to the decline of Alpujarras.

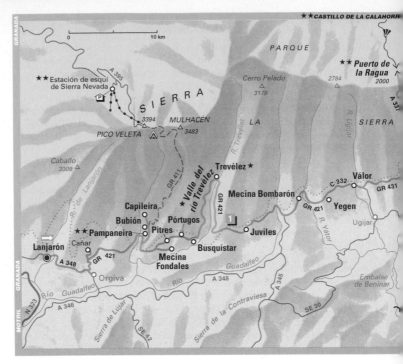

# Driving Tours 🏛 See map.

## The Granada Alpujarras 1 ★★

### From Lanjarón to Bayárcal

▷ *100km/62mi (127km/79mi with excursion to Puerto de la Ragua) – allow 2 days.*

**Lanjarón**
Lanjarón, gateway from Granada, is one of the most accessible towns in the Alpujarras. Famous for its medicinal water, it attracts thousands of visitors every year. The other attraction is a 16C **castle**, guarding the entrance to the valley.
The A 348 road offers magnificent views of the arid and imposing Sierra de Lújar.

▷ *9km/5.5mi from Lanjarón, before Órgiva, take A 7210, which crosses the northern slope of the Alpujarras. 🏛 Be cautious on this narrow mountain road.*

Before Pampaneira, the road passes through three villages, **Cañar**, with its impressive views, Carataunas and Soportújar, none of which are on the main tourist track.

**Pampaneira★★**
*Leave your car at the town entrance.* Pampaneira is in the **Poqueira Valley**★★. It preserves its traditional atmosphere. The main street, where shops offer local products, leads to the **plaza de la Libertad**, dominated by the 17C Baroque Iglesia de la Santa Cruz. Stroll the narrow streets to appreciate the charms of Pampaneira, and stop at a traditional loom where Alpujarras rugs *(jarapas)* are made. The **Visitor Centre** *(Centro de Visitantes)*, can organise excursions. 🕐 *Open 10am-2pm and 5-7pm (mid-Sep-mid-Apr 10.30-2pm and 4-6pm).* ☎ *958 76 31 27.*

▷ *Continue along A 7210. After 2km/1.2mi, turn to Bubión and Capileira.*

## Bubión

At 1 296m/4 250ft, Bubión was a centre of the *morisco* rebellion. Rugged whitewashed walls and flat rooftops are reminiscent of North Africa.

## Capileira

At 1 436m/4 710ft, Capileira is the highest village in the valley. Its 16C parish church has an attractive Baroque retable. A museum, the **Museo Alpujarreño de Artes y Costumbres Populares**, recreates 19C Alpujarran. ◷ *Open Tue-Fri, 11.30am-2.30pm; Sat, 4-7pm (8pm in summer).* ◷ *Closed Mon.* ☎ *958 76 30 51.*

▷ *Return to the junction with A 7210.*

## Mecina Fondales

Several excursions are possible from Mecina Fondales along the valley of the River Trevélez. A minor road leads to the village of Ferreirola. The name refers to the iron found throughout this region.

▷ *Continues through an area of outstanding beauty to enter the Trevélez Valley.*

*A narrow street in Pampaneira*

B. Kaufmann / MICHELIN

### Pitres

This is the largest of the seven settlements of the *taha* – the Moorish district – of Pitres, **Capilerilla**, Mecina, Mecinilla, Fondales, Ferreirola and Atalbéitar.

### Pórtugos

The **Fuente Agria** is a spring of iron-rich water behind the hermitage of Nuestra Señora de las Angustias, at the exit to the village. Tradition says that the water from one of the five pipes has a unique taste – you can test the theory! Opposite, steps lead to **El Chorreón**, a fall of waters reddened by minerals.

---

## Trevélez cured ham

Ever since **Queen Isabel II** extolled the virtues of its **cured ham** *(jamón)* in the 19C, the name of Trevélez has been synonymous with this gastronomic treat. The secret of its drying sheds *(secaderos)* lies in their special climatic conditions (dry and cold) and the exclusive use of sea salt. White-coloured pigs are bred to produce these large hams (up to 10kg/22lb in weight), which are slightly rounded in shape.

---

### Busquístar

This quiet, Mozarabic village of gleaming white houses is the first in the spectacular **Trevélez Valley**★. The road ascends to Trevélez itself.

### Trevélez★

Trevélez is the highest town in Spain (1 600m/5 250ft in the *barrio alto*). **Mulhacén**, towering above, is the highest peak on the Iberian Peninsula (3 482m/11 424ft).

▸ *Beyond Trevélez, the narrow A 7208 descends to Torvizcón and the A 348 which crosses the southern Alpujarras. Follow GR 421 eastward to Juviles.*

### Juviles

Green valleys yield in this region to a wilder landscape. The 16C **Iglesia de Santa María de Gracia** is one of the prettiest churches in the Granada Alpujarras.

▸ *Upon leaving Bérchules, bear left onto A 348.*

### Mecina Bombarón

A drier, Mediterranean vegetation dominates, particularly in the **Contraviesa** area to the south, famous for its wines. The village, formerly Mecina Buenvarón, is divided by small ravines. Upon leaving, note the Roman bridge over the River Mecina.

---

## Alpujarran houses

The local architecture is perhaps the best example of the region's Moorish past. Visitors who have set foot in North Africa will be surprised by the strong similarities, with the predominance of south-facing houses searching for the warmth of the sun and often following the relief of this mountainous landscape. The houses are usually built on different levels, forming spaced terraces and steep narrow streets acting as a conduit for rainwater. Traditionally they comprise two floors, the walls of which are completely covered with lime. Their most typical feature is the flat roof, known as a *terrao*, made using large beams of chestnut and battens *(alfarjías)*, on top of which a layer of bluish-grey clay *(launa)* is added. Upon contact with water, this layer of clay solidifies to provide a waterproof covering. In the past, these flat roof terraces were used as meeting areas, although nowadays they are predominantly used for storage or for drying clothes, curing food etc.

## Yegen

A plaque marks the house of **Gerald Brenan** – the author of *South from Granada*, a marvellous portrayal of the traditions and customs of the Alpujarras – who spent seven years here between 1923 and 1934.

## Válor

Along with many other churches in this area, the 16C **Iglesia de San José** is, typically, in Mudéjar style. Note the late-18C fountain in the square. The leader of the *morisco* rebellion of 1568, Don Fernando de Córdoba (**Abén Humeya**) came from Válor, the largest town in the area.

# Address Book

## SIGHTSEEING

**Centro de Interpretación del Parque Nacional de Sierra Nevada (NEVADENSIS)**, in **Pampaneira**, plaza de la Libertad (☎ 958 76 31 27). This visitor centre organises hikes, climbing trips, and horseback rides.

**Centro de Información del Puerto de la Ragua** (☎ 958 76 02 31). Cross-country skiing and dog-sledding can be arranged here. www.laragua.net

**Rustic Blue**, in **Bubión** *(Barrio la Ermita,* ☎ 958 76 33 81*).* This rural tourism operator books accommodation and outdoor activities. www.rusticblue.es

## WHERE TO STAY

⊜ **Hotel La Fragua** – *Barrio Medio, San Antonio, 4, Trevélez* – ☎ 958 85 86 26 – *www.hotellafragua.com* – ⊙ *Closed 10 Jan-10 Feb -24 rooms*. Two buildings, one traditional, the other newer, with mountain views. Private bathrooms, but basic. A separate bar-restaurant has lovely views.

⊜ **Hotel España** – *Avenida de la Alpujarra, 42, Lanjarón* – ☎ 958 77 01 87 – *www.lanjaron.biz* – ⊙ *Closed in January* – ⊠ – *36 rooms (including VAT)*. This early-20C hotel in the centre hosted García Lorca and bullfighter Manolete. Rooms have extremely high ceilings, some have balconies.

⊜⊜ **Alquería de Morayma** – *Along A 348, 3.5km/2.3mi from Cádiar towards Torvizcón* – *www.alqueriamorayma. com* – ⦿ – ☎ 958 34 32 21 – *13 rooms, 5 apartments*. Rustic rooms in this country hotel look onto mountains and the village of Cádiar. Regional restaurant-bar.

⊜⊜ **Villa Turística de Bubión** – *Barrio Alto, Bubión* – ☎ 958 76 39 09 – *www.villabubion.com* – ⦿ – *43 units*. A village of regional-style cottages. Units have kitchen and fireplace. The restaurant, one of the best in the area, specialises in kid, trout and sausages.

⊜⊜⊜ **Hotel Alcazaba de Busquístar** – *4km/2.5mi S from Trevélez towards Juviles* – ☎ 958 85 86 87 – *www.alcazabadebusquistar.com* – ⦿ – *51 units*. Regional materials predominate. Rooms are spacious; terraces have superb views over the sierra.

## SHOPPING

**Jarapas** – Local rugs *(jarapas)*, originally of joined brightly coloured sections, are now woven whole. Two workshops in Pampaneira are: **Hilacar** *(2 km N* – ☎ 956 76 32 26*)* and **La Rueca** *(Avenida de la Alpujarra, 2* – ☎ 958 76 30 14*).*

## LOCAL SPECIALITIES

**Cured hams** are best purchased in Trevélez, where there are several drying sheds.

*Cured hams, Trevélez*

H. Champollion / MICHELIN

▷ *Follow the A 7208 for 11km/7mi.*

## Laroles

Laroles stands at the foot of the Ragua Pass. Note the unusual tower of its parish church. The hamlets of Picena and Cherín are visible to the south.

▷ *2km/1.2mi beyond Laroles by an extremely narrow road is Bayárcal, first village in the Almería Alpujarras. The road northward to the Ragua Pass is the only link between the north and south slopes of the Sierra Nevada (closed in winter).*

## Puerto de la Ragua★★

The road ascends a gently to the summit (2 000m/6 559ft) amid a high mountain landscape, then narrows and descends abruptly to the Guadix Plateau, offering magnificent views of the **Castillo de la Calahorra** ★★ (👁 *see GUADIX*).

▷ *Head back towards Bayárcal.*

# The Almería Alpujarras ②★

## From Bayárcal to Alhama de Almería *73km/45mi – allow 3hr*

## Bayárcal

The highest village in Almería (1 275m/4 182ft), Bayárcal includes one of the largest oak groves in the province. Explore on foot and enjoy superb views. Statues in the 16C Mudéjar-style **Iglesia de San Francisco Javier** include Saint Francis Xavier, an *Immaculate Conception* by Alonso Cano and an *Ecce Homo*.

## Paterna del Río

*7km/4.5mi east of Bayárcal.* The village is surrounded chestnut, oak and poplar forests. The **Iglesia de San Juan Bautista** has an interesting Mudéjar *artesonado* ceiling.

## Laujar de Andarax

The capital of the Almerían Alpujarras is by the source of the River Andarax, south of the sierra. Several 16C-17C mansions and fountains adorn the streets. Poet **Francisco Villaespesa** (1877-1936), admirer of symbolist Rubén Dario, was born here.

**Iglesia Parroquial de la Encarnación** – This 16C brick church has a Baroque altarpiece with a statue of the Immaculate Conception attributed to Alonso Cano.

**Ayuntamiento** – The façade of the 18C town hall, also of brick, is sober and harmonious. The **Pilar de los Cuatro Caños**, a public fountain, dates from the 17C.

### Abén Humeya

The leader of the 1568 *moriscos* revolt in the Alpujarras, **Abén Humeya** was assassinated in Laujar by his followers on 20 October 1569. Once the revolt had finally been quashed in 1571, the *moriscos* were expelled from Spain.

**Source of the River Andarax** – *1.5km/1mi from Laujar. Follow the "Nacimiento" signs, to the left of the square.* This is an attractive picnic area.

▷ *Head east along the A 348.*

## From Laujar to Canjáyar

This road runs through the fertile Andarax Valley between terraces of orange trees, prickly pears and vineyards which grow the prized Almería grape.
The 20km/12mi stretch from Laujar de Andarax to Canjáyar passes **Fondón** and **Almócita**, villages of whitewashed houses with attractive parish churches.

H. Champollion / MICHELIN

*Canjáyar*

The road offers a delightful view of hill-side **Padules** and its 16C church.

### Canjáyar
Whitewashed Canjáyar, at the foot of the Ermita de San Blas, retains a Moorish air.

▶ *Continue along A 348. After 3km/2mi take the turn-off to Ohanes.*

### Ohanes road★
The winding road up to Ohanes (958m/3 142ft) offers spectacular **views**★, and no trace of habitation. The panorama even encompasses the faraway Sierra de Gata.

**Ohanes** – Ohanes enjoys a magnificent **site**★ dominating the vine-planted Andarax Valley, a blanket of white against the verdant backdrop, punctuated by a stone church. Narrow, winding streets seem suspended against the intense blue sky.

▶ *Return to A 348 and continue to Alhama.*

### Alhama de Almería
Contrasts abound around Alhama: the desert-like Tabernas and the lush Andarax Valley lie to one side, the Sierra de Gádor to the other. The village has its own source of mineral waters at around 46°C/115°F, several noble mansions and a café, the Tertulia, from the early 20C. Alhama was the birthplace in 1838 of **Nicolás Salmerón**, the president of the First Republic, who resigned rather than sign a death warrant. Before leaving, by all means try the local ring-shaped pastries *(rosquillas)*.

---

## A strange devotion

In many places such as Laujar, Fondón, Ohanes and Canjáyar, small hermitages known as *ánimas* (souls) are visible as you come into or leave the village. These small chapels are adorned with an altar containing a picture representing the Virgen del Carmen extracting souls from flames with the help of angels. The entrance doorway often has a peephole to enable visitors to peer inside.

---

### WHERE TO STAY
⬭ **Hotel Almirez** – *Laujar de Andarax, on A 348 towards Berja* – ☎ *950 51 35 14 – 20 rooms.* A good choice for spending a night, but not a lot of money. In a little hamlet, it offer simple rooms and an attractive rustic restaurant.

### LOCAL SPECIALITIES
A **rosé wine** is produced in Laujar by a number of private estates and one organic producer, the Cortijo del Cura, located on the outskirts of the town.

# ANDÚJAR★

POPULATION: 35 803.

Situated in the centre of Spain's olive-growing region are Andújar's narrow, winding streets, 15C and 16C churches and houses, and vestiges of monumental 9C Moorish walls. In the woods and streams of nearby **Parque Natural Sierra de Andújar** is the popular Santuario de la Virgen de la Cabeza (Shrine of the Virgin of the Head). *Plaza Santa Maria, Torre del Reloj, 23740 Andújar,* ☎ *953 50 49 59*

▶ **Orient Yourself:** Andújar sits in the depression of the Guadalquivir Valley, toward the west of the province of Jaén, 76km/47mi E of Córdoba along A 4.

🕓 **Organizing Your Time:** Take a few hours to see Andújar or a day or more if you linger at the Parque Natural de la Sierra de Andújar.

🖒 **Also See:** MONTORO (36km/22mi W), CÓRDOBA, JAÉN (45km/28mi SE) and LINARES (39km/24mi E).

## A Bit of History

Ancient Iberian Isturgis came under the Romans and Moors, and was reconquered by Fernando III in 1225. Francisco de Quevedo here planned a journey for Felipe IV; Cosimo de' Medici, and his entourage passed through, as did British traveller Joseph Townsend and French writer Prosper Merimée.

## Visit

### Iglesia de Santa María

This church, probably started in the 13C, was not completed until the 17C, hence its eclectic styles. The interior, a mixture of pointed, circular and groined vaults, holds an *Assumption of the Virgin* by Pacheco *(left-side apse chapel)*, an Immaculate Conception by Giuseppe Cesari, a manuscript signed by St John of the Cross, and, above all, **Christ in the Garden of Olives**★★ by El Greco, in a chapel enclosed by a fine 16C **grille**★ by Maestro Bartolomé. This huge canvas depicts Christ in an elegant red tunic, illuminated from the sky, and the Apostles St Peter, St James and St John, who appear to be dozing at his feet.

### Ayuntamiento

🕓 *Open Mon-Fri, 8am-2.30pm.* 🕓 *Closed Sat-Sun and public hols.* ☎ *953 50 49 59.*
The mid-17C **town hall** *(ayuntamiento)* retains its former Corral de Comedias, used for theatrical performances.

### Iglesia de San Miguel

The imposing silhouette of this church dominates the plaza de España (or plaza del Mercado). It holds unusual 17C and 18C murals, and an exceptional choir and a fine partition screen, both adorned with delicately carved reliefs.

### Palacio de Los Niños de Don Gome

🕓 *Open Jul to mid-Sep, 10.30am-1pm; mid-Sep to Jun, 7-9pm.* 🕓 *Closed, Sun, Mon and public hols.* ☎ *953 51 31 78.*
This fine 16-17C palace is topped with a sober tower with Indian-influenced decoration. Inside, note the attractive patio portico and original stable.

## Address Book

### WHERE TO EAT – TAPAS

**Mesón Ana Las Perolas** – *Serpiente, 6* – ☎ *953 50 67 26* – *www.lasperolas. com* – *Closed Monday and in July* – . Ana Domínguez is a local character known for her cuisine. Specialities are pork, rabbit and beef stews (*guisos*) served in small pots (*perolas*), as well as venison, boar, and other game. Friendly atmosphere.

**Los Naranjos** – *Guadalupe, 4* – ☎ *953 51 03 90* – Closed second half of July, Sundays in summer, Tuesdays rest of year – . This centrally located restaurant is known for value. The coffee shop and modest dining area have separate entrances.

### WHERE TO STAY

**Hotel Del Val** – *Hermanos del Val, 1* – ☎ *953 50 09 50* – *www.hoteldelval. com* – – *79 rooms*. Right at the entry to town, the hotel has modest rooms, pool and gardens, and a fine restaurant with regional dishes.

### SHOPPING

Andújar is famous for its ceramics, such as ashtrays, bowls, plates etc.

### LOCAL SPECIALITIES

The region is renowned for such dishes as *ajo blanco* (a sauce made from garlic and breadcrumbs), *flamenquines* (fried veal and ham rolls), and asparagus (*espárragos*).

## Iglesia de San Bartolomé

The main attraction of this late-15C church is the façade. Its three stone **Gothic portals** bear elegant and exquisitely carved ornamental features.

## Torre del Reloj

The clock tower, along with part of the calle Silera and the Fuente Sorda and Tavira towers, was long thought to be part of the Moorish walls, but is now dated 16C.

# Excursions

## Villanueva de la Reina

*14km/9mi SE*. This tranquil town sits on the banks of the Guadalquivir between the Sierra Morena rising to the north and the horizontal plain. In the old quarter is the 18C **Iglesia de Nuestra Señora de la Natividad**.

## Parque Natural de la Sierra de Andújar★

*Leave Andújar to the north along A 1208. Park visitor centre:* open Jun to mid-Oct, Fri, 6-8pm, Sat-Sun and public hols, 10am-2pm and 6-8pm; otherwise, Thu, 10am-2pm and 4-6pm, Fri, 4-6pm, Sat-Sun and public hols, 10am-2pm and 4-6pm. Closed Mon-Wed, 1 and 6 Jan and 25 Dec. ☎ 953 54 90 30.

The access road winds up through an impressive landscape of holm oaks, cork oaks, wild olives and arbutus, offering magnificent **views**★★ of the surrounding area.

This protected park in the low foothills of the Sierra Morena above the Guadalquivir Valley spreads over 60 800ha/150 240 acres. It alternates from open pasture, grazed by fighting

### Oak groves

Although the landscapes of Jaén are dominated by the ubiquitous olive tree, the province is also home to a number of holm oak forests, most notably in the Sierra de Andújar. These noble trees adopt a different appearance depending on the light; this ability has undoubtedly spawned a famous local legend which says that the oak trees dance at night, but are then petrified by the first rays of sunshine early in the morning.

bulls, to dark ravines with dense vegetation ideal for deer, lynx and wild boar. The Jándula and Yeguas rivers are popular sport fishermen, while the extensive network of marked paths criss-crossing forests and thickets carpeted in wild jasmine and mastic trees are a haven for hikers.

**Santuario de la Virgen de la Cabeza** – *Museum:* ◷ *open Sat noon-1.30pm, Sun and public hols, 10am-2pm and 4-6pm; Mon-Fri by arrangement.* ☎ *953 54 90 15.*

The sanctuary is situated at the heart of the park near a hunting reserve, 32km/20mi from Andújar. According to tradition, the Virgin Mary appeared to a shepherd as a head. A chapel was built here, and later a monastery which was destroyed in the Spanish Civil War. It is one of Andalucía's principal sites of pilgrimage to the Virgin, especially on the last Sunday in April.

**Bailén**

*23km/14mi NE on A 4*. The town was the scene of a Peninsular War **battle** in 1808. Spanish troops under General Castaños defeated the French, commanded by Dupont, turning the tide against French presence on Spanish soil.

Bailén whitewashed houses and pleasant squares are typically Andalusian. The **Iglesia de la Encarnación**, a 16C church with Gothic and Renaissance influences, holds the tomb of General Castaños.

# ANTEQUERA★

POPULATION: 40 239.

Antequera (Roman *Anticaria*) is the Andalusian ideal: cobblestone streets, whitewashed houses with flower-decked balconies and wrought-iron grilles, monumental churches, and attractive avenues. The bell tower of the Iglesia de San Sebastián, with its fine Mudéjar brickwork, is emblematic. Antequera was conquered by Fernando of Aragón in 1410. Its heritage buildings reflect its 16C-18C splendour. ▯ *Plaza de San Sebastián, 7, 29200 Antequera,* ☎ *952 70 25 05, oficina.turismo@antequera.es.*

▶ **Orient Yourself:** In the heart of Málaga province, 7km/4.5mi from A 92 linking Granada and Sevilla, Antequera extends below the Sierra del Torcal, opposite the imposing Peña de los Enamorados rock.

🕔 **Organizing Your Time:** Take a morning to a day in Antequera, longer to explore our suggested discovery routes through the countryside.

🖒 **Also See:** MÁLAGA (55km/34mi S), COSTA DEL SOL, OSUNA (74km/46mi NW), LUCENA (52km/32mi N), CABRA (63km/39mi N), and LOJA (43km/27mi E)

## Visit

### Alcazaba

🔑 *Closed for restoration.*

*Antequera at nightfall*

The fortress is accessed via an avenue offering expansive **views**★ of the Sierra del Torcal, the Antequera plain, and painted roofs and graceful church towers. Te first fortress in Moorish Granada to fall to the Christians (1410), it changed hands soon after. The 15C walls enclose a pleasant garden. The most interesting remaining towers are the Torre de la Estrella, the Torre Blanca and, above all, the Torre del Homenaje (or Torre del Papabellotas), crowned by a small chapel housing the Antequera bell.

## Colegiata de Santa María★

🕐 *Open Tue, 10.30am-2pm and 4.30-6.30 pm (9-11pm in summer), Sat-Sun and public hols, 10.30am-2pm;* 🕐 *Closed summer afternoons, 1 and 6 Jan, Good Fri, 1 May, 23 Aug, 12 Sep, 24-25 and 31 Dec.* ☎ *952 70 25 05 (tourist office).*

This 16C collegiate church, at the foot of the castle gardens, is a fine example of early Renaissance style, mixed with earlier Gothic elements. Access is through the 16C **Arco de los Gigantes** (Giants' Arch), which has incorporates Roman tablets and sculptures discovered around town. The monumental church has three aisles and Mudéjar vaults separated by semi-circular arches on Ionic columns. The splendid **façade**, inspired by Roman triumphal arches and adorned with slender pinnacles, is worthy of note, as is the rectangular chancel, with its Gothic-Mudéjar vault.

## Iglesia del Carmen

🕐 *Open Jul to mid-Sep, 10am-2pm and 5-8pm (10.30pm Wed-Fri), Sun and public hols, 10am-2pm; otherwise, 10am-2pm and 4-7pm, Sun and public hols, 10am-2pm.* ⊕ *€1.50.* ☎ *952 70 25 05 or 609 53 97 10.*

### Peña de los Enamorados

This impressive rock rises up halfway along the road linking Antequera and Archidona. It has given rise to a romantic legend which tells of Tagzona, the daughter of the Moorish leader of the area, who had fallen hopelessly in love with Tello, a young Christian imprisoned near Antequera. They made the decision to elope but were discovered by the guards of Tagzona's father, who chased them to the very top of a rock on the outskirts of the town. Without any hope of escape, and with the arrows of Moorish marksmen bearing down on them, the two lovers launched themselves hand-in-hand into the void below, sealing their love for each other for eternity.

## Address Book

### WHERE TO EAT

El Escribano – *Plaza de los Escribanos, 11* – ☎ *950 70 65 33* – ⏰ *Closed evenings in winter and Mondays all year.* El Escribano is located up by the Moorish castle. Enjoy such regional plates as partridge paté.

Lozano – *Avenida Principal, 2 – 2.5km/1.5mi E on old Málaga road* – ☎ *952 84 27 12* – *www.hotellozano.com* – ▤ – *Rooms available: €56/70.* The industrial area is unattractive, but Lozano is one of the best restaurants in Antequera. Specialities are meat and fish dishes, served in a large dining room.

### WHERE TO STAY

Parador de Antequera – *García del Olmo* – ☎ *952 84 02 61* – *www.parador.es* – *to re-open late 2006 – 55 rooms.* A modern *parador* with gardens on the outskirts of Antequera.

### LOCAL SPECIALITIES

A rich culinary tradition includes *porra antequerana* (similar to *gazpacho*), pigs' trotters with chickpeas *(manos de cerdo con garbanzos)* and the almond-based *bienmesabe*, a Moorish-influenced dessert.

### FESTIVALS

Renowned **Holy Week** celebrations peak on the night of Good Friday, with a moving "farewell" *(despedida)* in plaza de San Sebastián by the brotherhoods of Santa Cruz de Jerusalén (Holy Cross of Jerusalem) and Dulce Nombre de Jesús (Divine Name of Jesus), both founded in the 16C.

---

The church is all that remains of a Carmelite convent. Built in the 16C and 17C, it has a wide single nave and Mudéjar *artesonado* ceiling. The interior is profuse with paintings and polychrome stuccowork; note the fine 18C **retable** at the high altar by Antonio Primo, of wood without polychrome adornment.

### Museo Municipal

*Guided tours, 30min, Jul to mid-Sep, Tue-Sat, 10am-1.30pm and 8.30-10.30pm, Sun, 11am-1.30pm; otherwise, Tue-Sat, 10am-1.30pm and 4.30-6.30pm, Sun, 11am-1.30pm.* ⏰ *Closed Mon and public hols.* ☞ *€3.* ☎ *952 70 40 21.*

The municipal museum in the 17C **Palacio de Nájera** (interesting lookout tower) holds noteworthy artefacts. The **Ephebus of Antequera**★, a 1C bronze Roman sculpture, represents a naked boy whose hands held an object now lost. Note the lightness of the work, as well as the child's sublime expression.

### Convento de las Descalzas

*Guided tours, 30min, in summer, Tue-Fri, 10.30am-1.30pm and 6-7.30pm, Sat, 10am-12.30pm and 6-7.30pm, Sun, 10am-noon; otherwise, Tue-Fri, 10.30am-2pm and 5-7pm, Sat, 10am-12.30pm, Sun, 10am-noon.* ⏰ *Closed Mon, public hols and in Aug.* ☞ *€3 (museum).* ☎ *952 84 19 77.*

The façade in Antequera Baroque is a highly original ensemble of a portal with a semicircular arch resting on *estípites* and figures which support a cornice with beautifully sculpted plant motifs and grotesque masks. Inside is an interesting collection of old paintings.

### Convento de la Encarnación

This 16C convent, with its single aisle and lofty chancel, follows the pattern of Mudéjar churches in Granada. The pendentives of the arch on calle Encarnación depict the Angel and the Virgin Mary. The 18C sculptures are interesting.

## "May the sun come out in Antequera..."

At the beginning of the 15C, Antequera still found itself under Moorish domination, at a time when Christian troops continued their advance south to conquer further territory in al-Andalus. Unsure of what the best military strategy should be, the Infante, Don Fernando of Aragón, was confronted one night by an apparition of a beautiful young girl surrounded by lions who said to him: "Tomorrow, may the sun come out in Antequera and may whatever God ordains happen." The following day, 16 September 1410, Christian troops took the town of Antequera, which they dedicated to St Euphemia, the virgin and martyr from Chalcedon who so inspired Don Fernando. Henceforth he became known as *el de Antequera*. Since this time, the Spanish phrase *Salga el sol por Antequera* (May the sun come out in Antequera) has become a popular saying which serves as an inspiration for people to face up to whatever challenges present themselves in life.

### Iglesia de San Sebastián

The interesting main portal of this 16C church is Plateresque. Its graceful 18C steeple, in four sections, is emblematic of Antequera. Works of art include a 15C sculpture of the Virgin of Hope and paintings by Mannerist Antonio Mohedano.

### Iglesia de San Agustín

Built by Diego de Vergara, who designed Málaga Cathedral, this 16C church has a single aisle, pointed Gothic vaulting and a fine 17C-18C tower. Niches in the Mannerist portal hold religious images. On the high altar, canvases by Mohedano narrate the story of St Augustine.

### Palacio Municipal

The unusual neo-Baroque façade of this ex-Franciscan monastery was added only in 1953. The cloister has two elegant galleries: the lower on semicircular arches and arris vaulting, the upper level with large windows and broken pediments. The Baroque staircase has a stucco-adorned vault and polychrome marble decoration.

### Convento de Nuestra Señora de los Remedios

This 17C church, dedicated to the patron saint of Antequera, has a Latin-cross plan with two side chapels. Sumptuous ornamentation is based on Franciscan themes and plant motifs. The fine gilded retable has a niche *(camarín)* decorated with delicate stuccowork, housing a 16C Virgin of the Remedies.

### Real Convento de San Zoilo

Outstanding features in this 16C late-Gothic convent include include rich polychrome stucco decoration highlighting plant and geometric motifs; a Mudéjar *artesonado* ceiling, an altarpiece comprising 16C Renaissance panels and the so-called Green Christ *(Cristo Verde)*, a Renaissance statue attributed to Pablo de Rojas.

### Convento de Belén

The main nave of this richly decorated 18C convent has a barrel vault interspersed with lunettes. Semicircular arches separate the side aisles. On either side of the transept, topped by a semicircular cupola, stand two chapels; the one on the Epistle side contains a stucco-adorned niche *(camarín)* with a statue of Christ by José Mora. The nuns are renowned for their pastries which can be purchased by visitors.

### Menga and Viera dolmens★

*To the left on the way out of Antequera by the A 354, towards Granada.* ◐ *Open 9am-6pm, Sun, 9.30am-2.30pm.* ◑ *Closed Mon, 1 and 6 Jan, 28 Feb, 1 May, and 25 Dec.* ▭ *No charge.* ☎ *952 70 25 05.*

These enormous Bronze Age burial chambers are at the foot of the Cerro de la Cruz, a small hill. The builders entered laterally to slide in stone slabs. The entry gallery of the **Menga dolmen** (2500 BC), 25m/82ft long and 2.70m/9ft high, holds 10 vertical and five horizontal monoliths. The spacious main oval chamber contains seven monoliths on each side and a large stone at its head. The third vertical monolith on the left side reveals human figures and solar symbols. At the end of the **Viera dolmen** (2200 BC) is a cube-shaped burial chamber, with four monoliths and large stone slab.

*Menga dolmen*

B. Kaufmann / MICHELIN

## Excursions

### El Romeral dolmen★

*4km/2.5mi northeast. Leave Antequera on the A 354. Turn left at signposted crossroads.*
🕐 *Open in summer, Tue-Fri, 9am-6pm (to 3pm Tue), Sun, 9.30am-2.30pm; otherwise, 9am-5.30pm (to 3.30pm Tue), Sun, 9.30am-2.30pm.* 🕐 *Closed Mon, 1 and 6 Jan, 9 Apr, 1 May, 16 and 20 Aug, 1 Nov, and 6, 24, 25 and 31 Dec.* ☎ *952 70 25 05.*
The El Romeral dolmen, more complex than others in the area, dates from 1800 BC. It consists of projecting ashlar stone walls, two circular chambers and a gallery. The first chamber has a false ceiling and is enclosed by a large monolithic slab; a carved door leads to a second room with an altar-like structure.

### Parque Natural de El Torcal★★

*14km/9mi southeast. Take C 3310 towards Villanueva de la Concepción, then bear right onto a signposted road.* 🅿 *Reception centre closed for renovation.* ☎ *952 70 25 05.* The park's 12ha/30 acres hold some of Spain's most unusual scenery, chasms, obelisks and other strange formations created by erosion. Flora, including Spanish squill and Venus's navelwort, is particularly impressive in spring, when the colour and scent of wild flowers and plants are a botanist's delight.
Two signposted walks start at the reception centre. The shorter *(1hr there and back)* La Losa footpath leads to the Maceta corrie *(torca)* and passes the Ventanillas viewpoint *(mirador)*. **Views**★★ are quite exceptional. The longer walk *(3hr there and back)* traverses the Chamorro chasm *(sima)*, the Pizarro Rock *(peñón)* and the Los Topaderos trail *(vereda)*.

### Archidona

*19km/11mi northeast. Leave Antequera on A 354. After the Peña de los Enamorados, follow A 92 to exit 163.* This town in the Sierra de Gracia, at the foot of the Pico de Conjuro peak, recalls Moorish times.

**Plaza Ochavada**★ – This octagonal square is a symbol of the town. Built in the 18C by architects Francisco Astorga and Antonio González, it melds French urban planning with traditional Andalusian architecture. The façades of the buildings fronting the square mix red-brick arches and pilasters and whitewashed masonry, embellished by flower-decked balconies. This unusual square was once used for bullfights.

**Ermita de la Virgen de Gracia** – This small 18C chapel is in the upper town in the old Moorish castle, of which only a few walls, the keep, vestiges of a cistern and the restored Puerta del Sol (Sun Gateway) remain. There are three naves, a hemispherical dome and a stuccoed elliptical cap; ornamental features of the original mosque remain. Views of Archidona and surroundings from here are delightful.

**Iglesia de Santa Ana** – ⏰ *Visits by prior arrangement.* ☎ *952 71 40 82.* This predominantly Gothic construction includes several Baroque features, such as the fine 18C façade. The triangular-based tower is capped by a pyramidal pinnacle with glazed green and white roof tiles. The interior contains interesting works of art.

**Convento de las Mínimas** – The Baroque doorway of this former 18C convent is flanked by a polygonal red-brick tower with glazed ceramic decoration.

**Iglesia de las Escuelas Pías** – *Visits by prior arrangement.* ☎ *952 71 40 82.* This church houses a venerated statue of Jesus of Nazareth.

### Laguna de la Fuente de Piedra★
*22km/13mi northwest. Take the A 354, then the A 92 towards Sevilla. Turn right at the Km 132 exit and continue along A 6211 to Fuente de Piedra, then follow the signposts.* This large lagoon is the habitat for a variety of flora (saltwort, *suaeda vera*, rushes etc). Fauna includes one of the largest colonies of flamingoes in Europe, storks, gulls, cranes and egrets. The spectacle of these birds in flight or massed on the water is quite remarkable, particularly in the late afternoon.

## Driving Tour

# Valle del Guadalhorce★

### From Antequera to the Cueva de Ardales  *70km/44mi SW*

*Allow half a day.* The Guadalhorce River meanders through the Serranía de Ronda and the Montes de Málaga to the Guadalteba-Guadalhorce Reservoir *(embalse).* It traverses a landscape of olive groves and fields between plain and mountains, hills dotted with whitewashed houses, vegetable plots and rocky walls, offering superb **views**.

▷ *Leave Antequera on avenida de la Legión. Turn right onto the A 343 towards Álora.*

The **road** winds its way through delightful landscapes, passing through the Abdalajís Valley, before heading south to Álora.

### Álora★
Home of the haunting *malagueña*, Álora perches on a hillside along the River Guadalhorce, at the foot of Monte Hacho. It is a maze of narrow streets lined by low, whitewashed houses, overlooked by a castle, with fine views.

▷ *On the way out of Álora, take the MA 404 towards El Chorro.*

### Desfiladero de los Gaitanes★★
The **winding road**★ crosses superb mountain scenery to the incredible Garganta del Chorro defile. This astonishing gorge is the main attraction in the Parque de Ardales. Leave your car at the El Chorro campsite and continue on foot along a tarmac track *(30min there*

> ☺ **A Bit of Advice** ☺
>
> Given the dangerous nature of the defile and to ensure your safety, we recommend that you go no farther than the metal bridge suspended high above the El Chorro defile.

*and back)* which climbs to a metal bridge offering magnificent **views**★★★. One has the sensation of being suspended in mid-air far above the bed of the river flowing through a rock formation. A flimsy catwalk of wood and rope, the Camino del Rey, skirts the rockface to join a bridge in a worse state of repair.

▶ *Return to the road and continue towards Ardales. At a signposted junction, bear left onto a narrower track.*

This scenic winding **road**★★ crosses tranquil mountain landscapes before it reaches the Tajo de la Encantada Reservoir *(embalse)*.

▶ *Leave your car on the road and follow the marked path; allow 15min each way.*

### Bobastro ruins

It was from Bobastro that General Omar Ben Hafsun, of noble Visigothic lineage, opposed the Umayyads. The rebellion against the Emirate of Córdoba lasted from 880 to 917. Today only the ruins of the *alcázar* walls remain, along with several caves and an unfinished 10C church set in a sandstone outcrop. which exemplifies the synthesis of Hispano-Roman, Visigothic and Islamic art.

▶ *Return to MA 444. After 2km/1.2mi, turn right toward the Parque de Ardales information post (puntos de información) in front of the Conde de Guadalhorce reservoir.*

### Embalse del Guadelteba-Guadalhorce★

*Park information centre:* ⏲ *open 9am-10pm.* ☎ *952 11 24 01 or 607 39 21 41.*

This reservoir *(embalse)* is in the heart of the Parque de Ardales, an area of dark woods, light-coloured stone rocks and plentiful camping areas. Along with the neighbouring Gaitejo, Tajo de la Encantada and Conde de Guadalhorce reservoirs, it is a perfect escape to nature. Footpaths skirt the reservoir and criss-cross landscapes where not a soul can be seen. The silence, particularly in winter, the pure air and perfect climate are the main attractions. The views from the hills overlooking the reservoir are spectacular.

▶ *From the dam, take MA 444 towards Ardales. Before reaching the village, follow A 357 towards Málaga; the cave is located 3km/2mi farther on.*

### Cueva de Ardales★

*Guided tours (3hr, to be booked 3 weeks in advance) summer, Tue, Thu, Sat-Sun; rest of year, Sat-Sun.* ☞€5. ☎ *952 45 80 46.*

The cave, running 1 600m/5 250ft, contains evidence of occupation from the Paleolithic period to the Bronze Age. It has exceptional wall paintings (54 representations of animals and 130 symbols), particularly a female deer, its legs and heart painted bright red.

# ARACENA★

POPULATION: 6 500.

The whitewashed houses of Aracena rise in tiers on a hillside, overlooked by remains of a Templar castle. The **Museo al Aire Libre de Escultura Contemporánea**, an exhibition of modern art in streets and squares, adds a touch of modernity. ℹ *Pozo de la Nieve, 21200 Aracena,* ☎ *959 12 82 06.*

▶ **Orient Yourself:** Aracena lies close to Extremadura in the northeast corner of Huelva province, at the heart of the Parque Natural de la Sierra de Aracena.

🕓 **Organizing Your Time:** Allow several hours to a day for Aracena, depending on you (and any kids') taste for caves.

**Kids Especially for Kids:** Caves and kids go together. All will enjoy the Grutas.

👁 **Also See:** Parque Natural de la Sierra de ARACENA Y PICOS DE AROCHE, Parque Natural de la SIERRA NORTE DE SEVILLA, MINAS DE RIOTINTO (34km/21mi S), SEVILLA (93km/58mi SE) and HUELVA (108km/67mi SW).

# Sights

### Gruta de las Maravillas★★★

*Guided tours (45min), 10am-1.30pm and 3-6pm. €7.70. 959 12 83 55 (advance booking advised).*

Enter the aptly named Cave of Marvels, over 100m/330ft deep (and the setting for w the film *Tarzan and the Mines of King Solomon*) from the town centre. Underground lakes mirror the limestone ceilings to superb effect. Points of interest include the "organ chamber" *(salón de los órganos)*; the "cathedral chamber" *(sala de la catedral)* with a Virgin and Child formation; "Sultana's bath" *(baño de la sultana)*; and the stunning **"God's Crystalware Chamber"** ★★ *(salón de la Cristalería de Dios)*. The **Museo Geológico Minero**, a geological and mining museum, is part of the complex. 🕓 *Open 10am-6.30pm. No charge.* ☎ *959 12 83 55.*

H. Champollion / MICHELIN

*Gruta de las Maravillas*

## Address Book

### WHERE TO EAT

🍴 **José Vicente** – *Avenida Andalucía, 53 –* ☎ *959 12 84 55 – Closed Tue and mid-Jun to mid-Jul –* 🍽. One of the best restaurants in the province, serving only fresh products. The menu in the small, tastefully decorated restaurant includes locally picked cep mushrooms and pork dishes.

### WHERE TO STAY

🛏 **Hotel Los Castaños** – *Avenida de Huelva, 5 –* ☎ *959 12 63 00 – www. loscastanoshotel.com –* 🅿 *– 33 rooms.* This attractive, centrally located, Andalusian-style hotel has modern, tasteful rooms, some of which face onto a large inner patio, and a fine restaurant.

🛏 **Finca Valbono** – *Carboneras road (1.5km/1mi NE) –* ☎ *959 12 77 11 – www.fincavalbono.com –* 🅿 🍽 🛏 ♿ *– 6 rooms, 20 apartments, restaurant* 🍴. This country hotel complex has a choice of standard rooms, bungalows and private houses which sleep up to eight. Facilities here include a swimming pool, horse-riding, a handball court and a terrace, from where groups of the famous pata negra pigs can be seen. Bicycles are also available for hire.

### LOCAL SPECIALITIES

The many bars *(mesones)* dotted around Aracena offer ample opportunity to try the local cuisine, particularly the renowned **serrano ham** *(jamón serrano)*.

## Castle

🕐 *Open by appointment.* ☎ *959 12 82 06 (tourist office) or 959 12 88 25.*
This fortress dominates Aracena and the countryside. Groves of chestnut trees extend in the distance, pine groves surround the walls of the castle, built over a 9C Almohad fortress. The compound includes a Gothic church and a **Mudéjar-style tower** – once a minaret – with *sebka* panelling similar to that on the Giralda in Sevilla.

## Iglesia de Nuestra Señora del Mayor Dolor

The Church of Our Lady of Great Suffering was built between the 13C and 14C on a site affording superb **views**★★. It contains a sculpture of the Virgin Mary, the town's patron saint, as well as a recumbent statue by Pedro Vázquez.

## Plaza Alta

This tranquil square, the hub of local life, borders several notable buildings, including the Iglesia de Nuestra Señora de la Asunción and the Cabildo Viejo.

**Iglesia de Nuestra Señora de la Asunción** – This solemn 16C-17C Renaissance-style church has a well-preserved façade with fine decoration and large windows.

**Cabildo Viejo** – The 15C former municipal storehouse and town hall houses the **Centro de Información del Parque Natural Sierra de Aracena y Picos de Aroche**, providing information on the park and area. 🕐 *Open 9.30am-6.30pm.* ☎ *959 14 32 06*

# Parque Natural de la Sierra de ARACENA Y PICOS DE AROCHE★★

This superb nature park with of mountain landscapes and picturesque villages is a sensory pleasure. Vast forests punctuated by slender peaks offer delightful views of the sierra, while the rush of flowing water blends with the wind whistling through the treetops.

▶ **Orient Yourself:** This isolated park, accessible from Huelva on N 435 and Sevilla via N 433 and A 66, extends across northern Huelva province, bordering Portugal to the west and Extremadura to the north.

🕐 **Organizing Your Time:** Allow a day to drive from Aracena to Aroche.

▥ **Especially for Kids:** Between the castle-mosque of Almonaster La Real and herds of precious pigs, kids should be amused.

---

### WHERE TO STAY

⊜⊜ **Galaroza Sierra** – *On the N 433 to the west of Galaroza* – ☎ *959 12 32 37* – *www.hotelgalaroza.com* – ▣ ▤ – *22 rooms, 7 bungalows.* A quiet, up-to-date hotel with a rustic air. Restaurant.

⊜⊜ **Posada de Cortegana** – *On the El Repilado-La Corte road, 2.5km/1.6mi out* – ☎ *959 50 33 01* – *www.posadadecortegana.com* - ⬛ ▤ – *40 rooms.* The Posada, a complex of several bungalows, enjoys a shady rural setting 1km/0.6mi along a dirt road amid flocks of sheep and herds of *pata negra* pigs.

**Also See:** Parque Natural de la SIERRA NORTE DE SEVILLA, MINAS DE RIOTINTO, SEVILLA and HUELVA.

## Driving Tour

### From Aracena to Aroche *64km/40mi – allow one day.* ⏱ *See plan.*

**Aracena★** – ⏱ *see ARACENA*

▶ *Follow A 470 west as far as Alájar.*

### Alájar★
This whitewashed village, nestled at the foot of a church with a pointed belfry, is popular with walkers. The area around Alájar is a miniature of the park's attractions: dark cork and holm oak forests, steep rugged rocks and stunning views.

> ### Pata negra cured ham
> Pata negra from Jabugo is considered the king of cured hams. This exquisite delicacy has a sublime aroma and taste…and a price to match!

**Peña Arias Montano** – This impressive rock *(peña)* several kilometres to the north of Alájar provides yet more superb **views★★** of this extraordinary landscape. It s name recalls the learned **Benito Arias Montano**, tutor to Felipe II, diplomat and royal librarian. He retired to a contemplative existence in Alájar. The **Ermita de Nuestra Señora de los Ángeles**, a chapel, can be seen on a rocky outcrop.

▶ *Head north from Alájar to Fuenteheridos, then bear left onto N 433.*

### Jabugo
This isolated mountain village is world-famous for its prized **cured hams** *(jamones)* and **sausages** *(embutidos)*, which are available locally.

▶ *Follow N 435 south, then bear left onto a minor road.*

### Castaño del Robledo
Hikers come to this village to walk trails through groves of chestnut trees, to scale peaks and to admire birds of prey gliding through the air.

▶ *Continue south along N 435, then bear right onto A 470, heading west.*

### Almonaster La Real★
Almonaster is a pleasant surprise in dense stands of chestnut, eucalyptus, cork and holm oak. The exceptional **site** comprises a labyrinth of quiet streets and mansions where time has stood still. The local gastronomy is based on pork products. A major attraction is the *Cruces de Mayo* festival in May. A **park information point** is in the **town hall**. ◷ Open 9.30am-6.30pm. ☎ 959 14 32 06.

*Mezquita in Almonaster La Real*

**Mezquita★** – ⏰ *Open Sat-Sun and public hols, 11am-7pm.* 🎟 *No charge.* The 10C mosque is one of the few Caliphal structures left in this area. The reddish walls provide superb mountain views. An unusual bullring is visible to one side; the castle-fortress in the mosque enclosure offers **views** of the town below.

**Iglesia de San Martín** – This sober church is a mix of Gothic and Mudéjar styles.

▶ *Head northwest along A 470 for 7km/4.5mi.*

## Cortegana

Major activities in this pleasant town include processing meat and cork and making scales and pottery. Heritage buildings include the **Iglesia del Salvador**, an elegant 16C Gothic-Mudéjar church, the Gothic-Renaissance **Iglesia de San Sebastián** and, in particular, a medieval **castle**, which affords impressive **views.** It is also an information point, which retraces the evolution of local defensive systems. ⏰ *Open 10am-1pm (summer, to 2pm) and 4.30-6.30pm.* ⏰ *Closed Mon.* 🎟 *€1.25.* ☎ *959 13 16 56.*

▶ *From Cortegana, follow the N 433 northwest for 14km/9mi.*

## Aroche

Aroche is one of the oldest towns in the area, evidenced by the **Piedras del Diablo** (Devil's Stones), dolmens in a delightful setting 3km/2mi to the southeast along H 9002, near the chapel *(ermita)* of San Mamés. A maze of narrow, twisting alleyways, mansions, old buildings and small workshops specialising in saddles climb up to the **castle★**, a sober 12C construction used as a refuge by King Sancho IV the Brave. It houses a bullring, as well as a park information point dedicated to the black vulture, a species in danger of extinction. The park has one of the biggest breeding colonies of this bird of prey in Spain. ⏰ *Visits by prior arrangement.* ☎ *959 14 02 61.*

A visit to the 13C **Iglesia de Nuestra Señora de la Asunción** and the **Convento de los Jerónimos**, a Hieronymite monastery, are also recommended.

## Medieval festivities

On 9-12 August every year, the streets of Cortegana provide the backdrop for theatre performances, processions, medieval banquets, re-enactments of scenes of daily life in the Middle Ages and concerts of sacred Andalusian music, attracting thousands of visitors of all ages.

# ARCOS DE LA FRONTERA★★

POPULATION: 27 897.

Arcos enjoys a remarkable clifftop **setting**★★ seemingly about to plunge into the deep valley of the River Guadelete. Its Renaissance and Baroque mansions and whitewashed houses are adorned with wrought-iron grilles and balconies. *Plaza del Cabildo, 11630 Arcos de la Frontera, ☎ 956 70 22 64, turismo@ayuntamientoarcos. org; Plaza de San Sebastián, 7, 11630 Arcos de la Frontera, ☎ 952 70 25 05.*

▶ **Orient Yourself:** Arcos de la Frontera is the western gateway to the White Villages. The best **views**★ are from A 382, approaching from Jerez de la Frontera, and the A 372 linking Arcos with El Bosque and Grazalema.

◔ **Organizing Your Time:** Take at least half a day to absorb the charms of Arcos.

▣ **Parking:** Park in the lower town (paseo de Boliches) to best appreciate Arcos on foot.

⚲ **Also See:** PUEBLOS BLANCOS DE ANDALUCÍA, JEREZ DE LA FRONTERA, El PUERTO DE SANTA MARÍA, CÁDIZ and MEDINA SIDONIA.

## A Bit of History

The Roman colony on this site was Arx-Arcis, "fortress on high ground", though some have it that the town's name derives from Arcobrigán, the arch of Brigus, grandson of Noah. Arcos was capital of a taifa kingdom in the 11C. Following an initial incursion by Fernando III, it was finally conquered by Alfonso X in 1264.

## Walking Tour *Allow 2hrs.*

Ascend the cuesta de Belén, a hill which connects the bustling 19C heart of Arcos with the upper town, the nucleus of the medieval city, with steeply sloping narrow alleyways and whitewashed houses. Pass through the Puerta de Jerez, one of the gateways to the walled Moorish city. Beyond **callejón de Juan del Valle** note the 15C Gothic-Mudéjar **façade**★ of the **Palacio del Conde del Águila** to the right, fronted by a magnificent doorway with an *alfiz* surround decorated with finely worked tracery.

### Holy Week

On **Good Friday**, a traditional procession winds its way through the streets of Arcos as part of the Semana Santa celebrations. Included in this religious ritual are the armaos – local men dressed in Roman costume who parade proudly through the town wearing helmets and armour and carrying standards and lances.

▶ *Continue to the right on calle Nueva, which runs parallel to the castle wall.*

### Plaza del Cabildo

The tower of the **Iglesia de Santa María** dominates the square, which is also lined by the town hall, the *parador* in the former magistrate's house (Casa del Corregidor), and the castle, now privately owned. The terrace on the west side offers a magnificent **view**★ of the plains below and the Iglesia de San Pedro.

### Iglesia de Santa María de la Asunción★

◔ Open in summer, Mon-Fri, 4-7pm, Sat, 10am-2pm. ◑ Closed Sun and public hols. ⊜€1.50. ☎ 956 70 00 06.

This church was built around 1530 above an earlier 14C church, itself erected on the site a mosque. Its **west façade**★, the work of Don Alonso de Baena, is an extraordinary example of Plateresque art. The interior, accessed via the neo-Classical south façade, has a basilical plan with three aisles separated by robust columns supporting star vaults with tiercerons. In the high altar, a 17C **retable** by Jerónimo Hernández and Juan Bautista Vázquez represents the Ascension of the Virgin. Hidden behind the high altar is the polygonal apse of the earlier Mudéjar church. The **frescoes**★ *(The Coronation of the Virgin)* which decorated the earlier high altar were transferred to the wall of the Evangelist nave *(to the left of the altar)* in the 1960s.

Continue along the west façade into the evocative callejón de las Monjas. The flying buttresses were added in the 17C to counteract the movement of the walls. Pass the **Renaissance façade**★ of the Convento de la Encarnación, and continue along calle del Marqués de Torresoto. Note the 17C Classical-style patio of the **palace-residence of the Marquess of Torresoto** at n° 4. The small square at the end of the street, plazuela Boticas, is fronted by the **Convento de las Mercedarias Descalzas**, where the nuns sell pastries, and the unfinished 18C Jesuit house, now the town market.

*Façade of the Palacio del Mayorazgo*

Hidalgo–Lopesno Marco Polo

▶ *Calle Boticas and calle Nuñez de Prado lead to the other main section of the town.*

---

## Address Book

### WHERE TO EAT

☺☺ **Restaurante El Convento** – *Marqués de Torresoto, 7 – ☎ 956 70 32 22 – www.webdearcos.com/elconvento – ▦ - ① Closed 7-22 Jan and first week of Jul.* Opposite the Hotel Marqués de Torresoto (which owns it). Traditional decor and a columned patio. Specialities include local dishes and game in season.

### TAPAS

**Alcaraván** – *Calle Nueva, 1.* Within the walls of the castle and easily identified by the numerous flowerpots on its façade. Grilled meats, stuffed peppers and lamb stew are just some of the dishes on the menu, which diners can enjoy to the strains of flamenco music. Alcaraván is the name of a poetry prize awarded in Arcos de la Frontera since the fifties.

### WHERE TO STAY

☺☺ **Marqués de Torresoto** – *Marqués de Torresoto, 4 – ☎ 956 70 07 17 – www.hmdetorresoto.com - ▦ - 15 rooms.* This 17C palace has a central location in the historical centre. It features a Baroque chapel and an attractive arcaded patio. Antique furniture decorates the rooms.

☺☺ **Hotel El Convento** – *Maldonado, 2 – ☎ 956 70 23 33 – www.webdearcos.com/elconvento – ▦ - 11 rooms – ① Closed 2 weeks in Jan.* As the name suggests, this hotel is housed in a former 17C convent, located in a narrow street in the centre of Arcos. Rooms are quiet; most have views of the valley.

Close to the Iglesia de San Pedro stand the **Capilla de la Misericordia**, a chapel with a blind pointed arch, and the **Palacio del Mayorazgo**, a palace which houses a conservatory of music and is adorned with an ornate Renaissance loggia.

### Iglesia de San Pedro

🕐 *Open Mon-Sat, 10.30am-2pm and 4-7pm, Sun and public hols, 10am-1.30pm (mass is held from 11.30am to 12.30pm).* ⊜ *€1.* ☎ *956 70 11 07.*
This early 15C church for many years rivalled Santa María. The façade is crowned by a large neo-Classical tower. The interior consists of a single nave with a pointed vault with tiercerons.
A ceramics shop is hidden behind the Plateresque façade of n° 7 calle San Pedro.

▷  *Continue along calle Cadenas.*

The street has two interesting palaces. To the left, in calle Juan de Cuenca, is the palace-residence of the same name; a little farther on, in plaza del Cananeo, stands the former palace of the Marquess and Marchioness of Torresoto.

▷  *Continue along calle Bóvedas.*

On the corner with calle Boticas, note the Casa de los Gamaza.

▷  *Continue along calle Boticas to the plazuela de Boticas, then follow the charming calle de los Escribanos (delightful wrought-iron balconies) back to plaza del Cabildo.*

## Additional Sight

### Convento de la Caridad★
The convent stands in plaza de la Caridad, outside the medieval walls in the *barrio bajo* (lower town). It was built in the middle of the 18C and exudes a strong colonial influence. The entrance to the church is preceded by an attractive atrium.

# LA AXARQUÍA★

This area offers both tranquil inland villages and lively coastal resorts, along with a delightful climate. Until the 18C, marauding Barbary pirates forced the inhabitants into the mountains. Watchtowers still exist along the coast. Vineyards line mountain slopes, and orchards of fruit and subtropical crops, some in plastic greenhouses, cover valley floors.

▷  **Orient Yourself:** La Axarquía extends southwards along the slopes of the Sierra de Almijara, at the eastern extremity of Málaga province. The A 7-E 15 links the towns along this stretch of coastline, while  minor roads run inland.
🕐 **Organizing Your Time:** Allow a day to drive to Nerja, with stops, then return.
▥ **Especially for Kids:** Play in the sand and surf of Torox Costa.
⚫ **Also See:** MÁLAGA, ALHAMA DE GRANADA, Las ALPUJARRAS and GRANADA.

## Driving Tour

# From Málaga to Nerja *99km/62mi including excursions inland*

**Málaga** –👆 *See MÁLAGA.*

▶ *Leave Málaga along A 7 – E 15 to the east. Take the Cueva del Tesoro after the first Rincón de la Victoria exit.*

### Cueva del Tesoro or Cueva del Higuerón★
🕓 *Open 10.45am–5.15pm.* ☜€4.25. ☎ *952 40 61 62.*
Tradition says that treasure *(tesoro)* was hidden here in Moorish times, though none has been found. The cave, once under water, was created by erosion. Some of the shapes within its chambers could have inspired Antoni Gaudí in Barcelona.

### Rincón de la Victoria
The town is a popular seaside resort with a large number of tourist apartments and hotels, as well as a sandy beach over 3km/2mi long.

▶ *Return to A 7 – E 15 and continue east to exit 272.*

### Torre del Mar
This large seaside resort with its extensive beach is the closest to Vélez-Málaga.

▶ *Head north along A 335.*

*Rincón de la Victoria.*

B. Kaufmann/MICHELIN

### Vélez-Málaga
The capital of La Axarquía is dominated by the keep of its former fortress, destroyed by Napoleon's troops. The **Barrio de la Villa**, a district of Moorish origin at the foot of the tower, offers superb views. It is a maze of steep, narrow streets, whitewashed houses and a 16C Mudéjar-style church, the Iglesia de Santa María, with a fine bell tower. Access is from plaza de la Constitución, fronted by the Iglesia de San Juan Bautista, crowned by an attractive belfry, and containing a number of paintings and remnants of the old walls.
In the centre, the 17C Palacio de los Marqueses de Beniel, with sober façade, is the town hall *(ayuntamiento)*.

## The Axarco

Within the Euro Zone, one region in particular, namely La Axarquía, has steadfastly refused to succumb to Europe's new currency, creating its own currency, the *axarco*, which has been in circulation since 1988. While visitors and locals alike can still pay in euros, most shops accept the local currency, which on one side bears the portrait of an Arab botanist who introduced citrus fruits to Andalucía in the 13C, and on the other that of Felipe II. The dangers of counterfeiting are eliminated by the fact that each note is signed in ballpoint pen by its creator, Antonio Gámez, a descendant of a family of *moriscos* who escaped the massacre ordered by Felipe II in the 16C. Subdivided into *axarquitos*, the *axarco*, which is worth 60 cents, can be purchased in the region's town halls and, somewhat surprisingly, its banks.

▷ *Return to A 7 – E 15. At exit 277, follow signs to Algarrobo.*

## Algarrobo

Algarrobo's whitewashed houses rise on a cliff 190m/623ft above the sea. Typically Moorish narrow streets wind up to the Ermita de San Sebastián, a chapel with sea views.

▷ *Return to A 7 – E 15. Shortly before the junction with the coast road, go left toward the Necrópolis de Trayamar.*

## Necrópolis de Trayamar

What remains of this large necropolis includes Punic and Phoenician tombs, some from the 8C and 7C BC.

▷ *Continue along the coast. Two watchtowers come into view.*

## Torrox

In Torrox Costa (the resort section) close to the lighthouse *(follow "faro" signs)*, excavations have revealed Roman basins used in the production of *garum* (👍 *see TARIFA)*; some were used as burial urns. The beaches here are particularly pleasant.

▷ *Continue north, heading inland.*

## Address Book

👍 *For coin ranges, see the Legend on the cover flap.*

### WHERE TO EAT

🍽 **Chiringuito de Ayo** – *Paseo Antonio Mercero (Playa Burriana) - Nerja - ☎ 952 52 22 89 - www.ayonerja.com* . A long-standing favorite, it was even the locale for a TV series. It specialises in paella and has a large terrace on Burriana beach.

🍽🍽 **Pepe Rico** – *Almirante Ferrándiz, 28 – Nerja – ☎ 952 52 02 47 – ⏱ Closed early Jan-early Feb*. This Swedish-run restaurant on a pedestrian street has a cosy dining room with fireplace (and oil paintings), as well as apartments for rent *(🍽🍽)*. Specialities include Swiss suckling pig and duck in wine.

### WHERE TO STAY

🛏 **Hotel Rural Cortijo Amaya** – *Torrox Costa – Take the N 340 for 1.5km/1mi, then go right 1km/0.6mi – ☎ 952 53 02 45 – www.cortijoamaya.com -* 🅿 ▦ *– 14 rooms*. An old farmhouse set into the hillside with views of the Mediterranean and the surrounding countryside. Simple, comfortable rooms, plus a well-maintained garden with a swimming pool and tennis courts.

🛏🛏 **Hostal Marissal** – *– Paseo Balcón de Europa, 3 - Nerja - ☎ 952 52 01 99 - www.hostalmarissal.com -* ▦ *- 22 rooms*. This *hostal* has a prized location at the entry to the famed Balcony of Europe, with fine city view from its well-kept rooms. Coffee shop and restaurant.

🛏🛏 **Nerja Princess Hotel** – *Los Huertos, 46 bis – Nerja – ☎ 952 52 89 86 - www.hotelnp.com -* 🅿 ⌇ ▦ *– 20 rooms. Closed in Nov*. This small hotel with discreet façade is minutes from the Balcón de Europa. It features a marble entrance, attractive rooms and a pleasant pool. Good value.

🛏🛏🛏 **Hotel de Campo Molino de Santillán** – *8 km towards Macharaviaya (MA 106)– Rincón de la Victoria – ☎ 902 12 02 40 - www.molinodesantillan.es -* 🅿 *- 12 rooms*. This former mill is located in a bucolic setting at the end of a country lane. Arrive by daylight.

## Parque natural de las sierras de Tejeda y Almijara

The Tejeda and Almijara mountain ranges form a line of rocky escarpments rising to an altitude of 2 068m/6 783ft (Pico Maroma), creating a natural barrier between the provinces of Málaga and Granada. Covering an area of 40 600ha/100 300 acres to the south of Alhama de Granada, the majority of the park is located in the area of La Axarquía.

The magnificent yet harsh landscape here is characterised by steep, pine-covered slopes inhabited by wild goats, sharp crests, deep ravines, winding streams and villages with a palpable *morisco* feel, which in days gone by provided shelter for the famous brigands who roamed the region. The towns of Frigiliana and Nerja are located on the southern boundary of the park.

### From Torrox to Cómpeta
This winding road climbs along the spurs of the Sierra de la Almijara, dotted with whitewashed villages A bend in the road affords a delightful view of **Cómpeta**.

▷ *Return to A 4 – E 15 via the same road, then continue for 8km/5mi.*

### Nerja★
Nerja is an attractive whitewashed town of Moorish origin perched above the Mediterranean. The coast below the Sierra de Almijara is characterised by steep cliffs and delightful beaches. Numerous bars, outdoor cafés, restaurants and nightclubs have made Nerja one of the most popular summer resorts along the Costa del Sol.

**Balcón de Europa★** – This magnificent *mirador* (viewpoint) in old Nerja is on the site of the old castle. It is a landscaped square overlooking the sea with a view to Africa on clear days. The whitewashed 17C Iglesia del Salvador, with its impressive bell tower, stands alongside.

### Cueva de Nerja★★
*4.5km/3mi east towards Motril.* ◷ *Open Jul-Aug, 10am-2pm and 4-8pm; Sep-Jun, 10am-2pm and 4-6.30pm.* ◷ *Closed 1 Jan and 15 May.*⊛€6, children 6-12, €2.50.* ☎ *952 52 95 20.*

Discovered in 1959, this enormous cave is set in the marble of the Sierra de Almijara. Pottery, ceramics, human remains and wall paintings, some exhibited in the first few rooms, indicate that the caves were inhabited during the Palaeolithic era.

The cave is impressive in the scale of its chambers and its spectacular stalactites and stalagmites. The **Sala de la Cascada** (Cascade Chamber), also known as the **Sala del Ballet** (Ballet Chamber), takes its name from the formations on the right-hand side. A **Festival of Music and Dance** is held here in the second or third week of July.

*Cueva de Nerja*

H. Champollion/MICHELIN

▷ *Head north from Nerja, following MA 105 inland.*

*Frigiliana*

### Frigiliana★

This charming *pueblo blanco* extends across the southern slopes of the Sierra de la Almijara. Its **Morisco-Mudéjar quarter★★** is a superb ensemble of meticulously maintained whitewashed houses. Flowers add an extra dash of colour. Panels of *azulejos* on several walls recall battles here between Moors and Christians.

# AYAMONTE★

POPULATION: 17 000.

Ayamonte has an openness characteristic of port towns. The noise of the fleet unloading its catch and the hubbub of fish auctions blend in with the lively conversation in waterside cafés. Colonial-style houses were built by Spanish emigrants who returned from the Americas at the end of the 19C. ⓘ *Puente Internacional (bridge to Portugal), 21400 Ayamonte, ☎ 959 50 21 21, turismo@ayto-ayamonte.es*

> ▶ **Orient Yourself:** At the Guadiana, Ayamonte is a gateway to Portugal.
> ⏱ **Organizing Your Time:** Most visitors just past through, but the shopping and a visit to Isla Cristina could take up most of a day.
> ♨ **Also See:** HUELVA (60km/37mi E), COSTA DE HUELVA, La RÁBIDA and MOGUER.

## Visit

### Iglesia de las Angustias

Nestled between old houses, this 16C church with a colonial air has a spacious triple-nave interior, crowned by a tower which dominates Ayamonte.

## Address Book

### WHERE TO EAT

Casa Barberi – *Plaza de la Coronación* – ☎ 959 47 02 89 🕒 *Closed Tue.* The Casa Barberi on the main square has been run by the same family since 1917. Paellas are a specialty.

Acosta – *Plaza de las Flores, 13 – Isla Cristina* – ☎ 959 33 14 20 - 🔲. A family-run restaurant on a pleasant square. Fish and seafood are a good value.

Casa Rufino – *Avenida de la Playa – Isla Cristina* – ☎ 959 33 08 10 🕒 *Closed Christmas week and in Jan.* This fish and seafood eatery just a stone's throw from the sea offers a special menu *(tonteo)* consisting of eight fish dishes (€103 for four people). Ample desserts and wide selection of wines.

### LOCAL SPECIALITIES

Among local specialties are *pestiños* (a type of honey fritter) and *coca ayamontina*, a flat biscuit-like cake.

### FESTIVALS

Ayamonte and the surrounding area come to life at **Carnival**, with processions, masked balls and dances into the early hours.

## Convento de San Francisco

This 16C Renaissance monastery has an elegant belfry, Mudéjar polychrome wood ceiling, columns decorated with old inscriptions and a large retable.

## Iglesia del Salvador

This 13C building with fine stuccowork was erected on the site of an old mosque.

## Muelle de Portugal

Boats depart from this dock *(muelle)* to cross the river to Portugal and Sanlúcar de Guadiana.

# Excursions

## Isla Cristina

*14km/9mi SE. Take N 431 towards Lepe. Before El Empalme, go right on A 4201.* Houses in Isla Cristina's old quarter have *azulejo* decoration. A marina, protected marshes and attractive beaches are attractions.

## Isla Canela

*7km/4.5mi SE on H 921.* A popular resorts with sandy beach, apartments and golf.

## Punta del Moral

*9km/5.5mi southeast on H 921.* This small resort has numerous beach bars and restaurants, and is favored by fishing enthusiasts.

# BAENA

The houses of Baena extend in a white swathe amid undulating groves famous for the the local virgin olive oil. The old *barrio alto* is dominated by the tower of Santa María la Mayor parish church; the *llano* is Baena's modern, commercial heart. The drum *(tambor)*, emblem of Baena, plays a major part in celebrated and lively Holy Week festivities. *Plaza de España, 9, 14850 Baena, ☎ 957 66 50 10/15.*

▶ **Orient Yourself:** Baena is in eastern Córdoba province along the N 432.
♿ **Also See:** MONTILLA, AGUILAR DE LA FRONTERA, CABRA, LUCENA, PRIEGO DE CÓRDOBA, MARTOS and CÓRDOBA (62km/39mi NW).

## The unmistakable odour of olive oil
There's no escaping the aroma of this golden liquid. The acclaim of Andalusian *aceite de olivo* dates to Roman times. The oil produced in Baena is among the best in the region, certified by its *denominación de origen* label. It uses the *picuda* olive and is ideal for the table, for frying and as an ingredient in Andalusian stews.

## Walking Tour
## Barrio Alto

In the Middle Ages, this upper section of narrow streets was the Moorish quarter.

### Iglesia de Santa María la Mayor
The church, on the site of a mosque, dates from the 16C and has been repeatedly altered. The simple Plateresque portal (Portada del Ángel)has square decoration around the doorway. The slightly leaning bell tower is the former minaret, and now comprises two Baroque sections crowned by a green and blue *azulejo* spire.

### Iglesia del Convento Madre de Dios
🕐 *Open for services only at 1pm (7pm Thu). ☎ 957 67 09 10.*
This convent, closed to the public, was founded in the early 16C by Don Diego Fernández de Córdoba, fifth Lord of Baena. Renaissance influence is evident in the originally Gothic structure. The interesting **east end**★ is partly the work of Hernán Ruiz II, though the design is by Diego de Siloé. Note the sculpted decoration of Apostles and angels in the half-dome.
The exterior is fronted by an attractive late-Gothic portal.

## Visit
## Llano District

### Casa del Monte
This imposing three-storey building with its wide façade dates from 1774. It occupies one side of plaza de la Constitución or Coso, which is dominated by the town hall.

### Iglesia de Guadalupe
*Beside plaza de España.* The chancel of the 16C church has a fine **Mudéjar**

### Illustrious sons
Juan Alfonso de Baena, the 16C troubadour who wrote the *Cancionero de Baena*, the de los Ríos family, the writer and politician José Amador, and Demetrio, the architect who initiated the restoration of León Cathedral in northern Spain.

artesonado★ ceiling and 18C Baroque altarpiece. The **Capilla de la Virgen de Guadalupe**, a side chapel, has a Baroque altar covered with Mudéjar *artesonado* work.

### Antiguo Convento de San Francisco

*Now a rest home. On the outskirts towards Córdoba, left after the petrol station.* ⓒ *Open Mon, Tue and Thu, 10am-1pm and 5-7.30pm, Fri from 8am.* ☏ *957 67 01 42.*

The 18C **Baroque church**, with its Latin-cross ground plan, is crowned with barrel vaults The unusual oval cupola above the transept is arranged transversely. Frescoes cover the walls. A Baroque altarpiece has pride of place in the east end. A 18C **Nazarene Christ** is said to have been fired at during the Civil War without any damage.

## Excursions

### Zuheros★

*17km/10.5mi S by N 432, A 318 CV 241.* Picturesque Zuheros has a superb **setting**★★, enhanced by freshly whitewashed houses on cobbled, flower-decked streets.

**Plaza de la Paz** – This impressive viewpoint at 622m/2 040ft provides stunning **views**★★ of hills carpeted in olive groves, with Baena in the distance.

**Museo Arqueológico** – The archaeological museum displays artefacts from prehistory to the Roman period, discovered at the Cueva de los Murciélagos.

**Castle** – The Romans founded a fortress on this site. The accessible square tower and battlements are Moorish in origin, while the remains opposite are from a 16C Renaissance palace. *Visits to Museo Arqueológico and castle:* ☞ *guided tours (40min), daily, 10am-2pm and 4-6pm (Fri, 5-7pm).* ⓒ *Closed 1 Jan and 25 Dec.* ☞€1.80. *Reservation advised.* ☏ *957 69 47 75 (tourist office).*

### Cueva de los Murciélagos

*4km/2.5mi east of Zuheros on a signposted road.* ☞ *Guided tours (1hr), 12.30-4.30pm (5.30pm in summer), Sat-Sun and public hols at 11am, 12.30pm, 2pm, 4pm (5pm in summer) and 5.30pm (6.30pm in summer). Advance booking.* ⓒ *Closed 1 Jan and 25 Dec.* ☞€4.80. ☏ *957 69 45 45.*

B. Kaufmann / MICHELIN

*Zuheros above a sea of olive groves*

The road leading up to the cave offers more delightful **views**★★.
The cave is a superb formation with several chambers of impressive stalactites and stalagmites. It contains important archaeological remains from the Neolithic period, including drawings, engravings, a burial chamber tools, ornaments and pieces of ceramic, dating from between 4300 and 3980 BC.

## Luque

*5km/3mi northeast of Zuheros along CO 240. Leave your car in the main square.* The village is crowned by a Moorish fortress, restored and modified. The **Parroquia de la Asunción**, a 16C Renaissance church attributed to Hernán Ruiz II and Hernán Ruiz III has an elegant tower and belfry adorned with columns and a conical roof. The chancel houses an 18C Baroque retable dominated by an Assumption.
The remains of the **castle** are visible on a rocky crag behind the town hall. A staircase leading to the base of its walls offers an attractive panorama of Luque.

# BAEZA★★

POPULATION: 17 691.

Baeza extends across a low hill, surrounded by fields of cereal crops and olive groves stretching to the horizon, a setting immortalised by poet Antonio Machado: "Oh land of Baeza, I shall dream of you when I cannot see you." Churches, monuments and mansions of delightful golden stone recall the splendour of this peaceful provincial town during the 16C and 17C. The best time to visit Baeza is during the solemn processions of **Holy Week** or **Corpus Christi**. ▯ *Plaza del Pópulo, 23440 Baeza, ☎ 953 74 04 44, otbaeza@andalucia.org.*

▶ **Orient Yourself:** Baeza is at the centre of the province of Jaén, just north of the River Guadalquivir and close to the Parque Natural de Cazorla (to the east).

🕐 **Organizing Your Time:** Spend most of a day strolling and enjoying Baeza.

## Address Book

### WHERE TO EAT

▭▯▯ **Vandelvira** – *San Francisco, 14* – ☎ *953 74 81 72 - www.vandelvira.es* - ▤.*Closed Sun eve and Mon.* An elegant restaurant in the 16C Monasterio de San Francisco; enter via the impressive cloister and dine upstairs. Cuisine based on olive oil.

### WHERE TO STAY

▭ **Hostal El Patio** – *Conde de Romanones, 13* – ☎ *953 74 02 00* - ▱ - *15 rooms.* A somewhat dark and antiquated *hostal* in a heritage building, but with a redeeming patio – as the name suggests – and clean, well-maintained rooms.

▭ **Hotel-Palacete Santa Ana** – *Santa Ana Vieja, 9* – ☎ *953 74 07 65 – www.palacetesantana.com - 28 rooms.* A 16C mansion in the heart of the historical quarter with several delightful patios and pleasant rooms.

▭▯ **Hotel Fuentenueva** – *Carmen, 15* – ☎ *953 74 31 00 – www.fuentenueva.com* - ▤ - *13 rooms.* Central, charming, contemporary, each room is different. Garden and coffee shop.

### LOCAL SPECIALITIES

Try *bacalao al estilo de Baeza* (salt cod), *cocido mareado* (a bean stew with garlic, onions and tomatoes), and the *ochíos*, made from a dough of bread and oil and sprinkled with paprika.

🔔 **Also See:** ÚBEDA (9km/5.5mi E), Parque Natural de las Sierras de CAZORLA, SEGURA Y LAS VILLAS (55km/34mi E), LINARES (27km/17mi NW) and JAÉN (48km/30mi SW).

## A Bit of History

Originally a Bronze Age settlement, Baeza developed under the Romans into the town known as *Biatia*. Under the Visigoths in the 7C it was an episcopal see. Later it became the capital of a taifa kingdom. Following reconquest by Fernando III the Saint in 1227, Baeza was a centre for the christianisation of al-Andalus. In the 16C and 17C, the town enjoyed its period of greatest splendour. Handsome buildings shaped the centre, and a university was established, to be closed in the 19C. During these two centuries, intellectuals, architects and poets took up residence, including St John of the Cross, who completed his celebrated **Spiritual Canticle** here. Between 1912 and 1919, writer and poet Antonio Machado taught French at the new university.

## Architectural Centre★★★

*Allow half a day – route marked on town plan*

### Plaza del Pópulo★

In the centre of this small square is the **Fuente de los Leones** (Fountain of the Lions), built using stones from the ruins of nearby Cástulo. The central figure is said to be Imilce, the wife of Hannibal. The square is fronted by the former abattoir *(carnicería)* and the Casa del Pópulo, the former court. The **Arco de Villalar** (arch) commemorates the victory of Carlos I (Holy Roman Emperor Charles V) over the *comuneros* in 1521. Alongside, the **Puerta de Jaén** projects onto the Casa del Pópulo via an attractive quarter-circle balcony; this gateway marks the emperor's visit on his way to Sevilla to marry Isabel of Portugal.

| BAEZA | | |
|---|---|---|
| Roads | | |
| Aguayo | Y | 2 |
| Barbacana | Z | 3 |
| Cardenal Benavides Pas. | Y | 5 |
| Compañía | Z | 6 |
| Conde Romanones | Z | 7 |
| Córdoba Puerta de | Z | 9 |
| Gaspar Becerra | Y | 12 |
| General Cuadros | Y | 13 |
| José M. Cortés | Y | 15 |
| Magdalena | Y | 16 |
| Obispo Mengíbar | Z | 17 |
| Sacramento | Z | 20 |
| San Andrés | Y | 21 |
| San Felipe Neri Cuesta | Z | 23 |
| San Francisco | Y | |
| San Gil Cuesta de | Z | 25 |

| | | |
|---|---|---|
| Antigua Carnicería | Z | A |
| Antigua Universidad | Z | E |
| Antigua Universidad | Z | E |
| Ayuntamiento | Y | H |
| Casas Consistoriales Atlas | Z | K |
| Ruinas de San Francisco (Auditorio) | Y | R |
| Seminario de San Felipe Neri | Z | S |

**Antigua carnicería** (Former abattoir) – This elegant 16C Renaissance building, seat of the former Tribunal de Justicia, bears a large escutcheon of Charles V.

**Casa del Pópulo** – The former seat of the Caballeros Hijosdalgos de Baeza (Noble Knights of Baeza) and the Audiencia Civil (Civil Tribunal) houses the **tourist office**. The edifice has harmonious proportions and refined decoration. The façade, adorned by medallions and large windows, is fronted by six doors to clerks' chambers.

*Detail on the pulpit of Baeza Cathedral*

### Plaza de Santa María
The **fountain** decorated with caryatids and atlantes is by Ginés Martínez. To one side stands the 17C **Seminario de San Felipe Neri**, whose sober façade still bears the inscriptions of students written in bull's blood to celebrate graduation. To the left is the **Casas Consistoriales Altas** or Casa Cabrera, emblazoned with the coats of arms of Juana the Mad and Philip the Fair between two attractive mullioned windows.

### Cathedral★
🕐 *Open Jun-Sep, 10am-1.30pm and 5-7pm; Oct-May, 10am-1.30pm and 4-6pm. No charge.* ☎ *953 74 41 57.*
Fernando III ordered the cathedral built over the destroyed mosque. In mid-afternoon, its silhouette casts a mysterious shadow over the narrow cobbled streets behind.

### Exterior
The Renaissance-style façade contrasts with the west side's 13C Gothic-Mudéjar Puerta de la Luna (Moon Doorway), and 14C Gothic rose window. In the south wall is the 15C Puerta del Perdón (Pardon Doorway).

### Interior★★
The severity of Castilian architecture combines harmoniously with graceful Andalusian features. Andrés de Vandelvira planned the 16C reconstruction, crowning the three aisles with oven vaults. The Capilla Dorada (Gold Chapel) has delicate Italianate relief; the Capilla de Santiago (St James's Chapel) on the left side has a fine antique setting; while the Capilla de San José is flanked by caryatids. The fine

## The patios of Baeza

Baeza is a monument in itself, offering surprise after surprise in the form of elegant palaces, monumental churches, enchanting nooks and crannies and exquisite architectural detail. The town's patios – havens of peace and quiet hidden behind the attractive wrought-iron grilles of some of the town's most delightful buildings – are an essential part of any visit. Every season highlights a different aspect: a blaze of colour in spring; an oasis of cool in summer; the brightness in which they are bathed in the clear light of autumn; and their dazzling architecture, best seen in winter.

**Capilla del Sagrario** (Sacrarium Chapel) at the end of the north aisle holds a Baroque silver **monstrance**, carried in procession on Corpus Christi. Note the Plateresque door to the sacristy, with its delicate reliefs, the polychrome metal **pulpit** (1580) in the transept, the Baroque retable, and the monumental iron **grille** by Maestro Bartolomé in the nave. Four Mudéjar chapels in the cloisters have decorative plant motifs *(atauriques)* and Arabic inscriptions.

### Palacio de Jabalquinto★

🕙*Open 9am-2pm.* 🚫*Closed Sat-Sun and public hols. No charge.*

The Flamboyant Gothic former residence of Juan Alfonso de Benavides, the Capitán de Lorca, has an exceptional **façade★★**, attributed to Juan Guas and Enrique Egas. It is best seen in late afternoon when the shadows accentuate its details. Stylish features of the day include projecting pinnacles, stone fleurons, elaborate escutcheons etc. Inside is a spacious Renaissance patio with marble Corinthian columns and a monumental Baroque staircase.

*Façade, Palacio de Jabalquinto*

B. Kaufmann/MICHELIN

### Iglesia de Santa Cruz

This small Romanesque church has a Gothic chapel, and murals in the apse.

### Former university (Antigua universidad)

🕙 *Open 10am-1pm and 4-6.30pm. No charge.* ☎ 953 74 01 50.

To reach the university, pass through the Arco del Barbudo, along with the Puerta de Jaén the only vestige of the old walls. Founded in the 16C by Rodrigo López and Juan de Ávila, the university closed in 1875. Antonio Machado wrote his more melancholic poetry in the handsome Renaissance-style **patio**.

### Plaza del Mercado Viejo or Plaza de la Constitución

This hub of town life, is surrounded by the **Antigua Alhóndiga** (old corn exchange) and the 18C Baroque **Casas Consistoriales Bajas**, a former civic building. A number of traditional bars and cafés stand side-by-side beneath its arcades.

### Ayuntamiento★

The town hall was formerly the law courts and prison. It is Plateresque, with two floors separated by a wide cornice. Armorial bearings can be seen on the façade.

### Ruins of the Convento de San Francisco

Before the convent suffered disasters and pillage, it was considered one of Vandelvira's major works. The monumental transept and apse, fasciated columns and majestic altarpieces give an idea of the beautiful 16C church. It is now an **auditorium**.

### Palacio de Montemar (or Palacio de los Condes de Garcíez)

This 16C palace has large Gothic windows and a Plateresque inner patio.

### Iglesia de San Pablo

This church has a Renaissance façade and three wide aisles supporting Gothic pillars. It has several painted panels and a statue of *Christ of the Expiration*.

## Additional Sights

### Iglesia de San Andrés
🕐 *Open for services at 7.30pm (also 11.30am Sun and public hols).* ☎ *953 74 06 78.*
Following the Reconquest, Fernando III created in this church the Company of the Two
Hundred Crossbowmen of St James, noblemen from Baeza who showed allegiance
only to the king. The doorway is Plateresque. Note the **sacristy**, with its collection
of nine **Gothic wood tablets**★, the colours of which bear witness to the technical
expertise of Andalusian artists of the time.

### Convento de la Encarnación
This convent, in transitional Renaissance-Baroque style, is still occupied by Carmelite
nuns. It is where St John of the Cross completed his *Spiritual Canticle*.

# BAZA

POPULATION: 20 113.

Native Iberians established Basti in the 4C BC. Excavations outside the present
town unearthed the famous **Lady of Baza** (Dama de Baza) sculpture of a goddess.
With the expulsion of the *moriscos* at the end of the 16C, Baeza declined. The only
remnants of the former Moorish city are the baths and the maze-like layout of
several streets. ▯ *Plaza Mayor, 18800 Baza,* ☎ *958 86 13 25, turismobaza@terra.es.*

▸ **Orient Yourself:** Baza is south of the Negrat Reservoir, just north of the attractive
Parque Natural de la Sierra de Baza (🔍 *see Excursion*). The A 92 dual carriageway
provides excellent road links with Granada, the provincial capital, to the SW.

🕐 **Organizing Your Time:** Allow a couple of hours.

🔍 **Also See:** GUADIX (48km/30mi N), GRANADA and Sierra de los FILABRES.

## Walking Tour

### Colegiata de Santa María de la Encarnación★
This fortress-like collegiate church, built over the destroyed mosque, stands behind an
unusual wall of buttresses. There are three aisles of equal height and no transept.

### Cascamorras
This *fiesta* dates back to the 15C when, according to legend, an inhabitant of Guadix who was working in an Mozarabic chapel near Baza discovered a statue of the
Virgin. However, the problem soon arose as to which town would keep the statue.
The courts decided that the Virgin would remain in Baza, with the proviso that a
fiesta in her honour would take place once a year in Guadix. Unfortunately, when
the time came for the residents of Guadix – headed by a figure known as Cascamorras – to assert their rights and reclaim the Virgin Mary, they were chased out
of Baza by locals brandishing sticks. Upon their return to Guadix, they were further punished by townspeople angry at their failure. Nowadays, on **6 September**,
a resident of Guadix in multi-coloured attire plays the part of Cascamorras, and
attempts to reach the **Iglesia de la Merced** to steal the image. During the course
of his journey, he is jostled and provoked by the inhabitants of both towns.

The **plaza Mayor** is fronted by the Renaissance former town hall, now the **Museo Municipal**, which displays a reproduction of the Dama de Baza. (The original is in the Museo Arqueológico in Madrid.) ◷ *Open in summer, 10am-2pm and 5-7pm, Sun, 11am-2pm; otherwise, 10am-2pm and 4-6.30pm, Sat-Sun, 11am-2pm.* ◷ *Closed 1 Jan and 25 Dec.* ☜€1.20. ☎ *958 70 35 55.*

▶ *Leave the plaza Mayor through the Arco de la Magdalena, an arch beside the 18C bell tower. Follow calle Zapatería to the left to the former "morisco" quarter.*

The narrow alleyways are lined by several buildings of interest: the Mudéjar **Iglesia de San Juan Bautista**; the **Convento de la Merced**, housing the *Virgin of Piety.*

Plaza Mayor

▶ *Return to the Arco de la Magdalena. Follow calle Zapatería.* To the left, the **former abattoirs** *(carnicerías)*, date from 1568. *Continue to plaza de Santo Domingo.*

The **Convento de Santo Domingo** is in a state of poor repair. The better-preserved 17C cloister is concealed the inside an early-20C building, once a theatre.
*Follow calle Dolores.* The façade of the 17C-18C **Iglesia de los Dolores** has an unusual Baroque portal framed between two sturdy Solomonic columns.

▶ *Continue on calle Dolores, then bear left onto calle del Agua as far as calle Caniles.*

### Moorish baths (Baños árabes)★
*In calle Caniles. If closed, go to calle Caniles, 19 and ask for Mateo or Manuela.*
These simple baths, in the old Jewish quarter next to the Iglesia de Santiago, date from the Caliphal period (10C) and are some of the oldest in Europe.

## Excursion

### Parque Natural de Sierra de Baza
*15km/9.5mi towards Guadix along A 92, then 5km/3mi to the Visitor Centre in Narváez.*
◷ *Open in summer, Wed-Sun, 10am-2pm and 6-8pm; otherwise, open Tue-Wed and Fri-Sun, 10am-2pm and 4-6pm. No charge.* ☎ *958 00 20 05 or 670 94 28 89.*
Despite limited infrastructure, this park offers interesting walks. Several peaks in the Sierra de Baza exceed 2 000m/6 560ft.

# BELALCÁZAR

POPULATION: 3 879.

Formerly Gaete, Belalcázar, adapted its name in the 15C (from Bello Alcázar, a reference to its prominent fortress). Nobles of the most prominent family include Sebastián de Belalcázar, who founded Quito and conquered Nicaragua. *Plaza de la Constitución, 11 (town hall), 14280 Belalcázar, ☎ 957 14 60 04.*

- ▶ **Orient Yourself:** Belalcázar lies in the north of Córdoba province, close to the River Zújar, the border with Extremadura.
- ⏱ **Organizing Your Time:** Allow at least half a day.
- 🅿 Park in plaza de la Constitución.
- Kids **Especially for Kids:** The castle will keep kids busy.
- ⚲ **Also See:** FUENTE OBEJUNA (54km/34mi SW) and CÓRDOBA (131km/82km SE).

## Visit

### Iglesia Parroquial de Santiago
⏱ *Open at 6.30 and 7.30pm (7.30 and 9pm in summer), Sun, 11am for mass.*
The austere, granite parish church of St James, at one end of the square, dates from the 16C and 17C, An incomplete bell tower rises above its centre and sturdy buttresses support its walls.
The church is designed for preaching, with its single nave and side chapels set between buttresses. The east end was rebuilt after the Spanish Civil War. The roof, modified after a collapse, is untrue to the original proportions. Note the hewn stone arches of several chapels.

### Town Hall
This 19C granite building dominates Belalcázar's attractive main square. It features a clock in its central section.

- ▶ *Follow calle Sebastián de Belalcázar to the right of the church.*

The **Fuente del Pilar** (1570) was once a drinking trough. From here there is a superb view of the castle.

### Castle★
Belalcázar's dominant structure rose in the late 15C where a Roman fortress might have stood. It is quadrangular with towers in the corners and the centre of its walls. Brackets run along the upper walls and towers.
The keep is notable for its with its imosing proportions. Lookout posts bear the chequered escutcheons of the Sotomayor family, lords of the castle.
Belalcázar also has several noble mansions such as the Casa Grande and the Casa de la Administración de los Osuna. A Roman bridge survives on the outskirts.

### "La Chiquinina" romería

The pilgrimage *(romería)* of Nuestra Señora de Gracia de la Alcantarilla, the patron saint of Belalcázar, nicknamed La Chiquinina, is held on the last weekend in April. On Saturday morning, participants head to a chapel 20km/12mi from the town, returning with the image of the saint before sunrise on Sunday. Were they to fail in this endeavour, the statue of the Virgin Mary would become the property of the town of Monterrubio de la Serena, in the province of Badajoz.

### Convento de Santa Clara

*0.8km/0.5mi towards Hinojosa del Duque, along a road signposted to the left.*
⏰ *Open daily, 11am-1pm and 4-6pm.*
☎ *957 14 61 24.*

The late-Gothic convent, one of the largest in the province, was founded as a monastery in 1476, and converted to a nunnery in 1483, forcing the monks to found the **Convento de San Francisco**, now in ruins. The east end, under a *Christ of the Column,* features a star vault with frescoes between the ribs. The three damaged sculptures in the doorway arch represent Christ, Mary Magdalene and St Clare.

---

### Local pastries

Pastry-lovers should not miss a visit to the convent of the Poor Clares. The nuns have developed something of a reputation for their sweet delicacies. Specialities include *flores de almendra* (literally, almond flowers) and *repelaos* (made to order with eggs and almonds). ⏰ *Open 9.30am-1.30pm and 4.30-6.30pm.*

---

## Excursion

## Hinojosa del Duque

*8.5km/5mi S.* The church in this small town is the most important monument in the north of the province.

▶ *Follow directions to the Catedral de la Sierra.*

### Parroquia de San Juan Bautista★

⏰ *Open 11.30am-noon.* ☎ *957 14 18 31.*

Known as the *Catedral de la Sierra*, the church was built in the 15C and 16C by Cordoban architects Hernán Ruiz I, Hernán Ruiz II and Juan de Ochoa. The impressive **northeast façade**★ has a fine Renaissance portal with Corinthian columns. The **sacristy** has magnificent **cresting** and windows decorated with armorial bearings, scallop shells etc. The **bell tower** (1590) is a nesting place for a family of storks.

The stone used **inside** to construct arches, pillars and vaulting contrasts with the whitewashed walls. The central nave is crowned by a fine *artesonado* ceiling and the chancel with a star vault.

In the main square, to the right of the church's façade, is the **Iglesia de la Virgen del Castillo**, converted from church to exhibition hall.

### Convento de las Madres Concepcionistas

This convent was built in the 16C. The sober **south façade**, a series of sturdy buttresses between arches, is crowned by a graceful belfry popular with storks.

# Parque Natural de CABO DE GATA-NÍJAR★★

Cabo de Gata–Níjar park includes cliffs, wild beaches, delightful coves and azure skies. The landscape is sprinkled with prickly pears, agave and species able to survive in this desert-like region registering the lowest rainfall in Spain.

▶ **Orient Yourself:** The park is south of the volcanic Sierra del Cabo de Gata running southwest-northeast parallel to the coast.
⏰ **Organizing Your Time:** The driving tour takes a day
🧭 **Also See:** COSTA DE ALMERÍA and ALMERÍA.

# Visit

## Níjar
*North of the park*
This once-Moorish town sits on the southern slopes of the Sierra de Alhamilla, in view of the agricultural plain of **Campo de Níjar** below. Irrigation has transformed the surrounding landscape. Whitewashed houses and cobbled alleyways are the essence of Andalucía.

**Handicrafts** – Blue and green **pottery** produced from clay and marl is popular, as are *jarapas*, colourful cotton and wool rugs and blankets.

## Iglesia Parroquial
The 15C parish church by the square bears Felipe II's coat of arms – the two-headed eagle – on its bell tower. The interior contains fine *artesonado* work.

## Watchtower (Torre-vigía)
Walk from the church to the market square *(plaza del Mercado)*, with its 19C ceramic fountain and hundred-year-old elm trees, then ascend a steep and stony path *(the last few metres are somewhat difficult)* to the hilltop watchtower for a commanding **view** of the Níjar plain, with Cabo de Gata and the Mediterranean in the distance.

*Traditional rugs*

B. Kaufmann/MICHELIN

### ☺ A Bit of Advice ☺

Underwater fishing is prohibited within the park. Authorisation is not required for scuba-diving; however, solo divers need a permit from the Consejería de Medio Ambiente of the Junta de Andalucía. Contact an area scuba-diving centre for further information.

## Address Book

### WHERE TO STAY

**Hostal Puerto Genovés** – Balandro – San José – ☎ 950 38 03 20 - www.puertogenoves.com - 🖩 - 18 rooms. This small, family-run *pensión* just 200m from the sea has spotless modern rooms, albeit without a phone. Bar with billiards table.

**Las Salinas de Cabo de Gata** – Almadraba de Monteleva – 4km/2.5mi SE of El Cabo de Gata – ☎ 950 37 01 03 - www.hotellassalinas.com - 🖩 - 20 rooms - 🕐 Closed in Oct. In a peaceful setting within the Parque Natural del Cabo de Gata, this hotel, with bedrooms overlooking the beach or saltpans, is an ideal base from which to explore this unique area.

### SCUBA-DIVING

Tranquil, crystal-clear waters, pleasant temperatures, a richness of species, fascinating caves and basalt columns and breathtaking underwater scenery have made Parque Natural de Cabo de Gata one of Europe's most important marine reserves and a paradise for scuba-divers. Underwater enthusiasts can choose from several sites: Cala San Pedro, Playazo de Rodalquivar, Cala del Embarcadero (in Los Escullos) etc.

## Driving Tour

# Park★★ *90km/56mi – allow one day*

▶ *From Níjar, take A 7-E 15 towards Almería and exit at Km 467. Before reaching Retamar, follow a road heading southwest.*

Cross a desert-like terrain, with sea to the right and the sierra in the distance.

▶ *Upon reaching a junction, bear right.*

The seaside village of **San Miguel de Cabo de Gata** comes into view.

### Saltpans
The Cabo de Gata saltpans *(salinas)* extend 4.5km/3mi southeast from Salinas, covering 300ha/740 acres. This protected area attracts thousands of migratory birds. *To make the most of a visit here, binoculars are extremely helpful.*

### Cabo de Gata
The road winds up to the lighthouse *(faro)*, above clear water and volcanic formations called **The Finger** (El Dedo) and **Mermaids' Reef** (Arrecife de las Sirenas). A viewpoint (Mirador de las Sirenas) and an information point adjoin the lighthouse.

▶ *Return to the junction and take the road to the left.*

### Centro de Visitantes Amoladeras
*Open in summer, 10am-2pm and 5.30-9pm; otherwise, 10am-3pm. Closed Mon, 1 and 6 Jan, Holy Week, mid-Jul to mid-Sep, 25 and 31 Dec. No charge. ☎902 88 64 52.*
The nearby visitor centre provides detailed park information and has a bookshop. The inland road passes a number of fields under plastic, typical of the Almerian landscape. To the right is the **CEMA** (Michelin Tyre Experimentation Centre), where the company's new tyres are put to the test.

▶ *13km/8mi farther on, take the turn-off to Los Escullos.*

### Los Escullos
This small fishing port nestles alongside a delightful long beach with an 18C watchtower known as Calahiguera.The road to Rodalquilar passes the **Isleta del Moro** cove and the viewpoint **Mirador de las Amatistast**.

### Rodalquilar
This mining settlement was abandoned in the 1960s. The dirt track leading to the **Playa del Playazo** skirts a chain pump, the 16C Rodalquilar or Las Alumbreras tower, and the 18C coastal battery of San Román.

▶ *Return to the Los Escullos junction and follow signs to San José. At nearby Pozo de los Frailes is an information point.*

### Blood Wedding

It was in 1928, at the Cortijo del Fraile, near Rodalquilar, that the tragic event occurred that was to inspire **Federico García Lorca** to write his famous play, *Blood Wedding*. The play recounts the tale of a young woman who fled with her cousin on the day of her wedding. This course of action was to end in the dramatic assassination of her lover.

*Playa de los Genoveses*

### San José

The whitewashed houses of this small resort ascend from an attractive beach. Note the half-domed cupolas which cool interiors. There is a small marina.

**Beaches** – Two superb beaches are on the edge of San José. **Playa de los Genoveses**★ lines a wide bay 2km/1.2mi from the centre to the left of a dirt track; the **Playa de Monsul**★, 2.5km/1.5mi from San José nestles between mountain spurs descending to the sea, a sand dune at one end, a rock in its centre, and a cove beyond.

# CABRA

POPULATION: 20 057.

Cabra is a swathe of white across its sierra, amid rolling hills set with olive groves. Its imposing castle and the slender tower of the parish church rise on a hill above town. 🄸 *Calle Santa Rosalía, 2, 14940 Cabra, ☎ 957 52 01 10.*

▶ **Orient Yourself:** Cabra is in the southern part of Córdoba province, inside the limits of Parque Natural de las Sierras Subbéticas.
💧 **Also See:** LUCENA, PRIEGO DE CÓRDOBA, BAENA, MONTILLA and AGUILAR DE LA FRONTERA.

## Walking Tour

### Plaza Alta

From plaza Vieja, take the street up to an esplanade fronted by the parish church and the castle remains. On the way, note the stone benches with embedded fossils.

### Parroquia de la Asunción y Ángeles

Cabra's main church, modified over the years, was once a mosque, hence the five aisles. The colourful brick tower and the marble Baroque side portal, adorned with *estípites* and Solomonic columns, stand out. The marble-like altarpieces, the stalls, and the cover of the baptismal font, a work by Benlliure, notable inside.

### Torre del Homenaje

The castle of the Counts of Cabra was a Moorish fortress rebuilt after the Reconquest. Nowadays, the restored keep is part of a school, the Colegio de las Madres Escolapias. Walk into the patio of the school *(knock first at the gate)*. An octagonal room reveals neo-Mudéjar decoration.

### Barrio de la Villa

This quarter *(barrio)* spreads out behind the church, within the town walls. Calle Villa extends as far as a lookout garden encircled by the battlements.

### "El Cerro" Moorish quarter

*On the Cuesta de San Juan.* Narrow lanes and whitewashed houses and arches, including the **Puerta del Sol** (Sun Gate), recall Cabra's Moorish past.

### Iglesia de Santo Domingo

The church belongs to a convent founded in the 15C. The façade retains two 18C Baroque marble portals. The simple main doorway is adorned with balustered Solomonic columns.

### Instituto Aguilar y Eslava

An image of the Immaculate Conception ornates the elegant 17C red marble doorway. The *Iglesia de la Virgen de la Soledad* dates from the 18C.

### Seigniorial mansions

A number of fine noble houses stand in the centre of Cabra.

### Museo Arqueológico

*Calle Martín Belda.* ⏱ *Open Mon-Fri, 11am-2pm and 6-7pm, Sat-Sun and public hols by prior arrangement.* ☎ *957 52 01 10.*
This regional museum is adapted for the visually impaired.

### Parque Alcántara-Romero

The Paseo, as it's called, was laid out in the mid-19C.

## Excursions

### Ermita de la Virgen de la Sierra★

*Take the road towards Priego de Córdoba. After 5km/3mi, bear left at a signposted junction.* The road climbs for 7km/4.5mi through an arid and rocky landscape, where the major hazard is wandering sheep. The sanctuary is in a delightful **setting**★, at the highest point of the Sierra de Cabra (1 223m/4 011ft), affording expansive **views**★★. The chapel dates to the Middle Ages and was rebuilt in the 16C. It features a *camarín* housing a sumptuously dressed Virgin of the Sierra.

### Parque Natural de las Sierras Subbéticas

**Centro de Acogida Santa Rita** – *Along A 340.* Stop at this reception centre, at the Mojón Pass, for information on trails and camping grounds. The terrain can be divided into three areas: The Macizo de Cabra is a limestone massif which includes several naturally sculpted rocks – Lapiaz de Las Lanchas, Los Hoyones and La Nava (at the foot of the Ermita de la Virgen de la Sierra) – and the **Cueva de los Murciélagos** (*see BAENA*). The Sierra de Rute and Sierra de la Horconera ranges contain the park's most spectacular scenery, culminating in the Pico de La Tiñosa (1 570m/5 150ft).

# CÁDIZ★★

POPULATION: 143 129.

Touched by water on three sides, Cádiz is Spain's longest-established seafaring city, settled for over 3 000 years. It is also one of Andalucía's most delightful and engaging provincial capitals, with charming parks and squares, orderly if attractively dilapidated 19C streets, and a quietly confident air. Only February's exuberant Carnival, the best on the Peninsula, punctuates the usual tranquillity. Visitors discover a friendly, cosmopolitan city, scarce of monuments, but rich in spirit, an unheralded Spanish treasure. 🖪 *Avenida Ramón de Carranza, 11006 Cádiz,* ☎ *956 25 86 46; plaza de San Juan de Dios, 11, 11005 Cádiz, ☎ 956 24 10 01.*

▶ **Orient Yourself:** A near-island, Cádiz is joined to Spain by a narrow causeway, the Atlantic to the south and west, the Bay of Cádiz to the north and east.
⚑ **Also See:** SANLÚCAR DE BARRAMEDA, El PUERTO DE SANTA MARÍA, VEJER DE LA FRONTERA, MEDINA SIDONIA (44km/27mi E), JEREZ DE LA FRONTERA (35km/22mi NE) and ARCOS DE LA FRONTERA (60km/37mi NE).

## A Bit of History

Cádiz might well be Europe's oldest city. It was colonised in 1100 BC by Phoenicians from Tyre who landed on an islet almost surrounded by water and founded Gadir ("fortress"). This first settlement extended from the castle of Santa Catalina to the island of Sancti Petri. The trading outpost was initially a dependency of Tyre and later of Carthage, it came under Roman rule in 206 BC, as Gades. Trade developed through Gades between Baetica and Rome, but apparently declined under the Visigoths and Moors. The city fell to Fernando III the Saint in 1240. His son, Alfonso X the Wise, transformed Cádiz into a strategic port. The Pópulo district was developed and protected by walls. Three of the four original gateways remain: **Arco de los Blancos**, **Arco del Pópulo** and **Arco de la Rosa**. In the late 15C, Cádiz expanded into the present-day district of Santa María. The Earl of Essex sacked Cádiz in 1596. During the 17C, Cádiz underwent considerable growth, as testified by the numerous examples of Baroque architecture still visible today. Its greatest glory, however, followed the transfer of the Casa de Contratación (Exchange) from Sevilla to Cádiz in 1717, it became the port of entry for all goods from America.

O. Torres/MARCO POLO

## Walking Tour

The best way to discover the delightful squares, gardens and old streets of Cádiz is on foot. These two itineraries include the city's most characterful districts and its major sights (*see plan*).

*Carnival in Cádiz*

# Address Book

## TRANSPORT

**Airport** – The airport at Jerez de la Frontera is just 30min away on A 4. ☎ *956 15 00 00/83.*

**Trains** – The station is in plaza de Sevilla, near the centre and port. Trains operate to major cities. Provincial trains run every 30min or so. ☎ *956 25 43 01 (railway station)* or *902 24 02 02 (RENFE).*

**Inter-city buses** – Three depos are: **Transportes Generales Comes** *(Plaza de la Hispanidad, 1)* serves Cádiz province and Sevilla. ☎ *956 20 53 09 or 956 80 70 59.*

**ransportes Los Amarillos** *(Avenida de Ramón de Carranza, 31)* serves the provinces of Sevilla and Málaga. ☎ *956 28 58 52.*

**Secorbus** *(Plaza Elios, 1)* serves Sevilla and Madrid. ☎ *956 25 74 15.*

**Local buses** – The main stops are in plaza de España and close to the port. A single-journey ticket costs €0.85, while a ten-trip ticket is on sale for €5.70. ☎ *956 21 31 47 or 956 28 38 04.*

**Taxis** – ☎ *956 21 21 21/22/23.*

**Horse-drawn carriages** – In summer, hire carriages in plaza de San Juan de Dios for a one-hour trip. The cost is approximately €25.

## SIGHTSEEING

**Information** – The city publishes a monthly cultural guide, *Cádiz entre columnas,* free from hotels, etc.

## WHERE TO EAT

**Terraza** – *Plaza de la Catedral, 3* – ☎ *956 26 53 91* – ◷*Closed Mon in winter, Sun in summer.* Unpretentious but pleasant, specialises in fish and seafood at its central location.

**La Marea** – *Paseo Marítimo, 1* – ☎ *956 28 03 47* - ▦. Right on the beach in an area of bars, specializing in seafood and rice dishes.

**El Faro** – *San Félix, 15* – ☎ *956 21 10 68 - www.elfarodecadiz.com* - ◷*Closed 24 Dec evening.* High-end tapas bar. Modern, wooden decor, refined cuisine, regional emphasis.

## TAPAS

**Joselito** – *San Francisco, 38* – ☎ *956 26 65 48* – ◷ *Closed Sun in summer.* Central tapas bar with two entrances, one with a pleasant sheltered terrace. Enjoy king prawns, rice dishes and stews.

**Aurelio** – *Zorrilla, 1* – ☎ *956 22 10 3* – ◷ *Closed Mon (except Jul-Sep).* A small popular tapas bar next to the plaza de Mina where the emphasis is on fish and seafood.

**El Cañon** – *Rosario, 49* – ☎ *956 28 50 05.* A small, traditional bar dating back to the 19C with a counter selling cured hams and local wines. **La Manzanilla**, on the opposite pavement, is the ideal place to try the wines of the area.

**El Nuevo Almacén** – *Barrié, 17 (by plaza El Palillero)* - ☎ *956 22 10 33* - ◷*Closed Sun.* A fine tapas bar, but also an Iberian-style delicatessen offering the best regional sausage, cheeses, chocolates.

**Taberna Manteca** – *Corralón de los Carros, 66* – ☎ *956 21 36 03* ◷*Closed Sun eve and Mon.* The faded posters on the walls are a reminder that the owner of this traditional-style bar is a former bullfighter. The Manteca is renowned for its good selection of chorizos, hams and sausages.

## WHERE TO STAY

**Hostal Fantoni** – *Flamenco, 5* – ☎ *956 28 27 04 - www.hostalfantoni. net* - ▭ ▦ *- 12 rooms (some without a bathroom).* Why spend a fortune when you can stay in this simple, pleasant *hostal*? Take a room with bathroom overlooking a pedestrian way.

**Hostal Bahía** – *Plocia, 5* – ☎ *956 25 91 10* - ▦ *- 21 rooms.* Modern rooms in this small hotel in the old quarter are good for the price.

**Hotel Francia y París** – *Plaza de San Francisco, 6* – ☎*956 21 23 19 - www. hotelfrancia.com* - ▦ *- 57 rooms.* An early 20C hotel on a charming square, in period style with quite adequate room.

**Hospedería Las Cortes de Cádiz** – *San Francisco, 9* – ☎ *956 22 04 89 - www.hotellascortes.com* - ℗ ▦ ♿ *- 36 rooms.* This 19C house in the old quarter is well maintained. Rooms around a patio are individually decorated on historical themes.

## TAKING A BREAK

**Café Parisien** – *Plaza de San Francisco, 1* – ☎ *956 22 36 77* ◷ *Open 9am-11pm.*

This indoor-outdoor café on a quiet square is popular with people of all ages. The café also serves meals. **Taberna La Manzanilla** – *Feduchy, 19* - ☎ *956 28 54 01* - *www.lamanzanilladecadiz.com* - ⏰ *Open 9am-3pm and 6-10pm (Sat-Sun mornings only)*. This little tavern has been redolent of manzanilla since 1900 and has the barrels to prove it.

### GOING OUT FOR THE EVENING

During the winter, social life is concentrated around the **commercial centre**. The summer action is at **Playa de la Victoria** and its **Paseo Marítimo**. In this beach area, popular bars are in **calle General Muñoz Arenillas**. The **Punta de San Vicente** at the other end of the city is another popular area. **El Café de Levante** – *Rosario, 35* – ⏰ *Open 4pm-3am*. This quiet café with modern decor in the old quarter attracts a mixed crowd for quiet chats. **La Cava** – *Antonio López, 16* - ☎ *956 21 18 66* - *www.flamencolacava.com* - ⏰*Closed Mon and in Jan - show and drink: €22, from 9.30pm, all day in summer*. Enjoy a drink along with song, flamenco and more by local talents. **La Mirilla** – *Plaza Asdrúbal, 7-8* - ☎ *956 25 17 12* – Have a drink or a coffee from the extensive list, with ocean view. **O'Connell's** – *Sagasta, near plaza de San Francisco* – ⏰ *Open 1pm-3.30am*. This Irish pub is popular with locals and visitors. Beers, and whiskey, of course. **Yunque**– *Muñoz Arenillas, 5* – ⏰ *Open 10pm-4am*. In the area frequented by young people in summer, Yunque attracts a more mature crowd with danceable music for all tastes.

### SHOWS

The **Gran Teatro Falla** *(plaza Falla)* organises theatre and concerts throughout the year, while **cultural centres** (El Palillero, El Bidón, La Viña and La Lechera) host exhibitions and workshops. Flamenco concerts are occasionally held at the **Baluarte de la Candelaria** *(alameda de Apodaca)*.

### SHOPPING

The most typical shopping area in Cádiz is the old part of the city. The long, narrow streets and squares, particularly **San Francisco**, **Columela**, **Compañía** and **Pelota**, in addition to **calle Ancha** and **plaza de San Antonio**, are crammed with traditional stores and more modern boutiques.

Shops in the old quarter sell traditional cakes and pastries. Try such local specialities such as *pan de Cádiz* at **Horno Compañía** *(calle Compañía, 7)*.

**Markets** – Arts and crafts markets are regular events in the city. Head to the Sunday market near the **Arco de Pópulo**, or the market known as **El Piojito** (Little Flea)on avenida de la Bahía on Monday mornings, where you can buy virtually anything.

### FESTIVALS

The **carnival** in Cádiz, held during February, is renowned throughout Spain.

# Around the Santa María and Pópulo Districts 1

This walk passes through two gypsy quarters where the traditions of flamenco, guitar and dance are part of everyday life. The Pópulo district is the early medieval section, while Santa María developed in the 15C beyond the Arco de los Blancos. Despite their attractiveness, they remain the poor and rundown. Restoration projects have been undertaken in recent years on the houses – many from the 17C.

## Plaza de San Juan de Dios

This 16C square, formerly plaza de la Corredera, is, along with plaza de San Antonio, the oldest in the city. Its strategic position facing the port made it the hub of Cádiz life; for a long time the square was also the site of the city's market. On one side stands the neo-Classical façade of the **town hall** dating from 1799, a work by Torcuato Benjumeda; next to it is the Baroque tower of the **Iglesia de San Juan de Dios**. The **Tourist Office** *(n° 11)* is housed in an attractive neo-Classical building.

▸ *Take calle Sopranis, to the left of the Iglesia de San Juan de Dios.*

## Calle Sopranis

The street contains some of the best examples of Baroque civil architecture in Cádiz. The façades of n°s 9-10 (known as the Houses of the Lilacs because of the doorway decoration) and the staircase in the patio of n°s 17-19 are particularly noteworthy. At the intersection with Calle Plocia, to the left, is the iron-and-brick former **tobacco factory**, a superb example of 19C industrial architecture, now the city's conference centre *(Palacio de Congresos)*. Opposite stands the **Convento de Santo Domingo**.

▸ *Follow calle Botica as far as calle Concepción Arenal.*

## Cárcel Real★

The royal jail was the first neo-Classical building in the city. It was built in 1792 by local architect Torcuato Benjumeda. The centre of the single-section façade is an avant-corps, similar to a triumphal arch. Four Tuscan-style engaged columns and two lions flank the royal escutcheon. The interior, restored in 1990 for use as law courts, is set around one large central patio and two side ones.

▸ *Take calle Santa María to the church of the same name.*

CÁDIZ

### Iglesia de Santa María

This 17C church was part of the old Convento de Santa María. Its façade can be seen at the end of the street of the same name. This Mannerist edifice is a work by Alonso de Vandelvira, the son of the famous Renaissance architect Andrés de Vandelvira, although the influence of Juan de Herrera can be detected. Its belfry is topped with an *azulejo*-adorned spire. Inside, note the dynamism of the Baroque altarpiece, as well as the **Delft ceramics** covering the base of the Capilla del Nazareno.

The marble Casa Lasquetty in calle Santa María (n° 11) is an example of early-18C civil architecture.

Cross calle Félix Soto to the 18C **Arco de los Blancos**, an arch formerly known as the Puerta de Tierra which leads into the working-class Pópulo district.

▶ *Pass through the arch and continue along calle Mesón Nuevo to plazuela de San Martín.*

### Casa del Almirante

This fine Baroque palace was built by Admiral (almirante) Don Diego de Barrios at the end of the 17C. The most important feature is the double-section Genoa marble **doorway**★★, with its combination of Tuscan and Solomonic columns on the lower and upper storeys respectively.

▶ *Turn left along calle Obispo José María Rancés to the small plaza de Fray Félix.*

In the religious centre, the Iglesia de Santa Cruz stands on the site of the destroyed mosque. Note the Baroque Casa de Estopiñán on plaza de Fray Félix (n° 1).

### Iglesia de Santa Cruz (Catedral Vieja)★

This late-16C church was the city's second cathedral. The sober exterior is broken only by the glazed ceramics covering its umbrella cupolas. The finely proportioned interior consists of three aisles separated by robust Tuscan-style columns.

### Teatro Romano

🕐 *Open 10am-2pm.* 🕐 *Closed Mon and public hols. No charge.* ☎ *956 21 22 81.*
The Roman theatre, located immediately behind the Iglesia de Santa Cruz, preserves much of its seating area and several underground galleries.

▶ *From plaza de Fray Félix take charming callejón de los Piratas to the Catedral.*

*Façade, Cádiz Cathedral*

## Cathedral★★

🕒 *Open Tue, Thur 4.30-7pm; Wed, Fri 4.30-6.15pm; Sun, 11am-1pm.* ✆€4 *(including entrance to the museum).* ☎ *956 28 61 54.* Cadíz Cathedral's construction started in 1722, in a pure Baroque style, but was only completed in 1883. The brightness and movement of its lines are particularly evident in the concave and convex featuresof its façade. Two towers crowned by pavilions look like astronomical observatories. The large half-orange cupola, which appears to float high above the city when sea mist envelops Cádiz in winter, was completed in 1844. The interior, with its Latin cross ground plan and ambulatory, is surprisingly light and spacious.

▶ *The popular calle de la Pelota leads to plaza de San Juan de Dios.*

# From Plaza de San Juan de Dios to the Cathedral ②

▶ *Follow calle Nueva, then turn left onto calle Cristóbal Colón.*

### Casa de las Cadenas
The marble **doorway**★ of this late-17C Baroque mansion was made in Genoa. The building is similar to the Casa del Almirante, but for the pair of Solomonic columns framing the main entrance.

▶ *Continue along calle Cristóbal Colón, turn right onto calle Cobos then left along calle Nicaragua to plaza de la Candelaria.*

### Plaza de San Juan de Dios

This square is popular with locals and visitors alike. Enjoy a break from sightseeing at two of the city's most popular cafés: the traditional-style Novelty Café, and La Caleta, with its boat-shaped counter.

### Plaza de la Candelaria
The major features around the square are the late-19C iron- and glass-fronted building at n° 6, and the small Isabelline-style palace at n° 15. Note to one side of the square the birthplace of politician Emilio Castelar, whose bust adorns its centre.

▶ *From the square, continue along calle Santo Cristo as far as calle Nueva. Continue to plaza de San Agustín.*

### Plaza de San Agustín
The Baroque church and an attractive neo-Classical **patio**, now part of a school, are all that remain of the Convento de San Agustín.

▶ *Take calle Rosario.*

### Oratorio de la Santa Cueva★
🕒 *Open Tue-Fri, 10am-1pm and 5-8pm (4.30-7.30pm in winter), Sat-Sun, 10am-1pm.* 🕒 *Closed Mon and public hols.* ✆€2. ☎ *956 22 22 62.*
This small neo-Classical jewel is a feast of decoration. The upper, elliptical part consists of a cupola illuminated by lunettes, supported by Ionic columns. Three 1795 **canvases**★★ by Goya, recently restored, decorate this chapel.

### Plaza de San Francisco
The 16C **Iglesia de San Francisco**, with its simple façade and separate 18C tower, stands to one side of this small square. The interior was restored in the 18C in Baroque style with the addition of stucco and rocaille work. Below the pendentive-supported false ceiling, note the angels, attributed to Pedro Roldán.
On the corner of calle Sagasta and callejón del Tinte stands an **elegant building** with attractive windows. This Baroque edifice was modified in the 19C in Isabelline

## Cádiz in 1777

In 1777 Carlos III entrusted the military engineer Alfonso Ximénez and the ubiquitous Sabatini to produce a 1:250 scale **model**★ of the city of Cádiz. This apparent royal whim was to result in a magnificent 25m²/270sq ft maquette made from mahogany, ebony and marble. Such was the precision of this superb work that even the smallest detail is represented on it. The majority of buildings standing today can be made out on the model, which also provides an insight into the development of several open spaces within the city, such as the plaza de Mina and the plaza de la Catedral. The model is one of the exhibits at the **Museo Iconográfico e Histórico de las Cortes y Sitio de Cádiz** *(calle Santa Inés, 9)*.

style. Continuing along callejón del Tinte, note the fine example of neo-Classical architecture at n° 2, and the impressive, thousand-year-old dragon tree opposite.

### Plaza de Mina★
The 19C saw the creation of several squares on land expropriated from religious orders. One was the plaza de Mina, created in 1838 on the vegetable garden of the nearby Convento de San Francisco. Today, it is one of the city's most charming squares with a colonial feel, verdant appearance and fine examples of Isabelline-style architecture. In particular, note the houses at n°s 11 and 16, as well as the neo-Classical palace housing the **Museo de Cádiz**★ (*see description under Visit*).

### Plaza de San Antonio
This spacious square is one of the oldest in Cádiz. Despite its lack of ornamentation, it was a popular place of residence for the local bourgeoisie in the 1600s; even in the 19C it was considered the city's main square. Over the centuries it has been used for events as diverse as bullfights and festivals. The Baroque façade of the **Iglesia de San Antonio** is to one side, while the rest of the square is fronted by elegant 19C buildings and, at n° 15, the Casino de Cádiz, with its impressive neo-Mudéjar patio.

▶ *Continue along calle San José to plaza San Felipe Neri. Note the attractive example of Art Nouveau architecture at n° 34 calle San José.*

### Oratorio de San Felipe Neri
🕐 *Open Mon-Sat, 10am-1.30pm.* 🕐 *Closed Sun and public hols.* ⊜€1.20. ☎ 956 21 16 12.
This Baroque oratory is one of the few churches in Andalucía with an elliptical ground plan. It was built between 1688 and 1719. The cupola was badly damaged in the Lisbon earthquake of 1755. Inside on the lower level are eight richly decorated chapels and a high altar with an altarpiece dominated by an unusual **Immaculate Conception** in which the Virgin Mary is dark-skinned – sadly the artist was killed in an accident while creating this work. The Tuscan-ordered upper level, in the form of a bullfighting tribune, supports a lightweight cane-framed cupola. It was here that the Cortes gathered in 1812 to proclaim a liberal constitution following the invasion of San Fernando by French troops.

▶ *Follow calle Santa Inés to calle Sagasta.*

### Iglesia de San Lorenzo
Blue and white *azulejos* decorate the polygonal tower of this sober church.

▶ *Return to calle del Hospital de Mujeres.*

## Hospital de Mujeres★

🕐 *Open Mon-Sat, 10am-1pm.* 🕐 *Closed Sun and public hols.* ✑€1. ☎ *956 22 36 47.*
The Hospital for Women is one of the major Baroque buildings in Cádiz. In order to overcome space limitations, the architect designed a narrow façade, behind which the building widens. It is laid out around two patios linked via an extraordinary Imperial-style **stairway**★★ with a cane-framed vault above it. The 18C *Vía Crucis* created from Triana *azulejos* in the patio is particularly attractive. The church *(ask at the porter's lodge for access)* contains a painting of **St Francis** by El Greco.

## Torre Tavira★

✑✑*Guided tours (20min), mid-Jun to mid-Sep, 10am-8pm; otherwise, 10am-6pm; last admission 30min before closing.* ✑€3.50, €2.50 for children. ☎ *956 21 29 10.*

This tower, in the highest part of the city, was designated official watchtower in 1778, from which the entry and departure of ships was controlled by a complex system of semaphores. The very first **camera obscura** in Spain, an ingenious device capturing real-time images of the city's movements, was installed in the tower in 1995.

### Watchtowers

A city like Cádiz, with narrow streets and high buildings, breeds a longing for height, to gain additional natural light, space and views which were in short supply for the majority of the population. During the 17C and 18C, the merchants of Cádiz built over 160 towers to watch over the arrival of their ships and, above all, to act as a symbol of their prosperity and prestige. They are differentiated by their final touches.

▷ *Head down to plaza del Mercado. The plaza de las Flores is located behind the brick Correos (main post office).*

## Plaza de las Flores

The Square of the Flowers is also known locally as the plaza Topete. The numerous flower and plant stalls, cafés and shops contribute to the delightful atmosphere in one of the city's liveliest squares. A number of shopping streets, such as Calle Columela and Calle Compañía, branch off from here.

# Visit

## Casa de la Contaduría (Museo Catedralicio)★

🕐 *Open 10am-1pm and 4.30-7pm; Sats, 10.30am-1pm.* 🕐*Closed Sun, Mon and public hols.* ✑€4 (includes entrance to the cathedral). ☎ *956 25 98 12.*
This complex of four buildings has been superbly restored to house the cathedral museum. The 16C **Mudéjar patio**★ is particularly fine. The museum displays a variety of liturgical objects, vestments and documents, including a letter bearing the signature of St Teresa of Jesus. Other objects of interest are the 16C **Custodia del Cogollo**★, a gold-plated silver monstrance attributed to Enrique Arfe, and the so-called 17C **Custodia del Millón**, named for its numerous precious stones.

## Museo de Cádiz★

🕐 *Open Wed-Sat, 9am-8.30pm (Sat, to 8pm); Sun, 9am-2pm.* 🕐 *Closed Mon and public hols.* ✑€1.50, no charge for citizens of the European Union. ☎ *956 21 22 81.*
The city museum is housed in a small neo-Classical palace with a sober façade built midway through the 19C. The clearly presented archaeological displays are worthy of special note, in particular the section dedicated to the Phoenicians. Two **anthropomorphous sarcophagi**★★ in white marble from the 5C BC imitate Egyptian models and were almost certainly carved by Greek craftsmen. In the fine arts section, the star exhibit is the collection of nine **panels**★ painted by Zurbarán

## Ancient art

Important archaeological finds are displayed in many of the region's museums. The Museo Arqueológico in **Granada** contains the most impressive finds from the Phoenician necropolis at Almuñecar, as well as Egyptian alabaster and Greek and Phoenician vases, while the archaeological section in the Museo Provincial in **Cádiz** displays several magnificent Egyptian sarcophagi, an impressive small statue of the god Melkart, and various anthropomorphous sarcophagi of Phoenician origin. The kingdom of Tartessus is magnificently represented in the provincial museum in **Huelva**, although the Museo Arqueológico in **Sevilla** has by far the most complete collection from this legendary civilisation of southern Spain, with a number of quite extraordinary exhibits from the Carambolo, Ebora and Mairena treasures. Iberian art also has pride of place in the Museo Provincial in **Jaén**, whose exhibits include pre-5C BC carvings from Porcuna, including warriors, men and women in ceremonial costume, high priests etc.

between 1638 and 1639 for the sacrarium in the Cartuja monastery in Jerez. Note the artist's mastery of light and shade.

### Parque Genovés★

The park was formerly known as the paseo del Perejil. Nowadays, it is the city's main green area and delightful for a quiet stroll. The former barracks of Carlos III opposite have been converted into the main building for the University of Cádiz.

### Castillo de Santa Catalina

🕐 *Open 10am-2pm and 5-8; Sat, 10am-2pm.* 🕐 *Closed Sun and public hols. No charge.* ☎ *956 22 63 33.*
This castle is situated at the far end of La Caleta beach. Built by Cristóbal de Rojas in 1598 following the sacking of Cádiz by the Earl of Essex, this fortification has an unusual star shape. It is currently under restoration.

### Playa de la Caleta

Once the city's natural harbour, this is now the only beach in the old part of Cádiz. At one end, on a small island connected to the city by a small causeway, is the **Castillo de San Sebastián**, a castle built in the 18C and still used by the military. Legend has it that this was the site of the temple of Kronos. In 1925, **Balneario de la Palma**, a spa building, was built in the middle of the beach.

### Barrio de la Viña

This working-class district (barrio), created in the early 18C away from the port area and shops in a part of the city exposed to the elements, is one of the most colourful quarters of Cádiz. Today, it is renowned as the setting for the **Cádiz carnival**★★, without doubt liveliest in Spain, which takes place in February.

**Iglesia de la Palma** – This circular Baroque-style church was built at the beginning of the 18C. A number of tapas bars nearby serve excellent fish.

### Baluarte de la Candelaria

Built in the 17C, this bulwark (*baluarte*) formed part of the defensive wall which enclosed and protected Cádiz on three sides and was initially a platform for cannons. In the 19C, it underwent significant renovation, particularly its inner

### 😊 A Bit of Advice 😊

#### The Mackerel season

Summer is the season for this tasty blue fish, which is sold on the streets of the Barrio de la Viña. A good place to try mackerel is the simple bar on the plaza del Tío de la Tiza.

façade, resulting in its present-day neo-Classical appearance.

## Iglesia del Carmen

This is the most Latin American of the city's churches and provides clear evidence of the reciprocal influences between Spain and her colonies. It was built in the mid-18C, with the main interest centred on its **Baroque façade**★. The sober marble doorway is brought to life by the two exuberant belfries decorated with volutes and *estípites*.

*Belfry, Iglesia del Carmen*

B. Kaufmann / MICHELIN

## Excursions

### San Fernando

*9km/5.5mi southeast along CA 33.* For centuries, San Fernando and Cádiz have always enjoyed close ties. San Fernando began to develop as a military and commercial outpost in the 18C, when Cádiz was enjoying its greatest splendour. In 1766 Carlos III transferred the headquarters of the Navy here, since which time the town has been inextricably linked with the Spanish armed forces. Between 1810 and 1811, members of parliament convened here to promulgate the first Spanish constitution; in recognition of its resistance to the French during the Peninsular War, Fernando VII conferred the name of **San Fernando** upon the city.

On calle Real, the focal point of San Fernando, are the town hall *(ayuntamiento)*, the **Iglesia del Carmen** and the **Museo Histórico Municipal**. ⏱ *Open in summer, Mon-Fri, 10am-2pm; otherwise, 10am-2pm and 6-9pm.* ⏱ *Closed Sat-Sun and public hols. No charge.* ☎ *956 94 42 54.*

The neo-Classical **Iglesia Mayor**, dedicated to St Peter and St Paul, and the Teatro de las Cortes, where members of parliament sat in 1881, are in the nearby plaza de la Iglesia.

The city's most important civil building is the **Observatorio Astronómico de la Marina**, a naval observatory built in neo-Classical style in 1753 by Jorge Juan. This observatory was the predecessor of the observatory in Madrid. *Guided tours by appointment.* ☎ *956 59 93 66 or 956 94 42 26 (tourist office).*

A Roman bridge, the **Puente de Suazo**, is visible upon leaving San Fernando. Until recently, the bridge was the only link to the rest of Spain.

### Chiclana de la Frontera

*25km/15.5mi southeast along the C 33 and A 48.* Though surrounded by saltpans and countryside, Chiclana is a prime beach destination. The delightful **Playa de la Barrosa**★★, an 8km/5mi stretch of fine sand, is just 7km/4.5mi away. The beach has a number of hotels and excellent recreation facilities, particularly in **Sancti Petri** and **Novo Sancti Petri**. Chiclana's attractive main square *(plaza mayor)* is dominated by the imposing neo-Classical **Iglesia de San Juan Bautista**, a work by Torcuato Cayón.

# CARMONA★★

POPULATION: 25 326.

Carmona, one of Andalucía's oldest towns, was founded by Carthaginians, and played an active political role during Roman occupation and under Moors and Christians. The past lives on in the old quarter's elegant palaces, seigniorial houses and solemn places of worship. *Plaza de las Descalzas, 41410 Carmona, ☎ 954 14 22 00; Arco de la Puerta de Sevilla, 41410 Carmona, ☎ 954 19 09 55.*

▷ **Orient Yourself:** Carmona, on a plateau overlooking a fertile plain irrigated by the River Corbones, is 40km/25mi east of Sevilla via A 4 – E 5.

🕐 **Organizing Your Time:** Allow half a day to visit Carmon's old quarter.

🅿 **Parking:** Leave your car in the lower part of town, near the Puerta de Sevilla.

🜨 **Also See:** ÉCIJA (53km/33mi E), MARCHENA (27km/17mi SE), OSUNA and ESTEPA.

| CARMONA | | | Duquesa Pas. de la | BY | 27 | Quintanilla | BY | 49 |
|---|---|---|---|---|---|---|---|---|
| Arquillo de la Judería | AY | 2 | El Salvador | BY | 70 | María Auxiliadora | BY | 52 |
| Arquillo de San Felipe | BYZ | 4 | Fermín Molpeceres | BY | 32 | Marqués de las Torres Pl. | BY | 53 |
| Bernardo Enrique Cerezo | AY | 6 | Fernando Barrera | BY | 35 | Palenque Pl. del | AZ | 58 |
| Blas Infante Pl. de | AZ | 9 | General Chinchilla | BZ | 37 | Portugal Av. de | AZ | 60 |
| Cenicero Ronda del | AZ | 12 | General Freire | BY | 39 | Raso de Santa Ana | AY | 62 |
| Costanilla del Postigo | AY | 15 | José Arpa | AY | 42 | Sacramento | BY | 69 |
| Cristo Rey Pl. de | BY | 17 | Juan Caballero Pl. de | AY | 44 | San Bartolomé | AZ | 71 |
| Descalzas Pl. de Las | BY | 21 | Juan de Ortega | ABY | 45 | Santa María da Gracia | BY | 73 |
| Dolores Quintanilla | BY | 23 | La Fuente | AZ | 36 | Sevilla | AZ | 75 |
| Domínguez Pascual | BYZ | 24 | Lonja Alta Carlota | | | Torno de Madre de Dios | AZ | 79 |

| Casa de los Lasso | BY | E | Casa de los Rueda | BY | K |
|---|---|---|---|---|---|

## Walking Tour

## Old Quarter★

### Walls

The Moorish-arched **Puerta de Sevilla**★ in the lower fortress *(alcázar de abajo)*, served as an entrance to the old quarter, where sections of Carthaginian walls remain. The **Puerta de Córdoba**★ has two superb octagonal towers of Roman origin.

### Iglesia de San Pedro★

🕐 *Open Thu-Mon, 11am-2pm; and Mon, Thu and Fri, 4-6pm.* 🕐 *Closed Tue-Wed.* 👝 *€1.20.* ☎ *954 14 12 70.*

The 15C Church of St Peter, on the paseo del Estatuto, has a fine **bell tower**★, similar to the Giralda in Sevilla, hence the nickname "Giraldilla". The **Capilla del Sagrario** (sacrarium) is richly decorated, and there is an extraordinary 16C green ceramic **baptismal font**. The church was heavily restored during the Baroque period

### Convento de la Concepción

The convent contains charming **cloisters** and a Mudéjar-style church.

▶ *Walk through the Puerta de Sevilla.*

*Parador, Carmona*

Paradores

*Puerta de Sevilla*

### Iglesia de San Bartolomé

This Gothic church, rebuilt in the 17C and 18C, has a basilical plan and graceful neo-Classical tower. One chapel is covered with Renaissance *azulejos*.

### Iglesia de San Felipe★

A fine 14C Mudéjar church with a handsome tower, *artesonado* work bearing the coat of arms of the Hurtado de Mendoza family, and chancel with 16C *azulejos*.

### Plaza Mayor or Plaza de San Fernando

This attractive square is fronted by elegant Mudéjar and Renaissance mansions.

### Ayuntamiento

🕐 *Open daily, 8am-3pm.* ☏ *954 14 00 11.*

The interesting Baroque town hall in the heart of the old quarter has an attractive Roman **mosaic** in its courtyard.

### Iglesia del Salvador

🕐 *Open Fri-Tue, 10am-2pm and 4.30-6.30pm.* 🕐 *Closed Wed-Thu, 1 Jan and 25 Dec.* ⊘*€1.20.*

This large Baroque building on plaza de Cristo Rey was built with a Latin-cross plan between the 17C and 19C. Note the impressive Churrigueresque **altarpiece** and the paintings, retables and religious gold and silverware from the 17C and 18C.

### Iglesia de Santa María la Mayor★

🕐 *Open in summer, 10am-2pm and 6-7.30pm; otherwise, 9am-2pm and 5-7pm.* 🕐 *Closed Sat afternoon, Sun and in Aug.* ⊘*€3.* ☏ *954 19 14 82.*

This large 15C Gothic church replaced a mosque in calle San Ildefonso. Despite its restoration in Renaissance and Baroque style, it retains the Patio de los Naranjos (Orange Tree Patio) and beautiful horseshoe arches of the Moorish building. Note the 6C **Visigothic calendar** on one column. A monumental **Plateresque altarpiece**★ exquisitely depicts sculpted scenes of the Passion. Side chapels hold magnificent retables such as the Christ of the Martyrs behind 16C **Plateresque grilles**.

### Convento de las Descalzas★
This magnificent example of 18C Sevillian Baroque has a Latin-cross ground plan, a tower with a double campanile and *azulejo* decoration.

### Convento de Santa Clara
🕐 *Open by prior arrangement.* ☎ *954 14 21 02.*
The 15C Convent of St Clare has two pleasant cloisters and a Mudéjar church with canvases by Valdés Leal, and a fine collection of female portraits in the style of Zurbarán.

## Visit

### Alcázar de Arriba
This old Roman fortress offers superb **views**★ of the countryside. It was extended by the Almoravids, and later converted into the palace of Pedro I. A **parador** now stands in the parade ground. Only fragments remain of the original structures.

### Roman necropolis★
*At the end of calle Jorge Bonsor, on the road from Sevilla.* 🕐 *Open mid-Jun to mid-Sep, Tue-Fri, 8.30am-2pm, Sat, 10am-2pm; otherwise, Tue-Fri, 9am-6pm, Sat-Sun 10am-2pm.* 🕐 *Closed Mon, and Sun in summer. No admission charge.* ☎ *954 14 08 11.*
This impressive site from the 1C AD holds over 300 tombs, mausoleums and cremation kilns. The **Tumba del Elefante** (named for an elephant statue) holds three dining rooms, while the **Tumba de Servilia** is the size of a villa.

### Seigniorial mansions
A number of 17C and 18C noble residences are dotted around the town's squares. Of these, the most attractive are the Casa de los **Rueda**, Casa de los **Domínguez**, Casa del **Barón de Gracia Real**, Casa del **Marqués del Saltillo**, Casa de los **Lasso** and the Casa de las **Aguas**. These elegant mansions add a refined air to Carmona and provide an interesting contrast with the older buildings in the heart of the old quarter.

## Excursions

### Viso del Alcor
*12km/8mi southwest along A 392.* This town of Celtic origin is at the highest point in the Sierra de los Alcores. The **Iglesia de Santa María del Alcor** is a Mudéjar church with Renaissance cupola in the presbytery and a collection of 17C paintings from the Venetian School. The 15C **Iglesia de la Merced** holds 17C and 18C altarpieces.

### Mairena del Alcor
*16km/10mi SW along A 392.* The remains of a Moorish fortress overlook Mairena del Alcor. The Mudéjar-style **Iglesia de la Asunción** has a handsome 17C-18C **main altarpiece**.

### Alcolea del Río
*17km/10.5mi north. Take SE 122 towards Guadajoz then SE 129.* Alcolea has two old water mills. The Iglesia del Cristo is an 18C Baroque building. The fine 15C Mudéjar **Iglesia de San Juan Bautista** holds an image of the Virgen del Consuelo (Virgin of Solace).

# CAZORLA★

POPULATION: 8 527

Cazorla – ancient Roman Carcesa – lies in the heart of the **Parque Natural de las Sierras de Cazorla, Segura y Las Villas**★★★. The town's streets, lined by whitewashed houses with balconies replete with flowers, are perfect for a quiet stroll, for browsing and shopping, and as a backdrop for whiling away time over a drink on a *terraza*. 🖬 *Calle Juan Domingo, 2, 23470 Cazorla,* ☏ *53 24 26 24.*

▶ **Orient Yourself:** Cazorla is below the Peña de los Halcones, in the Sierra de Cazorla.
👣 **Also See:** Parque Natural de las Sierras de CAZORLA, SEGURA y LAS VILLAS, ÚBEDA (46km/29mi NW) and BAEZA (55km/34mi NW).

## Visit

### Castillo de la Yedra
*By car via the street that follows the River Cerezuelo.* ☾ *Open Wed-Fri, 9am-10pm; Tue, 3-10pm; Sun and public hols, 9am-3pm.* ☾ *Closed Mon. No charge.* ☏ *953 71 00 39.*
The Roman fortress above Cazorla was rebuilt in turn by Moors and Christians. The **views** from the keep are delightful. A chapel contains a life-size Romanesque-Byzantine image of Christ, surrounded by 12 paintings of the the the Apostles.

### Plaza de Santa María
In this pleasant square at the heart of the old quarter is the monumental **Fuente de las Cadenas**, a Renaissance-style fountain. The ruins of the Iglesia de Santa María, a church designed by Vandelvira and now used as an auditorium, stand to one side.

## Address Book

### WHERE TO EAT
◉◉◉ **La Sarga** – *Plaza del Mercado* – ☏ *953 72 15 07* – 🍽 – ☾ *Closed Tue and in Sep.* This cosy restaurant in the centre serves regional specialties high-quality products. Friendly service, mountain views.

### TAPAS
**La Montería** – *Corredera, 20* – ☏ *953 72 05 42* – ☾ *Closed Jan-Mar.* A popular bar decorated with stuffed animals. The excellent tapas on offer include cured hams, cheeses and venison.

### WHERE TO STAY
◉ **Guadalquivir** – *Calle Nueva, 6* – ☏ *953 72 02 68* - *www.hguadalquivir. com* - 🍽 👣 – *11 rooms.* This small hotel's main advantage is its central location.

◉◉ **Villa Turística de Cazorla** – *Ladera de San Isicio* – ☏ *953 71 01 00* - *www.villacazorla.com* - 🖬 🍽 👣 – *32 apartments.* This apartment-hotel compound set amid orchards imitates a picturesque village. Pool, castle views.
◉◉ **Molino La Fárraga** – *150m from Santa María ruins, calle de la Torre* – ☏ *953 72 12 49* - *www.molinolafarraga.com* - 🛏 🍽 – *9 units.* ☾*Closed 11 Dec-Feb.* This rustic hotel in an 18C mill has castle and mountain views, a pool, and a garden crossed by a stream.

### FESTIVALS
On the night of **14 May**, the *romería* of San Isicio, Cazorla's houses are adorned with *caracoladas*, oil-filled snail shells affixed with clay and lit up to form attractive geometric displays.

**Ayuntamiento**
Cazorla's town's hall is the impressive former Convento de la Merced (Convent of Mercy), with a large arcade on the ground floor and a graceful tower.

**Iglesia de San Francisco**
The church was part of a 17C Franciscan monastery. It contains a statue of the locally venerated Santísimo Cristo del Consuelo (Holy Christ of Solace).

# Parque Natural de las Sierras de CAZORLA, SEGURA Y LAS VILLAS★★★

This magnificent park of cliffs, gorges and a complex river network includes the source of the River Guadalquivir. Altitude and humidity favour dense Mediterranean-type mountain vegetation. Villages in the park preserve traditional culture and crafts. *Carretera del Tranco (Km 48.3), 23379 Torre del Vinagre, ☎ 953 71 30 40; Juan Domingo, 2, 23470 Cazorla, ☎ 953 72 01 15.*

▶ **Orient Yourself:** Spain's largest nature reserve, in the Cazorla, Segura and Las Villas ranges, was created in 1986. It covers 214 300ha/529 500 acres at altitudes between 600m/1 950ft and 2 017m/6 616ft.
🕐 **Organizing Your Time:** Allow a day for each suggested itinerary.
👶 **Also See:** ÚBEDA (46km/29mi NW of Cazorla) and BAEZA (55km/34mi NW).

## Driving Tours
*See suggested route on the map*

### Sierras de Cazorla, Las Villas y El Pozo
*92km/67mi – allow one day*

### From Cazorla to Tíscar 1

**Cazorla★** – 👶*see CAZORLA*

▶ *Head west along A 319. At a crossroads, bear left onto A 315 towards Quesada.*

**Quesada**
Set amid olive groves, Quesada was the birthplace of painter Rafael Zabaleta (1907-60). His work, shown in the **museum,** captures the light of the region and the character of locals. 🕐 *Open 11am-2pm and 5-7pm (4-8pm in winter)* ⊛€3. ☎ *953 73 30 25.*
The **Cañada de las Fuentes**, a ravine at 1 400m/4 592ft, is the **source of the River Guadalquivir** *(access via a track off A 315, to the north of Quesada).*

## Flora and fauna
The park's high levels of precipitation have resulted in abundant vegetation. Flora here includes the beautiful Cazorla violet, an endemic species that appears in forests of black pine, holm and downy oak; hazel and holly. Native fauna includes wild boar, stags, mountain goats and deer; predators such as the genet, stone marten, wildcat and fox; aquatic fauna such as the otter; and numerous fish species, including trout, barbel, carp and black perch. The park is also home to a variety of birdlife (golden eagle, peregrine falcon, kite, osprey etc).

## Address Book

### SIGHTSEEING

It is advisable to head to one of the **information points**, to plan a route that takes in the breathtaking landscapes. The largest information point is at the Torre del Vinagre; others are at **Cazorla**, Segura de la Sierra and Siles. Mountain-bikers, horse-riders and hikers can follow the extensive network of forest tracks and marked footpaths criss-crossing the park.

The itineraries described in this chapter are given as a guideline only; many others are possible depending on specific interests and on the direction of approach.

### WHERE TO STAY

⌂⌂ **Sierra de Cazorla** – *On the outskirts of La Iruela, heading towards the park –* ☎ *953 72 00 15 - www.hotel-sierradecazorla.com –* ▤ *– 59 rooms.* The outdoor pool and superb mountain views make up for the simply functional rooms.

⌂⌂⌂ **Parador de Cazorla** – *Lugar Sacejo – Sierra de Cazorla – 26 km E of Cazorla –* ☎ *953 72 70 75 - www.parador.es – 34 rooms.* �🕐*Closed 19-31 Dec and in Jan.* In the heart of the Parque de Cazorla, close to an old hunting reserve. The facilities and location are ideal for nature-lovers.

---

Wall paintings from the Palaeolithic era can be seen on Cerro Vitar (hill) and in the Cueva del Encajero (cave), just a short distance from the town.

### Tíscar★

*20km/12mi southeast of Quesada on C 323.* Below the statue of the Virgin in the **Santuario de Tíscar** is the impressive **Cueva del Agua**★, where a torrent emerges between rocks. 🕐 *Open for worship only. Jun-Sep, 11am-1pm and 5-7pm; Oct-May, 11.30am-1pm and 4.30-6pm.* ☎ *953 71 36 06*

## From Cazorla to the Embalse del Tranco de Beas ②

▶ *Leave Cazorla NW along A 319.*

### La Iruela

La Iruela was settled by Carthaginians in the 3C BC. The Iglesia de Santo Domingo, a Renaissance-style church designed by Vandelvira, stands at its centre. The remains of a Templar castle offering superb **views**★★ of the Guadalquivir Valley.

### From La Iruela to the Embalse del Tranco★

The first 17km/10.5mi of the winding A 319 afford **spectacular views**★★. The Parador de **El Adelantado** is reached via a branch road *(8km/5mi)* up through forests ,

▶ *Continue along A 319 running parallel to the river.*

### Torre del Vinagre – The Centro de Interpretación (information centre)

has a hunting museum and a botanical garden that displays native species. 🕐 *Open 11am-2pm and 4-6pm (to 7pm in spring, 9.30pm in summer).* ☎ *953 71 30 40.*

*La Iruela Castle and the Sierra de Cazorla*

A game reserve, **Parque Cinegético de Collado del Almendral**, 15km/9.5mi farther along A 319, has lookout points where wildlife (deer, mouflons, mountain goats etc) can be seen through binoculars early in the morning. *For further information, call* ☎ *953 71 01 25 (tourist office).*

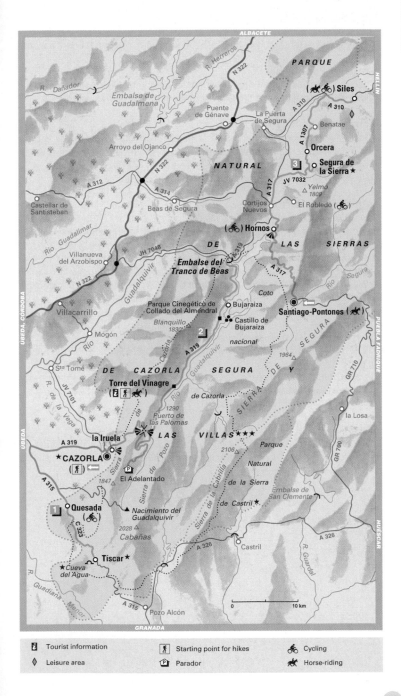

| | | |
|---|---|---|
| 🗺 Tourist information | 🧍 Starting point for hikes | 🚴 Cycling |
| ◇ Leisure area | 🅿 Parador | 🐎 Horse-riding |

**Embalse del Tranco de Beas** – Several camping areas, hotels and watersport facilities are located near this reservoir on the River Guadalquivir. The ruins of a Moorish castle stand on **Isla de Bujaraiza**, an island opposite a viewpoint.

# Sierra de Segura

## From Santiago-Pontones to Siles ③
*79.5km/49.5mi – allow half a day*
This itinerary passes through whitewashed towns with a distinct Moorish flavour.

## Santiago-Pontones
A number of archaeological sites lie within this mountain municipality, such as the **Cueva del Nacimiento** and the **Cuevas de Engalbo**, caves with wall art.

## Hornos
*27km/17mi NW of Pontones along the A 317.* The remains of the fortress rise above a cliff. There are spectacular **views**★ of the Tranco Reservoir and Guadalquivir Valley. An arts and crafts market is held on the first Saturday of every month.
Follow A 317 north, then bear right at a signposted junction.

## Segura de la Sierra★
*24km/15mi northeast of Hornos.* This village straddles a hill at 1 240m/4 067ft under its Mudéjar **castle**, partially intact. The keep offers a sweeping **panorama**★★. In the central maze of alleyways are the **town hall**, with its fine Plateresque doorway; the **parish church**, containing an alabaster statue of the Virgin and a recumbent Christ attributed to Gregorio Hernández; an unusual square bullring: the imperial fountain *(fuente imperial)*, bearing the escutcheon of Charles V: and, above all, the **Moorish baths** *(baños árabes)*, with horseshoe arches and star-shaped vault lights.

## Orcera
*7.5km/4.5mi northwest of Segura along JV 7020.* The most interesting feature of this village is the pentagonal plaza del Ayuntamiento, fronted by the Iglesia de Nuestra Señora de la Asunción, with its sober Renaissance portal, and the Fuente de los Chorros, a 15C fountain. The three Santa Catalina towers, the only remaining vestiges of the former Moorish fortress, are visible on the outskirts of Orcera.
Follow JV 7020 beyond Benatae, then take JV 7021.

## Siles
*21km/13mi northeast of Orcera.* The village has sections of its old walls. The nearby reserve of Las Acebeas is close to the source of the River Los Molinos.

# CÓRDOBA★★★

POPULATION: 310 388.

Magnificent Córdoba bespeaks the brilliance of the Roman, Moorish, Jewish and Christian civilisations, most notably through its *Mezquita*, its mosque-cathedral masterpiece. The delightful Jewish quarter *(Judería)* overflows with charm with its evocative narrow streets and quaint small squares embellished with wrought-iron grilles, flower-filled patios and shrines illuminated by attractive lanterns.
🛈 *Calle Torrijos, 10, 14003 Córdoba, ☎ 957 47 12 35, otcordoba@andalucia.org*

▸ **Orient Yourself:** Córdoba is on the River Guadalquivir at the centre of Córdoba province, between the ranches of the Sierra de Córdoba and Olive and wheat country. The city N IV – E 5 mortorway runs to Sevilla, 143km/89mi SW. southwest. Granada is located 164km/102mi to the SE along N 432.

⚐ **Also See:** MONTORO (42km/26mi NE), ANDÚJAR (76km/47mi E), MONTILLA, AGUILAR DE LA FRONTERA and ÉCIJA.

## A Bit of History

## The month of May

Córdoba is most beautiful in its month of vibrant celebrations. *Times may vary from year to year; contact the city's tourist office.*

**Cruces de Mayo** – During the May Crosses (first days of the month), flower-decked crosses dot the city in this contest involving the city's guilds and civic groups.

**Concurso de Patios** – In this competition in early May, patios of houses and mansions are transformed into breathtaking floral displays.

**Concurso Nacional de Arte Flamenco** – Spains's most talented flamenco singers, dancers and guitarists compete every three years *(next in 2007)*.

**The Feria** – This annual fair features entertainment at outdoor stands *(casetas)*, the dancing of *sevillanas*, and the consumption of tapas and *fino*.

## CÓRDOBA

| | | | |
|---|---|---|---|
| | Alfonso XII | CY | |
| | Alfonso XIII | BY | |
| **Roads** | Amador de los Ríos | AZ | 5 |
| Abéjar | América Av. de | AY | |
| Agustín Moreno CZ | Ángel Saavedra | ABZ | 7 |
| Alcázar Av. del AZ | Arenal Pte del | CZ | |
| Alfaros BY | Barcelona Av. de | CY | |
| | Barroso | AZ | |

| | | |
|---|---|---|
| Blanco Belmonte | AZ | 13 |
| Buen Pastor | AZ | 15 |
| Cádiz Av. de | BZ | |
| Cairuán | AZ | |
| Campo de la Verdad Av. | CZ | |
| Capitulares | BY | 17 |
| CapuchinosPl. de los | BY | |
| Cárcamo | CY | |

CÓRDOBA

0    200 m

# Address Book

## TRANSPORT

**Airport** – ☎ 957 21 41 00. Córdoba airport only serves domestic routes. The closest international connections are at Sevilla airport (☎ 954 44 90 00), 140km/88mi to the west. The cities are connected by both bus and train.
**Reservations:** ☎ 901 33 31 11 (domestic); 901 33 32 22 (international).
**Trains** – Plaza de las Tres Culturas – ☎ 957 49 02 02. Córdoba has high-speed service to Madrid on the AVE (Alta Velocidad Española) train. Journey time is under two hours. There are many trains in the region and to destinations throughout Spain.
**City buses** – AUCORSA – Avenida Libia, 61 – ☎ 957 76 46 76. A single journey costs €0.80, a ten-trip ticket €5.40. Transfers are at no charge. entitle passengers to transfer from one bus to another. Monthly passes available.
**Inter-city buses** – Glorieta de las Tres Culturas – ☎ 957 40 43 83.
**Taxis** – ☎ 957 76 44 44.
**Horse-drawn carriages** – Hire carriages by the Mezquita (Calle Torrijos) or in campo Santo de los Mártires.

## SIGHTSEEING

**Not to be missed:**
– the Mezquita illuminated at night;
– the view from atop the Torre de la Calahorra;
– the Mezquita's minaret from calleja de las Flores.

## WHERE TO EAT

◒ **Taberna los Faroles** – Velázquez Bosco, 1 – ☎ 957 48 56 29. Lanterns illuminate the patio at night, hence the tavern's name. Specialities include salmorejo (like gazpacho)and rabo de toro (braised oxtail). A fresh atmosphere is enhanced by the azulejos on the walls.
◒◍ **Almudaina** – Jardines Santos Mártires, 1 – ☎ 957 47 43 42 - www.restaurantealmudaina.com – ◷ Closed Sun (Jun-Sep); Sun evenings the rest of the year. An attractive restaurant by the Alcázar with exquisite regional decor, serving specialties of Córdoba.
◒◍◍ **El Caballo Rojo** – Cardenal Herrera, 28 – ☎ 957 47 53 75 - www.elcaballorojo.com. A Córdoba classic, alongside

the Mezquita, with a small entrance patio and traditional decor.
◒◍◍ **Bodegas Campos** – Lineros, 32 (near plaza del Potro) – ☎ 957 49 75 00 - www.bodegascampos.com – ◷ Closed Sun evening. The restaurant in venerable wine storehouses (bodegas) is set around several patios. The bar decorated with photos of famous visitors.
◒◍◍ **El Churrasco** – Romero, 16 – ☎ 957 29 08 19 - www.elchurrasco.com – ◷ Closed in Aug. A regional restaurant with pleasant patio and bar for an aperitif or a snack. Grilled meats are the house speciality. Several exquisite rooms are available (◒◍◍◍).

## TAPAS

Córdoba does full justice to Andalucía's great tapas tradition with bars offering a huge selection of tapas and the chance to salmorejo (a type of local gazpacho), rabo de toro (braised oxtail), embutidos (local sausage) and sherries (finos, amontillados, olorosos).
**Taberna San Miguel-Casa El Pisto** – plaza San Miguel, 1 - ☎ 957 47 01 66 - €9 - ◷Closed Sun and in Aug. Founded in 1886, plastered in bullfight posters, indispensable locale for tapas.
**Taberna Casa Pepe de la Judería** – Romero, 1 (between the Zoco and the Mezquita) – ☎ 957 20 07 44 - www.casapepejuderia.com. This bar opened in 1928 and still looks like 1928. Tapas rooms are around a patio, the restaurant is upstairs.
**Casa Gaudí** – Avenida Gran Capitán, 22 - ☎ 957 47 17 36 - A modern tavern serving beverages (including teas and coffee) as well as tapas from 8am into the early hours.
**Casa Salinas** – Puerta de Almodóvar, 2 – ☎ 957 29 08 46 - www.cuevasromanas.com – ◷ Closed Wed and in Aug. This cosy, traditional bar has a small patio, tile decoration, celebrity photos.
**La Bacalá** – Medina y Corella (near the Mezquita) – ☎ 630 37 56 82. Bar with a terrace on a little square, often with flamenco music. The specialty is cod.
**Taberna Guzmán** – Judíos, 9 (opposite the synagogue) – ☎ 957 29 09 60 – ◷ Closed Thu. A traditional bar with lots of character, azulejo decoration,

bullfighting mementoes and posters advertising the local *feria*. Good local sausages and cheeses.

**Taberna Salinas** – *Tundidores, 3 (plaza de la Corredera)* – ☎ *957 48 01 35 - www. tabernasalinas.com -* 🕐 *Closed Sun and in Aug.* Traditional 19C Córdoboa tavern with covered patio. Specialties: eggs with prawns and ham, fried aubergine, *rabo de toro*.

## WHERE TO STAY

🛏 **Hostal La Milagrosa** – *Rey Heredia, 12* - ☎ *957 47 33 17 - www. lamilagrosahostal.com -* 🅿 *- 8 rooms*. A good address in the old city near the Mezquita, with plant-filled patio and airy rooms, all with full bath.

🛏 **Hotel González** – *Manríquez, 3* – ☎ *957 47 98 19 – 16 rooms*. Rooms off the patio in this 16C palace, between the Mezquita and the Judería, are spacious and well appointed.

🛏 **Hostal Séneca** – *Conde y Luque, 7* – ☎ *957 47 32 34 – 12 rooms –* 🕐*Closed 2 weeks in Aug and in winter*. Close by the Mezquita, the Seneca fills quickly, despite plain rooms, some sharing bathrooms. Reserve.

🛏 **Hotel Maestre** – *Romero Barros, 4-6* – ☎ *957 47 24 10 - www.hotelmaestre. com – 26 rooms*. One of Córdoba's better values, near the plaza del Potro, with spacious if plain rooms. The owners have another hotel and apartments nearby.

🛏 **Mezquita** – *Plaza de Santa Catalina, 1* – ☎ *957 47 55 85 - hotelmezquita@ wanadoo.es – 21 rooms*. Opposite the main entrance to the Mezquita. Spacious, attractive rooms, good for the price.

🛏🛏 **Albucasis** – *Buen Pastor, 11* – ☎ *957 47 86 25 - www.hotelalbucasis. com – 15 rooms –* 🕐 *Closed 7 Jan-7 Feb*. Basic hotel with large rooms in a typical house in the Judería. Access via a patio.

🛏🛏🛏 **NH Amistad Córdoba** – *Plaza de Maimónides, 3* – ☎ *957 42 03 35 - www.nh-hotels.com – 84 rooms*. A reliable chain hotel in two 18C mansions close to the city's Moorish walls. Spacious public areas and a large Mudéjar patio, attractive large rooms.

🛏🛏🛏 **Hotel Casa de los Azulejos** – *Fernando Colón, 5 - Córdoba -* ☎ *957 47 00 00 - www.casadelosazulejos.com -* 🅿

*Taberna San Miguel "El Pisto"*

▦ ♿ *- 8 rooms –* 🕐 *Closed 24-25 Dec*. Charming hotel in a traditional house with plant-filled patio, large rooms, wrought-iron bedsteads, and designer baths.

## GOING OUT FOR THE EVENING

Córdoba's bars and nightclubs are around the avenida del Gran Capitán in the centre and in the El Brillante residential area.

**Cafetería Siena** – *Plaza de las Tendillas* ☎ *957 47 46 08 -* 🕐 *Open 8am-midnight* 🕐 *Closed Sun*. A long-established café in Córdoba's main square, with one of the city's most popular outdoor terraces.

**El Puentecillo** – *Poeta Emilio Prados - Córdoba - www.elpuentecillo.com* – 🕐 *Open 9.30pm-5 am in summer, midnight-5am winter*. On the way up to the El Brillante district, attracts a low-key, older set, good for starting the night.

**Málaga Café** – *Málaga, 3* – ☎ *957 47 62 98* – 🕐 *Open Mon-Thu, 4pm-2am, Fri-Sat, 4pm-4am, Sun 4-10pm*. A quiet, comfortable café near plaza de las Tendillas in the centre. Good for passing time.

**Sojo** – – *Benito Pérez Galdós, 3-* ☎ *957 48 39 98 -* 🕐 *Open 8am-midnight*. Avante-garde Sojo serves everything from breakfast to late-hour drinks, as well as art exhibits and installations. The clientele is mid-20s and up.

## SHOWS

Córdoba is a provincial capital with a buzzing social and cultural life. During the winter, the **Gran Teatro** *(avenida Gran Capitán, 3* – ☎ *957 48 02*

37) hosts a regular season of concerts and theatre. In addition, the Filmoteca de Andalucía *(calle Medina y Corella, 5 – www.cica.es/filmo)* organises a varied programme of cinema.

The town hall *(Ayuntamiento)* publishes *Qué hacer en Córdoba,* available free around town, lists cultural events.

## SHOPPING

Córdoba's main shopping streets are concentrated around plaza de las Tendillas. These include pedestrians-only calle José Cruz Conde and Conde de Gondomar. The larger department stores along avenida Ronda de los Tejares include El Corte Inglés. The Eroski shopping centre is next to the municipal stadium in the Arcángel district.

Traditional crafts in Córdoba include the famous *cordovans* (embossed leatherwork) and gold and silver filigree, on sale in shops throughout the city. La Purísima, a jeweller's located in the area behind the Alcázar, has an excellent reputation for its high-quality filigree products.

The municipal market or *Zoco Municipal* (☎ 957 20 40 33), around a small square and old lanes in the *Judería* includes ceramics, leather, pottery etc (🕐 *open Mon-Sat, 10am-8pm).*

**Neighborhood markets** are held almost every day. The best is held Sunday mornings next to the municipal stadium.

# A glorious past

**Roman Córdoba** – Córdoba became a Roman colony i n 152 BC and was the capital of Baetica until almost the end of the Empire. Leading intellectual figures included **Seneca the Rhetorician** (55 BC-AD 39); his son, , **Seneca the Philosopher** (AD 4-65); and the poet **Lucan**, Seneca the Philosopher's nephew, companion to Nero in his student days. Christian Córdoba produced **Bishop Ossius** (257-359), counsellor to Emperor Constantine and staunch opponent of Arianism in the Council of Nicaea.

**Muslim Córdoba** – Emirs from Damascus established themselves as early as 719. Following internecine struggles, Abd ar-Rahman I , sole survivor of the Umayyads, created an **independent emirate**. In the 9C, under Abd ar-Rahman II, the city underwent great cultural development, led by the Iraqi poet Ziryab.

**The Caliphate** – In 929, Abd ar-Rahman III proclaimed himself independent Caliph of Córdoba.Commerce, agriculture, and the city expanded, enhanced by an extensive network of roads. The 10C, a period characterised by peace and prosperity, brought with it unprecedented cultural splendour. Jewish, Christian and Muslim communities enriched each other and lived in peace. Córdoba became the capital of the entire Western world, with a population exceeding 250 000 inhabitants, perhaps much more. The city had some 3 000 mosques, a multitude of markets and baths and a complex sewage system. The university, the library created by Al-Hakam II – largest of the period – and sumptuous buildings amazed visitors inspired artists.

**A kingdom of taifas** – The Caliphate dissolved amid power struggles early in the 11C. Al-Andalus fragmented into small warring kingdoms, the **reinos de taifas**. However, artistic and cultural life continued unabated in the Caliphal tradition. Until its reconquest in 1236, Córdoba was itself a taifa. Astronomy, mathematics, medicine and philosophy flourished. The writings of the **Averroës** (1126-98) on the works of Aristotle had a major impact, while the Jew **Maimónides** (1135-1204) stood out as a philosopher and physician. His *Guide of the Perplexed*, in which he establishes conciliation between faith and reason, found favour with Jews and Muslims, and also influenced Christian scholars, particularly St Thomas Aquinas.

**Christian Córdoba** – On 29 June 1236, **Fernando III the Saint** reconquered the city. The arrival of the Christians had a large impact on Córdoba's architecture with the construction of 14 parish churches.In 1486 **Columbus** presented in Córdoba the plans for his expedition to the Indies to the Catholic Monarchs.

## Special Feature

# Mezquita-Catedral★★★

🕐 *Open Jan-Dec, 10am-5.30pm (Feb and Nov, to 6pm; Jul-Oct, to 6:30pm Tuesdays; Apr-Jun, to 7:30pm). Last admission 30 min before closing.* 💶 *€8.* ☎ *957 47 05 12.*
The mosque-cathedral, one of the world's most extraordinary buildings, was built between the 8C and 10C above the Visigothic basilica of San Vicente. Following the Reconquest, Christians erected a Gothic cathedral in the very heart of this Muslim place of worship. The Mezquita incorporates religious and architectural features of the two faiths, in a harmony of distinct, yet equally magnificent, parts.

### Mezquita (Mosque)

A world masterpiece of Islamic art, the Mezquita follows the plan that draws its inspiration from the house of the Prophet Muhammad in Medina. A crenellated square perimeter encloses a patio for ritual ablution, the prayer hall and the minaret. The first Muslims in Córdoba shared the Visigothic church of St Vincent with Christians. Soon, however, Abd ar-Rahman I (758-88) razed the church and around 780 began the construction of a splendid mosque with 11 aisles each opening onto the Patio de los Naranjos. Marble pillars and stone came from Roman and Visigothic buildings. Innovations included the superimposition of tiers of arches to gain height and space. In 848 Abd ar-Rahman II had the mosque

### The unique structure of the Mezquita

During the Moorish period, Córdoba had around 3 000 mosques. The one admired by visitors today was the main mosque, used for Friday prayers. Enlargements were carried out in line with the growth in the city's population.

The Mezquita has a structure totally different to that found in Christian churches and as such could be extended without affecting the building's architectural style. Its simple structure, with parallel aisles, enabled further aisles to be built, while retaining the overall unity.

*Interior of the Mezquita*

extended to the present-day Capilla de Villaviciosa (Villaviciosa Chapel); in 961 Al-Hakam II built the *mihrab* (prayer-niche); and in 987, Al-Mansur added eight aisles (recognisable by their red brick pavement).

## Patio de los Naranjos

This spacious and enchanting patio, with porticoes on three sides, is named for the orange trees *(naranjos)* planted after the Reconquest. The ir allure and aroma are part of the Mezquita's charm. Before prayer, Muslims would perform their ritual ablutions here. Several Mudéjar fountains remain, along with the 10C **Al-Mansur basin (1)**.

## Interior

*Entrance through the Puerta de Las Palmas.* A spectacular forest of columns and arches greets the worshipper. Colour and shade play a fundamental role. Horseshoe-shaped

B. Kaufmann/MICHELIN

arches are in alternate red (brick) and white (stone) voussoirs, while greys and pinks predominate in columns.

The doorway leads into the wide main aisle, leading to the *mihrab*. Aisles run perpendicular to the sacred walls of the *qiblah,* which unusually faces south, not toward Mecca.

After the Reconquest, chapels were built by the Christians in the west nave. These include the 17C marble-covered **Capilla de la Purísima Concepción (2)**.

In 833 **Abd ar-Rahman II** removed the wall of the *qiblah* to extended the 11 aisles.

The decoration was so striking that it was re-used in the extraordinary renovations carried out under **Al-Hakam II**. The aisles were further extended. All the columns and capitals were hand-carved for this part of the building. The rich ornamentation centred on the **mihrab**★★★ is the jewel in the Mezquita's crown. Its octagonal niche

Pta de Sta Catalina    Magistral González Francés

Pta del Caño Gordo

PATIO

DE LOS

NARANJOS

Pta del Perdón    Pta de las Palmas

Minaret

CATHEDRAL

Cardenal Herrero

Corregidor Luis de la Cerda

★★★ Mihráb

Pta de los Deanes    Torrijos

N

0    40 m

**Periods of construction**

785    848    961    987

was decorated by Byzantine artists who also created the superb mosaics in the magnificent **cupola**★★ before it. The three ribbed domes of the **maksourah (3)** – the Caliph's enclosure – rest on unusual multifoil arches with interwoven ribs, oriental in origin. The ceiling of the Capilla Real (Royal Chapel) followed the same design. **Al-Mansur** was responsible for the largest expansion of the mosque. With no more clearance on the river side, eight aisles were added to the east.

## Christian features

With conversion of the Mezquita to a church, the aisles on the side of the Patio de los Naranjos were walled up, with the exception of the Puerta de las Palmas. In order to build the **first cathedral (4)**, columns were removed and a Gothic *artesonado* ceiling supported by pointed arches was erected in their place. Alfonso X was responsible for the chancel in the **Capilla de Villaviciosa** or **Lucernario (5)**, and built the **Capilla Real**★ **(6)**, decorated in the 13C with Mudéjar stucco which nevertheless retained harmony with the rest of the monument.

## Cathedral

In the 16C, despite opposition from the cathedral chapter, Bishop Don Alonso Manrique received authorisation to build a cathedral in the middle of the mosque. However, in spite of the talent of the architects Hernán Ruiz I, Hernán Ruiz II and Juan de Ochoa, and the beauty and richness of their creation, Emperor Carlos V could not hide his anger at the result: "You have destroyed something

### Decoration: everything except the human form

Because of their religion, Muslims could not incorporate the human body in decorative features. As a result, they maximised the use of plant and geometric motifs. Marble panels, sections of carved stucco and mosaics combine to produce unparalleled splendour. Given the sacred character of the Word, the other fundamental characteristic of Muslim art is the use of script, in the form of verses from the Koran. A superb example can be seen on the entrance arch to the *mihrab*, on which the rectangular surround *(alfiz)* bears inscriptions in Kufic (early Arabic) script.

unique," he said, "to build something commonplace."

The styles of the 16C and 17C can be seen alongside each other in Hispano-Flemish arches and vaults, a Renaissance dome, Baroque vaulting above the choir and a Baroque high altar. Enrichments include two **pulpits**★★ **(7)** in mahogany, marble and jasper by Michel de Verdiguier.

The **choir (8)** is spectacular, in particular the Baroque **choir stalls**★★ by Pedro Duque Cornejo (c 1750). In exquisitely carved mahogany, they offer a complete iconographic programme, depicting saints, scenes from the lives of Christ and Mary, and the Old and New Testaments, in which the Ascension of Christ, in the centre, stands out. Note also the two impressive organs from the 17C and 18C.

### Callejita del Pañuelo

This attractive alleyway *(callejita)*, accessed via the plaza de la Concha *(very close to the Mezquita, along Martínez Rücker)*, is one of Córdoba's most delightful sights. Although its official name is calle Pedro Jiménez, it is known as Pañuelo (handkerchief) because at its narrowest point it has the width of a man's handkerchief placed diagonally. It comes to a dead end in a slightly wider, yet equally charming section with a small fountain, an attractive doorway and wrought-iron grilles.

**Treasury**

*To the left of the mihrab.* The Baroque treasury *(tesoro)*, by Francisco Hurtado Izquierdo, is in the **Capilla del Cardenal** (Cardinal's Chapel) **(9)** and two adjoining rooms. A monumental 16C **monstrance**★ by Enrique Arfe and an exceptional Baroque figure of Christ in ivory stand out in this collection of liturgical objects.

*Detail, cathedral vaults*

B. Kaufmann/MICHELIN

### Exterior

The **minaret** built under Abd ar-Rahman III is enveloped in a Baroque tower dating from the late 16C and early 17C. To the side, the 14C Mudéjar **Puerta del Perdón** (Pardon Doorway), a doorway faced with bronze, opens onto the street.

A small shrine to the much venerated **Virgin of the Lanterns (10)** is set into the north wall. Behind a metal grille and adorned with lanterns, it is a copy of a work by Julio Romero de Torres. Its illumination at night is particularly attractive.

It is well worth walking around the exterior of the Mezquita to admire the elegant decoration on its entrance gates, most of which have now been permanently sealed. Particularly notable for their decoration are the two gates on calle Torrijos – the Puerta de San Esteban, created by Abd ar-Rahman I and one of the very first gates to the mosque subsequently modified by Abd ar-Rahman II – and the Puerta de Palacio.

## Walking Tour

## Around the Mezquita★★ 1

The suggested itinerary begins alongside the walls of the Mezquita, follows the Guadalquivir, then heads into the delightful whitewashed maze of the **Judería.**

### Calleja de las Flores

This narrow street in the Judería is typically Cordoban with its arches and abundance of flowers *(flores)* and flowerpots. The street ends at a small square with a fountain, where visitors can enjoy one of the best views of the Mezquita's tower.

### Palacio de Exposiciones y Congresos

The conference and exhibition centre is the former Hospital de San Sebastián. It was later used as the city's orphanage and nowadays also houses the **tourist office**.

Its **doorway**★, with fine sculptures on the tympanum and jambs, dates from the early 16C. The wall is adorned with an ornamental border and fretwork, thistle leaves and stringcourses. The sober brick patio is entirely devoid of decorative features.

### Museo Diocesano de Bellas Artes

*Next to the Palacio de Exposiciones y Congresos.* ⊙ *Open Jul-Aug, Mon-Fri, 9.30am-3pm, Sat, 9.30am-1.30pm; Sep-Jun, Mon-Fri, 9.30am-1.30pm and 4-6pm, Sat, 9.30am-1.30pm.* ⊙ *Closed Sun and public hols.* ✍€1.50 *(no charge to holders of Mezquita tickets).* ☎ 957 49 60 85.

The **Fine Arts Museum** is in the 18C Bishops' Palace (Palacio Episcopal) built atop the former Moorish fortress. It has an interesting patio and a double Baroque black marble staircase topped by a fine cupola with stucco decoration.

The exhibition rooms, on the second floor, display sculptures, paintings, religious books and tapestries, some of which date back to the 13C. The highly restored Baroque chapel of Nuestra Señora del Pilar (Our Lady of the Pillar), can also be visited *(entrance from the patio, to the right of the staircase).*

### Triunfo de San Rafael

This, the most impressive of all the city's monuments to St Raphael, dates from the second half of the 18C. The archangel can be seen on top of the monument, with sculptures of various allegorical figures at its base.

### An oasis of greenery

The centre of Córdoba is not just a maze of narrow, winding streets, for one of the city's main thoroughfares has a wide stretch of greenery running through its centre. This oasis of peace and tranquillity links the avenida del Conde de Valledano, paseo de la Victoria and avenida de Cervantes.

## St Raphael

Devotion to the archangel Raphael has been a deep-rooted feature of the city for many centuries. It is rare to find a family without at least one member named after him. Even the local football stadium is called El Arcángel. This devotion has its origins in the 16C, following an apparition of St Raphael *(San Rafael)*, who came forward as the protector of the city. Several original monuments, known as *triunfos* (literally "triumphs"), have been erected around the city to honour Córdoba's patron saint.

### Puerta del Puente

This imposing monument has the appearance of a triumphal arch, having lost its original function as an entrance gateway on the north bank of the river. It was built in the 16C to a classical design with large fluted Doric columns, entablature, frieze and a curved pediment with an escutcheon supported by two warriors. The decoration can be seen on the side facing the river.

### Puente Romano

The Roman bridge rises above the waters of the Guadalquivir between the Puerta del Puente and the Torre de la Calahorra (which houses the Museo Vivo de al-Andalus; 👜 *see description under Visit*). The bridge was built under Emperor Hadrian, and rebuilt on several occasions, most importantly under the Moors. The river's watermills, of Moorish origin, can be seen to the right.

A statue of **St Raphael** towards the middle of the bridge, on a low, altar-like wall, was erected in 1651, following a serious epidemic. It is usually adorned with candles and flowers, highlighting its importance as a place of devotion.

H. Belmenouar/MICHELIN

▶ Cross the bridge, then follow calle Amador de los Ríos to the Campo Santo de los Mártires.

*A waterwheel (noria) on the Guadalquivir*

Excavations at the Campo Santo de los Mártires have uncovered vestiges of **Caliphal baths**. The walls of the **Alcázar de los Reyes Cristianos**★ (👜 *see description under Visit*) soon come into view on the left-hand side.

The **Caballerizas Reales**, royal stables situated next to the Alcázar, were founded by Felipe II in the 16C. The present building dates from the 18C. Although it is closed to the public, it is well worth a look inside if the entrance happens to be open as you pass by.

At the end of the street, after the arch, enter the **San Basilio district**, famous for its charming patios. One of the most attractive is at n° 50, calle San Basilio, seat of the Cordoba Patio Association.

▶ Return to the Campo Santo de los Mártires, then head along calle Cairuán.

### City walls and Puerta de Almodóvar

The pedestrianised calle Cairuán runs parallel to the walls of the Judería, which were just a small part of the defence system protecting the city. This well-preserved section, built from ashlar stone, contrasts with the tapestry of greenery provided by the numerous cypress trees.

The Puerta de Almodóvar (Almodóvar Gate) provides access to the Jewish quarter. Its origins date back to Moorish times, although it was heavily restored in the early 19C, when an inner doorway was added. A statue of Seneca can be seen to the left of the gateway. The illumination of this area at night adds to the charms of this delightful quarter.

▷ *Walk through the Puerta de Almodóvar and head into the Jewish quarter.*

# La Judería★★

Time seems to have stood still in the old Jewish quarter with its whitewashed alleyways with their flower-filled patios, wrought-iron grilles and typical bars.

### Calle Judíos

The Street of Jews, parallel to the walls, is one of the Judería's most famous thoroughfares. Look for the Bodega Guzmán, a charming bar at n° 7, and the **Casa Andalusí**, a 12C Moorish house at n° 12, which exhibits Moorish paper-making tools.

### Sinagoga

🕐 *Open Tue-Sat, 10am-2pm and 3.30-5.30pm; Sun and public hols, 9.30am-1.30pm.* 🕐 *Closed Mon.* ⊷€0.30 *(no charge for citizens of the European Union).* ☏ *957 20 29 28.*

Along with the two in Toledo, this is one of the few medieval synagogues preserved in Spain. Built in the early 14C, it consists of a small square room with a balcony on one side for women. The upper parts of the walls are covered with Mudéjar stucco and Hebrew inscriptions. The decorative motifs used are geometric and vegetal.

### Zoco

*25m/30yds farther along.* Access to the former Moorish **souk** is under the brick arches of a narrow alleyway. Shops on the way to two delightful patios sell a range of Cordoban handicrafts.

A monument to **Maimónides**, the acclaimed Jewish philosopher and physician, stands in the tiny plaza Tiberiades, just a few metres farther along calle Judías.

### Plazuela de Maimónides

This small square is fronted by the Casa de las Bulas, which contains the city's bullfighting museum, the **Museo Taurino** (*⚲ see description under Visit).* Note the fine mansion opposite the museum, and the Hotel NH Amistad (*⚲ see Address Book)* to the right.

## The Jews and Córdoba

The Jews arrived in Córdoba before the Moors and soon became influential, particularly in trade and the teaching of the sciences. Following the Moorish invasion, which was generally well received on their part, the city's Jewish population tended to concentrate in the area now referred to as the Judería (*Jewish quarter)*, mainly consisting of the streets close to the Puerta de Almodóvar, and built a fine synagogue in calle Judíos. When Fernando III reconquered the city in 1236, the Jews maintained their influence, largely as a result of the prestige of their academies. However, as the Catholic church consolidated its power, their position in society became more complicated. In the middle of the 13C they were forced to destroy their synagogue and soon after were compelled to pay taxes for the upkeep of the Catholic Church. They were blamed for every epidemic and disaster, until 1492, when Isabel la Católica ordered their expulsion from Spain.

▶ *Take calle Cardenal Salazar. This typical narrow alleyway climbs slightly to the plazuela del Hospital del Cardenal.*

## Facultad de Filosofía y Letras

The Faculty of Philosophy and Letters is the former Hospital del Cardenal Salazar. Built in the early 18C, it has a Baroque stone façade bearing a cardinal's escutcheon. From **calle Romero** *(to the rear of the square)*, the tower of the Mezquita is now visible. This street, along with **calle Deanes**, into which it runs, and the **Judería**, are part of the tourist area surrounding the Mezquita with its myriad souvenir shops.

# San Andrés and Santa Marina Districts★ 2

## Templo Romano

*Calle Capitulares, on the corner of calle Claudio Marcelo.* The imposing columns of this 1C AD Roman temple provide a reminder of the splendour of Córdoba under Roman rule. All are fluted and crowned with Corinthian capitals. The temple originally had a front portico raised on a podium and ten columns on each side, seven along the inner sanctuary *(cella)*.

## Iglesia de San Pablo★

🕐 *Open daily, 9-9.30am, 10.30am-1pm, 5.30-6.30pm and 8.30-9pm.* 🕐 *No visits during religious services.* ☎ 957 47 12 00.

The Church of St Paul is part of the former Convento de San Pablo, built to commemorate the reconquest of Córdoba on 29 June 1236, the feast day of St Paul. The Baroque doorway on calle Capitulares was built in 1706. Solomonic columns flank the entrance arch which bears an image of St Paul. The doorway leads to the atrium, which opens onto the façade. The church has a carillon instead of a bell tower.

The well-proportioned interior has three wide aisles which have retained features of the transitional Romanesque-Gothic style despite subsequent restoration. The Mudéjar **artesonado ceiling**★ is worth particular note.

The chapel to the left of the presbytery contains the 18C image of **Nuestra Señora de las Angustias** (Our Lady of Anguish), by the great sculptor Juan de Mesa, who also carved the Christ of Great Power in Sevilla. The luxuriously dressed Virgin, her face awash with tears, holds the body of Christ in her arms.

Note also, in the Epistle nave, a 15C **Mudéjar chapel** with fine *artesonado* work, the walls of which are completely covered with stucco above a frieze of *azulejos*.

▶ *Head down calle de San Pablo and turn right into calle Villalones.*

## Palacio de los Villalones

This impressive stone mansion has an interesting façade crowned by a gallery. The Plateresque-style decoration is concentrated around the bays. The palace is said to be the setting for a sad, and rather improbable legend from the 17C in which the beautiful daughter of a magistrate disappeared in the basement of the palace. In spite of numerous excavations, her father was never able to find her. It is said that the young girl's ghost inhabits the house at night.

▶ *Exit onto plaza de San Andrés.*

## Plaza de San Andrés

Alongside this small square with orange trees and fountain is the **Casa de los Luna**, also known as the Casa de Fernán Pérez de Oliva. Built in the 16C, it has two unusual corner windows. An escutcheon and a plain window can be seen above the door, which bears a Plateresque-style orle. Another Fernandine church, the 13C **Iglesia de San Andrés**, is to the left. It was rebuilt in the 18C. The graceful brick tower dates from this later period.

▷ *Follow calle Hermanos López Dieguez, then head along calle Enrique Redel as far as plaza de Don Gome.*

This square is dominated by the magnificent **Palacio de Viana**★★, accessible via a fine angled doorway *(see under Visit)*.

▷ *Take calle Santa Isabel to plaza de Santa Marina.*

## Iglesia de Santa Marina de Aguas Santas

The 13C Church of St Marina of the Holy Waters was one of 14 built under Fernando III following the reconquest of the city. The austere **façade**★, divided by four heavy buttresses, shows the beauty and strength of unadorned stone. The trumpet-shaped portal with its smooth, slightly pointed mouldings corresponds to the early ogival style.

Opposite the church, in plaza del Conde Priego, stands a **monument to Manolete** (b Córdoba 1917 – d Linares 1947), a bullfighting legend who spent his childhood here. The wall to the left is part of the **Convento de Santa Isabel**.

> ## ☕ A Sweet Treat ☕
>
> **Traditional Santa Isabel pastries:**
> The nuns from the Convento de Santa Isabel are famous for their delicious sweets and pastries, which include almond (*almendrados*), sultana (*sultanas*) and local Córdoba specialities (🕐 *open 9am-12.45pm and 5-7.15pm*).

▷ *Turn around and head along calle Rejas de Don Gome.*

Note the imposing belfry on the Iglesia de San Agustín.

▷ *Continue calle Pozanco, and follow it to plaza de San Rafael.*

On the elongated **plaza de San Rafael** is the **Iglesia de San Rafael**, with its large neo-Classical façade.

▷ *Take the street to the right of the church as far as plaza de San Lorenzo.*

## Iglesia de San Lorenzo★

🕐 *Open daily, 10am-1pm and 5.30-8.30pm.* ☎ *957 48 34 79.*

This church, one of the finest in the city, appears to stand on its own, as if to highlight its charms. Another of the Fernandine churches, its construction began in the late 13C and early 14C in early Gothic style. The original and attractive façade comprises a highly unusual portal which is rarely seen in this region, with three slightly pointed arches and a magnificent, finely worked **rose window**★. The tower is part of the façade: the section extending to the top of the nave was part of an older tower. The colour of the stone enhances the overall charm of the church.

The sober interior consists of three aisles with wooden ceilings and pointed arches on cruciform pillars. The chancel has Gothic vaulting. Illumination is provided by three high and narrow windows. Several 14C wall paintings remain at the apsidal end.

# From Plaza de las Tendillas to Plaza de Colón ③

## Plaza de las Tendillas

This spacious square is at very heart of Cordoban life. The equestrian statue of Gonzalo Fernández de Córdoba, known as El Gran Capitán, is the work of Mateo Inurria. Jets of water gush upwards to the delight of children on hot days.

## Iglesia de San Nicolás de la Villa

🕐 *Open daily, 10.30-11.30am, and at 6.30pm, 7.30pm and 8.30pm.* 🕐 *No visits during religious services.* ☎ *957 47 68 32.*

The church was built after the Reconquest in the late 13C and early 14C. The peculiar 15C Mudéjar-style **tower**★ on the façade has a square base supporting a lofty octagonal structure with a ledge along the top. A modern set of bells breaks its architectural harmony. Small reliefs depict people and the legend of patience and obedience. The simple portal was added in the 16C.

The nave is topped by a wooden ceiling, while the side aisles have more modern vaulting. The apsidal end has its original pointed vaulting. The richly decorated **Capilla del Bautismo** (Baptism Chapel), with baptism relief and oval cupola, is a mid-16C addition.

▶ *Return to plaza de las Tendillas and follow calle V. Ribera and calleja Barqueros.*

## Iglesia de San Miguel★

🕐 *Open for worship at 7am, noon and 7pm.*

The 13C church is in the plaza de San Miguel, a popular gathering place. The lovely Romanesque ogival façade is set off by sober architectural features. Buttresses support the central section, which is embellished with a doorway of simple ogival archivolts and a large rose window.

The interior has three short naves, with a wooden ceiling above the central aisle; the chancel has pointed vaults with ribs set with jagged indentations. The 18C altarpiece is in red marble. Mudéjar features survive in the Capilla del Bautismo *(Epistle nave)*.

Behind the church, look out for one of Córdoba's oldest bars, the *Taberna San Miguel "El Pisto"*. It is well worth a quick look inside, with or without tapas.

▶ *Follow calle San Zoilo, behind the church, and then head along calle Conde de Torres.*

## Plaza de los Capuchinos★

The impressive calvary of **Christ of the Lanterns** in this austere square was sculpted in the late 18C and was part of a *vía crucis* (Stations of the Cross). The Iglesia de los Capuchinos and the church of the former 18C Hospital de San Jacinto, containing a venerated, and luxuriously dressed Virgin of Pain, also front the square.

▶ *Exit the square via calle Cabrera and head to plaza de Colón.*

## Plaza de Colón

This pleasant square named for Columbus has an attractive fountain and gardens.

**Palacio de la Diputación**★ – The provincial Parliament building began as the 18C Convento de la Merced (Convent of Mercy). It also served as a hospital for French troops in the Peninsular War. The large yet attractive façade in three sections is painted to imitate marble. The white marble doorway is decorated by two Solomonic columns, a pediment and two belfries. The patio *(entrance through the left-hand door)* is decorated in the same style as the main façade. Note the marble staircase, and the Baroque, stucco-adorned church *(access via the middle door)*.

**Torre de la Malmuerta** – This magnificent 15C octagonal tower, once used as a noble prion, is in fact a turret which retains the arch connecting it to the defensive wall. The name recalls the wrongful death *(mal muerta)* of a woman at the hands of her husband, who was forced to build this tower in her memory.

# Visit

### Palacio de Viana★★

🕐 *Guided tours (1hr), Jun-Sep, Mon-Sat, 9am-2pm; Oct-May, 10am-1pm and 4-6pm, Sat, 10am-1pm.* 🕐 *Closed Sun, public hols and first two weeks of Jun.* ✍€6 (€3 patios only).* ☎ *957 49 67 41.*

This palace with its adjoining outbuildings is a fine example of 14C to 19C Cordoban civil architecture. It covers 6 500m²/70 000sq ft, half of it the 12 patios and the garden. The palace is owned by the Caja Provincial de Ahorros, a savings bank.

Enter from plaza de Don Gome, through an angled doorway. The interior is enhanced by the 16C Renaissance main staircase with magnificent Mudéjar *artesonado*. Several rooms also have fine *artesonados*.

Córdoba is famous for its **patios**, including the 12 superb examples in this palace.

*Entrance to the Palacio de Viana*

B.Kaufmann/MICHELIN

---

## Palacio de Viana collections

**Ground floor:**
 ◆ **Porcelain** of different provenances from the 17C to 20C.
 ◆ **Arquebuses.**

**First floor:**
 ◆ **Azulejos:** 236 pieces of ceramic from the 13C to 19C.
 ◆ **Cordoban leather:** the best collection of its kind, comprising articles of embossed leather and cordovans from the 15C to 19C.
 ◆ **Tapestries:** Flemish, French and Spanish – some based on cartoons by Goya.
 ◆ **Flags.**
 ◆ The **library** contains over 7 000 books from the 16C to 19C.

---

### Museo Arqueológico Provincial★★

🕐 *Open 9am-8.30pm; Tu, 2.30-8.30pm; Sun and public hols, 9am-2.30pm.* 🕐 *Closed Mon.* ✍€1.50 (no charge for citizens of the European Union).* ☎ *957 47 40 11.*

Andalucía's leading archaeological museum is in the superb 16C Renaissance **Palacio de los Páez**. It has an interesting **façade**★ depicting warriors, escutcheons etc, though it is somewhat eroded.

The **ground floor** exhibits prehistoric and Iberian objects – such as zoomorphic sculptures – as well as Visigothic remains. The **Roman collection**★ around the patios includes toga-clad sculptures, reliefs, sarcophagi, mosaics, capitals and column tambours.

The **first floor galleries** display Hispano-Moorish ceramics, bronzes – the 10C **stag**★ *(cervatillo)* from Medina Azahara entirely decorated with plant motifs – and a unique collection of Moorish and Mudéjar well copings. The unusual **capital of the musicians** is decorated with human figures with mutilated heads.

## Alcázar de los Reyes Cristianos★

🕐 *Open 10am-2pm and 4.30-6.30pm, Sun and public hols, 9.30am-2.30pm.* 🕐 *Closed Mon.* 🎟️*€4 (no charge Fri).* ☎ *957 42 01 51.*

This fortress-residence was built by Alfonso XI in the 14C. The *alcázar* was the head-quarters of the Inquisition until 1821.

On display are the exceptional 3C AD **Roman sarcophagus**★, with an outstanding treatment of facial features and fabric, and an interesting collection of **mosaics**★. The **baths** *(downstairs, to the right, at the end of the corridor)* are Moorish in design. Cross the Mudéjar patio to visit the delightful Moorish-style **gardens**★ with their terraces, pools, fountains, cypress trees and flowers of every colour and scent.

## Torre de la Calahorra: Museo Vivo de al-Andalus

🕐 *Open May-Sep, 10am-2pm and 4.30-8.30pm; Oct-Apr, 10am-6pm.* 🎟️*€4.50.* ☎ *957 29 39 29.*

This Moorish fortress is at the southern end of the Puente Romano. Originally, its two towers were linked by a single arch; in the 14C, they were enlarged, and later modified again. The tower has been used variously as a prison for nobles, a barracks, and even a school.

It now houses an **audio-visual museum** dedicated to the history of the Córdoba Caliphate – a period of cultural, artistic, philosophical and scientific prosperity. The museum also contains an impressive **model**★ of the Mezquita in the 13C. Enjoy fine **views** of the city from atop the tower.

*Torre de la Calahorra*

## Museo Municipal Taurino

*Plazuela de Maimónides.* 🔑*Closed for remodeling until 2007.* ☎ *957 47 05 12.*

The **bullfighting museum** is housed in the 16C Casa de las Bulas. Access is via two attractive patios: the Mudéjar-influenced entrance patio, and the finely proportioned main patio. The collection includes engravings, posters, photographs and mementoes of Córdoba's most famous matadors, including Lagartijo, Guerrita, Machaquito and Manolete.

## Plaza del Potro

The elongated plaza del Potro takes its name from the small statue of a colt *(potro)* crowning the fountain at one end. This fountain dates from the 16C; on the opposite side is a monument to San Rafael. The square was once the site of the city's lively horse and mule fair.

The **Posada del Potro**, a charming inn described by Cervantes in *Don Quixote*, faces the square. It is now a cultural centre that mounts temporary exhibitions. 🔑*Closed for renovation.* ☎ *957 48 50 01.*

The entrance to both the Museo de Bellas Artes and the Museo Julio Romero de Torres is through a patio-garden opposite the fountain.

### Museo Julio Romero de Torres★

*To the right of the patio.* 🕐*Open 10am-2pm and 5.30-7.30 pm; Sun and public hols, 9.30am-2.30pm. Last admission 20 min before closing.* 🕐*Closed Mon.* 🎟️*€3 (no charge Fri)*☎ *957 49 19 09.*

This mansion, the birthplace of Julio Romero de Torres (1880-1930), houses a collection of his paintings, many of beautiful, dark-skinned women.

The ground floor contains a number of posters advertising *ferias* of the past; the upper floor exhibits his attractive female portraits such as *La Chiquita Piconera* (The Charcoal Girl), which manifest a magnificent psychological treatment of the feminine world (note the gaze of his subjects). Several canvases have religious themes, such as *The Virgin of the Lanterns*, a copy of which hangs in an altar outside the Mezquita. Follow calle San Francisco as far as calle San Fernando. To the left, after an 18C arch, is the **Iglesia de San Francisco**. The church belongs to a convent of great historical importance, although only a part of a cloister, to the left, now remains.

## Museo de Bellas Artes

*To the left of the patio.* ◷ *Open Tue, 2.30-8pm; Wed-Sat, 9am-8.30pm; Sun and public hols, 9am-2.30pm.* ◷ *Closed Mon, Tue morning, 1 and 6 Jan, 1 May, 24 Oct, 1 Nov and 25 Dec.* ᔕ€*1.50 (no charge for citizens of the European Union).* ☎ *957 47 13 14.*

The **Fine Arts Museum** displays works ranging from the 14C to the 20C, predominantly by local artists. It is the former Hospital de la Caridad, founded in the 15C and home to the museum and the School of Fine Arts by the second half of the 19C. The staircase, covered by a fine Mudéjar *artesonado* ceiling, has 16C and 17C murals. Of particular interest are: an *Immaculate Conception* by Juan Valdés Leal, in the former church; the collection of modern Cordoban and Spanish art dating from the second half of the 19C and first half of the 20C by the likes of Ramón Casas, José Gutiérrez Solana, Rusiñol and Zuloaga; and sculptures by the Cordoban artist Mateo Inurria.

## Plaza de la Corredera

This large, porticoed, rectangular square, accessed via vaulted passageways, recalls the main squares found in Castille. For centuries it was an important meeting-place and the setting for *autos-da-fé*, fiestas, executions, markets and, well into the 19C, bullfights. The **calleja del Toril**, a narrow alleyway, was used as a bull enclosure. This sober square has undergone significant restoration. The square visible today dates from the 17C. On Saturdays, its usual tranquillity is broken by the hustle and bustle of a busy **market**.

## Museo Regina

Near the plaza de la Corredera, this modern building is a musem of jewelry, a craft historically connected with the city. The permanent exhibition shows the fabrication processes. A hall for temporary exhibits occupies the remains of a 16C building.

## Mausoleo Romano

This Roman mausoleum, discovered in 1993 during work in the Jardines de la Victoria, is a robust, circular monument from the 1C AD, the golden age of Roman Córdoba.

## Iglesia del Colegio de Santa Victoria

The monumental columns decorating the façade of this church can be seen at the end of plaza de la Compañía. Part of the Santa Victoria school *(colegio)*, it is built in the neo-Classical style and dates from the middle of the 18C. Ventura Rodríguez was involved in its construction and designed the dome.

# Excursions

# Medina Azahara★★

*Leave Córdoba by A 431 (west of the map). After 8km/5mi bear right onto a signposted road.* Once on the road, the ochre mass of the 15C **Monasterio de San Jerónimo de Valparaíso** *(private residence;* ⊶ *not open to the public)*, comes into view.

The palace-city of Medina Azahara was built at the behest of Abd ar-Rahman III in 936. Chronicles of the day contain many references to its amazing luxury and splendour. The city had only just been completed when it was razed to the ground by the Berbers in 1013 during the war with the Caliphate of Córdoba, and thereafter it served as a source of construction materials. Archaeological excavations began in 1911. Although little more than 10% of the original city remains, it is still possible to imagine what this sumptuous city must have been like.

Medina Azahara is built in terraces: the upper terrace contained the Alcázar, with the residences of the Caliph and other dignitaries, as well as administrative and military dependencies; gardens and the large reception room were in the middle terrace, and a mosque (excavated) and other buildings were below.

## Tour

*Follow the signposted itinerary.* ◕ *Open May-Sep, Tue-Sat, 10am-8.30pm, Sun, 10am-2pm; Oct-Apr, Tue-Sat, 10am-6.30pm, Sun, 10am-2pm.* ◔ *Closed Mon and public hols.* ◉*€2.* ☎ *957 32 91 30.* The tour starts outside the north wall, marked by square towers. Access is via an angled doorway, typical of Islamic defensive architecture.

## Upper terrace

The **residential quarters** are to the right. The rest of the upper dwellings were built around two large square patios. To the west, at the highest point of the Alcázar, is the **Casa Real** or Royal Quarters *(Dar al-Mulk)* (◔━ *currently under restoration and not open to the public).*

To the left of the entry door are the **official quarters**. The **Casa de los Visires** *(Dar al-Wuzara)* comprises a suite of rooms. A large basilica-like hall is surrounded by dependencies and patios. The viziers held their civil audiences in the large hall. The garden in front is modern.

Several streets lead uphill to the impressive **portico**, the façade of a large parade ground. Only a few of the 15 magnificent arches remain; this was the monumental entrance to the Alcázar, through which ambassadors would enter.

### Middle terrace

The remains of the **mosque**, which stood on the lower terrace, are to the left, along the path leading down. The five aisles are at right angles to the rectangular patio, as is the base of the minaret in the northwest wall of the patio.

The middle terrace, overlooking the gardens, is dominated by the jewel of this site: the restored **Abd ar-Rahman III Room** (Salón de Abderramán III), the decoration of which gives an idea of the city's splendour in the 10C. Only the finest materials were used. Beautiful horseshoe arches with alternating voussoirs are supported by grey and blue marble, contrasting with the large white marble flagstones used for the floor paving. Note the geometric and plant motif decoration on the magnificent carved stone wall panels, including stylisations of the tree of life, a common theme in Hispano-Islamic art.

Opposite this room is the **Pabellón Central** or central pavilion, once used as a waiting room for those granted an audience with the Caliph. It is in the centre of the gardens and is surrounded by four small pools.

## Castillo de Almodóvar del Río★★

*25km/15mi west of Córdoba along A 431.* The name Almodóvar originates from the Arabic *al-Mudawwar,* "the round one", a clear reference to the castle hill. In the 8C, under Moorish rule, a large fortress stood here. Almódovar was subsequently under the rule of various taifa kingdoms before its reconquest by Fernando III in 1240.

▶ *Follow the road skirting town and continue to the fortress along a dirt track.*

The present **castle** was erected in the 14C in Gothic style and is considered one of the most important in Andalucía because of its beauty and excellent state of repair. It was restored at the beginning of the 20C when a neo-Gothic mansion was added. The town nestles below on the south bank of the River Guadalquivir.

From the castle the **views**★ of the river and the Cordoban countryside are quite magnificent. There are two walled enclo-

### Princess Zaida

Every 28 March a woman dressed in white appears, wailing from one of the towers. It is said that this is the ghost of Princess Zaida, who was taken prisoner by the Almoravids, and died from grief in the castle's dungeon upon hearing of the death of her husband in battle.

*Castillo de Almodóvar del Río*

B. Kaufmann/MICHELIN

sures – one in the form of a barbican – with eight towers of varying proportions. The largest, the *torre del homenaje* (keep), is in fact a turret. ◑*Open 11am-2.30 p.m and 4-7pm (summer, 8pm); Sat-Sun and public hols, 11am-7pm (summer, 8pm).* ◑*Closed 1 Jan and 25 Dec.* €5. ☎ *957 63 40 55.*

## Embalse de la Breña

*5km/3mi northwest of Almodóvar. Head back towards the town and take a signposted turning to the left.* The road winds across hills carpeted in olive trees to the **Embalse de la Breña**, a reservoir used by the private Córdoba sailing club. On the return journey, appreciate the magnificent silhouette of the Castillo de Almodóvar.

## Lals Ermitas

*13km/8mi northwest of Córdoba on the El Brillante road; 10km/6mi from Medina Azahara. by A 431, then left at the first crossroads (follow signs to "Ermitas").* From either direction, the **views**★ of the sierra and the surrounding countryside are quite delightful.

These 13 hermitages *(ermitas)* and a church in a wild, mountainous location date from the 18C, although the hermit tradition in the area goes back centuries.

In the beautiful paseo de los Cipreses (Cypress Avenue), the skull and short poem on the **Cruz del Humilladero** serve as a reminder of the transitory nature of life. Past the cross, the **Ermita de la Magdalena** is to the left, along with the hermits' cemetery and the church in the distance. Entering the vestibule of the **church** *(on the right)*, note the skull once used as a cup and plate. The rich decoration of the church – the result of donations – contrasts with the hermits' austere existence. Behind the high altar, in the room used as a chapterhouse, note also the attractive frieze of lustre *azulejos*.

The rest of the hermitage spreads over the hillside. Back at the entrance, a path leads to the **Balcón del Mundo**. From this viewpoint, dominated by an enormous Sacred Heart (1929), enjoy a magnificent **panorama**★★ of Córdoba and its surrounding countryside. To the right, the view extends to the hilltop Castillo de Almodóvar del Río.

## Driving Tour

## From Córdoba to Fuente Obejuna *131km/71mi*

**Córdoba**★★★ – *see CÓRDOBA*

▶ *Head north from Córdoba along N 432. After 30km/18mi, turn left at a crossroads onto CP 81 and continue for a further 17.5km/11mi to Obejo.*

### Obejo

The 13C **Iglesia Parroquial de San Antonio Abad** is to the left, alongside the remains of a long-forgotten fortress. This small parish church is particularly charming. Three aisles separated by stilted arches rest on pillars and columns. Note the last two columns on the left-hand side, topped by **capitals**★ with plant motifs of Moorish origin. Several of the bases are in fact inverted capitals. The church's most noteworthy external feature is its sober and rustic Mudéjar tower. *If closed, the person living opposite the church will show you around.* ☎ *957 36 90 68.*

▶ *Rejoin N 432.*

*View of Bélmez and its castle*

The road traverses olive groves to the river. Past the bridge, views are impressive, especially when the oleander is in full bloom. The **road**★ crosses mountain pastures populated by flocks of sheep, and oak forest where a deer might appear. Views of the River Guadalbarbo on this tortuous ascent are memorable.

▶ *At a crossroads, continue straight on for 2.5km/1.5mi.*

## El Vacar

The ruins of an imposing rectangular fortress stand atop a hill to the right, looking down on the Puente Nuevo reservoir to the west. Two dirt tracks heading off the main road, 100m/110yd and 200m/220yd respectively, before El Vacar, lead to an esplanade providing a clearer view of the sober, bare walls of this 10C edifice.

▶ *Return to N 432 and head northwest.*

## Espiel

This picturesque village of cobbled streets and whitewashed houses has a town hall from 1792 which used to serve as a public granary. Espiel's 16C parish church, named after St Sebastian, is topped by a bell tower, a favourite nesting place for storks.

▶ *Continue for 21km/13mi along N 432 to Bélmez.*

## Bélmez

The road crosses fields of sunflowers to this town at the foot of a rocky outcrop crowned by a Moorish **castle** which was rebuilt after the Reconquest.
Alongside the 19C town hall stands the **Museo Histórico de Bélmez y del Territorio Minero**, in a former public granary. The museum retraces mining activities which date back to the 18C following the discovery of a rich seam of coal in the area. Today, the town is home to a mining school. ⊙ *Open Mon-Sat, 10am-2pm and 6-9pm.* ⊙ *Closed Sun and public hols. Free entry.* ☎ *957 58 00 12.*

**Castle** – The keep and walls, the latter punctuated with cylindrical and prismatic towers, are largely intact. To reach the castle, follow the road from the square, opposite the 18C **parish church**. To the right, after 50m/55yd, note the **Ermita de la Virgen del Castillo** (Chapel of the Virgin of the Castle). A ramp ascends to the foot of the castle walls *(5min)*. The more daring can continue up along a difficult path between the rocks to the first section of wall; note the cistern *(aljibe)* on the left-hand side. Steps lead from a patio to the terrace behind this first section. Beyond ((⌂) *only*

## "Who killed the Knight Commander?"

**Lope de Vega** (1562-1635) immortalised the town in his play *Fuenteovejuna*, in which he relates how the inhabitants, pushed to the breaking point by the atrocities committed by the Knight Commander Fernán Gómez de Guzmán, rebelled and subsequently murdered him. The judge dispatched to the town by the Catholic Monarchs to investigate the crime was only able to elicit the reply "Fuenteovejuna, señor" to his question "Who killed the Knight Commander?". Upon hearing of the outrages committed by the *comendador*, Isabel and Fernando approved the town's conduct. This episode has remained as an example of unity and rebellion against tyranny.

*recommended for those with a good head for heights)*, the upper part of the castle offers magnificent **views** of Fuente Obejuna and its surroundings.
The nearby **Embalse de Sierra Boyera** is a popular base for water sports enthusiasts.

## Fuente Obejuna

*23km/14mi west along N 432.*
A scenic drive through wooded landscapes leads to the small town of Fuente Obejuna, on a hill near the source of the River Guadiato. It is well worth strolling through this historic town to admire the Renaissance mansions which witness to past glories.

### WHERE TO STAY

⊜ **Hotel El Comendador** – *Luis Rodríguez, 25 - Fuente Obejuna -* ☎ *957 58 52 22 - www.hotelcomendadorfuenteobejuna.com - cerrado 2ª quincena sep -* 🍽 *- 13 rooms.*Centrally located with large, comfortable rooms, some with valley views. One of the few restaurants in the town is here.

### Plaza Mayor

In the upper section of the town is the impressive, irregular , largely granite square, fronted by the town hall and parish church.

**Iglesia de Nuestra Señora del Castillo** – This 15C church contains several interesting works of art within its frescoed walls. The presbytery houses a magnificent **Renaissance retable**★ with high-relief sculptures of scenes from the Life and Passion of Christ. It is dominated by the 14C statue of the Virgin of the Castle, which was discovered in a niche in the old castle walls. ◷ *Open in summer, Mon-Sat, 8.30-9.30pm, Sun and public hols, 8.30-10am; otherwise, Mon-Sat, 7-8pm, Sun and public hols, 8.30-10am.* ◷ *If closed, call* ☎ *957 58 41 63.*
The Sacrarium Chapel *(Capilla del Sagrario,* left of the chancel) is adorned with *azulejo* panelling. A 16C late-Gothic **retable** with seven tablets is dedicated to the Virgin Mary. A second, Baroque retable, dominated by the Virgin of the Rosary, is in the chapel to the right. The exterior has a doorway with four semicircular stilted arches on three columns with acanthus leaf capitals, possibly of Roman origin.

### Casa Cardona

This unusual Modernist-style mansion house was built between 1906 and 1911.

# COSTA DE ALMERÍA★

This coast is characterised by extensive beaches, coves lapped by crystal-clear waters, fishing villages turned into pleasant resorts, and areas of outstanding, almost virgin, natural beauty. Add a superb climate with little rainfall and sunshine almost all year and the result is a location that is becoming one of the region's most popular tourist destinations.

▶ **Orient Yourself:** The Costa de Almería along the southeastern Iberian Peninsula from Adra to Mojácar, and includes the provincial capital, Almería. The A 7- E 15, just in from the coast, is the principal highway.

🕐 **Organizing Your Time:** Allow a day or two to drive through picturesque villages, in addition to an extended beach stay.

🧒 **Especially for Kids:** Some of the most popular beaches are on this coast.

👁 **Also See:** TABERNAS, Sierra de Los FILABRES, GUADIX (109km/68mi NW of Almería), and Las ALPUJARRAS.

## Driving Tours

### From Adra to Almería 1 *117km/73mi – allow half a day*

#### Adra

This resort in a fertile plain was a Phoenician and Roman outpost, and the last place yielded by the Moors. Adra has a fishing port, a marina, a good beach and several 17C and 18C mansions. The Iglesia de la Inmaculada Concepción contains a *Christ of the Expiration*, attributed to Alonso de Mena. The Torre de los Perdigones, a 45m/147ft-high tower originally part of a 19C lead foundry, is now the tourist office.

▶ *Head north along A 347.*

#### Berja

The Roman Virgi (which evolved into *vergel*, meaning "orchard"), at the foot of the Sierra de Gádor, has a number of handsome noble Renaissance mansions and fountains, and the remains of a Roman amphitheatre.

▶ *Head back towards Adra, then follow A 7 – E 15 towards Almería.*

*The "Sea of Plastic" near Berja*

## Address Book

### WHERE TO EAT

⊜⊜⊜ **Náutico Almerimar** – *in the Almerimar marina – 10 km/6mi S of El Ejido –* ☎ *950 49 70 73.* ⊙ *Closed Mon and 7-31 Jan.* A famous fish and seafood restaurant, terrace with marina views.

⊜⊜⊜ **Al-Baida** – *Avenida Las Gaviotas, 94 – Roquetas de Mar –* ☎ *950 33 38 21 –* ⊙ *Closed Wed and in Mar.* A well-known local eatery serving fish and seafood. Simple decor, plus an aquarium containing live lobsters.

### WHERE TO STAY

⊜⊜ **Hotel Hesperia Sabinal** – *Avenida Las Gaviotas – Roquetas de Mar –* ☎ *950 33 36 00 –* 🅿 *– 522 rooms.* In the heart of the beach area. A large hotel complex with spacious rooms overlooking the sea.

The road offers attractive **views** of the Sierra de la Contraviesa to the left, with the Cerrón peak (1 238m/4 060ft) in the foreground.

After a bend in the road, the plastic-covered fields of the **Campo de Dalías** come into view. Between Adra and Almería, highway passes plastic greenhouses which produce several crops a year, in addition to early grapes, vegetables and flowers.

### Almerimar

This modern tourist complex also has a golf course and marina.

▷ *Return to N 340 – E 15 and turn off onto A 391 at Km 429.*

### Roquetas de Mar

This fishing village has been transformed into a lively resort. The remains of the old castle can be seen by the lighthouse *(faro)*. Roquetas has a fishing port and marina, golf course and a water park.

The **Urbanización Roquetas de Mar** *(3.5km/2mi)* has attractive beaches of fine sand and a long palm-lined promenade with views of the Gulf of Almería and Cabo de Gata. The avenida del Mediterráneo teems with shops and restaurants.

▷ *Head back along A 391 and turn right at El Parador.*

### Aguadulce

This large and popular beach resort is in an area of abundant vegetation just 11km/7mi from Almería. The nature reserve of Punta Entinas–Sabinar, an area of sand dunes and marshland, is to the southeast. Juniper bushes, bulrushes and canes predominate in this unusual landscape.

### From Aguadulce to Almería

The road follows the coast, hugging cliff tops and tunneling through rock. The approach to Almería offers views of the city, the bay, the port and the fortress.

**Almería** – *see ALMERÍA*

# From Almería to Mojácar ② *132km/82.5mi – allow one day*

**Níjar** – *see Parque Natural de CABO DE GATA-NÍJAR*

**Parque Natural de Cabo de Gata-Níjar**★★ – *see Parque Natural de CABO DE GATA-NÍJAR*

## Agua Amarga

The houses of this seaside village appear after a bend in the road. The resort's attractive and well-maintained beach is framed by two rocky promontories.

## From Agua Amarga to Mojácar Playa

*32km/20mi – allow 45min.* This stretch of road offers attractive views of the coast, including several watchtowers. After a short distance, a branch road to the right heads up to the Mesa Roldán lighthouse *(faro)* and fortified tower *(1.5km/1mi)*. Back on the main road, pass a power station, the port of Endesa and a beach, the Playa de Marinicas. Opposite, the whitewashed **Casa del Laberinto** or Casa de André Block, built in the 1960s, is frequently featured on postcards and posters.

## Carboneras

This fishing village developed around a 16C castle, the **Castillo de San Andrés**, built by the Marquess of Carpio. A small **market** is held Thursdays.
Between Carboneras and the Castillo de Macenas *(13km/8mi)*, the road traverses an arid mountain landscape with the occasional delightful view of the Mediterranean, culminating in the **Torre-vigía del Rayo**, a watchtower.

## Castillo de Macenas

This coastal watchtower dates from the 17C. Views extend to the south to the **Torre del Perulico** which, like many other watchtowers, was built by the Moors in the 13C and 14C. A dirt track parallel to the coast runs south past the tower to several nudist beaches, including the Playa de Bordonares *(3km/2mi)*.

## Mojácar Playa

The Mojácar municipality includes 17km/10.5mi of beaches and coves. Mojácar Playa is a modern resort of whitewashed tourist developments.

B.Kaufmann / MICHELIN

*Torre del Perulico*

## Mojácar★

This enchanting town, inhabited since antiquity, enjoys a superb **setting**★ on a promontory, with delightful views of the Mediterranean just to the east and the unusual rock formations of the surrounding plain. The old hillside quarter has a Moorish character, with narrow, cobbled streets lined by whitewashed houses adorned with floral arrangements. The town was only reconquered by the Christians in 1488.
A significant foreign community, particularly from northern Europe, gives Mojácar a cosmopolitan feel. The many small restaurants, outdoor cafés and craft shops attract tens of thousands of visitors every year, particularly in summer.

## The town

*Leave your car in the lower part of town.* The beauty of Mojácar mainly resides in the charm of its well-maintained buildings and its superb vistas. It is ideal town for aimless wandering aimlessly, with surprising discoveries at every turn.
The best starting point is the pleasant **plaza Nueva**, fronted by the 18C Ermita de Nuestra Señora de los Dolores, a former chapel and now a shop. The *mirador* on the square is the perfect viewpoint. Below are the remains of Mojácar la Vieja, the

original town.Cuesta del Castillo, a street to the left of the square, heads up to the **castle mirador**; nothing remains of the castle but its views to the coast.

Calle de la Iglesia to the right of plaza Nueva leads to the **Iglesia de Santa María**, its ochre-coloured walls standing out against white houses. Built after the Reconquest, it has fortress-like walls, a bell tower to one side, and buttresses on the other. Several picturesque narrow streets surround the church.

**Calle de Enmedio**, parallel to calle de la Iglesia, is lined by small restaurants and bars. This street passes in front of plaza del Ayuntamiento, from where it is possible to walk down to the 15C **Puerta de la Ciudad** (Town Gate), once part of the defensive walls. Walk through to the charming **plaza de las Flores** (of the Flowers).

▶ *Rejoin the coast road and continue north.*

## Garrucha

*5.5km/3.5mi north.* This former fishing village with excellent beaches becomes lively in summer. Garrucha has a marina and promenade. An 18C fortified watchtower can still be seen along the coast to the south of the resort.

▶ *Head north from Garrucha along C 3327.*

> ### 😊 A Bit of Advice 😊
>
> **Boat trips**: For those wishing to take to the water, excursions to Mojácar Bay, Carboneras and the Parque Natural de Cabo de Gata-Níjar are all available from Garrucha *(contact the tourist office for further information,* ☎ *950 13 27 83).*

## Vera

The plaza Mayor is fronted by the fortress-like 16C **Iglesia de la Encarnación**, a church with four solid corner towers. To the left stands the 19C **town hall** with a sober stone doorway; note the standard hanging in the council room, presented by the Catholic Monarchs. The **Museo Histórico Municipal** next door has sections devoted to the archaeology, history and ethnography of Vera. ⏱ *Open Mon-Fri, 10am-2pm and 5-8pm; Sat, 10am-2pm.* ⏱ *Closed Sun and public hols. No charge.* ☎ *950 39 30 16.*

Along the coast is the Vera Natura nudist resort.

## Cuevas de Almanzora

*6km/4mi northwest via A 8303 and then A 7 – E 15.*

The town of Cuevas de Almanzora is neara lake in an area rich in mineral deposits and archaeological remains. The town prospered in the 19C following the discovery of silver in the nearby Sierra de la Almagrera. Mansions in the old quarter, as well as the Capilla del Carmen in the Iglesia de Nuestra Señora de la Encarnación testify to the wealth of this period.There are cave dwellings close to the town.

A water park is located along the road to Vera.

### Castle

The 16C castle was expanded with the addition of a neo-Classical building, the Casa de la Tercia, now the municipal library. The walled enclosure is visible.

### Museo Antonio Manuel Campoy

The museum, named for a newspaper art critic, is in a restored part of the castle. Campoy's private collection of contemporary Spanish art (paintings, sketches and engravings), firearms and numerous personal mementoes are displayed. ⏱ *Open Jul to mid-Sep, 10am-1.30pm; otherwise, Tue-Sat, 10am-1.30pm and 5-8pm, Sun, 10am-1.30pm.* ⏱ *Closed Mon and public hols. No charge.* ☎ *950 45 80 63.*

### Museo de Arqueología

The archaeological museum in the castle focuses on the El Argar culture. Finds from nearby Antas and Fuente Álamo are on display.
Upon leaving the castle note the cave dwellings to the left.

### Huércal Overa

*25km/15mi north along N 340–E 15.* A Moorish fortress stands atop a hill on the outskirts. The 18C **Iglesia de la Asunción** holds an interesting Baroque altarpiece and the sculptures (some by Salzillo) borne in **Holy Week** processions, when three religious brotherhoods *(cofradías)* compete in pomp and ceremony.

# COSTA DE HUELVA★

The Huelva coast, running southeast from Portugal, is a succession of sun-blessed beaches interrupted by deltas where the Guadiana, Guadalquivir and Tinto enter the Atlantic. Relatively undeveloped, it forms part of the Costa de la Luz (Coast of Light). Columbus departed from this coast on his voyage of discovery.

▶ **Orient Yourself:** The Costa de Huelva extends from Ayamonte, at the mouth of the River Guadiana, to the Parque Nacional de Doñana. The A 49-E 1 highway runs between Ayamonte and Huelva, while the N 442 and A 494 embrace the coast.

◔ **Also See:** LA RÁBIDA, El ROCÍO and SANLÚCAR DE BARRAMEDA.

## Driving Tours

### Parque Nacional de Doñana to Palos de la Frontera ☐1 *49km/30mi – allow half a day*

**Parque Nacional de Doñana★★★** *– See Parque Nacional de DOÑANA*

▶ *Head south from the El Acebuche information centre along A 483. Turn right in Torre de la Higuera towards Matalascañas.*

The road to this resort crosses an attractive section of the Doñana National Park.

### Matalascañas

Matalascañas is one of the busiest resorts in Andalucía, with numerous apartment blocks, nightclubs, outdoor bars and a huge range of leisure facilities.

▶ *Return to Torre de la Higuera and head northwest along A 494.*

### Mazagón

The fine sands of **Playa de Mazagón** extend 10km/6mi from the mouth of the River Tinto to the Torre del Loro. This quiet beach offers good-quality campsites and chalet complexes and a marina, and just as important, no high-rises. The Parador de Mazagón commands delightful **views** of this Atlantic coastline.

▶ *Continue northwest along A 494.*

## Palos de la Frontera★

Columbus sailed from this picturesque small town on his voyage of discovery in 1492. It is also the birthplace of the Pinzón brothers, who accompanied Columbus. The charm of Palos lies in its whitewashed houses, narrow alleyways and lively atmosphere, best enjoyed in charming squares.

### Casa-Museo de Martín Alonso Pinzón

☛ *Closed for restoration.* ☎ *959 35 01 99.*
The home of the native navigator guards his personal mementoes (signed letters, navigational equipment etc), as memorabilia relating to the seaplane Plus Ultra , which flew from Palos de la Frontera to Buenos Aires in 1926.

### Iglesia de San Jorge

◷ *Open Apr-Sep, Tue-Fri, 10am-2pm and 5-9pm, Sat-Sun and public hols, 11am-8pm; Oct-Mar, Tue-Sun, 10am-7pm.* ◷ *Closed Mon, 1 and 7-31 Jan, and 24-25 and 31 Dec.*◷*€3.* ☎ *959 53 05 97.*

## Address Book

### WHERE TO EAT

The main square in **Matalascañas** is lined by lunch and dinner places. Two Andalusian-style restaurants are particularly recommended: **Manolo León**, which specialises in meat dishes, and **Manolo Vázquez**, whose menu is dominated by fish and seafood. In **Punta Umbría**, the plaza del Mercado is a good place to find fresh seafood.

⊝⊜ **Caribe II** – *Calle Nao – El Rompido* – ☎ *959 39 90 27.* The terrace with port views is ideal a leisurely lunch. Specialities include squid *(calamares)*, red mullet *(salmonete)*, crayfish *(langostinos)* and lobster *(bogavante)*.

⊝⊜ **El Remo** – *Avenida de Conquistadores, 123 – Mazagón (on the way to Matalascañas) –* ☎ *959 53 61 38 - www.restauranteelremo.com.* One of the best restaurants in the area. A pleasant terrace with upholstered chairs and a bar overlooking the beach. The menu includes fish, seafood and grilled meats.

⊝⊜⊜ **Miramar** – *Miramar, 1 – Punta Umbría –* ☎ *959 31 12 43 - www.restaurantemiramarsl.com.* Recently remodeled with large, airy dining areas, the Miramar serves excellent fish and rice dishes.

### WHERE TO STAY

⊝ **Hotel Santa María** – *Palos de la Frontera, near the Monasterio de Santa María de la Rábida –* ☎ *955 53 00 01 – 18 rooms.* A small hotel with a large restaurant offering views of the Tinto estuary. Unfortunately, just one double room enjoys a view of the river.

⊝⊜ **Hotel La Pinta** – *Rábida, 79 – Palos de la Frontera –* ☎ *959 35 05 11 – 30 rooms.* A delightful small hotel with adequate rooms in the centre of Palos.

⊝⊜ **Hotel Carabela Santa María** – *Avenida de Conquistadores – Mazagón –* ☎ *959 53 60 18 - www.hotelcarabela-santamaria.com -* ▣ ▤ ⏦ – *73 rooms.* This hotel is on the way in along the Huelva road. Modern rooms, a bar and a restaurant.

⊝⊜⊜ **Pato Amarillo** – *Urbanización Everluz – Punta Umbría –* ☎ *959 31 12 50 www.hotelpatoamarillo.com -* ▣ ⏋ – *120 rooms.* ◷*Closed 1 Nov-15 Mar.* Many rooms have pleasant sea views. Garden, bar and restaurant.

⊝⊜⊜ **Hotel Cortijo Golf** – *Sector E, Parcela 15 – Matalascañas –* ☎ *959 44 87 00 –* ⏋ ⏦ – *126 rooms.* The hotel, distinguishable by its towers, has a large swimming pool, two restaurants, regional-style bar and comfortable rooms. Organised activities in summer.

⊝⊜⊜⊜ **Parador de Mazagón** – *Playa de Mazagón, 7km/4mi SE along A 494 –* ☎ *959 53 63 00 - www.parador.es -* ▣ ▤ ⏦ – *62 rooms.* This modern *parador* dominates Mazagón beach. Rooms with terrace and panoramic views. Dining specialties include sea bass *(lubina)*, lobster *(langosta)*, crayfish *(langostinos)*, prawns *(gambas)* and loin of pork *(solomillo de cerdo)*.

*La Flecha de El Rompido*

This fine 15C Gothic-Mudéjar church fronts an attractive small square. Columbus prayed here on the morning of his departure (3 August). Behind the church, La Fontanilla, a fountain crowned by a small Mudéjar shrine, supplied the water for the three caravels, the *Niña*, the *Pinta* and the *Santa María*.

# From Huelva to Ayamonte 2 *77km/48mi – allow one day*

**Huelva★** – *See HUELVA*

▷ *Head west along A 497 towards Punta Umbria.*

## Punta Umbría
*Punta Umbría can be reached in summer by ferry from Huelva.* This former rest centre for miners is in the salt marshes of the Paraje Natural de las Marismas del Odiel nature reserve. Nowadays it is a popular resort with a small marina and attractive beaches lined by pine groves. The daily early-morning fish auction is worth seeing, as is the fishermen's procession to honour the Virgin Mary on 15 August every year. The **Paraje Natural de Enebrales de Punta Umbría**, is a protected area of sand dunes in a landscape dominated by savin, juniper, mastic and hawthorn.

▷ *Head back along the same road. After 7km/4.5mi, leave A 497 at El Portil.*

## El Portil
This section of coast is one of the province's busiest resort areas. The nearby **Reserva Natural de la Laguna de El Portil**, a lagoon of outstanding beauty, is home to a variety of birds, including the grey heron and grebe.

▷ *Continue northwest along A 4104.*

## El Rompido
This small fishing port has a pleasant dune-lined beach popular with summer visitors. The **Paraje Natural Marismas del Río Piedras y Flecha de El Rompido★**, is a protected salt marsh *(marisma)* off the road towards La Antilla. This reserve is home to the black-headed gull, pintail, oystercatcher and common egret.

▷ *Head north along A 4106.*

## Cartaya

The **plaza Redonda** is a tranquil square adorned with orange trees and elegant wrought-iron street lamps. Around the square are the 16C Iglesia de San Pedro, with its *azulejo*-decorated campanile, the town hall and the Casa de Cultura.

▶ *Continue along N 431, heading southwest to Lepe.*

## Lepe

The town is in an area that produces strawberries, figs and melons.

▶ *Head south.*

## La Antilla

Crowds flock to La Antilla's delightful beaches, yet the quiet town of older houses remains sedate, in contrast to nearby Islantilla, a modern complex of apartment blocks and a luxurious golf course. At the mouth of the River Piedras is **El Terrón,** worth a visit to watch fishermen and to enjoy seafood.

▶ *Return to Lepe and follow N 431 to the west.*

**Ayamonte★** – *See AYAMONTE*

# COSTA DEL SOL★★

The Sun Coast stretches along the Mediterranean from Tarifa on the Straits of Gibraltar to the Cabo de Gata, a headland east of Almería. Visitors are drawn to a wonderful climate, sandy beaches, whitewashed towns and villages and activities for every taste. Sadly, most of the charming fishing communities have been transformed beyond recognition since the tourist boom of the 1970s. This stretch of coastline comes to life during the summer. Over the past decade or so, luxurious holiday complexes have sprung up, many close to the dozens of golf courses that dot the coast, giving rise to a new nickname, the **Costa del Golf.**

▶ **Orient Yourself:** The Málaga coast stretches from Sotogrande to Torremolinos, southwest of Málaga. The Serranía de Ronda mountain range protects the coast from weather inland. The A 7-N340 is the main coastal highway.

🕐 **Also See:** ALGECIRAS, RONDA (50km/31mi N of San Pedro de Alcántara), MÁLAGA (9km/5.5mi NE of Torremolinos) and ANTEQUERA (55km/34mi N of Málaga).

## Driving Tours

### From Torremolinos to Sotogrande

*234km/146mi- allow two days.* 🕐 *See itinerary on map.*

## Torremolinos

Torremolinos has experienced huge growth since it first attracted artists in the 1950s. Traditional architecture has given way to hotels and tourist complexes for visitors attracted by the sunny climate, miles and miles of beaches, and endless choice of leisure activities. The **calle de San Miguel** is the commercial hub, but it's also here that you'll find the last of the windmills for which the town was named. The **paseo**

# Address Book

## TOURIST OFFICES

**Benalmádena** – *Avenida Antonio Machado, 10 – Benalmádena Costa* – ☎ 952 44 12 95 – www.benalmadena.com

**Estepona** – *Avenida San Lorenzo, 1 – 29680 Estepona* – ☎ 952 80 09 13 –www.estepona.com

**Fuengirola** – *Avenida Jesús Santos Rein, 6 – Fuengirola* – ☎ 952 46 74 57 –www. fuengirola.org

**Marbella** – *Glorieta de la Fontanilla – 29600Marbella* – ☎ 952 77 14 42 – www. pgb.es/marbella (also on motorway)

**Torremolinos** – *Plaza Blas Infante, 1 – 29260 Torremolinos* – ☎ 952 37 95 12 – *Playa de las Comunidades Autónomas – Playa del Bajondillo – 29620 Torremolinos* – ☎ 952 37 19 09.

## TRANSPORT

**Airport** – The only airport along the Costa del Sol is 9km/6mi from Málaga towards Torremolinos *(information: ☎ 952 04 88 84/04; arrivals: ☎ 952 04 88 45/44; departures: ☎ 952 04 88 04/42).* Buses serve coastal resorts, and the suburban train line *(tren de cercanías)* connects with points as far as Fuengirola *(see Trains)*. Taxis are also an option. A hired car is also a good choice, given the coastal sprawl and excellent roads.

**Trains** – Long-distance trains depart only from the Málaga station *(Explanada de la Estación – ☎ 952 36 05 60; RENFE office in Málaga – ☎ 902 24 02 02).*

Local trains operate every 30 min to Fuengirola via the airport, La Colina, Torremolinos and Benalmádena, from 6.33am to 11.15pm. Top ticket price is about €2.

**Benalmádena** – *Avenida de la Estación* – ☎ 952 12 80 84.

**Fuengirola – Avenida Juan Gómez "Juanito"** – ☎ 952 47 85 40.

**Marbella** – *Calle Strachan, 2* – ☎ 952 21 31 22.

**Torremolinos** – *Avenida de la Estación* – ☎ 952 12 80 85.

**Inter-city buses** – The **Portillo** company operates comfortable buses to major towns and many points between. Every town or city also has a station for buses to Spanish and foreign destinations.

**Benalmádena – Portillo** bus routes connect the three parts of Benalmádena with Torremolinos from 7am to 10.30pm. Tickets can be purchased on board or at the booth in avenida Antonio Machado (near McDonald's).

**Estepona** – Avenida de España (☎ 952 80 29 54).

**Fuengirola** – Matías Sáenz de Tejada at calle Alfonso XIII (☎ 952 47 50 66).

**Marbella** – Buses depart from avenida Ricardo Soriano, 21 (☎ 952 77 21 92) to destinations in Spain and abroad.

**Taxis – Benalmádena** – ☎ 952 44 15 45/11 00.

**Estepona** – ☎ 952 80 29 00/04.

**Fuengirola** – ☎ 952 47 10 00.

**Marbella** – ☎ 952 77 44 88/00 53.

**San Pedro de Alcántara** – ☎ 952 77 44 88.

**Torremolinos** – ☎ 952 38 06 00.

**Local buses** – *Málaga bus information* – ☎ 922 36 72 00.

**Benalmádena** – A regular bus service operates between Benalmádena Costa, Benalmádena Pueblo and Arroyo de la Miel, stopping frequently en route. A one-way ticket costs €1.05

**Torremolinos** – Two bus lines (L1 and L2) cover Torremolinos. A one-way ticket costs €1.05.

**Fuengirola, Marbella and Estepona** – There is no local bus service in these three resorts.

**Marinas** – Every major resort has a marina for pleasure craft. The main ones are:

**Puerto Banús** – *6km/3.6mi from central Marbela* – 915 moorings for boats ranging from 8m/26ft to 50m/164ft. Puerto Banús, home to some of the world's most luxurious sailing craft, is one of the resort's most popular attractions.

**Puerto Marina** – This newer marina in Benalmádena is one of the largest moorings for pleasure craft on the Costa del Sol with a capacity for 1 000 boats. Other marinas are in Estepona, Marbella and Fuengirola.

## WHERE TO EAT

**La Carihuela**, the pedestrian zone of **Torremolinos**, has dozens of bars and restaurants,as well as shops and hotels. Outstanding restaurants include **Casa**

**Juan** for seafood and **El Roqueo**, a classic with a sea-view terrace.

**El Balcón de la Virgen** – *Calle Remedios, 2 (old town) – Marbella – ☎ 952 77 60 92 92 - www.hosteleriamalaga.com/elbalcondelavirgen – Open for dinner only – ⏰Closed Sun and 20 Dec-20 Jan.* In an attractive street lined by an endless succession of restaurant terraces in the old quarter. The restaurant, recognisable by the image of the Virgin Mary on the façade, is popular with tourists. Andalusian cuisine.

**Casa Eladio** – *Virgen de los Dolores, 6 (old town) - Marbella - ☎ 95 277 00 83 - ⏰Closed Thu and 10 Jan-10 Feb.* A longstanding family-run restaurant, good for real Spanish cooking at an attractive price. Regional specialties are *ajo blanco* (like gazpacho) and *pellejo de patata* (potato peel).

**Los Rosales** – *Damas, 12 - Estepona - ☎ 952 79 29 45 - www.infhos.com/losrosales - ⏰Closed in Nov.* In an alley by the picturesque plaza de las Flores, an unpretentious seafood eatery with a good tapas bar.

## TAPAS

**Altamirano** – *Plaza Altamirano, 3 – Marbella - ☎ 952 82 49 32 - ⏰ Closed Wed and 10 Jan-20 Feb.* This unpretentious restaurant on a small square in the old quarter specialises in fish and seafood. *Azulejo* decoration on the façade.

**La Rada** – *Avenida de España and calle Caridad, Neptuno bldg – Estepona – ☎ 952 79 10 36.* A must for visitors. A pleasant atmosphere and delicious fish and seafood.

**La Venencia** – *Avenida Miguel Cano, 15 – Marbella – ☎ 952 85 79 13.* A bar with a regional air, close to the sea with barrel tables on the pavement. Always busy.

## WHERE TO STAY

**Hostal El Pilar** – *Plaza de las Flores, 10 – Estepona – ☎ 952 80 00 18 - www.ainte.net/hostalelpilar 20 rooms.* Time seems to have stood still in this pretty Andalusian house on Estepona's main square, with black and white family photos on the walls and an imposing staircase leading to the basic but pleasant bedrooms.

*J. Malburet/MICHELIN*

Puerto Banús

**Hostal Guadalupe** – *Calle Peligro, 15 – Torremolinos – ☎ 952 38 19 37 - www.hostalguadalupe.com10 rooms.* A *pensión* in a narrow street just 50m/55yd from the beach. Basic, but spotless rooms. Rates rise in August.

**Mediterráneo Carihuela Hotel** – *Calle Carmen, 43 – Torremolinos – ☎ 952 38 14 52 - www.usuarios.lycos.es/hotelmediterraneo – 33 rooms (rooms with sea views are slightly more expensive).* Located in one of the liveliest and most attractive parts of Torremolinos. Modest rooms with terraces overlooking the promenade.

**Hotel Lima** – *Avenida Antonio Belón, 2 – ☎ 952 77 05 00 - www.hotellimamarbella.com – 64 rooms.* Comfortable, just 60m/66yd from the beach and 100m/110yd from Marbella's old quarter.

**Hotel La Fonda** – *Calle Santo Domingo, 7 – Benalmádena – ☎ 952 56 83 24 - www.fondahotel.com– 26 rooms.* A charming hotel in the Sierra de Castillejos, overlooking the Mediterranean.

*B. Kaufmann/MICHELIN*

La Carihuela

Spacious rooms, indoor pool, patios and terraces with views of the hills and sea.

⊜⊜ **Hotel La Morada Más Hermosa** – *Montenebros, 16 (old town) - Marbella -* ☎ *95 292 44 67 - www.lamoradamasher-mosa.com – 6 rooms.* A personalized hotel on a lane bursting with plants. Charming rooms are individually decorated in country Andalusian style. Room nº 2 has a pleasant terrace, room nº 5 a wooden canopy.

⊜⊜⊜ **Tropicana** – *Calle Trópico, 6 – Torremolinos – ☎ 952 38 66 00 - www.hotel-tropicana.net – 84 rooms.* A quality hotel with exotic architecture, private beach, swimming pool with garden and a restaurant (Mango).

⊜⊜⊜ **Hotel El Fuerte** – *Avenida El Fuerte – Marbella – ☎ 952 86 15 00 - www.fuertehoteles.com – 233 rooms, 2 suites.* This high-end seaside hotel by the sea has its own tropical gardens is just minutes from Marbella's old quarter.

## GOING OUT FOR THE EVENING

In **Benalmádena**, life centres on the Puerto Marina and nearby plaza Solymar. Bars in plaza de la Mezquita de Arroyo de la Miel are also popular, although the marina and port area are mainstays, attracting visitors 24 hours a day. Benalmádena has its own casino, the **Casino Torrequebrada** (☎ *952 44 60 00),* as well as the **Tívoli World** amusement park in the Arroyo de la Miel district (🕐 *open daily, Apr-Dec – ☎ 952 57 70 16)* which in summer features concerts by major artists.

**Maracas** – *Puerto Marina – Benalmáde-na - ☎ 649 88 11 32 - www.maracas-bar.com – 🕐 Open 11am-5am.* This spacious, multi-functional bar with tropical decor in the port area is popular for a coffee on the terrace, a cocktail or for dancing until dawn. Attracts a mixed age group day and night.

**Monet** – *Puerto Marina – Benalmádena – 🕐 Open 10am-4am.* A café by day and pub by night. Views of the port and a large terrace with wicker chairs. A pleasant location for an early-evening drink. At night, drinks are served at the two bars, one outside, the other indoors, with dancing.

**Tabú** – *Puerto Marina – Benalmádena – 🕐 Open 11am-6am.* This is a marina-view café, bar and disco in one, with Caribbean-inspired decoration and a huge choice of fruit juices and cocktails popular with young and old alike. Salsa classes for women on Thursdays and Sundays.

**Disco Kiu** – *Plaza Solymar – Benalmáde-na Costa – 🕐 Open midnight-7am.* An enormous 80s-style nightclub with various rooms devoted to salsa, mainstream pop and house. Popular with a young international crowd.

**Calle Real**, in the town centre, and the **Puerto Deportivo** (marina) are the hub of life in **Estepona**. In the afternoon and evening the port is pleasant for a quiet drink on one of the many terraces. At night, the action tends to move to the quieter bars on calle Real, then on to harbourside bars in the early hours. Pop and rock concerts are organised on the beach in summer.

**Jazz Pub** – *Puerto Deportivo (marina), Control Tower – Estepona – 🕐 Open 4pm-3am.* A quiet, welcoming bar with comfortable chairs and a pleasant terrace popular with an older crowd. An excellent cocktail list and intimate concerts on Friday and Sunday evenings.

**Melodie Cool** – *Calle Real, 25 – Este-pona – 🕐 Open 6pm-4am.* This small bar with its spectacular, futuristic design attracts an eclectic young crowd. An excellent bar list, including a range of beers, coffees and cocktails.

**Chico Diez** – *Puerto Deportivo (marina), no. 27 – Estepona – 🕐 Open daily in summer; 10pm-5am at weekends in winter,* attracts a more varied age group.

**Ático** – *Puerto Deportivo (marina), upper level – Estepona – 🕐 Open daily in summer; 10pm-6am at weekends in winter.* Plaza de la Constitución is at the heart of **Fuengirola**, and of its nightlife. Nearby calle Miguel de Cervantes, calle Emancipación and the Paseo Marítimo Rey de España are also popular areas. Between July and September the town organises many activities, including art shows, concerts and theatre.

**Café La Plaza** – *Plaza de la Constitución, 9 – Fuengirola – ☎ 952 46 33 59 – 🕐 Open Mon-Sat, 8am-2am.* The La Plaza café is in a traditional house on the main square. Pleasant decor and a local clientele of all ages. Breakfast and tapas are served.

**Pijama** – *Calle Cervantes, 14 – Fuengirola* – 🕐 *Open daily in summer; 10.30pm-5am at weekends in winter.* A small venue with interesting decor and lively atmosphere. Popular with 20-somethings who tend to liven things up between midnight and 3am.

**El Piso** – *Avenida Conde de San Isidro, 24 (entrance on calle Estación) – Fuengirola* – 🕐 *Open Mon-Sat, 10pm-3am.* 🕐*Closed in winter.* Overlooking the main square. Quiet, warm ambience and old-style decoration. Flamenco and Latin music on Tuesdays, Wednesdays and Thursdays. Perfect for relaxed conversation.

**Mahama** – *On the ring road, in Mijas Costa* – 🕐 *Open Jul-Aug, 10pm-7am; Fri-Sat in Sep, 10pm-7am.* Mahama is laid out in Andalusian style out around a patio with greenery and fountains, with quiet areas an enormous dance floor, and all-night grill. Locals of all ages drop in, getting younger as the night ages.

**Marbella** offers year-round activities. In the **old quarter** *(casco histórico)* are picturesque narrow streets and squares with plenty of attractive places for a drink or bite to eat, particularly around plaza de los Naranjos. Marbella's teenagers hang out near the **marina** *(puerto deportivo)*. Trendiest and most lively is **Puerto Banús**, which caters to all ages and tastes. Some of the best-known night-spots, however, are along the main coast road *(autovía)*.

In summer, the **Auditorio** in Parque de la Constitución is a venue for concerts and theatre, while the **Galería Municipal de Arte** *(plaza José Palomo)* and the **Museo del Grabado Español Contemporáneo** *(calle Hospital Bazán)* host art exhibitions. Lastly, the **Casino de Marbella** *(in the Hotel Andalucía Plaza,* ☎ *952 81 28 44 – www.casinomarbella.com)* stages shows.

**Sinatra Bar** – *Puerto Banús – Marbella* - ☎ *952 81 90 50* – 🕐 *Open 9am-3am.* Pleasant terrace and tremendous marina views, popular with foreigners under 40. Good for yacht-watching over drinks.

**La Abadía** – *Calle Pantaleón (by plaza de los Naranjos) – Marbella* – 🕐 *Open mid-May to mid-Sep and during Holy Week, 9pm-4am.* In a small, attractive alleyway in the pedestrianised old part of town. Worth the effort to find. The 20-35 crowd starts the night between midnight and 2am.

**Café del Mar/The Club** – *Hotel Puente Romano, on the Cádiz road – Marbella – Café del Mar:* 🕐 *open 10pm-4am; The Club: midnight-6.30am.* These luxurious clubs overlooking the Mediterranean try to keep their guests all night, for a relaxed drink, followed by dinner and dancing.

**Olivia Valère** – *On the Istán road – Marbella* – 🕐 *Open 9pm-7am.* The most exclusive and luxurious venue on the Costa del Sol, a new Moorish palace, with patios, terraces and gardens offering a variety of atmospheres for a quiet drink or dinner. *The* place to be seen with the rich and famous.

**Oh! Marbella** – *Hotel Don Carlos, on the Cádiz road – Marbella-* ☎ *952 83 54 77* – 🕐 *Open 11pm-6am, Jul-Aug and Holy Week.* Stupendous dance floor, terrace with Mediterranean views, popular with visitors. Cover charge varies.

**Torremolinos** is popular with foreign tourists all year, though visitor numbers increase significantly in summer. The town hall organises shows and concerts all year; check the postings in the town hall *(ayuntamiento)* or a tourist office. Most bars and nightclubs are in calle San Miguel, plaza Costa del Sol and avenida Palma de Mallorca, although many locals and tourists head to the nearby marina (Puerto Marina) in Benalmádena, for a greater variety.

**El Molino de La Torre** – *Calle Cuesta del Tajo, 8 – Torremolinos* – 🕐 *Open noon-midnight.* A café-restaurant with spectacular views of the coast.

## SHOPPING

Of the three parts of **Benalmádena**, Benalmádena Costa , which includes the marina, has the most shops. Look for crafts stalls in the narrow streets and small squares behind the marina. Avenida de Antonio Machado is also a busy. In Arroyo de la Miel, calle de las Flores has more traditional shops.

A typical **market** selling a vast array of products is held Friday mornings in the car park of Tívoli Park; on Sundays, there's a second-hand market in the same place.

In Benalmádena Pueblo, look at the Casa del Artesano, in plaza de España, particularly on Saturdays.

The main shopping street in **Estepona** is the pedestrianised calle Real, between avenida Juan Carlos I and calle Terraza.

A Wednesday morning **market** is held on avenida Juan Carlos, while craftsmen sell their wares on Sunday mornings by the marina.

In **Fuengirola**, most shops are on or near plaza de la Constitución, avenida Matías Sáenz de Tejada and Ramón y Cajal

On Tuesdays, the showground (recinto ferial) is the setting for the largest **market** on the Costa del Sol. A flea market selling second-hand goods is held here on Saturday mornings.

**Marbella** is one of the best places for shopping on the Costa del Sol. All the top brands are represented. Most high-end stores are in Puerto Banús, and in the centre of Marbella, along avenidas Ricardo Soriano and Ramón y Cajal. The best shopping centre on the Costa del Sol is found in Puerto Banús.

**Markets** are part of Marbella life. The Monday market next to the football sta-

*Plaza de los Naranjos, Marbella*

dium and the Saturday morning market next to the Nueva Andalucía bullring (plaza de toros, near Puerto Banús) are large and varied.

There are many boutiques on calle San Miguel, a busy and noisy pedestrianised street in **Torremolinos. Look for traditional stores nearby,** such as the pastelería at calle Isabel Manoja, 4, founded in 1908, where local cakes (tortas) are sold. The Cuesta del Tajo, a hill with impressive sea views, features stalls of more traditional wares and souvenirs.

A Thursday morning **market** is held in El Calvario.

**Marítimo**, an attractive tree-lined promenade along the beach, boasts dozens of restaurants. **Pueblo Andaluz** is a new district of old-looking bars and cafés.

▶ *Head southeast along N 340.*

## Benalmádena

Just before Benalmádena Costa are the highrises of **Arroyo de la Miel**. Benalmádena is a summer destination at the foot of the Sierra de Mijas, though it is busy with expatriates even in winter. There are excellent beaches, golf courses, a marina and myriad restaurants, nightclub, bars and cafés. The **old quarter** (casco antiguo), a few kilometres inland, preserves the Andalusian charms of whitewashed houses and flower-decked windows. The **Museo Arqueológico**, displays pre-Columbian artefacts; the 16C Torremuelle, Torrequebrada and Torrebermeja **watchtowers** can be visited. ○ Open in summer, 9.30am-1.30pm and 5-8pm; otherwise, 9.30am-1.30pm and 4-7pm; Sun and public hols 10am-2pm. ○ Closed Mon, 1 and 6 Jan, Good Friday, 1 May, and 24,25 and 31 Dec. No charge. ☎ 952 44 85 93.

▶ *Take the A 368. Mijas is 8km/5mi to the west.*

**Mijas★** – ⌖ see MIJAS

▶ *Follow the A 387 northeast to Alhaurín el Grande.*

*Alhaurín el Grande*

## Alhaurín el Grande

This elegant town lies on a hill in the Sierra de Mijas, amid market gardens, lemon and orange orchards and olive groves. The old quarter is a maze of cobbled streets lined by whitewashed houses. The **Arco del Cobertizo** is a Moorish gateway, and the **Ermita de la Vera Cruz** is an unusual 20C chapel built in neo-Gothic style.

▶ *Follow A 366 northwest.*

## Coín

Coín is situated amid citrus groves. Its massive 16C **Iglesia de San Juan** contains a fine Baroque altarpiece and colourful *azulejos* on the spandrels and cornice. Other churches include the 15C **Iglesia de Santa María de la Encarnación**, incorporating a minaret; the **Iglesia de San Andrés**, with its rich *artesonado* work; and the Iglesia del Santo Cristo de la Veracruz, which belonged to a Trinitarian convent.

▶ *Return to Alhaurín el Grande. Take A 387, and then A 3108.*

## Fuengirola

Fuengirola is another of the major resorts, with 7km/4.5mi of beaches, and many hotels, restaurants and leisure facilities attracting visitors all year. The **Castillo de Sohail** dominates the town from on high. The castle has 10C merloned towers and its original walls. The **Santa Fe de los Boliches** district includes **archaeological remains** – some 1C AD baths and the vestiges of a Roman villa – and the **Museo Abierto**, an outdoor gallery with murals by well-known artists (Sempere, Rafael Peinado, Elena Asins etc).

▶ *Head along A 7 to Marbella.*

## Marbella★★ – *see MARBELLA*

## Excursion inland to Tolox – *see MARBELLA*

▶ *Return to A 7 and head west.*

**Puerto Banús★★** – see MARBELLA

## San Pedro de Alcántara

This old town was once populated by laborers from the cotton and sugar cane plantations owned by the Marqués del Duero. Today, it is a large resort. Remains from the past include **Las Bóvedas** – unusual thermal baths with an octagonal floor plan and vaulted rooms – and the **Basílica de Vega del Mar**, a 6C palaeo-Christian temple containing tombs with valuable funerary objects. *Guided tours (1hr 45min), Tue and Thu at noon (visit also includes Las Bóvedas). Reservations recommended. ☎ 952 78 13 60.*

A winding **road**★★ links San Pedro de Alcántara with **Ronda**★★ (see RONDA).

▷ *Head north along A 6205.*

## Benahavís

This inland village is on the banks of the River Guadalmina, close to the impressive Las Angosturas Canyon (cañón). The remains of the Castillo de Montemayor, and several old watchtowers bespeak Moorish origins. Benahavís has an extraordinary number of restaurants for a village its size, many British-run.

▷ *Return to San Pedro de Alcántara and continue southwest along the A 7.*

## Estepona

Estepona, at the foot of the Sierra Bermeja range, is one of the Costa del Sol's major resort areas. Its hotels and beaches stretch for 20km/12mi. The marina has a capacity of 900 boats, and there are a golf course, a scuba-diving centre, and the usual clubs and boutiques.

There are watchtowers from the 15C and 16C are along the coast near town.

*One of the many beaches along the Costa del Sol*

### Old quarter★
Despite modern encroachments, this district preserves the charm of an Andalusian village, its narrow streets lined by whitewashed houses adorned with wrought-iron balconies decked in flowers. The **castle ruins** include two towers, the Torre del Reloj and El Vigía. The picturesque **plaza de las Flores**★, or Flower Square, is one of Estepona's most famous sights.

### Iglesia de Nuestra Señora de los Remedios
The 18C Church of Our Lady of Remedies highlights colonial influence. Part of an ex-Franciscan convent, it has three aisles separated by semicircular arches on pilasters. Its most outstanding feature is its Baroque **portal**★★, with unusual decoration representing the sun, the moon and the stars. The church is crowned by a tower in four sections, with a pyramidal ceramic spire.

### Plaza de Toros
Estepona's bullring is out of the ordinary in that it is asymmetrical.

▶ *Take N 340 to San Luis de Sabinillas, then bear left on A 377.*

### Manilva
Hillside Manilva, surrounded by vineyards, is just a few kilometres from the Mediterranean. The 18C **Iglesia de Santa Ana**, has an unusual mixtilinear arch over the portal.

**Beaches** to the south include Playa de la Paloma, Playa del Salto de la Mora and Playa Negra between San Luis de Sabinillas and **Puerto Duquesa**.

▶ *Continue north along A 377, then bear right on MA 546.*

### Casares★
The houses in this small settlement seem suspended above a promontory in the

> ### Paraje Natural de Sierra Bermeja
>
> The main attractions of this area of natural beauty in the hills behind Estepona are the reddish rock formations and the Spanish fir – a tree only found in Andalucía. To get to the park, follow MA 557 towards Jubrique.

Sierra Crestenilla. Casares was one of the last mountain strongholds of the Moors in Málaga province. The birthplace of Andalusian nationalist **Blas Infante** (1855-1936), is at n° 51, calle Carrera.

The old **Moorish quarter**★ retains its labyrinthine plan and low houses with reddish-coloured roofs. The 17C Iglesia de San Sebastián with an elegant Baroque tower stands by the plaza de España. The remains of a former Moorish fortress stand above the old quarter stand alongside the 16C Iglesia de la Encarnación, badly damaged during the Spanish Civil War.

▶ *Return to A 377 and continue north.*

### Gaucín
The whitewashed houses and narrow streets of Gaucín lie on a rocky hill in the heart of the Serranía de Ronda. The **views**★ from the remains of the old castle are particularly spectacular. Gaucín is well known for its unfermented grape juice *(mosto)* and its *aguardiente*, a fiery brandy.

### Benadalid
*12km/8mi northeast along A 369.* This village in the shelter of a rocky outcrop is surrounded by olive and almond groves. *Azulejos* along the streets narrate anecdotes of local history. A Moorish fortress, in ruins, has its three flat cylindrical towers.

▶ *Return to San Luis de Sabinillas and rejoin N 340.*

### Puerto Duquesa
*2km/1.2mi south.* This lively marina teems with bars, restaurants and outdoor terraces. Nearby is the sober Castillo de Sabinillas (castle).

### Sotogrande
These luxury housing complexes and elegant homes are next to the famous Sotogrande golf course, which has hosted the prestigious Ryder Cup tournament.

# Parque Natural de DESPEÑAPERROS★

This natural gateway to Andalucía is a spectacular gorge (desfiladero) carved by the River Despeñaperros through the Sierra Morena. At 1 000m/3 300ft, it is a superb belvedere from which to enjoy magnificent **views**★★★ of vertical walls of slate and the deep precipices that cut the park. According to tradition, Christians threw the defeated Moors into the ravine after the Battle of Las Navas de Tolosa, hence its unusual name (*despeñaperros* translates as "where dogs are hurled").

▶ **Orient Yourself:** The Parque Natural de Despeñaperros in northern Jaén province is reached by the A 4 – E 5 highway linking Madrid with Sevilla and Córdoba.

⚲ **Also See:** LINARES, ÚBEDA, ANDÚJAR and JAÉN.

# Visit

The best way to enjoy the impressive natural beauty of Despeñaperros; is to follow planned **itineraries** on foot or by car. ▯ *For information, call* ☎ *953 12 50 18.*
The 6 000ha/14 800 acres include oak (holm, cork and gall) forset and umbrella pine rising above a dense arbutus, mastic and myrtle. This vegetation is an exceptional habitat for wolf, lynx, stone marten, genet, deer and wild boar, as well as the griffon vulture and the spectacular imperial eagle. The route from Arroyo del Rey passes through a landscape of vertical drops and strange formations created by erosion. In "Los Órganos", where the rocks look like gigantic organ pipes. The Las Correderas section is popular with hunting and fishing enthusiasts.

## Santa Elena

This small town in the park, along with La Carolina, is the starting point for a number of excursions.
Local sights include the **Collado de los Jardines** (*5km/3mi N towards Aldeaquemada*), an Iberian sanctuary, and the Cueva de los Muñecos (*3km/2mi W towards Miranda de Rey*), a cave with impressive wall paintings of animals. The **Paraje Natural de la Cascada de Cimbarra**, 4km/2.5mi NW, is famous for its spectacular waterfalls (*cascadas*) and the canyons (*gargantas*) of the River Guarrizas.

# Excursion

## La Carolina

*10km/6mi S of Santa Elena via the A 4 – E 5.* La Carolina owes it name to the 1767 plan of Carlos III aimed at repopulating the Sierra Morena introduced. Its wide, streets bespeak a planned city. The mystical theologian and poet **St John of the Cross** lived in La Carolina in the 16C. He is recalled by a statue in plaza del General Moscardó.
Iglesia de la Inmaculada Concepción – ◷ *Open mid-Jun to Aug, 8am-8.30pm; Sep to mid-Apr, 8am-8pm; mid-Mar to mid-Jun, 8am-9pm; Sun and public hols, from noon.* ☎ *953 66 00 37.*
The church is built above the vestiges of the Convento de La Peñuela, where St John of the Cross stayed. Its simple portal leads to an amply proportioned interior containing a fine 15C image of the Virgen de los Dolores (Virgin of Pain) and a *Martyrdom of St Dominic*, a work from the Ribera School.

## Palacio del Intendente Olavide

This palace belonged to Don Pablo de Olavide, in charge of populating the area. The monumental neo-Classical façade bears the royal coat of arms.

## Jail

The old jail (*cárcel*), a neo-Classical building, is where General Rafael del Riego was held in 1820 before his execution in Madrid for for leading a liberal revolt in Andalucía.

# Parque Nacional de DOÑANA★★★

Salt marshes, coastal dunes and dry, undulating scrub lands *(cotos)* combine in this exceptional park. A vast wetland, at its best in spring and autumn, it is a winter paradise for over 150 African and European birds. Apart from bird-watchers, Doñana attracts thousands to admire the contrasting landscapes of subtly moving sand dunes, marsh, and forests inhabited by lynx, deer, horses and wild boar.

▸ **Orient Yourself:** The park encompasses the right bank of the River Guadalquivir between the provinces of Huelva and Sevilla.

🕓 **Organizing Your Time:** Take at least a day to savour Doñana

👣 **Also See:** SANLÚCAR DE BARRAMEDA, JEREZ DE LA FRONTERA (22km/14mi SE of Sanlúcar de Barrameda), El PUERTO DE SANTA MARÍA and El ROCÍO.

## A Bit of History

Doñana is one of Europe's largest national parks, covering 73 000ha/180 400 acres. It is named for Doña Ana Gómez de Mendoza y Silva, wife of the seventh Duke of Medina Sidonia and the daughter of the famous Princess of Éboli, established a hunting reserve here in the 6C. There are three **ecosystems.**

The 27 000ha/66 700 acres of **salt marshes** are the ideal habitat for wintering birds. Characteristics are a high salt content and unusual features such as **caños** (depressions formed by water), *lucios* (a permanent lagoon), *paciles* and *vetas* (mounds of land rising above water, favoured areas for saltwort).

The **sand dunes,** parallel to the Atlantic, are advancing at 6m/20ft per year. The land between dunes is known as a corral *(enclosure)*, while sand-levelled trees are *cruces* (crosses).

The **cotos**, orignally hunting reserves, are dry, undulating areas covered with shrub sand aromatic plant such as heather, rockrose, rosemary and thyme.

Alongside these ecosystems is the **vera**, strips of land between woodlands and marshes. **Lagoons** include Santa Olalla, a nesting place for ducks, geese and swans, and La Dulce, filled with crustaceans – tasty fare for the park's pink flamingoes.

**Parque Natural Entorno de Doñana** – This nature reserve on the periphery of the national park covers 54 500ha/134 700 acres including the saltpans of Sanlúcar. Eucalytpus and pine predominate, though it does contain marshland and lagoons.

## Visit

### Visitor Centres

*Entry to the park is rigorously controlled. Excursions into the park depart from four visitor centres and last approximately 3hr 30min. It is advisable to book visits in advance.*

R. Corbel/MICHELIN

*Pink flamingo*

### El Acebuche
🕐 *Open Jun-Sep, 8am-9pm; Oct-May, 8am-7pm.* 🕐 *Closed 1 and 6 Jan and 25 Dec.* ☎ *959 44 87 11.*
All reservations are handled here. There is an exhibition on the park's wetlands. Walks from this centre provide a closer look at the aquatic birds found in the lagoon.

### La Rocina
🕐 *Open Jun-Sep, 9am-9; Oct-May, 9am--7pm.* ☎ *959 44 23 40.*
La Rocina is just a few kilometres from El Rocío, along the Almonte-Matalascañas road. It is the starting point of the popular **Charca de la Boca trail** *(14km/9mi)*, which leads to a various hides for bird-watching, including "El Paraguas" (The Umbrella).

### El Acebrón
🕐 *Open Jun-Sep, 9am-3pm and 4-9pm; Oct-May, 9am-3pm and 4-7pm.* 🕐 *Closed 1 and 6 Jan and 25 Dec.* ☎ *959 50 61 62.*
This centre exhibits the "Man and Doñana" presentation on the evolution of the park and man's presence in it. The upper floor affords fine views. El Acebrón is the starting point of a 12km/8mi forest walk.

### José Antonio Valverde
🕐 *Open Jun-Sep, 10,30am-7pm; Oct-May, 10.30am-6pm.* 🕐 *Closed 1 and 6 Jan and 25 Dec.* ☎ *959 95 90 96.*

This modern structure in the La Gallega section of Aznalcázar has large windows for bird observation. Audio-visual presentations are given as well.

## Park Excursions

### On foot
Marked trails run from each information centre. Park attendants will provide information on level of difficulty and expected duration. Wear comfortable shoes.

### By four-wheel drive
Book in advance. Two visits per day are organised, in the morning and mid-afternoon, with official park guides. Itineraries vary by season and individual preferences.

### By horse
Horseback tours and horse-drawn carriages are available by arrangement, with optional picnic for groups. This interesting alternative can either be made on horseback or by horse-drawn carriage. Picnics are included for larger groups.

### By boat
Excursions from Sanlúcar de Barrameda (&see SANLÚCAR DE BARRAMEDA).

# ÉCIJA ★

POPULATION: 37 113

This elegant Baroque churches, convents, palaces, mansions and soaring bell towers of Écija date from its economic peak in the 18C. Luis Vélez de Guevara (1579-1644), the author of *El Diablo Cojuelo*, was born here. Écija bears the unlikely nickname of "frying pan of Andalucía", so named for its summer heat. *Plaza de España, 1, 41400 Écija, ☎ 95 590 29 33.*

▶ **Orient Yourself:** Écija is along the River Genil, halfway between Córdoba (to the NE) and Sevilla (to the W), on the A 4 – E 5 highway.
🕐 **Organizing Your Time:** Take at least half a day to discover Écija on foot.
🅿 **Parking:** Leave your car in the Plaza de España and visit on foot.
& **Also See:** OSUNA (34km/21mi S), ESTEPA (38km/24mi SE), MARCHENA (38.5km/21mi SW), CARMONA (53km/33mi W), SEVILLA, PALMA DEL RÍO (29km/18mi NW) and CÓRDOBA.

## Visit

▶ *Follow signs to the town centre (centro ciudad).*

### Plaza de España
This square, called **El Salón** (Drawing Room), is the hub of Écija. Facing it are the **Iglesia de Santa Bárbara** (impressive choir stalls); the **Convento de San Francisco**; and the town hall.

### Festivals
September is the month for fiestas in Écija. On the 8th, there is a solemn procession in honour of the town's patron saint, the Virgen del Valle (Virgin of the Valley). The 21st is the Feria de San Mateo, celebrated with fiestas, bullfights, demonstrations of horsemanship etc. The Festival de Cante Jondo attracts leading flamenco performers.

## Town Hall

The council chamber retains two **Roman mosaics**★. The 16C coffered wooden ceiling was transferred from the Convento de San Pablo y Santo Domingo.

# Churches, Convents, Towers★

## Torre de San Juan★

The Baroque18C tower of the Church of St John, set with *azulejos,* is one of the most beautiful in Écija.

## Iglesia de Santiago★

🕒 *Open 10.30am-12.45pm and 6-7.30pm .*

| ÉCIJA | | | Cordero | BY | 22 | Paloma | AY | 50 |
|---|---|---|---|---|---|---|---|---|
| | | | Doctor Sánchez Malo | | | Pilarejo | BY | 51 |
| **Roads** | | | Av. del | AZ | 24 | Platería | BY | 53 |
| Almonas | AY | 3 | Emigrantes Av. de los | AY | 25 | Puerta Palma | AY | 56 |
| Amapola | BZ | 5 | Emparedamiento | AZ | 27 | Rojas | BY | 57 |
| Arabella | BY | 7 | General Weyller | BY | 30 | Santa Brígida | BZ | 59 |
| Cadenas | BY | 13 | Ignacio Soto | AZ | 35 | Santa María Pl. | AY | 63 |
| Cañaveralejo | AZ | 15 | José Canalejas | AY | 39 | Santiago | AZ | 67 |
| Canovas del Castillo | AZ | 14 | Juan de Angulo | BY | 42 | Secretario Armesto | AY | 69 |
| Capuchinos | AZ | 17 | María Auxiliadora Av. de | AY | 45 | Sor Ángela de la Cruz | AY | 71 |
| Cintería | AY | 19 | Mas y Prat | AY | 47 | Zayas | AY | 73 |
| Compañía | AY | 20 | Miguel de Cervantes Av. de | BZ | | | | |
| Conde | AY | | Morería | AY | 48 | | | |

| Ayuntamiento | AZ | H | Convento de San | | | Palacio de los Marqueses | | |
|---|---|---|---|---|---|---|---|---|
| Convento de las Teresas | AZ | C | Francisco | AZ | A | de Santaella | AZ | P² |
| | | | Palacio de Benamejí | AZ | P¹ | Palacio de Valdehermoso | BZ | P³ |

The portal and tower of the Church of St James are Baroque; the remainder is Gothic-Mudéjar. Three harmoniously proportioned aisles have wooden ceilings, the apse has Gothic vaulting. The Gothic **retable**★ illustrates the Passion and Resurrection of Christ.

### Iglesia de Santa María

🕐 Open 10am-1pm and 6-9pm (Oct-Apr, 10am-1pm and 5.30-7pm). ☎ 954 83 04 30.

This 18C church on plaza de Santa María has a handsome Baroque portal crowned by a large arch and a **tower** adorned with blue *azulejos*. Archaeological finds are displayed in the cloisters.

### Convento de las Teresas

This 14C-15C Mudéjar palace has a **portal** with *alfiz*, heraldic and rope decoration.

### Iglesia de la Concepción

🕐 Open Mon-Fri 10am-1pm and by appointment. ☎ 95 590 29 33.

Simple, red-brick Renaissance doorway, fine Mudéjar-style *artesonado* work.

### Iglesia de los Descalzos

o━ Closed for restoration.

The sober exterior belies the exuberantly adorned **interior**★ of this church of this masterwork of Écija Baroque. Fine **stuccowork** adorns vaults and the cupola.

*Torre de San Juan*

B. Kaufmann/MICHELIN

### Convento de los Marroquíes

The convent is famous for its **belfry**★, and for *marroquíes,* biscuits baked and sold by the nuns.

### Iglesia de Santa Cruz

🕐 Open 10.30am-1.30pm and 6-10pm (5-10pm in summer). ☞€2 (sacred art museum). ☎ 954 83 06 13.

On the plaza de la Virgen del Valle. Note the remains of an earlier church, and **Renaissance tower**. The neo-Classical church holds a 13C image of the **Virgin of the Valley**, the patron saint of Écija, and a 5C **Christian sarcophagus**★. The museum exhibits 16-19C sacred art.

## Palaces★

Take note of inlaid columns on the corners of buildings, houses adorned with coats of arms, patios, and small squares fronted by fine civil edifices.

### Palacio de Peñaflor

Now a cultural centre, the palace has a slightly curved **façade**★ with iron balcony and fresco decoration, and handsome pink marble doorway.

### Palacio de Valdehermoso

*Calle Caballeros.* Note the column shafts on the lower section of the fine 16C **Plateresque façade**★. To the left, admire the view of the **Torre de San Juan**.

### Palacio de Benamejí
*Calle Cánovas del Castillo.* ○ *Open Jun-Sep, Tue-Sun, 9am-2pm; Oct-May, Tue-Sun, 9.30am-1.30pm and 4.30-6.30pm.* ○ *Closed Mon, 1 Jan, 1 May and 25 Dec. No charge.* ☎ *955 90 29 19.*
This elegant, Baroque 18C brick and marble palace, now the **Museo Histórico Municipal,** comprises two storeys with curves throughout.

### Palacio de los Marqueses de Santaella
*Close to the Palacio de Benamejí.* ✍ *Private club; request permission for brief access.* Past the entrance is a magnificent **fresco-adorned cupola**★ above the staircase.

# ESTEPA★

POPULATION:11 654

**Lovely Estepa straddles the slopes of the Cerro de San Cristóbal (St Christopher's hill) in the Sevillian countryside, crowned by castle remains and the Iglesia de Santa María de la Asunción. It once was the seat of the Knights of the Order of Santiago.** ▯ *Avenida. Andalucia, 102, 41560 Estepa,* ☎ *95 591 39*

▸ **Orient Yourself:** Estepa, on the slopes of the Sierra de Becerrero, is halfway between Sevilla (to the W) and Granada (to the SE) on the A 92 highway.

◔ **Also See:** OSUNA (24km/16mi W), ÉCIJA (38km/24mi NW) and ANTEQUERA (50km/31mi SE).

## Visit

## El Cerro★

*Drive up to the Cerro de San Cristóbal.*
The esplanade surrounded by pine trees is lined by several buildings of interest.

### Walls
Moorish walls, rebuilt in the 13C by the Order of Santiago (St James), once circled the hill. Towers and sections remain.

### Keep
The massive square 14C *torre del homenaje* rises from the fortress ruins.

### Iglesia de Santa María de la Asunción
*Next to the castle ruins.* Theis 15-16C fortress church has wide buttresses and an unusual military-style tower. Nowadays, it is rarely used.

### Balcón de Andalucía
The esplanade commands magnificent **views**★★ to the surrounding countryside and the town rising to the elegant Torre de la Victoria.

---

### ☺ A Sweet Treat ☺

**Cakes and pastries**
Like many towns and villages in Andalucía, Estepa is renowned for its exquisite cakes with their traditional anise, sesame and almond flavourings, such as *polvorones, mantecados* and the yuletide treat, *dulces navideños.*

### Convento de Santa Clara

This 16C brick and masonry convent, alongside the Iglesia de Santa María, houses an order of enclosed nuns. Its a simple Baroque doorway with heraldic decoration.

## The Town

### Torre de la Victoria★

This handsome 18C tower survives its church and convent, now gone. A stone podium acts as a base for this brick construction, which comprises five sections.

Note the narrow charming, cobbled **calle Torralba**, its entrance framed by an arch, heading off to the right of the tower.

### Iglesia del Carmen★

*Calle Mesones, next to plaza del Carmen.* This 18C church, a jewel of Andalusian Baroque, has an original stone and black ceramic **portal**★ and a fine belfry.

### Casa-Palacio del Marqués de Cerverales

*Calle Castillejos. Private residence.* Estepa's finest civil building was erected in the 18C. Solomonic and balustered columns, escutcheons and assorted figures adorn the doorway and main balcony. Bays are framed by pilasters, while the upper storey has a truncated pediment, decorated with a human face.

The **Iglesia de la Asunción**, to the right, holds interesting paintings.

*Portal, Iglesia del Carmen*

# Sierra de los FILABRES★

The Sierra de los Filabres range is renowned for its stark landscape, majestic natural formations, and some of Europe's clearest skies. The roads that wind among the quarries of Macael marble are accompanied by discarded blocks that imitate the mountains of this desolate landscape.

▸ **Orient Yourself:** The Sierra de los Filabres rises east of the Sierra Nevada and north of the Sierra Alhamilla.

○ **Organizing Your Time:** Allow several hours for either of the drives.

⚑ **Also See:** MOJÁCAR, SIERRA NEVADA, BAZA, GUADIX and GRANADA.

## Driving Tours

### The Land of Marble *79km/49mi – allow 2hr 30min*

Marble from these mountains was used to build the Alhambra in Granada, among other magnificent buildings. The town of **Macael** is the economic centre here.

▷ *Head north from Macael along AL 841 to Olula del Río. From here, follow A 334 east, then turn right.*

## Cantoria

A viewpoint at the entrance to this whitewashed village commands surrounding fmarket gardens, orchards and olive groves. Stop at the Casa del Marqués de la Romana, a noble mansion, and the Iglesia de Nuestra Señora del Carmen. The old rail station is unchanged since the last train chugged out in the 1980s.

In **Almanzora** (5.5km/3.4mi E) is the Palacio del Marqués de Almanzora, a noble residence arranged around a central patio. Turn right towards Albánchez.

## Albánchez

*11.5km/7.2mi S by the A 8200.* The whitewashed houses of this village climb the hillside amid a landscape of thyme, broom and anthyllis.

Beyond Albánchez, the road passes mountains and open-cast marble quarries to reach **Cóbdar**, popular with mountaineers who come to climb the marble rock known as Los Calares. 🔠 A pleasant 3km/1.8mi walk takes in the remains of an old mill and fortress *(follow a path parallel to the river at the exit to Cóbdar)*.

▷ *From Cóbdar, head towards Alcudia de Monteagud, then turn right.*

## Chercos

This marble-quarrying village has an old quarter, known as El Soto.

3km/1.8mi to the south is **Chercos Viejo**★ (🅿 *leave your car at the entrance to the village)*. Wander its cobbled lanes, under the remains of an old fortress *(alcazaba)*. Prehistoric carved stones have been discovered on the outskirts.

▷ *Head back along the road from Cóbdar to Alcudia de Monteagud.*

**Alcudia de Monteagud** retains 19C threshing floors and its old public washery.

## Tahal

This well-kept whitewashed village dominated by the silhouette of its sturdy 15C Moorish castle is situated at the confluence of several ravines.

▷ *Return to Macael along A 349.*

# The Blue Sky Road

## Gérgal

Gérgal is situated on a fold of the Sierra de Los Filabres, some 50km/31mi to the north of Almería, and is crowned by a castle in a perfect state of repair. To reach the fortress *(o— private property – closed to visitors)*, follow the road bearing right to Las Aneas upon exiting the village. The fortification comprises a square crenellated tower with smaller cylindrical turrets overlooking the whitewashed village at its feet. The main feature of architectural interest is the parish church, with its Mudéjar *artesonado* ceiling in the main nave. The outlying area is particularly arid, in keeping with the rest of this part of the province.

## The road up to Calar Alto★

*Allow 1hr 30min excluding a visit to the Astronomical Observatory. Follow A 92 for 5km/3mi, then bear right onto AL 871 for a further 26km/16mi to Calar Alto.*

The road winds up through the Sierra de los Filabres to an altitude of 2 168m/7 111ft. Past Aulago, to the right of the road, no further villages are encountered. The arid landscape gradually gives way to an extensive planted pine woodland.

The superb **views**★ on both sides of the road encompass the city of Almería and Cabo de Gata to the south, the Sierra Alhamilla to the southeast, the Almanzora Valley to the north and the lofty peaks of the Sierra Nevada to the west. On the summit of Calar Alto, the characteristic domes of an **astronomical observatory** can be seen (🕐 *open to visitors one day a week*). The centre is the ideal location from which to observe the night skies as it has the best visibility in Europe with over 200 cloud-free nights per year. 🕐 *Visits on Wed by prior arrangement.* ☎ *950 63 25 00.*

*Dome, Astronomical Observatory*

B. Kaufmann/MICHELIN

# GRANADA★★★

POPULATION: 241 471

"Give him alms, woman, for there is no greater grief than to be blind in Granada." This saying, inscribed in the Alhambra, evokes the beauty of this city, its delightful **setting**★★★ and its monuments, the jewel of which is the Alhambra itself, one of the most magnificent artistic creations of humankind. Granada, in the garden plain watered by the rivers Genil and Darro, rises onto the hills of the Albaicín, Sacromonte and Alhambra, Christian and modern below, Moorish above, in a perfect symbiosis of art and history, under the snow-capped ridge of the Sierra Nevada. Once you've wandered its alleys and squares, experienced the sunsets, strolled its lively streets, you will agree that Granada is not only beautiful, it is unforgettable. 🛈 *Plaza Mariana Pineda, 18009 Granada,* ☎ *958 24 71 28, infotur@dipgra.es.*

▶ **Orient Yourself:** Granada is at the junction of the A 44 – E 902 and the A 92 motorways, connecting the city with Jaén, Antequera and Málaga.

🕐 **Organizing Your Time:** Allow at least two days.

🖢 **Also See:** MONTEFRÍO (52km/32mi NW), ALCALÁ LA REAL (54km/34mi NW), SIERRA NEVADA (SE), LAS ALPUJARRAS (SE), GUADIX (57km/35mi E), ALMUÑÉCAR (76km/48mi S) and JAÉN ( 94km/59mi N).

## Fiestas and Festivals

**Toma de Granada** – The first important festival in the busy Andalusian calendar, on 2 January, commemorates Boabdil's surrender to the Catholic Monarchs. A procession climbs to the Alhambra, where the bell in the Torre de la Vela is rung. Tradition has it that young women who take part will be wed within the year.

**San Cecilio** – The day of St. Cecil (1 February), the city's patron, is celebrated by a pilgrimage *(romería)* to the Sacramonte district. Wine and broad beans *(habas)* are given out. It's also a time to sing, and dance traditional *sevillanas*.

**Semana Santa** – Uniquely in Andalucía, Granada's Holy Week is a time of restraint. Processions file along the steep, cobbled Official Route *(Carrera Oficial)*. Valuable Baroque statues by masters such as Diego de Siloé and Pedro de Mena test the capacities of the *costaleros* (carriers), who kneel to squeeze floats into the cathedral.

**Las Cruces de Mayo** – For the May Crosses, flower-decked crosses adorn streets.

**Corpus Christi** – Granada's annual *feria* with bullfights and amusements, coincides with the solemn Corpus Christi procession through streets carpeted in flowers.

**Festivals** – The calendar includes the International Theatre Festival (*May, Teatro Manuel de Falla*), the International Music and Dance Festival (*Jun-Jul, Alhambra; www.granadafestival.org*), and the International Jazz Festival (*Oct-Nov*).

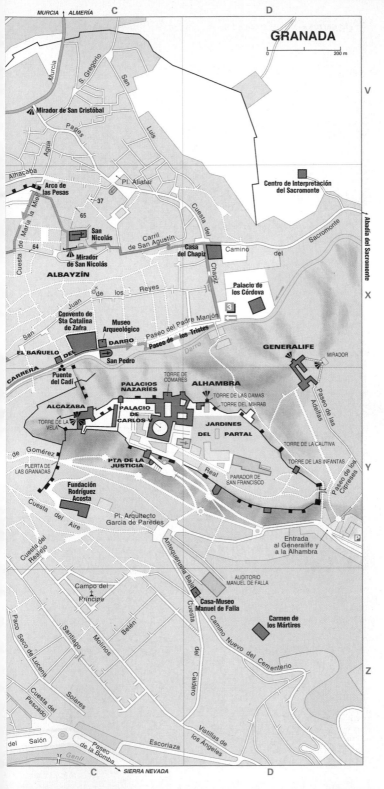

# GRANADA

0    200 m

MURCIA · ALMERÍA

Mirador de San Cristóbal

Centro de Interpretación del Sacromonte

Arco de las Pesas

San Nicolás

Mirador de San Nicolás

Casa del Chapiz

Camino

Palacio de los Córdova

ALBAYZÍN

Convento de Sta Catalina de Zafra

Museo Arqueológico

EL BAÑUELO

DARRO

San Pedro

Paseo del Padre Manjón

Paseo de los Tristes

GENERALIFE

MIRADOR

Puente del Cadí

PALACIOS NAZARÍES

TORRE DE COMARES

ALHAMBRA

TORRE DE LAS DAMAS

TORRE DEL MIHRAB

ALCAZABA

PALACIO DE CARLOS V

TORRE DE LA VELA

JARDINES DEL PARTAL

TORRE DE LA CAUTIVA

PTA DE LA JUSTICIA

TORRE DE LAS INFANTAS

PUERTA DE LAS GRANADAS

Fundación Rodríguez Acosta

Pl. Arquitecto García de Paredes

PARADOR DE SAN FRANCISCO

Entrada al Generalife y a la Alhambra

AUDITORIO MANUEL DE FALLA

Campo del Príncipe

Casa-Museo Manuel de Falla

Carmen de los Mártires

SIERRA NEVADA

# GRANADA

**Streets**

| Street | Code | Ref |
|---|---|---|
| Adelfas Pas. de las | DY | |
| Agua | CV | |
| Aire Cuesta del | CY | |
| Alhacaba Cuesta de la | BCX | |
| Alhamar | AZ | |
| Alhóndiga | AY | |
| Aliatar Pl. | CX | |
| Ancha de Capuchinos | AV | |
| Ancha de la Virgen | BZ | 3 |
| Ángel Ganivet | BZ | |
| Antequeruela Baja | CDYZ | |
| Arandas Los | AX | |
| Belén | CZ | |
| Bib-Rambla Pl. | ABY | |
| Bomba Pas. de la | CZ | |
| Caidero Cuesta de | DZ | |
| Calderería Nueva | BY | |
| Campillo Pl. de | BZ | |
| Capitán Moreno Av. | AV | |
| Capuchinas | AY | 12 |
| Cárcel Alta | BY | 13 |
| Cárcel Baja | BY | |
| Carmen Pl. del | BZ | 16 |
| Casino Acera del | BZ | |
| Ceniceros | BX | |
| Chapiz Cuesta del | DX | |
| Cipreses Pas. de los | DY | |
| Colón Gran Vía de | BXY | |
| Conde las Infantas | AY | 22 |
| Constitución Av. de la | AV | |
| Darro Carrera del | CXY | |
| Darro Acera del | BZ | |
| Duende | BZ | |
| Duquesa | AXY | |
| Elvira | BXY | |
| Escoriaza | CDZ | |
| Escudo de Carmen | BY | |
| Escuelas | AY | |
| Genil Carrera del | BZ | |
| Gomérez Cuesta de | BCY | |
| Gracia | AY | |
| Gracia Pl. de | AZ | |
| Gran Capitán | AXY | |
| Horno de la Charca | CX | 37 |
| Horno de Abad | AY | 36 |
| Isabel la Católica Pl. de | BY | 38 |
| Isabel la Real | BX | |
| Larga San Cristóbal | BV | |
| Lobos Pl. de los | AY | |
| Lozano | BZ | |
| Madrid Av. de | AV | |
| Málaga | AY | |
| Maria la Miel Cuesta de | CX | |
| Mariana Pineda Pl. de | BZ | |
| Marqués de Falces | BX | 40 |
| Mesones | AY | |
| Molinos | CZ | |
| Murcia Carret. de | BCV | |
| Navarrete | AX | 44 |
| Navas | BYZ | |
| Nueva Pl. | BY | |
| Nueva del Santísimo | AX | 46 |
| Nueva San Antón | AZ | 47 |
| Obispo Hurtado | AY | |
| Paco Seco de Lucena | CZ | |
| Padre Manjón Pas. del | CDX | |
| Pages | CV | |
| Paseo de los Tristes Pas. de los | CDX | |
| Pavaneras | BY | |
| Pedro Antonio de Alarcón | AZ | |
| Peña Partida | CY | |
| Pescado Cuesta del | CZ | |
| Picón Carril del | AY | 52 |
| Portón de Tejeiro | AZ | |
| Príncipe Campo del | CZ | |
| Puentezuelas | AYZ | |
| Real Puerta | BYZ | |
| Real | DY | |
| Realejo Cuesta del | CY | |
| Recogidas | AZ | |
| Rector López Argüeta | AX | |
| Reyes Católicos | BY | |
| Sacromonte Camino del | DX | |
| Salón Pas. del | BCZ | |
| San Agustín Carril de | CX | |
| San Antón | ABZ | |
| San Antón Pl. de | AZ | 61 |
| San Antonio Cuesta de | BV | |
| San Antonio Camino de | BCV | |
| San Cristóbal Veredilla de | BV | |
| San Gregorio Cuesta de | BX | |
| San Gregorio | CV | |
| San Ildefonso Acera de | BV | |
| San Jacinto | BZ | |
| San Jerónimo | AXY | |
| San Juan de Dios | AX | |
| San Juan de la Cruz Pl. | BY | 63 |
| San Juan de los Reyes | CX | |
| San Luis | CV | |
| San Matías | BY | |
| San Miguel Bajo Pl. de | BX | |
| San Nicolás Cuesta de | CX | 65 |
| San Nicolás Camino Nuevo de | CX | 64 |
| Santa Ana Pl. de | BY | 66 |
| Santa Bárbara | AX | |
| Santa Escolástica | BY | 67 |
| Santa Paula | AXY | |
| Santiago | CZ | |
| Santo Domingo Callejón de | BZ | 68 |
| Solares | CZ | |
| Solarillo de Gracia | AZ | |
| Tablas | AY | |
| Tendillas de Santa Paula | AX | 73 |
| Tinajilla | AX | 76 |
| Tovar Pl. | BY | 77 |
| Trinidad Pl. de la | AY | |
| Triunfo Pl. del | ABX | |
| Universidad Pl. de la | AX | 78 |
| Varela | BZ | |
| Ventanilla | AX | |
| Vistillas de los Ángeles | DZ | |
| Zenete | BX | |

| Place | Code | Ref |
|---|---|---|
| Abadía del Sacromonte | DX | |
| Albayzín | CX | |
| Alcaicería | BY | |
| Alcazaba | CY | |
| Alhambra | DY | |
| Arco de las Pesas | CX | |
| Baños árabes (El Bañuelo) | CX | |
| Capilla Real | BY | |
| Carmen de los Mártires (Jardines) | DZ | |
| Cartuja | BV | |
| Casa de los Duques de Abrantes | BY | |
| Casa de los Pisa-Museo San Juan de Dios | BY | B³ |
| Casa de los Tiros | BY | B² |
| Casa de Porras | BX | B¹ |
| Casa del Chapiz | DX | |
| Casa-Museo Manuel de Falla | DZ | |
| Catedral | ABY | |
| Centro de Arte José Guerrero | BY | D |
| Centro de Interpretacíon del Sacromonte | DX | |
| Chancillería | BY | |
| Colegio de San Bartolomé y Santiago | AX | C |
| Convento de Santa Catalina de Zafra | CX | |
| Convento de Santa Isabel la Real | BX | |
| Corral del Carbón | BY | |
| Curia eclesiástica | BY | F |
| Fundacíon Rodríguez Acosta | CY | |
| Generalife | DX | |
| Hospital de San Juan de Dios | AX | |
| Hospital Real | AV | |
| Huerta de San Vicente | AZ | |
| Iglesia de los Santo Justos y Pastor | AX | |
| Iglesia de San José | BX | |
| Iglesia de San Juan de Dios | AX | |
| Iglesia de San Nicolás | CX | |
| Iglesia de San Pedro | CX | |
| Iglesia de Santa Ana y San Gil | BY | |
| Iglesia de Santo Domingo | BZ | |
| Iglesia del Sagrario | BY | K |
| Jardines del Partal | DY | |
| Jardines del Triunfo | AV | |
| Jardines y Torres de la Alhambra | DY | |
| Madraza o Antiguo Ayuntamiento | BY | |
| Mirador de San Cristóbal | CV | |
| Mirador de San Nicolás | CX | N² |
| Monasterio de San Jerónimo | AX | |
| Monumento a la Immaculada Concepción | AV | R |
| Museo Arqueológico | CX | |
| Palacio Arzobispal | BY | S |
| Palácio de Carlos V | CY | |
| Palacio de los Córdova | DX | |
| Palacios Nazaríes | CY | |
| Parque de las Ciencias | BZ | |
| Puente del Cadí | CXY | |
| Puerta de la Justicia | CY | |
| Universidad | AXY | U |

# Address Book

## TRANSPORT

**Airport** – *Málaga road* – ☎ *958 24 52 00* The airport bus departs from the convention centre (Palacio de Congresos, ☎ *958 27 86 77/958 13 13 09).*

**Trains** – The station is on avenida de Andalucía (☎ *958 27 12 72).* Service to the province and major Spanish cities.

**RENFE (Spanish Rail)** – *Calle Reyes*

**Cars** – Getting around by car is difficult, especially for those unfamiliar with local restrictions. Use public transport or taxis, or walk.

**City buses** – Buses serve all major monuments and suburbs. Ticket, €1, 9-trip ticket €5.45 (☎ *900 71 09 00).*

**Bus station** – *Carretera de Jaén* – ☎ *958 18 54 801.* Service to Andalucía, Spanish cities and some European capitals. The Sierra Nevada bus leaves from the Ventorrillo bar, paseo de Violón, by the la Virgen bridge (☎ *958 27 31 00).*

**Taxis** – ☎ *958 15 14 61, 958 28 06 54*

**Horse-drawn carriages** – These can be hired near the Puerta Real.

## SIGHTSEEING

**Bonoturístico** – This pass includes the Alhambra, Generalife, cathedral, Capilla Real, La Cartuja, Monasterio de San Jerónimo and the Parque de las Ciencias, and ten bus journeys for €22.50. Valid for 7 days

The pass can be purchased at the Alhambra and Capilla Real, or the Caja de Ahorros de Granada bank *(60, plaza de Isabel la Católica).* Your Alhambra visit must be reserved at time of purchase. Information: Caja General de Ahorros de Granada, ☎ 902 100 095.

## WHERE TO EAT

🍽️ **Mariquilla** – *Calle Lope de Vega, 2* – ☎ *958 52 16 32* – ⏰ *Closed Sun evening, Mon and 15 Jul-31 Aug.* The Mariquilla is one of the best restaurants in Granada. Cosy, with paintings of Granada.

🍽️ **Chikito** – *Plaza del Campillo, 9* – ☎ *958 22 36 64 - www.restaurantechikito.com* – ⏰ *Closed Wed – Reservations recommended.* Hugely popular restaurant-bar. Artists and intellectuals such as García Lorca met here in the 1930s. Renowned for local specialities and its superb cured hams.

🍽️ **La Ermita en la Plaza de Toros** – *Avenida Doctor Olóriz, 25 (at the bullring)* – ☎ *958 29 02 57.* Unusual bullring location, exposed brick, wooden tables, rustic chairs, bullfighting memorabilia . . . not to mention typical Andalusian cuisine. Restaurant one flight up, tapas bar on the ground floor.

🍽️ **Mirador de Morayma** – *Calle Pianista García Carrillo, 2* – ☎ *958 22 82 90 - www.alqueriamorayma.com/mirador* – ⏰ *Closed Sun Jul-Aug, Sun evening rest of year.* One of the most romantic Granada restaurants, with planted terrace, Alhambra views and rustic decor. Local specialities are broad beans with ham *(habas con jamón)* and lamb chops *(chuletas de cordero).*

🍽️ **Ruta del Veleta, in Cenes de la Vega** – *Sierra Nevada, road, 8km/5mi from Granada* – ☎ *958 48 61 34 - www.rutadelveleta.com.* Elegant and popular. Dozens of ceramic jugs hang from the ceiling.

## TAPAS

**Bodegas Castañeda** – *Almireceros, 1-3* – ☎ *958 21 54 64.* Patrons crowd into this typical *bodega* for delicious hot and cold tapas. Metres from plaza Nueva.

**La Trastienda** – *Placeta de Cuchilleros, 11* - ☎ *958 22 69 95.* Descend a couple of steps to get to an 1836 grocery with tapas counter. Excellent *chorizo* at the bar in the pleasant room to the rear.

**Pilar del Toro** – *Hospital de Santa Ana, 12* – ☎ *958 22 54 70.* Stop in just to see the 17C premises with iron gate and large Andalusian patio to the right. **Casa Enrique** – *Acera del Darro, 8* – ☎ *958 25 50 08* – ⏰ *Closed Sun.* This small 1870 tavern is a hallmark and meeting point of Granada. Fine wine cellar, delicious cheeses and cured hams.

## WHERE TO STAY

🛏️ **Hotel Los Jerónimos** – *Calle Gran Capitán, 1* – ☎ *958 29 44 61 - www.hotelosjeronimos.com – 30 rooms.* Adequate, modern, good value; room 502 has a terrace with Alhambra views.

🛏️ **Hotel Los Tilos** – *Plaza Bib-Rambla, 4* – ☎ *958 26 67 12 - www.hotelosjeroni-*

mos.com - *30 rooms*. Modest, renovated, on a square filled with flower stalls, just a few metres from the cathedral. Terrace and views.

**Hotel Maciá Plaza** – *Plaza Nueva, 4 –* ☎ *958 22 75 36 - www.maciahoteles. com – 44 rooms*. Four-storey building on a central square at the foot of the Alhambra. Standard-quality rooms with wicker furniture.

**Hotel América** – *Calle Real de la Alhambra, 53 –* ☎ *958 22 74 71 - reservas@hotelamerica.com – 17 rooms –* 🕐 *Closed Nov-Mar*. A small family hotel superbly located within the Alhambra. Cosy and welcoming.

**Hotel Palacio de Santa Inés** – *Cuesta de Santa Inés, 9 –* ☎ *958 22 23 62 - www.palaciosantaines.com – 35 rooms*. 16C Mudéjar-style building in the Albaicín district, some rooms with Alhambra views, charming patio.

**Carmen de Santa Inés** – *Placeta de Porras, 7 –* ☎ *958 22 63 80 - sinescar@teleline.es – 9 rooms*. Albaicín Moorish villa. Elegant rooms, Alhambra views from the breakfast pergola.

**Parador de Granada** – *Alhambra -* ☎ *958 22 14 40 - www. parador.es -* 🔥 *36 rooms*. Superb. The Alhambra parador is the 15C Convento de San Francisco. Fine views of the Generalife gardens and Sierra Nevada.

## TAKING A BREAK

**El Tren** – *Carril del Picón, 22 –* 🕐 *Open 8am-10pm*. This unusual café—a model train runs on suspended tracks here—is warm and friendly. Extensive choice of teas, coffees and cakes, varied clientele.

**Café Central** – *Elvira, 3 (plaza Nueva) -* ☎ *958 22 48 98* – A classic Granada café on two levels, good for breakfast or a break, assorted coffees and teas.

## GOING OUT FOR THE EVENING

Granada has varied bars, cafés, nightclubs and discos. Calle Pedro Antonio de Alarcón (popular with university students), and the carrera del Darro, close to the Alhambra and Albaicín district, attract a younger crowd.

**Bohemia Jazz Café** – *Calle Santa Teresa, 17 –* ☎ *958 25 12 35 - www. bohemiajazzcafe.com –* 🕐 *Open 3pm-2am (3am Fri-Sat)*. Perfect for a drink (or ice cream, tea, coffee) and low-key

chat to a jazz backdrop. The pianos are collectors' items.

**Tea Houses** – *Calderería Nueva* – Calle Calderería Nueva, between downtown and the Albaicín, transports you to an Arab souk. Pervane offers sweets, teas, coffees and shakes. Kasbah has carpets and cushioned seating, befitting a Moorish guest.

**El Tercer Aviso** – *Plaza de Toros, 1-18* – 🕐 *Open 4pm-5am*. This large café, popular with the 25-45 crowd, is located on several floors, each with its own atmosphere, right in the bull ring.

**La Fontana** – *Carrera del Darro, 19* – 🕐 *Open 4pm-3am*. Antique-adorned heritage house below the Alhambra, inviting, ideal for a quiet drink, coffee, or tea from an extensive menu.

**El Camborio** – *Sacromonte, 47 (on Sacromonte hill) –* 🕐 *Open Tue-Sat, midnight to 6am*. For 30 years a leading nighttime haunt, four connecting cellars with danceable music for finishing the night. Borderline neighborhood, take a taxi.

**Sala Príncipe** – *Campo del Príncipe, 7 -* ☎ *958 22 80 88 - www.salaprincipe. com –* 🕐 *Open Thu-Sat*. This large venue hosting leading Spanish groups is the place to be seen for the city's in-crowd.

## SHOWS

Granada's cultural traditions run deep. Events are programmed all year. The drama season at Teatro Alhambra *(calle Molinos, 54 –* ☎ *958 22 04 47)* is complemented by quality concerts at the Auditorio Manuel de Falla. Shows and exhibitions are listed in the city's cultural guide available at tourist offices.

Paradores

*Patio, Parador de San Francisco*

## SHOPPING

Granada's principal shopping area is along the main avenues in the city centre and in nearby pedestrian streets. Gran Vía de Colón, calle Reyes Católicos and calle Recogidas have a mix of traditional shops, modern boutiques and the occasional shopping centre, such as the Neptuno in calle Recogidas.

The former Moorish silk market, the Alcaicería, is a maze of alleyways in the same area, by the cathedral. Here you'll find souvenir and craft shops, in a Moorish atmosphere. Also in this part of the city, flower stalls add a delightful splash of colour to plaza de Bib-Rambla. Typical crafts of Granada include inlaid wood, particularly on small objects such as boxes and jewellery cases, and pottery. Examples of these can be found in the Alcaicería.

Every Sunday a **market** selling wares of every description is held at the Campo de la Feria on the carretera de Jaén.

*Shopping in the Alcaicería*

B. Kaufmann/MICHELIN

## LOCAL SPECIALITIES

The Alcaicería has a number of pastry shops *(pastelerías)* selling *piononos*, the traditional delicacy of Granada. Those on sale at the Pastelería Flor y Nata, in calle Reyes Católicos, are worthy of their long-established reputation.

# Bit of History

Following early Iberian settlement, Romans founded Illiberis on the Albaicín hill. But the city was of little importance until the arrival of the Moors in the early 8C.

**Moorish Granada** – In 713, Tarik's troops conquered the city, which extended across the Alhambra and Albaicín hills. Granada was part of the Cordoban Caliphate. In 1013, it became the capital of a kingdom (taifa). The **Zirite dynasty** strengthened defences and built the El Bañuelo baths and a bridge, the Puente de Cadí.

In 1090, Granada fell to the **Almoravids**, then in the mid 12C to the **Almohads**. Despite frequent conflicts, the city underwent considerable development. Drainage and sewerage systems were built, and fortifications strengthened.

**Nasrid kingdom** – The ascendancy of the Nasrids in 1238 heralded the city's Golden Age. Mohammed ibn Nasar, the dynasty's founder, acknowledged his position as the vassal of Christian monarch Fernando II, ensuring stability and calm.

The kingdom at this time encompassed Almería and Málaga, and part of Cádiz, Sevilla, Córdoba and Jaén. Granada, prospered, expanded, and embellished itself. Yusuf I (1333-53) and Mohammed V (1353-91), under whose rule the

### The tears of Boabdil

Having handed over the keys to Granada, Boabdil, the last Nasrid king, began his journey into exile. At the place that has gone down in history with the name of The Moor's Sigh *(Suspiro del Moro)*, he stopped to cast a final glance at his beloved city, but was unable to hold back his tears. His mother is said to have turned on him: "You weep like a woman for what you could not hold as a man."

Alhambra's Nasrid palaces were built, transformed Granada into one of the leading cities of the period.

The **15C** was marked by in-fighting. Territory was gradually yielded to the Christians. Following a long siege, the Catholic Monarchs took Granada on 2 January 1492, bringing to a close eight centuries of Moorish domination on the Iberian Peninsula.

**Christian Granada** – Under the Christians, the city's *morisco* population concentrated on the Albaicín. By the end of the 15C the first conflict had broken out following the decree to force baptism upon Muslims. In 1568 rebel leader Abén Humeya, fled to the Alpujarras mountains, where he was subdued by Don Juan of Austria, on the orders of Felipe II. Following this episode, all *moriscos* were expelled from Granada.

During the **16C** and **17C**, the city was transformed. The maze of Moorish lanes gave way to wider streets and spacious squares. The cathedral, Chapel Royal, Charles V's palace, Exchange, Royal Hospital, chancery and Carthusian monastery were built.

In the **18C**, and particularly the **19C**, Granada bewitched numerous visitors. Romanticism forged a new myth for a city long accustomed to praise. Its beauty, mysticism and exoticism became a literary theme for Victor Hugo, Alexandre Dumas and Washington Irving, who penned his famous *Tales of the Alhambra*.

In the 19C Granada received unwelcome visitors. The French sacked the city and even tried to raze the Alhambra, but only destroyed some towers and wall sections.

**Granada today** – The city is the capital of an agricultural and ranching province, lively all year round, its atmosphere generated by the students of its respected university, and thousands of visitors. *Granadinos* believe that their city has the perfect location: on the doorstep of the Sierra Nevada with its sun-blessed ski slopes, just an hour's drive from the Mediterranean, offering the perfect escape in summer.

# Special Features

## Alhambra and Generalife★★★

*Allow half a day.* 🅟 *Purchase tickets in advance to avoid long lines (any BBV bank branch or www.alhambratickets.com).* 🕒 *Open Mar-Oct, 8.30am-8pm (and 10-11.30pm Tue-Sat); Nov-Feb, 8.30am-6pm (and 8-9.30pm Fri-Sat).* ✍€10; last ticket sale 1hr before last entry. Ticket for Alhambra and Generalife gardens specifies entry time to the Nasrid palace. ☎ 958 22 75 25 or 902 44 12 21. Book small-group theme visits Mon at ☎ 902 22 44 60.

Access on foot is along cuesta de Gomérez, from plaza Nueva. Enter by the Puerta de Granadas (Pomegranate Gate, built by Machuca under Charles V), to reach the **shrubbery**★. By car or bus, branch from the Sierra Nevada road where signposted.

### Alhambra★★★

The Calat Alhambra (Red Castle), one of the most remarkable fortresses ever built and the finest Moorish palace standing anywhere, sits atop the highest hill in the city. "La Sabika (as the hill was called) is the crown on Granada's head... and the Alhambra (may God protect her) is the ruby on the crown" wrote the poet Ibn Zamrak (1333-93).

Visitors are spellbound by the splendour of its architecture which incorporates delightful gardens and running water into the overall plan, thus exemplifying

### Key dates

The most accepted chronology for the construction of the Alhambra and Generalife is as follows:

 ◆ late 12C: external walls;

 ◆ 14C: the Generalife, then the Nasrid palaces, built during the reigns of Yusuf I (1333-54) and Mohammed V (1354-59 and 1362-91).

ALHAMBRA

0      40 m

N

**i** Tourist information\*
**Toilets**
**Shop**

BULWARK

Torre de
los Hidalgos

Torre de la Vela

Torre de las Armas

Torre de la Pólvora

Torre de la Sultana

Jardín de los Adarves

**ALCAZABA ★**

Torre del Adarguero

Torre Quebrada

Keep

Turret

Plaza de los Aljibes

Puerta del Vino

Torre de las Gallinas

Patio
de
Machuca

Torre de los Puñales

Torre de Comares

**★ MUSEO DE LA ALHAMBRA**

**NASRID PALACES ★★★**

Mexuar

Oratory

Cuarto
Dorado

**CARLOS V's PALACE ★★**

Museo de Bellas Artes

Patio de los Arrayanes

Sala de la Barca

Salón de Embajadores

Peinador de la Reina

Carlos V's quarters

Puerta de la Justicia ★

Sala de los Abencerrajes

Patio de los Leones

Sala de los Reyes

Sala de Dos Hermanas

Baños Reales

Jardín de Lindaraja

Mirador de Lindaraja

SANTA MARIA

Calle Real

JARDINES DEL PARTAL

251

a Koranic Eden like no other building. But its beauty is full of contradictions. Sumptuous appearances belie the poverty of the materials. It is curious that a power in decline should build a masterpiece and that the Alhambra would be so respected by usurpers.

## Nasrid Palaces (Palacios Nazaríes)★★★

These palaces are the nucleus of the Alhambra. Nothing on their exterior presages their rich and original *mocárabe* vaults, domes, friezes and stuccowork.

The buildings are around three courtyards: the Patio del Cuarto Dorado (Courtyard of the Golden Room), the Patio de los Arrayanes (Myrtle Courtyard) and the Patio de los Leones (Lion Courtyard). The use of small interconnected passageways heightens the impact as one passes from one architectural masterpiece to the next.

### The Mexuar

The tour begins in the rectangular **Mexuar**. Four columns support a stucco-adorned entablature. A frieze of *azulejos* and a calligraphic border cover the walls decorated with coats of arms. This room probably was a council chamber. Note the small oratory leading off the room to the rear.

### Patio del Cuarto Dorado (1)

The magnificent south wall is a compendium of Nasrid art. This outstanding wall-façade comprises *azulejos* with geometric decoration, panels with vegetal features, calligraphic borders, a *mocárabe* frieze, a carved wood cornice and a large eave, all arranged around two doors and five windows.

Opposite is the Cuarto Dorado, with tiled panelling, fine stuccowork and a beautiful wooden ceiling. The **view**★ of the Albaicín from its windows is quite magnificent.

*Mirador de Lindaraja, Alhambra*

B. Kaufmann/MICHELIN

### Patio de los Arrayanes

The entry to the Myrtle Courtyard is to the left of the south wall. This delightful patio has a long, narrow pool. A myrtle border reflects the mass of the **Torre de Comares**; the latter contrasts slender porticoes that give onto the **Sala de la Barca**, under a magnificent wooden vault with a quarter sphere at each end. Walls are adorned with the coats of arms of the Nasrids and calligraphy. This room leads to the **Salón de Embajadores** (Hall of Ambassadors), an audience chamber. The decoration is exquisite: magnificent lustre *azulejo* panelling, delicate stucco with plant and geometric motifs, and calligraphic strips with religious and poetic inscriptions. The remarkable **dome**, above latticework windows, comprising over 8 000 pieces of multi-coloured wood, represents the seven heavens of the Koran. Lattice-covered niches on three sides allowing light to filter through.

### Patio de los Leones

The justly famous Lion Courtyard dates from the reign of Mohammed V. The 11C fountain at its centre, supported by 12 rough stone lions, is surrounded by arcades of slender columns which lead to sumptuous state apartments. Two elegant pavilions on columns project over the sides of the courtyard.

The **Sala de los Abencerrajes** to the south is where the Abencerrajes were slaughtered and their heads piled in the fountain. The room has a stalactite ceiling and a splendid star-shaped lantern cupola illuminated by 16 windows.

The **Sala de los Reyes**, or Kings' Chamber, on the east side, comprises three square sections covered with *mocárabe* cupolas. The vaulting in the alcoves depicts pastimes of Moorish and Christian princes. It probably dates from the late 14C.

The **Sala de Dos Hermanas** (Hall of Two Sisters), is famed for a honeycomb cupola, and fine *azulejos* and stuccowork. A legend attributes its name to two sisters imprisoned within its walls. Beyond are the **Sala de los Ajimeces** and the **Mirador de Lindaraja**, both resplendent with stuccowork and honeycomb decoration. It looks onto the 16C Patio de Lindaraja.

A corridor passes the cupolas of the Royal Baths *(Baños Reales* to the left, ⚷ *currently closed to visitors).* Continue to an open gallery with delightful **views**★ of the Albaicín; descend the stairs to the Patio de la Reja **(2)** and the Patio de Lindaraja.

▷ *Cross the Patio de Lindaraja to enter the Jardines del Partal.*

## Gardens and perimeter towers★★

To the east are the **Jardines del Partal**, terraced gardens which descend to towers punctuating the walls. The first is the **Torre de las Damas** (Ladies' Tower), built by Yusuf I at the beginning of the 14C, preceded by a graceful *artesonado* portico. The Torre del Mihrab and the former Nasrid mosque *(mezquita)* are to the right. The Torre de la Cautiva (Captive's Tower), also dating from the reign of Yusuf I, and the later Torre de las Infantas (Infantas' Tower), have sumptuous internal decoration.

▷ *Enter the Palacio de Carlos V from the Jardines del Partal.*

## Charles V's palace (Palacio de Carlos V)★★

Emperor Charles V commissioned **Pedro Machuca**, who had studied under Michelangelo to build this palace in 1526. The simplicity of its Classical plan – a circle in a square – and the harmony of its lines confer a majestic beauty.

On the main doorway of the lower leve of dressed stone, note the medallions and superb bas-reliefs representing the triumph of peace (at the centre) and battles (to the side). The upper storey bears the escutcheon of Spain.

The outstanding feature is the **circular patio** (31m/102ft in diameter), fronted by Doric and Ionic (upper tier) columns. The patio's simplicity and its beautiful proportions combine to create a masterpiece of the Spanish Renaissance.

The palace contains two museums:

### Museo de la Alhambra★

*Entrance to the right of the vestibule.* This pleasant museum exhibits ceramics, wood carvings, panels of *azulejos* and *alicatados*, stuccowork, bronzes, fabric etc. Outstanding objects include a 10C ablutions basin, known as the Pila de Almanzor, decorated with lions and stags, the famous **blue** or **gazelle amphora**★, a delicate 14C masterpiece, unusual ceramics representing animals, and replicas of household objects.

### Museo de Bellas Artes (Fine Arts Museum)

*Entrance on the upper storey.* Paintings from the 15C and 16C include religious works by renowned artists such as Sánchez Cotán, Siloé, Alonso Cano and Pedro de Mena, and a magnificent still-life, *Thistle and Carrots*★★, by Sánchez Cotán, the equal of Zurbarán.19C and 20C galleries contain works by Rodríguez Acosta, Muñoz Degrain, López Mezquita and Manuel Ángeles Ortiz, including more avant-garde exhibits.

### Puerta del Vino

The Wine Gateway, built by Mohammed V, is purely monumental.

▶ *Pass through the gateway to reach the Alcazaba.*

## Alcazaba★

To the left of the Plaza de los Aljibes (Cistern Court) stands the Alcazaba, the oldest part of the Alhambra, with its defensive walls. Three towers overlook the courtyard: the Torre del Adarguero, the Torre Quebrada and the Torre del Homenaje (keep). View the Alhambra wood from the Jardín de los Adarves on the south side. At the remains of the **Torre de la Vela** (Watchtower) the Catholic Monarchs first hoisted their flags. The tower provides a magnificent **panorama**★★ of the palace, Granada and the Sierra Nevada. To the west are the **Torres Bermejas** (Red Towers). These were built in the late 8C and early 9C, and subsequently modified.

## Puerta de la Justicia★

Built by Yusuf I, the massive Justice Gateway is set in a tower in the outer walls. It comprises a large horseshoe arch and a wide strip of delightful *azulejos* with an image of the Virgin and Child from the 16C.

## Generalife★★

The name Generalife name derives from *Yannat al-Arif*, possibly "most noble of gardens". Terraced **gardens** in which running water plays a predominant role surround a palace. An avenue of cypress trees leads to the new gardens and an auditorium – the setting for Granada's annual Festival of Music and Dance.

The central **Patio de la Acequia**, a long pool *(acequia)* lined with water jets, has a pavilion at either end. A *mirador* alongside affords superb views of the Alhambra. The Sala Regia in the rear pavilion (reached through a portico) has fine stuccowork.

The Patio de la Sultana, enclosed on one side by a 16C gallery, owes its names to the so-called **"Sultana's cypress tree"**.

In the gardens above is the famous **escalera del agua**, or water staircase. *Exit the gardens by Paseo de las Adelfas (Oleander Avenue) and paseo de los Cipreses.*

*Generalife gardens*

B. Kaufmann/MICHELIN

# Cathedral Quarter★★ 1 *Allow 2hrs*

## Cathedral★

*Entrance on Gran Vía de Colón.* ◷ *Open Apr-Sep, 10.30am-1.30pm and 4-8pm, Sun, 4-8pm; Oct-Mar, 10.45am-1.30pm and 4-7pm, Sun, 4-7pm.* €3. ☎ *958 22 29 59.*

---

## A meeting-place for lovers

According to legend, it was by this cypress tree that the wife of the sultan Boabdil and a leader from the rival Abencerraje family would meet. Upon hearing of these secret liaisons, the sultan ordered a massacre of the members of the Abencerraje family in the room of the palace that now bears their name.

Construction of the cathedral began at the center of the Moorish city in 1518 and continued for almost two centuries. A Gothic cathedral like Toledo's was planned. But Diego Siloé, who replaced Enrique Egas as head of the project in 1528, introduced the Renaissance style to the building.

### Interior

*Enter by the ambulatory.* Five lofty aisles lead to an ambulatory. Enormous square pillars with engaged half columns support large sections of entablature, thereby considerably increasing the overall height. The vaulting above is Gothic.

The **high altar**⋆ *(capilla mayor),* richly decorated, is circular and unusually high. The space above the vaulted arches, between chancel and ambulatory, was to house royal tombs; these niches were later covered by portraits of Doctors of the Church. The lower columns have ledges with statues of Apostles and saints, while the second tier contains seven paintings by Alonso Cano of scenes from the life of Mary. Note the **silver tabernacle** in the centre of the presbytery, and the pulpits at each side.

A large **main arch** linking the chapel with the aisles frames statues of the Catholic Monarchs at prayer by Pedro de Mena. Above are two medallions of Adam and Eve, by Alonso Cano. The 18C **organs** between the first two pillars are impressive.

The right transept arm opens to the **north portal of the Chapel Royal**⋆, dominated by a Gothic-style Virgin and Child, by Enrique Egas. Above, Fernando and Isabel's emblems, the yoke and arrow, flank their coat of arms. To the left note the large altarpiece dedicated to St James on horseback, by Alonso de Mena.

The large marble retable in the **Capilla de la Virgen de las Angustias** (Chapel of the Virgin of Anguish) shows the Virgin with the dead Christ in her arms. The **Capilla de Nuestra Señora de la Antigua** contains a fine 15C statue of the Virgin and Child in a magnificent early-18C Baroque altarpiece by Pedro Duque Cornejo. The ambulatory contains an interesting collection of choir books from the 16C to 18C.

The small **Museo Catedralicio** (museum) exhibits silverware, tapestry, vestments, an image of the Virgin of Bethlehem, a bust of St Paul by Alonso Cano, and a bust of the Virgin and Child by Pedro de Mena.

In the **sacristy** is a delightful image of the Virgin, by Alonso Cano.

**Exterior** – Exit the cathedral onto calle Cárcel Baja, where there are two doorways by Siloé. On the lower section of the **Puerta del Perdón** (Pardon Doorway), Faith and Justice hold a tablet. Two magnificent royal escutcheons, of the Catholic Monarchs and Emperor Charles V, adorn the buttresses. The **Portada de San Jerónimo** (St Jerome portal) has a semicircular arch between Plateresque pilasters. The façade facing plaza de las Pasiegas was designed by Alonso Cano in 1667.

## Madraza (Former University)

*In calle Oficios, opposite the Chapel Royal.* The Madraza (Muslim university) was built in the 14C by Yusuf I. The Catholic Monarchs installed Granada's civil administration here. The Baroque façade, with adorning escutcheons, is from an 18C reconstruction. Across the inner patio, stands the Moorish **oratory**, an attractive hall of polychrome stuccowork, *mocárabe* decoration and an octagonal dome adorned with a lantern.

## Capilla Real (Chapel Royal)★★

○ *Open Apr-Oct, 10.30am-1pm and 4-7pm, Sun and public hols, 11am-1pm and 3.30-6.30pm; Nov-Mar, 10.30am-1pm and 3.30-6.30pm.* ○ *Closed 2 Jan (morning), Good Fri and 12 Oct (morning).* ◉€3. ☎ *958 22 92 39.*

The Catholic Monarchs commissioned the Chapel Royal as their burial place. Enrique Egas began the project in 1506 and completed it 15 years later. It is a masterpiece of the Isabelline Gothic style, in its stylistic unity and ornamentation.

Outstanding **exterior** features are the fine pinnacles and elegant **cresting.** The lower section is adorned with the letters F and Y for Fernando and Ysabel. Access is via the old Lonja (Exchange).

The **Lonja** is a graceful 16C Plateresque building. Decorative columns support arches. The city's coat of arms is on the lower section. The upper floor gallery bears the emblems of the Catholic Monarchs and Charles V on the carved sills.

B. Gardel/HEMISPHERES

*Detail on the magnificent screen by Master Bartolomé of Jaén*

The **interior** consists of a single nave with side chapels, and ribbed vaults. A blue fringe with a gilded inscription adorns the upper walls. Heraldic features on the walls and wrought-iron grilles are profuse. A spectacular 16C **screen**★★★ by Master Bartolomé of Jaén encloses the chancel. Note the escutcheon and yoke and arrow of Fernando and Isabel, and scenes of the life of Christ on the upper section.

The two double **mausoleums**★★★ in the chancel, one of the Catholic Monarchs, the other of their daughter, Juana la Loca (Joan the Mad), and her husband, Felipe el Hermoso (Philip the Handsome), are outstanding. The first, the work of Domenico Fancelli, was carved in Genoa in 1517 from Carrara marble, and is decorated with reliefs of Apostles and medallions. The second was carved by Bartolomé Ordóñez in 1519 on a pedestal decorated with religious scenes. The royal remains are in four simple coffins in the chapel's crypt.

> ## A historic place of rest
>
> The importance of the reign of the **Catholic Monarchs** cannot be underestimated, with their influence extending far beyond the Iberian Peninsula. This was particularly true of the discovery of America, to which they had given their financial and political support. Their marriage was also to have a determining effect on the history of Spain, by uniting the kingdoms of Castilla and Aragón into a political and geographical entity that would provide the basis for the future Spanish state and bring the country into the modern age. However, their reign is overshadowed by less glorious events, including the expulsion of Jews from the country and the establishment of the Spanish Inquisition.

The magnificent Plateresque **retable**★ with lifelike figures from the Gospels was sculpted by Felipe Vigarny between 1520 and 1522. The lower register of the predella depicts the siege of Granada. Note the statues of the Catholic Monarchs at prayer.

### Museum
*Access by the north arm of the transept.* Objects of incalculable historical value include **Queen Isabel's sceptre and crown, King Fernando's sword**, plus an outstanding **collection of paintings**★★ by Flemish (Rogier van der Weyden, Memling), Italian (Perugino, Botticelli) and Spanish (Bartolomé Bermejo, Pedro Berruguete) artists. In the rear of the museum are the **Triptych of the Passion** by the Dirk Bouts and two sculptures of the Catholic Monarchs at prayer by Felipe Vigarny.

### Centro de Arte José Guerrero
*In calle Oficios.*
This magnificent late 19C building is a centre of modern art. Its galleries show works by Spanish and foreign artists. The third floor is devoted to Granada painter José Guerrero (1914-1991), associated with the abstract movement in American art.

### Curia
The doorway of this 16C Plateresque-style building is adorned with an archiepiscopal escutcheon. To the left is the simple **Palacio Arzobispal**, or Archbishop's Palace.

### Iglesia del Sagrario
🕐 *Open for worship, Mon-Sat, at 11am and 8pm, Sun and public hols at 11.30am, 12.30, 1.30-7pm (8pm in summer. ☎ 958 22 85 74.*
This 18C church was built over the city's main mosque.

### Plaza Bib-Rambla
This central square with central Neptune fountain is the setting for a number of colourful flower stalls.

### Alcaicería

The restored area of the Moorish silk market, with winding alleyways, arches and oriental decoration, is now a centre for craft and souvenir shops.

### Corral del Carbón

This 14C Moorish storehouse has a harmonious doorway with a horseshoe arch adorned with an *alfiz* surround and inscription. Two panels with *sebka* decoration. flank the window. The doorway has *mocárabe* vaulting.

### Casa de los Duques de Abrantes

*In placeta Tovar, to the left of the Corral del Carbón.* This 16C building has a simple Gothic-influenced doorway with heraldic decoration.

### Plaza de Isabel la Católica

The Monument to the Santa Fe Agreement (1892) in this square, by Mariano Benlliure, shows Columbus presenting his plans to Queen Isabel.

### Casa de los Tiros

This mid-16C palace has an unusual stone façade with five nearly round sculptures of figures in warrior dress. It houses a museum of 19C Granada. The Cuadra Dorada salon has a splendid Renaissance **artesonado ceiling**★ with famous figures in relief.

## Walking Tour

## Carrera del Darro★ ②  *Allow 1hr*

This delightful street runs along the River Darro through through an older, village-like area. Simple stone bridges providing access to Granada's legendary hills, the Alhambra and Albaicín. Start with a look at **plaza Nueva** and **plaza de Santa Ana.**

### Chancillería

The 16C on plaza Nueva former chancery now houses Andalucía's High Court of Justice. The Classical façade combines elements that presage the Baroque. The balustrade is an 18C addition. The harmonious **patio**★ is attributed to Siloé.

*Carrera del Darro*

### Iglesia de Santa Ana y San Gil
*Plaza de Santa Ana.* This small 16C church was designed by Diego de Siloé. The bell tower has *azulejo* decoration. The nave and chancel have Mudéjar ceilings. A 16C fountain, the **Pilar del Toro**, attributed to Siloé, bears Granada's coat of arms.

▶ *Follow carrera del Darro.*

### El Bañuelo★
🕐 *Open Tue-Sat, 10am-2pm.* 🕐 *Closed Sun, Mon and public hols. No charge.* ☎ *958 02 78 00.*
The Moorish baths are opposite the ruins of 11C **Puente del Cadí** (bridge). Part of a tower and horseshoe arch remain. The 11C baths are some of the best preserved in Spain. Note star-pierced vaults with octagonal skylights. The arcades in the last two rooms have Roman, Caliphal and Visigothic capitals.

### Convento de Santa Catalina de Zafra
This 16C convent has a Renaissance-type doorway with semicircular arch framed by pilasters and with medallions on the spandrels.

### Casa Castril
The **archaeological museum** (🔖 *see under Visit*) in the Casa Castril (1539) has a **Plateresque doorway★**, adorned with heraldic motifs, shells, animals, etc.

### Iglesia de San Pedro
*Opposite the museum.* The 16C Church of St Peter is along the Darro under the Comares Tower *(torre)*. The two portal sculptures are St Peter holding the keys and St Paul.

### Paseo de los Tristes
This avenue offers unforgettable nighttime **views**★★ of the illuminated Alhambra rising above. Café terraces provide the perfect spectator seats.

## Albaicín★★ ③ *Allow 1hr 30min*

This hill district, Granada's most famous quarter, offers magnificent views of the Alhambra at every turn. A maze of narrow alleyways wind up between the palisades of small villas known as *cármenes*, through delightful squares past picturesque street corners. Explore on foot.

### Cármenes

This is the name given to the small villas found in the Albaicín. They are a more modern version of a type of Moorish residence or *carmen* which would have consisted of a house and its adjoining kitchen garden *(huerto)*.

### Palacio de los Córdova
*At the foot of the Cuesta del Chapiz.* An avenue of cypress trees in the garden leads to the Municipal Archives, a palace with Renaissance doorway.

### Casa del Chapiz
*Entrance along camino de Sacromonte.* 🕐 *Open Mon-Fri, 8am-8pm (to 3pm Jun-Sep).* 🕐 *Closed Sat-Sun and public hols.* ☎ *958 22 22 90.*
Now the School of Arabic Studies, this is a combination of two Moorish houses from the 15C and 16C, with patios and galleries. The gardens offer Alhambra **views**★. Continue up along cuesta de San Agustín, between typical *cármenes*.

### Mirador de San Nicolás
This terrace in front of the **Iglesia de San Nicolás** enjoys magnificent **views**★★★, of the breathtaking ochre-coloured Alhambra and the outline of the Sierra Nevada.

▷ *Pass before the church; follow callejón de San Cecilio to the end, then turn right and continue through the Arco de las Pesas.*

## Arco de las Pesas
This simple 11C arch alongside the pleasant plaza Larga was part of the walls of the old fortress. It has a typically Moorish structure with an angled entrance.

▷ *Return through the arch. From plaza de Minas, head along cuesta de María de la Miel, then turn right onto camino Nuevo de San Nicolás.*

## Convento de Santa Isabel la Real
Enter this 16C monastery to admire the church's fine, pinnacled Gothic portal bearing the coat of arms and yoke and arrow emblems of the Catholic Monarchs.

## Plaza de San Miguel Bajo
A Christ of the Lanterns stands here. Alongside is the church of San Miguel Bajo. Follow the street opposite the church. The lower town comes into view.

▷ *Turn left and left again along calle Bocanegra, then right along calle San José.*

## Iglesia de San José
The 16C church incorporates a 10C minaret from a mosque as a bell tower.

▷ *Continue heading down, then look to the right immediately after some steps.*

## Casa de Porras
This mansion has a simple stone doorway with heraldic decoration.
A delightful typical villa, the Carmen de los Cipreses (cypress trees), can be seen opposite. The trees that have given the house its name are visible from the street.

▷ *Descend cuesta del Granadillo and the extremely narrow cuesta Aceituneros to where you started.*

# From the University to the Royal Hospital★ ④ *Allow 2hr*

## University
The Baroque seat of the university since the 18C is on plaza de la Universidad; the statue of founder Charles V is in the centre of the square. The building, with Solomonic columns, is now the Faculty of Law.

## Iglesia de los Santos Justo y Pastor
The church, on the same square, once belonged to the Jesuits. Its 18C Baroque portal includes reliefs of St Francis Xavier and St Francis Borgia. The upper tier shows the conversion of St Paul. The wall paintings inside are of interest.

## Colegio de San Bartolomé y Santiago
This college dates from 1621. To the left is the cupola of the Iglesia de los Santos Justo y Pastor. The elegant patio has slender Doric columns and basket-handle arches.
From the corner of calle de la Duquesa and Gran Capitán, admire the monumental **apse** in the church of the **Monasterio de San Jerónimo**★ *(entrance on López de Argueta; ⓘsee description under Visit)*. The **Hospital de San Juan de Dios** in calle San Juan de Dios was built between the 16C and 18C. .

## Iglesia de San Juan de Dios★
This is one of Granada's main Baroque churches, from the early 18C. On the **façade**★, between bell towers, the lower niches hold images of archangels Gabriel and Rap-

hael; the upper section features St. John of God, St. Ildefonsus, and St. Barbara. The **interior**, reached by a carved mahogany doorway, has a Latin-cross ground plan, elevated cupola, and chancel. The massive Churrigueresque altarpiece is of gilded wood. The **camarín** (chapel) behind is accessed via a door to the right of the altar. The middle of three lavishly ornamented rooms houses the tabernacle with the urn containing the remains of the saint – the founder of the Order of Hospitallers, who died in 1550. (⚅ *See under Visit, Casa de los Pisa*).

## Monumento a la Inmaculada Concepción

This 17C monument to the Immaculate Conception stands in the **Jardines del Triunfo** (Triumph Gardens). The statue of a crowned Virgin Mary surrounded by beams of light is by Alonso de Mena.

## Hospital Real

The 16C former Royal Hospital is now the university Rectorate, designed by Enrique Egas in the form of a cross in a square with four patios. Plateresque windows adorn the upper storey. Note the yoke and arrows – emblems of the Catholic Monarchs – over the 17C marble doorway; above it a Virgin and Child is flanked by the statues of Fernando and Isabel. The sculptures are the work of Alonso de Mena. The two patios in the left wing are decorated with heraldic motifs. Stairs lead from the right-hand patio to the library *(biblioteca central)*, which has an open framework and a wooden coffered dome at its centre.

# Visit

## Monasterio de San Jerónimo★

*Entrance on calle López Argüeta.* ⏲ *Open Apr-Oct, 10am-1.30pm and 4-7.30pm; Nov-Mar, 10am-1.30pm and 3-6.30pm.* ⊛ €3. ☎ *958 27 93 37.*
Construction of the monastery, begun in 1496, involved two architects: Jacopo Fiorentino (Jacopo l'Indaco), until 1526, and Diego Siloé, afterward.
Note the **façade** of the church. The upper section shows the coats of arms of the Catholic Monarchs. A fine window is flanked by medallions and grotesque animals.
Plateresque and Renaissance doorways open onto the large **cloisters** completed in 1519 to plans principally by Diego de Siloé. Pillars with foliated capitals support semicircular arches on the lower tier and basket-handle arches above. The church wall has a Plateresque window and the magnificent escutcheon of El Gran Capitán.

### Church★★

Past the fine Siloé-designed **Plateresque doorway** are surprisingly rich interior elements: vaults and domes with high reliefs, a magnificent main retable and murals, an ensemble masterpiece of Spanish Renaissance architecture. Construction began during the Gothic period. The transept and apse were completed under Siloé in Renaissance style. The widow of Gonzalo Fernández de Córdoba financed the building to create a mausoleum for her husband, El Gran Capitán.
Note the apse and the dome with fan vaulting and numerous busts and statues. The vault above the high altar depicts Christ accompanied by Apostles,

B. Kaufmann/MICHELIN

*Detail on the church façade*

angels and saints. The large **retable**★★ of the Granadine School portrays God the Father above clouds on the crowning piece. Statues of El Gran Capitán and his wife at prayer are to the side; a simple stone slab marks the burial place of Don Gonzalo.

## La Cartuja★

🕐 *Open daily, Apr-Oct, 10am-1pm and 4-8pm; Nov-Mar, Mon-Sat, 10am-1pm, Sun and public hols, 10am-noon.* €3. ☎ 958 16 19 32.

Construction of the Carthusian monastery began early in the 16C. Enter the atrium through a Plateresque portal. The church's façade is unpretentious, with the shield of Spain visible above and a statue of St Bruno over the portal. Some of the outbuildings hold paintings by Carthusian monks Sánchez Cotán and Vicente Carducho.

## Church

The church is exuberant with Baroque stucco (1662) and paintings. The areas in the nave reserved for monks and lay brothers are separated by a gilded screen by Sánchez Cotán: *The Baptism of Christ* and *Rest after the Flight into Egypt*.

The Assumption, below the baldaquin, is by José de Mora. Behind is the overwhelmingly exuberant early 18C Baroque **sacrarium**, decorated by Francisco Hurtado.

## Sacristy★★

This Baroque masterpiece (built 1727-1764) masks its structure in a sea of stucco, and cornices all arranged to create an extraordinary effect of light and shadow. Lanjarón marble is used extensively. The magnificent door and the cedarwood furnishings inlaid with tortoiseshell, mother-of-pearl and silver, are by a Carthusian monk, José Manuel Vázquez.

*Sacristy, La Cartuja*

B. Kaufmann/MICHELIN

## Museo Arqueológico

🕐 *Open Wed-Sat, 9am-8.30pm; Tue, 2.30-8.30pm; Sun, 9am-2.30pm.* 🕐 *Closed Mon and public hols.* €1.50 *(no charge for citizens of the European Union).* ☎ 958 22 56 03.

The archaeological museum is in the Casa Castril (1539), a Renaissance palace with a fine **Plateresque doorway** ★. It exhibits 9C BC Egyptian alabaster vases found in Almuñécar, numerous Roman artefacts and Moorish decorative objects. The *Dama de Baza* is a copy of the original in the Museo Arqueológico Nacional in Madrid.

## Casa de los Pisa – Museo de San Juan de Dios

La Pisa family here cared for St. John of God, founder of the Order of Hospitalers, until his death in 1550. The museum displays paintings (Alonso Cano, Flemish), images, and silver and gold objects belonging to the order.

## El Sacromonte

Sacromonte hill rises alongside the Albaicín quarter, opposite the Generalife. **Flamenco shows** are frequently staged in this gypsy district.

## Abadía del Sacromonte

*End of Camino del Sacromonte, bus n° 34, then walk up the steep road.*

Remains found here in the 16C were identifed as those of Cecil, patron saint of Granada. At the hill, and an abbey was built. The museum here displays a lovely 15C Flemish panel of the **Virgin of the Rose**★ by Gerald David; a marble Calvary said to be by Alonso Cano as well as the **Libros plúmbeos** (leaden books), inscribed sheets found with St. Cecil. The **santas cuevas** (holy caves) contain a number of chapels.

## Centro de Interpretación del Sacromonte
*Buses 31 and 34*
A museum in these cave houses in the Barranco de los Negros (canyon) is dedicated to the story and customs of the inhabitants of these unusual dwellings.

## Fundación Rodríguez-Acosta★
The paintings of José María Rodríguez-Acosta (1886-1941) are shown in a *carmen* (Moorish-style house). The **museum**★ dedicated to archaeologist Manuel Gómez-Moreno. exhibits his personal collection: Romanesque and Gothic works, paintings by Zurbarán&, Ribera&, Alonso Cano&, and Chinese and Aztec artifacts.

## Casa-Museo Manuel de Falla
🕐 *Open 10am-1.30 pm.* 🕐 *Closed Mon and public hols.* €3. ☎ *958 22 21 88.*
Manuel de Falla (1876-1946), composer of such famous works as *Love, the Magician*, was a passionate admirer of Granada, which he only came to know after 40. This 16C house, where he lived from 1919 to 1939, is unchanged.

## Carmen de los Mártires
🕐 *Open in summer, Mon-Fri, 10am-2pm and 5-7pm (4-6pm in summer), Sat-Sun and public hols, 10am-6pm.* 🕐 *Closed in Aug. No charge.* ☎ *958 22 79 53.*
The Carmelite monastery is situated on the Alhambra hill. Terraced **gardens**★ are a beautiful setting for a stroll, with their Romantic 19C decor and views of the city.

## Iglesia de Santo Domingo
This Renaissance-style 16C church in the plaza de Santo Domingo retains some Gothic features. The stone portico comprises three semicircular arches adorned with the initials of the Catholic Monarchs, their shield and that of the Emperor Charles V.

## Parque de las Ciencias★
🕐 *Open Tue-Sat, 10am-7pm; Sun and public hols, 10am-3pm.* 🕐 *Closed Mon, 1 Jan, 1 May, second half of Sep, and 24-25 Dec.* €4.50. ☎ *958 37 78 10.*
This complex houses a planetarium, astronomical observatory and a tropical butterfly collection. *Explora* is the area for visitors three to seven.

## Huerta de San Vicente
*Guided tours (30min), Apr-Sep, Tue-Sun, 10am-1pm and 5-8pm; Oct-Nov, Tue-Sun, 10am-1pm and 4-7pm.* 🕐 *Closed Mon and public hols.* €2. ☎ *958 25 84 66.*
This was the summer home of Federico García Lorca (1898-1936), one of the greatest of Spanish poets and writers, conserved as it was during his life.

# GUADIX★

POPULATION: 20 322.

Guadix is perfectly framed by clay hills, backdropped by the **Sierra Nevada.** This mysterious *pueblo* conceals secrets in its troglodyte dwellings, evidenced by a the forest of white chimneys poking up from an underground world.
This crossroads between eastern and western Andalucía was settled by a suc-cession of peoples. It reached its peak during Moorish rule; its fortress *(alcazaba)* survives from those days, though most buildings date from the 17C and 18C.
🛈 *Avenida Mariana Pineda, 18500 Guadix, ☎ 958 66 26 65; otguadix@andalucia.org.*

▶ **Orient Yourself:** Guadix is at the centre of a basin *(hoya)*, 57km/35mi from Granada along A 92. It is a starting point for visiting the Alpujarras (via Puerto de la Ragua, 30km/18mi to the SE) and the east of the province (Baza, Orce etc).
🕐 **Organizing Your Time:** Spend several hours, or a memorable cave night
👶 **Also See:** GRANADA (W), BAZA (4km/28mi NW), SIERRA NEVADA and Las ALPU-JARRAS (S).

## Visit

### Plaza de la Constitución
This pretty arcaded square dates from the 16C and 17C; along one of its sides stands the **town hall**, built at the beginning of the 17C during the reign of Felipe III.

### Cathedral
🕐 *Open Mon-Sat, 10.30am-1pm and 4-6pm. ☞€2 (Thu, no charge) ☎ 958 66 51 08.*
Work began on the cathedral in 1597 to designs by **Diego de Siloé**, and continued until 1715. This is reflected inside, where the Gothic entrance aisles give way to an immense Renaissance dome adorned with a large lantern covering the false tran-sept. The **Capilla de San Torcuato** *(second chapel to the left of the retrochoir)* was designed by Diego de Siloé. Its entrance arch is called a "bull's horn" because its width decreases as it curves. The **Fach-ada de la Encarnación★** *(façade, facing the square)*, exemplifies the theatricality and movement of Baroque architecture. Three horizontal registers increase in complexity as they converge.
Behind the cathedral, in calle Santa María, stand the 16C **Palacio Episcopal** (Bishop's Palace), the Hospital de la Cari-

### The name Guadix

Originally known as **Acci** (hence the name *accitanos* given to modern residents of the Guadix), the name of this former Roman camp changed to the more poetic Guadh-Haix, which translates as "the river of life", during the period of Moorish occupation.

dad and **Palacio de Villalegre** (1592), which has an attractive Renaissance doorway flanked by two solid brick towers.

## Barrio de Santiago★

This is one of the most characteristic districts with seigniorial mansions such as the **Palacio de Peñaflor** in which an unusual **balcony** decorated with wood can be seen. The mansion is built around a beautiful Renaissance patio. The seminary *(seminario menor)* next door provides access to the former Arab **alcazaba** (fortress) dating from the 11C. Although the fortress is in poor condition, a tour of it provides the best views of Guadix and the town's troglodyte district. ⚫━ *Closed for restoration.* ☎ *958 66 93 00.*

Back in calle Barradas, flights of steps lead to plazuela de Santiago. At the end of this small square is the **Iglesia de Santiago**, its lovely Plateresque **doorway**★ crowned with the shield of Charles V, recognisable by the two-headed eagle and the Golden Fleece. The Mudéjar ceiling inside is especially worthy of note. ⓒ*Visits by prior arrangement.* ☎ *958 66 10 97/08 00.*

**Calle Ancha**, which leads off this square, has a number of fine 19C seigniorial mansions.

## Barrio de las Cuevas★

The cave district is situated in the highest part of Guadix, amid a landscape of streams, gullies and small brown hills. The caves are built on different levels, so that those dwellings hollowed into the side of hills often have their entrance on top of the roof of another cave. Solitary caves can occasionally be seen in an isolated location, occupying a single hillside.

## Cueva-Museo

ⓒ *Open 10am-2pm and 4-6pm, Sun and public hols, 10am-2pm.* ⓒ *Closed Sun and public hols.* ⚫€1. ☎ *958 66 93 00.*
The cave-museum re-creates life in a cave dwelling during the 19C. Several rooms exhibit farming and shepherds' tools from the region.

## Museo de Alfarería

*In the Mozarabic district of San Miguel.* ⓒ *Open in summer, Mon-Sat, 10am-1.30pm and 4-8.30pm, Sun and public hols, 11am-2pm; otherwise, Mon-Sat, 10am-1.30pm and 5-9pm, Sun and public hols, 11am-2pm.* ⚫€2. ☎ *958 66 47 67.*

*Barrio de las Cuevas*

## Cave dwellings

The special characteristics of the clay soil found in the **Guadix Basin** have made the construction of these unusual dwellings possible. Clay has the property of being easy to work and yet hardening upon contact with air. The end result is a cave which is impermeable, thermally insulated, and which maintains a constant temperature (18°C/64°F) all year round, making it cool during the hot summer months and warm during the cold winters. Guadix alone has around 2 000 inhabited caves, while one of the largest groups of cave dwellings in Europe exists in the surrounding area. The origin of these dwellings is uncertain, although it would appear that most of them were built after the Christian Reconquest and the progressive segregation imposed upon the area's *morisco* population. In Guadix, these inhabitants were gradually expelled from the Santa Ana district and subsequently occupied the cave dwellings in the troglodyte district visible today.

This pottery museum is housed in a cave of Moorish origin which has retained some of its historical features, including a well dating from 1650 made from Arab bricks and a large earthenware jar from 1640 buried in the floor and possibly used to store wine. The museum clearly demonstrates the rich tradition of pottery in Granada province, including the famous **accitano pitchers**.

### Barrio de Santa Ana

The town's Moorish quarter is a network of narrow alleyways, lined by whitewashed houses decked in flowers and aromatic plants. The **Iglesia de Santa Ana**, built on the site of a mosque in the 15C, can be seen at the heart of the *barrio*. Next to the façade is a Renaissance fountain dating from 1567.

## Excursions

### Purullena

*6km/4mi on the Granada road*. The **road**★★ from Guadix crosses a beautiful landscape of tufa rock. Purullena is known for its cave dwellings and its ceramic shops which can be seen on both sides of the road running through the village. The spa of **Cortes y Graena** is reached after 6km/4mi. The road continues to **La Peza** (13km/8mi), passing through an attractive landscape of low-lying clay hills.

### La Calahorra★

*18.5km/11.5mi southeast on A 92*. Hidden behind the peaks of the Sierra Nevada, like an island surrounded by a sea of almond trees, La Calahorra has retained much of its historic past. One of the most spectacular approaches is the route across the Sierra Nevada via the **Ragua Pass**★★, along which the contrast between the Sierra and the Altiplano can be appreciated to the full. This isolated village, crowned by an impressive fortress, stands much as it did as the capital of the Marquisate of Zenete.
The desolate landscape of the Minas del Marquesado, mines which were abandoned in 1997, is visible 4km/2.5mi from the village.

#### Castillo de la Calahorra★★

 Guided tours, Wed, 10am-1pm and 4-6pm. No charge. ☎ 958 67 70 98.
Despite the castle's robust military appearance, enhanced by four cylindrical towers, one of Spain's most beautiful **Renaissance patios**★★ is hidden inside. The patio was built at the beginning of the 15C in the artistic style of the Italian *quattrocento* and is laid out in a square plan with two sections joined by a splendid **staircase**★★ comprising three flights of stairs. The decoration, particularly on the doorways and capitals, uses the full range of classical features, including mouldings, candelabra, flowers and storiated columns.

# HUELVA★

POPULATION: 150 000

This capital of the westernmost province of Andalucía lies a few kilometres inland amid marshland and channels. Associated with Columbus, Huelva cultivates its links with Latin America. The climate and nearby beaches make it a poular summer destination. 🅸 *Avenida de Alemania, 12, 21001 Huelva, ☎ 959 25 74 03, othuelva@andalucia.org.*

▸ **Orient Yourself:** Huelva is between the mouths of the River Tinto and River Odiel, at a crossroads of routes to Portugal, Cádiz, Extremadura and Sevilla.
🕓 **Organizing Your Time:** Allow several hours, or a full day with nearby sites.
🕭 **Also See:** AYAMONTE, MOGUER, La RÁBIDA, El ROCÍO and SEVILLA (82km/51mi E).

## A Bit of History

Mineral deposits have attracted settlers since ancient times. Phoenicians and Greeks mixed with native groups to give rise to the kingdom of Tartessus, possibly centred on present-day Huelva, then known as Onuba. As Muslim Guelbar, the town developed a range of artisanal activities, such as glazed pottery. Following an unsettled period after the reconquest, the Dukes of Medina came into control. Huelva was marked forever by the arrival of **Christopher Columbus**. As the cradle of discovery and a key port, it underwent commercial expansion; but the 1755 Lisbon earthquake and the devastating early 19C War of Idependence precipitated Huelva's commercial decline. Nowadays, it's the gateway to Parque Nacional de Doñana, and the site of a chemicals complex.

## Visit

### Cathedral
🕓 *Open for services, Mon-Sat, 7pm; Sun and public hols, 11am and 7pm. ☎ 959 24 30 36.*
The main features of this 1605 building, are its Renaissance façade, the sculpture of Christ of Jerusalem and the carving of the Virgen de la Cinta, the patron saint of the city, by Martínez Montañés.

### Iglesia de San Pedro
The **church of St Peter** is at the end of the pleasant paseo de Santa Fe. It is painted a characteristic Huelva white. The bell tower is emblematic of the city.

### Iglesia de la Concepción
Badly damaged during the 1755 earthquake, this Renaissance church is being rebuilt. It contains interesting choir stalls and a number of paintings by Zurbarán.

*The port*

B. Kaufmann/MICHELIN

## Address Book

### WHERE TO EAT

⊜⊜ **Jeromo** – *Plaza de la Merced, 6 – ☎ 959 26 16 18 – Ⓒ Closed Mon, 25 Dec, 1 Jan*. On a noisy square, Jeromo is one of the best fish and seafood restaurants in the city. Highly recommended despite its plain decor.

### TAPAS

**Taberna El Condado** – *Sor Ángela de la Cruz, 3 - ☎ 959 26 11 23 - Ⓒ Closed Sun and Mon mornings-*. A typical tapas bar with barrels used as tables. Good selection of sausages, grilled fish and seafood.

### WHERE TO STAY

⊜ **Los Condes** – *Alameda Sundheim, 14 – ☎ 959 28 24 00 - www.hotelloscondes. com – 54 rooms*. On one of the city's main avenues. Although the building lacks charm, rooms are spacious, modern and clean, and a good value.

⊜⊜⊜ **Monte Conquero** – *Pablo Rada, 10 – ☎ 959 28 55 00 - www.hotel-esmonte.com – 164 rooms, 2 suites*. A large hotel with all modern comforts in one of Huelva's liveliest streets. Private garage.

### TAKING A BREAK

**Pastelería Dioni** – *Palacio, 3 - ☎ 959 24 06 32*. Good place for a break: coffee and pastry shop, tea room upstairs, and almost always full.

### SHOPPING

A wide range of shops can be found in the pedestrianised streets around the Iglesia de la Concepción.

---

### Santuario de Nuestra Señora de la Cinta

Ⓒ *Open for services, Mon-Sat, 7.30pm; Sun and public hols, 1.30 and 7.30pm*. ☎ 959 25 11 22.
Columbus stayed in this building at the end of the elegant paseo del Conquero, on the outskirts of Huelva. The beautiful *azulejos* are by Daniel Zuloaga.

### Museo Provincial

Ⓒ *Open 9am-8pm (Tue, 2.30-8.30pm); Sun and public hols, 9am-2pm. No charge.*
Ⓒ *Closed Mon*. ☎ 959 25 93 00.
Exhibits relate the history of Huelva, notably of the Tartessian civilisation

### Barrio Reina Victoria★

The English-style houses in this district were built for the families of employees of the Río Tinto Company Limited.

### Monumento a la Fe Descubridora

This large sculpture to the Spirit of Discovery is by American artist Gertrude Vanderbilt Whitney. It was erected in 1929 on Punta del Sebo, directly opposite the city.

## Excursions

### Paraje Natural de las Marismas del Odiel★★

*2km/1.2mi SE. Leave Huelva along avenida Tomás Domínguez*. This marsh *(marisma)* is a World Biosphere Reserve, home to over 200 bird species, despite nearby chemical plants. Viewing is spectacular, particularly in February and March. Visit El Burro and Isla de Enmedio sections by **canoe**. Ⓒ *Open Fri-Sun and public hols, 10am-2pm and 4-6pm (8pm in summer). Reserve with reception office,* ☎ 959 50 90 11 or 660 41 49 20.

### San Juan del Puerto

*12km/7.5mi NE along A 472*. The Renaissance **Iglesia de San Juan Bautista** houses a Christ of Mercy, a 16C polychrome sculpture by Juan de Oviedo.

# HUÉSCAR

POPULATION: 8 013

Huéscar is a good base for exploring the east of the province of Granada, known for its archaeological sites and its contrasts, from the semi-desert region around **Orce** to the snowy winter peaks of the **Sierra de la Sagra** and Sierra Seca. The town of Huéscar was founded in 1241 by the **Order of St James**, fell to the Moors, and was reconquered by **Fernando the Catholic** in 1488.

▶ **Orient Yourself:** Huéscar is perched on a high plateau at an altitude of 960m/3 150ft, southeast of the Sierra de la Sagra and the Sierra de Segura.

🕐 **Organizing Your Time:** Allow half a day for Huéscar, including walks.

🚲 **Also See:** BAZA (47km/29mi SW), VÉLEZ BLANCO (56km/35km SE) and the Parque Natural de las Sierras de CAZORLA, SEGURA Y LAS VILLAS.

## Sights

### Plaza Mayor
The town's main square is fronted by the town hall and a number of 19C houses. Note the unusual Art Nouveau-style house in one of the streets leading into the square.

### Colegiata de la Encarnación
Construction of this collegiate church started in the early 16C. The dominant Renaissance style is most notable in the large polygonal ceiling above the transept.

## Excursions

### Galera
*8km/5mi south along A 330.* Between the 13C and 15C, Galera was a border town which changed hands regularly between the Moors and Christians; this history is reflected in its layout. The lower, Christian town, is ordered and built in a square pattern in contrast to the upper town, with its Moorish maze of alleyways, and cave dwellings. Galera is the site of the 6C BC **Iberian necropolis of Tutugi**, and the Argar settlement of **Castellón Alto**, dating from 1600 BC. 🕐 *Open Sat-Sun and public hols, 10.30am-1pm and 4-6pm; midweek by prior arrangement.* ☎ *958 73 92 73.*
The Iglesia de la Anunciación dates from the 15C.

### Orce★
*16km/10mi southeast of Huéscar. Follow A 330 and bear left onto SE 34 before Galera.* Orce is situated in the eastern part of the Baza Basin, in an impressively wild and desertic landscape which undergoes surprising changes of light and colour. The elegant stone tower of the 16C **parish church** and the recently restored **Palacio de los Segura**, also dating from the 16C, stand out among

**WHERE TO STAY**

🍽 **Molinos de Portillo**
– 2.5km/1.5mi along Santas road
– ☎ 958 34 45 04 - www.molinode-portillo.com - 🚲 – 7 rooms – 🕐 Closed 23-25 Dec. This inn takes up an early 20C flour mill, with simple, comfortable rooms. Tranquillity is assured. The restaurant serves grilled meats.

🍽🍽 **Casas-Cueva** – *Iglesia, 4 – Galera* – ☎ 958 73 90 68 - www.casas-cueva.es – 32 caves. Original and reasonably priced, off-beat accommodation with magnificent views of the unique landscape. Pleasant caves with all mod cons, plus a welcome bottle of wine.

whitewashed houses. The palace has a simple façade and an elegant patio supported by stone columns.

### Museo Municipal de Prehistoria y Paleontología

🕐 *Open Jun-Sep, Mon-Sat, 11am-1pm and 6-8pm; Oct-May, Mon-Sat, 11am-2pm and 4-6pm.* 🕐 *Closed Mon.* ⊜€1.50. ☎ 958 74 61 01.

The museum of prehistory and palaeontology is in the **Castillo-Alcazaba de las Siete Torres**, a 16C Christian fortress with seven towers *(torres)*, largely restored. The museum exhibits numerous bones and stones from the region's archaeological sites, including a piece of skull which made the town famous at the beginning of the 1980s, and an infant humerus, possibly 1.5 million years old. If this date is confirmed, this would be the oldest hominid palaeontological discovery in Europe.

### Fuencaliente

*2km/1.2mi from Orce, on the Galera road.* Water gushes from this spring in a desert landscape at a constant 18°C/64°F. It's a pleasant spot to cool off in the summer.

### Castril

*22km/14mi west along A 326.* Castril is a typical mountain village at the foot of an impressive cliff, surrounded by the beautiful and largely unknown **Parque Natural de la Sierra de Castril**. The village is thought to have its origins in a Roman military camp; its name comes from the Arabic *qastal*, or fortress. After the definitive reconquest in the 15C, Castril became part of the seigniory of Hernándo de Zafra, who established the town's famous glassworks, which closed in 1878. Today, pieces of green and yellow glass are collector's items; some are in the Museo Arqueológico de Granada. The 15C **parish church** is particularly worthy of note.

### Parque Natural de la Sierra de Castril★

This nature park is the extension of the neighbouring Sierra de Cazorla. Its most notable characteristic is its spectacular relief, mainly the result of woodcutting for the glassworks. ⟋⟍A walk of around two hours starting in the lower part of Castril skirts the river and continues around the outskirts of the village. For information on walks in the area, contact the **Visitor Centre** *(Centro de Visitantes)*, which also houses an interesting ethnographical museum. 🕐 *Open in summer, Wed-Sun and public hols, 9am-2pm and 6-8pm; otherwise, Thu, 10am-2pm, Fri, 4-6pm, Sat-Sun and public hols, 10am-2pm and 4-6pm. Other days of the week by prior arrangement.* ☎ 958 72 00 59.

# IZNÁJAR ★

POPULATION: 5 200

Iznájar's **magnificent site**★, atop of a hill that juts out into the **Iznájar Reservoir** *(embalse)*, offers a foretaste of its charms. Picturesque houses line steep whitewashed streets leading to the upper part of the town, which is dominated by the ochre-coloured stone of the church and the remains of the Moorish castle.
🏛 *Calle Julio Burell, 14970 Iznájar,* ☎ *957 53 40 33.*

▶ **Orient Yourself:** Iznájar is in the Sistema Subbético mountain range at the southern tip of Córdoba province, near the borders of Málaga and Granada.

🕐 **Organizing Your Time:** Allow what you'd spend on a country getaway.

👁 **Also See:** PRIEGO DE CÓRDOBA (26km/16mi N), LUCENA (35km/22mi NW), CABRA (46km/29mi NW) and MONTEFRÍO (40km/25mi NE).

*Iznájar and its reservoir*

## Walking Tour

The countryside surrounding Iznájar is never far from view. Several street corners provide stunning **views**. The panorama from the castle and church quarter takes in far-distant landscapes carpeted in olive groves.

### Castle
The origins of the castle date back to the 8C. The Moors called this strategic site Hisn Ashar. The remains of sections of wall and several towers are still visible.

### Biblioteca Municipal
The municipal library is housed in the former granary, built during the reign of Carlos III.

### Parroquia de Santiago
This 16C Renaissance-style parish church was built with large pieces of ashlar stone. It is topped by a truncated tower.

### Mirador de la Cruz de San Pedro
*At the end of calle Cruz de San Pedro.* This mirador offers **views**★ of the fortress and church, the lake and the town.
The lower part of the town is the site of the **Museo Etnográfico**, an ethnographical museum displaying a collection of implements, ploughing tools and other instruments used to work the land, and the **Casa de las Columnas**, with heraldic decoration on its façade. ○ *Open 10am-2pm.* ○ *Closed Sat-Sun and public hols. No charge.* ☎ *957 53 40 33.*

### Embalse de Iznájar
The 30km/18mi-long Iznájar Reservoir, also known as the Lago de Andalucía (Lake of Andalucía), dams the waters of the River Genil. The eastern section of the lake is part of Granada province. The Playa de Valdearenas, on its shoreline, is a popular beach for swimmers and water sports enthusiasts.

# JAÉN ★

POPULATION: 107 413

Spain's olive capital rises onto Cerro de Santa Catalina (St Catherine's Hill). Jaén is a storehouse of artistic heritage, from its Moorish castle to numerous Renaissance buildings, many designed by Andrés de Vandelvira. *Calle Maestra, 13 bajo, 23002 Jaén, ☎ 953 24 26 24, otjaen@andalucia.org.*

▸ **Orient Yourself:** Jaén extends along the crescent at the base of the Sierra de Jabalcuz. The A 44 – E 902 links Jaén with Granada (94km/59mi S).
🕐 **Organizing Your Time:** Take at least a full day to savour Jaén.
**Kids Especially for Kids:** The castle is *the* site.
👁 **Also See:** MARTOS (24km/15mi SW), BAEZA (48km/30mi NE), ÚBEDA (57km/36mi NE), PRIEGO DE CÓRDOBA (67km/42mi SW), ALCALÁ LA REAL and GRANADA.

## A Bit of History

Jaén was called *Aurigi* following conquest by Roman general Publius Cornelius Scipio in 207 BC, then *Djayyân* (on the caravan route), and *Geen* under the Moors. Fernando III the Saint turned Jaén into a bastion upon its reconquest in 1246. Jaén declined after the final Christian victory. Olive oil has brought an upturn in fortunes.

## Visit

### Town Centre *Allow half a day*

#### Cathedral★★
🕐 *Open in summer, daily except Sun afternoon, 8.30am-1pm and 5-8pm; otherwise, 8.30am-1pm and 4.30-7pm.* €3. ☎ *953 23 42 33 or 953 22 46 75.*
Towering over old Jaén, built in the 16C and 17C to plans by Andrés de Vandelvira, this is one of the most extraordinary Renaissance buildings in Andalucía.

*Partial view of the cathedral façade*

## Main façade★★

On the lower tier of the sumptuous façade, fine reliefs represent the Assumption of the Virgin, the archangel St Michael, and St Catherine. Sculptures on the full **balustrade**★ represent King Fernando, the four Evangelists and the Doctors of the Church.

## Interior★★

The domed transept is a magnificent work by Pedro del Portillo and Juan de Aranda. Admire the wash of light into the huge building. The **choir stalls**★★ are by José Gallego and Oviedo del Portal, disciples of Alonso Berruguete. The altarpiece includes the Gothic **Virgin of La Antigua**★. The **Veil of the Holy Face**★, used by Veronica to wipe the face of Christ on his way to Calvary, bears His features. Note the *Annunciation* by Cellini and a *Visitation* attributed to Titian. The most outstanding side chapels are the Capilla de San Fernando *(left of the high altar,* fine statue of Our Father Jesus of Nazareth); Capilla del Santísimo Sacramento (Baroque altarpiece and image of St. Benedict by Pedro Duque Cornejo, 18C); and Capilla de la Virgen de las Angustias (sculptures by José de Mora).The chapter house *(sala capitular)* holds a fine 16C *Sagrada Familia* by Pedro Machuca.

## Museum

The Museo Catedralicio is in the **sacristy** (by Vandelvira). *Access by right transept.* Exhibits include a Flemish *Virgin and Child*, two **Ribera** canvases, choir books, gold and silverwork, and candelabra by Maestro Bartolomé. ○ *Open in summer, 10am-1pm and 5-8pm; otherwise, 10am-1pm and 4-7pm.* ⊛ *€3.* ☏ *953 23 42 33.*

## Iglesia del Sagrario

In this sober, late-18C neo-Classical church designed by por Ventura Rodríguez, beside the cathedral, is an *Assumption of the Virgin*, painted by Salvador Maella.

## Convento de Santa Teresa (Convento de las Descalzas)

The Convent of Poor Clares (or Discalced Nuns) has a *Spiritual Canticle* handwritten by St John of the Cross. **Pastries** produced by the nuns here are the major attraction.

## Palacio Provincial

An ex-Franciscan monastery houses the provincial administration *(Diputación Provincial).* The internal patio is fronted by a double gallery of columns.

## Iglesia de San Bartolomé

Past the sober façade of this 16C-17C church is a wonderful **Mudéjar artesonado ceiling**. A processional during Holy Week displays The Christ of the Expiration.

## Iglesia de San Ildefonso★

○ *Open 9am-noon and 5-8pm; Sun and public hols 9am-2pm. No visits during religious services.* ☏ *953 19 03 46.*
The second-largest church in Jaén is from the 14C and 15C. A mosaic in the main Gothic portal shows the *Descent of the Virgin of the Chapel*. A Renaissance portal is by Vandelvira; an 18C neo-Classical portal by Ventura Rodríguez. The magnificent **main altarpiece** is by Pedro and Julio Roldán, the fine tabernacle by Pedro Duque Cornejo. An altar holds the **Virgen de la Capilla**, Jaén's patron saint.

## Convento de las Bernardas

○ *Open 9.30am-12.45pm and 4.30-8pm.* ○ *Closed Holy Week.* ☏ *953 24 38 54.*
A small church in this 16C convent houses in its transept the paintings of the *Annunciation* and the *Assumption of the Virgin*, works by the Italian artist Angelo Nardi.

## Address Book

### TRANSPORT

**Airport** – The nearest airport is in Granada (☎ *958 24 52 00)*, 50min to the south along the fast N 323 highway.

**Trains** – Direct routes from the station on paseo de las Culturas (☎ *953 270202)* to Madrid, Córdoba, Sevilla and Cádiz.

**Inter-city buses** – Buses run from the central station on plaza de Coca de la Piñera (☎ *953 25 01 06)* to every provincial capital in Andalucía and to major cities around Spain.

**Local buses** – A single bus ticket costs €0.75, and a ten-trip ticket €5.10. ☎ *953 21 91 00/88.*

**Taxis** – ☎ *953 22 22 22.*

**Horse-drawn carriages** – These can be hired at several central locations.

### SIGHTSEEING

Get to know Jaén's *barrios*: **La Magdalena**, at once Moorish and Christian; **San Juan**, the hub of nightlife; and **Santa María**, for heritage buildings.

✆ *For coin ranges, see the Legend on the cover flap.*

### WHERE TO EAT

⊜⊜ **Mesón Río Chico** – *Nueva, 12* – ☎ *953 24 08 02* – 🕐 *Closed Sun evening, Mon and in Aug.* A cellar on a street of bars and restaurants. *Raciones* de fish, *flamenquines* (ham and cheese rolls), mussels and more. More formal dining upstairs, fair prices.

⊜⊜ **Mesón Nuyra** – *Pasaje Nuyra* – ☎ *953 24 07 63* – 🕐 *Closed Sun evening and first two weeks of Jul.* This traditional cellar restaurant is close to calle Nueva. The menu includes suckling pig *(cochinillo)* and sirloin steak *(solomillo de vaca).*

⊜⊜⊟ **Casa Vicente** – *Francisco Martín Mora, 1* – ☎ *953 23 22 22* – 🕐 *Closed Sun evening, Mon and in Aug.* The dining rooms in this traditional home surround an attractive patio. Fine regional cuisine, steps from the cathedral.

### TAPAS

**La Manchega** – *Bernardo López, 8* – ☎ *953 23 21 91* – 🕐 *Closed Tue.* This bar, started in 1886, makes no concession to current fashions and serves an excellent selection of sausage tapas and wine.

### WHERE TO STAY

⊜ **Hotel Husa Europa** – *Plaza Belén, 1* – ☎ *953 22 27 00 - www.husa.es* – *37 rooms.* This modern hotel lacks charm, but rooms are functional, comfortable, and well equipped. Its central location makes it a good vaule. Bikes for rent.

⊜⊜⊟⊟ **Parador de Jaén** – *Carretera del Castillo de Santa Catalina (4.5km/2.8mi W)* – ☎ *953 23 00 00 - www.parador.es* – *45 rooms.* Jaén's *parador* is in the 13C Moorish fortress above town, with magnificent views of mountains and olive groves. Worth stopping by for dinner or drinks.

### TAKING A BREAK

**Ábaco** – *Avenida Muñoz Grandes, 5* – ☎ *953 27 68 71* 🕐 *Open 4pm-5am.* Modern, meticulously decorated bar for a quiet afternoon drink or dancing at night, popular with a range of ages.

**Café-Bar del Pósito** – *Plaza del Pósito, 10* – 🕐 *Open 9am-1.30am.* Close by the cathedral, mixes jazz and flamenco, attracts under-40s. Art exhibitions held.

**Chubby-Cheek** – *San Francisco Javier, 7* - ☎ *953 27 38 19 - www.chubbycheek. com* – 🕐 *Open 4.30pm-2am.* A café which lives and breathes jazz. Concerts on Thursday evenings. A pleasant place for a coffee or quiet drink. Clientele changes with the hour.

**Trujal** – *Calle Hurtado, 21* - ☎ *953 23 44 84* – 🕐 *Open 4pm-3am.* This bar in the San Ildefonso area is for thirtysomethings. Cosy, rustic, candle-lit.

### ENTERTAINMENT

For an up-to-date list of cultural events in Jaén and around the province, consult *Agenda Turístico-Cultural*, published monthly by the town hall and available from tourist offices. The booklet is also on-line at *www.promojaen.es*. The **Teatro Darymelia**, in calle Maestra (☎ *953 21 91 80)*, organises an excellent programme of theatrical events.

### SHOPPING

Jaén's main shopping streets are located around **plaza de la Constitución**.

Calle Virgen de la Capilla, calle San Clemente and paseo de la Estación are the main commercial arteries, along with other adjoining streets lined by small shops and the occasional large department store, such as **El Corte Inglés**, in calle Roldán y Marín.

**Markets** – An open-air *mercadillo* selling a wide selection of food, clothes and other goods is held on Thursday mornings at the fairground *(recinto ferial)* near Alameda de Calvo Sotelo.

## LOCAL SPECIALITIES

Gastronomic specialities include *pestiños* (honeyed doughnuts) and *pipirrana*, a type of cold soup made with garlic, green peppers, ripe tomatoes and breadcrumbs, and of course exquisite olive oil.

## FESTIVALS

No description of Jaén is complete without mention of its **Holy Week** celebrations, when dramatic Andalusian religious songs fill the streets.

### Real Monasterio de Santa Clara

The outstanding feature of this 13C monastery, the oldest in the city, is its church, with an unusual 16C bamboo image of Christ.

### Iglesia de San Juan

This post-reconquest church has a noteworthy collection of Gothic carvings.

### Capilla de San Andrés★

◷ *Open 10am-noon.* ☎ *953 23 74 22.*
This 16C Mudéjar chapel with Judaic features, on a steep street, was commissioned by Gutierre González Doncel, treasurer to Pope Leo X. The **Capilla de la Purísima Inmaculada**★★ (Chapel of the Immaculate Conception) is a Plateresque masterpiece. The gilded chapel **screen**★ is by Maestro Bartolomé (16C), a native of Jaén.

### Palacio de Villardompardo

◷ *Open Tue-Fri, 9am-8pm (last admission 30min before closing); Sat-Sun, 9.30am-2.30pm.* ◷ *Closed Mon and public hols. No charge.* ☎ *953 24 80 00 (ext 4166).*
This elegant 16C palace with arcaded **patio**★ was the residence of Fernando de Torres y Portugal, Viceroy of Peru and Count of Villardompardo. The **Museo de Artes y Costumbres Populares** in several rooms illuminates the lives of everyday folk through farm tools, household objects and clothing; the **Museo Internacional de Arte Naïf**, devoted to naive art, shows a fine collection of paintings and sculptures.

### Moorish Baths★★

The *Baños Árabes*, situated deep below the palace, are the largest that remain in Spain. As you enter, note the 11C remains from the period of construction, protected under glass. An excellent restoration allows appreciation of Moorish architectural mastery. Light delicately penetrates the shadows to create a pleasant sensation of calm. Its 450 sq m²/ 4 842 sq ft of baths comprise a barrel-vaulted entrance hall with star-shaped skylight and alcoves at either end; a cold room; a larger warm room, roofed with a handsome hemispherical cupola on pendentives; and a hot room (*left of the warm room*) next to the boilers.

*Moorish Baths*

H. Belmenouar/MICHELIN

## JAÉN

### Real Monasterio de Santo Domingo

🕐 *Open in summer, 9am-1pm; otherwise, 8.30am-2pm.* ☎ *953 23 85 00.*

This royal monastery, founded by Juan I above a Moorish palace, became headquarters of the Inquisition. The Renaissance façade is by Vandelvira. In the 17C inner **patio**★, a delicate gallery of arches rests on paired columns. Window openings are finely carved. Historical archives (**Archivo Histórico Provincial**) are kept here.

### Iglesia de la Magdalena

This lovely 16C Isabelline church retains the patio of a mosque and its ritual pool. The fine *Calvary* is by Jacopo I'Indaco, the 18C relief of *La Magdalena* by Mateo Medina. The 19C fountain opposite (*Fuente del Raudal*) once provided drinking water.

### Monasterio de Santa Úrsula

🕐 *Open by prior arrangement.* ☎ *953 19 01 15.*

The convent's church has a fine Mudéjar *artesonado* ceiling. By all means, try the traditional **candied egg yolks** *(yemas)* produced by the nuns of Santa Úrsula.

## Outside the Centre

### Castillo de Santa Catalina★

*5km/3mi W. Best approached by car.* 🕐 *Open in summer, 10am-2pm and 5.30-9.30pm; otherwise, 10am-2pm and 3.30-7.30pm.* 🕐 *Closed Mon.* ⊚ *€3.* ☎ *953 12 07 33.*

This once-Moorish hilltop fortress (now a parador) became the starting point for the monumental walls of Jaén (of which only the Baroque 17C **Puerta del Ángel** and the arches of **San Lorenzo** and Consuelo remain). Remaining sections include the **Capilla de Santa Catalina** in a turret, accessed via a delicate horseshoe arch; and the graceful keep, affording stupendous **views**★★ of Sierra de Jabalcuz.

### Museo Provincial

🕐 *Open Wed-Sat, 9am-8pm; Tue, 3-8pm; Sun and public hols, 9am-3pm.* 🕐 *Closed Mon.* ⊚ *€1.50 (no charge for EU citizens).* ☎ *953 25 06 00.*

The main building from 1920 incorporates the façades of the former public granary *(pósito)* – note the reliefs of wheat and a bread basket – and of the Iglesia de San Miguel, both from the 16C. The 6C BC set of **Iberian carvings from Porcuna**★ (bulls, sphinxes, high priests and warriors) is the outstanding exhibit in the archaeological section *(ground floor)*. Roman items include the **Bruñel** mosaic, striking in its complexity and use of colour. The marble **sarcophagus from Martos**★ is a magnificent palaeo-Christian work between columned porticoes representing seven miraculous scenes from the life of Jesus. The fine arts section *(upstairs)* displays works by Pedro Berruguete, Alonso Cano, José and Federico de Madrazo, Mariano Benlliure and Antonio López *(Women in Dialogue)*.

## Excursions

### La Guardia de Jaén

*10km/6mi southeast along A 44 – E 902.* Impressive **views** from the Moorish fortress above the village take in the Cerro de San Martos and distant fields and orchards.

### Parque Natural de la Sierra Mágina

*35km/22mi east. Take avenida de Granada, follow A 316 and A 320 towards Mancha Real, then JV 3242.* 🔲 **Centro de interpretación de Jodar**. ☎ *953 78 76 56.*

This park is part of the Cordillera Subbética, between the Guadalquivir Depression and the Sierra de Lucena. Its 19 900ha/49 127 acres of mostly oak forest are a habitat for the imperial eagle, peregrine falcon and mountain goat.

# JEREZ DE LA FRONTERA★★

POPULATION: 181 602

Jerez, horses and sherry go together. Horses dominate the local festivals. The aroma of sherry wafts through streets and alleyways. Jerez boasts one of the finest architectural heritages of the province and with Sevilla is the birthplace of flamenco. The traditional Andalusian dance, the *bulería*, takes place in the town's humble gypsy quarters. 🏠 *Alameda Cristina (Los Claustros bldg),* ☎ *956 32 47 47, turismoinfo@aytojerez.es*

▶ **Orient Yourself:** Jerez is 35km/22mi from the provincial capital, Cádiz, 30km/19mi from Arcos de la Frontera, and 90km/56mi from Sevilla along A 4 – E 5.
🕐 **Organizing Your Time:** Allow a day or more for sherry tasting and the sea.
Kids **Especially for Kids:** The zoo is a good stop.
👣 **Also See:** EL PUERTO DE SANTA MARÍA, CÁDIZ, SANLÚCAR DE BARRAMEDA, ARCOS DE LA FRONTERA and PUEBLOS BLANCOS DE ANDALUCÍA.

## A Bit of History

### The ABCs of sherry

The **Sherry appellation** covers the triangle between **Jerez**, **Sanlúcar** and **El Puerto de Santa María**. Wines from this area earn **Denominación de Origen Jerez-Xerez-Sherry** status and are regulated by the Consejo Regulador.

**Albariza** – A light-coloured soil containing loam of marine origin. Its ability to retain moisture makes it ideal for grape cultivation.
**Palomino** – 95% of the grapes grown in Jerez are of the Palomino variety, introduced to the region during the time of Alfonso X.
**Pedro Ximénez** – This grape variety was introduced in 1680 by a Flemish soldier.
**Botas** – Three types of barrels are used: *bocolles*, *toneles* and *botas*. The *botas* (500 litres), made from American oak, are most common.
**Sobretabla** – This is the youngest wine which is placed in the first *criadera*. This is the fermented must fortified to bring the alcohol level to 15%.
**Flor del vino** – This layer of surface yeast both ferments and prevents oxidisation.
**Solera and Criaderas** – The *solera* is the row of casks *(barricas)* closest to the floor, with the oldest wine. The rows above are *criaderas*. The wine descends from the top level (first *criadera*) to the *solera*, a process known as "running down the ladder".

### 13C Jerez

The capture of Sevilla in 1248 by Fernando III the Saint led to the opening up of the Lower Guadalquivir Valley to Christian troops, who subsequently occupied cities such as Arcos, Medina and Jerez de la Frontera. Jerez finally came under Castilian control on 9 October 1264, the feast day of St Dionysius. During this period, the city was surrounded by a rectangular wall, built by the Almohads, with a perimeter of more than 4km/2.5mi; remains of this defensive structure can still be seen in calle Porvera and calle Ancha. Three gates led into the city, which was divided into six parishes or *collaciones* (Cádiz only had one), named after the four Evangelists, St Dionysius (the city's patron saint) and the Saviour. The suburbs of San Miguel and Santiago, as well as the Dominican and Franciscan monasteries, stood outside the walls. From the 13C onwards, the city played a key role in the defensive border system established between the Christian and Nasrid kingdom.

### Types of sherry
**Fino** – This is a dry wine which is light and straw-like in colour, with an alcohol content of 15%. An excellent accompaniment to fish and seafood.
**Amontillado** – An amber sherry, dry and aromatic. About 17% alcohol.
**Oloroso** – Dark in colour with a sharp aroma. Around 18% alcohol.
**Cream** – A sweet, dark sherry produced from *oloroso,* a perfect dessert wine.
**Pedro Ximénez** – The sweet ruby wine made from the Pedro Ximénez grape.

### The main sherry bodegas
**Pedro Domecq** – *Calle San Ildefonso 3, Jerez,* ☎ *956 15 15 00, www.domecq.es.* *Guided tours Mon-Fri 9am-1pm.* €4. The 18C El Molino *bodega* is impressive.
**González Byass (Tío Pepe)** – *Calle Manuel María González 12, Jerez, www.gonzalezbyass.es.* *Guided tours daily (1hr), Mon-Sat, 11am-5pm.* €7. ☎ *956 35 70 16.* Founded in 1835. The La Concha *bodega* was designed by Eiffel in 1892; barrels in La Constancia bear famous signatures. Original tasting room.
**Williams & Humbert** – *Highway 4 Km 642, www.williams-humbert.com* *Guided tours Mon-Fri, 9am-3pm; later by arrangement.* €4.50. ☎ *956 35 34 06.* Museum.
**Sandeman** – *Calle Pizarro , 10, Jerez, www.sandeman.com.* *Guided tours Mon-Fri 11am-3pm.* €4.15. ☎ *956 30 26 26.*
Learn about sherry and other *bodega* tours at www.sherry.org.

## Walking Tour

## Historic Jerez★★

The itinerary below starts in the medieval quarter, with visits to several "churches of the Reconquest" *(most open during services, from 7pm),* followed by the medieval districts of San Miguel and Santiago, now lively with outdoor cafés and shops.

### Plaza del Mercado
The Moorish market once stood on this square in working-class San Mateo. The surviving façade of the Renaissance **Palacio de Riquelme** stands out like a stage set. The **Museo Arqueológico** (👁 *see under Visit)* and **Iglesia de San Mateo** are here.

*Detail, main façade of the cathedral*

# Address Book

## TRANSPORT

**Airport** – La Parra airport (☎ 956 15 00 00/1 83) is located 7km/4.5mi from the city along A 4. Best access by taxi.

**Trains** – Plaza de la Estación (☎ 956 34 23 19). Services to Sevilla, Madrid, Barcelona and, most frequently, Cádiz.

**RENFE (Spanish State Railways)** – Ticket office at calle Tonería, 4 – ☎ 956 33 79 75 or 902 24 02 02.

**Local buses** – A single ticket costs €0.90, a 10-trip ticket €6, monthly passes available. ☎ 956 14 36 08/9.

**Inter-city buses** – The station is on calle Cartuja (☎ 956 34 52 07).

**Taxis** – ☎ 956 34 48 60.

**Horse-drawn carriages** – Horse-drawn carriages can be hired, stopping at the min sites of interest.

## WHERE TO EAT

🍽🍽 **Gaitán** – Gaitán, 3-5 – ☎ 956 16 80 21 - www.restaurantegaitan.com – ⏲ Closed Sun. Respected restaurant serving innovative regional cuisine. The elongated dining room is replete with decoration.

🍽 **San Juan** – Plaza Melgarejo – ☎ 956 32 64 71 – ⏲ Closed Mon and in summer – reservation advised. Pleasant Italian restaurant arranged around a glass-covered patio. Attractive decor with enormous canvases of a fradmented David by Michelangelo, and recycled theatre seats. Try fresh stuffed pasta or sirloin à la San Juan.

🍽🍽 **Tendido 6** – Circo, 10 – ☎ 956 34 48 35 35 - www.tendido6.com – ⏲ Closed Sun. Next to the bullring. One of the best restaurants in Jerez, serving Andalusian meat and fish specialities on a covered patio, also a tapas bar.

🍽🍽🍽 **La Taberna Flamenca** – Angostillo de Santiago, 3 – ☎ 956 32 36 93 - www.latabernaflamenca. com – ⏲ Closed Sun-Mon Nov-Apr. A large tavern located in a former wine storehouse. Dinner is served from 8pm; flamenco show May-Oct, Tue, Wed, Thu and Sat, starting at 2.30pm; Nov-May 10pm and Thu at 2.30pm.

## TAPAS

**Juanito** – Pescadería Vieja, 8-10 – ☎ 956 33 48 38 - www.bar-juanito.com – ⏲ Closed feria week. On a pedestrian way teeming with outdoor cafés, the venerable Bar Juanito serves award-winning tapas. Quintessentially Andalusian: azulejos and bullfighting paintings and posters adorn the walls.

**El Gallo Azul** – Larga, 2 - ☎ 956 32 61 48. Brilliant choice for a break and drink amongst the to-and-fro of the heart of Jerez. Lovely columned façade.

## WHERE TO STAY

🛏 **Nuevo Hotel** – Caballeros, 23 - ☎ 956 33 16 00 - www.nuevohotel.com - 27 rooms. This 19C mansion was one of the first hotels of Jerez. Rooms are modest but large, around a central patio; n° 208 has fine plasterwork of Moorish inspiration.

🛏 **Serit** – Higueras, 7 – ☎ 956 34 07 00 - www.hotelserit.com - ♿ – 35 rooms. Central, homey, functional and up-to-date; 7 rooms in annex have wood floors and wrought-iron furniture.

🛏🛏 **Hotel Doña Blanca** – Bodegas, 11 - ☎ 956 34 87 61 - www.hotel-donablanca.com - 30 rooms. Great location: Andalusian style building right downtown. Large, comfortable rooms.

🛏🛏🛏 **Hotel Jerez** – Avenida Alcalde Álvaro Domecq, 35 – ☎ 956 30 06 00 - www.jerezhotel.com - 🅿 🖥 ♿ – 126 rooms. A large hotel of a high standard with rooms overlooking the garden or the swimming pool. It is 1.5km/1m from the city centre.

## TAKING A BREAK

**Baños Árabes Hammam Andalusí (Moorish Baths)** – Salvador, 6 - ☎ 956 34 90 66 - www.hammamandalusi.com - ⏲ Open 10am-10pm, 2hr sessions, by reservation. Return to days gone by in these candle-lit, carefully re-created baths with Moorish decor. Treatments and a tea house with Cathedral views.

## GOING OUT FOR THE EVENING

**Bereber** – Cabezas, 10 – ☎ 956 34 42 46 - www.tablaodelbereber.com - dinner show: 9pm-midnight (€95 by reservation). ◒Open 4pm-2am. The indispensable nightspot; spaces carefully decorated in Andalusian or Moorish style, include coffee shop, bar, discos in adjacent cellars, and a flamenco *tablao*.

**Kapote** – *Avenida Álvaro Domecq, 13 (Yeguada bldg) - ☎ 956 31 28 75 - www.kapote.es - ◒ Open 4pm-dawn*. Modern locale in bullfighting dress. Lively for terrace sitting, or late dancing.

**La Carbonería** – *Letrados (behind the town hall) - ☎ 956 16 87 01 - ◒ Open 4.30pm-3am*. An avant-garde bar with a young clientele. Recommended for a late afternoon or early evening drink.

## LEISURE

**Teatro Villamarta** – *plaza Romero Martínez – ☎ 956 32 73 27 – www.villamarta.com*. Opera, theatre, flamenco. Jerez is famous for flamenco clubs *(peñas flamencas)*, such as **Peña Tío José de Paula** *(calle Merced, 11 – ☎ 956 30 32 67/01 96)*, and **Peña el Garbanzo** *(calle Santa Clara, 9 – ☎ 956 33 76 67)*.

## SHOPPING

The main shopping district is around pedestrianised calle Larga. At one end, in plaza Estévez, is a traditional market. Two harness shops are recommended: **Arcab** *(avenida Duque de Abrantes – ☎ 956 32 41 00)* and **Duarte** *(Lancería, 15 – ☎ 956 34 27 51)*.

Buy sherry from a specialised establishment, such as La Casa del Jerez *(Divina Pastora, 1 – ☎ 956 33 51 84)*.

**Market** – The **mercadillo** offers a wide selection of goods on Monday mornings in the **Parque González Hontória**, the site of the city's annual horse fair.

## FESTIVALS

The **Festival de Jerez**, dedicated to flamenco, is at the end of April. The famous **Feria del Caballo** (horse fair) takes place in May in the Parque González Hontória. The **Fiesta de la Vendimia** (vine festival) and the **Fiesta de la Bulería**, devoted to Andalusian song, are in September.

**Iglesia de San Mateo** – One of the first churches built by Alfonso X in the 13C replaced a mosque. The present buttressed building dates from the 15C.

▷ *Follow calle Cabezas to plaza de San Lucas.*

## Iglesia de San Lucas
Baroque additions hide the medieval origin of this church. The tower is striking.

▷ *Follow calle Ánimas de San Lucas. Turn left into calle Santa María to plaza Orbaneja. Take calle Liebre to plaza Carrizosa. Admire the striking façade of an 18C mansion with curved balcony. Return to plaza Orbaneja and follow calle San Juan.*

## Iglesia de San Juan de los Caballeros★
This 15C church has a façade added in the 17C. A magnificent nine-sided 14C **polygonal apse**★, is topped by a ten-rib cupola with jagged decoration. Nearby, the **Centro Andaluz de Flamenco** is on plaza San Juan.

▷ *Take calle Francos and turn left into calle Canto. Continue to plaza Ponce de León.*

The Plateresque **Palacio de los Ponce de León** has a lovely corner **window**★★.

## Convento de Santa María de Gracia
*In plaza de Ponce de León.* ◒ *Open 9.30am-12.45pm and 4.45-5.30pm.* Pastries are sold, and tocino de cielo is made on request.

▷ *Follow calle Juana de Dios Lacoste, then left onto calle Almenillas. Cross calle Francos and follow calle Compañía from beside the church to the Iglesia de San Marcos.*

## Iglesia de San Marcos
Over the single nave visible today in this 15C church is a beautiful 16C **star vault**. A 19C panel representing St Mark hangs above a 17C polygonal **retable**★.

## Plaza de Rafael Rivero
This small square is bordered by the Palacio de los Pérez Luna, with its beautiful late-18C **doorway**, and next to it, the Casa de los Villavicencio, with an attractive patio.

### Tocino de Cielo
This delicious dessert (literally "heavenly bacon") is thought to have its origins in the Jerez wine-cellars, where local wine-producers once used beaten egg whites to clarify their wine. Not knowing what to do with the left-over egg yolks, they gave them to the neighbouring convents, where the nuns used them to make these delicious custard puddings.

▶ *Follow calle Tornería as far as plaza de Plateros.*

## Plaza del Plateros
This was a medieval commercial centre – note nearby streets named *Sedería* (silk dealers) and the like. The **Torre Atalaya** is an early 15C watchtower.

## Plaza de la Asunción★
A 20C sculpture is of the Assumption. The Renaissance **Casa del Cabildo**★★ (town hall, 1575) is adorned with figures.

**Iglesia de San Dionisio** – The Mudéjar-influenced Church of St Dionysius honors the patron of Jerez. Rather clumsy, it is adorned with odd modillions at roof level.

▶ *Follow calle José Luis Díez down to plaza del Arroyo.*

## Palacio del Marqués de Bertemati★
The façade is one of the most impressive in Jerez. The first section of the **left doorway**★ represents the secular world; the second portrays the religious world.

## Cathedral★★
🕐 *Open Mon-Fri, 6-8pm; Sat-Sun and public hols, 11am-2pm.* ☎ *956 34 84 82.*
The Colegial del Salvador was the first church built after the Reconquest. The present building was constructed in the 18C, along with new streets and squares. The tiled **cupola**★ above the transept is visible from much of the city.

## Alcázar★
*In the Alameda Vieja.* 🕐 *Open May to mid-Sep, 10am-8pm (last admission 30min before closing); mid-Sep to Apr, 10am-6pm.* 🕐 *Closed 1 and 6 Jan and 25 Dec.* ⌧ *€2.50.* ☎ *956 32 69 23.* ⌧ *€4.50 (combined ticket for Alcázar and Camera Obscura).*
There is an excellent **view**★★ of the cathedral. The old Moorish fortress was part of the 4km/2.5mi 12C Almohad wall. Access is via the angled **Puerta de la Ciudad** (City Gateway), a typical Almohad structure. Along the walls are the keep and the 15C Torre de Ponce de León (👁 *see description of the interior under Visit*).

## Plaza del Arenal
The square has been a meeting place since Moorish days. The monument, by Mariano Benlliure, honors **Miguel Primo de Rivera**, dictator of Spain in the twenties.

▶ *Take calle San Miguel, which provides a good view of the Iglesia de San Miguel.*

## Iglesia de San Miguel★★
The 1480 Hispano-Flemish **San José façade** is the oldest part. St Joseph is flanked by two imposing Flamboyant pillars. The three-tiered Baroque tower is topped

with a Jerez-style *azulejo* roof. The highly decorated transept and main chapel are covered by an elaborate star vault. The extraordinary late-Renaissance **retable**★ is by Martínez Montañés, with Baroque additions by Juan de Arce. Attached to the church is the Baroque-style **Capilla Sacramental** (Sacramental Chapel).

▶ *Return to plaza del Arenal and follow calle Lencería as far as the popular Gallo Azul building. Calle Larga leads to the Convento de Santo Domingo.*

## Convento de Santo Domingo
This Dominican monastery founded under Alfonso X houses exhibitions.

## Casa Domecq★
This is an elegant late-18C Jerez Baroque-style palace with a highly decorative marble **doorway**★. Note the graceful iron balustrade on a curving cornice.

## Visit

# Museos de la Atalaya (Museums)

### Palacio del Tiempo★★
🎧 *Guided tours Tue-Sun, 10am-3pm (Mar-Oct, also 6-8pm, holiday Monday mornings). €6. ☎ 902 18 21 00.*
This remarkable **clock museum**, in the 19C neoclassical Palacete de la Atalaya, is surrounded by gardens where peacocks roam. The collection numbers some 300 timepieces.

### Misterio de Jerez
Also in the Atalaya gardens, the Mystery of Jerez, in a 19C *bodega,* uses state-of-the-art technology to delve into Jerez wine, so closely linked to the soul of the city.

### Real Escuela Andaluza del Arte Ecuestre★
🎧 *Guided tours (30min), Mon, Wed and Fri, 11am-2pm (and Tue from Nov-Feb). Horse show Tue and Thu at noon. ☒ Closed Sat-Sun and public hols. Visit only: €8. Horse show: €17 or €23 (€23 or €30 during the Feria). ☎ 956 31 80 08.*
The **Royal Andalusian School of Equestrian Art**, occupies a 19C French-style palace, built by **Charles Garnier**. The tour takes in the museum and school. The **show**★★ – music, riders in 18C costume, and magnificent Cartujana horses – is a spectacle not to be missed. The adjacent **Museo del Enganche** displays magnificent coaches.

### Alcázar
📖 *See Walking Tour for description.* The **mosque**★★ is in unadorned early Almohad style. Over the prayer room is a delightful **octagonal cupola**. 12C Roman-style baths are across the garden.

| | | | | | | | |
|---|---|---|---|---|---|---|---|
| Alcázar | AZ | | de Flamenco | AY | E | Misterio de Jerez | AY |
| Bodega Domecq | AZ | B² | Convento de Santa María | | | Museo Arqueológico | |
| Bodega González Byass | AZ | B⁴ | de Gracia | AY | F | de Jerez | AY M |
| Bodega Harvey | BZ | B⁶ | Convento de | | | Palacio de Riquelme | AY V |
| Bodega Sandeman | ABY | B⁸ | Santo Domingo | BY | | Palacio del Marqués | |
| Bodega Williams | | | Iglesia de San Dionisio | BZ | K | de Bertemati | AZ R |
| & Humbert | BY | B¹⁰ | Iglesia de San Juan | | | Palacio del Tiempo | AY |
| Cabildo | BZ | C² | de los Caballeros | AY | | Real Escuela Andaluza | |
| Casa de los | | | Iglesia de San Lucas | AY | | de Arte Ecuestre | BY |
| Ponce de León | AY | C⁶ | Iglesia de San Marcos | ABY | | Teatro Villamarta | BZ T |
| Casa Domecq | BY | C⁴ | Iglesia de San Mateo | AZ | | Yeguada de la Cartuja | BZ |
| Catedral | AZ | | Iglesia de San Miguel | BZ | | Zoo-Jardín Botánico | AY |
| Centro Andaluz | | | La Cartuja | BZ | | | |

### Camera Obscura

The second camera obscura of its type built in Spain is housed in the tower of the **Palacio de Villavicencio**. An optical system provides a unique **view**★★ of Jerez. This is an ideal first stop on a tour of the city.

### Museo Arqueológico

🕐 *Open mid-Jun to Sep, Tue-Sun, 10am-2.30pm; Oct to mid-Jun, Tue-Fri, 10am-2.30pm and 4-7pm, Sat-Sun and public hols, 10am-2.30pm.* 🕐 *Closed Mon, 1 and 6 Jan, Good Fri and 25 Dec.* ☜ *€2 (no charge first Sun of every month).* ☎ *956 32 63 36.*

The Jerez archaeological museum is in a restored 18C mansion. The outstanding exhibit is an elegant **Greek helmet**★ dating from the 7C BC, found in the River Guadalete. Simple marble Copper Age **cylindrical idols**★ discovered in Cerro de las Vacas (Lebrija) and Torrecera, manage to portray remarkable expression.

### Iglesia de Santiago

The 15C church of St James in the Santiago district was built over a 13C chapel. Sturdy buttresses culminate in pinnacles. The Hispano-Flemish main façade is typical of this period. The portal bears the coat of arms of the Catholic Monarchs.

### Zoo-Botanical Garden

🅺🅸🅳🆂 🕐 *Open Jun-Sep, 10am-8pm; Oct-May, 10am-6pm.* 🕐 *Closed Mon except public hols.* ☜*€6.30, €4.10 (child).* ☎ *956 15 64 65.*

The zoo and garden in the north of the city make up one of the most pleasant parks in Jerez. More than 400 species include lions, tigers and elephants.

## Excursions

### La Cartuja★

*6km/3.5mi southeast along A 381 on the Medina Sidonia road.* 🕐 *Open for prayer 8am and 5.30pm.* 🕐 *Closed Mon.* ☎ *956 15 64 65.*

Construction of the Carthusian monastery started in 1478. The Renaissance doorway leads to a paved courtyard. At its end is a four-part church **façade**★★★, adorned with the saints of the Order, an Immaculate Conception and, above the rose window, the figure of St Bruno, the founder of the Order.

### Yeguada de la Cartuja (La Cartuja Stud Farm)★

*Leave Jerez on the Medina Sidonia road. The Finca Fuente del Suero is at km 6.* ☜ *Guided tours (2hr), Sat 11am-1pm. €12.50, €7.50 (child).* 🕐 *Closed 15 Dec-15 Jan.* ☎ *956 16 28 09.*

On Saturdays, the public can visit the state-run **Cartujana** stud farm and get a close-up look at the training of these magnificent beasts. The visit also includes a tack exhibit and an opportunity to admire a team of mares.

### Montecastillo Golf Club

*Next to the racetrack.* One of the best courses in Spain, site of the **Volvo Masters** since 19997. *For information on facilities and green fees, consult www.montecastillo.com*

### Jerez Racetrack (Circuito de Jerez)

*10km/6mi east along A 382 towards Arcos.* Site of the motorcycle Grand Prix. *For event information, consult www.circuitodejerez.com or call* ☎ *956 15 11 00.*

### Lebrija

*32km/20mi north along A 4, then left at El Cuervo on A 484.*

The birthplace of **Elio Antonio de Nebrija** (1442-1522), the first lexicographer of the Spanish language, is in an area of marshland alongside the Guadalquivir Estuary.

### Iglesia de Santa María de la Oliva

🕐 *Open 10am-2pm and 6-9pm.* ☎ *955 97 23 35.*

This church, converted from a mosque in 1249, fronts the attractive plaza del Rector Merina. The stylistic mix includes Mudéjar horseshoe arches , Gothic windows in the side chapels; the Renaissance transept and apse; and Baroque bell tower. It has a statue of the Virgin, and a fine **main altarpiece** by Alonso Cano.

### Iglesia de Santa María del Castillo

⚷ *Closed for restoration.*

The church, beside the ruins of the old Moorish castle in the upper town, is Mudéjar in style with fine original *artesonado* work and a patio from the former mosque.

### Capilla de la Vera Cruz

🕐 *Open Mon-Fri, 8-9.30pm.* 🕐 *Closed Sat-Sun and public hols.* ☎ *955 97 54 53.*

This interesting 17C neo-Classical chapel on plaza de España, the hub of local life, houses an exquisite **crucifix** carved by Martínez Montañés.

| Júas |
|---|
| Created by Lebrija's citizens, these rag dolls are ceremoniously burned on the night of St John (23-24 June) as the centrepiece of this Andalusian festival in honour of John the Baptist. |

# JIMENA DE LA FRONTERA

POPULATION: 8 949

Amid a magnificent landscape, dominated by its Moorish castle, this delightful town straddles the slopes of the Cerro de San Cristóbal above the River Hozgarganta. Only the red-brick neo-Classical bell tower of the **Iglesia de Santa María La Coronada** breaks the sea of white. Jimena was a border outpost between Christians and Nasrids (hence *de la frontera*) until reconquest in 1454 by the Trastamara king, Enrique IV. Smugglers and highwaymen frequented this area of difficult access from the 19C until after the Spanish Civil War. A growing British community has settled here over the past few decades.

▶ **Orient Yourself:** Jimena stands at the eastern end of the **Parque Natural de los Alcornocales** (*see Excursions).* Access from the north is via a spectacular landscape of forests of cork, holm and gall oak, which near Jimena gives way to pastures for fighting bulls.

🕐 **Organizing Your Time:** Stop for an hour or two.

👁 **Also See:** RONDA, PUEBLOS BLANCOS DE ANDALUCÍA and ALGECIRAS (including Gibraltar).

### WHERE TO STAY

**El Anón** – *Consuelo, 34-40* – ☎ *956 64 01 13 – www.andalcuia.com/jimena/hostalanon – 12 rooms.* 🕐 *Closed 15-26 Jun and 9-24 Nov.* Small rooms, numerous steps, flower-decked patios, a typical restaurant and swimming pool with views of the mountains are the main features of this charming hotel. Highly recommended.

**Hotel La Almoraima** – *Near Castillo de Castellar, on A 369 between N 340 and Jimena de la Frontera* – ☎ *956 69 30 02 02 - www.la-almoraima.com – 24 rooms.* This magnificent country hotel is in the middle of a huge park. The ex-17C convent, later a ducal hunting lodge is soberly decorated in rustic style. Peace and quiet guaranteed.

# Visit

### Iglesia de la Misericordia

This simple, 15C Gothic church with a single nave has been sensitively restored to house the **Centro de Información del Parque Natural de los Alcornocales**, providing a wealth of information on the park. ○ *Open 11am-1pm and 3-5pm (4-7pm in summer), Sat-Sun and public hols, 10am-1pm and 3-4pm.* ☎ *956 64 02 77 or 956 41 00 07.*

### Castle

This 13C Moorish castle-fortress is atop Cerro de San Cristóbal, where Roman Oba might have stood. Access to the main enclosure is through the double horseshoe arch of the imposing turret-watchtower. The esplanade on the hill is occupied by the town cemetery, several large water tanks and the castle enclosure, dominated by its austere **keep** *(torre del homenaje)*.

> ## Turrets
>
> One of the innovations of Almohad military architecture was the construction of turrets *(torres albarranas)*, which were often built in a forward position separate from the main body of the fortification, yet connected to it via an arch or a wall. These turrets served as watchtowers and were permanently guarded. The most famous of these is the **Torre del Oro** in Sevilla.

# Excursions

### Laja Alta wall paintings★

ⓘ *Visitors must engage a local guide.* These wall paintings are some of the most interesting in Cádiz province as well as some of the best preserved, mainly due to their recent discovery and difficult access. The paintings on rock include six Phoenician sailing vessels of extraordinary beauty that have been dated to around 1000 BC.

### Castillo de Castellar★

*29km/18mi south along A 369 to Almoraima, then bear right.* The Nasrids built this village-fortress in the 13C to protect the recently created kingdom of Granada. For two centuries, Castellar de la Frontera (as it was known) saw frontier battles until its reconquest in 1434. In the early 1970s, following the construction of the **Embalse de Guadarranque**, a reservoir which flooded the local area, most inhabitants moved to Nuevo Castellar, 7km/4mi to the south. The road to old Castellar winds up past whitewashed houses through a landscape of outstanding beauty to this half-abandoned village. Entry to the village, totally enclosed in the fortress, is via the gateway to the palace of the Dukes of Arcos.

### Parque Natural de los Alcornocales★

*Several roads criss-cross the park, including the A 375 from Alcalá de los Gazules, CA 503 from Arcos de la Frontera, and A 369 from San Roque (Algeciras). Others come over the Puerto Galis. For information on the park, call* ☎ *956 41 33 07.*
The typical vegetation here includes wild olive trees and, notably, the cork

*A typical street in Castillo de Castellar*

Hidalgo-Lopesino/MARCO POLO

## Cork

The extraction of cork *(corcho)* is a process that calls for the experience and skill of the *corchero* or cork-stripper. The exploitation of Andalusian cork oak began in the 1830s, since when there has been little change in working methods. The instrument used to strip the cork is a special hatchet which cuts large strips of bark known as *panas*. This is the most delicate phase of the whole operation as any damage to the tree might affect the regeneration of the bark, a process which normally takes ten years. Once the cork is stripped, the collectors and splitters take over; it is their job to prepare the cork ready for transport by the muleteers. Cork oaks are considered ready for exploitation once they have reached 30 years and a diameter exceeding 60cm/2ft. As the lifespan of a cork oak is about150 years, each tree normally yields around 10 harvests. Stripping normally takes place between June and September, when the cork oak is best able to regenerate itself.

oak, which covers almost half the park's area to form Europe's largest cork oak forest.

🔢 Many paths and trails include old cattle tracks. Two of the best walks here are to La Sauceda *(about 5hrs)* and the more strenuous ascent of **El Picacho** *(about 3hrs)*.

# LINARES★

POPULATION: 58 410

This old mining settlement, birthplace of guitar master Andrés Segovia (1893-1987) is the second largest town in Jaén province, sited amid olive groves at the foot of the Sierra Morena along a Roman road. Linares has sights and monuments of interest to visitors, including an excellent archaeological museum.

▶ **Orient Yourself:** Linares is southwest of several reservoirs, 14km/9mi from the A 4 – E 5 highway from Madrid. N 322 provides a road link with nearby Úbeda.
🕐 **Organizing Your Time:** Allow a couple of hours in town.
🖾 **Also See:** ÚBEDA (27km/17mi E), BAEZA (22km/14mi SE), ANDÚJAR (44km/27mi W) and JAÉN (45km/28mi SW).

## A Bit of History

Linares is associated with famed bullfighter **Manolete**, killed in the ring here in 1947. It originated as Roman *Linarium*. Conquered by Fernando III the Saint in the mid-13C, it became a lead and silver mining centre in the 18C during the reign of Carlos III. In recent times, mining has been on the decline.

## Sights

### Museo Arqueológico★
🕐 *Open Jun 15-Sep, Tue-Sat 9am-2pm; otherwise 10am-2pm, Sat-Sun, 4-7pm.* 🕐 *Closed Mon and public hols (and Sun in summer). No charge.* ☎ *953 54 40 04.*
The archaeological museum in the elegant Palacio Dávalos (note the graceful watchtower) exhibits pieces from the Bronze Age to the Middle Ages. One of the finest

is a 1C AD bronze **Nike from** nearby Cástulo, with delicately sculpted robes. The collection of **6C BC statuettes** of Astarté is also of interest.

### Iglesia de Santa María la Mayor
This magnificent 16C building is a mix of Romanesque, Gothic and Renaissance styles. Note the doors of several side chapels *(the first and second on the right)*, and the fine **main altarpiece**, depicting scenes from the Old Testament.

### Hospital de los Marqueses de Linares
The exuberant neo-Classical architecture of this 20C building contrasts with the elegant simplicity of the square of the same name. The crypt of the Marquess and Marchioness of Linares inside is by Coullaut Valera.

### Palacio de Justicia
The façade of this imposing 18C building is profuse with sculptures which combine in a superb composition. Scenes are both religious themes and of daily life.

### Iglesia de San Francisco
The austere exterior, crowned by a spire and flanked by a graceful bell tower, contrasts with the beauty of the fine Baroque **retable** at the high altar.

### Ayuntamiento
The monumental 18C town hall by the square has an attractive porticoed atrium.

## Excursions

### Ruins of Cástulo
*7km/4.5mi NE along A 312 towards Arquillos.* Cástulo was founded by the Greeks and prospered as a lead and silver mining center under Phoenicians and Romans. Imilce, wife of the Carthaginian general Hannibal, was born here. Artefacts of those days have been unearthed.

### Baños de la Encina
*11km/7mi NW along A 1200.* This quiet village amid olive groves and the gentle hills of the **Parque Natural de la Sierra de Andújar**★ *(see ANDÚJAR)*, is overlooked by a strategic **Moorish fortress**. Vestiges of the former mosque are visible. It is well worth climbing any one of the watchtowers to enjoy the superb **views**.

# LOJA

POPULATION: 20 143

Loja stands on a hill overlooking the plain of the River **Genil**, halfway between Málaga and Granada. The town is dominated by its Moorish fortress, which defended the plain extending eastward towards Granada. Loja was razed on several occasions during the Reconquest, and fell definitively to the Catholic Monarchs in 1486. **General Narváez**, the authoritarian behind Queen Isabel II, was born here in 1800. *Calle Comedias 18300 Loja,* ☎ *958 32 39 49.*

▶ **Orient Yourself:** Loja is on the Route of the Nasrids, south of the Iznázar Reservoir. The town is linked to Granada (55km/34mi to the east) and Antequera (44.5km/28mi to the west) by the A 92 highway.

**WHERE TO EAT**

Nearby **Riofrío** has had an excellent reputation for its trout since the 17C. For dessert, try another local speciality, the cakes known as **roscos de Loja**.

To catch your own dinner, head to the **Coto Intensivo de Pesca**, a fishing area open all year. *For permits, information and reservations, contact the Albergue de Pescadores (fishermens lodge) de Riofrío, ☏ 958 32 31 77/11 56.*

**WHERE TO STAY**

⊝⊜⊜⊜ **Barceló La Bobadilla** – *18 km/11mi west by A 92, exit 175 toward Sevilla – ☏ 958 32 18 61 – www.la-bobadilla.com – 62 rooms.* This luxury hotel on an estate covering 350ha/865 acres hosts the rich, famous and powerful. The estate is a village in itself and even has its own chapel and monumental organ.

🕐 **Organizing Your Time:** Take a few hours to see Loja.

👣 **Also See:** ALHAMA DE GRANADA, IZNÁJAR, PRIEGO DE CÓRDOBA, MONTEFRÍO and GRANADA.

## Walking Tour

### Old Quarter

Loja's historical centre of alleyways with evocative names is accessed by the Cuesta del Señor hill or by circling the impressive 16C-18C **Iglesia de la Encarnación**. Above stand the **alcazaba**, a fortress with an intact keep; the simple, 17C residence of the Christian Governors *(Caserón de los Alcaides Cristianos)*; the Torre Ochavada (tower) and, on the parade ground, the remains of a cistern *(aljibe)*. Calle Moraima leads to the outer limits of the medieval quarter. The view from the Mirador Arqueológico of the **Iglesia de San Gabriel**, a fine 16C Renaissance church, is impressive. Its façade, attributed to **Diego de Siloé**, is a striking Renaissance work. ⚲ *The fortress is currently closed for restoration. ☏ 958 32 39 49 (tourist office).*

In plaza de Abajo, formerly plaza Joaquín Costa, note the 13C **Puerta de Jaufín**, the gate that provided access to the fortress. To the side stands the old granary *(pósito)*, a building that has only retained its lower section.

*Bell tower, Iglesia de la Encarnación*

B. Kaufmann/MICHELIN

# LUCENA

POPULATION: 35 564

Set amid olive groves just west of the Parque Natural de la Sierra Subbética, Lucena is one of the most prosperous towns in Córdoba province. Its most interesting monument is the Iglesia de San Mateo, with its exuberant Capilla del Sagrario. ▯ *Calle Castillo del Moral, 14900 Lucena, ☎ 957 51 32 82, turlucena@ turlucena.com.*

▶ **Orient Yourself:** Situated on the southern fringes of Córdoba province, Lucena is near the A 45-N 331 (2km/1.2mi to the W), linking the town with Antequera and Aguilar de la Frontera; and the A 340, connects to Priego de Córdoba. The scenic A 331, heading southeast, offers delightful views of the Iznájar Reservoir and surrounding countryside (& *see Excursions*).

🕐 **Organizing Your Time:** Allow half a day for Lucena, more with drives nearby.

🚗 **Also See:** CABRA (12km/8mi NE), AGUILAR DE LA FRONTERA (20km/12mi NW), PRIEGO DE CÓRDOBA (34km/21mi E) and ANTEQUERA (51km/32mi S).

## Visit

### Iglesia de San Mateo★
*Plaza Nueva, opposite the town hall.* 🕐 *Open in summer, 7.30am-1.30pm and 7-9pm; otherwise, 7.30am-1.30pm and 6.30-9pm.* ☎ *957 50 07 75.*
Hernán Ruiz I and II were both involved in the design of this transitional Gothic-Renaissance church.

### Exterior
The interplay of features gives dynamism to this large church. Buttresses frame the fine, classically inspired Renaissance portal. A tower stands to the left; the Capilla del Sagrario (Sacrarium Chapel), with characteristic cupola, is to the right.

### Interior
The interior is spacious and harmonious. The nave has wooden ceilings; the triple apse has Gothic vaulting. Polychrome reliefs on the five panels of a magnificent Renaissance **retable**★ narrate Gospel and Old Testament scenes.

### Capilla del Sagrario★★
*In the Epistle nave, at the foot of the church.* The walls and cupola of this early 18C Baroque jewel are covered with polychrome **stuccowork**★★ in an ensemble of unparalleled exuberance. Every type of ornamental feature is used, including geometric and plant motifs, angels, bishops, saints etc.

### Castillo del Moral
This restored old medieval fortress retains two of its towers. It is said that Boabdil was imprisoned in the octagonal Torre del Mora. The square-shaped Torre de las Damas is the former keep.

---

### Roman, Moorish, Jewish

This historic town date to the Roman period, although it was under the Moors in the 10C and 11C that Lucena enjoyed considerable development. It became an important Jewish enclave known as "The Pearl of Sefarad" and was home to a prestigious Hebrew university. In the 18C it experienced an economic and artistic revival, developing into one of the most prosperous towns in the province.

### Iglesia de Santiago

🕐 *Open 9am-1pm and 6.30-9pm.* ☎ *957 50 05 45.*

The Church of St James was built over a razed synagogue. The brick façade, with late-Gothic portal, is supported by buttresses. Inside, ogival arches rest upon brick pillars that appear twisted by the weight, creating an unusual impression of fragility. The church also houses a sculpture of Christ tied to a column, by Pedro Roldán.

Other churches in Lucena are the **Iglesia de San Juan de Dios** and the **Iglesia de San Agustín**, both with handsome Baroque portals. The Iglesia de San Agustín has one of the few elliptical ground plans to be found in Andalucía.

### WHERE TO EAT

🍴 **Araceli** – *Avenida del Parque, 10* – ☎ *957 50 17 14* – 🕐 *Closed last two weeks of Aug.* Ordinary in appearance, this is the town's best restaurant, specialising in fish and seafood.

### WHERE TO STAY

🛏🛏 **Hotel Santo Domingo** – *Juan Jiménez Cuenca, 16* – ☎ *957 51 11 00* – *www.husa.es* – *30 rooms.* A luxury hotel with large, comfortable rooms, housed in a former 18C convent.

## Excursion

### Santuario de la Virgen de Araceli★

*6km/4mi S, last section with a steep 20% gradient.* Thhis sanctuary is at the highest point of the Sierra de Aras. There is an impressive **view**★ of olive groves, with the mountains acting as a backdrop.

## Driving Tour

### The road from Lucena to Iznájar

*35km/22mi along C 331.* Cross a charming landscape of olive orchards and mountains to **Rute**, (*20km/12.5mi*) famous for its anise liqueur A donkey sanctuary is on the outskirts. The **road**★ (*15km/9.5mi*) continues with views to the right of the reservoir (*embalse*) and **Iznájar**★ (🔎 *see IZNÁJAR*), impressively positioned on top of a hill.

# MÁLAGA★

POPULATION: 534 683

The bustling capital of the Costa del Sol is characterised by elegant promenades, impressive monuments, an active marina and port, and charming residential quarters with villas that bespeak 19C prosperity. Málaga's skyline is dominated by the Gibralfaro, or Lighthouse Hill, crowned by a Moorish fortress. 🛈 *Pasaje de Chinitas, 4, 29015 Málaga,* ☎ *952 21 34 45,www.malagaturismo.com, otmalaga@ andalucia.org; Plaza de la Marina, 11, 29001 Málaga,* ☎ *952 12 20 20.*

▶ **Orient Yourself:** Málaga is at the mouth of the River Guadalmedina, between Parque Natural de los Montes de Málaga and the sea, 59km/37mi east of Marbella. Its airport, serving the Costa del Sol, is one of the busiest in Spain.

🕐 **Organizing Your Time:** Take several days for Málaga, more for a beach vacation.

🧒 **Especially for Kids:** The Alcazaba fortress and Senda El Retiro aviary and zoo.

👁 **Also See:** COSTA DEL SOL and ANTEQUERA (48km/30mi N).

# Address Book

## TRANSPORT

**Pablo Picasso International Airport**
– The airport is 10km/6mi SW along the coast road (☎ 952 04 88 04).
The Portillo company operates buses between from the city centre every 25min. The local train to Fuengirola stops at the airport (every 30min). Taxis are also widely available at the airport.

**Trains** – The rail station (☎ 952 36 05 60 or 902 24 02 02) is along esplanada de la Estación and serves Spain's major cities. The Fuengirola train runs through Torremolinos, Benalmádena and other towns and resorts along its route.

**RENFE** (Spanish State Railways) – *Calle 50 61*) is on paseo de Los Tilos. Travellers have a wide choice of departures to Spain and cities abroad.

**City buses** – The local bus network (SAM) is comprehensive. A single journey costs €0.95, and a 10-trip ticket €5.90. ☎ 952 35 72 00 or 902 52 72 00. A private company, **Portillo**, provides periodic services to the major resorts and towns along the Costa del Sol.

**Taxis** – ☎ 952 32 00 00 or 952 33 33 33.

**Horse-drawn carriages** – These can be hired at a number of places around the city for tours of the main sites.

**Ferries** – Málaga's port is mainly commercial, although a passenger service operates to Morocco. Málaga is a popular port of call for cruise ships.

## WHERE TO EAT

🍽🍽 **El Chinitas** – *Moreno Monroy, 4-6* - ☎ 95 221 09 72 - www.chinitas.arrakis. es. A restaurant emblematic of Málaga with old-time photos, ceramics, and paintings. Lovely terrace on a pedestrian street, three floors of dining.

🍽🍽 **El Campanario Ignacio** – *Paseo de la Sierra, 36* – ☎ 952 20 24 48 – 🅿 – 🕐 *Closed Sun eve and Mon.* Ignacio, the owner, is at the stove. Great bay views, and a mix of updated classic dishes and the chef's creations.

🍽🍽🍽 **Restaurante-Museo La Casa del Ángel** – *Madre de Dios, 29 (facing Teatro Cervantes)* - ☎ 95 260 87 50 - www.lacasadelangel.com – 🕐 *Closed Mon and 2 weeks in Jun.* Angel Garó

combines art and tradition in an ambience that captivates the senses. Enjoy delicious cuisine surrounded by originals by Picasso, Dalí, and Miró.

## TAPAS

**Orellana** – *Moreno Monroy, 5* – ☎ 952 22 30 12 – 🕐 *Closed Sun.* Short on decor, but the Orellana is one of the city's best-known and liveliest tapas bars.

**La Posada de Antonio** – *Granada, 33* – ☎ 952 21 70 69. This bar decorated with barrels is at the heart of Málaga's nightlife area. Regional dishes and meats grilled in view. A favourite meeting point for young *malagueños*.

**Bar La Mesonera** – *Gómez Pallete, 11.* This small bar fills up with stars and the rich and famous before and after flamenco performances at the Teatro Cervantes opposite. Delicious tapas and a colourful Andalusian atmosphere.

## WHERE TO STAY

🛏 **Hotel Castilla y Guerrero** – *Córdoba, 7* - ☎ 95 221 86 35 - www.hotelcastillaguerrero.com – 36 rooms. Plain but a good value, adequate bathrooms. Up one flight.

🛏🛏 **California** – *Paseo de Sancha, 17* – ☎ 952 21 51 64 - www.hotel-california. net – 24 rooms. A stone's throw from the sea, ten minutes from the old city. Old-fashioned, with cosy rooms.

🛏🛏 **Hotel Monte Victoria** – *Conde de Ureña, 58* - ☎ 952 65 65 25 - www. hotelmontevictoria.com – 8 rooms. Reservation advised. Family villa hotel, its garden-terrace enjoys fine city views. Impeccable rooms. On a narrow, inclined street (hard to park), 15 min on foot from the historic centre.

🛏🛏 **Hotel Don Curro** – *Sancha de Lara, 7* – ☎ 95 222 72 00 – www. hoteldoncurro.com – 118 rooms. The Don Curro occupies a seventies tower in the city centre. Cosy and comfortable rooms, plus a popular games room.

🛏🛏🛏🛏 **Parador de Málaga-Gibralfaro** – *Castillo de Gibralfaro* – ☎ 952 22 19 02 – 38 rooms. Málaga's charming *parador* dominates the hill. Have a drink on the bar terrace and enjoy delightful views of city and coast.

## TAKING A BREAK

**Café Central** – *Plaza de la Constitución, 11* – 🕐 *Open 8am-10pm.* A centenary coffee house frequented by faithful regulars. Pleasant terrace on the square, but don't miss the large tea room.

**Casa Aranda** – *Herrería del Rey, 2* – ☎ *952 22 12 84* - 🕐 *Open 9am-9pm.* This lively, atmospheric café has taken over every building on its street. Great place for chat over *chocolate con churros*.

## GOING OUT FOR THE EVENING

The central area around the cathedral and calle Larios has numerous lively old bars, mainly frequented by Málaga's younger generations and foreign visitors, and quieter cafés or *teterías*. In summer, locals tend to spend more of their time along the paseo Marítimo. The more exclusive bars and clubs are in the upscale El Limonar district at the foot of the mountains.

**El Pimpi** – *Calle Granada, 62* – 🕐 *Open 11.30am-3am.* A Málaga tradition, on a pedestrian way in the old town. This old-time tavern is good for a quiet beer, coffee or tapas in the afternoon and early evening; and for lively nights, with the occasional burst into song in a wine cellar-type atmosphere.

**La Tetería – Tetería Alcazaba** – *Calle San Agustín, 9 and 21* – 🕐 *Open 4pm-midnight.* Two small bars, popular with a younger set, in a pedestrianised street. The Moorish feel and aroma of the many teas add to the atmosphere.

**Siempre Así** – *Calle Convaleciente, 5* – ☎ *952 21 54 12* - 🕐 *Open Thu-Sat, 10pm-5am.* This central bar is a favorite of the city's jet set. From midnight onwards the dance floor fills with people dancing to rumbas, *sevillanas* and the latest flamenco hits.

## BEACHES

Málaga is blessed with a series of beaches, from La Malagueta and Las Acacias to Playa del Palo, 5km/3mi to the east. All have excellent facilities and a wide choice of bars and restaurants.

*Parador, Málaga*

Paradores

## ENTERTAINMENT

**Teatro Cervantes** (*calle Ramos María* – ☎ *952 22 41 00/09*), which opened in 1870, offers an extensive programme of theatre and concerts.

## SHOPPING

The main shopping streets are concentrated between calle Puerta del Mar (which runs into plaza de Félix Sáez and becomes calle Nueva) and **calle Marqués de Larios**. Many street vendors also have their pitch here. Look for shops selling the typical puff pastry cakes (*hojaldres*), a local speciality. A good selection of more modern stores, as well as two large department stores of the El Corte Inglés chain, are just outside the historical centre in calle Armengual de la Mota.

Large hypermarkets such as Pryca and Continente are on the city's outskirts.

## MARKETS

A colourful market with everything from second-hand clothes to antiques is held on Sunday mornings near the La Rosaleda football stadium.

## LOCAL SPECIALITIES

**Ajoblanco** – If you happen to be in Málaga in summer, make sure you try fried fish (*pescaíto frito*), as well as one of the city's traditional dishes, *ajoblanco*, a local variant of *gazpacho*. The ingredients for this refreshing chilled soup include almonds, garlic, breadcrumbs, salt and olive oil. It is normally served with Moscatel grapes.

## FESTIVAL

Málaga is home to the Festival of Spanish Film, the most important of its kind.

## Local Fiestas

**Semana Santa** – Málaga, like all Andalucía, celebrates Holy Week to the full, with processions rooted in the 16C.

Huge floats, known as *tronos* (thrones), are erected in the open. The moment at which these floats are lifted and subsequently "rocked" is one of the most spectacular of the entire week.

The most important **processions** during Holy Week are: Señor de los Gitanos (Easter Monday), El Cautivo (Wednesday), Cristo de la Buena Muerte and Esperanza Perchelera (Maundy Thursday). The liberation of a prisoner is another highlight.

**The Feria** – The annual fair, commemorating Málaga's reconquest, is held the week of 15 August. It includes entertainment booths, copious eating and drinking, dancing, and general merriment by both locals and visitors.

## A Bit of History

**Antiquity** – Phoenicians founded Malaca in the late 8C or early 7C BC. Greek and Carthaginian trading posts followed. The Romans created a colony in the 3C BC. It exported wine, oil, raisins, cereals, salted meat and fish. Christianity came in the 4C.

**Moorish domination** – After 716, Málaga was ruled from Córdoba, then became part of the kingdom of Granada. The fortress *(alcazaba)* was built in the 11C, when the city developed its textile industry. Following periods of Almoravid and Almohad dominion, Málaga became the chief port of the Nasrids in Granada. In the 14C, the Gibralfaro fortress was

### Málaga wines

The city's wines were highly appreciated during Antiquity. Nowadays, the best-known Málaga wines are sweet or semi-sweet with an alcohol content of between 15% and 23%. The two grape varieties used in their production are Pedro Ximénez and Moscatel. The latter, which is also highly prized as a dessert grape, is used to produce a dessert wine known as **Málaga Dulce** (Sweet Málaga). Other wines made here include the smooth **Lágrima**, and **Pedro Ximénez**, which is created exclusively from the grape of the same name.

*View of the city and port from the Castillo de Gibralfaro*

B. Kaufmann/MICHELIN

rebuilt and extended by Yusuf I. Genoese developed the city's commerce and opened new trade routes.

**The Christian city** – Moorish Málaga fell in August 1487. In the 16C, under Felipe II, a new port brought renewed prosperity, heightened in the 18C by liberalised trade.

**19C** – The French held Málaga from 1810 to 1812. Liberal-absolutist conflics led to the execution of General Torrijos in 1831. The 19C was the era of the Industrial Revolution. Two wealthy families, the Heredias (iron and steel) and the Larios (textiles), developed factories. After a decline, tourism took up the slack in the 1950s.

## Sights

# Roman and Moorish Quarter

### Alcazaba★

🕐 *Open in summer, Tue-Sun, 9.30am-8pm; otherwise, Tue-Sun, 8.30am-7pm.* 🕐 *Closed Mon, 1 Jan and 24, 25 and 31 Dec.* ☞ *€2 (€3, including Castillo de Gibralfaro).* ☎ *952 22 51 06.*

Construction of the hilltop Moorish fortress started in 1040. One of the largest Muslim military installations preserved in Spain, it consists of a double enclosure with rectangular towers, all once connected to the city walls, now demolished.

Access is via a zig-zag ramp from calle Alcazabilla past sections of brick and masonry walls and through gateways, some of which re-used Roman columns. The Arco de Cristo (Christ's Arch), where mass was celebrated after the reconquest, leads to the Moorish gardens. The **views**★ from atop of the walls take in the city and port.

In the second enclosure is the former palace, Nasrid in style.

*The towers and ramparts of the Alcazaba*

### Teatro Romano

The terraces of the cavea, on the slope of the hill, are all that is left of this theatre at the foot of the Alcazaba (west side). Close by, the neo-Classical **Aduana** (Customs House) now houses provincial offices and an exhibit hall.

### Castillo de Gibralfaro

*Access: bus n° 35. Alight at paseo del Parque. Open in summer, 9am-8pm; otherwise, 9am-6pm.* ☞ *€2.* ☎ *952 22 51 06.*

The path around the hilltop remains of the 14C Gibralfaro Castle , built to protect the *alcazaba,* provides magnificent **views**★★ of the city and the port. The walled corridor connecting the Alcazaba with the castle was built in the 14C.

### Centro de interpretación de Gibralfaro

The former powder store is now a centre retracing military life in the castle from the 15C-20C. Exhibits include collections of uniforms, weapons, maps and navigational equipment.

# City Centre

Central Málaga has some delightful narrow streets and alleyways – many now closed to traffic – with an unmistakable Moorish air, such as **pasaje Chinitas**, a lively shopping area near pedestrianised **calle Marqués de Larios**, the old city's main street.

## Museo Picasso★★

🕐 *Open Tue-Sun, 10am-8pm (Fri-Sat, to 9pm); last admission 30 min before closing.* 🕐 *Closed Mon, 1 Jan, and 24 and 31 Dec.* ⊛ *€6; €4.50 exhibition; €8 combined; free last day of month, 3-8pm.* ☏ *902 44 33 77.*

The Picasso museum is in the 16C Renaissance Palacio de Buenavista with its fine *artesonado* ceilings. The permanent collection comprises more than 200 works from the collections of the artist's niece and grandson, Christine and Bernard Ruiz-Picasso. Oils, sketches, engravings, sculptures and ceramics, displayed chronologically, illuminate the artist's journey. Early works show his technical mastery, notably *Olga Kokholva with Mantilla* (1917, note the penetrating gaze). Among other significant canvases are *Mother and Child* (1921-1922); the delicious *Portrait of Pauo with White Cap* (1923); *Bust of Woman with Arms Crossed Behind Head* (1939), an expressive work with surrealist influences; and *Woman in Armchair* (1946).

## Cathedral★

🕐 *Open Mon-Fri, 9.30am-6.45pm; Sat, 9.30am-6pm; Sun and public hols, worship only.* ⊛ *€3.50.* ☏ *952 21 59 17.*

Construction took place between the 16C and 18C, hence the mix of styles: Renaissance predominates, the ground plan is Gothic, the ceilings and façade Baroque. The design is believed to be the work of Diego de Siloé, who was also responsible for Granada Cathedral, with the assistance of Andrés de Vandelvira.

### Exterior

The Baroque main façade, fronts plaza del Obispo. The tower on the right is unfinished, hence the nickname "La Manquita" (Missing One). Note the relief of the Incarnation (the Cathedral's name) on the middle portal.

### Interior

*Enter through the garden, left side of the cathedral.* The proportions are monumental: a hall-church ground plan with three aisles, side chapels and an ambulatory. The lofty naves rest on layers of columns, and are crowned by fine **oven vaulting★** bearing attractive decoration. Handsome 17C choir **stalls★**, were partly carved by Pedro de Mena. Note the two magnificent 18C Baroque organs, large choral stands, and the 17C marble pulpits with ecclesiastical escutcheons. The tabernacle at the high altar dates from the 19C.

Behind the choir is a lovely *Pietà* (1802) in Carrara marble by the Pisan brothers.

The **side chapels** hold notable works: in the Capilla de los Caídos, a *Dolorosa* by Pedro de Mena below a *Christ Crucified* by Alonso de Mena, both 17C; a huge canvas of the *Virgin of the Rosary* by Alonso Cano in the Capilla del Rosario; and a 17C *Immaculate Conception* by Claudio Coello in the Capilla de la Inmaculada Concepción.

In the **ambulatory**, the Capilla de Nuestra Señora de los Reyes boasts a *Virgin and Child*, and a sculpture of the Catholic Monarchs, by Pedro de Mena; the Capilla de Santa Bárbara has an impressive early-15C **Gothic retable★★**. The 18C Capilla de la Encarnación or Capilla del Sagrario (Sacrarium Chapel) is entirely of marble.

### Museo

*Enter from the ticket window, downstairs.* This small museum exhibits religious paintings, anonymous 16C and 17C sculpture, and silver and gold objects.

## El Sagrario
🕐*Open 9.30am-12.30pm and 6.30-9.30pm.* ☎ *952 21 19 35.*
This unusual 16C rectangular church in the cathedral gardens has a superbly sculptured Isabelline Gothic **side portal**★ *(giving onto calle Santa María).* The single-nave Baroque interior dates from an 18C renovation. The superb sculpted **altarpiece**★★ in the apse is Mannerist in style and crowned by an impressive Calvary.

## Palacio Episcopal
The 18C Baroque Bishop's Palace, on plaza del Obispo, has a beautiful pink and grey marble doorway adorned with Corinthian columns and broken entablatures. The upper niche houses a *pietà*. There is also an exhibit hall for the Andalusian council.

## Museo de Arte Sacro
The Abbey of Santa Ana hosts this collection of sacred art, including 17C-18C carvings with outstanding works by Pedro de Mena (*Ecce Homo, Child Jesus*).

## Iglesia de Santiago
🕐 *Open 9am-1pm and 6-9pm.* ☎ *952 21 03 99.*
The Church of St James, founded after the Reconquest, is on calle Granada, near plaza de la Merced. A brick tower is in primitive Mudéjar style with *sebka* decoration on its second section, and a portal (now sealed) with geometric *lacería* motifs. The 18C Baroque interior houses the venerated statue of **Jesus the Rich** in a chapel off the Evangelist nave. Pablo Picasso was baptised in this church.

## Plaza de la Merced
An obelisk recalls General Torrijos, executed in 1831 for defending liberal ideas. One of two identical buildings on the northeast side was the birthplace of Picasso.

### Museo-Casa Natal Picasso
🕐 *Open 10am-8pm; Sun, 10am-2pm.* 🕐 *Closed 1 Jan; 25 Dec.* ⊜€1. ☎ *952 26 02 15.*
Picasso was born in the mid-19C building at n° 15. The first floor displays a number of his drawings as well as photos, as well as ceramics.

## Iglesia de los Mártires
🕐 *Open 8am-1.15pm and 7-8pm (mass); public hols, 9am-1pm. .* ☎ *952 21 27 24.*
This 15C church is in a pedestrianised area of narrow streets. The surprising Baroque interior was created during an 18C restoration. An altarpiece with a small chapel *(camarín)* houses statues of St Paula and St Cyriacus, the city's patrons.
On calle Mártires nearby, a small square displays a typical **Christ of the Lanterns.**

## Museo de Artes y Costumbres Populares
🕐 *Open Mon-Fri, 10am-1.30pm and 4-7pm (mid-Jun to late Sep, 5-8pm), Sat, 10am-1.30pm.* 🕐 *Closed Sun and public hols.* ⊜ €2. ☎ *952 21 71 37.*
The Museum of Popular Arts and Traditions is in an attractive 17C inn, the Mesón de la Victoria. It provides insight into traditional rural and urban life.

## Mercado Central
The main market is a 19C iron structure on the site of the old Moorish dockyards.

## CAC Málaga
The former wholsale market is now the **Centro de Arte Contemporáneo de Málaga** (modern art centre). It holds 400 works donated from private collections, shown on a rotating basis. Notable are 20C Spanish paintings (by Sicilia, Broto, Barceló, etc.).

### Museo Interactivo de la Música

This underground (literally) museum has an entertaining and well-presented collection of musical instruments from different eras and regions. Some can be played.

### Paseo del Parque

This stretch of greenery is a botanical garden, a haven amid the urban bustle.
In **paseo de la Farola**, to the east, is the **statue of the Cenachero**, a fish peddler and Málaga character. The La Malagueta quarter, beyond, marks the beach area.

## Outside the City Centre

### Santuario de la Virgen de la Victoria★

*End of calle Compás de la Victoria.* ⓒ *Open 9am-12.30pm and 5-6.30pm, no visit during services, camarín and crypt by appointment.* ⊜ *€1.50.* ☎ *952 25 26 47.*
The church of this 15C sanctuary has a simple brick exterior and restrained Andalusian Baroque interior. The 17C carved altarpiece narrates scenes from the life of St Francis of Paola; in the Evangelist nave is a highly expressive *Dolorosa* by Pedro de Mena.
The **camarín**★★, at the centre of the main altarpiece, a masterpiece of exuberant Baroque architecture, is engulfed by stuccoed cherubs, acanthus leaves, etc.
The **crypt**★ for the Counts of Buenavista could not be more sombre, with its black background festooned with skeletons and skulls.

### Cementerio Inglés

*Avenida Pries, 1.* The **English cemetery**, first Protestant burial ground in Spain, was ceded to the British consul in 1829. Poet Jorge Guillén (1893-1984) is buried here.

## Excursions

### Finca de la Concepción★

*7km/4.5mi north.* ▰ *Guided tours (1hr 15min), mid-Jun to mid-Sep, 10am-7.30pm; mid-Sep to mid-Oct, 10am-5.30pm; mid-Oct to mid-Dec, 10am-4.30pm; mid-Dec to Mar, 10am-4pm; Apr to mid-Jun, 10am-6.30pm.* ⓒ *Closed Mon. €3.* ☎ *952 25 21 48.*
This magnificent garden was created in the middle of the 19C by Jorge Loring and his wife, Amalia Heredia, who brought tropical and subtropical species to Málaga on ships owned by her father. The delightful estate is a forest of greenery dissected by small streams and embellished with lakes, waterfalls and Roman remains.

### Senda El Retiro★

*15km/9.5mi SW. Follow airport signs. Bear onto A 366; past Churriana, turn right.* ⓒ *Open 10 am-6pm (8pm, 16 May-15 Sep). Last admission 4 hours before closing.* ⊜ *€20 (€40 annual pass); children and over 60, €15.* ☎ *952 62 35 40.*
Children and adults will enjoy the 17C estate of the bishop of Málaga, featuring **aviaries** with 150 species, aquarium, reptile house, and Andalusian village.

*Finca de la Concepción*

B. Kaufmann/MICHELIN

## Parque Natural de los Montes de Málaga

This park, situated just a few kilometres to the north of the city, covers an area of 4 762ha/11 767 acres of semi-mountainous landscape dissected by streams which have carved small valleys along their path. The typical vegetation here is predominantly Mediterranean with extensive repopulated woods of Aleppo pine. These plantations were created to prevent the flooding experienced by the city of Málaga over several centuries. The road to the park is dotted with viewpoints and roadside inns where visitors can enjoy the delicious local cuisine and wine.

The **historical garden**★ is made up of 17C and 18C gardens. The most spectacular sections are the French-influenced garden-court, with lion fountain and impressive **water staircase**; and the patio-garden with the Genoa fountain **(fuente de Génova)**.

# MARBELLA★★

POPULATION: 98 377

Marbella is the tourism centre of the Costa del Sol. A magnificent climate, superb beaches and leisure facilities have transformed a fishing port into a playground of seafront apartment blocks and inland holiday complexes. In the old quarter, whitewashed houses are adorned with wrought-iron grilles and displays of flowers. 🛈 *Glorieta de la Fontanilla, 29600 Marbella, ☎ 952 77 14 42, turismo@marbella.es; Plaza de los Naranjos, 29600 Marbella, ☎ 952 82 35 50, info@turismomarbella.com.*

▶ **Orient Yourself:** Between the Mediterranean and mountains to the north, Marbella, is on the A 7-N 340 highway, 32km/20mi NW of Málaga and its airport.
🕐 **Organizing Your Time:** Stay for as long as your beach vacation allows.
[Kids] **Especially for Kids:** Beaches here and along the coast.
👣 **Also See:** COSTA DEL SOL, MÁLAGA, RONDA and MIJAS (29km/18mi E).

## A cosmopolitan resort

Marbella is known as the most exclusive resort along the Costa del Sol, attracting the rich and famous. It is also a shoppers' paradise, particularly for luxury goods, and has developed a reputation for its health clubs and spas. Superb sporting facilities include famous golf courses. There are even mosques and a synagogue.

### TOURING TIP

If you are looking for a hotel, a restaurant, the best nightspots and shopping areas, or just somewhere for a quiet drink, consult the Address Book for *COSTA DEL SOL.*

## Walking Tour

### Old Town★ *Allow 2hr*

Marbella's old Moorish quarter is a maze of narrow, twisting alleyways lined by whitewashed old buildings, and shops, bars and restaurants.

*Plaza de los Naranjos*

## Plaza de los Naranjos★

This enchanting centre of the old quarter is perfect for unwinding at an outdoor café facing the 16C stone fountain, delightful floral displays and orange trees *(naranjos)*. Buildings around the square include the 16C **town hall**, with its wrought-iron balconies and handsome Mudéjar doorway, the 17C **Casa del Corregidor** (Magistrate's Mansion), with monumental stone **façade**★ and elegant balcony, and the 15C **Ermita de Nuestro Señor Santiago**, the first Christian church erected in Marbella.

## Iglesia de Santa María de la Encarnación

The church, in the square of the same name, is at the end of the busy calle Nueva, where a Moorish tower still stands. . This Baroque building has a splendid stone **portal** and large bell tower. It holds a carving of St Barnabas, the patron of Marbella, and a sumptuous organ, the **Órgano del Sol Mayor**.

## Museo del Grabado Español Contemporáneo★

🕐 *Open mid-Jun to Sep, Tue-Sat, 10am-2pm and 7-9pm; Oct to mid-Jun, 10am-2pm and 5.30-8.30pm.* 🕐 *Closed Sun, Mon and public hols.* ⊛€2.50. ☎ 952 76 57 41.
The Contemporary Spanish Print Museum, unique in Spain, is in the 16C former Hospital de Bazán. Works by Tàpies, Alberti, Chillida and Maruja Mallo are on display.

## Hospital de San Juan de Dios

This hospital in calle Misericordia dates from the Reconquest. Its oustanding features are the pleasant cloisters and the Mudéjar *artesonado* work in the chapel.

## Seigniorial mansions

Mansions in plaza Ancha and plaza de Altamirano include the 16C Casa de los Cano Saldaña, and the house of Ferdinand de Lesseps, of Suez Canal fame.

## Excursions

### Villa Romana de Río Verde

*2km/1.2mi west along A 7.* This 1C-2C Roman villa has attractive mosaic paving.

### Puerto Banús★★

*5km/3mi west along the A 7.* This superb marina shelters some of the world's finest sailing vessels. Alongside the moorings (and an impressive collection of fast cars), stand bars, restaurants, and luxury boutiques. The marina attracts visitors on summer evenings for a drink or meal and shopping in late-hours boutiques. By day, Puerto Banús is a quiet and pleasant place for a stroll and views down the coast.

### Istán

*15km/9.5mi northwest along A 6206. Follow signposts west from Marbella.* This former Moorish village is set along the River Verde among terraced fields of fruits and vegetables. The Iglesia de San Miguel, a 16C church, has an impressive belfry.

## Driving Tour

## Excursion Inland *51km/32mi, excluding return journey.*

▷ *Head north out of Marbella along A 355, and turn where signposted.*

### Ojén

This whitewashed village with old Moorish quarter is set amid orange and pine groves. The **Iglesia de Nuestra Señora de la Encarnación** is a 15C church with a single nave and a fine *artesonado* ceiling. Ojén is famous for its brandy *(aguardiente)*.

▷ *Return to the A 355, then bear left.*

### Refugio de Juanar

This refuge in a lovely setting offers stunning **views**★ over the Sierra Blanca.

▷ *Return to A 355 and continue north to Monda.*

### Monda

This village shelters below the remains of a Moorish fortress. The 16C **Iglesia de Santiago**, modified in the 18C, has profusely decorated vaulting in its triple nave.

▷ *Exit Monda via A 6207, bear left onto A 366, then continue along MA 412.*

### Tolox

Tolox lies in the sierra within the **Parque Natural de Sierra de las Nieves**. The 16C church, **Iglesia de San Miguel**, has three aisles separated by semicircular arches and topped by an attractive *artesonado* ceiling. The ceiling is elliptical, decorated with paintings. ○ *Open daily, 11am-2pm and 6-9pm.* ☎ *952 48 73 33.*
The Fuente Amargosa spa was built in 1867 in an area of exceptional beauty.

# MARCHENA

POPULATION: 18 018

This Sevillian country town prospered in the 15C and 16C under the Dukes of Arcos. The Iglesia de San Juan Bautista is from that period, while imposing towers recall Moorish times. Remains of settlements have been dated back to the Bronze Age. ⓘ *Calle San Francisco, 43, 41620 Marchena,* ☎ *955 84 51 21.*

▶ **Orient Yourself:** Marchena is 7.5km/4.5mi N of the A 92, east of Sevilla.
🕓 **Organizing Your Time:** Take a day to see Marchena and towns nearby.
ⓖ **Also See:** UTRERA (43.5km/27mi SW), CARMONA (27km/17mi NW), ÉCIJA (40km/25mi NE), OSUNA (37.5km/23mi SE) and SEVILLA (66.5km/41mi W).

## Walking Tour

### Arco de la Rosa
This 15C gateway in a remaining section of the town wall is a horseshoe arch framed by bastions.

### Iglesia de San Juan Bautista★★
The 15C Gothic-Mudéjar Church of John the Baptist fronts a pleasant square with several seigniorial doorways. The spire on the bell tower bears *azulejo* decoration. The **interior** comprises three central aisles with *artesonado* ceilings, and two side aisles – in 16C extensions – covered by arris vaults. Numerous **works of art** adorn the walls. In the presbytery is a sumptuously carved and painted early 16C **retable**★★★ narrating scenes from the life of Christ (paintings by Alejo Fernández, sculptural groups by his brother, Jorge). The 16C **grille** was made locally.The wrought-iron pulpits are 18C, as is the impressive choir **grille**. The 18C mahogany and cedar **choir stalls**★ were carved by Jerónimo de Balbás. The two organs are Rococo and neo-Classical.
The Capilla del Sagrario, a chapel to the left of the presbytery, has a magnificent 16C **carved retable**★★ by Roque Balduque and Jerónimo Hernández. Note the unusual Last Supper arrangement.
Noteworthy statues include an *Immaculate Conception* by Pedro de Mena *(first chapel in the Epistle nave)* and a *St Joseph and Child (chapel to the right of the apse).* The St Joseph figure is by Pedro Roldán.

### Museo Zurbarán, Orfebrería y Bordados★★
*Enter from church.* 🕓*Open by prior arrangement, 10.30am-1.30pm.* ⛔*€1.50.* ☎ *955 84 51 21 (tourist office).*
Nine paintings by this Baroque (1598-1664) include *Christ, The Immaculate Conception, St Peter, St James, John the Evangelist, John the Baptist, St Paul, St Andrew* and *St Bartholomew.* These were commissioned for the sacristy and date from same period as those in the Monasterio de Guadalupe, in Cáceres

*Iglesia de San Juan Bautista*

B. Kaufmann/MICHELIN

province. Also shown are a 16C silver monstrance 1.62m/4.9ft high, 15C-16C books, and 16C-17C embroidery and silverware.

▷ *Head up to the highest part of the town.*

## Plaza Ducal
The 18C former town hall with sober stone doorway faces this square, on a former castle parade ground. Parts of the nearby castle are well preserved. Pass through the Arco de la Alcazaba, an arch dating from the 11C.

## Iglesia de Santa María la Mayor or Iglesia de la Mota
The sombre Gothic-Mudéjar church lies within the ducal palace. Modifications are evident on the tower. The façade has a single trumpet-shaped doorway.
Nearby are the **Iglesia de San Agustín**, a church built during the transition from Baroque to neo-Classical, and the **Puerta de Morón**, a fortified tower that houses the tourist office and a museum dedicated to sculptor Lorenzo Coullault Valera.

# Excursions

## Paradas
*8km/5mi SW along SE 217.* Paradas was a stopping-point *(parada)* for caravans to Sevilla in the Middle Ages. The **museum** in the 16C Baroque **Iglesia de San Eutropio** displays religious gold and silverware, illuminated books, and an outstanding *Magdalena* by El Greco. ◷ *Open by prior arrangement.* ☎ *954 84 90 39.*

## El Arahal
*15km/9.5mi SW along SE 217.* In the old quarter of this tranquil town, small white-washed houses stand alongside elegant Baroque and neo-Classical buildings. Among them: the 18C Capilla de la Vera Cruz, in colonial style; the Mudéjar Iglesia de Nuestra Señora de la Victoria; the 17C **Iglesia de Santa María Magdalena**; and the **Iglesia de San Roque**, containing several 18C altarpieces.

## Morón de la Frontera
*27km/17mi S. Follow A 364 to Montepalacio, then A 361.* Morón de la Frontera surrounds the ruins of a Moorish castle. The Gothic **Iglesia de San Miguel** with neo-Classical portal features 18C Baroque details inside. The **Iglesia de San Ignacio** (or Iglesia de la Compañía, as it was built by Jesuits) houses outstanding Flemish canvases. The 16C Renaissance **Iglesia de San Francisco** contains paintings by **José Ribera.**

# MARTOS

POPULATION: 22 391

Martos, set amid endless olive groves, has a picturesque old quarter. Numerous 15C and 17C ancestral homes lend an elegant and seigniorial air.

▷ **Orient Yourself:** Martos is situated 26km/16mi SW of Jaén along A 316.
◷ **Organizing Your Time:** Allow an hour or two to stroll and sightsee.
⏱ **Also See:** JAÉN, BAENA, ALCALÁ LA REAL and CÓRDOBA.

# Visit

## Plaza de la Constitución
This graceful square is the heart of the old quarter.

## Iglesia de Santa Marta
🕐 *Open 9.30am-1pm and 6-8pm(9pm in summer).* 🕐 *No visits during services.* ☎ *953 55 02 68.*
Originally Gothic-Mudéjar, the church was remodelled in the 16C by Francisco del Castillo. The handsome **portal** is Isabelline. The sober interior has monumental pillars linked by arches with decorative plasterwork.

### An eventful past
The former Iberian settlement of *Tucci* was used by the Lusitanians and their leader, Viriatus, as a winter camp in 142 BC. A little over a century later, in 27 BC, Augustus transformed it into a colony for veteran legionaries; in the early days of Christianity, the town was the seat of a bishopric. Following five centuries of Arab domination, Martos was finally reconquered in 1225 by Fernando III the Saint, and was later ceded to the Order of Calatrava.

## Ayuntamiento
The late-16C Renaissance town hall, once a prison, is adorned with an elegant portico of semicircular arches and a balcony with reliefs.

## Fortaleza de la Virgen de la Villa
This fortress rises on the outskirts. Only two towers – the keep and the Torre de Almedina – remain, providing a clear idea of the immensity of the fortress in its prime.

## Fuente Nueva★
This large 16C Renaissance fountain by Francisco del Castillo, near the bullring, shows the influence of the Italian architect Vignola. It bears the town's coat of arms.

## Calle Real
Modernist buildings contrast with an old fortified tower, originally part of the defensive walls, and the Iglesia de las Madres Trinitarias, a Baroque church built in the 18C but damaged during the Spanish Civil War.

## Iglesia de San Francisco
The elegant colonial-style portal is the oldest feature of the Church of St Francis.

## Iglesia de Santa María de la Villa
Only the monumental four-storey tower remains from the original 13C church.

# Excursion

## Torredonjimeno
*7km/4.5mi N.* The historical quarter is to the right as you enter. Torredonjimeno is renowned for wrought-iron work – it has the only bell foundry remaining in Andalucía – as well as for *encebollado*, a stew of cod, tomatoes, onions, garlic and herbs.

### Treasure
In 1931, local farmworkers discovered a chest full of valuable objects from the Visigothic period. The "Treasure of Torredonjimeno", as it has come to be known, is now on display in the archaeological museums of Madrid and Barcelona.

## Old quarter
The 16C Renaissance **town hall** fronts the plaza. The 16C **Iglesia de San Pedro** is Renaissance-style with an occasional Mudéjar feature. The 13C **castle** covers a Roman and Visigothic fortress.

The slender, Gothic 16C **Iglesia de Santa María** is dedicated to the Immaculate Conception.

**Ermita de Nuestra Señora de la Consolación**
This Renaissance-style hermitage on the outskirts of town is a destination for several lively pilgrimages.

# MEDINA SIDONIA★

POPULATION: 10 872

Medina Sidonia is at the centre of Cádiz province close to the **Parque Natural de los Alcornocales**. From its elevated site, it is possible to make out **El Puerto de Santa María** and **Vejer de la Frontera** on a clear day. Steep, narrow alleyways lend a Moorish feel, though Roman remains are the main interest. *Plazuela de la Iglesia Mayor, 11170 Medina Sidonia, ☎ 956 41 00 05, zuyalmedina@eresmas.com.*

▶ **Orient Yourself:** Medina Sidonia is linked to Cádiz by A 390.
🕐 **Organizing Your Time:** Take a day for the signts and culinary treats.
👣 **Also See:** CÁDIZ, El PUERTO DE SANTA MARÍA, JEREZ DE LA FRONTERA, ARCOS DE LA FRONTERA and VEJER DE LA FRONTERA.

## Walking Tour

### Medieval Town

▶ *Climb calle Espíritu Santo as far as the Arco de la Pastora.*

### Arco de la Pastora
Built in the 10C, this is one of three surviving medieval gateways (with Arco del Sol and the **Arco de Belén**). The double, pointed horseshoe arch supported by two sturdy marble columns is probably Phoenician in origin.

### Iglesia Santa María la Mayor, la Coronada★
🕐 *Open 10am-2pm and 4-6pm; summer, 9.30am-2pm and 4-9.30pm.* 🕐 *Closed 1 Jan and 25 Dec.* ⊘ €2.50. ☎ *956 41 03 29.*
This 15C "aristocratic Gothic" church has a tower finished in 1623 in Baroque style. Access is via a patio from an earlier church, with strong Mudéjar influence. Note the impressive **Plateresque retable**★ at the high altar by Roque Boldaque, Juan Bautista Vázquez and Melchor de Turín, showing the life of Jesus, and the Virgin Mary, with the mystery of

### WHERE TO EAT
🍽🍽 **Mesón Rústico Machín** – 2.5km/1.5mi on Medina-Chiclana road – ☎ 956 41 13 47 – 🕐 Closed Wed. A regional restaurant offering fine valley views. Specialities include grilled asparagus, braised oxtail, *(rabo de toro)* and game in season.

### LOCAL SPECIALITIES
**Pastries** – Since Moorish times, Medina Sidonia has been famous for its delicious cakes and biscuits, including the ever-popular **alfajor** – a type of macaroon made with almonds, eggs and honey.
**Convento de Jesús, María y José** – ☎ 956 41 01 54. This convent in the **medieval quarter**, behind the Iglesia de Santa María Mayor, sells *alfajores* and *tortas pardas (a type of flat biscuit).* 🕐 Open 9.30am-12.15pm and 4.30-6.15pm.
**Convento de San Cristóbal** – Calle Hércules, 1 – ☎ 95 64 10 28. In the **modern town**, behind the municipal market. Alfajores, tortas pardas and *amarguillos.* 🕐 Open 10am-2pm and 4-6pm.

## A Phoenician, Roman, Visigothic, Moorish and Christian town

The name Medina Sidonia has evolved from two key periods in the town's history: the first under the Phoenicians; the second during the Moorish occupation of the region. The Phoenicians referred to their settlement here as Assido, while the Moors, who conquered the town in 712, named it Medina (city). Medina Sidonia was an important Roman town and the seat of one of the first Visigothic councils, the Assidonensis, in the 6C. Alfonso X the Wise reconquered it in the 13C, and in 1430 Juan II handed the town over as a dukedom to the Guzmán family. The seventh Duke of Medina Sidonia has gone down in history as the commander of the ill-fated Spanish Armada.

the coronation as its central theme. To the left of the high altar is the 17C statue of Nuestra Señora de la Paz (Our Lady of Peace), the town's patron saint. A monstrance of Mexican silver, by Martínez Montañés, is in the chapel to the right of the transept. A Plateresque doorway leads to the patio.

### Alcázar and old town

*Guided tours (20min), 10am-2pm and 4-6pm (5-7pm in summer). €2. Closed Mon, 1 Jan and 25 Dec. 956 41 24 04.*
The Moorish fortress *(alcazaba)* became a fortified Christian palace *(alcázar)* in 1264 with a triple walled enclosure and angled access gateway. The surrounding medieval district was abandoned in the 16C and used as a quarry. Some 16C houses and silos survive. The enclosure is guarded by the **Torre de Doña Blanca**, a watchtower which offers excellent views.

## Modern Town

Go through the 15C **Arco de Belén** (Bethlehem Arch), and cross to Medina Sidonia of the 16C-19C.

### Plaza de España
A neo-Classical 18C **town hall** fronts this triangular *plaza* .
Beside the 1871 **market** nearby, on plaza de la Cruz, is a late-17C Baroque church, the Iglesia de la Victoria.
**Calle de Fray Félix**★ (calle de la Loba) is lined by 18C and 19C houses adorned with charming balconies. Outside of the walls is the 16C Iglesia de Santiago, with its fine *artesonado*.

## Visit

### Archaeological site★
*Open 10am-2pm and 4-6.30pm (8pm Apr-Jun). €3.10. 956 41 24 04.*
This Roman drainage system dates from the 1C AD. Excavations offer a look at a a barrel-vaulted channel with tile flooring, which collected waters from smaller galleries. Cryptoporticoes, used to terrace the terrain, have been unearthed. The *cardo maximus* was the main Roman street.

## Excursions

### Ermita de los Santos Mártires Justo y Pastor
*On the ring road. Open daily, 10.30am-1.30pm and 5-8pm. 956 41 24 04.*

Founded by bishop Pimenio in 630, this hermitage is one of the oldest churches in Andalucía, with a large medieval tower possibly of Roman origin. The interior, of unpretentious beauty, re-uses Roman pieces in stelae and capitals.

### Castillo de Gigonza

*4km/2.5mi north of Paterna de Rivera.* Only the Moorish keep of this castle survives.

### Alcalá de los Gazules

*25km/15.5mi east along A 381.* This white hilltop town (named for its castle, *alcalá,* which survived until the 19C) is the gateway to the **Parque Natural de los Alcornocales**. In the upper section is the **Iglesia de San Jorge**, with its 18C Baroque tower and Gothic façade showing St George (San Jorge) on horseback. The 16C former **town hall** is the park visitor centre, the **Centro de Interpretación del Parque Natural de los Alcornocales**. The climb up to **El Picacho** and the Ruta de los Molinos (Route of the Windmills) are popular excursions. *Reception centre: ◷ open 10am-2pm and 4-6pm (summer, 5-7pm). ◷ Closed Mon, 1 Jan and 25 Dec. ☎ 956 41 24 04.*

### Benalup

*20km/12.5mi SE of Medina Sidonia on A 393.* This was the site of the **Casas Viejas** incident (the former name of Benalup). In 1933, anarchists disenchanted with agrarian reforms were brutally repressed by the government under **Azaña**.
**Cueva del Tajo de las Figuras** – *8km/5mi SE on A 5203 towards Algeciras, left-hand side.* These caves contain wall paintings from the post-Palaeolithic period. ◷ *Open 9am-3pm. ◷ Closed Mon-Tue and public hols exc. Sun. ☎ 956 42 41 29.*

# MIJAS ★

POPULATION: 37 490

**Picturesque Mijas, on a hill amid pines in the sierra, offers stunning views★ of the Costa del Sol. Its winding streets, charming nooks and crannies, flower-decked houses and numerous tiny squares draw thousands of annual visitors. Many purchase its renowned pottery, basketwork and woven goods.**

▸ **Orient Yourself:** The A 7-N 340, between Mijas and the Mediterranean, provides a fast road link to Málaga, 24km/15mi NE, and Marbella, 33km/21mi SW.

◷ **Organizing Your Time:** Take at least a morning or an afternoon to stroll.

👶 **Also See:** MÁLAGA and COSTA DEL SOL.

### WHERE TO EAT

⊖🍽 **El Olivar** – *Av. Virgen de la Peña, 6* – ☎ *952 48 61 96* – ◷ *Closed Sat and in Feb.* Andalusian country restaurant with windows to the sierra, best views from terrace.

⊖🍽🍽 **El Padrastro** – *Paseo del Compás, 22* – ☎ *952 48 50 00* – *Reservation recommended.* El Padrastro is unbeatable for panoramas of the town, coast and mountains. Original menu, romantic and candlelit at night.

### WHERE TO STAY

⊖🍽🍽 **Hotel Mijas** – *Urbanización Tamisa, 2* – ☎ *952 48 58 00* – *197 rooms, 4 suites.* Inspired by typical Andalusian architecture, dazzling white façade below the pines. Rooms are elegant with country wood decor. Good value.

# Visit

### Old Quarter★

This photographer's paradise is a network of bright streets lined by low-roofed houses decorated with wrought-iron balconies and grilles. Boutiques and souvenir shops can be found in calle de Charcones, calle de San Sebastián and calle de Málaga.

### Walls

Sections of the old Moorish walls can be discovered on walks in town.

### Iglesia de la Inmaculada Concepción

The 16C Church of the Immaculate Conception retains an imposing Mudéjar tower. One of the side chapels has attractive polychrome stuccowork adorned with plant motifs.

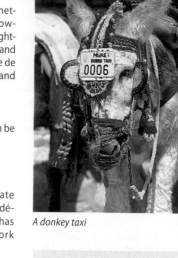
*A donkey taxi*

### Iglesia de San Sebastián

Built in the 18C, this single-nave church is crowned by a cupola with internal Rococo stuccowork decoration.

### Museo de Miniaturas

🕐 *Open 10am-7pm (summer, 10pm).* ⊗*€3.* ☎*952 48 59 00.*
The Miniatures Museum displays a *Last Supper* by Leonardo painted on a grain of rice, among other curiosities.

## The donkey taxi

This unusual form of transport is the most frequently used by visitors to the town. Although these colourfully decked-out animals travel at a less than breakneck pace, they are a popular aspect of local life.

### Museo Histórico-Etnológico

The old town hall houses a **museum** of agricultural and fishing tools and other items relating to old ways of life at home, on land and at sea. 🕐 *Open 10am-2pm and 4-7pm (5-7pm in summer).* ☎ *952 59 03 80.*

### Plaza de Toros

This small bullring has an unusual rectangular design and a **bullfighting museum** (*museo taurino*). 🕐 *Open in summer, 10am-7pm (summer, 10pm).* ⊗ *€3 (museum and bullring), €1.50 (museum only).* ☎ *952 48 55 48.*

### Santuario de la Virgen de la Peña

*At the entrance to the town.* 🕐 *Open 9am-9pm.* ☎ *952 48 50 22.*
This sanctuary was excavated out of rock by an order of monks in the 16C. The hermitage, dedicated to the town's patron saint, the Virgin of the Rock, has an attractive **mirador** (lookout) known as El Compás, providing delightful views of the valley and the Mediterranean.

# MINAS DE RIOTINTO★★

POPULATION: 5 500

This small community is set in a landscape of breathtaking colours, oak forests, and reservoirs and lakes, such as Cobre-Gossan, Campofrío and Agua. Excavated mountain slopes, deep-red in colour, bear witness to a mining tradition dating back to Antiquity. The British district of Bellavista, arts and crafts centres, and a number of pleasant hotels are attractions.

▶ **Orient Yourself:** Minas de Riotinto is in the Sierra de Aracena, near Parque Natural Sierra de Aracena y Picos de Aroche, 73km/45mi northeast of Huelva by the N 435, and 85km/53mi northwest of Sevilla.

🕓 **Organizing Your Time:** Allow a couple of hours in and around town.

🖐 **Also See:** ARACENA (35km/22mi N) and Parque Natural Sierra de ARACENA Y PICOS DE AROCHE.

## Special Features

## Parque Minero de Riotinto★★

This mining-themed park lies within the town and in the surrounding area.

### Museo Minero y Ferroviario★

🕓 Open 10.30am-3pm and 4-7pm. ☜ €2.40. ☎ 959 59 00 25.
The mining and railway museum is in the former British hospital. Exhibits include early-20C locomotives and the popular **Maharajah's carriage**★★★, built in England, for a planned journey to India by Queen Victoria. This work of art is a mass of carved wood and leather. The museum also displays artefacts of mining as far back as the Bronze Age, and a reconstruction of a **Roman mine**.

### The British in Riotinto

It is a strange sensation to discover the vestiges of Anglo-Saxon culture, so out of keeping with the character of the local population and landscape, in an isolated backwater such as Riotinto. It should be remembered, however, that at the beginning of the 20C, Britain had developed into a huge economic power, partly due to its colonial possessions and to the role played in this economic development by mining operations in outposts such as Riotinto.

### Corta Atalaya★★★

2km/1.2mi northwest. 🕓 Open 10.30am-3pm and 4-7pm. ☜€4.25. ☎ 959 59 00 25.
This huge open-cast mine is over 1 000m/3 280ft in length, 900m/2 950ft wide and 350m/1 150ft deep. The **views**★★★ of the striated crater from the lookout

### WHERE TO STAY

☞☞ **Santa Bárbara** – Cerro de Los Embusteros – ☎ 959 59 11 88 – 19 rooms, 1 suite. This recently opened hotel, with its modern, spacious rooms, is situated in the upper section of the town, from where it enjoys impressive views of the mountains and local open-cast coal-mines.

### LOCAL SPECIALITIES

Typical products from the area include *migas* (breadcrumbs fried in olive oil and garlic, and traditionally served with grilled sardines), *gurumelos* (a local cep mushroom), *pestiños* (honeyed doughnuts), and a whole variety of pork-based products.

B. Kaufmann/MICHELIN

*The impressive Corta Atalaya mine*

point are exceptional. Horizontal seams are cut in perfect straight lines by huge machines. Other facilities can be visited nearby, showing how gossan (mineralised iron) is extracted and transported in enormous vehicles capable of carrying up to 200 tons.

### Cerro Colorado★★
*2.5km/1.5mi NW.* The pit of the second largest mine in Riotinto is an unusual red colour. Unexpectedly beautiful, it appears to twinkle in the late afternoon sun.

### Tourist train★★
*By prior arrangement.* 🎫 *€8.50.* 📞 *959 59 00 25.*
The train runs from an old station to Cerro Colorado. Trips (10km/6mi or 23km/14.5mi) along the river on a line built at the end of the 19C to carry ore to Huelva for export to Great Britain. This journey in old-fashioned carriages offers surprises at every turn, including stunning glimpses of the reddish-coloured River Tinto as it winds through dense woods, views of the very first stations, and an impressive bridge, the Puente de Salomé, from which views of the river and surroundings are spectacular.

### Bellavista district
This district of Victorian-style houses, like one in Huelva, was built at the beginning of the 20C to accommodate the huge numbers of British workers. It is uninhabited, A Presbyterian church, social club and British cemetery remain.

## Visit

### Necrópolis de la Dehesa
*3km/2mi N along A 461.* 🕐 *Visits by prior arrangement,* 📞 *959 59 00 25.*
This large Roman cemetery dating from the 2C AD was part of the Corta de Lago settlement. Tombs bearing inscriptions and personal effects have enabled archaeologists to ascertain the social class of those buried here.

### Pozo Alfredo
*1km/0.6mi NW.* This underground mine, linked to Corta Atalaya, will be extended to a length of 600m/1 968ft. Only parts of this sizeable project can be visited.

## Excursions

### Nerva
*4km/2.5mi E along A 476.* A Roman tablet found here is dedicated to Emperor Nerva. The village is in a lunar landscape, where tailings, piled to the edges of reddish water, produces an acrid odour.

### Zalamea la Real
*12km/8mi W. Follow the A 461, then the N 435 after El Campillo.* The **road**★★ winds across mountain spurs past the Cobre-Gossan Reservoir *(embalse)* to Zalamea, renowned for anise-flavoured liqueurs. Visit the Iglesia de Nuestra Señora de la Asunción and the El Pozuelo dolmen.

### Valverde del Camino
*45km/28mi SW. Follow the A 461, then bear onto N 435 after El Campillo.* This community is famous for its shoes. Such is the renown of this local industry that many Andalusians make a special trip to Valverde to buy walking shoes, boots and footwear for dancers made to exacting standards.

# MOGUER★

POPULATION: 11 000

Elegant Gothic and Baroque houses line the quiet avenues of noble Moguer. This town is associated with Columbus, who sailed from nearby Palos de la Frontera. Fishing and agriculture are mainstays. Moguer is the birthplace of 1956 Nobel prizewinning poet **Juan Ramón Jiménez** (1881-1958), whose verses adorn *azulejo* panels. The town is also famed for its *pastelillos* of almond paste and candied fruit. ▪ *Calle Castillo, 21800 Moguer,* ☎ *959 37 23 77, turismo.moguer@terra.es.*

▸ **Orient Yourself:** Moguer, along the River Tinto, is 20km/12mi from Huelva.
◷ **Organizing Your Time:** Take a couple of hours in town, at least.
ċ **Also See:** LA RÁBIDA (10km/6mi SW), HUELVA and COSTA DE HUELVA.

## Special Features

### Casa-Museo "Zenobia y Juan Ramón"★
*Guided tours (45min), Tue-Sat, 10.15am-1.15pm and 5.15-7.15pm; Sun, 10.15am-1.15pm.* ◷ *Closed Mon and public hols.* ⊛ *€2.50.* ☎ *959 37 21 48.*
The traditional Andalusian home of Juan Ramón Jiménez and his wife Zenobia is now a museum *(museo)* displaying photographs, books and other memorabilia.

### Juan Ramón Jiménez
There were two sides to the poet. A contemporary of Lorca, he was a cultured man of letters, but also a passionate popular writer. The bitterness and anger of his literary assaults evaporated in his portrayals of Moguer and its ways and vocabulary.

### Casa Natal de Juan Ramón Jiménez
The poet's birthplace *(casa natal)* is in calle Ribera. Today, it is used as the setting for important literary contests. ○ *Visits by appointment.* ☎ *959 37 23 77 (Turismo).*

## Sights

### Monasterio de Santa Clara★
⬤ *Guided tours (40min), Tue-Sun, 11am-12.30pm and 5-7pm.* ○ *Closed Sun, Mon and public hols.* €2. ☎ *959 37 01 07.*
Columbus prayed at this 14C Gothic-Mudéjar monastery on the morning of 16 March 1493, in fulfilment of a promise made during a storm on the high seas. The interior, now occupied by an order of Conceptionist nuns, is made up of monastic rooms and porticoed patios with elegant balconies. Orange trees and even several banana trees are reminders of the lands touched by Columbus. The buttressed façade of the convent fronts the **plaza de Portocarrero**, an attractive square.

### Church
The **tombs of the Portocarreros**★, lords of Moguer, are an outstanding example of the Andalusian Renaissance, carved in Carrara marble by Giacomo, Michelangelo's master. Note also the 16C main altarpiece, a fine 17C carved depiction of the Immaculate Conception, and the set of **tombs**★ at the high altar, including that of Beatriz de Henríquez, who partly financed the voyage of discovery.

### Cloisters
This tranquil area is enclosed by galleries of pointed arches and includes the former infirmary – now a display of 16C-18C vestments – and the storeroom, which houses a 16C Gothic carving and a skullcup worn by Pope John Paul II.

### Choir and antechoir
The choir has exceptional 14C **Nasrid-Mudéjar stalls**★★. The arms of these magnificently carved stalls depict the lions of the Alhambra; the heraldic coat of arms of each nun adorns the seat backs. The antechoir has a fine Mudéjar-style *artesonado* ceiling and contains several 15C books of Gregorian chants.

### Calle Andalucía★
This attractive pedestrianised street runs from plaza del Cabildo to the **Archivo Histórico Municipal y Biblioteca Iberoamericana** (Historical Archives and Ibero-American Library), containing precious old documents. ⬤ *Guided tours (15 min) 11am-2pm.* ○ *Closed Sat, Sun and public hols.* ☎ *959 37 27 13.*
Along this street are the modern **Teatro Felipe Godínez**, a theatre with façade of *azulejos*; the chapel of the Hospital del Corpus Christi; the heritage houses along the **pasaje de Nuestra Señora de la Esperanza**; and the Convento de San Francisco.

### Convento de San Francisco
This 15C convent, built under the initiative of Pedro Portocarrero, was important in spreading Christianity to the New World. It has Mannerist cloisters, a 17C belfry and an interesting 18C Baroque main altarpiece.

### Ayuntamiento
The Renaissance town hall on plaza del Cabildo has a handsome porticoed **façade**★, with fine wood *artesonado* work and galleries comprising five semicircular arches.

### Iglesia de Nuestra Señora de la Granada

This 18C church, opposite the plaza del Marqués, holds a carving of Nuestra Señora de la Granada, protected by a baldaquin in the middle of the presbytery. The **bell tower**★, Moguer's principal landmark, remains from an earlier church.

# MONTEFRÍO ★

POPULATION: 7 030

Montefrío, one of the prettiest towns in western Granada province, enjoys an impressive **setting**★★ on two hills, islands in a sea of olive groves. Several Castilian kings failed to conquer Montefrío until the triumph of the Catholic Monarchs in 1486. 🅱 *Plaza de España, 1, 18270 Montefrío,* ☎ *958 33 60 04.*

▶ **Orient Yourself:** Montefrío, at the foot of the Sierra de la Parapanda, is linked with Granada (58.5km/36mi SE) via the A 92 and A 335.

🕔 **Organizing Your Time:** Allow several hours to stroll.

🖑 **Also See:** PRIEGO DE CÓRDOBA (34km/21mi NW), ALCALÁ LA REAL (24km/15mi N), IZNÁJAR (39km/24mi W), LOJA (42km/26mi SW) and GRANADA.

## Walking Tour

*Approximately 2hr*

### Iglesia de la Encarnación

This circular neo-Classical church on **Plaza de España**, the main square (near the tourist office and town hall), has an orange cupola visible from all over.

▶ *Climb up to the Villa section of town along calle del Arco Gracia.*

*Montefrío*

### Iglesia de la Villa★

🕐 Open 10am-2pm and 4-6pm. ☎ 958 33 60 04 (tourist office).

This hilltop church stands above the remains of a **Nasrid fortress**, of which the old cistern survives. The ubiquitous **Diego de Siloé** was responsible for the design.

---

**WHERE TO EAT**

🍽**Mesón Coronichi** – Avenida La Paz, 23 – ☎ 958 33 61 46. 🕐 Closed Mon and in July. A good place to sample local cuisine, including its speciality, relleno de carnaval, a type of meatball or sausage.

---

▶ Walk down to plaza de España; follow calle Enrique Amat to placeta del Pósito.

### Placeta del Pósito

The 18C former **granary** (pósito), of simple design, dominates this small square.

▶ From here, head up Monte del Calvario to the Iglesia de San Antonio.

### Iglesia de San Antonio

The **Iglesia de San Antonio de Padua** is a Baroque church with a handsome façade, and a three-sectioned retable with a statue of St Anthony. The church was part of a convent, which became a flour mill after the 19C confiscation of church property.

▶ From here, it is well worth walking along calle Cruz del Calvario for one of the best **views**★★ of the town.

## Excursions

### Peña de los Gitanos★

5km/3mi E of Montefrío along the Illora road. Pass the Mesón Curro on your right, continue to a sign for Peña de los Gitanos. Park, and continue on foot (15min).

🔺The track climbs gently through olive groves. Take the right fork past an abandoned mine. Cross a meadow, passing a dolmen to the right, to a second meadow with oaks. The best-preserved megalithic tombs are here. The most spectacular is to the right, behind some oaks. This **dolmen**★ has a corridor and burial chamber.

### Moclín

33.5km/21mi E. Follow the NO 26 to Illora, the NO 19 to N 432, left towards Alcalá la Real to Puerto López.

**Illora** is dominated by the 16C Iglesia de la Encarnación. Beyond, the hilltop **Castillo de la Mota**★ suddenly appears over Moclín. This Nasrid fortress holds a 16C granary (pósito), the Iglesia de la Encarnación, and the remains of the keep and a cistern.

# MONTILLA

POPULATION: 22 792

Montilla, set amid gently undulating hills in the province of Córdoba, is at the centre of a large wine-producing region, of the Montilla-Moriles appellation. Montilla enjoyed its period of greatest splendour in the 16C, when influential personalities such as the writer Inca Garcilaso de la Vega and St John of Ávila took up residence. Montilla's most important buildings date from this time. ▣ Capitán Alonso Vargas, 3, 14550 Montilla, ☎ 957 65 24 62, turismo@montilla.es.

▶ **Orient Yourself:** Montilla is situated 48.5km/30mi south of Córdoba via A 4 – E 5, N 331 and A 309.

◔ **Also See:** AGUILAR DE LA FRONTERA (10km/6mi S), LUCENA (30km/18.7mi SE), CABRA (30km/18.7mi SE), BAENA (41km/25.6mi E) and CÓRDOBA.

## A Bit of History

**Fiefdom of the Fernández de Córdobas** – Historians identify the town as the site of a battle between troops of Caesar and Pompey in AD 45. From 1375, Montilla is intimately linked to the **Fernández de Córdoba** family, who moved the family seat here from Aguilar. An illustrious family member was Gonzalo Fernández de Córdoba, known as **El Gran Capitán** (1453-1515), who took part in the capture of Granada. In 1508, King Fernando the Catholic ordered the razing of the castle at the town's highest point, to punish the disloyalty of Don Pedro Fernández de Córdoba.

## Sights

*Follow signs to the centre (centro). Leave your car in a signposted car park.*

### Iglesia Parroquial de Santiago

*Calle Iglesia.* This 16C parish church dedicated to St James was restored in the 18C, when the façade was much altered. It re-used materials from the nearby castle razed by Fernando the Catholic. The handsome brick tower is decorated with attractive blue *azulejos* around the bays, and the cupola is also covered with glazed ceramics. Explore the, narrow, cobbled streets around the church. At nº 2 calle Miguel Molina, the **Museo Histórico Local**, a museum, exhibits local artefacts from prehistory to the modern era. ◔ *Open Sun and public hols, 10.30am-1.30pm and 5-7pm.* ◔ *Closed Mon. No charge.* ☎ *957 65 41 94 / 957 65 59 81.*

### Iglesia de San Francisco Solano

*Calle San Francisco Solano.* This 17C-18C church stands where St Francis Solano was born in 1549. The peculiar **façade**★, of civil appearance, has a porticoed atrium, with semicircular arches on Doric columns. A statue of the town's patron is above the entrance. The tower was added in 1910. The bell tower and the spire above are totally covered by *azulejos.* See the main altarpiece inside.

## Wines of Montilla-Moriles

As a result of the region's continental climate, Montilla-Moriles wines have developed their own personality. The main grape variety grown here is Pedro Ximénez. Four different wines are produced: **fino** (an extra dry, slightly bitter wine, with an attractive light gold colour); **amontillado** (an older, amber-coloured fino with a nutty aroma); **oloroso** (a fragrant, velvety-textured wine almost mahogany in colour); and **Pedro Ximénez** (a sweet ruby-coloured wine which is an ideal accompaniment for a dessert). A visit to one of the bodegas such as Alvear, founded in 1729 and one of the region's oldest producers, is highly recommended.

B. Kaufmann/MICHELIN

### Ayuntamiento

*Calle Corredera.* The town hall was built on the site of the former Convento-Hospital de San Juan de Dios. Only the 18C church (now an exhibition hall), with its simple portal, remains. The town hall has an arcaded central patio.

### Convento de Santa Clara

Don Pedro Fernández de Córdoba, first Marquess of Priego, commissioned Hernán Ruiz the Elder to build this convent, completed in 1524 and later extended.
The façade of the **church** has a fine Flamboyant-Gothic **portal**★. The family escutcheon is above the door, alongside the niche housing an image of St Clare. The *artesonado* ceilings above the nave and main altarpiece are the highlights inside the church.
Upon leaving the convent, pass through an arch to the Llano de Palacio, the setting for the **Palacio de los Duques de Medinaceli** which was built by the Marquess and Marchioness of Priego as a residence following the destruction of their castle.

### Convento de Santa Ana

Only the 17C church with its simple doorway remains from the 16C convent. The main altarpiece includes an Immaculate Conception by renowned sculptor Pedro Roldán. The belfry, partially obscured by newer buildings, is decorated with *azulejos*.

### Casa-Museo del Inca Garcilaso

🕐 *Open Mon-Fri, 10am-2pm and 5-7pm (Dec-Mar, 4.30-6.30pm); Sat-Sun and public hols, 11am-2pm.* 🕐 *Closed afternoons in Jul-Aug. No charge.* ☎ *957 65 23 54.*
Inca Garcilaso de la Vega lived in this house between 1561 and 1591 and wrote several important works such as *La Florida* and *Los Comentarios Reales*. Now a museum, it is an interesting example of civil architecture from the period, with sober façade of golden-hued stone. Furniture inside is both original and reproduction.
Fine buildings in the centre include **La Tercia**, in plaza de la Rosa, the **Teatro Garnelo** (1921), the **Colegio de las Monjas Asuncionistas** (School of Assumptionist Nuns, the former residence of the Count of La Cortina), and the **Iglesia de San Agustín**.

# Excursions

## Espejo

*13.5km/8.5mi northeast along A 309*. Espejo's whitewashed houses, cobbled lanes and flights of steps stand on a hill beneath a castle amid a landscape of olive groves.

▷ *Leave your car in paseo de Andalucía and walk up to the castle.*

### Castle

☞ *Private property; closed to visitors*. The 15C castle with lofty keep belongs to the ducal house of Osuna. It is in the upper town, where **views**★ are magnificent.

The nearby **Iglesia Parroquial de San Bartolomé**, a Gothic parish church modified over time, contains works by Pedro Romaña (retable of St Andrés), an 18C Corpus Christi monstrance, and gold and silverwork.

## Montemayor

*14km/9mi northwest along the N 331*. A well-preserved 14C Mudéjar **castle** with impressive keep rises among the houses of Montemayor on a gentle hill.

### Iglesia de la Asunción

The **plaza de la Constitución** is lined by the town hall and this impressive 16C-17C church with Renaissance bell tower. The remains of a Roman mill are embedded in one of its walls. It has a richly decorated triple apse and three Baroque cupolas, a large 17C carved Renaissance altarpiece in the presbytery, and Baroque side chapels with rich stuccowork. The Capilla del Rosario (Rosary Chapel) contains interesting gold and silverwork, including a superb 18C altar frontal.

The **Museo de Ulía**, a museum in the former the ossuary and cistern, displays objects from the 5C BC to the 15C. ⓒ*Visits are only possible when the church is open*.

The delightful streets around the square display popular architecture, with picturesque corners and whitewashed houses, some with impressive doorways.

## Fernán Núñez

*18km/11mi northwest along the N 331*. This town, on the site of Roman Ulía, is named for its 13C founding noble.

### Palacio Ducal

This impressive ducal palace was built around a square in the 18C. The vermilion of its plasterwork and white mouldings on the windows inject life into the decoration.

### Iglesia de Santa Marina de Aguas Santas

The interior of this 18C church retains Baroque frescoes and stuccowork on the vaulting and cupolas.

## La Rambla

*16km/10mi NW along N 331 and A 386*. This town has a long pottery tradition. Miguel de Cervantes worked here as tax collector and treasurer for the royal storehouses.

### Iglesia Parroquial de la Asunción

Built during the Reconquest and rebuilt in the 18C, this parish church has a superb **Plateresque portal**★, the work of Hernán Ruiz I. Note the Baroque Capilla del Sagrario to the left of the chancel, with imitation marble retable and cupola, both of which are covered with plaster. Some of the statues in the church are attributed to Martínez Montañés: St Joseph with the Infant Jesus, St Ann with the Virgin Mary, John the Baptist, and St Rose.

Nearby, also in calle Iglesia, are the remains of a massive tower of the old **fortress**.

**Torre del ex-Convento de la Consolación**
This fine Baroque brick tower bears abundant decoration, particularly on its west side around the windows and bays.

**Colegio del Espiritú Santo**
The church belonging to this school houses a sculptural jewel which is the pride and joy of La Rambla's inhabitants: the wooden carving of **Jesus of Nazareth**★ bearing a cross on his shoulders, by Juan de Mesa. This impressive sculpture shows exceptional skill in its portrayal of the subject's emotion.

## Santaella
*32km/20mi west along N 331 and A 386.* Enjoy the view of this small town, under the Iglesia de la Asunción, from the main road. In the main square *(plaza mayor)* to the right of the town hall, the vestiges of a Moorish fortress are visible. The 18C Casa de las Columnas is to house the **Museo de Arqueología Local**, currently in the former granary. The museum contains a fine collection of exhibits, including the *Leona de Santaella* (The Santaella Lioness), Iberian votive offerings, an Ibero-Roman lion and a set of Visigothic monograms. ◷ *Open Sat, 5-7.30pm (6.30-9pm in summer); Sun and public hols, 11am-1pm. Other days by arrangement.* ☎ *957 31 32 44.*

▶ *Climb the ramp in front of the castle.*

Views from the top of the ramp take in the church and countryside.

**Iglesia de la Asunción**
Walk around the 16C-17C Church of the Assumption to appreciate its monumental stature. The Baroque **façade** is preceded by a wall, a windbreak which obstructs a full view. To the left, a **Renaissance tower** bears heraldic decoration. The wall on the northwest side retains its original decoration. Note the Mudéjar *artesonado* in the Capilla de las Ánimas, and several retables.
The 18C Baroque sanctuary of **Nuestra Señora del Valle**, housing the image of Our Lady of the Valley, the town's patron saint, can be visited on the outskirts.

# MONTORO★

POPULATION: 9 489

Montoro's impressive site, on a loop of the Guadalquivir, is best viewed from a bend on the main road, from where the full contrast between the reddish tones of its soil and the ochre and whitewash of its houses can be admired. The Baroque tower of the Iglesia de San Bartolomé rises majestically above the rooftops of this attractive town, which descend gently to the river, spanned by a graceful 15C bridge. ▮ *Plaza de España, 8, 14600 Montoro,* ☎ *957 16 00 89.*

▶ **Orient Yourself:** Montoro is situated at the eastern edge of the province of Córdoba, 44km/27mi east of Córdoba along the N IV – E 5, which runs parallel to the Guadalquivir.

◔ **Also See:** Neighbouring sights are described in the following chapters: ANDÚJAR (34km/21mi E) and CÓRDOBA.

# Walking Tour

*⊛Visitors are advised to leave their vehicle at the entrance to the town, as driving and parking in Montoro is particularly difficult.*

## Plaza de España★

This charming square at the very heart of the old town is lined by three interesting buildings: the Iglesia de San Bartolomé, the town hall and a fine seigniorial mansion. All three are built in the characteristic stone of the area and add a sense of harmony to the square's appearance.

## Iglesia de San Bartolomé

🕘 *Open 11am-2pm.* ☎ *957 16 00 89.* This handsome 15C church is the dominant feature of the square with its monumental Baroque bell tower standing proudly at the east end. Note the finely carved elegant Gothic-Mudéjar **portal★**, in the upper section of which the arch and a statue of the Virgin Child are framed by an *alfiz* surround. To the left of the doorway, embedded in the wall, a Visigothic slab can also be seen. Two coats of arms appear on the portal, while another adorns the Baroque window to the right of the façade. The triple-aisled interior contains some interesting marquetry, in addition to a delicately carved statue of the Virgin of the Rosary in a side chapel on the left-hand side.
The headless statue of the archangel Raphael stands alongside the church.

## Ayuntamiento

The Renaissance-style town hall is fronted by a harmonious two-storey façade bearing the coat of arms of the ducal house of Alba-Montoro. Between the façade and the vaulted arch on its left, note the stone commemorating the order given by Felipe III to build the old prison next door. The interior is crowned by some fine Mudéjar *artesonado* ceilings.

## Seigniorial mansion

*To the right of the church.* It was in this building that justice was formerly administered in Montoro. Four escutcheons can be seen on the second floor, while the heads of a man and woman above the doors denote the entrances through which the

*Montoro, nestling in a meander of the Guadalquivir river*

accused of each sex would have entered the building.

The area surrounding the square is a maze of narrow cobbled streets, picturesque nooks and crannies, and typical examples of popular architecture, with whitewashed houses framed by the traditional stone of the area providing a colourful contrast with the blue of the Cordoban sky. The **Casa de las Conchas** (House of the Shells) is an unusual modern building built in 1960 and, as the name would suggest, is completely covered by shells.

Walk along calle Bartolomé Camacho, next to the church in plaza de España, to the **Ermita de Santa María**, a 13C chapel, now home to the town's **Museo Arqueológico Local**. Upon returning to the square, there is an impressive view of the church tower. ⏱ *Open Sat-Sun and public hols, 11am-1pm; weekdays by prior arrangement.* ☎ *957 16 00 89.*

> ☺ **Local Crafts** ☺
>
> **Handicrafts:** A number of traditional handicraft workshops can still be found in calle Corredera, including the one run by the sons of Manuel Mohedo (n° 39), who specialise in harness-making.

## Sights

### Iglesia del Carmen

*Calle El Santo.* The façade of this church, built out of local stone, is dominated by the image of St John of the Cross. Inside, the three naves are overshadowed by an 18C Baroque **retable** in the chancel, with a Virgin and Child enthroned at its centre.

### Hospital de Jesús Nazareno

This hospital was built in the 17C and 18C, although it has undergone subsequent restoration on a number of occasions. It is now used as a rest home. The cupola of the church is brightly decorated in tones of blue and gold.

## Excursions

### Adamuz

*24km/15mi west. Take the E 5 motorway towards Córdoba. Exit at Km 367 and follow signs to Adamuz.*

The road passes through an area of abundant vegetation, following the wide course of the Guadalquivir until it crosses the river at El Salto. Continue along the opposite bank, before leaving the river behind and ascending a winding route towards Adamuz, set amid a landscape of olive groves.

The town's whitewashed streets are overlooked by the Gothic **Iglesia de San Andrés**, built in red sandstone in the late 14C and early 15C. The sober appearance of the church, enhanced by the absence of decoration, is counteracted only by its impressive bulk. The main civil building is the **Torre del Reloj**, a clock tower built by the Marquess of El Carpio in 1566, but subsequently restored.

### El Carpio

*19km/12mi southwest along E 5. Exit at Km 374.*

The houses of El Carpio rise up a hill dominated by a 14C tower, the Mudéjar-style **Torre de Garci Méndez**. The best view of this imposing brick tower can be enjoyed from plaza de la Constitución, a pleasant square fronted by a 17C parish church and adorned with orange trees and arrangements of flowers.

## Parque Natural de la Sierra de Cardeña y Montoro

*15km/9.5mi north along N 420.* The gentle features of this protected area to the south of the Sierra Morena give way to steeper landscapes and numerous ravines further to the west. The predominant tree species found here are holm oak, arbutus, the occasional downy oak, and areas replanted with pines. Local wildlife includes wolves, otters, lynx, wild boar, genet and deer. The numerous marked paths criss-crossing the area make the park very popular with hikers.

## Bujalance

*14km/9mi south along the A 309.* This pleasant town in the Cordoban countryside is set in a landscape dominated by the ubiquitous olive. It has preserved much of its popular Andalusian architecture, characterised by a number of noble mansions, most of which were built in the 17C.

▶ *Follow signs to the town centre (centro ciudad) and park next to the plaza Mayor.*

### Plaza Mayor

This sloping, triangular square, with its attractive orange trees, is overlooked by the tower of the Iglesia de la Asunción. The 17C **town hall**, with its heraldic decoration, encloses the upper part of the square, alongside a vaulted arch which leads to the Iglesia de la Asunción.

### Iglesia de la Asunción

*Entrance through the sacristy (the first house on the left upon leaving the square through the arch).*
The Church of the Assumption dates from the 16C, although an earlier church occupied this site. The ground plan is in keeping with the majority of Cordoban churches of the period: three aisles, no transept and a rectilinear apse with three rectangular chapels. The side aisles have retained their original wooden ceiling, unlike the nave which is topped by an 18C vault. The apsidal end has Gothic vaulting, with a star vault in the chancel with tierceron features to the sides.
Works of art in the church include the 16C carved and painted Renaissance altarpiece in the presbytery and the Baroque retable in the chapel on the right side of the apsidal end.
The outstanding feature of the exterior is the fine 18C Baroque **tower** which at 55m/180ft in height is the tallest in the province.

### Alcazaba

*Entrance to the left of the main façade of the church.* Despite the fact that this former Moorish fortress is now in ruins, the towers and curtain wall which were part of the external defences are still visible. Built during the reign of Abd ar-Rahman III, it was modified after the Reconquest. The castle's seven towers form the basis for the town's coat of arms.

### Iglesia de San Francisco

*From the plaza Mayor, head down calle E Sotomayor to calle Ancha de Palomino.*
The church is of new construction, with the exception of the portal and the fine Baroque tower. The earlier building, which was considered a jewel of Cordoban Baroque, was destroyed during the Spanish Civil War.

### Ermita de Jesús

*On the outskirts of the town. Follow calle San Antonio to the left of the façade of the Iglesia de San Francisco.* The chapel is situated in the Parque de Jesús, on top of a promontory affording a pleasant view of the olive groves that extend to the horizon. The style is 18C, although the chapel's origins are earlier. The Baroque portal is adorned with *estípites* and an abundance of minute decoration.

# OSUNA

POPULATION: 17 306

This elegant Andalusian town, built on a hill at the heart of the Sevillian countryside, has preserved a beautiful **monumental centre**★ inherited from its former status as a ducal seat. The dukedom was created in 1562 and the House of Osuna was to become one of the most powerful on the Iberian Peninsula. The prosperity that Osuna enjoyed in subsequent centuries is reflected in the fine examples of civil and religious architecture embellishing the town. *Calle Sevilla, 22, 41013 Osuna, ☎ 954 81 22 11.*

▶ **Orient Yourself:** Osuna rises above a gently undulating landscape to the south of the Guadalquivir depression, near the A 92 highway linking Granada (160km/100mi E) with Sevilla.

▷ **Also See:** MARCHENA (34km/21mi NW), ÉCIJA (34km/21mi N), ESTEPA (24km/15mi E), ANTEQUERA (67km/42mi SE), CÓRDOBA (85km/53mi NE) and SEVILLA (92km/58mi W).

## Walking Tour

## Monumental Centre★

▶ *Follow signs to the town centre (centro ciudad) and Zona Monumental.*

### Colegiata★

*Guided tours (45min), May-Sep, Tue-Sun, 10am-1.30pm and 4-7pm (10am-2pm, Jul-Aug); Oct-Apr, Tue-Sun, 10am-1.30pm and 3.30-6.30pm. Closed Mon, 1 and 6 Jan (afternoon), Maundy Thu, Good Fri, 24 (afternoon), 25 and 31 (afternoon) Dec. €2. ☎ 954 81 04 44.*

This imposing 16C Renaissance-style collegiate church stands impressively above the town. The façade is adorned with a handsome, finely sculpted Plateresque doorway.

### Interior

The **church** is composed of three elegant Renaissance aisles opening out onto several chapels and a Baroque apse with an interesting retable in the same style, bearing the coat of arms of the House of Osuna. The organ dates from the 18C.

The church contains several important works of art within its walls: *Jesus of Nazareth* by the "divine" Morales, a *Christ of Mercy* by Juan de Mesa, the superb tenebrist canvas, **The Expiration of Christ**★★, by **José Ribera**, "lo Spagnoletto", and an unusually small 16C organ, which is carried during religious processions.

The **sacristy** is adorned with 16C **azulejos** and some original **artesonado** work. Exhibits include several books of

### An Eventful History

Initially inhabited by the Iberians, who named it Urso, this elegant town was subsequently conquered by the Romans, under Caesar. Following the period of Moorish occupation, it was reconquered by Fernando III the Saint in 1239, and then ceded to the Order of Calatrava by Alfonso X the Wise in 1264. However, its period of greatest splendour is inextricably linked with the House of Osuna, under whose control it passed in 1562, when Felipe II granted the title of Duke of Osuna to the fifth Count of Ureña. The dukedom was responsible for the embellishment of Osuna, as well as its artistic and cultural development.

## WHERE TO STAY – AND EAT

**El Caballo Blanco** – *Granada, 1* – ☎ *954 81 01 84 – 13 rooms*. This motel-like residence is located in the heart of Osuna. Spotlessly clean rooms, all at street level. Good value for money.

**Palacio del Marqués de la Gomera** – *San Pedro, 20* – ☎ *954 81 22 23 – 18 rooms, 2 suites*. This 18C architectural jewel, which once belonged to the Marquess of La Gomera, has been transformed into a hotel with rooms that have been tastefully furnished and maintained.
The hotel's restaurant, **La Casa del Marqués** (⊜⊜), with its elegant patio, offers a refined menu of Andalusian cuisine.

Gregorian chants dating from the 16C, and four more **paintings by Ribera**★★: *St Jerome, The Tears of St Peter, The Martyrdom of St Bartholomew* and *The Martyrdom of St Sebastian,* all of which were painted between 1616 and 1618.
Additional works of art on view in other rooms include an *Immaculate Conception* by Alonso Cano, a silver processional cross (1534), Flemish paintings, gold and silver and vestments dating from the period in which the Colegiata was founded.

### Panteón Ducal★★

The ducal pantheon was built in Plateresque style in 1545 as the burial place for the Dukes of Osuna. It is approached by a delightful patio, designed in the same style. The chapel stands just below the Colegiata's main altar, and despite its tiny dimensions (8m/26ft long, 4.5m/15ft wide and 2.5m/8ft high), it comprises three aisles and a choir. It is crowned by a blue and gold polychrome coffered ceiling which has been blackened by candle smoke. The altarpiece, by Roque Balduque, represents the Burial of Christ.
The **crypt** beneath the chapel contains the tombs of the most notable Dukes of Osuna and the founders of the Colegiata (the parents of the first duke).

### Former university

The old university *(antigua universidad)*, created in 1548 and in existence until 1824, was founded by Juan Téllez, the Count of Ureña and father of the first Duke of Osuna. It is a large square building made of stone; the circular towers on its corners are crowned by spires decorated with blue and white *azulejos*. Note also the attractive inner patio.

### Monasterio de la Encarnación★

🕓 *Open in summer, Tue-Sun, 10am-1.30pm and 4.30-7.30pm; otherwise, Tue-Sun, 10am-1.30pm and 3.30-6.30pm.* 🕓 *Closed Mon.* ⊜€2. ☎ *954 81 11 21.*
This convent of discalced nuns was founded by the fourth Duke of Osuna in the 17C. Its outstanding feature is the magnificent **dado**★ of 17C Sevillian *azulejos* in the patio, dedicated to the five senses. This decoration continues up the stairs and on the patio's upper floor. The large collection of paintings, statuary and other objects of artistic interest includes a set of statues of the Infant Jesus, various pieces of gold and silverwork and an 18C Baroque altarpiece. The church is also Baroque in style. Like many convents in Andalucía, the nuns here produce and sell several types of delicious biscuits and pastries.

### Torre del Agua

*On the way down to the plaza Mayor.* This medieval defensive tower dates from the 12C-13C, although its origins can be traced to the Carthaginians. Nowadays, it is home to the town's **Museo Arqueológico**, displaying a range of Iberian and Roman objects discovered in Osuna, as well as reproductions of Iberian bulls and Roman bronzes (the originals can be seen in the Museo Arqueológico Nacional, Madrid). 🕓 *Open* *in summer, 10am-1.30pm and 5-7pm (10am-2pm, Jul-Aug); otherwise, 11am-1.30pm and 3.30-6.30pm. €2. ☎ 954 81 12 07.*

# The Town

The centre of Osuna has some fine examples of civil architecture, including an impressive array of Baroque **palaces and seigniorial residences**★★.

## Calle San Pedro★
In addition to several interesting town houses and churches, this street contains two magnificent palaces:

### Cilla del Cabildo
This original 18C Baroque edifice was designed by Alonso Ruiz Florindo, who was also responsible for the tower *(torre)* of the Iglesia de la Merced (& *see below*). In both buildings he incorporated unusual pilasters with individual decoration. Above the doorway, a somewhat curious copy of the Giralda (Sevilla) dominates the façade.

### Palacio de los Marqueses de la Gomera
This 18C Baroque palace has a striking cornice with a sense of movement created by volutes and waves, in addition to a beautiful stone doorway crowned by a large escutcheon. The building now houses a hotel and restaurant (& *see Address Book*).

*Cilla del Cabildo*

B. Kaufmann/MICHELIN

### Antiguo Palacio de Puente Hermoso
*Calle Sevilla, 44.* The handsome 18C Baroque **portal**★ adorning the façade of this former palace is embellished by the Solomonic columns on the lower tier adorned with fig leaves and bunches of grapes.
The street has several other notable civil and religious buildings.

### Palacio de los Cepeda
*Calle de la Huerta.* This palace is now the home of the town's law courts. It is a handsome 18C construction with an impressive main doorway and a fine cornice crowning the building. However, its most outstanding features are the *estípites* on the doorway and, in particular, the large coat of arms with the two halberdiers flanking it.

### Antigua Audiencia
*Carrera Caballos, 82.* Osuna's law courts were formerly housed in this sober building dating from the reign of Carlos III.

### Torre de la Iglesia de la Merceda
The church tower, designed by the same architect as the Cilla del Cabildo, is an impressive monument with a number of decorative elements.
Osuna's religious architecture is represented by numerous convents and churches (Santo Domingo, la Compañía, la Concepción etc), predominantly dating from the 17C and 18C.

# PALMA DEL RÍO

POPULATION: 18 948

Palma del Río, a tranquil town which has preserved substantial sections of its Arab walls, is situated on a plain, close to the confluence of the River Guadalquivir and River Genil. Approaching from Córdoba along C 431 the whitewashed Ermita de la Virgen de Belén, a chapel named after the town's patron saint, the Virgin of Bethlehem, can be seen on top of a small hill to the right. The views of the town from here are particularly impressive. A turning on the other side of the road leads to Palma del Río, reached after crossing a large iron and concrete bridge built in the 19C. *Plaza de Judá Levi, 14700 Palma del Río, ☎ 957 20 05 22; Calle Cardenal Portocarrero, 14700 Palma del Río, ☎ 957 54 43 70.*

▸ **Orient Yourself:** Situated at the eastern edge of the province of Córdoba, Palma del Río is linked to its provincial capital by A 453 and A 431.

▸ **Also See:** ÉCIJA (29km/18mi SE), CÓRDOBA (58km/36mi E) and CARMONA (52km/32mi SW).

## Sights

*Follow signs to the town centre (centro ciudad), then park near plaza de Andalucía.*

### Plaza de Andalucía

The town's main square is lined by three major buildings: the town hall, post office *(correos)* and law courts *(juzgados)*. The most interesting constructions in the square are the **Puerta del Sol** (Sun Gateway) and the 16C **Renaissance balcony**, which was part of the Palacio de los Portacarrero, above which rises the tower of the Iglesia de la Asunción. The palace originally stood through the arch on the right-hand side.

### Town walls★

These date from the 12C and formed part of an extensive walled enclosure built during the Almohad period to provide protection for the town. Substantial parts of the walls still remain intact, including several solid sections, in addition to several square towers and one octagonal one.

### Museo Municipal

○ Open mid-Jun to mid-Sep, Tue-Sat, 10am-2pm, Sun and public hols, 11am-2pm; mid-Sep to mid-Jun, Tue-Sat, 5-8pm, Sun and public hols, 11am-2pm. ○ Closed Mon. No charge. ☎ 957 64 43 70.
The municipal museum is in the former royal stables. It is divided into three sections, devoted to archaeology, ethnography and fine arts.

---

### El Cordobés

It was in Palma del Río that one of Spain's greatest bullfighters, Manuel Benítez Pérez, known as El Cordobés, was born. Between 1964 and 1971, he established himself as one of the most revered and talked-about matadors in the history of bullfighting with his endeavours both in and out of the ring, The awarding of the honorary title of "Caliph of bullfighting" by the city authorities in Córdoba in the presence of the province's highest dignitaries in November 2002 was a noteworthy achievement for this former outcast who in his younger years earned his living from theft and on more than one occasion was arrested by the Guardia Civil.

---

**WHERE TO STAY**

**Castillo** – *Portada, 47* – ☎ *957 64 57 10* – *48 rooms*. A modern, comfortable hotel in the centre of town.

**Hospedería de San Francisco** – *Avenida Pio XII, 35* – ☎ *957 71 01 83* – *21 rooms, 1 apartment*. A luxury hotel and **restaurant**, housed in a former 15C Franciscan monastery which has also been used as a religious university. The impressive guest bedrooms are all furnished with antiques. The restaurant, in the monks' refectory, serves Basque specialities.*(☺☺)*.

**LOCAL SPECIALITIES**

**A tradition of pottery** – The town's inhabitants believe that it is the quality of the clay used in the production of the local earthenware pots that keeps the water stored in them so cool. Other typical items of pottery from Palma del Río include wine pitchers, gazpacho bowls and flowerpots.

## Iglesia de la Asunción

🕐 *Open 11am-1pm.* 🕐 *Closed Thu.* ☎ *957 64 56 76 (Cultural Office).*

The Church of the Assumption was built in the 18C. The exterior is dominated by an elegant **tower**★, showing clear Écijan influence in the middle of the façade, above a red-brick Baroque portal. The rich decoration on the belfry (*estípites*, frets and Solomonic columns) is enhanced by the blue-tinged tones of its *azulejos*.

The **interior**★ is particularly harmonious with its wide nave and transept, above which rises a cupola, with pendentives decorated with stuccowork bearing plant motifs. The nave is supported by enormous pilasters, above which runs a cornice adorned with further stucco features. The wrought-iron balconies create a pleasant contrast, adding an element of dynamism to the overall effect. Side chapels open out from the nave, although the walls originally in place to separate them have since disappeared, leaving what now appears to be two narrow, corridor-like aisles. The church is presided over by a Baroque altarpiece.

## Iglesia y Convento de San Francisco

The church and convent were founded in the 16C, but underwent significant modification in the 17C and 18C. Noteworthy external features include the cupolas above the side chapels and the transept. A hospice *(hospedería)* stands alongside the church.

Other sights of interest in Palma del Río include the 18C Baroque **Capilla del Virgen del Rosario**, a chapel dedicated to the Virgin of the Rosary, in the Iglesia de Santo Domingo, and the **Hospital de San Sebastián** (now a retirement home), with its attractive patio and a church with a Mudéjar-influenced façade. Inside, note the unusual retable of the Virgin of Sorrow (Virgen de los Dolores) and a chapel with a fine dado of old *azulejos* and a Mudéjar *artesonado* ceiling.

# Excursions

## Jardines de Moratalla

*11km/7mi east along A 431.* Botanical enthusiasts will not want to miss the gardens (*jardines*) of this private estate, designed in 1918 by JN Forestier, the architect of the María Luisa Park in Sevilla.

## Hornachuelos

*18km/11mi northeast. Head along A 431 for 10km/6mi, then bear left onto CO 141.* This small whitewashed town in the sierra of the same name has preserved vestiges of the castle and walls built during the period of the Cordoban Caliphate. Several vantage points, including one in plaza de la Iglesia, offer impressive views of the mountains. Hornachuelos is renowned for its local gastronomy, which is based on venison and wild boar.

Walk along calle Palmera, so named after the palm tree *(palmera)* engraved on its pavement, to the 16C **Iglesia de Santa María de las Flores**, a church embellished with a handsome late-Gothic **portal** attributed to Hernán Ruiz I, and an 18C tower.

**Las Erillas** can be seen on the outskirts of Hornachuelos, heading east. This area of limestone has been eroded by water to produce some extraordinary rock formations such as the so-called *casas colgantes* or "hanging houses".

## Parque Natural de la Sierra de Hornachuelos

This park covers an area of 67 000ha/165 557 acres in the west of the province. Despite its relatively low altitude – its highest peak is the Sierra Alta (722m/2 368ft) – the scenery is grand: rivers running through the park have sculpted a landscape of gorges and lakes, one of which (El Retortillo) is popular with swimmers. The vegetation here is mainly holm, cork and gall oak and wild olives, with poplar, alder and ash closer to water. The park is a popular area for hunting, particularly for deer and wild boar; other species found here include the black vulture and the golden eagle, as well as otters, wolves and the rare Iberian lynx.

### Centro de Visitantes Huerta del Rey

*1.5km/1mi from Hornachuelos along CO 142.* ◷ *Open in summer, Tue-Sun, 10.30am-2.30pm and 4-7pm; otherwise, Tue-Sun, 10am-2pm and 4-7pm.* ◷ *Closed Mon.* ☎ *957 64 11 40 or 957 45 32 11.*

The Huerta del Rey visitor centre has a number of rooms devoted to interactive exhibitions on the park. Information is available on the extensive network of footpaths on offer to visitors, as well as details on camping permits. The centre is also able to organise tours of the park by donkey and jeep *(advance booking required).*

### San Calixto

*16km/10mi from the visitor centre along CO 142.* San Calixto was developed as part of Carlos III's land colonisation policy in the 18C. Its major buildings are the Palacio del Marqués de Salinas and its gardens, a 16C convent for discalced Carmelite nuns, and the Iglesia de Nuestra Señora de la Sierra, a church rebuilt in the 18C. The nuns from the convent have developed a reputation for their handicrafts, in particular embroidered table linen, trays decorated by hand and receptacles made from deerskin.

# PRIEGO DE CÓRDOBA★★

POPULATION: 22 196

The delightful town of Priego de Córdoba, nestled at the foot of the Pico de la Tiñosa (1 570m/5 150ft), is considered to be the capital of Cordoban Baroque, as borne out by the numerous buildings erected during this sumptuous period in the town's history. Priego reached its economic zenith in the 18C thanks to the silk industry, which was to generate untold artistic and cultural splendour.
🛈 *Calle Real, 46, 14800 Priego de Córdoba,* ☎ *957 59 44 27;* 🛈 *Calle Río, 3, 14800 Priego de Córdoba,* ☎ *957 70 06 25.*

▶ **Orient Yourself:** The town is situated at the heart of the Subbética Cordobesa mountain range, in an isolated area away from the region's major roads.
◔ **Also See:** Neighbouring sights are described in the following chapters: CABRA (29km/18mi W), LUCENA (36km/22mi W), ALCALÁ LA REAL (24km/15mi E), BAENA

(36km/22mi N), JAÉN (67km/42mi NE), GRANADA (79km/49mi SE) and ANTE-QUERA (85km/53mi SW).

# Walking Tour

▶ *Follow signs to the town centre (centro ciudad) and park near plaza de la Constitución, which is fronted by the town hall.*

## Hospital-Iglesia de San Juan de Dios

*In plaza de la Constitución, to the right of the town hall.* The hospital was founded in 1637 by Juan de Herrera and completed in 1717. The first feature of interest inside the building is the attractive cloistered patio. The handsome Baroque church, with its single nave and fine echini-adorned cupola above the transept, stands to the rear, on the right-hand side. Several broken cornices run along the upper sections of the side walls, providing the church with a certain dynamism. The building is completely whitewashed, with vegetal decoration arranged in bands or garlands. The Virgin of Mercy (Virgen de las Mercedes) presides over the main altarpiece, which is also Baroque.

▶ *Exit calle Ribera and head along paseo del Abad Palomino.*

## Castle

The significant remains of this sober and imposing fortress, of Moorish origin but modified in the 13C and 14C, can be seen from the **paseo del Abad Palomino**. The wall is punctuated with square towers, including the **keep**, with its paired windows. It is possible to walk around most of the outside of the castle, where houses can be seen built against the wall.

## Parroquia de la Asunción★

*Visits by prior arrangement.* ⊙ *Open in summer, Tue-Sat, 11am-2pm and 5.30-8pm, Sun, 11am-2pm; otherwise, Tue-Sat, 10.30am-1.30pm and 4-7pm (no visits during religious services).* ⊙ *Closed Sun afternoon and Mon.* ☎ *606 17 16 53.*
This 16C late-Gothic church was remodelled in the 18C in Baroque style. Note also the fine Renaissance portal on the right-hand side. The bright, spacious interior comprises three aisles crowned with arris vaults and decorated keystones, and an echini-adorned cupola above pendentives. The presbytery is dominated by an impressive carved and painted 16C Mannerist-style **retable**. In the chapels, several altarpieces and a Christ attributed to Alonso de Mena are also worthy of note.

## El Sagrario★★

This chapel, which opens onto the Evangelist nave, is a masterpiece of Priego and Spanish Baroque. Its ground plan consists of a rectangular antechamber leading into an octagonal space surrounded by an ambulatory, in the centre of which stands the chapel. Light plays an important part in the overall scene, and is intensified by the whiteness of the walls and ceiling, inundating the central area with a dazzling brightness and creating a magical atmosphere. The interior is enhanced by the sublime **plasterwork**★★★ by the local artist Francisco Javier Pedrajas (1736-1817), which covers the entire chapel. Pay particular attention to the keystone of the large cupola which is adorned with numerous small heads. Lower down, a sculpture of an Apostle

### Priego's native sons

Famous former inhabitants of the town include the politician **Niceto Alcalá-Zamora** (1877-1949), president of the Second Republic, and the Baroque artists Juan de Dios Santaella (1718-1802) and Francisco Javier Pedrajas (1736-1817).

can be seen against each pillar. The decoration combines plant motifs, rocaille work and scenes with characters illustrating themes found in both the Old and New Testaments. Despite the profuse decoration, the overall effect is one of lightness and delicacy, and is without doubt one of the highlights of a visit to Priego de Córdoba.

## Barrio de la Villa★★

Tucked away behind the church, this charming quarter dating back to medieval and Moorish times is characterised by narrow, winding streets and flower-decked whitewashed houses. The combination of myriad colours and scents has made the Barrio de la Villa one of Andalucía's archetypal sights. A leisurely stroll along calle Jazmines, calle Bajondillo, calle Reales and through plaza de San Antonio is particularly recommended.

## El Adarve★

To the north of the Barrio de la Villa, this delightful balcony looks onto the Subbética mountain range. The impressive **views**, attractive lamp posts, iron benches and contemplative atmosphere transport visitors back to bygone days.

▶ *Return to the beginning of paseo del Abad Palomino and follow carrera Álvarez.*

## Iglesia de la Aurora

The former 15C church was remodelled in the 18C by Juan de Dios Santaella in Baroque style, although it has preserved its 16C tower and belfry. It has a fine polychrome marble Baroque portal on two levels, presided over by the Virgin of the Aurora between two Solomonic columns. The single-nave interior has profuse Baroque decoration.

### Brothers of the Aurora

The brotherhood of the Iglesia de la Aurora keeps alive a time-honoured tradition every Saturday night, when it takes to the streets of Priego de Córdoba singing songs in honour of the Virgin.

▶ *Retrace your steps as far as plaza de San Pedro.*

## Iglesia de San Pedro

🕐 *Open 10am-1pm.*

The Baroque additions to this church were completed in 1690. The interior contains some interesting statuary, including an outstanding **Immaculate Conception**★ in the *camarín* behind the main altarpiece; this statue is attributed by some to Diego de Mora, and by others to Alonso Cano. The first chapel to the side of the Evangelist nave houses an image of the **Virgin of Solitude**, while the last chapel on the Epistle nave contains a delightful wooden **recumbent Christ** (1594) attributed to Pablo de Rojas, on display inside a glass urn.

▶ *Head along calle Pedrajas.*

## Carnicerías Reales

🕐 *Open 1-2pm and 7-10pm.*

The former royal abattoir and market was built in the 16C along Classical lines, and is a somewhat surprising addition to a town dominated by Baroque architecture. The simple stone doorway, presided over by the coat of arms of the Fernández de Córdoba family, is adorned with two unusual engaged columns. The square-shaped interior has a central patio and towers on its corners. To the rear, to the right of the window with views of the local countryside, a spiral staircase descends to the room where animals were slaughtered. Nowadays it is used as an exhibition hall.

▶ *Return to plaza de la Constitución, at the start of calle del Río.*

## Las Angustias

*If closed, knock on the door of the adjacent building; the nuns from the school will show visitors around.* Built in 1772 by Juan de Dios Santaella, the church's outstanding feature is the twin-sectioned polychrome doorway with its abundant broken lines. Note also the unusual Virgin and Child in the vaulted niche and the finely worked *estípites* on the lower section. The church belfry can be seen to the left side.

The inside of the church, which is surprisingly small in size, is Rococo. The area above the altar is covered by an attractive moulded dome above pendentives. On the gilded retable, the 18C middle sculptural group is from the Granada School and depicts the Virgin with the dead Christ in her arms. Also worthy of note are two terracotta sculptures by José Risueño beneath this work.

Follow **calle del Río**, which is lined by several seigniorial houses. The **birthplace of Niceto Alcalá-Zamora** (1877-1949), President of the Second Republic, is now home to the town's tourist office.

## Iglesia del Carmen

This 18C church was built in the transitional style between Baroque and neo-Classical. The façade combines elements of both styles, with a tower directly incorporated onto it. Last to be built, the portal is pure neo-Classical.

## Fuentes del Rey y de la Salud★★

*At the end of calle del Río.* Known as the Fountains of the King *(Rey)* and Health *(Salud)*, these fountains form the best-known sight in Priego de Córdoba.

*Fuente del Rey*

The older of the two, the **Fuente de la Salud★**, was sculpted in the 16C by Francisco del Castillo. It is a stone frontispiece built in Mannerist style with, at its centre, a small niche containing the Virgin of Health, hence its name. The green of the vegetation contrasts with the golden stone, helping to create a charming scene enhanced by the proximity of the lavish **Fuente del Rey★★**, which was completed at the beginning of the 19C. Both its dimensions and the richness of its design, characterised by curves and counter-curves, evoke the gardens of a Baroque palace. It is arranged on three levels with 139 jets spouting water from the mouths of masks. The sculptural groups are the work of Remigio del Mármol: the central work represents Neptune's chariot and Amphitrite. The lion fighting the snake on the top section is attributed to the neo-Classical sculptor J Alvarez Cubero.

▷ *Head along calle Obispo Pérez Muñoz as far as carrera de las Monjas.*

## Museo Histórico Municipal

🕐 *Open Tue-Sat, 10am-1.30pm and 5-7.30pm; Sun and public hols, 10am-1.30pm.*
🕐 *Closed Mon, 1 Jan, Good Fri and 25 Dec.* ☎ *957 54 09 47.*
This local museum, housed in the birthplace of the painter and illustrator Adolfo Lozano Sidro (1872-1935), displays a number of archaeological exhibits discovered in and around Priego de Córdoba.

Other Baroque churches of interest include the **Iglesia de las Mercedes** and the **Iglesia de San Francisco**, the latter fronted by a neo-Classical portal.

## Excursion

### Carcabuey

*8km/5mi west.* Carcabuey sits at the foot of a hill crowned by the ruins of a castle and chapel amid a delightful landscape of olive groves, behind which stands the impressive backdrop of the Subbética mountain range. *Follow the street with flights of steps, which comes out opposite the town hall, then continue along a cobbled ramp.* It is well worth climbing up to the castle precinct, inside of which a chapel, the **Ermita de la Virgen del Castillo**, can be seen. The views of the town and the surrounding countryside from this elevated spot are delightful. Walk around the right-hand side of the hermitage to see the remains of the castle, including its walls and turrets.

The **Iglesia de la Asunción**, a solid stone construction, dominates the upper part of the town. The most impressive feature of the church, which was built in the 16C and 17C, are the two imposing buttresses connected via an arch, and its brick tower.

A track leads from Carcabuey towards Luque across the **Parque Natural de las Sierras Subbéticas** (&see CABRA: Excursions).

# PUEBLOS BLANCOS DE ANDALUCÍA★★

### WHITE VILLAGES OF ANDALUCÍA

The route through the White Villages of Andalucía crosses one of the most beautiful, yet undiscovered parts of the Iberian Peninsula. Delightful whitewashed towns and villages with a maze of lanes, once Moorish, are often crowned by the ruins of a castle, and dominated by the silhouette of a bell tower.

▶ **Orient Yourself:** This area stretches between Ronda and Arcos in a region formed by four sierras (Grazalema, Ubrique, Margarita and Ronda).

🕓 **Organizing Your Time:** Allow at least three days to tour the Pueblos Blancos.

&  **Also See:** COSTA DEL SOL, ALGECIRAS (including Gibraltar), MÁLAGA (98km/61mi E of Ronda), JEREZ DE LA FRONTERA (24km/15mi W of Arcos de la Frontera).

## Driving Tour

This itinerary departs from **Arcos** and continues through the delightful **Sierra de Grazalema**, to **Ronda**, then skirts mountain folds on a road back to Arcos.

### Arcos de la Frontera★★ – &see ARCOS DE LA FRONTERA

▶ *Leave Arcos along A 372 heading east towards El Bosque.*

### Lime

A particular feature of Andalusian architecture is the use of lime. A number of theories have been put forward to explain this practice, the origins of which can be found in the Middle Ages. When used on walls, lime acts as a consolidating agent and an insulator against fierce heat; in times past it was also used as a disinfectant against disease.

Enjoy one of the best **views**★ of Arcos is from this road.

**Prado del Rey** (*7km/4.5mi N of El Bosque, turn before town*) was founded in the 18C by **Carlos III** ( "del Rey", of the King). Its orthogonal plan is unusual for the area.

## El Bosque

*30km/19mi E of Arcos.* The **Centro de Visitantes del Parque Natural Sierra de Grazalema** is here. A small botanical garden includes native species (Spanish fir, gall oak and cork oak). *Visitor centre,* 🕐 *Open 10am-2pm and 4-6pm (Apr-Sep, 6-8pm), Sat-Sun, 9am-2pm.* ☎ *956 72 70 29.*

From El Bosque, the direct road to Grazalema *(description below)* passes through **Benamahoma**, with a small **water museum** *(museo del agua)* in its old mill. The River Bosque originates here. An alternative route is via Ubrique.

## Ubrique

*12km/7.5mi SE of El Bosque along the A 373.* The **road**★ enters the heart of the Sierra de Grazalema in the most beautiful part of the tour. White Ubrique extends across Cruz del Tajo Hill, its **setting** one of the most attractive in the sierra. Ubrique specialises in leather goods. The 18C parish church of **Nuestra Señora de la O** dominates the upper section of the town beyond the **plaza del Ayuntamiento**.

▶ *Leave Ubrique on A 374 towards Benaocaz.*

The 2C AD **Roman settlement of Ocurri** is 2km/1.2mi outside of Ubrique, at Salto de la Mora. ⟿ *Guided tours (2hr), Sat-Sun and public hols at noon.* ⟿€4.50. ☎ *956 46 49 00 (tourist office).* The road continues through mountains to Benaocaz *(6km/4mi)* and Villaluenga del Rosario *(11km/7mi)*.

## Benaocaz

Benaocaz has an attractive town hall built in the 18C under Carlos III and a small museum, the **Museo Municipal**. 🕐 *Open Sat-Sun and public hols, 11.30am-1.30pm and 5-7pm; midweek by prior arrangement. No charge.* ☎ *956 12 55 00.*

## The Spanish fir

This species, a relic of the Tertiary Era, is the most common tree to be found in the local sierra. Known popularly as the Spanish pine, the Spanish fir *(pinsapo)* is a tree which is more commonly found in Mediterranean areas. Today, it is only found in the Sierra de Grazalema and the Serranía de Ronda in Spain, and the Rif mountains in Morocco. The Spanish fir was officially classified as an arboreal species in 1837 by the Swiss botanist Edmond Bossier. It can grow to a height of some 30m/100ft and attain a diameter of around 1m/3ft. Its branches, which grow horizontally, and its leaves, with their helicoidal shape, give the tree an unusual appearance which is quite unique in Spain.

▷ *Continue on the A 374.*

## Villaluenga del Rosario

This village, the highest in Cádiz province, is unspoilt, its cobbled streets lined by whitewashed houses. Oddities are a falling-down brick tower in the upper town, the neo-Classical façade of the cemetery entrance, and a **bullring** *(plaza de toros)* perched on an outcrop.

▷ *The road continues along the La Manga defile (desfiladero).*

## Grazalema

The approach to beautiful Grazalema (Moorish *Ben-Zalema*) is through the Los Alamillos Pass, revealing **Peñón Grande**, a peak rising to 1 000m/3 328ft behind the village. It is perhaps surprising to note that Spain's wettest village is not in the region of Galicia, in the northwest of the country, but here in the heart of Andalucía. This quirk of nature is due to the **föhn effect**, whereby warm clouds full of moisture from the Atlantic penetrate inland areas.

The tower of the **Iglesia de San Juan** is of Moorish origin. The tower of the 16C **Iglesia de la Encarnación** is Mudéjar in style. The 18C **Iglesia de la Aurora** is on **plaza de España**. Grazalema is known for basketwork and woollen blankets. Visit the **hand looms** at the entrance to the town. ○ *Open Mon-Thu, 8am-2pm and 3-6.30pm, Fri 8am-2pm (shop open Fri afternoon); Jul, Mon-Fri, 7am-3pm.* ○ *Closed Sat-Sun, public hols and in Aug. No charge.* ☎ *956 13 20 08.*

To bypass Ronda, take CA531 over the dramatic **Las Palomas Pass**, with its dramatic **views★**, to **Zahara de la Sierra**

## Ronda★★ – ◖*see RONDA*

▷ *Leave Ronda along the MA 428 towards Arriate.*

## Setenil★

This is the only village in this region with troglodyte dwellings built into the rock. Unlike Guadix, no chimneys are visible, just rows of houses which appear to support the weight of the rock above. Fine examples are the **Cuevas del Sol** (Caves of the Sun) and **Cuevas de la Sombra** (Caves of the Shade). The **tourist office** is in an

H.Champollion/MICHELIN

*Grazalema*

impressive building with 6C *artesonado* ceiling. ◷ *Open 10.30am (noon Sat-Sun and public hols)-2pm and 4-7pm (5-8pm Jun-Sep).* ☏ *956 13 42 61.*

Neighbouring Olvera is visible from a keep in the upper town. The **Iglesia de la Encarnación**, higher still, is Gothic in style, with neo-Gothic frescoes.

### Olvera

*13km/8mi NW from Setenil along CA 422.* The triangle-shaped 12C **castle** overlooking Olvera's hilltop **site**★★ defended the Nasrid kingdom until its conquest by Alfonso XI in 1327. ◷ *Open 10.30am-2pm and 4-6.30pm (to 7pm Mar-Oct).* ◷ *Closed Mon.* ⊷€2 *(museum).* ☏ *956 12 08 16 (tourist office).* The Iglesia de la Encarnación is neo-Classical. Olvera's **olive oil** is considered some of Spain's finest.

### Algodonales

*22km/14mi from Olvera along CA 342.* This is one of Spain's top hang-gliding spots.

### Zahara de la Sierra★

*6km/4mi south of Algodonales along CA 531.* Formerly "de los Membrillos" because of the local importance of quince *(membrillo)*, the village has a beautiful hilltop **setting**★★. The Nasrids of Zahara surrendered to Ponce de León in 1483. The view from the castle encompasses vegetable gardens and the **Zahara Dam** *(presa)* below and neighbouring Algodonales and even Olvera. The clock tower is from the 16C, the Baroque **Iglesia de Santa María de Mesa** dates from the 18C.

### Villamartín

Flat streets are decidedly uncharacteristic of the Pueblos Blancos. The **plaza del Ayuntamiento** is the hub; the **calle de El Santo** leads past seigniorial mansions such

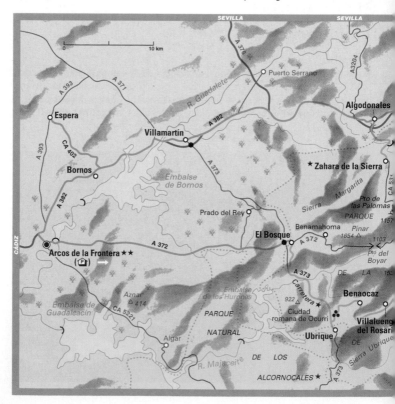

as the 19C **Casa-Palacio de Los Ríos**, and the 16C Casa-Palacio de los Topete. The street itself was remodelled for the **1929 Ibero-American Exhibition** in Sevilla. Calle de la Feria leads to the **Museo Histórico Municipal**. ⓧ *Open in summer, Tue-Sat, 10am-2pm and 4-6pm (6-9pm in summer).* ⓧ *Closed Mon and public hols.* ⌦ *€1.50.* ☎ *956 73 33 96.*

The **Alberite dolmen**, dating from around 4000 BC, is 4km/2.5mi to the south of Villamartín. It consists of a gallery 20m/65ft long formed by large stone slabs, and a funerary chamber. *For information, call* ☎ *956 71 50 15*

    ⓖ *1km/0.6mi from the town, along A 382 towards Jerez, is one of the largest tamarisk groves in Europe.*

## Bornos

*13km/8mi east of Villamartín along A 382.* Bornos extends gracefully along the reservoir *(embalse)* of the same name. Unlike neighbouring villages, it is not sur-rounded by mountains, nor is it completely white. It does, however, have some of the best architecture in the whole area. The plaza del Ayuntamiento is fronted by the **Castillo-Palacio de los Ribera**★, a castle-cum-palace which is now home to the **tourist office** and a workshop-school. The attractive Renaissance-style **patio**★ has an ogival balustrade running along the upper gallery, from where there is access to one of the village's hidden treasures: a garden laid out in the 16C, one of the first of its kind designed in pure Renaissance style. At one end, note the loggia-type gallery. ⓧ *Open 9am-2pm and 3-6pm; Apr-Sep, 11am-2pm and 3-10pm. No charge.* ☎ *956 72 82 74.*

Also on the plaza del Ayuntamiento is the **Iglesia de Santo Domingo**, a Gothic church built in the late 15C.

## Espera

*10km/6mi northwest along CA 402.* The village stands on a small outcrop in the middle of a fertile landscape. A Moorish castle, the **Castillo de Fatetar**, looks down from on high. Note the Baroque façade of a chapel, the Ermita del Cristo de la Anti-gua, next to it and the **Iglesia de Santa María de Gracia**, a church in the village.

▶   *Return to Arcos along A 393.*

# EL PUERTO DE SANTA MARÍA ★

POPULATION: 73 728

The mansions of El Puerto de Santa María were erected when the town prospered following the discovery and exploitation of the Americas. The ordered old quarter, predominantly built in the 18C and 19C, is best discovered on foot.
Modern El Puerto has the *joie de vivre* typical of Andalucía, Streets are thronged in summer with visitors from around Spain who come to enjoy superb gastronomy and a lively nightlife. *Calle Luna, 22, 11500 El Puerto de Santa María, ☎ 956 54 24 13, ptoturis@elpuertosm.es.*

▶ **Orient Yourself:** On the Bay of Cádiz, at the mouth of the River Guadalete, El Puerto de Santa María is linked by road with Cádiz via A 4.
🕐 **Organizing Your Time:** Allow a day for lingering in El Puerto de Santa María.
**Kids Especially for Kids:** The Castillo (castle) of San Marcos.
👣 **Also See:** JEREZ DE LA FRONTERA (12km/7.5mi N), CÁDIZ, ARCOS DE LA FRONTERA, SANLÚCAR DE BARRAMEDA (23km/14mi NW) and MEDINA SIDONIA.

## Visit

### Iglesia Mayor Prioral
🕐 *Open Mon-Fri, 8.30am-12.45pm (Sat, to noon; Sun, to 1.45pm) and 6.30-8.30pm. No charge. ☎ 956 85 17 16.*
This priory church was founded in the 13C; the building visible today is from the 15C in late-Gothic style. The **Portada del Sol** ★ (Sun Gateway), with its profuse Plateresque and Baroque decoration, opens onto plaza de España. The interior is in many styles as a result of renovations.

Follow calle Pagador, by the **Museo Municipal**, as far as calle Santo Domingo.
🕐 *Open Tue-Fri, 10am-2pm (Sat-Sun, 10.30am-2pm). 🕐 Closed Mon and public hols. No charge. ☎ 956 54 27 05.*

### Fundación Rafael Alberti
🕐 *Open 11am-2.30pm; mid-Sep to mid-Jun, Mon-Fri, 11am-2.30pm. 🕐 Closed Mon. €3. ☎ 956 85 07 11.*
The Rafael Alberti Foundation honors this poet (1902-99) from El Puerto. Photos, letters and copies of his works trace his life, and reflect Spain over the past 100 years.

### Casa-Museo Pedro Muñoz-Seca
Nearby is the house of another native son, Pedro Muñoz-Seca (1879-1936), author of *La venganza de don Mendo*. The exhibit recalls his life and work.

### Castillo de San Marcos
*Guided tours (30min), Jul-Sep, Tue-Sat, 10am-1.30pm; Jan-Jun, Tue, 12.30-1.30pm; Thu and Sat, 11.30am-1.30pm; Oct-Dec, by arrangement. €5. ☎ 956 85 17 51 (Bodegas Caballero).*
Alfonso X had the first castle-church built over the main mosque of Moorish

## The voyages of Columbus

It was from El Puerto de Santa María that **Columbus** departed on two occasions on his journeys of discovery to the Americas; **Juan de la Cosa** also created his **Mapamundi** in the town in 1500, the first map to show the recently discovered New World.

# Address Book

## TRANSPORT

**Airport** – The nearest airport is in Jerez de la Frontera, 20km/12mi along the main A 4 Cádiz-Madrid road. (☎ 956 15 00 00/01 83).

**Trains** – The station (☎ 956 54 25 85) is on plaza de la Estación. Trains between Cádiz and Sevilla stop in El Puerto de Santa María. Trains operate from Cádiz and Sevilla to every corner of Spain.

**Inter-city-buses** – The stop for all services is at the bullring (plaza de toros).

**Transportes Comes** (☎ 956 80 70 59) operates in the province and to Sevilla.

**Transportes Los Amarillos** (☎ 956 29 08 00) mainly operates to the provinces of Sevilla and Málaga.

**City buses** – Six lines serve El Puerto de Santa María (☎ 900 70 07 71).

## SIGHTSEEING

**El Vaporcito del Puerto** (Little Steamer) is the affectionate name for the *Adriano III* which plies the route between Puerto de Santa María (from plaza de las Galeras Reales, with its attractive 18C **fountain)** and Cádiz. Juan Fernández has operated the service since 1927. Prior to the opening of the Carranza Bridge, it was a vital link. The 40 min crossing offers visitors a different perspective of Cádiz. An evening bay cruise *(2hr)* operates in summer.
*Departures 9.15 and 11.15am, 1.15, 3.45 and 5.45pm (and 7.45pm Jun-Sep); evening cruise Jul-9 Sep at 9.30pm.* ○
*No service Mon (except public hols) and Oct-May. €3 (€5 return, €6 night cruise). ☎ 629 46 80 14.*

## WHERE TO EAT

**Ribera del Marisco** – The attractive **plaza de la Herrería** and Ribera del Marisco are the liveliest parts of El Puerto. Two well-known bars are **Romerijo 1** and **Romerijo 2** (www.romerijo.com), where fish and seafood can be bought by weight and eaten on the terrace. It is often difficult to get a table.

◡◻ **Los Portales** – *Ribera del Río, 13* - ☎ *956 54 18 12 - www.losportales.com.* Excellent seafood fresh from the bay, relaxed rustic regional ambience.

◡◻◻ **Casa Flores** – *Ribera del Río, 9* - ☎ *956 54 35 12 - www.casaflores.com.* You can't go wrong with *pescaito"* (fried fish), crayfish or prawns. The decor mixes sea and bullring.

◡◻◻ **El Faro del Puerto** – *Avenida de Fuentebravía* – ☎ *956 87 09 52* - *www.elfarodelpuerto.com* – ○ *Closed Sun evening exc Aug.* This high-end restaurant away from the noise of the town centre is one of El Puerto's most elegant establishments. International and Andalusian cuisine.

## WHERE TO STAY

◡ **Hostal Chaikana** – *Javier de Burgos, 17* – ☎ *956 54 29 02 - www.hostalchaikana.com* – *35 rooms.* Small, modern and spotless hotel in the centre.

◡◻◻ **Hotel Dunas Puerto** – *Camino de Los Enamorados* – ☎ *956 85 03 11* - *www.jale.com/dunas* – *62 rooms.* For those who prefer nature to the city. Bungalows with independent access in an area of greenery by the sea.

◡◻◻ **Hotel Los Cántaros** – *Curva, 6* – ☎ *956 54 02 40 - www.hotelloscantaros.com* – *39 rooms.* This well-maintained hotel, on a small square in the town centre, owes its name to the 17C pitchers discovered in its basement.

◡◻◻ **Monasterio de San Miguel** – *Virgen de los Milagros, 27* – ☎ *956 54 04 40 - www.hotelesjale.com* – *165 rooms.* This former Capuchin monastery dates from the 18C. Rooms are tastefully decorated and crowned by impressive vaulted ceilings. Swimming pool and garden.

## GOING OUT FOR THE EVENING

**Café-Pub Blanco y Negro** – *Ricardo Alcón, 10* - ☎ *956 54 15 59* – ○ *Open 5pm-dawn.* This former wine storehouse, tucked in an alleyway, is renowned for its locally roasted coffee. It occasionally hosts art and photography exhibitions and is popular with 25-and-overs.

**El Resbaladero** – *Micaela Aramburu (Castillo de San Marcos)* - *www.elresbaladero.com.* One of the liveliest spots in El Puerto. Well conceived for dancing to the latest, good DJs, theme parties.

**La Pontona** – *Parque Calderón (by Vaporcito ferry)* - ☎ *956 851 335 - www.*

lapontona.com - ◐ *Open 4pm-dawn.* An original, on the river, good for a coffee or a cocktail; splendid views up top.

## WINE CELLARS

No visit to El Puerto de Santa María is complete without a tour and tasting. **Bodegas Osborne**: call ☎ *956 86 91 00.* **Bodegas Terry**: the visit includes a tour of the **Carriage Museum** *(Museo de Carruajes).* Call ☎ *956 54 36 90.*

## SHOPPING

The main shopping district in the town centre is concentrated around three streets: **calle Luna**, **calle Palacios** and **calle Larga**. The first two head off from the **Iglesia Mayor Prioral** and are predominantly pedestrianised. This part of El Puerto is also pleasant for a stroll.

**Arte Sano** (◐ *Open Mon-Sat, 10am-2pm),* a boutique selling high-quality and original ceramics and basketwork, is located on calle Santo Domingo, parallel to calle Palacios.
A small **market** selling a whole range of goods is held every Tuesday on rotonda de la Puntilla.

## SPORT AND LEISURE

With its excellent beaches and leisure facilities, El Puerto de Santa María has developed into a popular summer resort. The rest of the year, visitors come here to visit its wine cellars, enjoy its delicious local tapas, and perhaps play a round of golf at one of the internationally renowned courses in the area.

---

**Alcanatif** in the 13C. It was modified during the 14C and 15C, and restored in the 20C.
The former fish exchange *(lonja de pescado)* can be seen behind the castle.

### Plaza del Polvorista
The **Palacio de Imblusqueta** on the square, a 17C mansion, is the town hall.

### Plaza de toros
◐ *Open Tue-Sun, 11am-1.30pm and 5.30-7pm (May-Sep, 6-7.30pm).* ◑ *Closed Mon and days preceding and following bullfights. No charge.* ☎ *956 54 15 78.*
The 1880 bullring, one of the largest in Spain, seats over 12 000. It is arcaded and solid on the outside, graceful inside.

### Monasterio de Nuestra Señora de la Victoria
*On the outskirts.* This monastery is austere but for its exuberant **portal**★, framed by two buttresses ending in pinnacles. A gable bears the Cerda family coat of arms. Once a prison, the monastery now hosts official ceremonies.

## Excursions

### Rota
*27km/17mi west.* Past an American military base, the 16km/10mi of beaches of Rota at the northern tip of the Bay of Cádiz are sheltered from strong coastal winds.

#### Old town★
Rota's old fishing village is between two beaches, **Playa de la Costilla**★ and Playa del Rompidillo. The **Parroquia**

### Local specialities
Rota's most typical dish is undoubtedly *urta a la roteña,* sea bream cooked with peppers, tomatoes, white wine and thyme. It is a traditional feature of one of the region's most unusual festivals, the **Fiesta de la Urta**, when locals compete to produce the best recipe for this dish. The festival has been held for the past 30 years and takes place in mid-August.

de **Nuestra Señora de la O** is a church with a fine late-Gothic **interior**★. The **Castillo de Luna**, a castle, is the town hall.

### Puerto Real

*10km/6mi south.* This royal port *(puerto real)*, founded by the Catholic Monarchs in 1483, prospered in the 18C, but the Napoleonic invasion in 1808 heralded a century of decline. The recent closure of local shipyards has also had a serious impact. Puerto Real is home to several faculties of the **University of Cádiz**. Its major monument is the **Iglesia de San Sebastián**, a church built in the middle of the 16C.

# LA RÁBIDA★

Whitewashed houses cluster around the La Rábida monastery just a few kilometres from Palos de la Frontera, and from Huelva. La Rábida is another town along the "Columbus Route". 🗓 *Plans, maps and other information on La Rábida are available from the* **La Casita de Zenobia** *information and reception centre.* 🕐 *Open 10am-2pm and 5-9pm, Sat-Sun and public hols, 11am-8pm; mid-Sep to mid-Apr, 10am-7pm.* 🕐 *Closed Mon, 1 Jan and 25 Dec.* ☎ *959 53 05 97.*

▸ **Orient Yourself:** La Rábida enjoys an impressive position at the mouth of the River Tinto. The monastery is the first stop on the local tour from the capital of the province (👆 *see Driving Tour* 9 *in the Planning Your Trip section*).

🕐 **Organizing Your Time:** Vist La Rábida for an hour or two from Huelva; conentrate on following the footsteps of Columbus.

👆 **Also See:** HUELVA, MOGUER (11km/7mi NE) and EL ROCÍO (57km/36mi SE).

## Visit

### Monasterio de Santa María de la Rábida

🕐 *Open Jun-Sep, Tue-Sun, 10am-1pm and 4-7pm (Aug, 4.45-8pm); otherwise Tue-Sun, 10am-1pm and 4-6.15pm.* 🕐 *Closed Mon.* 🚫 *€2.50.* ☎ *959 35 04 11.*

This 14C Mudéjar-Gothic Franciscan monastery has gone down in history as the place in which Christopher Columbus stayed. It was here, with the help of the Pinzón brothers and two monks, Antonio de Marchena and Juan Pérez, that he planned his voyage of discovery, as depicted in magnificent frescoes by **Daniel Vázquez Díaz** (1930) in rooms on the ground floor.

Before entering, note the large white stone monument, the Columna de los Descubridores (Discoverers' Column), in a large rotunda, depicting scenes from the Discoveries erected on the 400th anniversary of this momentous event.

#### Church★

The small church contains items of great artistic value: old frescoes in various chapels; polychrome wood *artesonados*, whose filigree work contrasts with the

B. Kaufmann/MICHELIN

*Monasterio de Santa María de La Rábida*

austere appearance of the building; several 18C paintings by Juan de Dios, representing scenes from the life; and, above all, the **Virgin of the Miracles**★, the monastery's patron, in a chapel to the left of the altar. Legend has it that Columbus and the crew of his three caravels prayed before this exceptional alabaster 14C figure, sculpted by an Andalusian workshop, on the two days before departure.

### Cloisters
The Mudéjar-style cloisters comprise two galleries of columns: the lower tier was built in the 15C, while the upper section, added in the 18C, contains models of the *Pinta*, the *Niña* and the *Santa María*. The cloisters retain the charm of Andalusian patios, with abundant vegetation and the gentle bubbling of water.

### Dining room
A whitewashed pulpit which was formerly used for readings by lectors can be seen to the side of this austere rectangular room.

### Chapter house
Tradition has it that the large table in this bright, spacious room was used by Columbus to plan his voyage with his advisors. Note the 18C Mudéjar *artesonado* ceiling.

### Sala de las Banderas
The Flag Room exhibits the flag of every country on the American continent as well as a small chest with earth from each. In a small room to the right is a **mapamundi**★, a work by Juan de la Cosa, which outlined the coast of America for the first time.

## Sights

### Muelle de las Carabelas★
Life-size replicas of the three caravels of Columbus are moored at this modern dock on the Tinto Estuary. A tour of the berths, storerooms and decks of these old vessels enables visitors to observe the detailed decoration and the firearms, anchors, and sails used by the crew. Audiovisual presentations are given in the building at the entrance to the dock. A small **museum** displays 15C navigational tools. ○ *Open 1-7pm.* ○ *Closed Mon and in Jan.* ◈€3. ☎ *959 53 05 97.*

### Muelle de la Reina
The small Queen's Dock, alongside the three caravels, is dominated by the monument to Icarus of the Triumph *(Ícaro del Triunfo)*, commemorating the first transatlantic flight by the Plus Ultra seaplane from Palos de la Frontera to Buenos Aires in 1926.

### Avenida de los Descubridores
This wide avenue, named in honour of the Great Discoverers, links Palos de la Frontera with La Rábida and is decorated with the coats of arms of every Ibero-American country. The Glorieta del Pueblo Argentino, a square named in honour of the Argentinian people, stands at the end of the avenue, with a glazed ceramic Aztec calendar as its centrepiece.

### Parque Botánico José Celestino Mutis
The botanical garden, dedicated to this Andalusian scientist, is a maze of leafy avenues, canals and bridges displaying the most typical plant species to be found on the five continents.

### Foro Iberoamericano de la Rábida
The Ibero-American forum is a building with a large open-air auditorium used as a venue for congresses, concerts and theatrical performances.

**Universidad Internacional de Andalucía**
This prestigious university is devoted to the study of American cultures.

**Plaza de Macuro**
A modern sculpture in the square recalls a crossing of the Atlantic by helicopter from Macuro, Venezuela, to La Rábida.

# EL ROCÍO

This small village of whitewashed houses and sandy streets is the site of the Iglesia de la Virgen del Rocío, the most venerated pilgrimage site in Spain. For all but one weekend of the year it is peaceful, inhabited by a few locals – many of whom use horses as their main mode of transport – second-homers (particularly from Almonte), and brothers of religious orders. During Whitsun weekend, however, the village's tranquility is broken when around a million pilgrims make their way here to show their devotion to the Virgin of the Dew (Virgen del Rocío).

▶ **Orient Yourself:** El Rocío, SW of Sevilla, is on the border of Parque Nacional de Doñana, in Almonte municipality. El Rocío is linked with the Costa de Huelva to the south via A 483, and the Parque Natural Sierra de Aracena y Picos de Aroche to the north via A 483, HV 5131 and A 461.

🕓 **Organizing Your Time:** El Rocío will take up from a few hours to a day, depending on religious interest.

🕹 **Also See:** COSTA DE HUELVA.

## El Rocío Pilgrimage

For those born outside Andalucía, the deep significance of the pilgrimage to El Rocío – the largest and most famous in Spain – is difficult to comprehend. But for hundreds of thousands, including an increasing number of pilgrims from outside Spain attracted by its beauty and significance, the journey here is an important annual event.

R. Mattes/MICHELIN

*A simpecado with pilgrims on their way to the Ermita*

According to tradition, the Church of the Virgin of the Dew was erected at the beginning of the 15C to house a statue found by a hunter in the hollow of an oak. In the mid-17C, during an epidemic, the church developed into a place of pilgrimage which attracted the devout from far and wide to implore the Virgin for good health. Almonte, nearest to El Rocío, and Villamanrique, became the first two towns to establish brotherhoods or religious associations, which now number around 100.

**"The Route"**
During the course of the week preceding Pentecost, members of each brotherhood make their way towards the shrine. These pilgrims follow long-established routes on foot, in carts adorned with colourful decoration and paper flowers, on horseback and even nowadays by jeep. Women wear the traditional *rociero* skirt, decorated with one or two pleated ruffles, and hats to offer protection against the hot sun; men tend to wear a white shirt, tight-fitting trousers and a Cordoban sombrero or cap. Almost everyone wears leather boots. A sprig of rosemary and the medallion of the brotherhood complete the attire. Each brotherhood follows its own *simpecado*, a silver cart pulled by oxen carrying a standard bearing the image of the Virgin of the Dew. At night the scene transforms into one of dancing and singing around open fires. The rosary is always recited at nightfall and mass is celebrated at dawn.

**The village of El Rocío**
Pilgrims arrive at El Rocío throughout **Saturday**, where they pay homage to the White Dove (*Blanca Paloma*) or to Our Lady of the Marshes (*La Señora de las Marismas*), two of the many names given to the Virgin Mary. **Sunday** is given over to masses, recitals of the rosary and socialising, culminating in the most eagerly awaited moment in the **early morning on the Monday of Pentecost**. Just before daybreak, youngsters from the nearby town of Almonte climb over the gate of the church and remove the statue of the Virgin, which they carry in procession through the streets, surrounded by a security cordon to prevent pilgrims from approaching. The night is long, full of emotion, fatigue and happiness, the culmination of a week of physical effort and devotion for which pilgrims have been preparing throughout the year.

## Driving Tour

### The Wine Route from El Rocío to Niebla
*36km/22mi. Allow half a day.*

The highlight of this itinerary is the tasting of excellent local white and sweet wines which fall under the Condado de Huelva appellation. It is well worth visiting the local *bodegas* to try specialities such as old *oloroso*, fruity whites, *mistela* (a flavoured brandy), *moscatel* and sweet orange wine (*vino dulce de naranja*).

### Almonte
*15km/9.5mi north of El Rocío along A 483.*
Almonte is one of the best-known towns in the province of Huelva thanks to the Parque Nacional de Doñana within its limits (👣 *see Parque Nacional de DOÑANA*), popular Matalascañas beach (👣 *see COSTA DE HUELVA*) and, in particular, the village of El Rocío. However,

---

**WHERE TO EAT**

⊜⊜⊜ **Aires de Doñana** – *Avenida de la Canaliega, 1* – ☏ *959 44 27 19* – 🅿. 🕐 *Closed Mon and during pilgrimage.* Rustic building with a straw roof; restaurant with views to Ermita and horses grazing nearby.

**WHERE TO STAY**

⊜⊜ **Hotel Toruño** – *Plaza del Acebuchal, 22* – ☏ *959 44 23 23* - *hoteltoruno@eremas.com* – *30 rooms*. A traditional house in the centre of the village decorated in local style. Some rooms have lovely views to the marshlands.

much of the town's prestige stems from wine, the aroma of which is ever-present. Whitewashed houses adorned with wrought-iron grilles and resplendent doorways are a typical feature of Almonte, as are the carts used to transport grapes at harvest time. The **plaza Virgen del Rocío**, the hub of town life, is a delightful haven of peace and tranquillity fronted by two of Almonte's main buildings: the parish church, an attractive example of colonial-style architecture, and the town hall, with its elegant gallery of arches on the upper floor.

## Bollullos del Condado

*9km/5.5mi north.* Every corner of this town appears to be devoted to wine production, with numerous old *bodegas* lining its well-maintained streets with their seigniorial air. Behind the impressive façades of these imposing buildings, visitors can learn more about ancestral wine-making techniques, and taste and purchase some of the excellent sweet and white wines produced in large vats and served in attractive earthenware cups. Bollulos is also home to several craft workshops producing iron utensils, carriages, gold embroidery and barrels, and boasts a number of bars and restaurants specialising in seafood. The **plaza del Sagrado Corazón de Jesús**, a picturesque square fronted by the **Iglesia de Santiago Apóstol**, with its Andalusian Baroque façade and tower, and the town hall, its attractive façade composed of two storeys of stilted arches, are worthy of note.

## La Palma del Condado

*4km/2.5mi north of Bollulos.*
Renowned for its excellent wines, this bright town is embellished with a number of seigniorial squares, elegant whitewashed houses and notable monumental buildings. The main event in the local calendar is the *Fiesta de la Vendimia*, the wine harvest festival held at the end of September, the origins of which date back to the 14C.

### Ayuntamiento

The former 16C Hospital of the Immaculate Conception was restored in 1929 in the Regionalist style employed for the Ibero-American Exhibition of the same year. It is now the town hall.

### Plaza del Corazón de Jesús

This attractive square, dominated by the statue of the Sacred Heart of Jesus (Corazón de Jesús), a work created in 1927 by local sculptor Antonio Pinto Soldán, is surrounded by elegant, colonial-inspired buildings.

### Plaza de España

This well-proportioned square is the centre of local life. One side of the *plaza* is bordered by the former Palacio del Señorío, the theatre and the Casa de los Arcos, while the opposite side is fronted by the Casa de Tirado, with an exquisite **grille** and *azulejos* which reproduce *Las Meninas* and *Las Hilanderas* by Velázquez. However, the most interesting construction on the square is the **Iglesia de San Juan Bautista**, a sober Baroque church, its impressive whitewashed façade crowned by a graceful tower used by storks as a nesting place.

### Iglesia del Valle

The *camarín* behind the main altar of this 15C Mudéjar-style church houses a statue of the Virgin of the Valley, the patron saint of La Palma del Condado.

## Niebla★

*8km/5mi southwest of La Palma del Condado along A 472. Several cultural itineraries depart from the tourist office, housed in the Hospital de Nuestra Señora de los Ángeles.*
🕐 *Open 9.30am-2pm and 4-6pm.* ☎ *959 36 22 70.*

This old settlement, dating back to the 8C BC, is located 29km/18km from Huelva. The historical centre of Niebla is graced with several old monuments of significant interest, in particular the series of **walls**★, one of the most complete of any in Spain. Erected during the period of Almohad domination in the 12C using clay from the banks of the River Tinto – hence their reddish colour – they run for a length of 2km/1.2mi and are punctuated by a total of 50 towers and five entrance gateways. The **Iglesia de Santa María de la Granada**, built on the site of the former mosque, combines features from the earlier construction, such as the peaceful patio of orange trees which opens onto the entrance of the church, with additional Gothic elements. The **alcázar** or **Castillo de los Guzmanes**, dating from the 15C, has retained several interesting vestiges of Moorish architecture. The **Iglesia de San Martín**, divided into two by a street, is a building formerly used both as a mosque and synagogue. On the outskirts of Niebla, the River Tinto is spanned by a large Roman bridge.

# RONDA★★

POPULATION: 35 788

Ronda stands at the heart of the Serranía de Ronda, split by the famous ravine (**tajo**★) of the River Guadalevín. Its isolation and legends of highwaymen made it an obligatory destination for 19C Romantic writers, and visitors continue to come all year. ⬚ *Plaza de España, 9, 29400 Ronda, ☎ 952 87 12 72, otronda@andalucia.org; Paseo Blas Infante, 29400 Ronda, ☎ 952 18 71 19, informacion@turismoderonda.es.*

▸ **Orient Yourself:** Ronda is 133km/83mi E of Cádiz via A 376, A 382 and A 4 – E 5, and hardly 50km/31mi to the Costa del Sol, S over the Sierra Bermeja range.

🕐 **Organizing Your Time:** Take a day, at least, to savour the charms that lured the Romantics, with walks through the old precincts of Ronda.

👣 **Also See:** COSTA DEL SOL, MÁLAGA (96km/60mi E), ANTEQUERA (94km/59mi NE) and ARCOS DE LA FRONTERA (86km/54mi W).

*Puente Nuevo*

# A Bit of History

**Ronda under the Moors** –Invaders under **Tarik-ibn-Zeyad** followed the Roman way from Gibraltar. They founded *Izna-Rand-Onda*, some 20km/12mi from old Roman **Acinipo**. Under the Umayyads, Ronda was the capital of a Moorish region *(cora)*, then became a taifa capital after the fall of the Caliphate. Ronda prospered under the Almohads and into the Nasrid era, and fell to the Christians in 1485.

# Walking Tour

## La Ciudad★★

The Moorish quarter of narrow alleys lined by mansions and whitewashed houses with iron balconies offers fine views of the countryside, and impressive churches.

### Puente Nuevo★
The New Bridge, a manificent 18C engineering feets, is the best place to start your visit. Take the path to the coffee shop of the *parador* for a superb view of the bridge, the Guadiaro valley, and the Sierra de Grazalema. A chamber under an arch, once a jail, now houses an exhibit on the bridge.

▶ *Cross the bridge and follow calle Santo Domingo.*

The Convento de Santo Domingo (left side) was the first construction by victorious Christians after 1485; on the right is the birthplace (in 1839) of Francisco Giner de los Ríos, who ran a school, the **Institución Libre de Enseñanza,** on liberal principles.

▶ *Head down calle Santo Domingo.*

## Casa del Rey Moro

According to legend, this was the mansion of Almonated, king of Ronda, who drank wine from the skulls of vanquished enemies. The current 18C building has Mudéjar-style brick towers and wooden balconies. A Moorish staircase, **La Mina**, descends to the river.

## Address Book

### SIGHTSEEING

The **River Guadalevín** ("river of milk") cuts Ronda in two: the Moorish quarter, **La Ciudad** (or Old Town); and the modern **Mercadillo** district. To the south, beyond the **Puerta de Almocabar**, and the Arrabal Nuevo (New District) is the San Francisco quarter, which grew in the 15C as a market outside the walls.

### WHERE TO EAT

☞ **Doña Pepa** – *Plaza del Socorro, 10 - ☎ 952 87 47 77 - www.dpepa.com – ⏱ Closed evenings of 24 and 31 Dec.* Enjoy Ronda's signature plates, such as *rabo de toro* (braised bull's tail) in an enchanting Andalusian ambience. Attractive prix-fixe menus offered.

☞☞ **Don Miguel** – *Plaza de España, 5 – ☎ 952 87 10 90 - www.dmiguel.com – ⏱ Closed Sun lunchtime from Jun-Aug.* A pleasant terrace with excellent views of the Puente Nuevo, the ravine and the River Guadalevín. Quality cuisine includes specialities such as *rabo de toro* (braised bull's tail), *solomillo de venado* (venison loin) and *cordero a la menta* (lamb with mint sauce). Rooms are available *(☞☞☞)*.

☞☞ **Casa Santa Pola** – *Santo Domingo, 3 – ☎ 952 87 92 08 - www.ronda.net/usuar/santapola – ⏱ Closed Sun in summer and Wed in winter.* A restaurant with several Moorish-style rooms overlooking the ravine, offering updated regional cuisine.

☞☞☞ **Tragabuches** – *José Aparicio, 1 – ☎ 952 19 02 91 - www.tragabuches.com – ⏱ Closed Sun evening and Mon.* This restaurant, considered by many locals to be the best in Ronda, is just a stone's throw from the *parador* and the bullring. Its kitchen, run by Sergio López, a prize-winning young chef, offers modern cuisine in an avant-garde setting.

### WHERE TO STAY

☞ **Hotel Virgen de los Reyes** – *Lorenzo Borrego, 13 – ☎ 952 87 11 40 – 52 rooms.* An inexpensive hotel with clean, simple rooms.

☞☞ **Alavera de los Baños** – *Hoyo San Miguel – ☎ 952 87 91 43 - www.andalucia.com/alavera – 9 rooms – ⏱ Closed Dec-Jan.* In the lower part of the town next to the Moorish Baths. Although this pleasant hotel is of recent construction, all the rooms are different. Other facilities for guests include a restaurant and terrace.

☞☞☞ **Hotel San Gabriel** – *Marqués de Moctezuma, 19 – ☎ 952 19 03 92 - www.hotelsangabriel.com – 21 rooms.* This is a delightful, magnificently decorated mansion dating from 1736. Ask for a room with a view to the charming patio.

☞☞☞☞ **La Fuente de la Higuera,** in **Los Frontones** – *5.5km/3.4mi along A 376 towards Sevilla, then bear right for 3.2km/2mi – ☎ 952 11 43 55 - www.hotellafuente.com – 11 rooms.* ⌷ This luxury country hotel in a restored manor combines the Mediterranean with Nordic efficiency. Reservations are essential.

### Jardines de Forestier★

🕐 *Open 10am-7pm (8pm, spring and summer); autumn and winter, 10am-6pm.* 🎫 *€4.* ☎ *952 18 72 00.*

In 1912 French landscaper **Forestier** (who later designed María Luisa Park in Sevilla) was commissioned to design these lovely gardens *(jardines)*. Despite narrow terrain, he managed to create a jewel. Three terraces combine Moorish features (fountains, water and *azulejos*) with the pergolas and parterres of Europe.

### Palacio del Marqués de Salvatierra

⚠ *Interior closed to visitors.* This small mansion is typical of noble 18C architecture, The **portal**★★ is exceptional. The door is flanked by pairs of Corinthian columns topped by an architrave decorated with medallions. Above, human figures with strong pre-Columbian influence substitute for columns.

*Detail on the façade of the Palacio del Marqués de Salvatierra*

▷ *Walk towards the old bridge. Beyond the Puerta de Felipe V, follow a stone path to the Moorish Baths.*

### Moorish Baths★

🕐 *Open 10am-6pm (7pm in summer); Sat-Sun and public hols, 10am-3pm.* 🕐 *Closed Mon, 1 Jan and 24 Dec.* 🎫 *€2.* ☎ *952 18 71 19 or 656 95 09 37.*

These 13C baths are some of the best preserved on the Iberian Peninsula. They were built close to the river along the Las Culebras stream *(arroyo)*, in the Arrabal Viejo, a district then popular with artisans and tanners. The first part of the building, unroofed, leads to the baths themselves, comprising three transversal rooms topped with barrel vaults and illuminated by star-shaped lunettes. The middle room, divided by horseshoe arches and brick columns, is the most impressive. The cauldron used to heat water for the baths is to the rear.

▷ *Climb a stone staircase parallel to the walls, then pass through a 13C gateway, the Puerta de la Acijara.*

### Minarete de San Sebastián★

*In plaza del Poeta Abul-Beca.* This graceful minaret is the only remnant of a 14C Nasrid mosque, which victorious Christians converted to a church. The lower stone section is Moorish; the upper brick section is Mudéjar in style. The horseshoe arch doorway is particularly noteworthy. This is the smallest minaret still standing in Andalucía.

### Museo del Bandolero

🕐 *Open 10.45am-3.30pm; Sat 10am-6.30 pm (8.30pm in spring and summer).* 🎫 *€3.* ☎ *952 87 77 85.*

Bandits, brigands and outlaws of Andalucía ride again in this museum, including legendary Diego Corrientes and José María el Tempranillo, who were variously perceived as wretches, romantic travellers or bloodthirsty murderers. A video *(in Spanish)* and documents reveal these Andalusian figures.

## The legend of Tragabuches

At the beginning of the 19C, a gypsy from Ronda by the name of José Ulloa, whose nickname was Tragabuches, developed a certain renown as a bullfighter. Alas, having returned home on the evening of a bullfight, he caught sight of the silhouette of a man sneaking out of the window of his house. Mad with rage, Tragabuches murdered his rival before throwing his wife out of the window and disappearing. It is said that he then joined the fearsome band of brigands known as the "seven sons of Écija", of which he was to become one of the most merciless.

▶ *Go down calle Armiñán to Espiritú Santo church.*

### Iglesia del Espíritu Santo
The fortress character of the late 15C Church of the Holy Spirit derives from its position by the town walls. The façade is elegant; the interior, remodelled several times, has a single nave crowned by a stellar vault with tiercerons.

### Puerta de Almocabar
This gateway of three horseshoe arches, now flanked by 18C towers, led to a cemetery (*al-maqabir* in Arabic). To one side note the **Puerta de Carlos V** (Charles V's Gateway) and opposite, beyond the walls, the **San Francisco district**, site of a 17C Franciscan convent.

▶ *Return and go left into plaza de la Duquesa de Parcent*

### Santa María la Mayor★
🕐 *Open 10am-6pm.* ⊛€2. ☎ 952 87 22 46.
The Collegiate Church of St Mary is, like many Andalusian churches from the period, dedicated to the Incarnation. It replaced the main mosque. Today, only the original Mihrab Arch *(in the entrance room)*, decorated with *atauriques* and calligraphic motifs, remains. Two interior sections are Gothic and Renaissance.

▶ *Take calle Manuel Montero.*

### Palacio de Mondragón (Museo de la Ciudad)★★
🕐 *Open 10am-7.30pm (6pm Nov-Mar). Sat, Sun and public hols 10am-3pm.* 🕐 *Closed 1 Jan, Good Fri and 25 Dec.* ⊛ €2. ☎ 952 87 84 50.
The palace foundations are from a 14C Moorish residence. The present building mixes Mudéjar (towers and patios) and Renaissance styles, the latter best seen on the doorway. The charming **Mudéjar patio**★★ retains traces of *azulejos* and stuccowork between its arches. The palace houses the town **museum**, with exhibits on history, ethnography, and the environment, including the the Serranía de Ronda.

▶ *Continue to plaza del Campillo.*

Follow the path heading down to the 18C **Arco de Cristo** (Christ's Arch), from where there is a magnificent **view**★★ of the **ravine** *(tajo)* and bridge.

▶ *Follow calle Sor Ángela to plaza del Gigante.*

The square is named for a barely discernible relief of Hercules on one of its 14C houses.

▶ *Return to calle Armiñán.*

## Museo Lara

🕐 *Open 10.30am-7pm (8pm in summer).* ⊚ €4. ☎ *952 87 12 63.*
Over the years, the owner, Juan Antonio Lara, has assembled an extraordinary eclectic
**collection**★ of superb 18C enamel clocks, fans, and an armoury. The museum is in the
Casa-palacio de los Condes de las Islas Batanes, fronted by an attractive façade.

▶ *Follow calle Armiñán to return to plaza de España.*

# El Mercadillo

This district, which grew in the 16C, connects to **La Ciudad** by the **Puente Nuevo**
(New Bridge) and the Puente Viejo (Old Bridge). El Mercadillo is the commercial area,
with pedestrianised streets such as calle Nueva, **calle Remedios**, calle Ermita and
the **plaza del Socorro**, a square fronted by attractive 19C and 20C buildings.

## Bullring (Museo Taurino)★

🕐 *Open 10am-6pm (7pm spring and fall, 8pm in summer).* 🕐 *Closed Fri-Sun during
Feria of Pedro Romero (Sep).* ⊚ €4. ☎ *952 87 15 39.*
The bullring, built in 1785 by the Real Maestranza de Caballería (Royal Institute of
Knights), is one of Spain's most beautiful, with a tradition to match. Note statues
immortalising Ronda's bullfighting dynasties, the Romero and Ordóñez families.
At 66m/216ft, it is the widest bullring anywhere. The twin-tier interior is neo-Clas-
sical with Tuscan columns and a stone barrier, but the overall effect is one of great
simplicity. The bullring also houses a **museum** devoted to bullfighting.

## Templete de la Virgen de los Dolores★

Built in 1734, this small temple is crowned by a plain vault resting on two columns and
two pilasters. Each column is adorned with four half-human, half-fantastic **figures**★
with arms interlinked and attached by the neck, all showing great expression.

## Iglesia de Nuestro Padre Jesús

The oldest part of this heavily restored church is the 15C Gothic tower-façade; the
roof dates from 1735. Opposite stands the **Fuente de los Ocho Caños** (Fountain of
the Eight Spouts), created during the reign of Carlos III in the 18C.

## Excursions

### Iglesia Rupestre de la Virgen de la Cabeza★

*2.7km/1.7mi south via ③ on the map and the A 369. Upon leaving the town, take a
signposted road to the right (after approx 700m/770yd) leading to the chapel.* 🕐 *Open
10.30am-2pm.* 🕐 *Closed Mon, 1 Jan and 25 Dec.* €2. ☎ *952 18 71 19 or 649 36 57 72.*
This small Mozarabic monastery, probably founded by Hispano-Visigoths in the 9C,
was erected on high ground on the opposite bank of the River Guadalevín, affording
one of the best **views**★★ of Ronda. The monastery, excavated from rock, occupies
almost 280m²/3 013sq ft. Inside the cave, the store, the monastic quarters and the
church are all clearly visible. The frescoes were painted in the 18C.
In the middle of August every year the Virgen de la Cabeza (Virgin of the Head) is cer-
emoniously taken from the collegiate church to the chapel next to the monastery.

### Ruinas de Acinipo

*19km/11.5mi northwest. Leave Ronda via ① on the map and A 376, then head along
MA 449 towards Ronda la Vieja.* 🕐 *Open 9am-3pm; Sun and public hols, 9am-2pm.*
👁 *Hours subject to change; call to confirm.* 🕐 *Closed Mon, Tue, 1 Jan and 24 Dec. No
charge.* ☎ *952 18 71 19.*

Known popularly as **Ronda la Vieja**, the ruined settlement retains a large 1C AD **theatre**, including part of the stage.

### Cueva de La Pileta★

*20km/12mi southwest. Leave Ronda via ① on the map and A 376, then take MA 555 towards Benaoján. From here, bear onto MA 501.* ✎✎ *Guided tours (1hr) in summer, 10am-1pm and 4-5pm (6pm in summer).* ◐ *Closed 1 Jan and 24 Dec.* ✎€7. ☎ 952 16 73 43.

The cave was discovered in 1905 by Don José Bullón Lobato when he was searching for bat droppings for use as fertiliser. The importance of the discovery was such that in 1912 studies were carried out here by the eminent prehistorians **Hugo Obermaier** and **Abbé Breuil**. The Pileta Cave is a limestone formation with over 2km/1.2mi of galleries; some 500m/550yd are open to the public. The red and black wall paintings span an extensive period of prehistory, with figurative motifs dating from the Palaeolithic era (20000 BC) and symbolic art from the Neolithic period (4000 BC).

## Driving Tour

## A 376 From Ronda to San Pedro de Alcántara★★
*49km/30.5mi – allow 1hr.*

This impressive road was built in the 1970s to connect the Serranía de Ronda with the Costa del Sol. Although it does not pass through any towns or villages, it runs between two of the most spectacular mountain ranges in Málaga province: to the left the **Parque Natural de la Sierra de las Nieves**; and to the right, the **Sierra Bermeja**. The road climbs gradually though a landscape of pines and Spanish fir to the Alijar Pass (410m/1 345ft), then descends steeply towards the coast.

### Parque Natural de la Sierra de las Nieves
This small nature park (18 500ha/45 713 acres), a **Biosphere Reserve**, is home to the **Spanish fir** *(pinsapo)*, as well as one of the largest **mountain goat** colonies on the Iberian Peninsula. The relief here is characterised by steep escarpments and a limestone landscape. One of the world's deepest chasms, known as **GESM** (Grupo de Exploraciones Subterráneas de Málaga), is located within the confines of the park.

# SANLÚCAR DE BARRAMEDA★

POPULATION: 61 382

The soil around Sanlúcar gives birth to one of Andalucía's best dry sherries, *manzanilla*. The old monumental quarter of Sanlúcar is occupied by numerous sherry *bodegas*; along the waterfront are shops and superb seafood restaurants. ⛊ *Calzada del Ejército, 11540 Cádiz,* ☎ *956 36 61 10, turismo@aytosanlucar.org.*

▶ **Orient Yourself:** Sanlúcar us at the mouth of the River Guadalquivir, near the southern end of Parque Nacional de Doñana, not far from Jerez de la Frontera (22km/14mi SE) and El Puerto de Santa María (23km/14.5mi SE).

◐ **Organizing Your Time:** Allow a half to a full day, more for a beach vacation.

**Kids** **Especially for Kids:** Make sure to include beach time.

**Also See:** JEREZ DE LA FRONTERA, El PUERTO DE SANTA MARÍA, CÁDIZ, MEDINA SIDONIA and VEJER DE LA FRONTERA.

## A Bit of History

**Looking seaward** – Sanlúcar's position ensured its rise in the 15C as a stopping point for galleys returning to Sevilla from the Americas. In 1519, **Magellan**'s expedition left to circumnavigate the globe, and here it returned three years later under **Juan Sebastián Elcano**. The fall from grace of the Duke of Medina Sidonia and the transition to larger ships unable to negotiate the sandbanks, heralded the town's decline. At the end of the 19C the sherry industry developed.

**Manzanilla** – This superb wine has a taste both penetrating and dry on the palate. From May on, the triangle between Sanlúcar de Barrameda, El Puerto de Santa María and Jerez is a swathe of leafy **Palomino** vines. The harvest is in September. This dry sherry is fortified to 15% and then transferred to American oak barrels, where the *solera* and *criadera* system applies (*see ABC of sherry under JEREZ*). The difference between *manzanilla* and *fino* sherry is due to Sanlúcar's climate: a layer of yeast *(flor)* remains in place during ageing– a minimum of three years for *manzanilla* .

**Bodega visits** – Guided visits are offered by several companies, including **Barbadillo** *(next to the castle)*, a local institution since the 18C, **Pedro Romero** *(calle Trasbola, 84)* and **La Cigarrera** *(plaza Madre de Dios)*. For information, call ☏ 956 38 30 32.

**The world's most beautiful racecourse** – The horse race that has taken place on the beaches of Sanlúcar for the past 150 years is one of Spain's most exciting events, in a spectacular setting, combining water, light and superb horsemanship. Its origins date to the 19C, a time when horse races were a novelty. It is thought to be one of the oldest races in the country, held every August at low tide, although the time and date vary. *More information can be obtained from the tourist office.*

## Address Book

### WHERE TO EAT

**Casa Bigote** – *Bajo de Guía, 10* – ☏ *956 36 26 96 – www.restaurante-casabigote.com* – ☉ *Closed Sun and in Nov.* This old tavern in the Bajo Guía river district is a gastronomic landmark. Run by the same family for 50 years, it is decorated with old photos, fishing mementos and antiques. Pride of place on the extensive menu is given to the excellent local fish and prawns.

### WHERE TO STAY

**Posada de Palacio** – *Caballeros, 11 (Barrio Alto)* – ☏ *956 36 48 40 - www.posadadepalacio.com – 34 rooms*

– ☉ *Closed Jan-Feb.* This family-run hotel is in an 18C mansion opposite the town hall *(ayuntamiento)* in the upper section of Sanlúcar. The rooms, around an attractive patio, are tastefully decorated with antiques.

**Tartaneros** – *Tartaneros, 8* – ☏ *956 38 53 93 – hoteltartaneros@telefonica.net – 22 rooms, 2 suites.* This attractive yellow early 20C mansion is decorated with columns and balconies.

### LOCAL FESTIVALS

Carnival *(February)*, Feria de la Manzanilla *(late May)*, horse race *(August)*.

## Tours

# From Plaza del Cabildo to the Barrio Alto *1hr*
*This itinerary includes the main sights of interest in the Barrio Alto (Upper Town).*

### Plaza del Cabildo
This large square with a 19C appearance, embellished with orange and palm trees. is the focal point of Sanlúcar. To one side is the 18C former **town hall** *(cabildo)*.

### Plaza de San Roque
This small square in one of the liveliest areas is the setting for a morning market.

### Iglesia de la Trinidad
🕐 *Open 9.30am-1.30pm.* 🕐 *No visits Sun or holidays.*
The Church of the Trinity is half-hidden on the square, on the side of the plaza de San Roque. This small church contains a magnificent 15C Mudéjar **artesonado**★★ ceiling. The 17C Baroque retable includes a fine statue of Our Lady of the Sorrows.

▶ *Continue along calle Regina.*

### Convento de Regina Coeli
This early 16C convent housed an order of Poor Clares. It has a handsome Pompeii-red façade. In the two elegant portals are statues of St Clare and the Virgin and Child.

▶ *Return to plaza de San Roque and follow calle Bretones. Head up cuesta de Belén, passing the municipal market along the way.*

### Covachas★
These are five recently restored ogee stone arches decorated with Gothic tracery and winged dragons. Eroded and mysterious, they were probably part of a 15C palace of the Dukes of Medina Sidonia.

### Palacio de Orleans y Borbón
*Entrance along calle Caballeros.* 🕐 *Open 11am-1pm and 4-6pm; Sun and public hols, 11am-1pm.* ⊛ €3. ☎ *958 66 51 08.*
This magnificent Moorish-style palace built in the 19C as a summer residence for the Duke of Montpensier, with delightful **gardens** offering attractive views, is now Sanlúcar's town hall.

### Parroquia de Nuestra Señora de la O
*Open for worship, Mon-Sat, at 7.30pm; Sun at 9am, noon and 7.30pm.*
The church was ordered built by Isabel de la Cerda y Guzmán, niece of Alfonso X the Wise. Its west façade shows a majestic 14C **Mudéjar portal**★★; the superb 16C **artesonado**★ ceiling is from the same period. The **Palacio de los Condes de Niebla**, residence of the Duchess of Medina Sidonia, stands alongside the church. ◈ *Guided tours, Sun, 10am-1.30pm.* ☎ *956 36 01 61.*

▶ *Walk along calle Luis de Eguilaz.*

At n° 21 note the **Casa de la Cilla**, an attractive small 18C Baroque palace now owned by the Barbadillo *manza-*

---

### Local pastries

**Convento de la Madre de Dios:** The nuns from this 17C convent with its attractive Renaissance façade are famed for their *tocino de cielo* (◈ *see JEREZ*), which is reputed to be among the best in the province. The entrance is on calle del Torno. 🕐 *Open daily except Sun 10am-1pm and 5-7pm.* The convent looks onto a pleasant colonial-style square.

*nilla* company. Enjoy strolling along callejón de las Comedias and calle Eguilaz, with their whitewashed façades and scent of *manzanilla*.

### Castillo de Santiago

The oldest section is the 13C keep, built by Guzmán the Good. The remainder is from the 15C. Isabel the Catholic, among other notables, stayed here.

## The Modern Town and Bajo de Guía

Barrio Bajo (Lower Town) is Sanlúcar's 16C expansion and the commercial hub.

### Iglesia de Santo Domingo

🕐*Open 10am-noon and 3.30-8pm. No visits during religious services.* ☎ *956 36 04 91.*
The former Convento de Santo Domingo from 1548 sheltered Dominicans returning from afar. A portal attributed to Cristóbal de Rojas leads to a cloistered atrium.

▶ *Continue along calle de Santo Domingo to plaza de San Francisco.*

The square is fronted by the imposing 17C **Iglesia de San Francisco**.

▶ *Follow calle de San Nicolás and avenida del Cabo Nobal to avenida Bajo de Guía.*

### Centro de Visitantes Bajo de Guía

*Open 10am-2pm and 4-7pm; Sat-Sun, 10am-2.30pm. No charge.* ☎ *956 36 07 15.*
This visitor centre is dedicated to the natural habitats of the Parque Nacional de Doñana on the opposite bank of the Guadalquivir.

### Centro de Visitantes Fábrica de Hielo

*Open in summer, 9am-8pm; otherwise, 9am-7pm.* ☎ *956 38 16 35.*
The Ice Plant (its former use) centre serves **Parque Nacional de Doñana**.

## Excursions

### Parque Nacional de Doñana★★★ – 👣 *see Parque Nacional de DOÑANA*

### Bonanza

*4km/2.5mi north along CA 9027.* Attend the daily fish auction held in nearby Bonanza just before 5pm for the frenetic action, and the coded language.

### Chipiona

*9km/5.5mi southwest along A 480.* **Playa de la Regla**★ and other beaches at this resort are delightful. The 16C **Parroquia de Nuestra Señora de la O** has an Isabelline north façade, the **Santuario de Nuestra Señora de la Regla** interesting *azulejos*. 🕐 *Open in summer, 8am-1.30pm and 5-7.30pm.* ☎ *956 37 01 89.*

---

### 😊 A Bit of Advice 😊

**Excursions by boat to the Doñana on board the Real Fernando:**
The boat departs from Sanlúcar de Barrameda and docks at La Plancha, where visitors will enjoy a short walk before returning to Sanlúcar. During the course of the trip, organised by the town hall in Sanlúcar, information is provided on the national park. Tickets can be purchased at the **Centro de Visitantes Fábrica de Hielo.**

---

### WHERE TO STAY

⊜⊜⊜**Cruz del Mar** – *Avenida de Sanlúcar, 1 – Chipiona –* ☎ *956 37 11 00 – 93 rooms – Closed mid-Nov to mid-Feb.* On the seafront with views across to the Parque de Doñana. A modern hotel offering a range of facilities including a pool, beach and fitness room. The local golf course is just 6km/3.5mi from Chipiona.

# SEVILLA★★★

POPULATION: 701,927

The city of art and history, Andalucía's capital, has managed to maintain its magnificent traditions without turning its back on modernity. It's said that Sevilla is a feminine city, secure in its charms and happy to display them to visitors. *Sevillanos* are passionate about where they live and take every opportunity to extol their city's virtues. Sevilla is more than a city: it is a way of embracing life to the full that is exuberant, festive and, above all, passionate. Sevilla is too many things to highlight in just a few words: it is the Guadalquivir, a river that has left its indelible mark on the city's history and acts as a mirror of itself; it is its impressive Holy Week and April Fair; it is Velázquez, Murillo, Don Juan Tenorio and Carmen; the scent of orange blossom; a lively gatherings of friends; and the dancing of *sevillanas* and bullfights. Sevilla is bright, it is colourful, and, in summer, it is extremely hot! *Avenida de la Constitución, 21 B, ☎ 954 22 14 04, otsevilla@andalucia.org, www.turismosevilla.org; Santa Justa station, ☎ 954 53 76 26*

▶ **Orient Yourself:** Sevilla lies in west-central Andalucía, an inland port on the Guadalquivir. The A 4-E5 motorway connects with Cádiz to the S and Córdoba to the NE. The E-1 runs toward Huelva to the W, and Portugal.
🅿 **Parking:** Leave your car and get around by bus, taxi, or on foot.
🅐 **Don't Miss:** The Giralda, the Real Alcázar, Parque María Luisa, a stroll in the Santa Cruz quarter and, if you can make it, the Feria de Abril and Holy Week.
🕐 **Organizing Your Time:** Two days are the minimum to see the Giralda, Cathedral, the Santa Cruz quarter, and your choice of shops, markets and streets.
**Especially for Kids:** Top destination is the Isla Mágica theme park.
♨ **Also See:** CARMONA (39km/24mi E), ÉCIJA (91km/57mi E), UTRERA (31mi/19km SE), MARCHENA (66km/41mi SE) and HUELVA (94km/59mi).

## Fiestas

In spring, Sevilla lives for two fiestas that have brought it international fame: Holy Week (Semana Santa) and the April Fair (Feria de Abril). For those yet to experience

*Plaza de España*

either, it is difficult to imagine their splendour or how *Sevillanos* embrace these two authentic, yet totally distinct expressions of the Sevillian soul.

**Semana Santa** – Holy Week is celebrated between Palm Sunday and Easter Sunday, in March or April, depending on the liturgical calendar. The origins of Sevilla's Semana Santa date back to the 16C, when the first brotherhoods or fraternities were formed to assist guild associations. Over 50 brotherhoods participate in the Holy Week processions, each carrying its own statue of Christ or the Virgin Mary.

The whole city comes onto the street to relive the Passion of Christ and the pain of his mother. The spectacle is impressive, with the streets and street corners of the city providing a magnificent backdrop to processions. In an extravagant religious ritual, breathtakingly beautiful statues are borne on floats exquisitely adorned with gold and silver, as popular fervour erupts in an atmosphere bordering on ecstasy.

**The processions** – These take place throughout the week. Every brotherhood departs from its own church or chapel and usually carries two floats or *pasos*: one bearing Christ, the other the Virgin Mary. They make one journey (*carrera*) to the cathedral and then return to their headquarters, always by way of calle Sierpes and the town hall. More than 100 floats wind through the city's streets, each accompanied by a band of musicians, and carried by *costaleros* – young men under the tutelage of an overseer (*capataz*) – who take immense pride in transporting these holy figures and demonstrate great skill and physical prowess in this feat of endurance.

A number of these famous processions take place on the **madrugá** (the early morning of Good Friday): El Silencio, La Macarena, La Esperanza de Triana, Los Gitanos and, on Friday afternoon, El Cachorro.

Some of the statues borne aloft in procession are priceless works by leading 17C sculptors, including *Jesus of Great Power* and *Christ of Love*, by Juan de Mesa; the *Christ of the Passion*, by Martínez Montañés; *La Macarena*, by an unknown artist; the *Holy Christ of the Expiration* ("El Cachorro"), by Francisco Antonio Gijón; and *Our Father Jesus of Nazareth*, by Francisco Ocampo.

**Feria de Abril** – Started in the mid-19C as an animal exchange, the April Fair soon developed into a colourful and lively celebration of pure enjoyment. It is the major fiesta held in Sevilla, a city with a reputation for partying like nowhere on Earth.

The April Fair takes place two or three weeks after Holy Week in the Los Remedios district, where a veritable city of light is created, illuminated by thousands of bulbs and fairy lights. Streets house traditional *casetas*. Festivities commence late Monday evening and in the early hours of Tuesday with the illumination of the fairground area, and continue until the closing fireworks display the following Sunday.

During the *feria* a high-spirited, good-humoured crowd throngs the streets. Famous *fino* sherry from Jerez and *manzanilla* from Sanlúcar flow in *casetas*. Tapas are eaten, and *sevillanas* are danced with great passion until the early hours.

During the day, the women of Sevilla do their best to upstage each other with the beauty and grace of their flamenco costumes as they dance, stroll the streets with friends and family, or wander around the *feria* area itself.

In the Feria parade, horsemen dress in tight-fitting costumes and wide-brimmed *sombreros cordobeses*. Carriages are drawn by horses with their colourful harnesses.

The calle del Infierno ("Hell Street") has attractions to delight young and old alike.

> ### 😊 A Bit of Advice 😊
>
> The Feria is created by *sevillanos* for *sevillanos;* many of the entertainment booths (*casetas*) are private and if you don't know anyone who can provide you with an introduction or ticket you may feel somewhat left out of proceedings.

**El Rocío** – The list of local fiestas would not be complete without mention of El Rocío (*see EL ROCÍO*). This religious pilgrimage, a combination of devotion to the Virgin and festive spirit, converges on a chapel in the village of El Rocío, south of Almonte in the province of Huelva.

## A Bit of History

*"Hércules me construyó, Julio César me rodeó de murallas y altas torres y el Rey Santo me conquistó"* (Hercules built me; Caesar surrounded me with walls and towers; and the King Saint conquered me), said the inscription on the former Jerez Gate (Puerta de Jérez), destroyed in the 19C. From its earliest days Sevilla's fate has been determined by its role as a river port. Although its origins are less than clear, the city probably was founded by Iberians. It became a Greek, Phoenician and Carthaginian colony, which was subsequently overrun by the Romans in 205 BC following a long siege.

**Romans and Visigoths** – Roman occupation was at first marked by factional disputes. Julius Caesar seized the city in 42 BC, fortified it, and transformed Sevilla into one of the main cities in Baetica.
In the 5C the Vandals invaded the region; they were expelled by the Visigoths who made the city their capital until the court was transferred to Toledo. The 6C saw the rise of a figure of major importance, the bishop St Isidore, author of *Etymologies*, who was to have great influence on medieval European culture.

**The Moors** – The Moorish conquest in 712 heralded a long period of Arab domination. During the Caliphate, the city came under the control of Córdoba; upon its fall in 1031 it became a taifa kingdom. During the reign of Al Mutamid, Sevilla experienced great cultural development. However, difficult relations with the Christian king, Alfonso VI, obliged Al Mutamid to seek aid from the Almoravids who subsequently seized the kingdom in 1091. In the 12C, the Almohads took control from the Almoravids and began a period of urban transformation that included construction of both the Giralda and the *mezquita* (mosque), on the site now occupied by the cathedral.

**The Reconquest** – On 23 November 1248, Fernando III the Saint reconquered Sevilla and established his court in the city, followed by Alfonso X the Wise and then Pedro I, who restored the Alcázar and took up residence there.

**16C: The Golden Age** – Following the discovery of America in 1492, Sevilla held a monopoly on trade with the New World and became the departure and arrival point for every expedition. Among those who sailed from Sevilla were Amerigo Vespucci, and Magellan, who set out in 1519 and whose expedition was the first to circumnavigate the globe. 1503 saw the founding of the **Casa de Contratación**, a body established to encourage, inspect and control trade with the Americas.
Sevilla began to amass great wealth, Foreign merchants and bankers heeded the call of American gold. Palaces were built, new industries were created and the smell of money and frenetic activity attracted hustlers, villains and people from every sector. The population of Sevilla almost doubled during the 16C, rising to some 200 000 inhabitants.

### No me ha dejado

The emblem on the city's coat of arms was given to Sevilla by Alfonso X the Wise (1221-84) to commemorate the loyalty and support he had received from the city. The figure of eight in the emblem, representing a skein of wool (madeja), creates the motto "No madeja do" or "No me ha dejado", which translates as "It has not forsaken me".

# Address Book

## TRANSPORT

**Airport** – San Pablo international airport, 8km/5mi along the A 4 towards Madrid, ☎ 954 44 90 00. Apart from taxis, buses operatesto the city centre and Santa Justa rail station (€2.30).

**Trains** – *Estación de Santa Justa, Avenida Kansas City,* ☎ *954 41 41 11.* Trains run to destinations in the province and throughout Spain, The AVE high-speed train connects Sevilla with Madrid in just 2hr 25min; Córdoba in 45min. *Information and reservations,* ☎ *902 24 02 02.*

**Inter-city buses** from **Estación Plaza de Armas** (☎ *954 90 77 37/80 40*) run to Sevilla province, Huelva, elsewhere in Spain, and Europe; from **Estación del Prado de San Sebastián** (☎ *954 41 71 11*) to localities in Andalucía.

**City buses** (☎ *954 22 81 77/53 60*) are the best way to get around. Fare is €1 (€5 for a 10-trip *abono* with transfer privileges within one hour).

**Taxis** – ☎ *954 58 00 00 and 954 62 22 22.*

## SIGHTSEEING

**Publications** – **Welcome Olé** and **The Tourist** are free from hotels and tourist sites. Sevilla's culture department publishes a monthly cultural brochure. The monthly **El Giraldillo** covers Andalucía's fairs, exhibitions and diversions. *www.elgiraldillo.es*

**Horse-drawn carriages** for visiting major sites can be hired in plaza de la Virgen de los Reyes, plaza de España, avenida de la Constitución and at the Torre del Oro.

**Boat trips on the Guadalquivir** run every 30min from the Torre del Oro (*1hr during by day, 1hr 30min at night*). A trip to the mouth of the river at Sanlúcar de Barrameda passes Parque Nacional de Doñana. ☎ *954 56 16 92.*

**Tourist bus** – The *bus turístico* from the Torre del Oro stops at each sight. Passengers get on and off at leisure.

## WHERE TO EAT

☞☞ **Bodegón La Universal** – *Betis, 2 (Triana)* – ☎ *954 33 47 46* – ◷ *Closed Wed.* Lovely view of Seville and bull ring from riverside terrace. Try a regional specialty before or after a stroll in Triana. Nicely decorated.

☞☞ **Corral del Agua** – *Callejón del Agua, 6* – ☎ *954 22 07 14 - www.andalunet.com/corral-agua* – ◷ *Closed Sun.* Pleasant, refreshing, on a quiet, alley. The terrace, with its abundant vegetation, is delightful in the heat of summer. Andalusian cuisine.

☞☞☞ **La Albahaca** – *Plaza de Santa Cruz, 12* – ☎ *954 22 07 14* – ◷ *Closed Sun.* Choose from three dining rooms in this mansion. Regional dishes, pleasant terrace.

☞☞☞☞ **Taberna del Alabardero** – *Zaragoza, 20* – ☎ *50 27 21 - www.tabernadelalabardero.com* – ◷ *Closed Aug.* This 19C mansion houses one of the best restaurants, a seven-room hotel (☞☞☞☞), tea room and a hotel school. Worth a visit just to look.

## TAPAS

### SANTA CRUZ DISTRICT

**Calle Mateos Gago** – This street by the Giralda is full of bars and restaurants. **Bodega de Santa Cruz** attracts a young crowd who spill onto the street. The **La Giralda** *cervecería* (*n°1*) is a most traditional bar with tasty *raciones*. **Bodega Belmonte** (*n°24*) is known for *lomo a la pimienta* (spicy loin of pork). **Las Teresas** – *Santa Teresa, 2* – ☎ *954 21 30 69.* A small, typically Sevillian tavern on a picturesque alley, one of the oldest in the Barrio Santa Cruz. Attractive early-19C decor. **Casa Plácido** opposite is good for hot and cold tapas.

### CENTRO

**El Patio de San Eloy** – *San Eloy, 9* – ☎ *954 22 11 48.* Unusual ensemble of small wine bar, a counter with all kinds of sandwiches (*bocadillos*), and *azulejo*-clad benches at the back, ideal for chatting. Packed at lunchtime.

### SANTA CATALINA

**El Rinconcillo** – *Gerona, 40* – ☎ *95 422 31 83 - www.elrinconcillo1670.com* - ◷ *Closed 17 Jul-9 Aug.* Old and attractive, dating to 1670, with 18C and 19C *azulejo* panelling and fine wooden ceiling. Prix-fixe menus from €12.

### ARENAL AND PLAZA NUEVA

**Bodega San José** – *Adriano, 10* – ☎ *954 22 41 05 .* A meeting point for bullfight fans, a real *bodega* with dirt floor and fumes from the immense casks.

**Casablanca** – *Zaragoza, 50* - ☎ *954 224 698* – ⏰ *Closed Sun*. Small bar, one of the most famous in Sevilla, full of locals.

**Bodeguita Romero** – *Harinas, 10* - ☎ *954 22 95 56* – ⏰ *Closed Mon and in Aug*. Next to the Maestranza bullring. Famous for its exquisite *pringá* (a meat stew eaten with bread). Regional decor.

### TRIANA

**Casa Cuesta** – *Castilla, 3* - ☎ *954 33 33 35* - *www.casacuesta.net* – ⏰ *Closed Tue*. Founded in 1880, this tapas bar has a rustic dining room and, in good weather, tables in the small square nearby.

**Kiosco de Las Flores** – *Betis* - ☎ *954 27 45 76* - ⏰ *Closed Sun afternoon and Mon*. This riverside tapas bar, long in the same family, specialises in fried fish, seafood and garlic shoots with eggs.

**Sol y Sombra** – *Castilla, 149-151* – ☎ *954 33 39 35* – *www.tabernasolysombra. com* - ⏰ *Closed all day Mon and Tue lunchtime*. This bustling bar, its walls covered with bullfighting posters, is rich with the odours of ham and cheese.

### WHERE TO STAY

If you're planning to stay for Holy Week or the Feria, verify the room rate. Prices can double or even triple at these times.

☎ **Hostal Sierpes** – *Corral del Rey, 22 (Santa Cruz)* - ☎ *954 22 49 48* - *www. hsierpes.com* - 🅿 – *35 rooms*. This 17C mansion on an alley in the Santa Cruz *barrio* has rooms around a patio, good for the price. Its tavern, Melquiades, serves inexpensive tapas.

☎ **Hotel Sevilla** – *Daóiz, 5* – ☎ *954 38 41 61* - *www.hotel-sevilla.com* – *35 rooms*. Excellent location in a pleasant small square near the Palacio de la Condesa de Lebrija, basic comfort at budget prices. The faded decor adds to the overall charm.

☎☎ **Hotel Londres** – *San Pedro Mártir, 1* – ☎ *954 50 27 45* - *www. londreshotel.com* – *25 rooms*. This charming Sevillian house has basic, clean rooms. Those with balcony are generally more pleasant and, despite the central location, are relatively quiet.

☎☎ **Hotel Simón** – *García Vinuesa, 19* – ☎ *954 22 66 60* - *www.hotelsimonse-villa.com* – *29 rooms*. This white mansion by the cathedral, arranged around a cool patio, seems to be from another era, with antiques and large mirrors. Rooms are comfortable, the best decorated with colourful *azulejos*.

☎☎ **Hotel Doña Blanca** – *Plaza P Jerónimo de Córdoba, 14* - ☎ *954 50 13 73* - *www.donablanca.com* – *19 rooms*. A mansion with distinctive red façade, reasonably priced given the decor and comfort. In the bustling area by the church of Santa Catalina.

☎☎ **Hostería del Laurel** – *plaza de los Venerables, 5 (Santa Cruz)* - ☎ *954 22 02 95* - *www.hosteriadellaurel.com* – *20 rooms*. The best feature is the location on one of Sevilla's most charming plazas. Comfortable rooms, Provençal furniture, and restaurant with regional dishes.

☎☎ **Hostal Van Gogh** – *Miguel de Mañara, 4* - ☎ *95 456 37 27* - *www. grupo-piramide.com* – *14 rooms*. Entirely Sevillian, despite the name: bull's head over the door, bright colours and geraniums on the balconies. Modest rooms, near the *barrio* of Santa Cruz.

☎☎☎ **Hotel Amadeus Sevilla** – *Farnesio, 6* - ☎ *954 501 443* - *www. hotelamadeussevilla.com* – *14 rooms*. A family of musicians transformed this magnificent 18C house in Santa Cruz. The decor highlights the building's elements. Also six rooms next door (☎☎☎) in "La Música de Sevilla".

☎☎☎ **Hotel Las Casas de la Judería** – *Callejón Dos Hermanas, 7* – ☎ *954 41 51 50* - *www.casasypalacios.com* – 🅿

*El Rinconcillo*

*– 119 rooms.* A pleasant surprise in the old Jewish quarter. Elegant, charming, traditional and full of colour, once the mansion of the Duke of Béjar.

⊜⊜⊜ **Hotel Doña María** – *Don Remondo, 19 –* ☎ *954 22 49 90 - www.hdmaria.com – 64 rooms.* Tastefully renovated with Giralda view. Even if you're not staying, spend some time on its delightful terrace.

⊜⊜⊜ **Casa Imperial** – *Imperial, 29 –* ☎ *954 50 03 00 - www.casaimperial.com – 18 rooms, 8 suites.* In a quiet street behind the Casa de Pilatos, an interesting largely 17C-18C Baroque-style mansion. Attractive main patio.

⊜⊜⊜ **Hotel Alfonso XIII** – *San Fernando, 2 –* ☎ *954 91 70 00 - www.alfonsoxiii.com –* 🅿 *– 147 rooms.* Built in 1928 in neo-Mudéjar style opposite the Alcázar gardens, Sevilla's most luxurious and famous hotel.

## TAKING A BREAK

**Horno San Buenaventura** – *Avenida de la Constitución, 16 –* ☎ *954 45 87 11 –* 🕐*Open 8am-10pm.* Part of a network of old furnaces (*hornos*) over six centuries old. Near the cathedral with a spacious and popular ground floor tea-room. Its cakes are justifiably famous.

**La Campana** – *Sierpes, 1 -* ☎ *954 22 35 70 - www.confiterialacampana.com –* 🕐*Open 8am-10pm.* One of Sevilla's classic coffee houses. Everyone from local seniors to tourists enjoys pastries served in a pleasant Rococo atmosphere.

## GOING OUT FOR THE EVENING

The most popular areas for a drink are the city centre and the attractive Santa Cruz and Arenal districts, all of which provide a magnificent historical backdrop. Working-class Triana, in particular calle Betis, across the Guadalquivir, is also lively, with bars and clubs with a local flavour. Sevilla's younger crowd prefers the Nervión district where many nightclubs stay open until dawn. The alternative crowd heads for Alameda de Hércules, a borderline neighbourhood at night, where interesting haunts include Fun Club, a popular concert venue, and the Habanilla café, with its large and unusual collection of old coffee pots.

In summer, the action moves down to the river, where several kilometres of bars and outdoor terraces are popular with people of all ages and tastes.

**Antigüedades** – *Calle Argote de Molina, 40 –* 🕐*Open 8pm-3am.* One of Sevilla's most colourful spots, this club changes decor according to what's on. Particularly popular with thirtysomethings. Very lively at about midnight.

**Café de la Prensa** – *Betis, 8 –* 🕐*Open 10pm-1am.* This riverside café attracts the young and intellectual with modern decor, and outside tables with priceless views of the Guadalquivir and old city. Perfect for drinks at any time.

**El Sonanta** – *Calle San Jacinto, 31 –* 🕐*Open 8.30pm-dawn.* This small bar across the river in Triana serves tapas by day and fills up with flamenco lovers by night. Live shows Thursdays and Fridays, flamenco festival twice yearly.

**El Tamboril** – *Plaza de Santa Cruz, 12 –* 🕐*Open 10pm-5am.* Tucked in a corner of the Santa Cruz district, this *taberna* hums into the early hours with a faithful clientele who might burst into an impromptu *sevillana* or *rumba*. The *Salve Rociera*, a prayer to Our Lady of El Rocío, is always sung at midnight.

**La Carbonería** – *Levíes, 18 –* 🕐*Open 8pm-4am.* A Sevilla institution, key to the alternative crowd. In various parts of this former coal warehouse in the Jewish Quarter (Judería), you can listen to an intimate recital around a fireplace, watch live flamenco, or view an art or photography exhibition. A must!

**Paseo de las Delicias** – Four venues on this avenue (Chile, Líbano, Alfonso and Bilindo) shine for summer bar-hopping

*The terrace of La Campana*

and outdoor dancing. In winter they are ideal for a quiet drink in María Luisa park, surrounded by the buildings of the 1929 Ibero-American Exhibition. The age range is between 25 and 40, but varies from one venue to the next.

**Sopa de Ganso** – *Calle Pérez Galdós, 8 – Open 1pm-2am, Fri-Sat until 6am.* The playlist and woodsy decor attract a crowd at night, including visitors; by day, pastries are the draw.

**Voulez-Bar / Wall Street** – *Calle Ramón y Cajal, 1-A (Viapol building) – Open Wed-Sat, midnight-6am.* These adjoining bars are in the city's favourite clubbing district, Nervión. Voulez-Bar organises salsa and flamenco concerts and occasionally books a leading band. At Wall Street, fluctuating drink prices are shown on screens all along the bar. Huge numbers of people 25 to 35 move back and forth throughout the night.

## ENTERTAINMENT

Sevilla is a lively and festive capital offering varied cultural activities all year.

**El Patio Sevillano** – *Paseo Cristóbal Colón, 11-A* – ☎ *954 21 41 20 - www. elpatiosevillano.com - shows: 7.30-9pm and 10-11.30pm by reservation - drink and show: €30; dinner and show: €55.* An institution since 1952, offering a flamenco retrospective. Near the bull ring, parking nearby.

**Tablao El Arenal** – *Rodó, 7 (El Arenal)* - ☎ *954 21 64 92 - www.tablaoelarenal. com - Open from 7.30pm. Shows 8.30pm and 10.30pm by reservation - drink and show: €33; dinner and show: €64.* One of Sevilla's most important *tablaos*, said by those in the know to feature flamenco at its purest.

**Teatro Central** – *Avenida José de Gálvez* – ☎ *955 037 200 - www.teatrocentral. com.* This modern theatre, built on Isla de la Cartuja for Expo'92, offers avant-garde theatre, concerts by some of the world's leading opera singers, and a season of flamenco.

**Teatro de la Maestranza** – *Paseo de Cristóbal Colón, 22* – ☎ *954 22 33 44 73 - www.teatromaestranza.com - box office: 10am-2pm and 6-8.30pm.* Full season of theatre, dance and opera with performances by international stars.

**Teatro Lope de Vega** – *Avenida María Luisa* – ☎ *954 59 08 53.* This theater concentrates on drama and flamenco.

**Baños Árabes-Tetería Aire de Sevilla** – *Aire, 15 (Santa Cruz) - 5 min. on foot from cathedral* - ☎ *955 01 00 24 - www. airedesevilla.com - Arab bath: 10am-2am in 2hr sessions. Tea house: Sun-Thu, 4pm-midnight and Fri-Sat, 4pm-2am.* This late 16C palace of the Viceroy of the Indies houses magnificent baths in the best of Andalusian-Moorish style, as well as an upstairs patio-tea room. Excellent for a break during your tour of the Santa Cruz neighborhood. Reserve for steam baths.

## SHOPPING

The most traditional shops are in the historic centre, particularly along calle Tetuán, in the plaza del Duque de la Victoria, calle de San Eloy and other pedestrian areas. Historic **calle Sierpes** has traditional and more unusual shops and boutiques, including several Foronda boutiques selling the hand-embroidered shawls created by this famous local artisan. The Ochoa pastry shop is perfect for breakfast or an afternoon snack, and has take-away pastries. The streets at right angles to Sierpes and those around the El Salvador church are popular with jewellery hunters, who are spoilt for choice in the plaza del Pan and the calle Alcaicería.

In the **Los Remedios** district across the river, calle Asunción has a number of leading brand-name stores.

In the modern Nervión district are two large shopping centres (El Corte Inglés and Nervión Plaza), and stores of leading clothing chains.

Another centre is the former **Plaza de Armas railway station**, an early 20C regionalist building that even includes a brewery, La Fábrica de Cerveza.

**Markets** – The "jueves" (Thursday) market in calle Feria is popular for antiques and second-hand goods. Sunday morning markets are held in plaza de la Alfalfa (a much-frequented livestock market); plaza del Cabildo (stamps and old coins); and along Alameda de Hércules (second-hand goods early in the day).

**The decline** – Following the plague of 1649, the city entered a period of decline, exacerbated by the transfer of the Casa de Contratación to Cádiz in 1717.

**20C** – During the 20C Sevilla hosted two major international exhibitions: the 1929 Ibero-American Exhibition and Expo'92, both of which had a significant effect on the layout of the city.

Expo'92 saw the realisation of a number of large projects, in particular the Isla de la Cartuja, where the fair was held. The Isla Mágica theme park and the Centro Andaluz de Arte Contemporáneo are now on the site.

## Visit

Sevilla's two most important monuments, the cathedral and the Alcázar, as well as its famous Santa Cruz quarter, are near each other in the centre of the city.

## The Giralda and Cathedral★★★

🕓 *Open Mon-Sat, 11am-5pm; Sun, 2.30-6pm. Restricted opening times on Tue of Holy Week, Maundy Thu and Good Fri.* 🕓 *Closed 1 and 6 Jan, 30 May, Corpus Christi, 15 Aug, and 8 and 25 Dec.* ⊜ *€7.50, no charge Sun.* ☎ *954 21 49 71.*

### Giralda★★★

Elegant and lofty, the Giralda is the symbol of Sevilla. Built at the end of the 12C, this brick minaret (96m/315ft), part of the mosque (*mezquita*), was once surmounted by three gilded spheres, which sadly fell off in a 14C earthquake. The belfry, three superimposed stages and balconies are 16C additions by Cordoban architect Hernán Ruiz. These were crowned with an enormous weather vane, the statue of Faith, known as the Giraldillo (from *girar*: to turn), from which the tower's name evolved.

The tower is a masterpiece of Almohad art, delicate yet restrained. This purist dynasty shunned ostentation, yet managed to create a harmonious style of beauty and simplicity. The decoration on each side is organised into three vertical registers with *sebka* panels. *Access to the Giralda is from inside the cathedral (see below).*

### Cathedral★★★

"Let us build a cathedral that will make them think us mad", the chapter is said to have declared in 1401 when it ordered the demolition of the mosque. The cathedral is impressive in its dimensions, and is considered to be the third largest in floor space in the Christian world after St Peter's in the Vatican and St Paul's in London. One of the last Gothic cathedrals built in Spain, it shows obvious Renaissance influence.

View the massive **exterior** to appreciate its size. The Cristóbal (or Príncipe), Asunción and Concepción (in the Patio de los Naranjos) doorways are modern (19C and 20C), yet respect the style as a whole. The Puerta del Nacimiento and Puerta del Bautismo, which open out onto the Avenida de la Constitución, include beautiful sculptures by Mercadante de Bretaña (1460). At the east end, admire the rounded Chapel Royal (*Capilla Real* – 1575), decorated with coats of arms and, on either side, the Gothic

### The "Seises" – A Fine Tradition

The Seises are a group of 12 brightly dressed choir boys who perpetuate a tradition dating back to the 16C, by which they sing and dance in front of the cathedral's high altar during the eight days following Corpus Christi and the Feast of the Immaculate Conception. Initially the group consisted of 6 (*seis*) boys, hence the name. They also accompany the **Corpus Christi** procession when this stops in the plaza del Ayuntamiento and the plaza del Salvador.

# SEVILLA

Puerta de Palos and Puerta de las Campanillas with Renaissance-style tympana in which Miguel Perrin has made full play of perspective.

### Interior

This universe of stone, stained glass and grilles is striking in its size and richness, while its extraordinary height is the result of tall, slender pillars. The ground plan consists of five aisles – the central nave being wider and higher – with chapels in the side aisles. The column shafts support simple Flamboyant Gothic pointed vaults, except in the central section. The vault of the transept, also Flamboyant, reaches to 56m/184ft. A **mirror (1)** on the floor enables a striking view.

### Climbing the Giralda

It is possible to climb up to the tower's belfry (70m/230ft) on a ramp with 34 sections. The ascent is not particularly difficult; take your time to admire views of the Patio de los Naranjos, the gargoyles and pinnacles of the cathedral and the Alcázar from the balconies on the way up. Your efforts will be well rewarded at the top with a magnificent **panorama**★★★ over the city.

### High Altar

The high altar (*capilla mayor*), rich in surprising decoration, is enclosed by a splendid 16C Plateresque **grille**★★, by Fray Francisco de Salamanca. The immense Flemish **altarpiece**★★★ (1482-1525), the largest in Spain, is profusely and delicately carved with colourful scenes from the lives of Christ and the Virgin Mary (except the predella, decorated with saints). The altarpiece has seven vertical panels, the widest is in the centre. Unfortunately, it is impossible to get close enough to admire one of the world's most impressive altarpieces.

### Chancel

In the main nave, partly hidden by a 16C grille by Fray Francisco de Salamanca is the *coro*, with fine 15C-16C choir stalls. The majestic organs are from the 18C. The **trascoro** (chancel screen) of multicoloured marble, jasper and bronze, is 17C.

### Treasury

The treasury in the 16C **Sacristía de los Cálices** (Chalice Sacristy) is surmounted by a fine vault. Interesting paintings exhibited are: *Santa Justa* and *Santa Rufina* by Goya, a Zurbarán, a triptych by Alejo Fernández and several canvases by Valdés Leal.

*Sevilla Cathedral*

The anteroom of the sacristy houses the **Tenebrario**, a 7.80m/25ft, fifteen-branch Plateresque candelabrum, used during Holy Week processions.

The main **sacristy** (*sacristía mayor*), a fine 16C room with a Greek cross plan, contains the impressive Renaissance silver **monstrance** (*custodia*) by Juan de Arfe, measuring 3.90m/13ft and weighing 475kg/1 045lb; a *Santa Teresa* by Zurbarán and *The Martyrdom of San Lorenzo* by Lucas Jordán can be seen on the rear wall.

### Chapter house

The fine 16C Renaissance chapter house (*sala capitular*) has an elliptical dome and a characteristic *Immaculate Conception* by Murillo.

### Capilla Real★★

⚬━ *Closed to visitors.* The Plateresque Chapel Royal, built during the reign of Charles V over an earlier chapel, is of monumental size. Square in shape, it is covered by an elegant, richly ornamented coffered dome with carved busts and contains a small apse, itself covered by a scallop shell decorated with figures. A wooden carving of the **Virgen de los Reyes**, patron saint of Sevilla, decorates the altar. Behind it, in a silver urn of great value, are the remains of Fernando III the Saint. On either side are the tombs of Alfonso X and of his mother, Beatrice of Swabia. The Capilla Real is enclosed by a majestic grille dating from 1771.

### Patio de los Naranjos

This exceptional rectangular patio is planted with orange trees (*naranjos*) and was used for ritual ablutions in the former mosque.

### Puerta del Perdón

The Almohad arch and the door leaves survive from the original mosque on this majestic portal. The impressive sculptures and the relief, representing the Expulsion of the Money Changers from the Temple, are from the 16C.

### Palacio Arzobispal

The residence of the Archbishop of Sevilla is in the attractive plaza de la Virgen de los Reyes, with its monumental lantern (and numerous horse-drawn carriages). The edifice has an elegant, late-Baroque façade from the beginning of the 18C.

### Plaza de Santa Marta

*Take the narrow callejón de Santa Marta, opposite the Palacio Arzobispal.* The alleyway offers the only access to this delightful small square of whitewashed façades, simple wrought-iron grilles and a small stone cross shaded by orange trees. The charming, hushed atmosphere is typical of so many of the city's squares.

### Archivo General de Indias

🕐 *Open 10am-4pm. No charge.* ☎ *954 50 05 28.*

The historical archives relating to the Spanish conquest of the Americas are housed in the former Exchange (*lonja*), built at the end of the 16C to plans by Juan de Herrera, architect of El Escorial. The archives were established here by Carlos III in 1785. This sober, Renaissance-style building has two floors with architrave bays. Note the sumptuous 18C pink and black marble staircase. Only the upper floor, with large rooms topped with elegant vaults, can be visited. It houses priceless documents on the conquest and colonisation of the Americas, as well as the signatures of Columbus, Magellan, Hernán Cortés, Juan Sebastián Elcano and others.

---

# Chapels and Altars

Once you have seen the cathedral's major works, take time to admire its chapels, which themselves contain numerous works of art.

◆ **Altar de Nuestra Señora de Belén (2)** (Our Lady of Bethlehem): north side, to the left of the Puerta de la Concepción. Fine portrayal of the Virgin Mary by Alonso Cano.

◆ **Capilla de San Antonio (3):** this chapel contains several interesting canvases dominated by Murillo's Vision of St Anthony of Padua, on the right-hand wall. Also worthy of note are *The Baptism of Christ*, also by Murillo, and two paintings of St Peter by Valdés Leal.

◆ **Altar del Santo Ángel (4)** (at the foot of the cathedral, to the left of the Puerta Mayor): this altar is dominated by a fine *Guardian Angel* by Murillo.

◆ **Capilla de San Hermenegildo (5)** (next to the Capilla de San José): the 15C alabaster tomb of Cardinal Cervantes sculpted by Lorenzo Mercadante.

◆ **Capilla de la Virgen de la Antigua (6)** (the next chapel): larger than the others and covered with an elevated vault. A fine 14C fresco of the Virgin adorns the altar.

◆ 19C funerary monument to **Christopher Columbus (7)**: the explorer's coffin is borne by four pallbearers bearing the symbols of Castilla, León, Navarra and Aragón on their chest.

◆ **Capilla de San Pedro (8):** the walls of this chapel are hung with a superb series of paintings by **Zurbarán** illustrating the life of St Peter.

## Plaza del Triunfo

Some of Sevilla's most impressive buildings surround this square. In the centre stands a "triumph" (*triunfo*) to the Immaculate Conception. Along the sides are the Archivo General de Indias; the cathedral (south side); the Alcázar; and the former Hospital del Rey, now the Casa de la Provincia.

# Real Alcázar★★★

*Entrance through the Puerta del León.* ◷ *Open Apr-Sep, Tue-Sun, 9.30am-7pm (Sun and pub hols, to 5pm); Oct-Mar, Tue-Sat, 9.30am-5pm (Sun and public hols, to 1.30pm). Last admission 1hr before closing.* ◷ *Closed 1 and 6 Jan, Good Fri, 25 Dec and for official ceremonies.* ⊛ *€7, Cuarto Alto: €4.* ☎ *954 50 23 24.*

Unusual for a royal residence, this magnificent palace is the result of several phases of construction from the 10C onwards, in a variety of architectural styles. All that remains of the 12C Alcázar of the Almohads are the Patio del Yeso and the fortified arches separating the Patio de la Montería from the Patio del León. In the 13C Alfonso X the Wise built the Gothic-style apartments known as the Salones de Carlos V. The nucleus of the palace was built by Pedro I the Cruel in 1362. This Mudéjar masterpiece was built by masons from Granada, as can be seen in the decoration, highly influenced by the Alhambra (ⓖ *see GRANADA*), which dates from the same period. Modifications were made by Juan II, the Catholic Monarchs, Charles V and Felipe II.

| | REAL ALCÁZAR | |
|---|---|---|
| 🏠 Shop | 🚻 Toilets | ☕ Café |

### Cuarto del Almirante

*To the right of the Patio de la Montería.* Isabel the Catholic founded the Casa de Contratación in the Admiral's Apartments in 1503. The Sala de Audiencias (Audience Hall) has an altarpiece, the **Virgin of the Navigators**★ (1531-36), by Alejo Fernández.

### Sala de la Justicia and Patio del Yeso

*To the left of the Patio de la Montería.* The Sala de la Justicia (Justice Chamber) was built in the 14C over the remains of the Almohad palace. Note the finely sculpted plasterwork (*yesería*) and the magnificent cupola.

### Palacio de Pedro el Cruel★★★

The façade of Pedro the Cruel's Palace is reminiscent of the Patio del Cuarto Dorado in Granada's Alhambra, with its *sebka* decoration, fragile multifoiled arches and a large epigraphic frieze beneath its carved wood overhang.

A small hallway leads left from the entry to the **Patio de las Doncellas**, around which are rooms for official functions. Note the exquisite *yesería* decoration over a gallery of foliated arches above paired columns; and magnificent 14C *azulejo* panels. The Italian upper storey was added under Charles V.

A number of Mudéjar rooms open onto this patio: **the Salón del techo del Carlos V (1)** (Carlos V's Room), the palace's former chapel, with splendid Renaissance ceiling with polygon caissons; the **Dormitorio de los Reyes Moros (2)** (Bedroom of the Moorish Kings), two rooms with blue-toned stucco and magnificent artesonado ceilings; and the **Salón de Embajadores (3)** (Ambassadors' Hall), the most sumptuous room in the Alcázar, with remarkable 15C half-orange cedarwood **cupola**★★★ with stucco decoration and exceptional azulejo panelling. The pendentives have decorative Moorish motifs (*mocárabes*). This room connects with the **Salón del techo de Felipe II (4)**, with its magnificent Renaissance coffered cedarwood ceiling.

The Salón de Embajadores leads to the smaller **Patio de las Muñecas (5)**, in the family area. Foiled arches with *alfiz* surround are clearly Granadan. The upper floors are from a 19C restoration. This patio opens to the Cuarto del Príncipe (Prince's Room).

▷ *From the Patio de la Montería follow Corredor de Carlos V, a low-vaulted gallery.*

### Palacio Gótico or Salones de Carlos V

The Baroque doorway to the Gothic Palace (or Charles V's Rooms) is to the rear of the **Patio del Crucero**. Built by Alfonso X, it was restored in the 18C after the Lisbon earthquake. In the Sala Grande is part of a collection of 17C **tapestries**★★ from the Real Fábrica de Tapices in Madrid relating the Conquest of Tunis in 1535. The 13C **Sala de las Fiestas**, or **Sala de las Bóvedas**, the oldest section, retains its original structure and groin vaults (*bóvedas*). It was here that Carlos V married Isabel of Portugal. The walls, with 16C *azulejo* panelling, are hung with the remainder of the tapestry collection. Large windows look onto enchanting gardens.

### Gardens★

The extensive gardens are a Paradise of sensations. Like the palace, they were created over different periods; Moorish, Renaissance and Baroque styles are all represented. Their terraces and ornamental basins occupy 80% of the Alcázar's total area.

---

## The Cuarto Real Alto

An optional 30min guided tour enables visitors to view the King and Queen of Spain's official residence in Sevilla. The various rooms, with their fine artesonado ceilings, contain an impressive display of 19C furniture and clocks, 18C tapestries and French lamps. Of particular note are the **Capilla de los Reyes Católicos** (Chapel of the Catholic Monarchs) – an exquisite oratory with a ceramic font, by Nicola Pisano – and the Mudéjar **Sala de Audiencias**.

Leave Carlos V's Rooms and pass the Mercurio Pool to reach the 17C **Galería del Grutesco**★, which masks the front of an old wall and affords the best views.
Lower down is the Jardín de las Danzas (Dancing Garden). From here, head to the baths (*baños*) of Doña María de Padilla, a large vaulted pool.
Beyond the 15C **Pabellón de Carlos V** (pavilion) is the labyrinth, with clipped hedges. A modern, English-style garden is to the right. A quiet wander with just the gentle bubbling of water in the background is unforgettable.
The Baroque *apeadero* (to alight from horses) leads to the Patio de Banderas.

### Patio de Banderas

The Flag Court was the parade ground (*patio de armas*) of the original Alcázar. This enclosed rectangle, with characteristic orange trees and a single fountain, is bordered by elegant façades, notably the silhouette of the Giralda.

# Barrio de Santa Cruz★★★

These delightful twisting streets, white-washed houses, flower-filled patios and shady squares are the quintessential *barrio* of Sevilla. In the Middle Ages it was the Jewish quarter (*Judería*). It had royal protection until the end of the 14C, when it was seized by Christians, who converted the synagogues into churches.
Today, it is a haven of peace and quiet in the heart of Sevilla, where time has stopped. Visitors will want to meander through its alleyways – resplendent in the bright sunshine, and equally delightful at night – to discover its many facets and its hospitality, particularly during the *paseo*.

## The Barber of Seville

The city was to provide the inspiration for this comic opera, created in 1816 by the Italian composer Gioacchino Rossini (1792-1868). Written in two acts, this masterpiece tells of the attempts of Bartolo, an elderly doctor, to marry his pretty ward, Rosina. His plans are foiled by another admirer, Count Almaviva, through the help of his acquaintance, Figaro, who also happens to be Bartolo's barber.

One of the best entrances to the quarter is through the **Arco de la Judería**, a covered alleyway leading centuries back in time to the Patio de Banderas. Continue to the **callejón del Agua**, which runs alongside the district's outer wall. A less theatrical yet equally interesting route upon leaving the Patio de Banderas is through the **calle Romero Murube**, continuing along the wall of the Alcázar to the plaza de la Alianza. Cross the square, and follow the street which becomes the twisting yet delightful **callejón de Rodrigo Caro**, ending up at the **plaza de Doña Elvira**, one of Santa Cruz's most typical squares with *azulejo*-adorned benches shaded by orange trees, a small stone fountain at its centre. The calle Gloria leads to the lively **plaza de los Venerables**.

### Hospital de los Venerables★

*Guided tours (25min), 10am-1.30pm and 3.30-7.30pm.* ⊘ *Closed 1 Jan, Good Fri and 25 Dec.* ⊙ *€4.75.* ☎ *954 56 26 96.*
Founded in 1675, this priests' hospital (now the seat of the Focus-Abengoa cultural foundation), by Leonardo de Figueroa, is one of the finest examples of the 17C Sevillian Baroque. Its attractive patio is decorated with 19C *azulejos*.
The **church**★, with its single nave and barrel vault with lunettes, is covered with **frescoes**★★ painted by Valdés Leal and his son Lucas Valdés. *The Last Supper* by Valdés the Younger and, above it, *The Apotheosis of San Fernando*, by Valdés the Elder, are at the apsidal end. The nave contains four Flemish works on copper and two smaller works painted on marble. Two fine statues by Pedro Roldán, *San Fernando* and *San Pedro*, are at the foot of the church. Organ concerts are held frequently.

## Don Juan

This legendary character, the archetypal seducer who shows no respect for any-one or anything, appears for the first time in Tirso de Molina's *The Trickster of Seville and His Guest of Stone* (1630). It is said that he may have found his inspira-tion for the character in Don Miguel de Mañara, the founder of the Hospital de la Caridad ( *see below*).

Although the character is known to the world of opera as Mozart's *Don Giovanni* and has been re-created time and time again over the centuries by writers of the stature of Molière, Dumas and Byron, none of whom could resist his attraction, the most well-known version in Spain is that of *Don Juan Tenorio* (1844) by Zorrilla, in whose memory the statue in the plaza de los Refinadores has been erected.

In the **sacristy** is a fresco by Valdés Leal on the theme of the triumph of the Cross. The balustrade appears to change position if you watch it as you move around the room. Admire also the anonymous 18C figures of Christ in ivory.

Above the attractive **main staircase**★ is an elliptical Baroque dome adorned with stuccoes bearing the papal arms. *The Presentation of the Infant Jesus in the Temple*, by Lucas Valdés, hangs on the wall.

### Streets and squares

Many street name are evocative: Mesón del Moro (Moor's Inn), Pimienta (Pepper) and Susona, from the legendary love of a Jewess and Christian man.

Follow calle Santa Teresa – at n°7 is where the artist Murillo lived (now an exhibition room) – or exit plaza de Alfaro to **plaza de Santa Cruz**. Amid the orange trees of the square stands an impressive iron cross, the 17C Cruz de la Cerrajería, where one of the city's favourite sons, Murillo, is buried. Gardens nearby carry his name.

Calle Mezquita leads to the majestic **plaza de los Refinadores**. Continue to the **plaza de las Tres Cruces**, a triangle with three columns upon which stand three wrought-iron crosses, via a narrow alleyway.

**Calle Mateos Gago**, which runs into plaza de la Virgen de los Reyes, has a number of popular tapas bars as well as several early-20C houses.

# Walking About

## Palacio de San Telmo and Parque de María Luisa★ [1]

### Palacio de San Telmo

This impressively wide late 17C palace is the seat of the Presidencia de la Junta de Andalucía (Regional Council). It was once a naval academy, then the residence of the Dukes of Montpensier, and a seminary. Its **main portal**★, one of the finest works of Sevillian Baroque, is by Leonardo de Figueroa. It is completely covered with reliefs and sculptures. Above, a statue of San Telmo is silhouetted against the sky.

### Hotel Alfonso XIII

( *See Where to Stay in the Address Book*.) The most famous of all Sevilla's hotels was built for the 1929 Ibero-American Exhibition in regionalist style with neo-Mudéjar features.

### University

The city's university is a fine building with classical, harmonious lines and impressive dimensions, built in the 18C as a tobacco factory (and entrenched in the Sevilla myth by Bizet's *Carmen*). The **portal** fronting calle San Fernando has paired columns, and is crowned by a pediment bearing a large coat of arms, and a statue of an angel of the apocalypse representing Fame. In the doorway arch are medallions of Columbus and Hernán Cortés. Inside are attractive patios and a monumental staircase.

## Parque de María Luisa★★

The popular park was a gift from the Infanta María Luisa Fernanda, Duchess of Montpensier. Once part of the gardens of the Palacio de San Telmo, it was landscaped for the 1929 Ibero-American Exhibition by Jean-Claude Nicolas Forestier, and enhanced with gazebos, pools and exhibition buildings, some of which remain.

### Gazebos, Statues and Fountains

The Parque de María Luisa is much more than just a collection of attractive buildings and long, tree-lined avenues. Its fountains, with their gentle murmuring of water, its gazebos and its statues of famous characters add an intimate, romantic air to this delightful park. The memorials to Gustavo Adolfo Bécquer and Cervantes, with its *azulejos* illustrating scenes from *Don Quixote* (*at one end of plaza de América*), are just two examples of the surprises awaiting visitors as they stroll around the gardens.

## Plaza de España★

This magnificent creation of Sevillian architect Aníbal González is semicircular, fronted by a canal where rowboats can be hired. The enormity of the plaza is striking, and the ceramics exquisite. Before the brick building with towers at either end are *azulejo* scenes, illustrating an episode from the history of each province of Spain.

## Plaza de América

Here are three buildings from the 1929 Exhibition by the same architect: the Isabelline Pabellón Real (Royal Pavilion); the Renaissance pavilion, now the **archaeological museum**★ (& *see Visit: Museo Arqueológico de Sevilla*), and the Mudéjar pavilion, now a museum of popular arts (& *see Visit: Museo de las Artes y Costumbres Populares*).

# The River Bank★ 2

The pleasant **paseo de Cristóbal Colón** parallels the river between the San Telmo and Triana bridges. Along it are the Torre del Oro and the Real Maestranza bullring and other impressive sights. It offers attractive views across to the Triana district.

## Torre del Oro

The splendid Gold Tower was built by the Almohads in the 13C, along with the Torre de la Plata or Silver Tower, as part of a defensive system. The main part of the tower is a dodecagonal stone structure crowned with merlons, topped by two levels in brick, the second added in the 18C. The interior houses the **Museo de la Marina**, with documents, engravings, boat models and other items of maritime life. ⏰ *Open Tue–Fri, 10am–2pm; Sat–Sun and public hols, 11am–2pm.* ⏰ *Closed Mon, public hols and in Aug.* ☞ €1. ☏ 954 22 24 19.

Cruises along the Guadalquivir depart from just below the tower.

Opposite the Torre del Oro is the **Teatro de la Maestranza**, with an unusual false façade. The Hospital de la Caridad, with an important art collection, is behind.

## Hospital de la Caridad★

The Hospital of Charity was founded in 1667 by Don Miguel de Mañara (1627–79). The white façade of the church,

*A typical horse-drawn carriage*

R. Mattes/ MICHELIN

dazzling in sunlight, has five murals of blue and white ceramics apparently based on drawings by Murillo: theological virtues predominate (Faith, Hope and Charity); the two below show St George slaying the dragon and St James (Santiago), the Moorslayer (👓 *see tour description under Visit*).

As you leave, the founder's statue is opposite; to the left is the **Torre de la Plata**.

▷ *Return to the paseo de Cristóbal Colón and continue towards the Puente de Triana.*

## La Maestranza

👓 *Guided tours, 9.30am-7pm.* ⊛€4. ☎ *954 22 45 77.*

Sevilla's famed *plaza de toros*, with attractive red and white façade, was built between 1758 and 1881. Unusually, the bullring itself is not quite circular. Triumphant bullfighters are carried on the shoulders of fans through the Puerta del Príncipe (Prince's Gate). The **museum** has an interesting assortment of posters, paintings, and costumes.

In front of La Maestranza, where the tragic finale of the opera played out, is a bronze statue to Carmen, the personification of passionate female love.

Before the Puente de Triana is the **Monumento a la Tolerancia**, a large sculpture with the stamp of Eduardo Chillida, who spent time here in April 1992.

### Carmen

This legendary character created by the French writer Prosper Merimée in 1845 was subsequently used by Bizet as the subject of his famous opera (1874), in which he narrates the story of a triangle of love and jealousy involving Carmen the cigar-maker, a soldier and a bullfighter.

## Triana★

Triana, one of the city's most colourful areas, is across the Puente de Triana (or Puente de Isabel II), a bridge built in 1845. It offers fine **views** of the Guadalquivir and the east bank. Triana is a fishermen's and merchants' quarter, which has also produced famous singers and bullfighters.

To the left of the bridge, the **plaza del Altozano** has a monument to bullfighter Juan Belmonte (1892-1962) a *trianero* (though born across the river), .

Enter the district by the **calle Pureza**. At n° 55, between simple, well-maintained houses, stands the **Capilla de los Marineros**, a chapel dedicated to sailors, with a statue of the **Esperanza de Triana** (Hope of Triana), one of the most venerated statues of the Virgin Mary, whose procession rivals that of La Macarena. A late 16C Christ of the Three Falls is to the right of the high altar.

## Parroquia de Santa Ana

*Calle Pureza.* A little farther on, the Iglesia de Santa Ana in the parish (*parroquia*) of the same name is the oldest in Sevilla. The original church, founded by Alfonso X the Wise in the 13C, was restored and altered in the 18C.

## Exterior

Because of modifications, there is no single style. The most striking feature is the tower, with multifoiled arches in the lower sections showing clear Mudéjar influence, and *azulejo* decoration in the upper part.

### The Ceramics Quarter

A number of ceramics workshops and boutiques can still be seen in the area near the plaza del Altozano occupied by the calle de Callao, calle Antillano and calle de Alfarería, perpetuating an artistic tradition which has always existed in this quarter. The façades of some of these shops and workshops are decorated with *azulejos* advertising the wares inside.

## Interior

*Entrance at the side, in calle Vázquez de Leca.* Three elevated aisles are covered with sexpartite vaults.

A **Renaissance altarpiece** in the chancel comprises a fine ensemble of sculptures and paintings dedicated to the Virgin Mary; several of the canvases are by Pedro de Campaña. A sculpture of St Anne and the Virgin and Child is in the central vaulted niche. The Child is modern; the other figures are from the 13C, but have been altered.

The retro-choir contains a delicate early 16C **Virgin of the Rose**, by Alejo Fernández. Admire the panelling and altar, decorated with *azulejos*, in the Evangelist nave.

### "El Cachorro"

The **Capilla del Patrocinio**, a chapel situated at the end of the calle Castilla in the most northerly section of the Triana district, is where the **Christ of the Expiration**, commonly known as "El Cachorro", is venerated. It is said that the artist, Francisco Antonio Gijón, used a sketch of a murdered gypsy known as "El Cachorro" for the face of Christ in this late-17C masterpiece. Once he had finished carving Christ, the sculpture was so realistic that when people saw it they immediately recognised the dead gypsy, hence its name.

## Calle Betis

Stroll this riverside street and enjoy a completely different perspective of Sevilla: the Torre del Oro and La Maestranza in the foreground, dominated by the majestic Giralda. Calle Betis is known for its traditional houses, bars and open-air kiosks. At night, with the moon reflected on the river, the street is plainly romantic.

# La Macarena and Calle San Luis★ 5 *Map p 380*

## Basílica de la Macarena

🕐 *Open 9.30am-2pm and 5-8pm.* 🕐 *Closed during Holy Week and one week before and after in preparation for religious processions.* ⊚ *Museum: €3.* ☎ *954 90 18 00.*

The Iglesia de Nuestra Señora de la Esperanza (Church of Our Lady of Hope), built in the middle of the 20C, contains one of Sevilla's most famous statues: **La Macarena**★. This carving of the Virgin Mary, the work of an anonymous 17C artist, looks down from the high altar. Sevillians say that only angels could have created such a work. The beauty of her tearful face unleashes fervour during her procession, in the early morning of Good Friday. A Christ under Sentence in a chapel on the Evangelist side of the church is also venerated, and carried alongside the Virgin.

The **museum** displays cloaks and skirts, as well as the impressive floats which bear La Macarena and Christ, conveying the splendour of these occasions.

The **Arco de la Macarena** stands opposite the church. This arch was part of the Arab walls. The remaining section continues as far as the Puerta de Córdoba (Córdoba Gate). The walls have barbicans and are punctuated with large, square fortified towers.

*Holy Week procession*

Ch. Sappa / RAPHO

## Hospital de las Cinco Llagas or Hospital de la Sangre

*Opposite the Arco de la Macarena*. The former Hospital of the Five Wounds (*llagas*) or Blood (*sangre*), is the seat of the Andalusian Parliament. Until the mid-20C, this Renaissance-style building was Sevilla's main hospital. It is sober and harmonious, with a tower on each end. Two floors open onto a green square. The white marble doorway is crowned by the escutcheon of the Five Wounds.

*Return to La Macarena*. Behind it is the 13C parish church of **San Gil**, which has undergone significant restoration over the centuries. Follow calle de San Luis.

## Iglesia de Santa Marina

This 14C brick church has a simple stone ogival portal with minor sculpted decoration and a sober Mudéjar tower with staggered merlons. A tour of the exterior reveals the church's sturdy buttresses and the large Gothic windows at the apsidal end.

## Iglesia de San Luis de los Francesesa

🕐 *Open Tue-Thu, 9am-2pm, Fri-Sat, 9am-2pm and 5-8pm.* 🕐 *Closed Sun, Mon and public hols and in Aug.* ☎ *954 55 02 07.*

This church, the work of Leonardo de Figueroa, is one of the best examples of Sevillian Baroque architecture. The **façade** is clearly compartmentalised: two storeys, with octagonal tower on each side, and central cupola with ceramic decoration.

The **interior**★★ is surprisingly exuberant, with murals on the magnificent cupola by Lucas Valdés and outstanding retables by Pedro Duque Cornejo. The fine *azulejos* complete this superb ensemble, which manages to combine a richness of decoration with harmony. Note also the unusual reliquary on the frontal of the chancel.

### Iglesia de San Marcos

The impressive 14C façade blends Gothic and Mudéjar features. The attractive **Mudéjar tower**★ stands out, clearly Giralda-influenced (multifoiled arches and *sebka* work on the upper frieze). The tower is brick, with the exception of the Gothic stone portal which has three 18C sculptures (God the Father, the Virgin Mary and an angel), which replaced the original works, and an elegant and unusual *sebka*-style frieze.

The whitewashed interior contains a handsome 17C sculpture of **St Mark** (*Evangelist nave*) and an 18C **Recumbent Christ** (*Epistle nave*).

In the **plaza de Santa Isabel** behind the church, admire the doorway of the convent of Santa Isabel. A relief depicts the Visitation of the Virgin to her cousin Elizabeth. The work, from the early 17C, is by Andrés Ocampo. The church is interesting, albeit somewhat difficult to visit as it only opens for daily mass first thing in the morning.

A little farther along stands the **Convento de Santa Paula**★, one of the most ornate convents in the city ( ☽ *see description under Visit*).

## Centro★ ⑥

### Plaza Nueva

This spacious square is on land previously occupied by the Convento de San Francisco. The equestrian statue is of Fernando III the Saint, the city's Christian conqueror. Tall palms, benches and street lamps attract locals and tourists.

### Ayuntamiento

The west front of the neo-Classical 19C town hall faces the square. The more interesting east side, on plaza de San Francisco, has an attractive Plateresque 16C **façade**★, the work of Diego de Riaño, adorned everywhere with delicate classical motifs (fantastic and grotesque animals, medallions with faces, escutcheons etc).

The palace opposite the town hall in plaza de San Francisco is the Caja de Ahorros San Fernando (savings bank). It was formerly the seat of the Royal Court of Justice (Audiencia). Its classical late-16C façade are attributed to Alonso de Vandelvira.

### Calle Sierpes

Sevilla's most famous street, now pedestrianised, is lined with shops traditional and modern. Sierpes is liveliest in the late afternoon and early evening when locals window-shop or enjoy pastries in its renowned *pastelerías*. When the sun is hottest, canopies are brought out to cool things off. The famous La Campana coffee and pastry shop, founded in 1885, is at the very end of Sierpes (corner of Martín Villa).

### Capilla de San José★

Ⓘ *Open 8am-12.30pm and 7-8.30pm; Sat, Sun and public hols, 9am-1pm and 6.30-8.30pm. No visits during services.* ☎ 954 22 31 42/32 42.

This chapel, a masterpiece of Sevillian Baroque, dates from the end of the 17C. Its 18C façade and belfry with bright blue azulejos can be seen from the corner of calle Sierpes and calle Jovellanos. St Joseph with the Infant Christ in his arms is on the portal. The exuberance of the Baroque decoration in the small interior is a surprise, particularly at the apsidal end. The large wooden **altarpiece** in the presbytery depicting

*Calle Sierpes*

G. Bludzin / MICHELIN

angels, saints and God the Father, is an ornamental outcry. The image of St Joseph in the centre is venerated here.

▷ *At the end of calle Sierpes, take calle Cuna, which runs parallel to it, to the east.*

The most impressive building along this street is the magnificent **Palacio de la Condesa de Lebrija**★ (👁 *see description under Visit*).

▷ *Continue along calle Cuna to plaza del Salvador.*

## Plaza del Salvador
The huge parish church of El Salvador looks over this large square, one of the most popular places for an afternoon drink and lively socialising, especially on Sundays.

### Iglesia del Salvador★
🕐*Open 9-10am and 6.30-9pm.* ☎ *954 21 16 79.*
This church, rising majestically on one side of the square, replaced the former main mosque, demolished in 1671. Construction lasted until 1712, to plans by José Granados; the cupolas were designed by Leonardo de Figueroa. The elegant façade of attractive pink brick and stone, is a fine example of the ornamental Baroque style. A sensation of vastness pervades the interior. There are three short aisles. Note the high lanterned cupola above the transept.
Some of the city's most notable **Baroque retables**★★ (all from the 18C) are inside. The one in the chancel, dedicated to the Transfiguration of the Lord, is the work of Cayetano Acosta. It covers the entire wall with unrestrained decoration.
The frontispiece of the **Capilla del Sagrario**, the sacrarium chapel which opens onto the left transept, takes the form of a gigantic retable. This is also the work of Cayetano Acosta, dedicated to the exaltation of the Sacred Host; it displays the same exuberance as the main altarpiece. Inside, the most interesting object is the 17C **Christ of the Passion**, by Martínez Montañés. Part of an opulent silver altarpiece, it conveys an image of serene suffering on the face of Christ. Another fine retable, by José Maestre, with a shrine dedicated to the Virgin Mary, is in the right transept.
The chapel to the right displays the 17C **Crucificado del Amor**, by Juan de Mesa, a moving interpretation of the suffering and solitude of Jesus on the Cross.

# From Plaza del Duque de la Victoria to Alameda de Hercules ⑦

**Plaza del Duque de la Victoria** is the commercial heart of this part of the city with several department stores and numerous smaller shops.
The church of the former Colegio de San Hermenegildo (1616-20) in nearby **plaza de la Concordia**, with a fine oval cupola, is a municipal exhibition centre.

▷ *Walk through plaza de Gavidia, with its statue of Daoíz, then take calle Cardenal Spínola, which leads into plaza de San Lorenzo.*

## Templo de Nuestro Padre Jesús del Gran Poder
🕐 *Open 8am-1.30pm and 6-9pm (Fri, 7.30am-10pm).* ☎ *954 91 56 72.*
This modern church (1965) in the Plaza de San Lorenzo houses the magnificent statue of **Jesus of Great Power**★ (1620). Juan de Mesa's masterpiece is housed in a shrine surrounded by red carnations, where the devout leave offerings. The slightly inclined face of Jesus realistically reflects His great fatigue and profound sadness. The 13C parish church alongside was modified in the 17C.
Follow calle Santa Clara, past the Santa Clara convent of an enclosed order of nuns (⊶*not open to visitors*). Take calle Lumbreras. Past the junction with calle Becas, turn

around to admire the **Torre de Don Fadrique**, all that remains of a palace. This battlemented tower, built in the 13C, shows both Romanesque and Gothic influence.

▶ *Continue along calle Lumbreras as far as Alameda de Hércules.*

### Alameda de Hércules
This boulevard was constructed in the 16C. Atop two 18C columns at the north end are lions bearing coats of arms; the columns at the south end are Roman, crowned by statues of Hercules and Caesar. A lively **flea market** is held Sunday mornings.

## Visit

## North of the Cathedral

### Museo de Bellas Artes★★★
*Entrance via the plaza del Museo.* ◷ *Open Wed-Sat, 9am-8.15pm; Tue, 2.30-8.15pm; Sun and public hols, 9am-2.15pm.* ◷ *Closed Mon, 2 and 6 Jan, 28 Feb, 13 and 14 Apr, 1 and 30 May, 15 Jun, 15 Aug, 12 Oct, 1 Nov, and 6, 8 and 25 Dec.* ⊚ *€1.50 (no charge for citizens of the European Union).* ☎ *954 2207 90.*
This excellent art gallery contains one of the largest collections of Spanish paintings from the Golden Age. It is in the former Convento de la Merced (17C), designed by Juan de Oviedo ; the Baroque doorway was added in the 18C. The museum is built around three delightful patios and a magnificent staircase, covered by a cupola decorated with Mannerist stucco designs.
The gallery displays significant works from the Middle Ages to the 20C.

### Room V★★★
*Ground floor.* This is undoubtedly the star attraction. The church, its walls decorated with paintings by the 18C artist Domingo Martínez, provides a stunning backdrop to an outstanding collection of work by Murillo and one of Zurbarán's masterpieces, *The Apotheosis of St Thomas Aquinas* (*in the nave*).
**Murillo** (1617-82), a master of both the pictorial technique and the use of light in his canvases, is the great painter of religious subjects and children. His characters, always very human, exude tenderness and gentleness in a world which avoids drama and excess. His canvases can be found in the transept and in the apse, where his monumental *Immaculate Conception*, with its energetic movement, holds pride of place. Around it are notable paintings of saints: *Santa Rufina* and *Santa Justa*, who are clutching the Giralda, and *San Leandro* and *San Buenaventura*. In the right transept, a kindly *Virgin of the Cloth* is particularly interesting (the child seems to move towards you). Note also *St Francis Embracing Christ on the Cross* and another Immaculate Conception, also known as *La Niña* (*The Child*). On the left-hand side, *St Anthony and Child*, *Dolorosa* and *St Felix of Cantalicio and Child* are all worth a closer look.

### Room X★★
*Upper floor.* This room is dedicated to works by **Francisco de Zurbarán** (1598-1664). This artist had a particular skill for

*The former church, dominated by Murillo's Immaculate Conception*

B. Kaufmann / MICHELIN

painting the shades of white of monks' habits and the pure cloth of Christ, as in the fine *Christ on the Cross*, in which the body of Christ, painted against a dark background, appears as if sculpted in relief. Zurbarán's compositions are simple and peaceful. A lack of correct perspective is seen in *St Hugh and Carthusian Monks at Table* which is otherwise quite outstanding. His preoccupation with the treatment of cloth, seen in his depiction of the Fathers of the Church in *The Apotheosis of St Thomas Aquinas*, is also evident in the splendid velvet brocade in *San Ambrosio*. Apart from his saints, his *Virgin of the Caves* and *San Bruno's Visit to Urbano II* are interesting. Sculptures in the same room include *St Dominic* by Martínez Montañés. Note the splendid *artesonado* ceiling in the inner room.

### Other rooms

**Room I** displays interesting medieval works. **Room II**, once the refectory, is dedicated to Renaissance art, in particular a fine sculpture of *St Jerome* by Pietro Torrigiani, a contemporary of Michelangelo. Other works of note include Alejo Fernández's *Annunciation*, with Flemish and Italian influence clearly evident, a painting by El Greco of his son *Jorge Manuel*, and a diptych of *The Annunciation and Visitation* by Coffermans. Two magnificent portraits of *A Lady and a Gentleman* by Pedro Pacheco are the highlights in **Room III**.

**Upper floor: Room VI** displays a fine collection of richly decorated female saints (anonymous, some by followers of Zurbarán) and two male saints. **Room VII** contains more works by Murillo and his disciples while **Room VIII** is devoted to the other great Baroque artist Valdés Leal, a more expressive and dramatic painter than Murillo. European Baroque is represented in **Room IX** by, among others, Ribera's powerful *St James the Apostle*, canvases by Brueghel and the supreme *Portrait of a Lady* by Cornelis de Vos. **Room XI**, devoted to 18C art, is enlivened by Goya's *Portrait of Canon José Duato*, and several works by Lucas Valdés. The following two rooms (**XII** and **XIII**) display 19C art, in particular superb portraits by Esquivel, while the final room (**XIV**) shows 20C canvases by Vázquez Díaz and Zuloaga, among others.

### Casa de Pilatos★★

🕐 *Open 9am-6pm (mid-Mar to mid-Sep, 9am-7pm).* ✎ *€8: ground floor: €5.* ☎ *954 22 52 98.*

The palace is one of Sevilla's most famous monuments. It is on the pleasant plaza de Pilatos to which it has lent its name. The statue in the square is of Zurbarán.

*Detail, Casa de Pilatos*

G. Bludzin / MICHELIN

Construction began at the end of the 15C. However, it was Don Fadrique, the first Marquess of Tarifa, who was responsible for most of the palace visible today. It is said that he took his inspiration from Pontius Pilate's house in Jerusalem, hence the name of the palace. It is a mixture of Mudéjar, Renaissance and Flamboyant Gothic styles, although the Mudéjar style predominates.

The delightful **patio** recalls an elegant Moorish palace with its finely moulded stuc-cowork and magnificent 16C lustre **azulejos**★★. Note the unequal arches and the different motifs of the *azulejo* panels. The fountain was carved in Genoa in the 16C. Statues in the palace include **Athena**, a 5C BC Greek original; the others are of Roman origin. Rounded niches in the walls hold superb busts of Roman emperors. The rooms around the patio have fine *artesonado* ceilings, panels of *azulejos*, sculpted plaster-work, groined vaulting and the palaeo-Christian sculpture of the Good Shepherd in the chapel, the oldest part of the house. The gardens can also be visited.

The sumptuous *azulejo*-adorned **staircase**★★ leading up from a corner of the patio has a remarkable half-orange **wooden dome**★.

On the upper floor, frescoes from the 16C represent characters from Antiquity. Several rooms have interesting ceilings, particularly one painted by Francisco Pacheco in 1603 illustrating the Apotheosis of Hercules.

A visit to the nearby **Convento de San Leandro** is particularly recommended. Although access to the church is difficult, it is still worth a visit to buy the convent's famous *yemas*, delicious sweets made with egg yolk and sugar.

## Convento de Santa Paula★

🕐 *Open Tue-Sun, 10am-1pm and 3.30-6.30pm.* 🕐 *Closed public hols and for certain religious ceremonies.* 🎟 *€2.* ☎ *954 53 63 30.*

This historic convent of an order of enclosed nuns, founded at the end of the 15C, with an elegant and lofty 17C belfry, is one of the finest in Sevilla. The Hieronymite nuns prepare tasty cakes and jams.

### Church★

*Entrance through the left-hand door with the azulejo depicting St Paula.* Note the inter-esting atrium and the fine **portal**★, worked on by Nicola Pisano and completed in 1504. The portal is made of brick with alternating twin-coloured rows and is profusely adorned with ceramics. In spite of the evident mixture of styles – Mudéjar in the use of brick, Gothic in the arches, and Renaissance in the medallions and cresting – the effect is of perfect cohesion and harmony. The escutcheon on the tympanum

*Presbytery vault, Iglesia del Convento de Santa Paula*

is of the Catholic Monarchs. The central medallion, attributed to Luca della Robbia, represents the Birth of Jesus.

The **interior**★, a single nave topped by a 17C a*rtesonado* ceiling, comprises a presbytery with Gothic vaults totally covered with delightful polychrome frescoes. Two niches on either side of the high altar contain the tombs of the Marquess and Marchioness of Montemayor, the benefactors of this church. The brother of the Marchioness is laid to rest in a separate niche. The main altarpiece dates from the beginning of the 18C, though it retains the image of St Paula, in the centre, from an earlier retable. Note the movement of the two lamp-bearing angels. Two altars in the nave, opposite each other, are dedicated to John the Evangelist and John the Baptist. Two finely carved sculptures are the work of Martínez Montañés. A Gothic Christ can also be seen in a large window in the Epistle nave. The enclosed choir is separated from the rest of the church by an iron grille.

### Museum★

(*Entrance at n° 11 on the plaza*). The museum is in several tall outbuildings. Two have fine *artesonado* ceilings. The museum contains objects of great value, including canvases by **Ribera** (*St Jerome* and *The Adoration of the Shepherds*), two works by Pedro de Mena (*Our Lady of Sorrows* and *Ecce Homo*), an Immaculate Conception by Alonso Cano, and a charming 17C crib with many figurines.

## Palacio de la Condesa de Lebrija★

🕐 *Open Mon-Fri, 10.30am-1.30pm and 4.30-7.30pm (8pm, 20 Apr-Sep), Sat, 10am-2pm.* 🕐 *Closed Sun.* ⊛ *€4 (€7 for both floors).* ☎ *954 22 78 02.*

This private residence provides an opportunity to visit a palace with a typically Sevillian layout, comprising a hallway, central patio and interior garden. inside, a pleasant surprise awaits: a floor that appears to be completely covered with Roman **mosaics**★ from nearby Itálica (📖 *see description under Excursions*). The patio floor depicting mythological scenes is particularly fine, as is the octagonal room with its volutes and large vases. The attractive patio also has elegant foiled arches, Moorish-influenced panelling and *alfiz* rectangular moulding, a colourful plinth of Sevillian *azulejos* and showcases displaying archaeological remains. The **staircase**★, rich in ceramic tiles, has a mahogany banister, marble steps and an outstanding Mudéjar marquetry ceiling, which originally graced a palace in Marchena.

The rooms and galleries on the upper floor are embellished with a mix of Renaissance, Baroque and romantic decorative features.

## Iglesia de la Magdalena

The church was built in the late 17C and early 18C according to designs by Leonardo de Figueroa. It is possible to discern the layout of the church from the exterior: aisles, transept and elegant dome ornamented with *azulejos*.

The **interior**★ contains a number of treasures. The ceiling paintings are the work of Lucas Valdés. A lanterned cupola rises majestically above the transept, while the exuberant Baroque altarpiece in the chancel dates from the early 18C; the paintings on the vaults illustrate allegories of saints. The **Capilla del Cristo del Calvario** (*to the right of the presbytery*) takes its name from *The Exposed Christ*, an 18C work by Francisco Ocampo. In the Epistle nave are the fine **high-relief of the Assumption** supported by four small angels, by Juan de Mesa (1619), and the Sacramental and Quinta Angustia chapels. The former contains two canvases by **Zurbarán**: *St Dominic in Soria* and *The Miraculous Healing of the Beatified Reginald of Orleans*. The **Capilla de la Quinta Angustia**★ is situated in the vestibule of the main entrance doorway. The magnificent sculpture at the altar, depicting a highly moving Deposition, is attributed to the followers of Pedro Roldán. Look up to admire the three Moorish-influenced cupolas. Ten canvases of saints by Valdés Leal hang on the walls of the chapel.

In the left transept, next to the door, stands a 16C sculpture of the **Virgin of the Fever**, an elegant and maternal Virgin with the Infant Christ in her arms.

## Around the Cathedral

### Hospital de la Caridad

🕐 *Open 9am-1.30pm and 3.30-7.30pm; Sun and public hols, 9am-1pm.* 🕐 *Closed on certain public hols.* 🎫 *€5.* ☎ *954 22 32 32.*

Enter the church via the hospital, with its harmonious double patio adorned with panels of *azulejos* representing scenes from the Old and New Testaments.

### Church★★

The single-nave Baroque church contains artistic gems commissioned by Mañara from Sevilla's leading artists of the period. The pictorial representations of Death and Charity would have created an example of the path that the brothers of Charity were expected to follow.

Two **paintings**★★ by **Valdés Leal** beneath the chancel tribune are quite staggering in their severity. In **Finis Gloriae Mundi**, Valdés Leal depicts with macabre realism a dead and half decomposed bishop and knight; the scales held in the hand of Christ refer to the moment of judgement. **In Ictu Oculi** (In the Blink of an Eye) is an allegory of death in which the skeleton has earthly symbols at its feet (a globe, a crown, books etc). An *Exaltation of the Cross*, by the same artist, can be seen above the choir.

In the nave, **Murillo** has illustrated the theme of Charity through several **works**★. The sense of submission to one's fellow man is exalted in the fine **St Isabel of Hungary Curing the Lepers**, and in **St John of God Carrying a Sick Man On His Shoulder**, in which the artist demonstrates his mastery of *chiaroscuro*. Two paintings of children on the side altars are also by Murillo. Another side altar has a 17C bleeding Christ casting a distressed gaze toward the sky, by Pedro Roldán. The two horizontal paintings facing each other in the transept are *The Miracle of the Loaves and Fishes* (representing the gift of food) and **Moses Smiting Water from the Rock** (representing the gift of water). The canvases in the dome of the transept are by Valdés Leal: in each echinus is an angel bearing the instruments of the Passion; the Evangelists are depicted in the pendentives. Note also the fine lamp-bearing angels.

At the main altar, a splendid Baroque altarpiece by Pedro Roldán has at its centre a fine sculptural group representing the **Holy Burial of Christ**★★ in which the artist has interpreted with great beauty the pain in the contained emotion of the faces.

### Iglesia de Santa María la Blanca★

This former synagogue was transformed into a church in the 14C; the simple Gothic portal is from this period, but the façade and the **interior**★ are 17C reconstructions. Three aisles are separated by semicircular arches resting on pink marble columns. The barrel vaults adorned with lunettes and the dome over the transept are completely covered with delightful plasterwork decoration. Baroque exuberance is balanced by the lightness of the columns, creating an effect which is both attractive and harmonious. The Evangelist nave contains a *Last Supper*, attributed to Murillo, which is surprising in its dramatic use of light, in keeping with the pure tenebrist style.

## South of the Cathedral

### Museo Arqueológico de Sevilla★

🕐 *Open Tue, 2.30-8.30pm; Wed-Sat, 9am-8.30pm; Sun, 9am-2.30pm.* 🕐 *Closed Mon and public hols.* 🎫 *€1.50 (no charge for citizens of the European Union).* ☎ *954 23 24 01.*

The archaeological museum, in a Renaissance pavilion in plaza de América, in Parque María Luisa, contains an interesting collection of prehistoric and Roman objects.

The prehistoric collection, on the ground floor, includes items discovered at archaeological excavations in the province. The exhibits in **Room VI** are particularly exciting, comprising the 7C-6C BC **El Carambolo treasure**★, a superb collection of gold jewellery of Phoenician inspiration with a surprisingly modern design, and the Goddess Astarte (8C BC), a small bronze statue bearing an inscription said to be the oldest script found on the Iberian peninsula.

The first floor is dedicated exclusively to the **Roman collection**★ (Rooms XII to XXV), largely discovered at Itálica (👁 *see Excursions*). Exhibits include magnificent sculptures and mosaics which provide an insight into the artistic development of the Romans in the region. Other displays show objects which re-create aspects of Roman civilisation.

Other items of interest include a Mercury with a large mosaic at his feet (Room XIV); an unusual collection of marble plaques with footprint markings offered at games ceremonies (Room XVI); a Venus in Room XVII; fine sculptures of Diana in Room XIX; and bronze plaques

> ### Hispano-Roman Ceramics
>
> The export of agricultural products to the Italian peninsula encouraged the development of the ceramics in Baetica, especially amphorae, of a type now known as Dressel 20. Over 70 kilns have been discovered in the lower Guadalquivir Valley.
>
> Other workshops, sited outside of towns to reduce the risk of fire, produced a widely used domestic pottery known as *sigillata hispanica*. Typical pieces were bright red in colour and decorated with plant or animal motifs.

from the Roman Lex Irnitana in the annexe. The oval room (Room XX) contains an impressive statue of Trajan, while Room XXV, dedicated to funerary art, has a variety of sarcophagi, columbaria and household objects.

### Museo de las Artes y Costumbres Populares

🕐 *Open Tue, 3-8pm; Wed-Sat, 9am-8pm; Sun and public hols, 9am-2.30pm.* 🕐 *Closed Mon.* ⊚ *€1.50 (no charge for citizens of the European Union).* ☎ *954 23 25 76/55 40.*
The Museum of Popular Art and Traditions, in the Mudéjar pavilion of María Luisa park, displays costumes worn for *romerías* and *fiestas*, models of workshops, musical instruments, farming tools, and a collection of posters for the April Fair.

# Isla de la Cartuja

### Isla Mágica★

🕐*Open daily 30 Mar to mid-Sep 4 (except for special occasions) and on a limited schedule in Oct and Nov. Open daily late Jun to mid-Sep, 11am-11pm (midnight on some days). Consult the Web site for opening times outside of this period. Prices vary according to season, check the Web site to confirm.* ⊚*Adults €25; children between 5 and 12 and over-60s €17.50.* ☎ *902 161716; www.islamagica.es.*
Isla Mágica (Magic Isle) theme park, spread over 40ha/99 acres on the island of La Cartuja, takes visitors on a journey back to the century of the Discoveries. The park's eight areas are: Sevilla, the Gateway to the Indies; Quetzal, the Fury of the Gods; The Balcony of Andalucía; The Gateway to America; Amazonia; The Pirates' Den; The Fountain of Youth; and El Dorado. Facilities and attractions include rides, street entertainers and souvenir shops, and a good selection of bars and restaurants.

### The following are some of the park's attractions:

- **Quetzal, the Fury of the Gods** – An exciting journey to the Mayan world. Ride a plumed serpent across Central America to escape the fury of the gods.
- **The Balcony of Andalucía** – An enjoyable stroll through this miniature world highlighting important monuments and geographical features of the region.
- **Anaconda** – A breathtaking water ride to satisfy the most intrepid of sailors.
- **Iguaçu** – These impressive waterfalls are bound to get your nerves tingling as you are propelled into a lagoon at speeds of over 50kph/32mph.
- **The Jaguar** – For an extra rush of adrenaline try this huge roller coaster with its vertigo-inducing descents that reach speeds of up to 85kph/53mph.
- **The Fountain of Youth** – This enchanting world of ponds and streams delights young children with the Tell-Tale Toad and the story-telling Tadpoles.

- **The Rapids of the Orinoco** – Challenge the river on an inflatable raft.
- **The House of Superstition** – A state-of-the-art film projected onto a gigantic spherical screen. Experience a whole new world of sensations.

## La Cartuja: Centro Andaluz de Arte Contemporáneo

🕐 *Open 21 Apr-Sep, Tue-Sat, 10am (11am Sat) to 9pm, Sun, 10am-3pm; Oct-Apr 20, Tue-Fri, 10am-8pm, Sat, 11am-8pm, Sun, 10am-3pm. Last admission 30min before closing.* 🕐 *Closed Mon and public hols.* 🎟 *€3 (no charge Tue for citizens of the European Union).* ☎ *955 03 70 70. Buses C-1 and C-2.*

The Andalusian Centre for Contemporary Art, in the former monastery of La Cartuja, is part of an unusual complex with a complicated history. The monastery was founded at the end of the 14C in honour of an apparition of the Virgin Mary in this district. It was visited by royalty and such notable figures as Columbus, who prepared his second journey of discovery here. The French converted it into a barracks during the Napoleonic invasion and it was later acquired by Charles Pickman, who set up a ceramics factory, which closed in 1982. The chimneys and kilns are still visible.

### Monastic buildings★

These mainly date from the 15C, 16C and 17C. Some have managed to preserve their original *azulejos*. The church is of particular interest with its delightful *azulejo* rosette, a sacristy with Baroque plasterwork and charming Mudéjar brick cloisters supported by slender marble columns. The monks' chapter house, containing a number of interesting tombs, and the long refectory with a superb 17C *artesonado* ceiling, are also well worth a visit.

### Museum

The museum's collection mainly comprises early-20C works by major names such as Miró and Chillida, and by young Andalusian contemporary artists.

## Excursions

### Itálica★

*9km/5.5mi NW along A 66 - E 803. Bear left after Santiponce.* 🕐 *Open Apr-Sep, Tue-Sat, 8.30am-8.30pm, Sun, 9am-3pm; Oct-Mar, Tue-Sat, 9am-5.30pm, Sun, 10am-4pm.* 🕐 *Closed Mon.* 🎟 *€1.50 (no charge for European Union citizens).* ☎ *955 99 73 76/65 83.*

The remains of Roman Itálica, founded by Scipio Africanus in 206 BC, stand on a cypress-shaded hill above the Guadalquivir Plain. Its golden age was in the 2C AD. Emperors **Trajan** (AD 53-117) and **Hadrian** (AD 76-138) were born here. Hadrian granted the title of colony, transforming Itálica into a monumental city. Its decline began under the Late Empire.

The excavated area is a district created under Hadrian, with streets laid out according to an orthogonal plan and lined by public buildings and luxurious private houses. Original **mosaics** of Neptune, birds, and planetary divinities have been preserved.

### Amphitheatre

This elliptical amphitheatre, one of the largest in the Roman Empire with a capacity for 25 000, is relatively well preserved. Sections of tiered seating and the pits beneath the arena remain.

The town of **Santiponce** stands on the oldest part of Itálica. The former Roman theatre can be seen at its centre.

### Bollullos de la Mitación

*18km/11mi west along A 49 towards Huelva to exit 11.*

### Iglesia de San Martín

🕐 *Open Mon-Sat, 7-9pm; Sun and public hols, 11am-noon and 5-7pm (for religious services).*

Plaza de Cuatrovitas is fronted by the town hall and the Church of St Martin, an 18C Baroque construction. The brick tower has detailed *azulejo* decoration. Inside, note the **retable** with four paintings by Zurbarán.

### Santuario de Cuatrovitas

*Head toward Aznalcázar. After 4km/2.5mi, bear left just after a pine grove, then go 2km/1.2mi along an unmetalled road.* 🕐 *Open Sat-Sun and public hols, 10am-1pm and 5-7pm (otherwise, contact the church warden in the house opposite).*

The drive to this simple sanctuary, one of few rural mosques still standing, is particularly pleasant. Built during the Almohad period, its most striking features are a brick **tower** and foliated horseshoe arch decoration. The interior contains a 16C ceramic altar frontispiece representing the Virgin and Child and the Four Evangelists.

### Alcalá de Guadaira

*20km/12mi SE along A 92. Park next to the Iglesia de Santiago.*

### Iglesia de Santiago

The Church of St James was built in the 15C and 16C. Elegant ceramic decoration covers the upper sections and the spire of the lofty bell tower. The presbytery is crowned with an unusual trumpet-shaped and coffered vault.

### Castle

Climb the stepped ramps next to the church. The remains of this important Almohad fortress stand atop a hill, dominating the town and rolling landscape. The walls and towers of the original outer enclosure can still be seen. This pleasant site is a leisure area with a children's park. The 14C-16C **Ermita de Nuestra Señora del Aguila**, a chapel with a solid brick tower topped by merlons, stands at its centre. Note the remains of a medieval fresco inside the chapel (*to the right of the presbytery*).

# SIERRA NEVADA★★

It surprises many visitors to find Europe's second-highest mountain range so far south. Rising above Granada, the Sierra Nevada's highest peaks are perpetually snow-capped. The many attractions include a superb ski resort and magnificent mountain landscapes characterised by steep valleys and breathtaking ravines. Fourteen (one-fifth) of the Sierra Nevada's peaks are over 3 000m/9 840ft high. The range covers 170 000ha/420 070 acres (90 000ha/222 390 acres of which are part of a national park, Parque Nacional de Sierra Nevada). Snow and ice have sculpted this this young mountain chain into a twisted profile. The highest peaks, Mulhacén (3 482m/11 424ft), Veleta (3 394m/11 132ft) and Alcazaba (3 371m/11 057ft) are all in the western part of the range.

▸ **Orient Yourself:** The Sierra Nevada range is SE of Granada, in a landscape crossed by scenic roads and delightful hiking routes.

🅿 **Parking:** Park in Pradollano, and continue by bus (*see below*).

🚡 **Don't Miss:** Unbelievable skiing and high mountain scenery.

🕐 **Organizing Your Time:** Take several days to ski.

**Especially for Kids:** The Sierra is tops for kids who love the outdoors.

🖐 **Also See:** GRANADA, GUADIX and Las ALPUJARRAS.

## Address Book

### BEFORE SETTING OUT

**Centro de Visitantes del Dornajo** – *Km 23, Sierra Nevada road.* ○ *Open in summer, 9am-2.30pm and 4.30-7pm; otherwise, 9am-2pm and 4.30-6pm.* ☎ *958 34 06 25.* The El Dornajo centre is an ideal starting-point, with its wide range of information on the park (models, exhibitions etc), an excellent bookshop and the introduction it provides to the region's gastronomy and arts and crafts. The centre also organises activities, including high-mountain hikes and bicycle hire.

**Punto de información del Puerto de la Ragua** – *Puerto de la Ragua road* – ☎ *958 76 02 31. www.laragua.net*

**Punto de Información del Parque Nacional de Sierra Nevada** – *In Pampaneira (plaza de la Libertad* – ☎ *958 76 31 27).* The **Nevadensis** agency (☎ 958 76 31 27) here also organises activities in the Sierra Nevada and Alpujarras.

**Mountaineering** – *Federación Andaluza de Montañismo – camino de Ronda,* *101 (edificio Atalaya), Granada* – ☎ *958 29 13 40 – www.fedamon.com*

### ACCESS

**By car** – The fastest route from Granada is along the A 395. In Pradollano visitors must leave their vehicles in the underground car park. A more attractive alternative is to combine the two suggested driving itineraries (⌖ *see Driving Tours*).

**By bus** – The BONAL company (☎ 958 27 31 00) operates several daily services from Granada to Pradollano, from the stop next to the Palacio de Congresos.

### WHERE TO STAY

◔◔◔ **Hotel Kenia Nevada** – *Virgen de las Nieves, 6* - ☎ *958 48 09 11 - www.kenianevada.com – 67 rooms.* An Alpine-style hotel with plenty of exposed stone and wood, and cosy rooms, as well as a pool. They organise skiing, hiking, hang-gliding, canyoning, and more.

## When to visit?

At any time! Winter options include downhill skiing, various excursions, and treks to some of the highest snow-capped peaks. In summer, hiking and horse riding are popular. Snow can start to fall in October and even into June; despite this, the Sierra Nevada is renowned for glorious sunny days for two-thirds of the year, when sun, snow and the blue sky combine to create a scene of almost unparalleled beauty.

# Hiking routes

Head for the visitor centre to obtain information on marked walks and the length of time needed. The most popular departure points are: the village of Güejar-Sierra, the El Dornajo visitor centre and the **Albergue Universitario** (University Hostal). The most interesting routes are the climb to the Laguna de las Yeguas lagoon and the ascents of Pico Veleta and Mulhacén.

## The "Ice Vendors"

The name *neveros* was given to those men who supplied ice to the city of Granada in bygone days. These fearless souls would climb up to the snow-capped peaks of the Sierra Nevada in groups of about ten men and with the help of mules and donkeys would load up and transport ice to the hospitals, shops and bars in the city. This activity was so important that even in the 18C operating licences existed and regulations were already in place. The trade in ice collapsed around 1920 with the establishment of the first ice factories.

## Sierra Nevada ski resort★★

The resort was built in 1964 and held a World Cup downhill race in 1977, but struggled financially. The situation improved as protective measures for the Sierra Nevada were put into place. Investments made for the 1996 World Skiing Championships transformed the resort. It has 84km/43.7mi of skiable trails, 80 runs and over 20 lifts, and offers weekend night skiing. A full range of apartment and hotel accommodation is available in Pradollano.

### Mulhacén

According to legend, the name of the highest peak on mainland Spain originates from a story which recounts that the king of Granada, Muley-Hacén, the father of Boabdil, is buried here. The king fell in love with a beautiful Christian maiden by the name of Zoraida, who, after the king's death in Mondújar Castle, had him buried on the highest peak of the Sierra Nevada to hide him from his enemies.

## Driving Tours

### From Granada to El Dornajo★★

*Possible only in summer – 1hr*
Leave Granada on the old mountain road (*carretera de la Sierra*). After 8km/5mi turn towards Pinos Genil. The road skirts the Canales Reservoir (*embalse*) to reach **Güejar-Sierra**. After Maitena, the road crosses and then follows the Genil, twisting sharply up to the Hotel del Duque, now a seminary, and the El Dornajo visitor centre.

### From El Dornajo to the Borreguiles crossroads ★★

From the El Dornajo Visitor Centre take the left fork to climb to the Collado de las Sabinas pass, a steep ascent punctuated with sharp bends. The view is of native pines, and of the Genil Valley. Continue to Pradollano, and the Borreguiles crossroads.

## Excursions

### Valle del Lecrín★

*Head S from Granada along the A 44-E 902, then turn off the main road in Dúrcal.* The little-known Lecrín Valley is a delight of orange groves and hillside villages.

### Dúrcal

This village of Moorish origin has a charming main square, the **plaza de España**.

### Nigüelas

Nigüelas is one of the prettiest settlements. The town hall is in the 16C Palacio de los Zayas. In the 14C **Las Laerillas oil mill** ★, presses, instruments, olive bins and, in particular, two large mills, can be seen. One is known as the *molino de sangre* (blood mill), because it was animal-powered (the other was hydraulically operated). ○ *Visits by prior arrangement.* ☎ *958 77 76 07 (town hall).*

### Mondújar

The Mudéjar-style church has an impressive tower. The neighbouring village of Lecrín (Arabic for "happiness") has given its name to the valley.
The road continues along the Torrente river valley, skirting Murchas, Restábal, **Melegís** and **Saleres**. The churches in Melegís and Saleres have managed to preserve Mudéjar *azulejos* on their towers.

# Parque Natural de la
# SIERRA NORTE DE SEVILLA

The park covers 164 840ha/407 320 acres of outstanding natural beauty in the Sierra Morena north of Sevilla. Along its rivers – the Viar, Huéznar and Retortillo – lush vegetation includes cork oak, horse chestnut, elm, holm oak and hazel. Fauna include wild boar, harrier eagles and tawny vultures

- ▷ **Orient Yourself:** The park is in the north of Sevilla province.
- ◷ **Organizing Your Time:** Allow a day for one of the drives through the park.
- ⚭ **Also See:** SEVILLA, CARMONA and Parque Natural SIERRA DE ARACENA Y PICOS DE AROCHE.

## Driving Tour

### From Lora del Río to Guadalcanal *90km/56mi – allow one day*

#### Lora del Río
*Situated outside the park.* This irregularly shaped town is situated on the Guadalquivir, at the base of the Sierra Morena foothills. Lora is peaceful and steeped in tradition. Its neatly maintained streets and buildings lend it a slightly solemn air.
Local delicacies include snails (*caracoles*), *sopeaos* (a variant of gazpacho), and *gachas con coscurros*, a flour-based pureé sprinkled with breadcrumbs fried in olive oil.

#### Iglesia de la Asunción
This 15C Mudéjar-Gothic church has undergone considerable restoration. Its 19C bell tower is one of the tallest in Sevilla province.

#### Ayuntamiento
The 18C Baroque town hall has a magnificent floral **façade**.

## Address Book

### SIGHTSEEING
The **Centro de Información del Parque** in Constantina has plans, maps and other documentation on activities in the park. ◷ *Open Jan-Mar and Oct-Dec, Fri-Sun and public hols 10am-2pm and 6-8pm; Apr-Sep, Fri-Sun and public hols 10am-2pm and 4-6pm. Also open Thu, 10am-2pm, Jan-15 Jun and 15 Oct-Dec.* ☎ 955 88 15 97.

### WHERE TO STAY
⊜ **San Blas** – *Miraflores, 4 – Constantina* – ☎ *955 88 00 77 - www.fp-hoteles.com – 15 rooms.* A country-style hotel with large, adequate rooms, and a small swimming pool on the terrace.
⊜⊜ **Posada del Moro** – *Paseo del Moro – Cazalla de la Sierra* – ☎ *954 88 48*

*58 - www.laposadadelmoro.com -* 🅿 ⌫ ⚭ *– 31 rooms.* A small, family-run hotel opposite Parque del Moro. The hotel also has a high-quality restaurant and a garden with swimming pool. Good value for money.
⊜⊜ **Las Navezuelas** – *Cazalla de la Sierra – On the A 432, 2km/1.2mi from the centre of Cazalla towards El Pedroso; then 0.5km/0.3mi on dirt track* – ☎ *954 88 47 64 - www.lasnavezuelas.com – 6 rooms, 2 suites, 3 apartments.* An attractive old olive oil mill from the 18C. The guest rooms are tastefully decorated, while the swimming pool offers a magnificent view of the Sierra Morena. A bucolic setting, where the only sound is the far-off bleating of sheep. A set dinner menu is available to guests.

### Casa de los Leones
This fine example of Baroque civil architecture has an impressive façade and an elegant patio.

### Casa de la Virgen
The doorway of this unusual late-18C palace is embellished with elegant marble columns.

### Santuario de Nuestra Señora de Setefilla
This handsome Mudéjar sanctuary, isolated in mountains outside Lora del Río, was rebuilt in the 17C. Its statue of the Virgin of Setefilla is venerated in a lively pilgrimage (*romería*) every 8 September.

## Constantina
*29km/18mi north along the A 455.* The town, surrounded by delightful forests and streams of crystal-clear water, is named for Roman emperor Constantine. Its centre is a mix of Moorish and distinctive 15C-17C noble edifices.

> ### Cep Mushrooms
> The area around Constantina is a paradise for mushroom-lovers. During the autumn, the town is inundated by visitors who come here to pick them or simply to enjoy them in one of Constantina's many bars and restaurants.

### Barrio de la Morería★
The Moorish quarter sits at the foot of the old fortress above Constantina. Steep, winding alleyways lined by whitewashed houses and connected by flights of steps preserve the enchantment and flavour of an Arab district. Two churches are worthy of note. The impressive **Iglesia de la Encarnación** is an elegant Mudéjar construction with handsome Plateresque façade. Outstanding stone decorative motifs on its portal (Puerta del Pardón) incude a delicate sculpture of the archangel Gabriel. The **Iglesia de Nuestra Señora de los Dolores** preserves notable Renaissance cloisters and an interesting Baroque retable at the high altar.

### Ermita de El Robledo
*5km/3mi NE of Constantina along the SE 156.* ○ *Open Mar-Sep, 9am-9pm; Oct-Feb, 10am-7pm.* ☎ *955 95 41 14.*
This isolated white Mudéjar chapel houses a statue of the Virgin of the Oak Wood.

## El Pedroso
*18km/11mi west of Constantina along the A 452.* El Pedroso, in a landscape of outstanding beauty, has two impressive religious buildings: the church of Nuestra Señora de la Consolación and the Ermita de La Virgen del Espino. The nearby hills of Monteagudo and La Lima offer **views** of the sierra.

## Cazalla de la Sierra
*17km/10.5mi north along the A 455.* This delightful town is hidden in the heart of the Sierra Morena amid holm and cork oak forests. The centre is characterised by picturesque streets fronted by attractive seigniorial houses with elegant stone façades. The town is renowned for its brandies.

### Plaza Mayor
This large square, the hub of Cazalla, is bordered by a singular array of 16C popular Andalusian architecture. Also note the fine Baroque façade of the the courts (*Juzgado*) and the 14C **Iglesia de Nuestra Señora de la Consolación**, its red-brick Mudéjar tower adorned with pointed and trefoil arch windows. The church interior is a mass of pillars, topped by Renaissance coffered vaults.

### Convento de San Francisco

The notable Baroque cloisters have slender columns supporting semicircular arches.

### Ruinas de la Cartuja

*3km/1.82mi north of Cazalla.* ☾ *Open 10am-2pm and 4-8pm.* ☾ *Closed 23-25 Dec.* ☞ *€3.* ☎ *954 88 45 16.*
The monumental ruins of the former 15C Carthusian monastery are in an attractive leafy woodland. The Mudéjar paintings in the cloisters are of particular note. The former monk-gatekeeper's lodge is now a small hotel.

### Alanís

*17km/10.5mi north of Cazalla along the A 432.* Alanís stands in a near-impregnable mountain area, at the foot of a medieval castle. The Casa de Doña Matilde Guitart has an elegant two-storey patio. The **Iglesia de Nuestra Señora de las Nieves**, a church originally Gothic, was rebuilt in neo-Classical style. The vault above the high altar is decorated with attractive frescoes. Exceptional Mudéjar **azulejos** are on view in the 16C Capilla de los Melgarejo.

### Guadalcanal

*11km/7mi northwest along the A 432.* This old fortified settlement retains interest-ing vestiges of its medieval walls. The Iglesia de la Asunción, a church built above a mosque, and the Ermita de Guaditoca, a chapel which hosts an important pilgrimage, are its most outstanding architectural features.

# TABERNAS

POPULATION 3 241

**Tabernas stands in the Almerian desert, in a near-lunar landscape of eroded hills, not unlike the American West. In the 1960s and 1970s, it provided the backdrop for a number of spaghetti westerns.** ▤ *Highway N-340, Km 364,* ☎ *950 52 50 30.*

▶ **Orient Yourself:** Tabernas is on the plain between the Sierra de los Filabres (N) and Sierra Alhamilla (S), 29km/18mi N of Almería via the N-340a and A-92.
☾ **Organizing Your Time:** Allow a few hours in Tabernas if passing through.
▦ **Especially for Kids:** Oasys and Hollywood sets.
⚲ **Also See:** ALMERÍA (29km/18km S), Sierra de los FILABRES (N) and COSTA DE ALMERÍA (S and E)

## The Tabernas Desert

The town's location between two ranges of mountains produces the so-called "orographic shadow" phenomenon, which explains the sparse rainfall in the area. As a result, the vegetation and fauna found in this part of Andalucía are adapted to conditions of extreme aridity. In general, flora, such as the hardy everlasting or curry plant, is small in size, while the local fauna mainly consists of insects, toads, scorpions and hedgehogs.

Spain's American West

## Visit

Tabernas is crowned by the partially restored ruins of its fortress (*access via a track next to the sports centre*), best viewed from the A 340a to the east.

Like many of the religious buildings in the area, the parish church, on a pleasant shady square, is built of brick. It has two simple Renaissance portals.

### Oasys, Parque temático del desierto de Tabernas (Tabernas Desert Theme Park)

*5km/3mi SW on A 370-N340A; follow signposts.* ⓢ *Open 10am-9pm.* ☎ *950 36 52 36.*
This leisure complex with a biodiversity theme also includes the old Mini-Hollywood set where *A Fistful of Dollars* and *A Place Called Trinity* were filmed. As you walk the dusty streets lined by wooden buildings such as a saloon, a bank and a water tank, you'll be transported to another era against a backdrop of bare, rocky mountains. You can still see brawls and shoot-outs in the best traditions of the Wild West today. Other old film sets can also be seen along the A 370.

## Driving Tour

### From Tabernas to Los Molinos del Río Aguas

*41km/25.5mi. Head east along the A 370-N340A. Bear right after 17km/10.5mi.*

### Lucainrena de las Torres

This former mining town is on the eastern edge of the Sierra de la Alhamilla. Its main attractions are its white streets, 18C parish church, a square with a centenary tree, and, on the outskirts, old iron-smelting furnaces. The tavern-museum, the Mesón Museo, displays works by local artists and traditional farming implements, and offers regional cuisine.

> ### Local Arts and Crafts
>
> Sorbas still maintains its tradition of pottery-making. It is particularly famous for its red ceramic earthenware, which is mainly used for cooking, due to its resistance to heat. Workshops producing this pottery can still be visited in the lower section of the town.

▶ *Return to the A 370 and continue 9km/5.5mi farther.*

## Sorbas

Sorbas is an attractive town on a clay escarpment encircled by a meander in the River Aguas. The best view of its picturesque **setting**★ is from Los Molinos del Río Aguas. Its cliff-clinging houses have made Sorbas known as "Little Cuenca", after the town of Cuenca in the region of Castilla-La Mancha.

🅿 *Leave your car in plaza de la Constitución, in the centre of the town.*

### Plaza de la Constitución

This square, the hub of Sorbas, is fronted by the 16C Iglesia de Santa María, the town hall, the house of Francisco García Roca (both from the 19C), and the 18C Palace of the Duke of Alba, built for one of the duke's administrators. The town has several **miradors** overlooking the river and plain. The houses built above the ravine are particularly impressive.

### Paraje Natural de Karst en Yesos

*On the AL 8203 towards Los Molinos del Río Aguas. For information:* ☎ *950 36 45 63.*
This reserve of thousands of limestone caves, formed by erosion of gypsum, is a must for adventure-seekers. Torch, helmet, outer clothing and boots are all available on site. A tour led by specialist guides, involving climbs, descents and crawling on all fours, enables visitors to see how gypsum crystallises into spectacular formations.

### Molinos del Río Aguas

*5km/3mi southeast of Sorbas along the A 8203.* This district is named for the numerous flour mills (*molinos*) once found here. Past the village, the road climbs to offer attractive views of the valley.
Several foreign families settled here in the 1960s and 1970s to develop solar cooking, water purification, and organic farming for desertic areas.
🚶 Pleasant walks along marked paths (*maximum 2hr*) provide an opportunity to see Roman irrigation ditches, the remains of flour mills and local gypsum furnaces.

# TARIFA

POPULATION 15 118

Tarifa is the most southerly town on the Iberian Peninsula, on the **Straits of Gibraltar** just 13km/8mi from the North African coast. Converging Atlantic and Mediterranean air masses and unspoilt beaches nearby have made it one of Europe's most important windsurfing centres. This charming little town, popular with an alternative crowd, exudes tranquillity and well-being with its small squares and enchanting nooks and crannies. 🅸 *Paseo de la Alameda, 11380 Tarifa,* ☎ *956 68 09 93, turismo@aytotarifa.com*

▶ **Orient Yourself:** Tarifa is along the N 340-E 5, SW of Gibraltar
🕐 **Organizing Your Time:** Wander the old quarter, then watch whales in the straits.
👣 **Also See:** ALGECIRAS (including Gibraltar, 21km/13mi NE), and VEJER DE LA FRONTERA (50km/31mi NW).

*The port of Tarifa*

## Walking Tour

Enter the old quarter by the particularly impressive **Puerta de Jerez**.

### Castillo de Guzmán el Bueno

🕐 *Open 11am-2pm and 4-6pm.* 🕐 *Closed Sun-Mon.* 👓 *€2.* ☎ *956 68 46 89.*

**Abd ar-Rahman III**, first Moorish governor to adopt the title of Caliph, attached great importance to the control of the Straits of Gibraltar, which led him to capture the strongholds of Ceuta and Melilla. He started construction of Tarifa's fortress in 960. The castle visible today is the result of later modifications by both Moors and Christians. Access is via the 13C **Almohad wall** (*coracha*); to the right, note the **Torre de Guzmán el Bueno**, a 13C turret, from which the Christian commander Don Enrique de Guzmán is said to have thrown down his dagger to besieging Moorish troops to execute his captured son rather than hand over the castle. Access is through a 14C angled doorway. A 14C church, the Iglesia de Santa María, stands within the walls.

▸ *Leave the castle and walk along calle Guzmán el Bueno to Plaza Santa María.*

### Plaza Santa María

Alongside this small square are the **town hall** and the Museo Municipal. An attractive *azulejo*-decorated fountain stands in the centre.
*Follow calle de la Amargura to plaza del Viento.* The **views**★★ of Africa across the Straits from the Mirador del Estrecho are superb.

### A Berber Name

The origins of the name Tarifa date from the time of the Moorish invasions when the Berber general **Tarif ibn Malluk** is said to have landed here in July 710 with 400 men. This incursion, the first Moorish expedition to set foot on the Iberian Peninsula, has spawned a number of legends. The reasons behind the invasion would appear to lie in a dispute between the Visigothic king, **Roderick**, and the descendants of the former king **Witiza**. Seeing the weakness of the Visigoths, the Moors, "invited" by the Witiza faction, disregarded the pacts they had made with them and embarked upon the conquest of the whole peninsula.

## Address Book

### EXCURSIONS IN THE STRAITS OF GIBRALTAR

Reservations are necessary for **whale- and dolphin-watching by boat**★.
**Turmares Tarifa** – *Av. Alcalde Juan Nuñez, 3* – ☏ *956 68 07 41* - *www.turmares.com* - €*25/40* - ⊙ *Closed in Dec.* A boat for larger groups provides underwater viewing; a smaller, faster boat is for the more daring.
**Whale Watch** – *Av. de la Constitución, 6* - ☏ *956 627 013* - *www.whalewatchtar-ifa.net* - ⊙ *Closed Nov-Holy Week.* €*25/40.* This whale-protection group organises sightings of whales, dolphins and orcas, according to the season.

### WHERE TO EAT

⊝⊝ **Mesón Juan Luis** – *San Francisco, 15* – ☏ *956 68 12 65* – ⊙ *Closed Sun.* A small restaurant in an old building on a pedestrianised street. Everything is pork based, with a surprisingly large

selection. The Rincón de Juan on the same street has a small terrace.

### WHERE TO STAY

⊝⊝ **Aparthotel La Casa Amarilla** – *Sancho IV el Bravo, 9* – ☏ *956 68 19 93* – *www.lacasaamarilla.net* – *8 apartments/3 studios.* This is an old house in the centre, next to the Iglesia Mayor de San Mateo. Apartments are all different and tastefully decorated. The proprietors also own the nearby Café Central, which is particularly lively in the evening.
⊝⊝ **Hotel La Codorniz** – *6.5km/4mi northwest along the Cádiz road* – ☏ *956 68 47 44* – *www.lacodorniz.com* – *35 rooms.* This lovely compound re-creates a traditional Andalusian inn. Standard rooms have balconies, others are in garden bungalows. The country-style restaurant has a good wine cellar and specialises in seafood.

## Iglesia Mayor Parroquial de San Mateo Apóstol

The parish church of St Matthew the Apostle was built in the early 16C in Flamboy-ant Gothic style. The main façade, completed in the 18C, is Baroque, with a broken pediment and imposing Solomonic columns. In the surprisingly spacious interior, the central nave is crowned by a star vault, the side aisles by groin vaulting. A small funer-ary stone from the Visigothic period is at the entrance to the Capilla del Sagrario. In plaza de Oviedo, opposite the church, are numerous cafés and bars for a break.

## Iglesia de San Francisco

The Church of St Francis is on the plaza del Ángel. The Baroque **tower-façade**★ consists of a large Franciscan cordon on two columns with Corinthian capitals.
A small cove next to Tarifa's port is known as **Playa Chica** (small beach). On the other side of Isla de las Palomas is a spectacular beach, **Playa de los Lances**★. Opposite, atop Santa Catalina Hill, note the unusual building dating from the early 20C.

## Excursions

### The road from Tarifa to Punta Paloma

*Follow the N 340 towards Cádiz.*
This short stretch parallels the sea **(Playa de los Lances)**, separated by a copse of pines. Campsites and hotels line the road, and it is possible to pull over for a swim. After 4km/2.5mi, a road to the right leads to a sanctuary, **Santuario de Nuestra Señora de la Luz**, named for Tarifa's patron saint. Two beaches, **Playa de Valdevaqueros**★ and the **Playa de Punta Paloma**, an impressive series of sand dunes, are a little farther along.

### Ruinas Romanas de Baelo Claudia★

*22.5km/14mi NW (15km/9.5mi by the N 340 towards Cádiz, then bear left and 7.5km/4.5mi on the CAP 2216.* ⊙ *Open Tue-Sat, 10am-7pm (6pm, Nov-Feb; 8pm, Jun-Sep), Sun and*

## Garum

Since time immemorial, the Cádiz coast has been one of the main areas for tuna fishing in the whole of Spain. Phoenicians and Romans alike took advantage of the movements of shoals of tuna to the Mediterranean during the spawning months of May and June. The technique used by the Romans, and still used in Cádiz province today, is known as the **almadraba**. Many of the Roman cities along the Andalusian coast, such as Baelo, were originally outposts whose primary function was the salting of fish. Once the tuna had been cut into sections, they were placed in large silos and covered with a layer of salt, where they would remain for several months before being transported throughout the Empire in a special type of amphora. The best-known and most expensive product from this industry was without doubt **garum**, a sauce produced from the head, entrails, blood and other remains of fish, and used as a condiment or even a main dish to which oil or vinegar would then be added.

*public hols, 10am-2pm. Last entry 30min before closing.* ⏱ *Closed Mon, 1 and 6 Jan and 24-25 and 31 Dec.* €1.50 *(no charge for European Union citizens).* ☎ *956 68 85 30.* The Roman city of Baelo Claudia was founded in the 2C BC as a salting factory. Emperor Claudius granted it the title of municipality in the 1C AD; the remains visible today date mostly from this period. Baelo was a walled city, accessed through large gateways; sections remain. Public buildings stood at the intersection of the two main streets: the decumanus maximus (running east to west), and the cardo maximus (north to south). Note the columns of the former basilica, the space occupied by the forum (marked by temples dedicated to the Capitoline Triad, Jupiter, Juno and Minerva), a theatre and a salting factory along the beach.

# ÚBEDA★★

POPULATION 32 524

**Úbeda is a town of monuments, one of Andalucia's architectural treasures, celebrated by illustrious travellers, with a great cultural tradition as well. It was home to writer Antonio Muñoz Molina and singer Joaquín Sabina. Antonio Machado called it "a queen and gypsy"; Eugenio d'Ors compared Úbeda to the most beautiful cities in northern Italy. Admire Úbeda's austere palaces, its elegant squares, and the fine detail where Andalusian art has reached its height. The Moorish quarter, the barrio de San Millán, delightfully contrasts the town's 16C masterpieces with its maze of narrow streets where hand-embroidered esparto matting, rugs, pottery and lanterns made of tin and glass can still be purchased.** 🛈 *Plaza Baja del Marqués, 4 (Palacio del Marqués de Contadero),* ☎ *953 75 08 97, otubeda@andalucia.org.*

▸ **Orient Yourself:** Úbeda stands in a plain set with olive groves at the centre of the province of Jaén between the Guadalquivir and Guadalimar Valleys. The town is linked with Jaén (57km/36mi SW) via the A 316 and Córdoba (146km/91mi W) via the N 322 and A 4 – E 5

⊙ **Don't Miss:** The gems of Úbeda's treasured old quarter.

⏱ **Organizing Your Time:** A day is the minimum one should spend in Úbeda.

⚲ **Also See:** BAEZA (9km/5.5mi W), JAÉN, LINARES (29km/18mi W), CAZORLA (45km/28mi SE), and Parque Natural de las SIERRAS DE CAZORLA, SEGURA Y LAS VILLAS (E).

# A Bit of History

Although its origins are Roman, it was the Moors who founded Ubbadat Al Arab, one of the major cities in Al-Andalus. In 1234, Fernando III the Saint reconquered the city. In the 16C, during the reigns of Charles V and Felipe II, Úbeda enjoyed its greatest splendour. Its citizens held important positions in the Empire, magnificent Renaissance buildings were erected, and members of the nobility took up residence.

ÚBEDA

> ## "Wandering through the Hills of Úbeda"
>
> According to legend, when Fernando III was laying siege to the town, one of his noblemen, who appeared not to relish the prospect of battle, appeared at his side only once the fighting was over. When asked by the king the reason for his late arrival, he replied that he had got lost in the many hills around Úbeda.

# Walking Tours

## Old Town★★ *Allow one day*

### Plaza Vázquez de Molina★★

This magnificent square, the monumental centre of Úbeda, is at the heart of the old quarter whose sumptuous buildings and delightful streets transport visitors to another era. It is lined by impressive buildings, including the Capilla del Salvador, Palacio de las Cadenas, Iglesia de Santa María de los Alcázares and the Casa del Deán Ortega, now a *parador*. Other buildings worthy of note are the **Cárcel del Obispo** (Bishop's Prison), so called as it was here that nuns were obliged to suffer the canonical punishments imposed by the bishop, the former granary (*pósito*), the **Palacio del Marqués de Mancera**, the Renaissance façade of which is crowned by a quadrangular tower, and the **Casa del Regidor**.

### Palacio de las Cadenas★

🕐 *Open 8am-1pm and 3-9pm.* ☎ *953 75 04 40.*

This palace was built by Vandelvira in the middle of the 16C at the behest of Don Juan Vázquez de Molina, nephew of Don Francisco de los Cobos, a leading political and cultural figure during the reigns of Carlos I and Felipe II. In 1566 it was adapted for use as a convent. It was subsequently a jail, and became the town hall in 1868. The name, Palace of the Chains, derives from the iron chains that once stretched across the entry. The **façade★★**, which bears the family coat of arms, unusually combines decorative Andalusian features with the harmony of classical architectural orders. Note the alternating bays and pilasters which are replaced on the upper tier by caryatids and atlantes in which the influence of the French sculptor Jamete is clear. Two elegant lanterns on the ends add a lighter touch.

Inside is a delightful Renaissance patio with refined arcades and a central fountain. On the upper floor, embellished with a colourful *artesonado* ceiling, is the **Archivo Histórico Municipal** (municipal archive), whose windows afford lovely views of the plaza area. The basement holds the **Centro Municipal de Interpretación Turística**, which illuminates Úbeda's heritage through models and panels, and also shows local pottery and ceramics. ⚷ *Closed for relocation.* ☎*953 75 04 40.*

### Iglesia de Santa María de los Alcázares★

⚷ *Closed for restoration.* The church was built in the 13C above the remains of a mosque. Its harmonious façade, crowned by two belfries, each with three large bells and a smaller one, enhances the plaza Vázquez de Molina. Of three doorways, the main one, the work of López de Alcaraz and Pedro del Cabo (17C), and the Puerta de la Consolada, on the left-hand side (late 16C) stand out.

> ### Calle Real
>
> This attractive thoroughfare, one of the most elegant in Úbeda, provides visitors with an insight into the town's architectural splendour during the 16C, when Úbeda was at its economic and artistic peak. The street is lined by monumental buildings, typical shops and refined decorative detail. Nowadays, calle Real is a favourite with residents of the city, who look upon it with great affection.

The interior, badly damaged during the Spanish Civil War, contains several beautiful **chapels**★ adorned with sculptures and profuse decoration, in particular the Capilla de La Yedra and Capilla de los Becerra, both enclosed by impressive **grilles**★ designed by Master Bartolomé. Sculptures in the church include a *Fallen Christ* by Mariano Benlliure and *Christ of the Bullfighters*, from a nearby convent.

The patio of the mosque was replaced in the 16C by handsome Renaissance **cloisters** of irregular shape with elegant pointed arches and groin vaulting.

### Casa del Deán Ortega

The *parador* is a 16C Renaissance building partly designed by Vandelvira. Behind the building's sober façade is a patio of considerable charm.

### Capilla del Salvador★★

🕐 *Open 4-6.30pm; Apr-May and Sep-Oct, 4.30-7pm; Jun-Aug, 10am-2pm and 5-7.30pm.* 🎟 *€3.* ☎ *953 75 81 50.*

Designed by Diego de Siloé in 1536 and built by Andrés de Vandelvira between 1540 and 1556, this chapel is one of the finest religious buildings of the Andalusian Renaissance. It was commissioned as a family pantheon by Don Francisco de los Cobos, secretary to Charles V, who, as a result of his vast fortune and artistic leanings, became a leading figure in 16C imperial Spain.

The main **façade** combines several ornamental motifs popular in Renaissance art: Christ's ascent to Mount Tabor appears above the door, while representations of St

---

## Convent Pastries

Delicious pastries such as *magdalenas* (madeleines) and *tortas de aceite* (olive oil tarts), and *pastas de té* biscuits and *roscos de ajonjolí* (sesame seed cakes), can be purchased from the Convento de las Carmelitas Descalzas and the Convento de Santa Clara respectively. They come with a seal of quality that has been developed with patience and care over the past 300 years.

Peter and St Paul can be seen on both sides. The intrados of the inner arch bears reliefs depicting figures from Greek mythology, and the Cobos and Molina escutcheons. The lavish **interior**★★ has a single nave, its vaulting outlined in blue and gold. The central part, intended for the tombs of Don Francisco de los Cobos and his wife, is separated from the remainder of the chapel by a monumental grille attributed to Villalpando. The presbytery, by Vandelvira, is a rotunda in which an immense 16C altarpiece includes a baldaquin with a sculpture of the Transfiguration by Alonso Berruguete; only the carving of Christ remains.

The **sacristy**★★, also by Vandelvira, is an architectural jewel, containing interesting decoration based on caissons, caryatids, atlantes and medallions, in which the stylistic influence of the Italian Renaissance is clear. Note the harmonious south doorway and the impressive grille enclosing the nave, a work by two local artists.

## Casa de los Salvajes

The 17C Renaissance House of the Savages – or Casa de Camarero Vago, for the steward (*camarero*) of Bishop Francisco de Yago who lived here – owes its unusual name to two figures in animal skins on the façade, supporting the bishop's coat of arms.

## Plaza del Primero de Mayo

Popularly known as the plaza del Mercado (Market Square), this *plaza* was the setting for bullfights, autos-da-fé, outdoor fairs, executions and theatre performances in days gone by. It is bordered by the former town hall and the Iglesia de San Pablo.

### Antiguo Ayuntamiento

The 17C former town hall shows clear Palladian influence. A lower tier comprises an elegant porch with three semicircular arches and paired columns. An upper register is in the style of a double loggia or porticoed gallery, from where the town's council presided over events in the square below.

## Iglesia de San Pablo★

🕐 *Open for worship, noon-1.30pm and 5-7pm; Sat, 12-1.30pm and 7-7.30pm.* 🕐 *Closed Mon and afternoons of public hols.*

The harmony of the main Gothic portal with Plateresque bell tower, contrasts with the south doorway (1511), featuring attractive Isabelline-style reliefs. On the southwest corner, to the left of the main façade, admire the Renaissance gallery. Two chapels stand out: the **Capilla de las Calaveras** (third on the right), with an impressive arch by Vandelvira, and the Isabelline **Capilla de las Mercedes**, enclosed by extraordinary **grilles**★★ created in Úbeda. Note the highly imaginative scene of Adam and Eve.

## Museo de San Juan de la Cruz

🕐 *Open 11am-12.45pm and 5-6.45pm.* 🕐 *Closed Mon.* €1.20. 📞 *953 75 06 15.*

The Museum of St John of the Cross is in the oratory of the same name – a Baroque room containing a sculpture of the saint. A guided visit through the monastery retraces the final days of this mystical poet who died in Úbeda.

### Casa del Obispo Canastero

This residence stands close to the **Puerta del Losal**, a 15C Mudéjar gateway that formed part of the town walls and provided access to the San Millán district. The Plateresque mansion is named after one of the numerous reliefs which decorate the façade, representing a bishop (*obispo*) holding a basket (*canasta*).

### Palacio de la calle Montiel

The palace is a fine example of early Plateresque in Úbeda. The handsome façade is emblasoned with the poorly preserved coat of arms of its former owners, indicating that the residents supported the *comuneros* who rose against Carlos V in the early 16C.

### Casa Mudéjar

The **Museo Arqueológico** in this restored 14C Mudéjar house displays artifacts ranging from the Neolithic era to Moorish occupation, all from Úbeda and the surrounding area. ○ *Open 9am-8.30pm; Tue, 2.30-8.30pm; Sun, 9am-2.30pm.* ○ *Closed Mon; Tue morning.* ≈€1.50 *(no charge for citizens of the European Union).* ☎ *953 75 37 02.*

### Palacio del Conde de Guadiana

Built in the early 17C, the Palace of the Count of Guadiana is crowned by a fine **tower**★ with angular balconies divided by small columns and galleries on the third floor.

### Iglesia de San Pedro

This church, sited on the tranquil square of San Pedro, retains its original Romanesque apse. Note the harmonious Renaissance façade and several Gothic chapels.

### Real Monasterio de Santa Clara

This monastery is the oldest Christian church in Úbeda (1290), although it also includes Renaissance and Gothic-Mudéjar features.

### Palacio de Vela de los Cobos

This palace was commissioned of Vandelvira by Don Francisco Vela de los Cobos, governor of Úbeda, in the mid-16C. Its Renaissance façade has an elegant arcaded gallery extending to the corners, where there are two unusual white columns.

### Palacio del Marqués del Contadero

Although the façade dates from the late 18C, its Renaissance features witness the endurance of that style in Úbeda. The upper floor has a blunt-arched gallery.

### Plaza de Santo Domingo

This pleasant square is bordered by two buildings of interest: the **Iglesia de Santo Domingo**, with its Plateresque façade, and the **Casa de los Morales**, a replica of which has been built in the Poble Espanyol (Spanish Village) in Barcelona.

## Outside the Old Town

### Casa de las Torres

The mansion of High Constable Dávalos has a Plateresque façade flanked by monumental square towers, with finely sculpted reliefs and gargoyles on the cornice.

### Iglesia de San Lorenzo

The main attraction of this church is the placement of its façade on the parapet of the old walls, where it is supported by the barbican of the Puerta de Granada.

### Palacio de la Rambla
This palace on one side of the elegant plaza del Marqués (now a hotel – *see Address Book*) includes two impressive life-size warrior figures supporting a coat of arms.

### Iglesia de la Santísima Trinidad
The portal, above which a sober, three-storey bell tower has been added, is one of the finest examples of Baroque decoration in Úbeda.

### Palacio de los Bussianos
This late-16C Renaissance palace has an attractive staircase leading to a delightful gallery of pointed arches on the first floor.

### Iglesia de San Nicolás
Although Gothic in style, the trumpet-shaped vault over the entrance was built by Vandelvira during the Renaissance period.

### Antiguo Hospital de Santiago
*Head out of town along calle Obispo Cobos.* Construction of the hospital was ordered by Don Diego de los Cobos, bishop of Jaén and a native of Úbeda. The façade, which is preceded by a large portico flanked by two towers, is a work of restrained size by Vandelvira. The only decorative features are the relief of St James the Moorslayer(*Santiago Matamoros*), above the doorway, and the glazed ceramic medallions on the cornice. A chapel houses an impressive wooden altarpiece. Note the double-arcaded **patio** and the elegant staircase under a coffered vault, the columns of which were carved from marble brought from Italy. The hospital houses the **Museo de la Semana Santa**, a museum dedicated to Holy Week celebrations. ◷ *Open Mon-Fri, 8am-10pm; Sat-Sun and public hols, 11am-2.30pm and 6-9.30pm.* ☎ *953 75 08 42.*

*Patio, Hospital de Santiago*

G. Bludzin / MICHELIN

## Excursions

### Sabiote
*9km/5.5mi northeast along A 1202.* This peaceful town has elegant houses and old, narrow alleyways. Sabiote was the place of residence of Alonso de Vandelvira, who built mansions here for the Mendoza, Melgarejo and Higuera Sabater families. Of interest are the 15C **Iglesia de San Pedro Apóstol**, a monumental Gothic church, and the castle outside the walls, once a Moorish fortress, restored by Vandelvira.

### Torreperogil
*10km/6mi east along N 322.* Torreperogil is a charming small town with a maze of medieval streets. The church, the Iglesia de la Asunción, has a handsome double-entrance portal with central column. A stone retable depicts the Deposition.

### Villacarrillo

*32km/20mi northeast along N 322.* This agricultural and industrial centre is one of the oldest settlements in the province, dating back to the Bronze Age.

### Iglesia de la Asunción

🕐 *Open daily, 7.30-9pm. If closed, ask next door.*

Another 16C work by Vandelvira, the church was erected on the foundation of an earlier castle, from which three monumental towers have survived. The ground plan consists of three aisles and side chapels covered with sober groined vaulting.

### Casa de la Inquisición

Despite its association with the Inquisition during the Middle Ages, this monumental three-storey building has a number of redeeming features, including several attractive wrought-iron balconies on the façade. The rooms are somewhat devoid of decoration.

# UTRERA

POPULATION: 45 947.

**Utrera is on a rise at the heart of the Sevillian countryside, amid eucalyptus groves and cultivated land. Although of Roman origin, it developed starting in the 16C, then ground to a halt with an epidemic in the middle of the 17C, leaving intact a historical centre with noteworthy monuments.** 🔖 *Rodrigo Caro, 3, 41710 Utrera,* ☎ *955 86 09 31. www.utrera.org*

▶ **Orient Yourself:** Utrera is at the crossroads of A 376 from Sevilla (33km/21mi NW) to the Costa del Sol (SE), and A 394, heading SW to Cádiz..

🕐 **Organizing Your Time:** Allow a couple of hours.

👣 **Also See:** SEVILLA, MARCHENA (38km/24mi NE) and OSUNA (68km/42mi E).

## Sights

### Castle

This fortress of Almohad origin was part of the defensive walls. Today, only a few sections and an arch, the Arco de la Villa – to which an upper, chapel-like section was added in the 18C – remain. An impressive keep and parade ground are within.

### Iglesia de Santa María de la Asunción or
### Iglesia de Santa María de la Mesa★

This Gothic church with additional Renaissance and Baroque features dominates a charming square. The handsome façade centers on a large splayed arch, above which rises a graceful Baroque tower. Outstanding features include **choir stalls** by Duque Cornejo (1744), the main altarpiece and the sepulchre of the Count of Arcos.

### Iglesia de Santiago

This triple-nave Gothic church dates from the 15C. Its severe, defensive look contrasts with the ostentatious Isabelline-Gothic decor of the **Puerta del Perdón** gateway.

### Plaza del Altozano★

This elegant square at the heart of Utrera is framed by an attractive three-storey 17C and 18C mansions with pitched roofs and delicate unbroken balconies.

## Ayuntamiento

The town hall, an 18C mansion on elegant plaza de Gibaxa, has a magnificent Rococo façade and period rooms. Note the furniture in the Salón Azul (Blue Room).

## Casa Surga

This late-18C mansion has a charming Baroque façade and rooms in period decor.

## Iglesia de San Francisco

🕐 *Open Mon-Sat, 7-8.30pm.* ☎ *955 86 09 31.*
This 17C late-Renaissance church has a large cupola adorned with paintings.

## Santuario de Nuestra Señora de la Consolación★

*Leave by avenida de Juan XXIII.* 🕐 *Open 9am-2pm and 4-6.30pm.* ☎ *954 86 03 30.*
This outstanding 17C and 18C Mudéjar-style sanctuary occupies a former Franciscan monastery. The impressive Baroque façade and the delicate *artesonado* work in the sanctuary are particularly worthy of note. On 8 September a popular pilgrimage (*romería*) is held in honour of the Virgin of Solace (*Consolación*).

## Excursion

### El Palmar de Troya

*13km/8mi south along the A 394.* The heretical Order of the Carmelites of the Holy Face, founded by the controversial priest Clemente Rodríguez (1946-2005), who proclaimed himself Pope in 1978, is headquartered here. The enormous church holds statues of venerated saints, presided by a sculpture of Our Crowned Lady of El Palmar. In the afternoon, mass is held in Latin in accordance with the liturgy in use before the Second Vatican Council.

### Suitable Dress

Women who wish to attend religious ceremonies at El Palmar de Troya will need to observe a strict dress code which requires them to wear trousers and to cover their head with a veil.

# VEJER DE LA FRONTERA★

POPULATION: 12 731

Vejer perches delightfully on a rocky crag dominating the valley of the River Barbate, just kilometres from the Atlantic coast. One of Andalucía's most picturesque *pueblos blancos*, it has some of the strongest Moorish roots, revealed by its maze of narrow, cobbled streets, and whitewashed houses enclosing verdant patios and crowned by flat terraced roofs. 🛈 *Marqués de Tamarón, 10,* ☎ *956 45 17 36, oficinaturismovejer@hotmail.com*

## The "Cobijado"

This name was given to the traditional garment worn by the women of Vejer up until the Spanish Civil War. Although its origins are uncertain, this simple black head-dress is also worn in a number of towns and villages in North Africa.

It is traditionally worn during the **Velada de Agosto**, a festival held in honour of the **Virgin of the Olive**, the town's patron saint, between 10 and 24 August every year.

- ▶ **Orient Yourself:** Vejer de la Frontera lies between Cádiz and Tarifa, the southernmost point in Spain. It is linked to both towns via N 340 – E 5 coastal route.
- 🕐 **Organizing Your Time:** Take two hours for sights, more for beach time.
- **Especially for Kids:** Coves and La Breña park are great for small swimmers.
- 👁 **Also See:** TARIFA (50km/31mi SE), MEDINA SIDONIA (26km/16mi N) and CÁDIZ (51km/32mi NW).

# Visit

*Guided tours (1hr 30min) of the town's major sights: €3. ☎ 956 45 17 36.*

## Walls

Four 15C gateways in walls built to protect against Nasrid attacks survive to this day. The **Arco de la Segur**, a basket-handle arch, is the entrance to Vejer's old quarter.

## Iglesia Parroquial del Divino Salvador

🕐 *Open 11am-1.30pm and 7.30-9pm (15 Apr-Oct, 8.30-10pm). ☎ 956 45 17 36.*
Vejer's parish church retains the minaret from the mosque that preceded it. The three-aisle **interior**★ manifests an odd mixture of styles. The oldest part of the church is the apsidal end, which combines Romanesque and Gothic features.

## Convento de las Concepcionistas

This 17C convent with a sober, Classical façade, sits in one of Vejer's most charming corners, beside the mysterious **Arco de las Monjas**. It is used for cultural programmes.

## Castle

Despite its poor state of repair, the fortress affords views that are particularly impressive. Access is via what looks like an ordinary neighbourhood patio.

## Casa del Mayorazgo

*Private house.* This 17C Baroque residence with a simple façade backs onto

H. Champollion/ MICHELIN

---

## Address Book

### WHERE TO EAT

🍽 **Trafalgar** – *Plaza de España, 31 – ☎ 956 44 76 38 – 🕐 Closed Jan-mid-Feb, Sun eve and Mon (except Jun-Sep).* This welcome culinary surprise specialises in delicious fresh fish in minimalist and rustic dining rooms. Tapas are also served at the entrance. Guests can dine on the terrace in summer.

### WHERE TO STAY

🛏 **Hostal La Posada** – *Los Remedios, 21 – ☎ 956 45 02 58 – 6 rooms, 6 apart-ments.* A family-run hotel with pleasant rooms, three with wonderful views of the valley. La Posada also has a number of apartments for rent (🛏🛏), some with a terrace.

🛏 **Hotel Convento de San Francisco** – *La Plazuela – ☎ 956 45 10 01 – 25 rooms – Restaurant 🍽🍽.* This former convent for Poor Clares dating from the 17C is in Vejer's old quarter. Rooms are soberly decorated and cosy, with high ceilings and exposed beams. The restaurant, El Refectorio, has good food.

the town walls. It is possible to climb one of the defensive towers from inside the building.

▶ *Arco de la Villa leads to plaza de España.*

## Plaza de España

Also known as plaza de los Pescaítos, for the fish decorating its fountain, this square is one of the liveliest and most attractive here. It is surrounded by palm trees, and several whitewashed houses which lend a colonial air, along with the town hall.

## Excursions

The coastal towns between **Chiclana** and **Zahara de los Atunes** are not Andalucía's most attractive, but the beaches are some of the area's most spectacular and under-developed, popular with those seeking sun, sea and peace and quiet.

### Conil de la Frontera

*15.5km/9.5mi northwest.* Like its neighbours along the Cádiz coast, Conil is a tranquil town where life almost comes to a standstill in winter. In summer it is transformed into a lively resort, whose main attractions are 14km/8.5mi of beach and low-key tourism. In the oldest

> ### Tuna Fishing
>
> The technique used locally to catch tuna, known as *almadraba*, derives from the Arabic word al-madraba. It involves a complex labyrinth of vertical nets, some of which reach lengths of several kilometres, which lead the tuna to a circular area of permanent or temporary netting. Tuna migrate through this part of the coast twice a year: on their way to the spawning grounds in the Mediterranean in spring, and upon their return to the Atlantic in the autumn.

section, between the sea and the **Puerta de Conil,** is an 18C colonial-style former church, the **Iglesia de la Misericordia**, now a school. A heavily restored tower, the Torre de los Guzmanes, is all that remains from the castle (*castillo*) in plaza de Santa Catalina. Also bordering the square are a chapel, the Capilla de Jesús, and the **Museo de Raíces Conileñas**, a museum of local ways. *Castle – ◷ Open mid-Jun to mid-Sep, 10.30am-2pm and 6-9pm; rest of the year 9am-2pm. No charge. ☎ 956 44 05 00. Museum – ◷ Open Jul-Sep, Tue-Sat, 11am-2pm and 8.30-11.30pm; Sun and public hols, 11am-2pm. ◉ €1, no charge Sun. ☎ 956 44 05 01.*

### Beaches

Coves, such as the **Cala del Aceite**, are north towards the port; longer, windy beaches—**Playa de la Fontanilla** and **Playa de los Bateles**—are to the south. **El Palmar**, considered Vejer de la Frontera's beach, is a few kilometres farther.

### Barbate

*10km/6mi south.* Although devoid of cultural interest, Barbate is a fishing port with a tuna industry, and bars and restaurants renowned for fish and seafood.

> ## The Battle of Trafalgar
>
> On 21 October 1805, Admiral de Villeneuve sailed out of Cádiz harbour with his Franco-Spanish fleet to confront the British, commanded by Nelson. After heroic combat, in which Nelson and the Spanish Gravina and Churruca were mortally wounded, Villeneuve's fleet was destroyed. The event sounded the death-knell for Napoleon's hopes of defeating the British, and confirmed the dominance of a victorious naval superpower.

### Parque Natural La Breña and Marismas de Barbate★

*Access from Vejer along A 5206 or from Barbate.* The main attractions of this nature reserve are its lovely coves, nestled between rocky cliffs, and beaches, bordered by umbrella pines. The best-known beach is the **Playa de los Caños de Meca★★**.

### Zahara de los Atunes

*20km/12mi SE.* This small fishing community (de los Atunes translates as "of the tunas") has some of the longest and most unspoilt beaches on the Costa de la Luz. The town was controlled from the 15C on by the Dukes of Medina Sidonia, who exploited the tuna industry. The dukes lost their domain in the 19C, by which time Zahara had been reduced to a village. A few ruins remain from its 15C castle. Today, the town lives mainly off fishing and tourism.

# VÉLEZ BLANCO

POPULATION: 2 190

In the foothills of the Sierra de María, Vélez Blanco's whitewashed houses extend across a hillside below a majestic Renaissance castle. It and nearby Vélez Rubio are linked with the Marquess of Vélez, a title bestowed upon Don Pedro Fajardo y Chacón by the Catholic Monarchs in 1506. Numerous archaeological remains include such significant sites as the Cueva de los Letreros, a cave containing rock paintings.

▶ **Orient Yourself:** Vélez Blanco is in northern Almería province, near Murcia.

◔ **Organizing Your Time:** Spend hours in town, or days in the nature park.

⚲ **Also See:** BAZA (77km/48mi SW) and Sierra de los FILABRES.

### The Indalo

The origins of this attractive figure, the symbol of Almería, can be found in the Cueva de los Letreros, for it was here, in the 19C, that wall paintings of human figures and animals dating from about 5000 BC were discovered.

## Visit

### Castle★

◔ *Open 11am-1.30pm and 4-6pm.* ☏ *950 41 50 01 (town hall).*
Construction of this impressive 16C fortress was ordered by the first Marquess of Vélez, who commissioned Italian artists for the project. Sadly, its charming Ren-

*Vélez Blanco*

aissance marble patio was sold to a French antique dealer, and ended up at the Metropolitan Museum in New York, where it is now displayed.

The castle is no traditional fortress, as shown by its large miradors offering superb views, and the numerous wall openings in its lofty walls. The Salón del Triunfo and the Salón de la Mitología originally contained wooden friezes depicting Caesar's triumph and the labours of Hercules. These are in the Musée des Arts Décoratifs in Paris.

## Centro de visitantes del Parque Natural de la Sierra de María

The visitor centre, in a converted grain storehouse, offers a wealth of information on both the park ( *see Excursions*) and the nearby Cueva de los Letreros.

## Churches

The town has two churches of interest. The 16C Iglesia de Santiago has fine Mudéjar *artesonado* work. The church of the Convento de San Luis bears the coat of arms of the Marquisate of Vélez above the portal, and has a large number of fountains.

# Excursions

## Vélez Rubio

*6km/3.5mi south*. Vélez Rubio extends across a small plain below the towers and dome of its parish church. Its two main streets, carrera del Carmen and carrera del Mercado, are lined with mansions, the Baroque church of the Convento de la Inmaculada, and the 17C Iglesia del Carmen, the oldest church in the town.

### Parroquia de la Encarnación★

🕐 *Open Tue-Sun, 5-8pm.* 🕐 *Closed Mon.*

Construction of this magnificent parish church was ordered by the 10th Marquess of Vélez in the 18C. Its monumental proportions come as something of a surprise. Two bell towers flank the richly decorated Baroque stone **portal**★, sectioned by pilasters and architraves. Note the coat of arms and a fine relief of the Annunciation. The main altarpiece and organ, both made of wood but without polychrome decoration, stand out. A St Antony of Padua, by Salzillo, dominates the altarpiece in the Capilla de la Encarnación.

The town hall, an 18C seigniorial residence, fronts the same square.

### Museo Comarcal Velezano

🕐 *Open 10.30am-2pm and 5-8pm.* 🕐 *Closed Mon. No charge.* ☎ *950 41 25 60.*

This museum devoted to local ways is in the former 18C Royal Hospital. It displays archaeological items from nearby, southeast Andalucía and even the Sahara.

## María

*9km/5.5mi northwest*. Of interest in this whitewashed village nestled in the Sierra de María are the 16C Mudéjar-style parish church, the 18C Edificio de la Tercia and a triple-spouted basin. The village also has an unusual public wash house.

A 16C chapel, the Ermita de la Virgen de la Cabeza, lies 3km/1.8mi outside María.

### Parque Natural de la Sierra de María★

The visitor centre, the **Centro de Visitantes Umbría de María**, situated 2km/1.2mi from María along A 317, is well worth a visit. 🕐 *Open Fri-Sun, 9am-1pm and 3-5pm.* 🕐 *Closed Mon-Thu.* ☎ *950 52 70 05.*

The reserve extends over 22 500ha/55 600 acres in the municipalities of Vélez Rubio, Vélez Blanco, María and Chirivel. The landscape here is steep – several sections are above 2 000m/6 560ft – and varied, with cereal crops, fields of thyme, forests of oak and pine, and even Spanish broom in the higher mountain areas. A number of recreational areas and shelters are dotted throughout the park.

# INDEX

# ACCOMMODATIONS

# INDEX

# INDEX

# MAPS AND PLANS

## PRINCIPAL SIGHTS

### TOWN PLANS

### PLANS OF MONUMENTS AND SITES

## COMPANION

## PUBLICATIONS

### MICHELIN MAP 578 ANDALUCÍA, COVERING THE WHOLE REGION

- a 1:400 000 scale map detailing sights and monuments described within this guide, street plans of Sevilla, Málaga and Granada, and a full index of place names

### MICHELIN ESPAÑA/PORTUGAL ROAD ATLAS

- similar in scale to Michelin map 578, but covering the whole Iberian Peninsula

### MICHELIN MAP 734 ESPAÑA/ PORTUGAL

- a 1:1 000 000 scale map of the Iberian Peninsula

### MICHELIN EUROPE ATLAS

- a 1:1 000 000 scale atlas of Western Europe in a single volume
- all major roads and 70 town/city maps
- driving regulations in force in each country

# Little Red Riding Hood

**B**ut Little Red Riding Hood had her regional map with her, and so she did not fall into the trap. She did not take the path through the wood and she did not meet the big bad wolf. Instead, she chose the picturesque touring route straight to Grandmother's house, and arrived safely with her cake and her little pot of butter.

## The End

With Michelin maps, go your own way.

# Legend

## Selected monuments and sights

◉ ⇒ Tour - Departure point

🏛 ♦ Catholic church

🏛 ♦ Protestant church, other temple

◼ ▢ ⛩ Synagogue - Mosque

▭ Building

■ Statue, small building

† Calvary, wayside cross

◎ Fountain

● ■ Rampart - Tower - Gate

✕ Château, castle, historic house

⁖ Ruins

◡ Dam

✿ Factory, power plant

☆ Fort

∩ Cave

▣ Troglodyte dwelling

🏚 Prehistoric site

▼ Viewing table

🌢 Viewpoint

▲ Other place of interest

## Special symbols

🦅 Civil Guard (Guardia Civil)

🅿 Parador (hotel run by the State)

🐂 Bullring

🌿 Olive grove

🌳 Orange grove

## Sports and recreation

🐎 Racecourse

⛸ Skating rink

≋ ▥ Outdoor, indoor swimming pool

🎥 Multiplex Cinema

⛵ Marina, sailing centre

⛺ Trail refuge hut

◻■■■◻ Cable cars, gondolas

◻+++++◻ Funicular, rack railway

🚂 Tourist train

◆ Recreation area, park

🎢 Theme, amusement park

🦌 Wildlife park, zoo

❀ Gardens, park, arboretum

🌐 Bird sanctuary, aviary

🚶 Walking tour, footpath

👶 Of special interest to children

## Abbreviations

**D** Provincial Council (Diputación)

**G** Central government representation (Delegación del Gobierno)

**H** Town hall (Ayuntamiento)

**J** Law courts/Courthouse (Palacio de Justicia)

**M** Museum (Museo)

**POL.** Police station (Policía)

**T** Theatre (Teatro)

**U** University (Universidad)

|                          | Sight | Seaside resort | Winter sports resort | Spa |
|--------------------------|-------|----------------|----------------------|-----|
| *Highly recommended* ★★★ | ★★★   | ♨♨♨            | ✱✱✱                  | ‡‡‡ |
| *Recommended* ★★         | ★★    | ♨♨             | ✱✱                   | ‡‡  |
| *Interesting*            | ★     | ♨              | ✱                    | ‡   |

## Additional symbols

| | |
|--|--|
| **🛈** | Tourist information |
| **═══ ═══** | Motorway or other primary route |
| **❶ ❶** | Junction: complete, limited |
| **╍╍╍** | Pedestrian street |
| **I ═════ I** | Unsuitable for traffic, street subject to restrictions |
| **┉┉┉ ╌╌╌** | Steps – Footpath |
| **🚆 🚉** | Train station – Auto-train station |
| **🚌 🚌 (S.N.C.F.)** | Coach (bus) station |
| **─┼─** | Tram |
| **Ⓜ** | Metro, underground |
| **P R** | Park-and-Ride |
| **♿** | Access for the disabled |
| **✉** | Post office |
| **☎** | Telephone |
| **⬚** | Covered market |
| **•╳•** | Barracks |
| **△** | Drawbridge |
| **ʊ** | Quarry |
| **✗** | Mine |
| **B F** | Car ferry (river or lake) |
| **🚢** | Ferry service: cars and passengers |
| **⛴** | Foot passengers only |
| **③** | Access route number common to Michelin maps and town plans |
| Bert (R.)... | Main shopping street |
| **AZ B** | Map co-ordinates |

## Hotels and restaurants

**Hotels-** price categories:

|          | Provinces   | Large cities |
|----------|-------------|--------------|
| ⬭        | <40 €       | <60 €        |
| ⬭⬭       | 40 to 65 €  | 60 to 90 €   |
| ⬭⬭⬭      | 65 to 100 € | 90 to 130 €  |
| ⬭⬭⬭⬭     | >100 €      | >130 €       |

**Restaurants-** price categories:

|          | Provinces  | Large cities |
|----------|------------|--------------|
| ⬭        | <14 €      | <16 €        |
| ⬭⬭       | 14 to 25 € | 16 to 30 €   |
| ⬭⬭⬭      | 25 to 40 € | 30 to 50 €   |
| ⬭⬭⬭⬭     | >40 €      | >50 €        |

| | |
|--|--|
| *20 rooms :* | Number of rooms |
| *"double rooms"* | Double occupancy only |
| ⇄ € 5.50 | Price of breakfast when it is not included in the price of the room |
| *100 apart/ room* | Number of apartments or rooms |
| *100 beds* | Number of beds (youth hostels, refuges, etc) |
| *150 sites* | Number of camp sites |

| | |
|--|--|
| ⊘ | No credit cards accepted |
| **P** | Reserved parking for hotel patrons |
| ⊸ | Swimming Pool |
| ▤ | Air conditioning |
| ♿ | Rooms accessible to persons of reduced mobility |

*The prices correspond to the higher rates of the tourist season*

**MICHELIN**

Michelin North America
One Parkway South – Greenville, SC 29615 USA
☎ 800-423-0485
www.MichelinTravel.com
michelin.guides@us.michelin.com

## Manufacture française des pneumatiques Michelin

Société en commandite par actions au capital de 304 000 000 EUR
Place des Carmes-Déchaux – 63000 Clermont-Ferrand (France)
R.C.S. Clermont-Fd B 855 200 507

No part of this publication may be reproduced in any form
without the prior permission of the publisher.

© Michelin, Propriétaires-éditeurs
Dépot légal novembre 2006 – ISSN 0763-1383
Printed in France: octobre 2006
Printing and Binding: AUBIN